トゥルル
RING
ルルルル
RING
MORIOH GRAND HOTEL
MORIOH GRAND HOTEL
トゥルル
RING
ルル
RING
ルルルル
トゥルル
RING
ル
324
ル
RING
トゥルルル ル
RIIING
ルル
RING

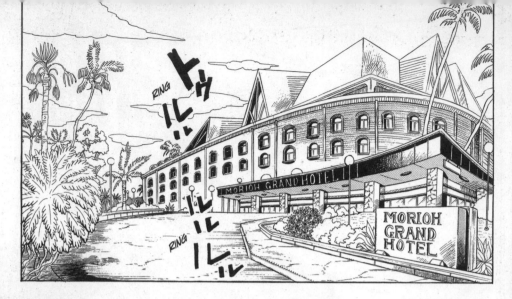

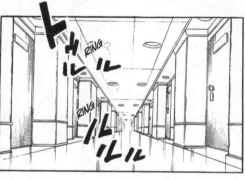

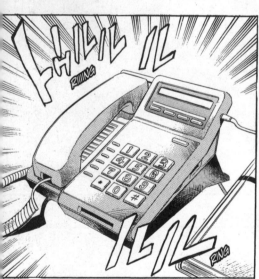

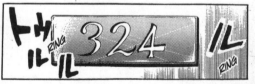

CHAPTER 19

KOICHI HIROSE (REVERB), PART 1

JoJo's
BIZARRE ADVENTURE

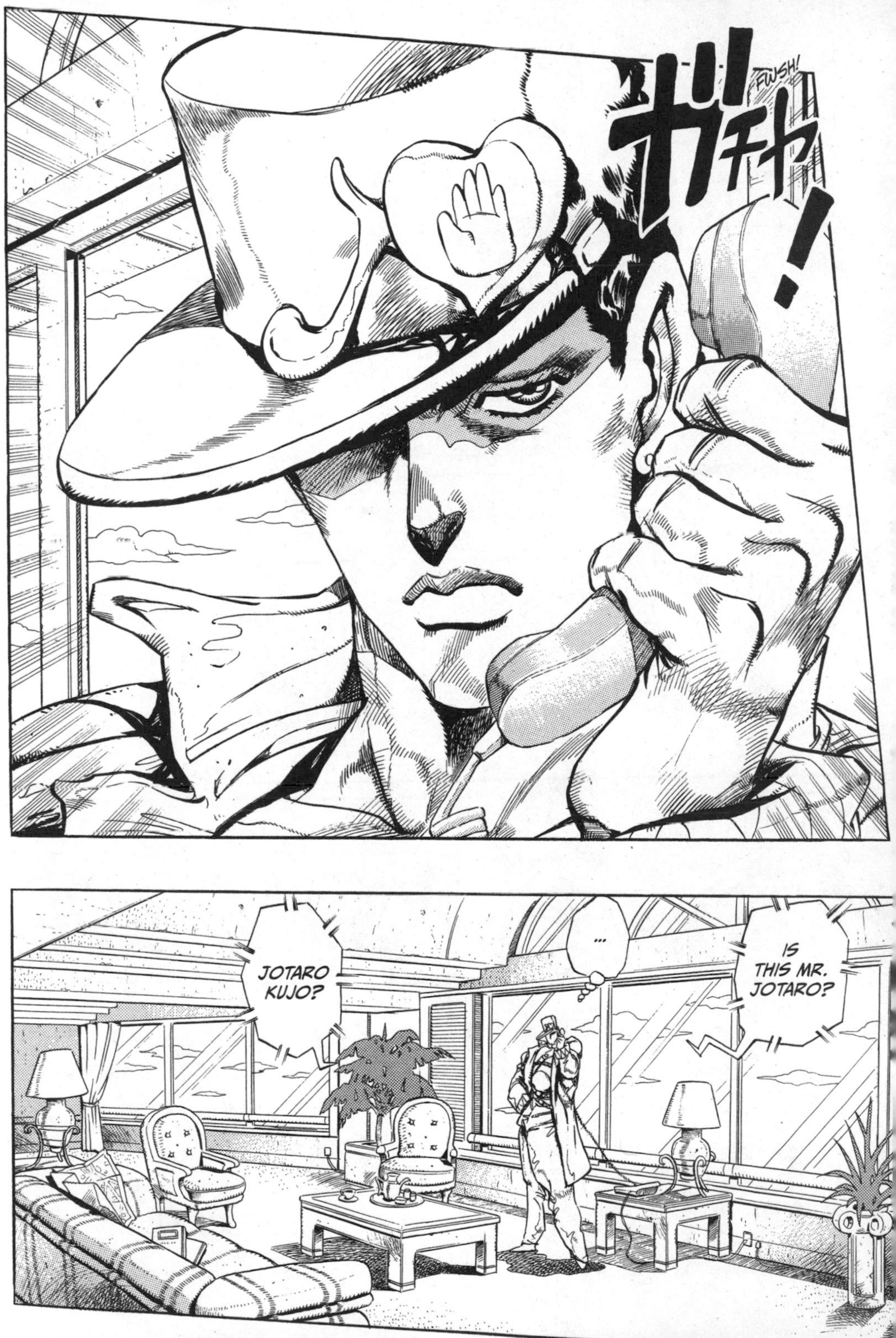
ガチャ!
FWSH!
IS THIS MR. JOTARO?
...
JOTARO KUJO?

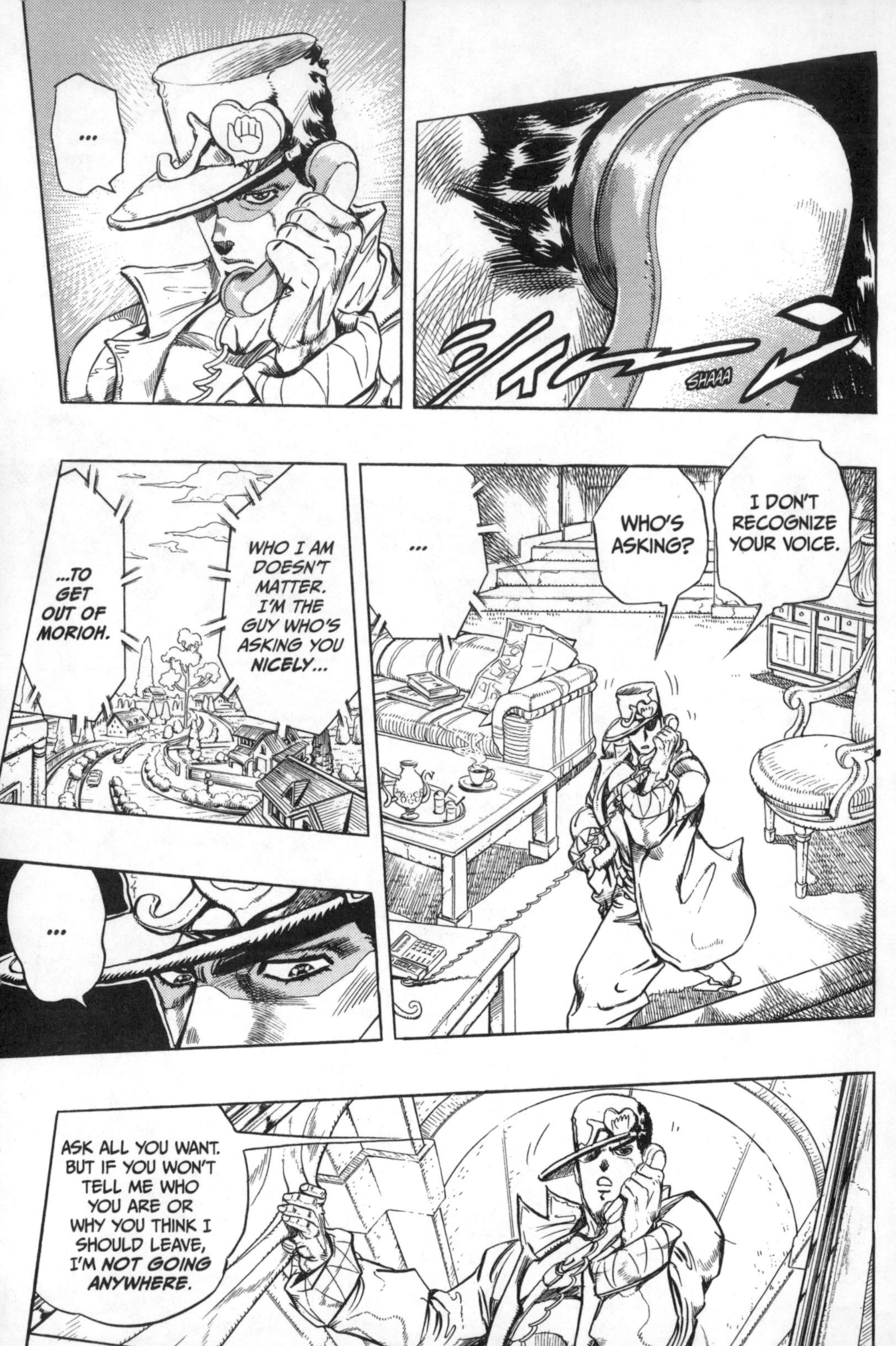
SHAAA
...
I DON'T RECOGNIZE YOUR VOICE.
WHO'S ASKING?
...
WHO I AM DOESN'T MATTER. I'M THE GUY WHO'S ASKING YOU NICELY...
...TO GET OUT OF MORIOH.
...
ASK ALL YOU WANT. BUT IF YOU WON'T TELL ME WHO YOU ARE OR WHY YOU THINK I SHOULD LEAVE, I'M *NOT GOING ANYWHERE*.

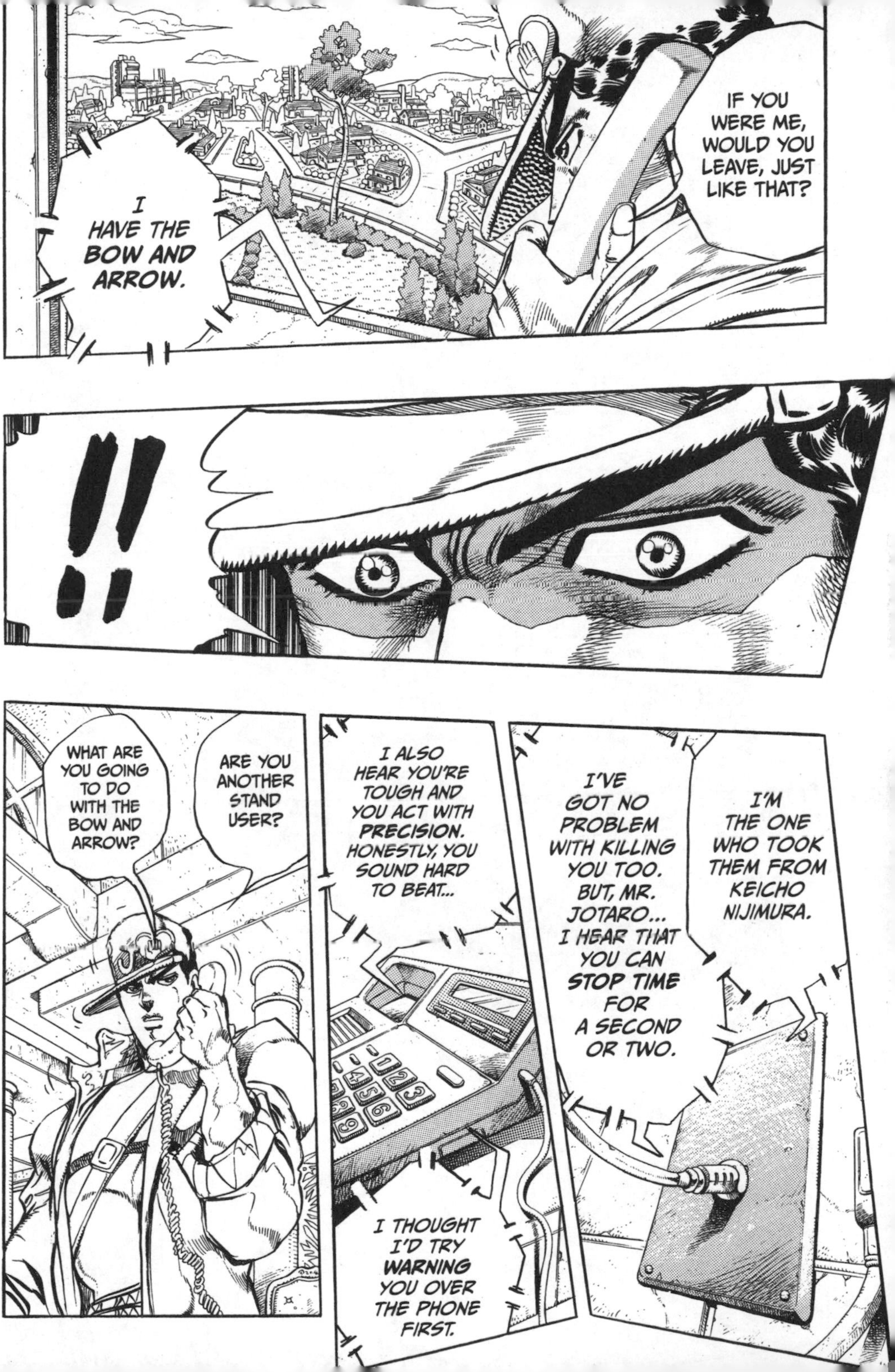
IF YOU WERE ME, WOULD YOU LEAVE, JUST LIKE THAT?
I HAVE THE BOW AND ARROW.
!!
I'M THE ONE WHO TOOK THEM FROM KEICHO NIJIMURA.
I'VE GOT NO PROBLEM WITH KILLING YOU TOO. BUT, MR. JOTARO... I HEAR THAT YOU CAN STOP TIME FOR A SECOND OR TWO.
I ALSO HEAR YOU'RE TOUGH AND YOU ACT WITH PRECISION. HONESTLY, YOU SOUND HARD TO BEAT...
I THOUGHT I'D TRY WARNING YOU OVER THE PHONE FIRST.
ARE YOU ANOTHER STAND USER?
WHAT ARE YOU GOING TO DO WITH THE BOW AND ARROW?

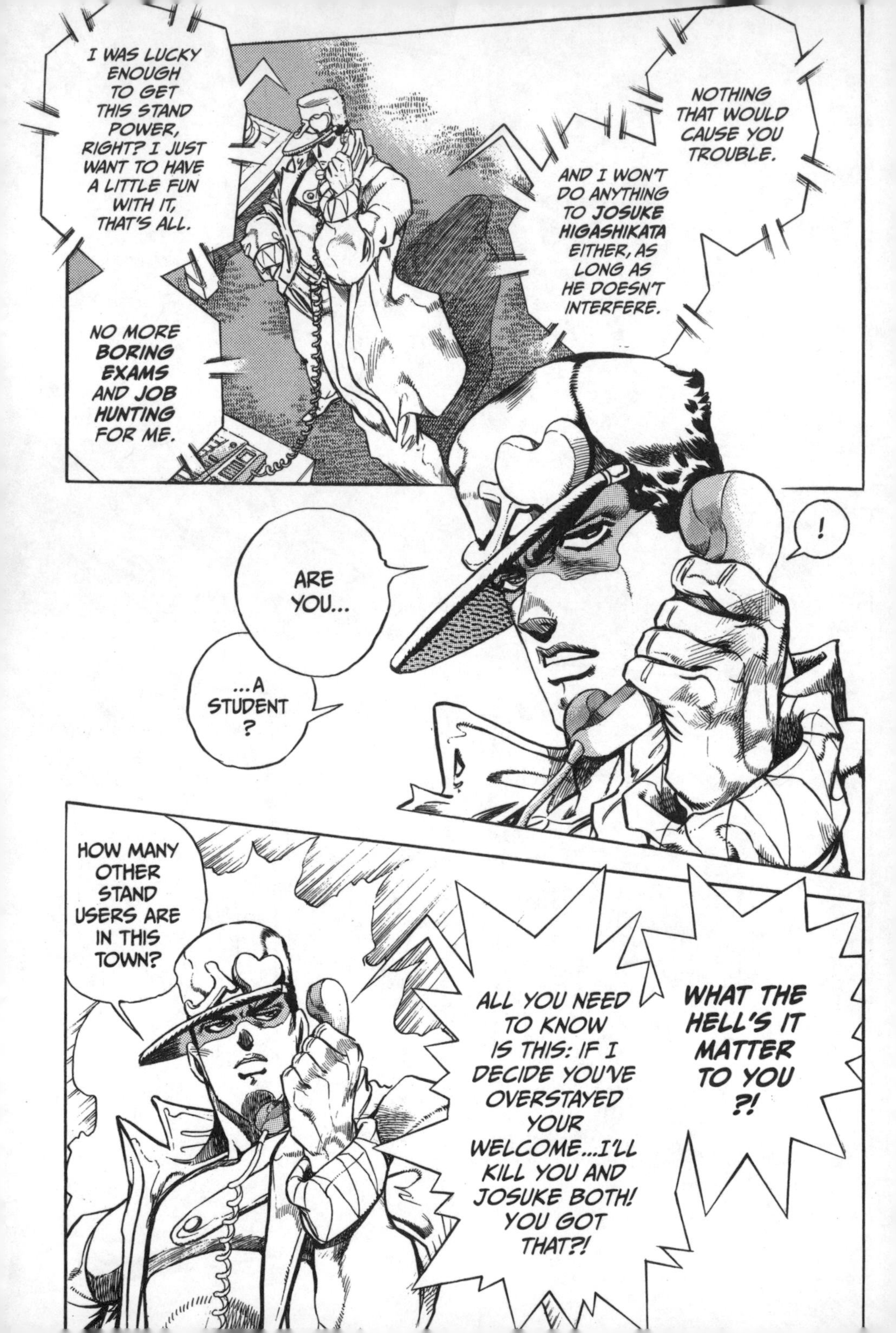
NOTHING THAT WOULD CAUSE YOU TROUBLE.
AND I WON'T DO ANYTHING TO JOSUKE HIGASHIKATA EITHER, AS LONG AS HE DOESN'T INTERFERE.
I WAS LUCKY ENOUGH TO GET THIS STAND POWER, RIGHT? I JUST WANT TO HAVE A LITTLE FUN WITH IT, THAT'S ALL.
NO MORE BORING EXAMS AND JOB HUNTING FOR ME.
!
ARE YOU...
...A STUDENT?
WHAT THE HELL'S IT MATTER TO YOU?!
ALL YOU NEED TO KNOW IS THIS: IF I DECIDE YOU'VE OVERSTAYED YOUR WELCOME...I'LL KILL YOU AND JOSUKE BOTH! YOU GOT THAT?!
HOW MANY OTHER STAND USERS ARE IN THIS TOWN?

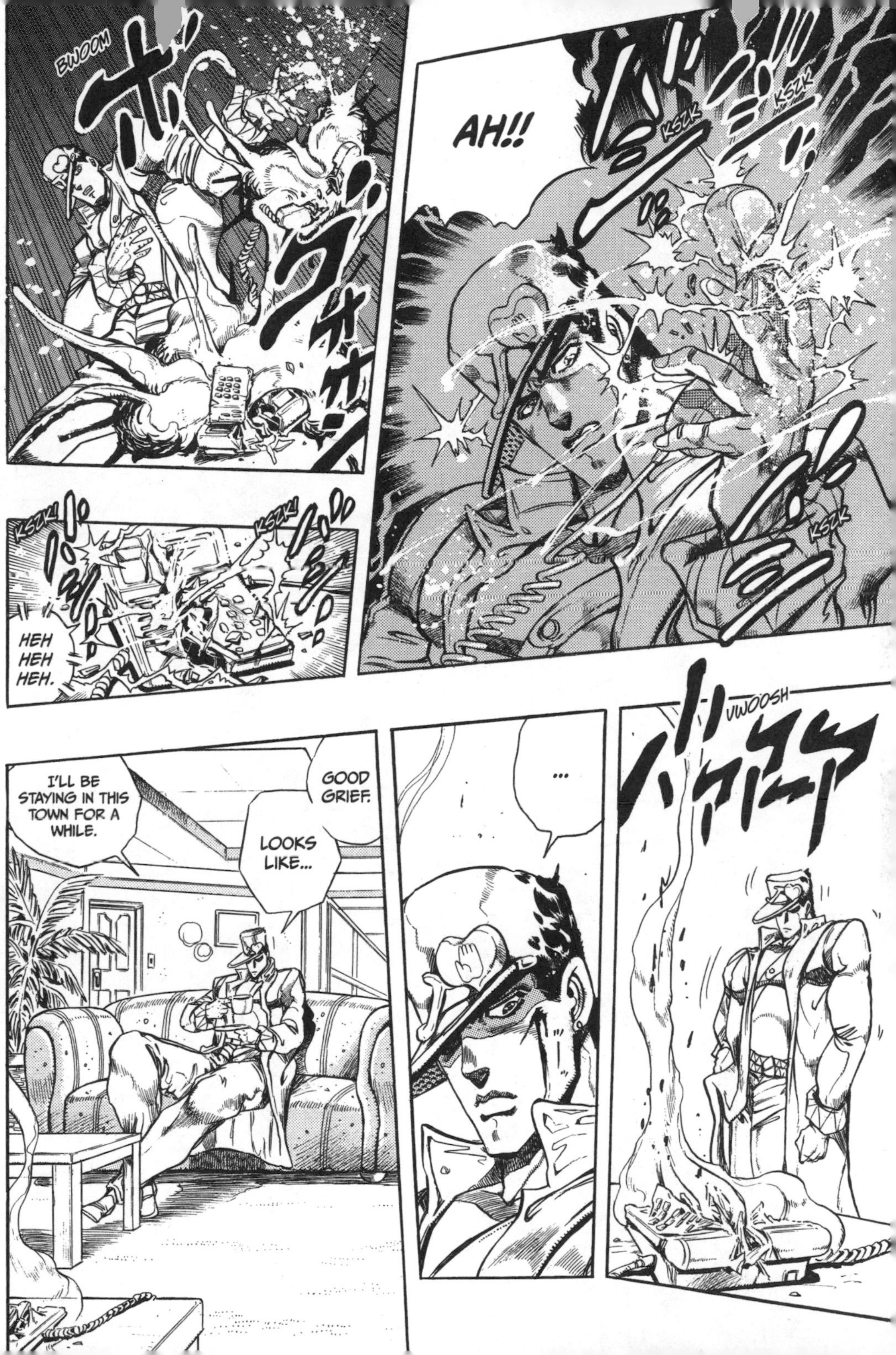
KSZK
KSZK
AH!!
KSZK
BWOOM
KSZK!
KSZK!
HEH HEH HEH.
VWOOSH
...
GOOD GRIEF.
LOOKS LIKE...
I'LL BE STAYING IN THIS TOWN FOR A WHILE.

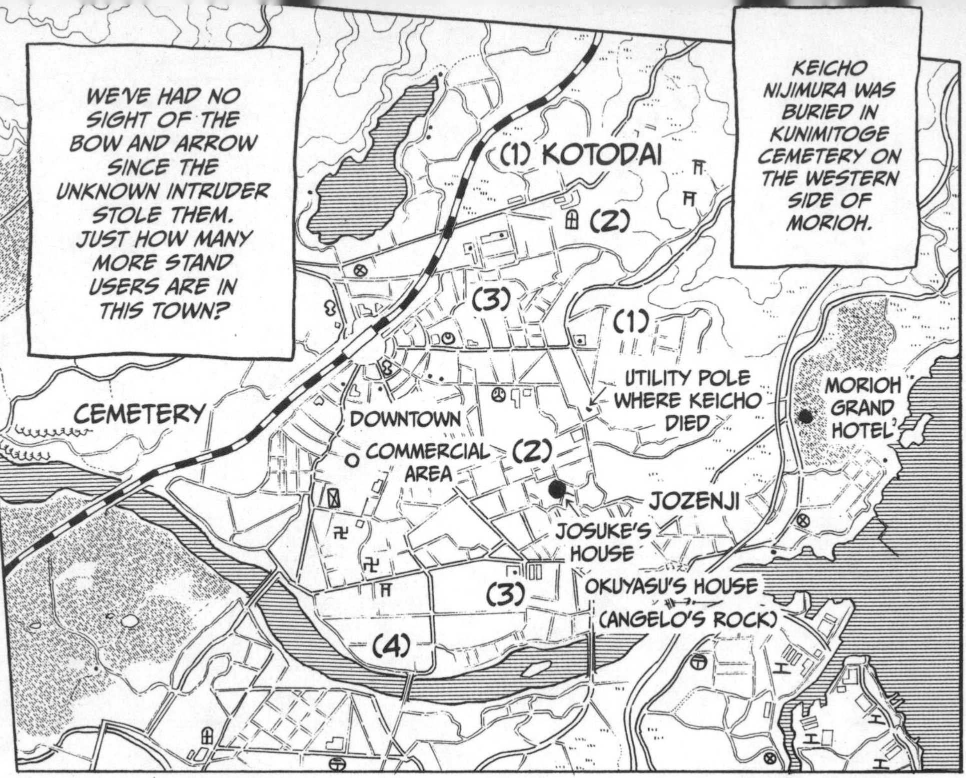
KEICHO NIJIMURA WAS BURIED IN KUNIMITOGE CEMETERY ON THE WESTERN SIDE OF MORIOH.
WE'VE HAD NO SIGHT OF THE BOW AND ARROW SINCE THE UNKNOWN INTRUDER STOLE THEM. JUST HOW MANY MORE STAND USERS ARE IN THIS TOWN?
(1) KOTODAI
(2)
(3)
(1)
MORIOH GRAND HOTEL
UTILITY POLE WHERE KEICHO DIED
CEMETERY
DOWNTOWN
COMMERCIAL AREA
(2)
JOZENJI
JOSUKE'S HOUSE
OKUYASU'S HOUSE (ANGELO'S ROCK)
(3)
(4)
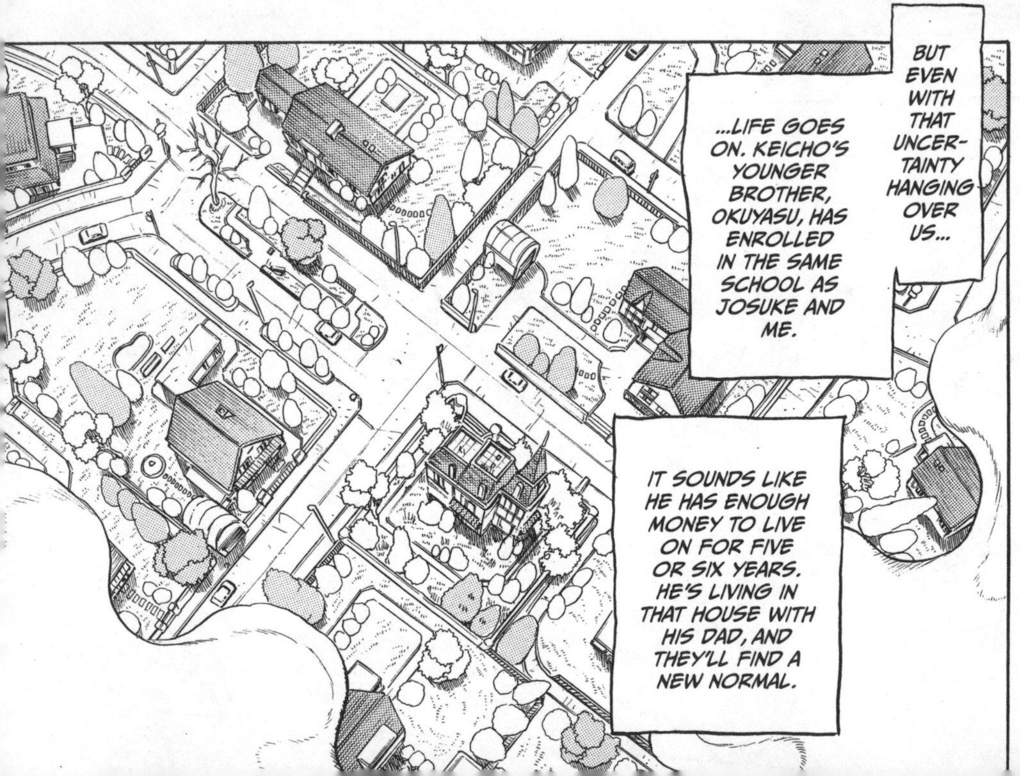
BUT EVEN WITH THAT UNCER-TAINTY HANGING OVER US...
...LIFE GOES ON. KEICHO'S YOUNGER BROTHER, OKUYASU, HAS ENROLLED IN THE SAME SCHOOL AS JOSUKE AND ME.
IT SOUNDS LIKE HE HAS ENOUGH MONEY TO LIVE ON FOR FIVE OR SIX YEARS. HE'S LIVING IN THAT HOUSE WITH HIS DAD, AND THEY'LL FIND A NEW NORMAL.

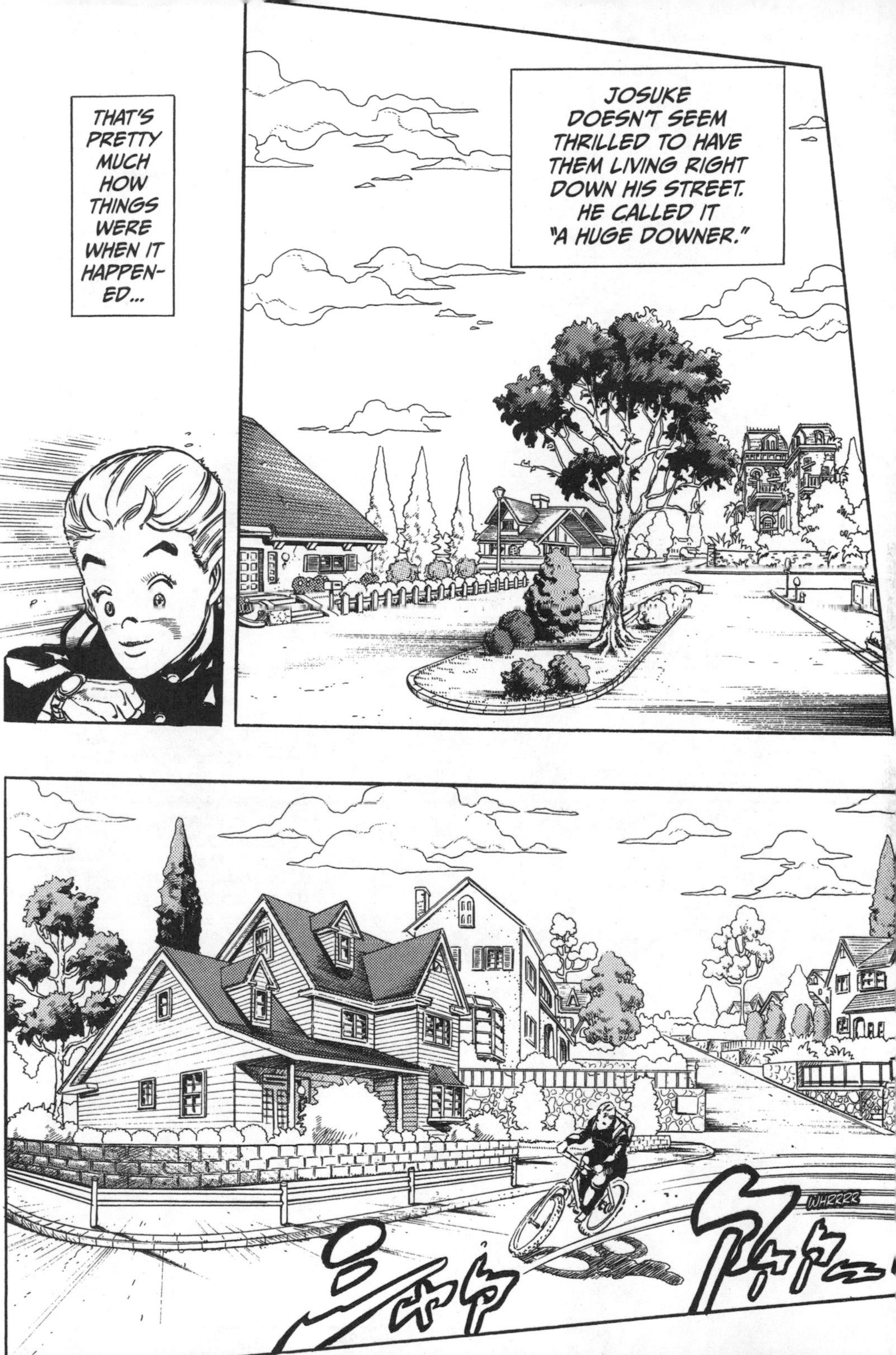
JOSUKE DOESN'T SEEM THRILLED TO HAVE THEM LIVING RIGHT DOWN HIS STREET. HE CALLED IT "A HUGE DOWNER."
THAT'S PRETTY MUCH HOW THINGS WERE WHEN IT HAPPEN-ED...
WHRRRR

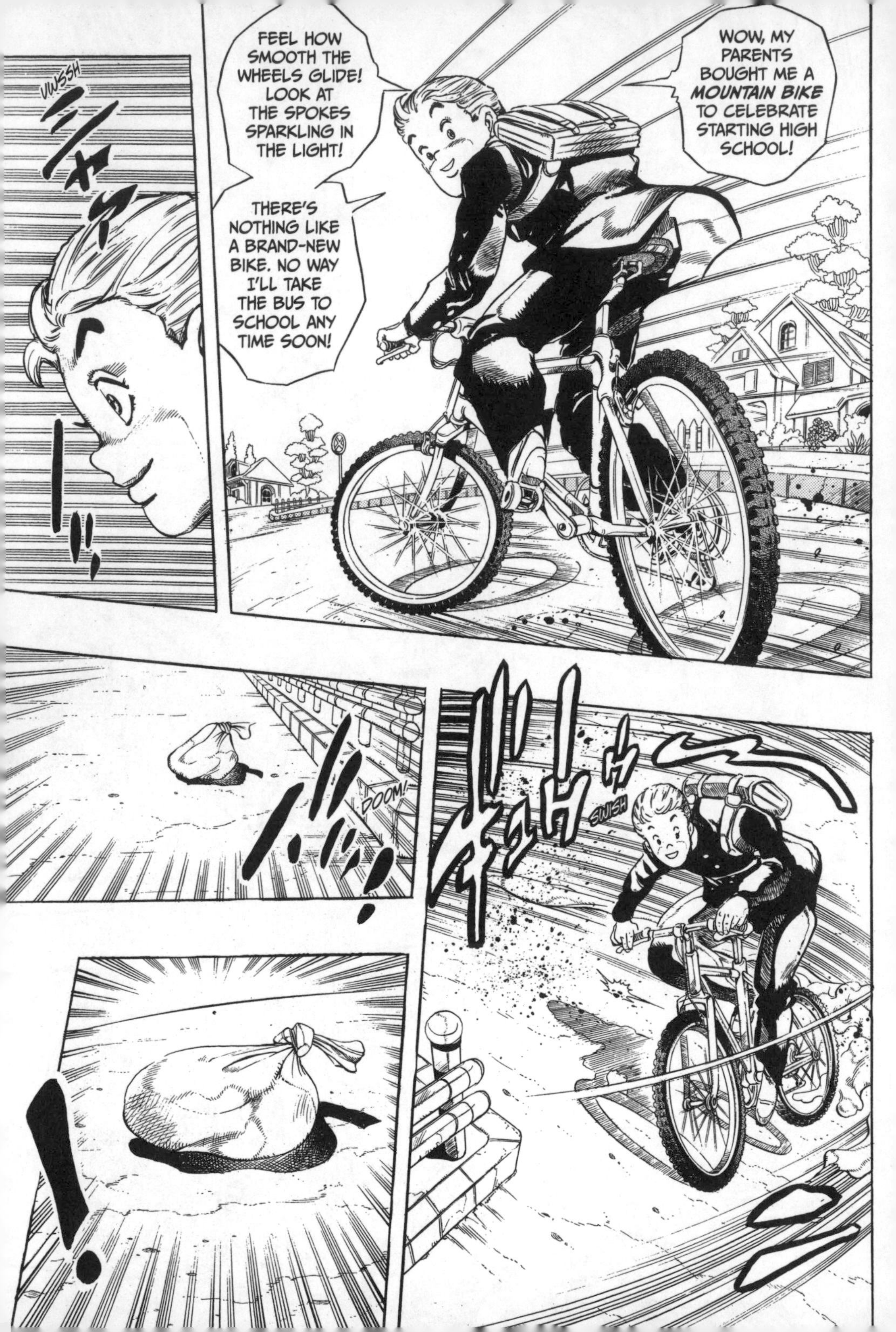
WOW, MY PARENTS BOUGHT ME A *MOUNTAIN BIKE* TO CELEBRATE STARTING HIGH SCHOOL!
FEEL HOW SMOOTH THE WHEELS GLIDE! LOOK AT THE SPOKES SPARKLING IN THE LIGHT!
THERE'S NOTHING LIKE A BRAND-NEW BIKE. NO WAY I'LL TAKE THE BUS TO SCHOOL ANY TIME SOON!
VWSSH
SWISH
DOOM!

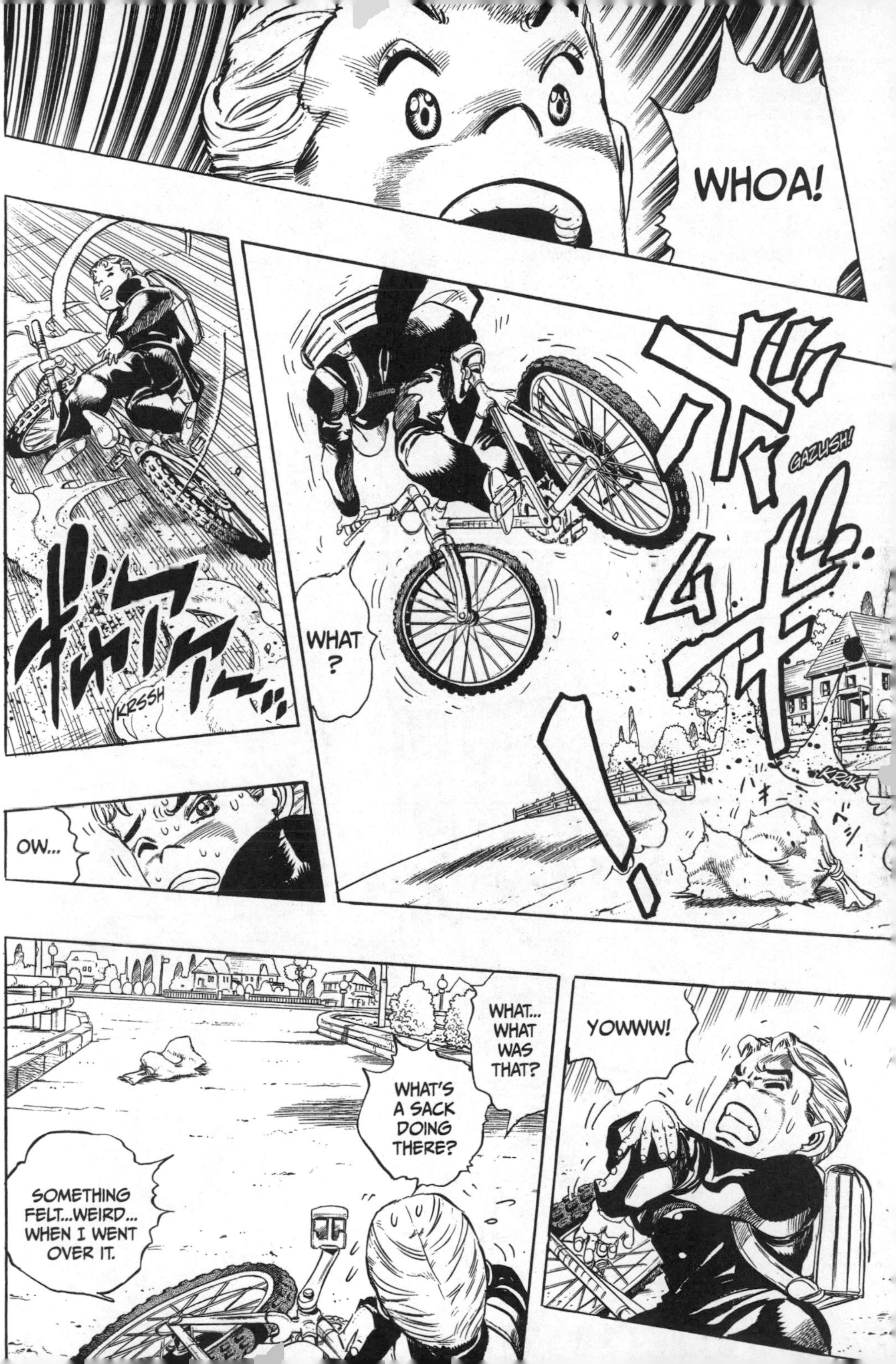
WHOA!
GAZUSH!
KRAK
WHAT?
KRSSH
OW...
YOWWW!
WHAT... WHAT WAS THAT?
WHAT'S A SACK DOING THERE?
SOMETHING FELT...WEIRD... WHEN I WENT OVER IT.

MEOW...
ME...
MEOWW!
M... EO... WW...
ME... OWWW!
ZUSHH
NO!
IT CAN'T BE...

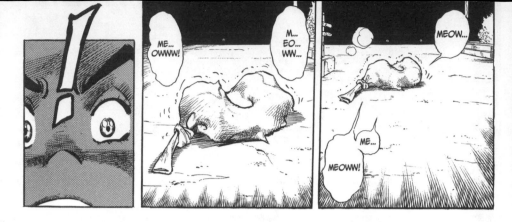

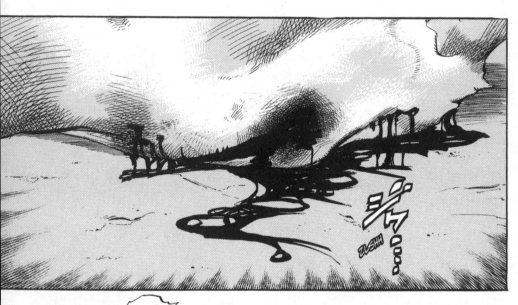

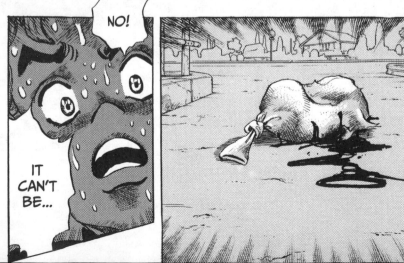

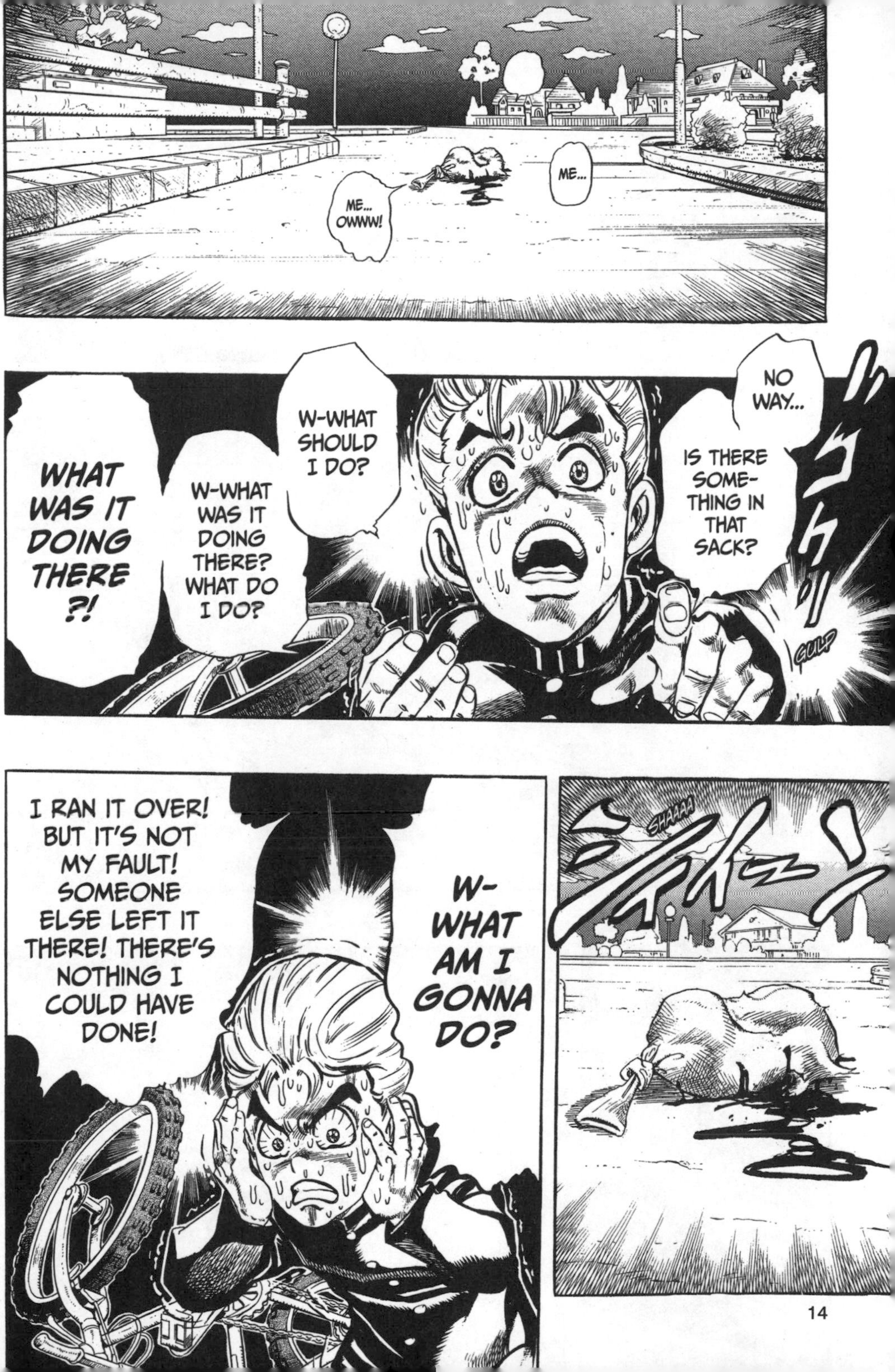

ME...
ME... OWWW!
NO WAY...
IS THERE SOME-THING IN THAT SACK?
GULP
W-WHAT SHOULD I DO?
W-WHAT WAS IT DOING THERE? WHAT DO I DO?
WHAT WAS IT DOING THERE?!
SHAAAA
W-WHAT AM I GONNA DO?
I RAN IT OVER! BUT IT'S NOT MY FAULT! SOMEONE ELSE LEFT IT THERE! THERE'S NOTHING I COULD HAVE DONE!

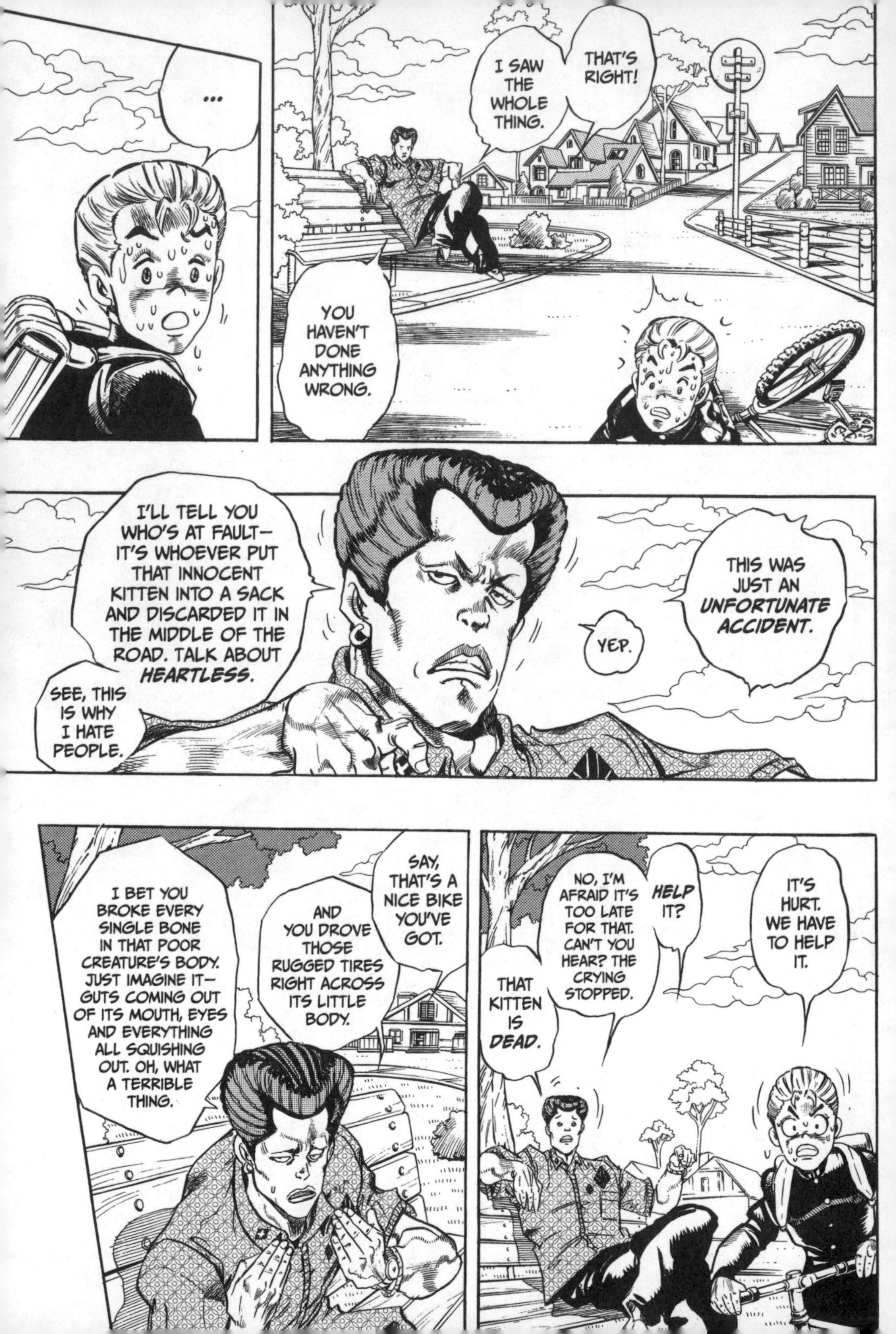
THAT'S RIGHT!
I SAW THE WHOLE THING.
YOU HAVEN'T DONE ANYTHING WRONG.
...
THIS WAS JUST AN *UNFORTUNATE ACCIDENT*.
YEP.
I'LL TELL YOU WHO'S AT FAULT— IT'S WHOEVER PUT THAT INNOCENT KITTEN INTO A SACK AND DISCARDED IT IN THE MIDDLE OF THE ROAD. TALK ABOUT *HEARTLESS*.
SEE, THIS IS WHY I HATE PEOPLE.
IT'S HURT. WE HAVE TO HELP IT.
HELP IT?
NO, I'M AFRAID IT'S TOO LATE FOR THAT. CAN'T YOU HEAR? THE CRYING STOPPED.
THAT KITTEN IS *DEAD*.
SAY, THAT'S A NICE BIKE YOU'VE GOT.
AND YOU DROVE THOSE RUGGED TIRES RIGHT ACROSS ITS LITTLE BODY.
I BET YOU BROKE EVERY SINGLE BONE IN THAT POOR CREATURE'S BODY. JUST IMAGINE IT— GUTS COMING OUT OF ITS MOUTH, EYES AND EVERYTHING ALL SQUISHING OUT. OH, WHAT A TERRIBLE THING.

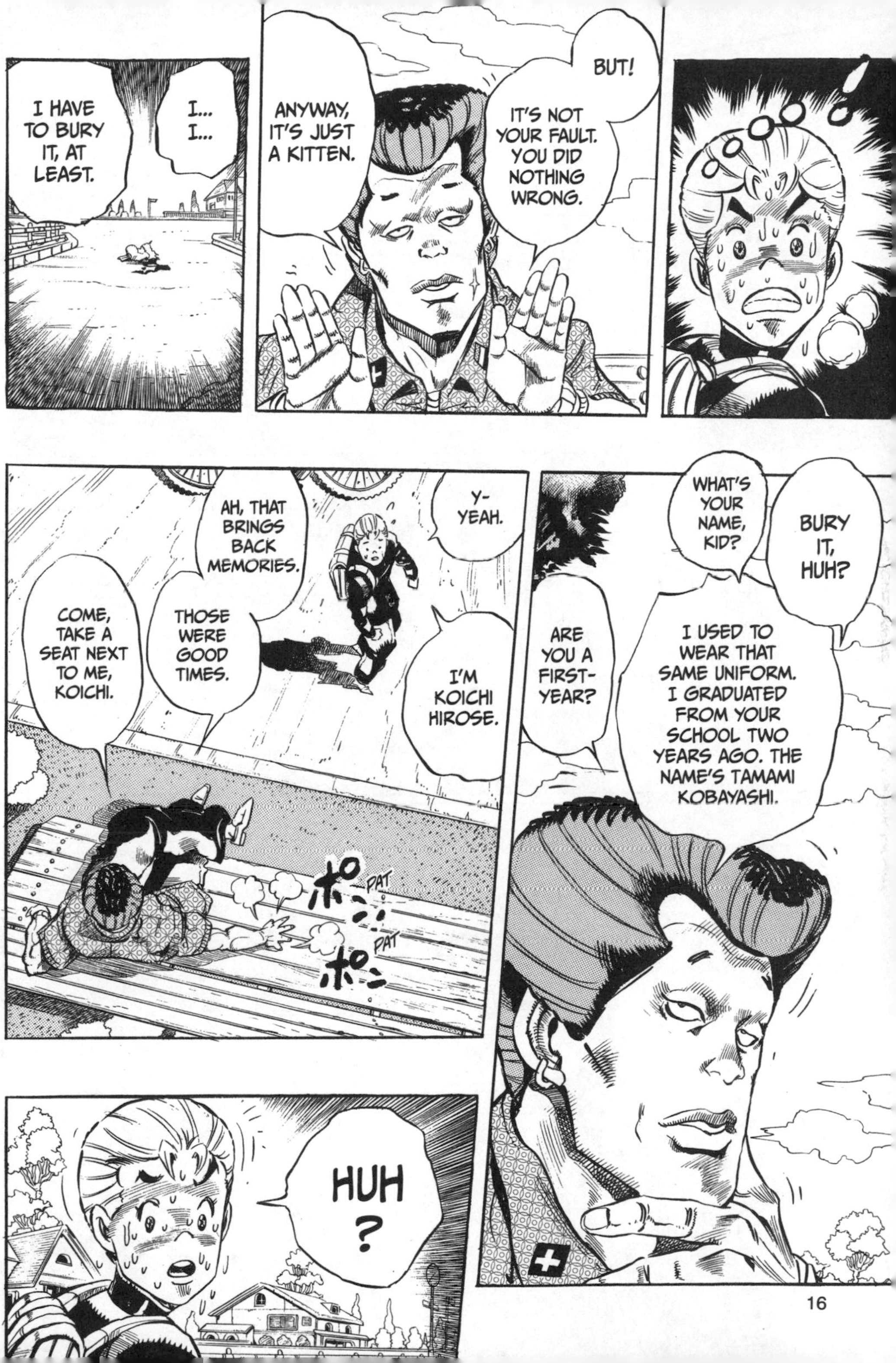
BUT!
IT'S NOT YOUR FAULT. YOU DID NOTHING WRONG.
ANYWAY, IT'S JUST A KITTEN.
I... I...
I HAVE TO BURY IT, AT LEAST.
BURY IT, HUH?
WHAT'S YOUR NAME, KID?
ARE YOU A FIRST-YEAR?
I USED TO WEAR THAT SAME UNIFORM. I GRADUATED FROM YOUR SCHOOL TWO YEARS AGO. THE NAME'S TAMAMI KOBAYASHI.
Y-YEAH.
I'M KOICHI HIROSE.
AH, THAT BRINGS BACK MEMORIES.
THOSE WERE GOOD TIMES.
COME, TAKE A SEAT NEXT TO ME, KOICHI.
ポン PAT
ポン PAT
HUH?

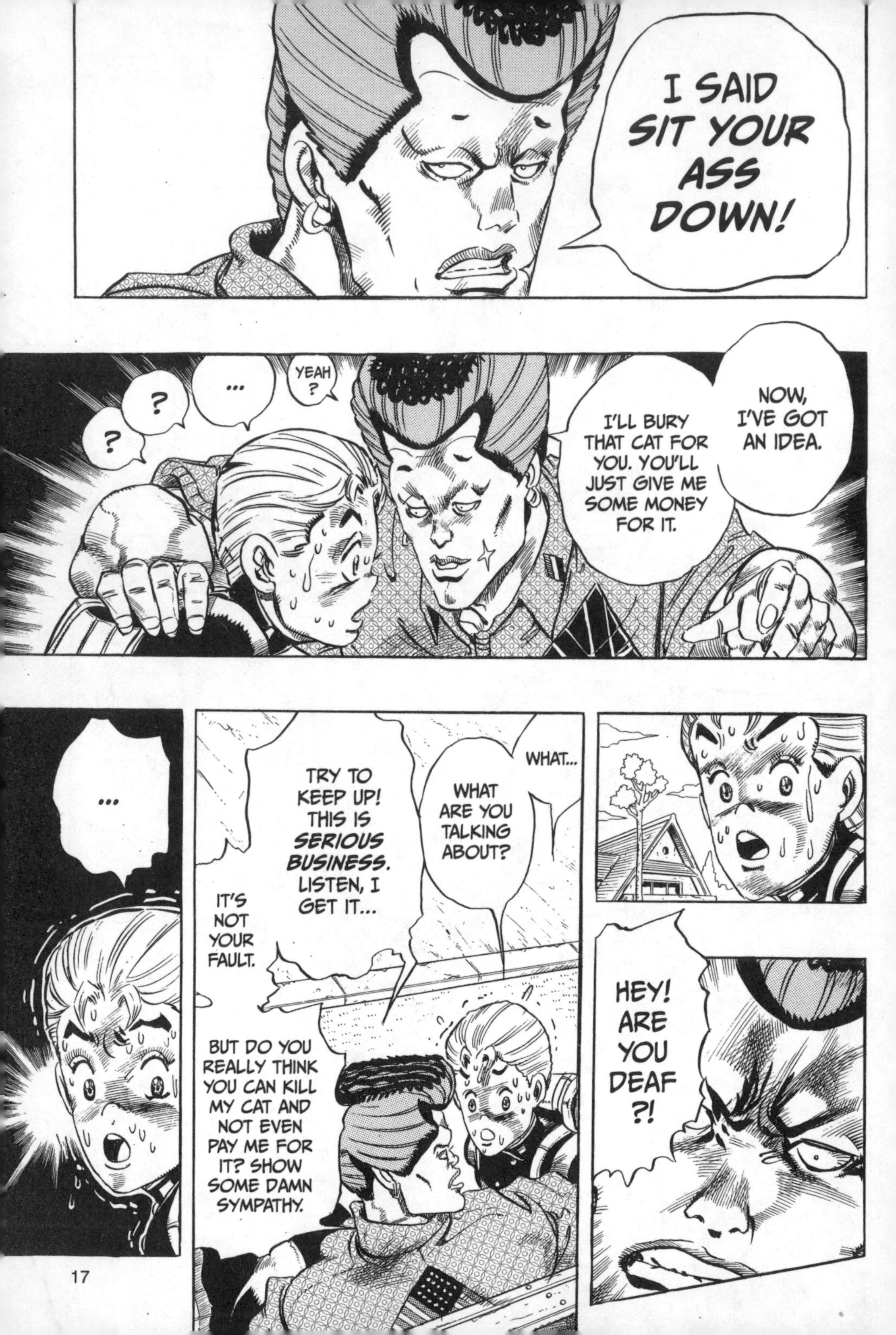

I SAID SIT YOUR ASS DOWN!
NOW, I'VE GOT AN IDEA.
I'LL BURY THAT CAT FOR YOU. YOU'LL JUST GIVE ME SOME MONEY FOR IT.
YEAH ?
...
?
?
HEY! ARE YOU DEAF ?!
WHAT...
WHAT ARE YOU TALKING ABOUT?
TRY TO KEEP UP! THIS IS SERIOUS BUSINESS. LISTEN, I GET IT...
IT'S NOT YOUR FAULT.
BUT DO YOU REALLY THINK YOU CAN KILL MY CAT AND NOT EVEN PAY ME FOR IT? SHOW SOME DAMN SYMPATHY.
...

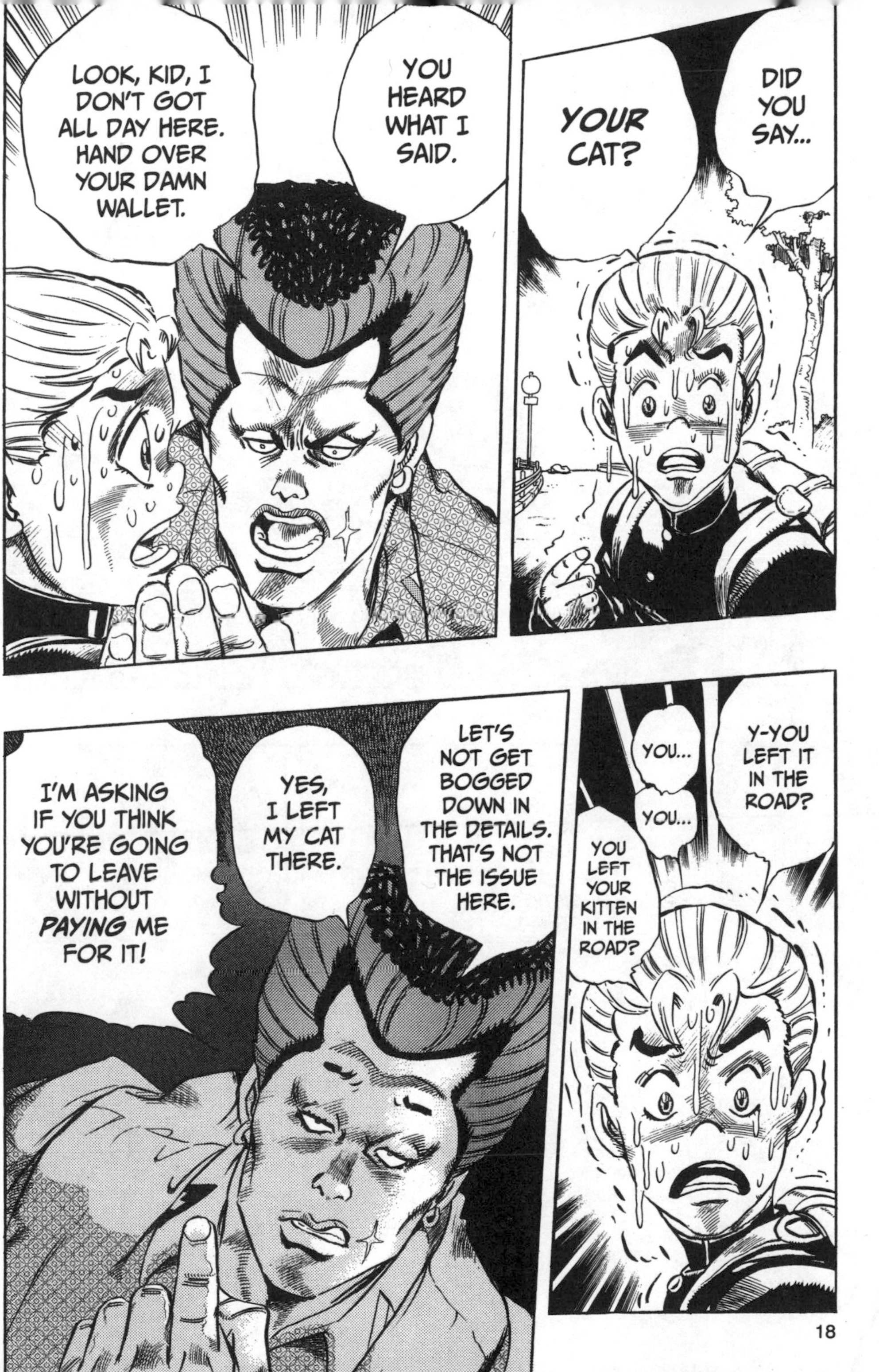
DID YOU SAY...
YOUR CAT?
YOU HEARD WHAT I SAID.
LOOK, KID, I DON'T GOT ALL DAY HERE. HAND OVER YOUR DAMN WALLET.
Y-YOU LEFT IT IN THE ROAD?
YOU...
YOU...
YOU LEFT YOUR KITTEN IN THE ROAD?
LET'S NOT GET BOGGED DOWN IN THE DETAILS. THAT'S NOT THE ISSUE HERE.
YES, I LEFT MY CAT THERE.
I'M ASKING IF YOU THINK YOU'RE GOING TO LEAVE WITHOUT PAYING ME FOR IT!

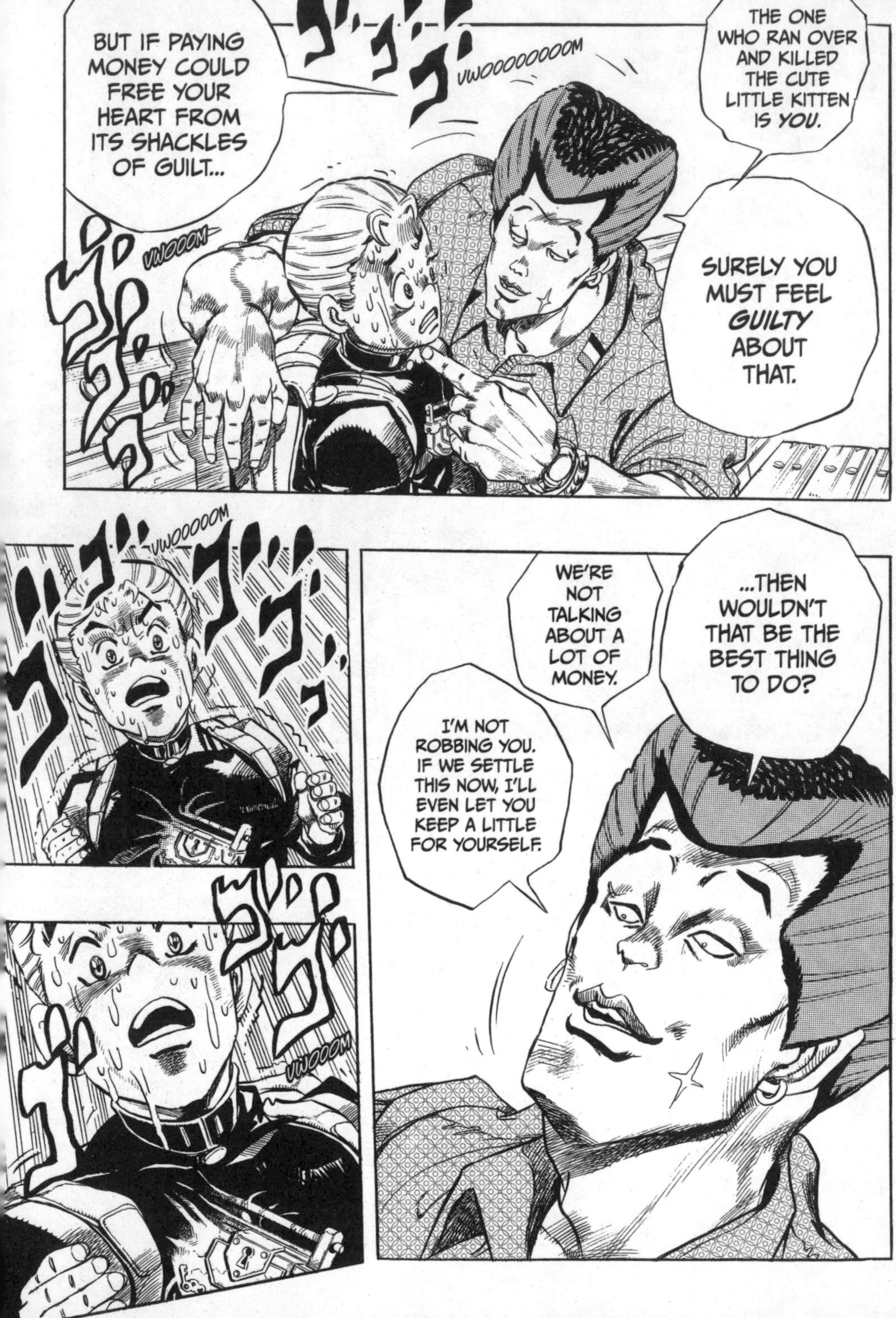
THE ONE WHO RAN OVER AND KILLED THE CUTE LITTLE KITTEN IS *YOU.*
VWOOOOOOOOOM
SURELY YOU MUST FEEL *GUILTY* ABOUT THAT.
BUT IF PAYING MONEY COULD FREE YOUR HEART FROM ITS SHACKLES OF GUILT...
VWOOOM
...THEN WOULDN'T THAT BE THE BEST THING TO DO?
WE'RE NOT TALKING ABOUT A LOT OF MONEY.
I'M NOT ROBBING YOU. IF WE SETTLE THIS NOW, I'LL EVEN LET YOU KEEP A LITTLE FOR YOURSELF.
VWOOOOOM
VWOOOM

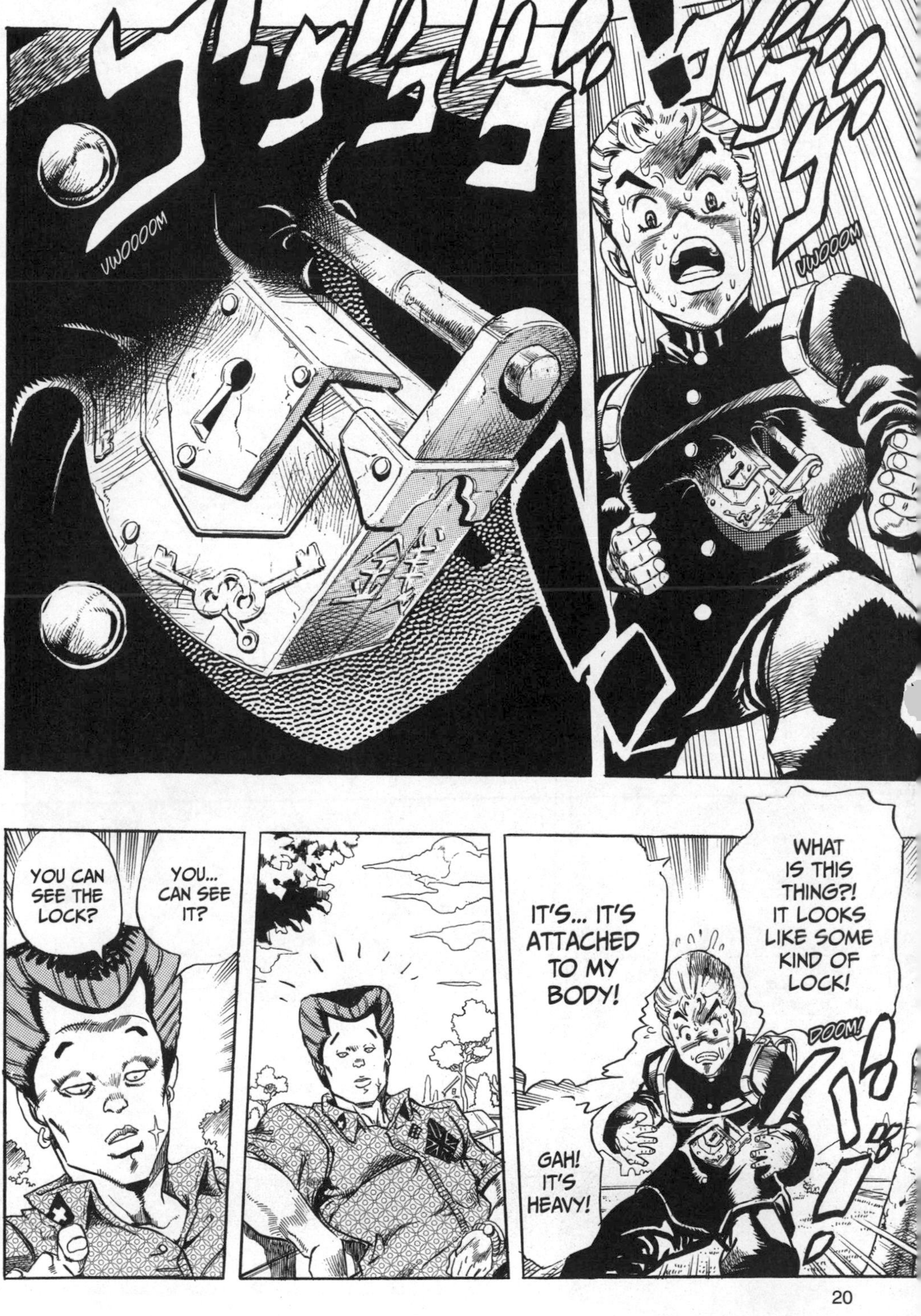
VWOOOM
VWOOOOM
WHAT IS THIS THING?! IT LOOKS LIKE SOME KIND OF LOCK!
IT'S... IT'S ATTACHED TO MY BODY!
DOOM!
GAH! IT'S HEAVY!
YOU... CAN SEE IT?
YOU CAN SEE THE LOCK?

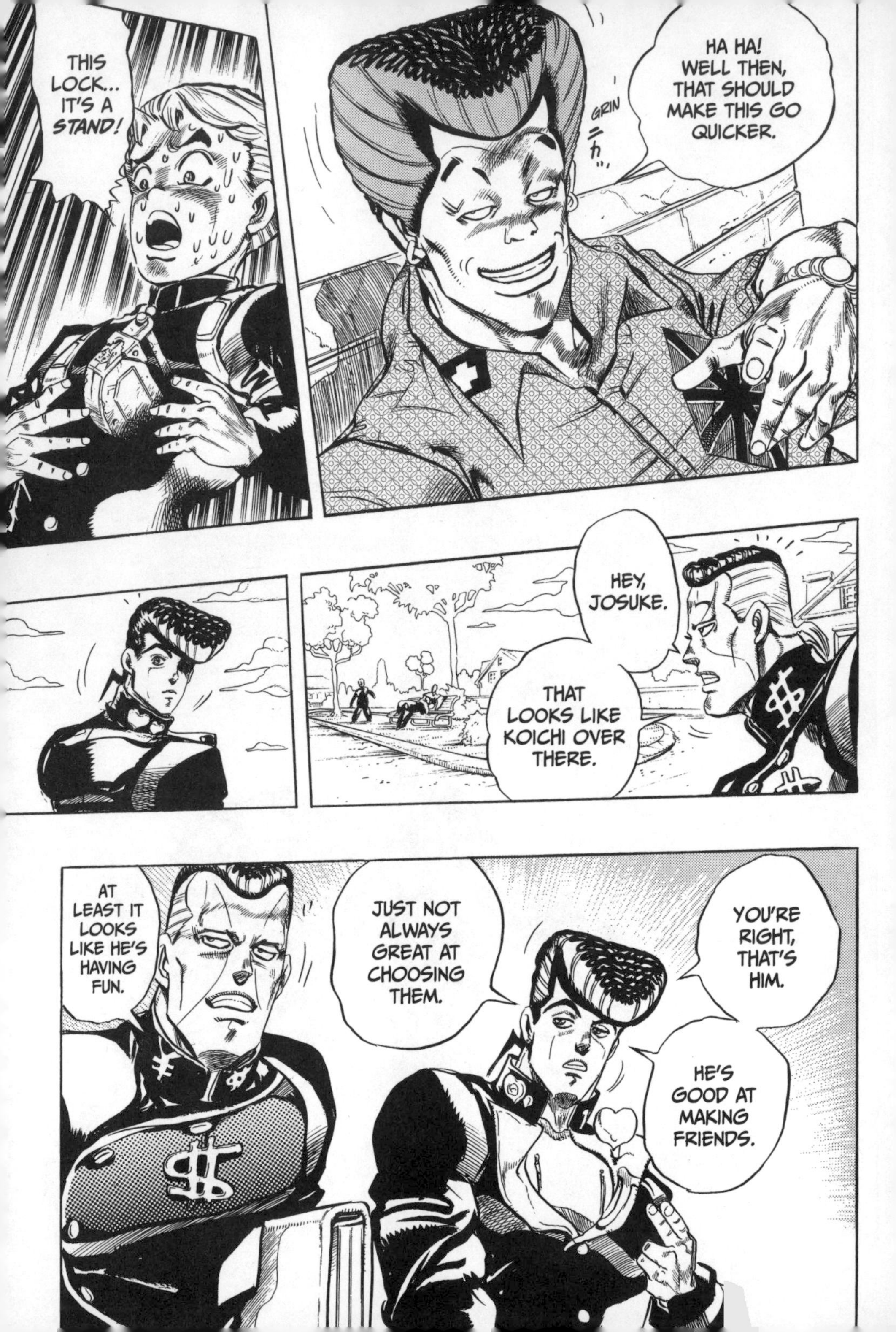
HA HA! WELL THEN, THAT SHOULD MAKE THIS GO QUICKER.
GRIN
THIS LOCK... IT'S A STAND!
HEY, JOSUKE.
THAT LOOKS LIKE KOICHI OVER THERE.
YOU'RE RIGHT, THAT'S HIM.
HE'S GOOD AT MAKING FRIENDS.
JUST NOT ALWAYS GREAT AT CHOOSING THEM.
AT LEAST IT LOOKS LIKE HE'S HAVING FUN.

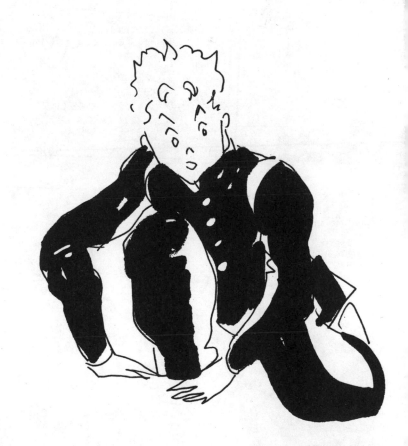

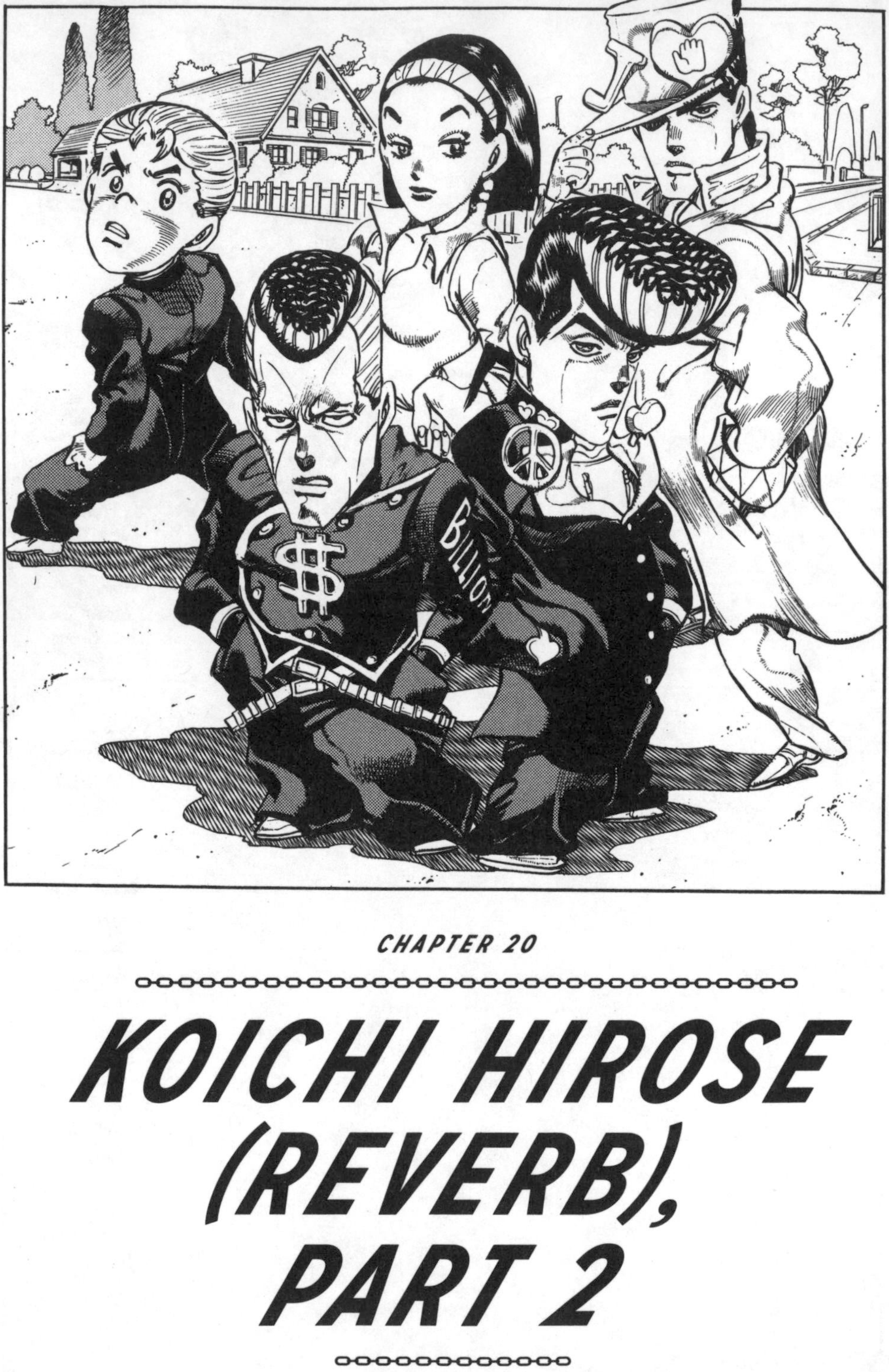
BILLION

CHAPTER 20

KOICHI HIROSE (REVERB), PART 2

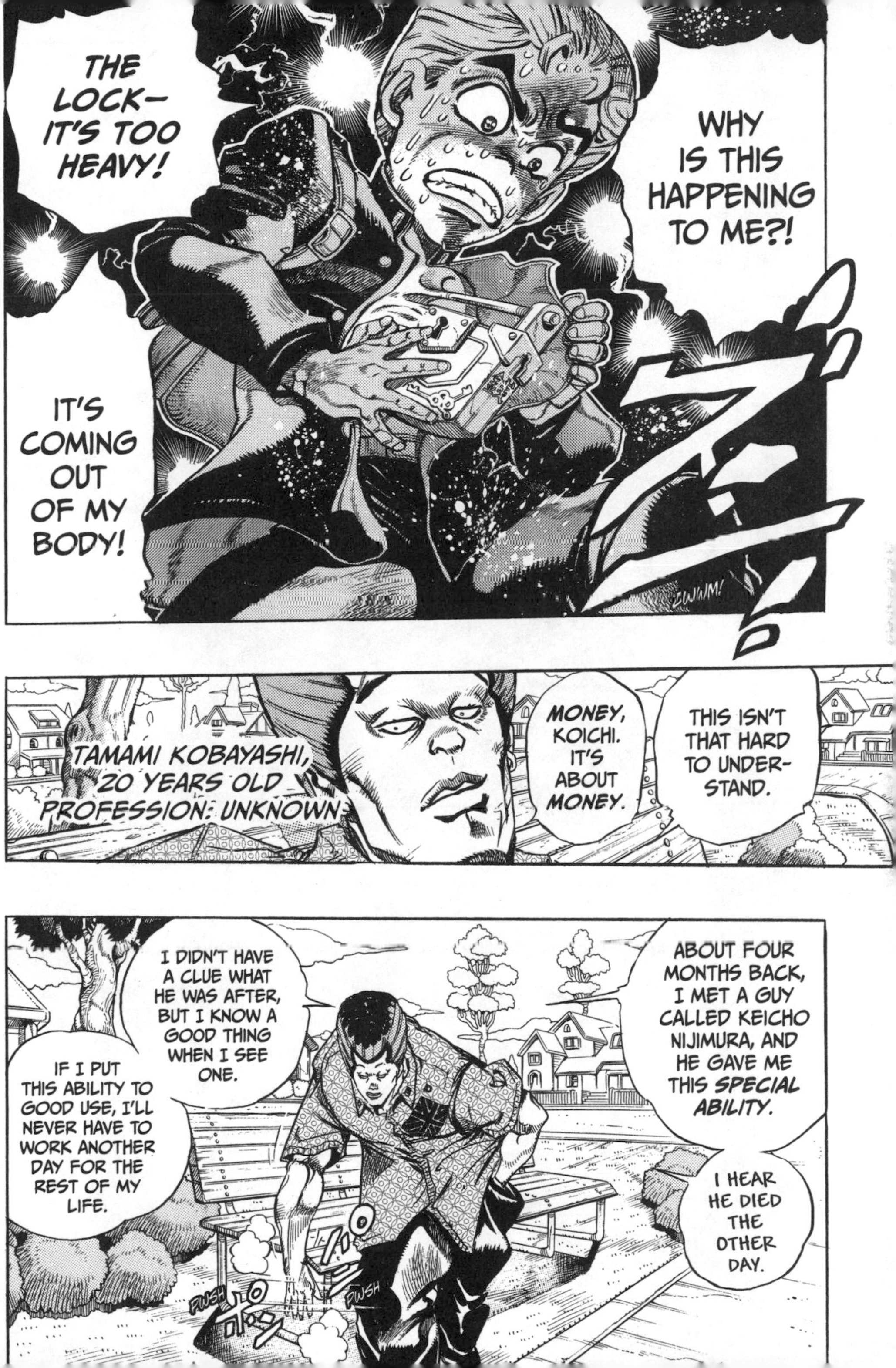
WHY IS THIS HAPPENING TO ME?!
THE LOCK— IT'S TOO HEAVY!
IT'S COMING OUT OF MY BODY!
THIS ISN'T THAT HARD TO UNDERSTAND.
MONEY, KOICHI. IT'S ABOUT MONEY.
TAMAMI KOBAYASHI, 20 YEARS OLD PROFESSION: UNKNOWN
ABOUT FOUR MONTHS BACK, I MET A GUY CALLED KEICHO NIJIMURA, AND HE GAVE ME THIS SPECIAL ABILITY.
I HEAR HE DIED THE OTHER DAY.
I DIDN'T HAVE A CLUE WHAT HE WAS AFTER, BUT I KNOW A GOOD THING WHEN I SEE ONE.
IF I PUT THIS ABILITY TO GOOD USE, I'LL NEVER HAVE TO WORK ANOTHER DAY FOR THE REST OF MY LIFE.
PWSH
PWSH

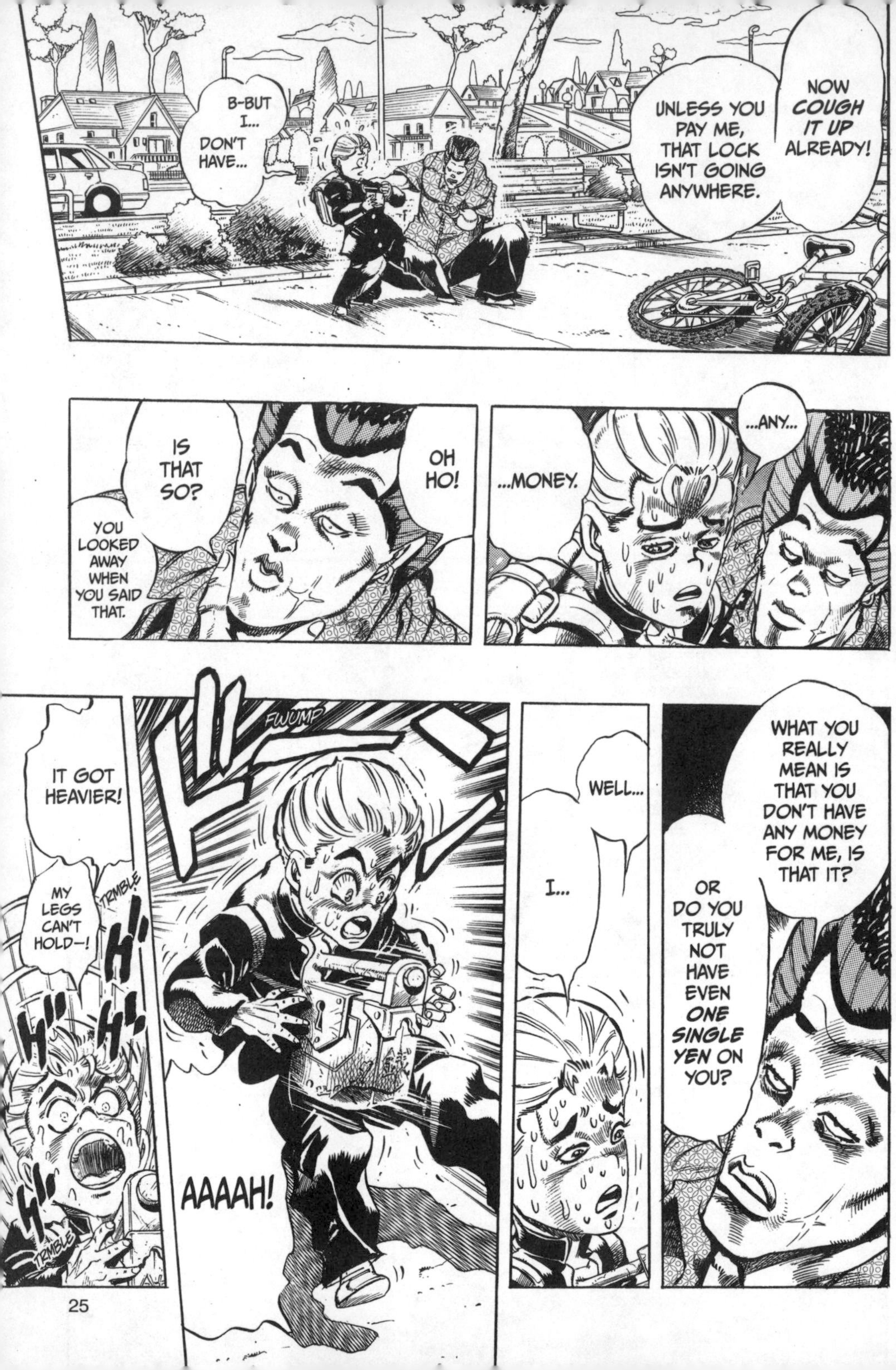
NOW *COUGH IT UP* ALREADY!
UNLESS YOU PAY ME, THAT LOCK ISN'T GOING ANYWHERE.
B-BUT I... DON'T HAVE...
...ANY...
...MONEY.
OH HO!
IS THAT SO?
YOU LOOKED AWAY WHEN YOU SAID THAT.
WHAT YOU REALLY MEAN IS THAT YOU DON'T HAVE ANY MONEY FOR ME, IS THAT IT?
OR DO YOU TRULY NOT HAVE EVEN *ONE SINGLE YEN* ON YOU?
WELL...
I...
FWUMP
AAAAH!
IT GOT HEAVIER!
MY LEGS CAN'T HOLD—!
TRMBLE
TRMBLE

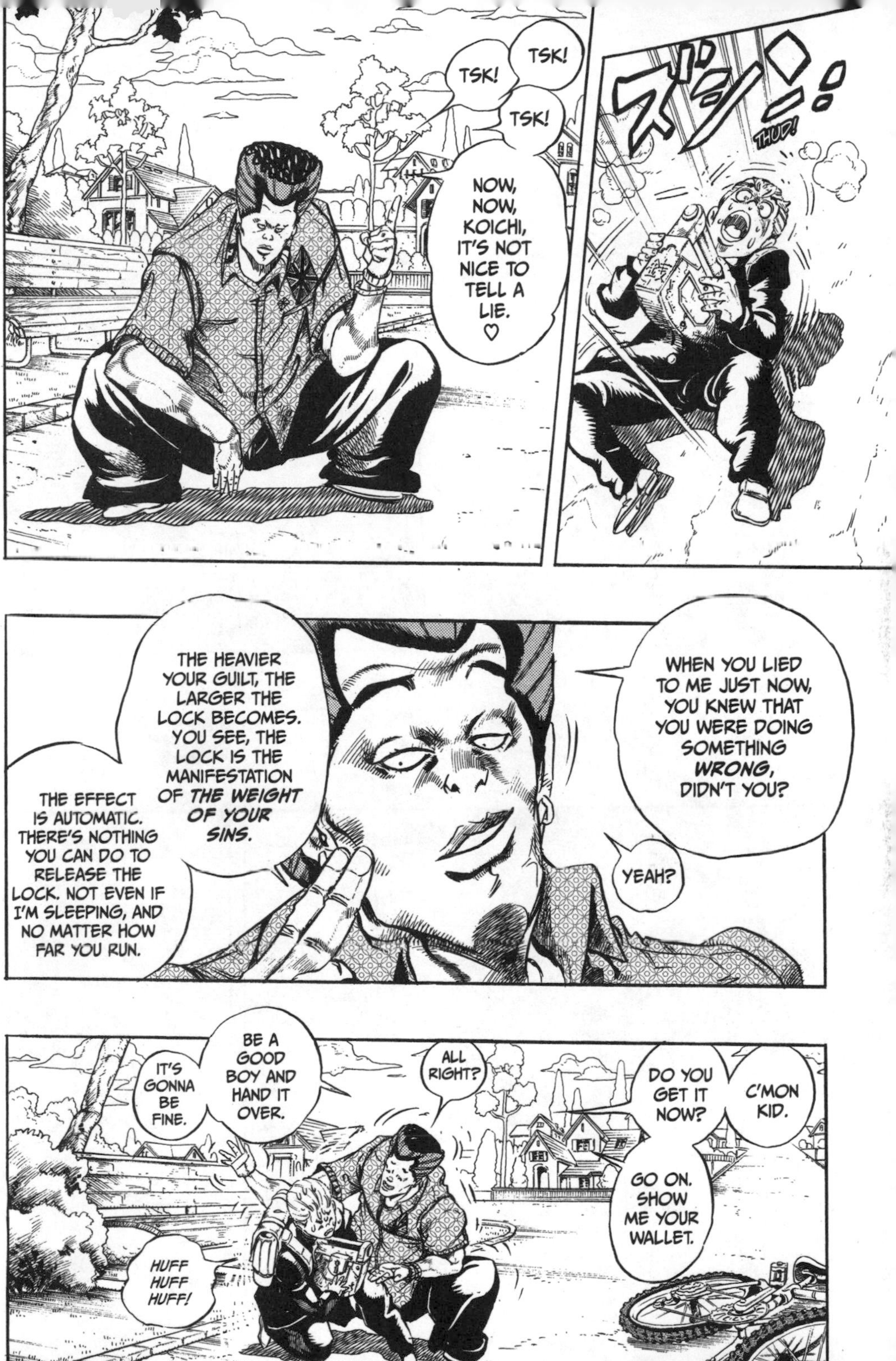
ズシン！
THUD!
TSK!
TSK!
TSK!
NOW, NOW, KOICHI, IT'S NOT NICE TO TELL A LIE. ♡
WHEN YOU LIED TO ME JUST NOW, YOU KNEW THAT YOU WERE DOING SOMETHING WRONG, DIDN'T YOU?
YEAH?
THE HEAVIER YOUR GUILT, THE LARGER THE LOCK BECOMES. YOU SEE, THE LOCK IS THE MANIFESTATION OF THE WEIGHT OF YOUR SINS.
THE EFFECT IS AUTOMATIC. THERE'S NOTHING YOU CAN DO TO RELEASE THE LOCK. NOT EVEN IF I'M SLEEPING, AND NO MATTER HOW FAR YOU RUN.
C'MON KID.
DO YOU GET IT NOW?
GO ON. SHOW ME YOUR WALLET.
ALL RIGHT?
BE A GOOD BOY AND HAND IT OVER.
IT'S GONNA BE FINE.
HUFF HUFF HUFF!

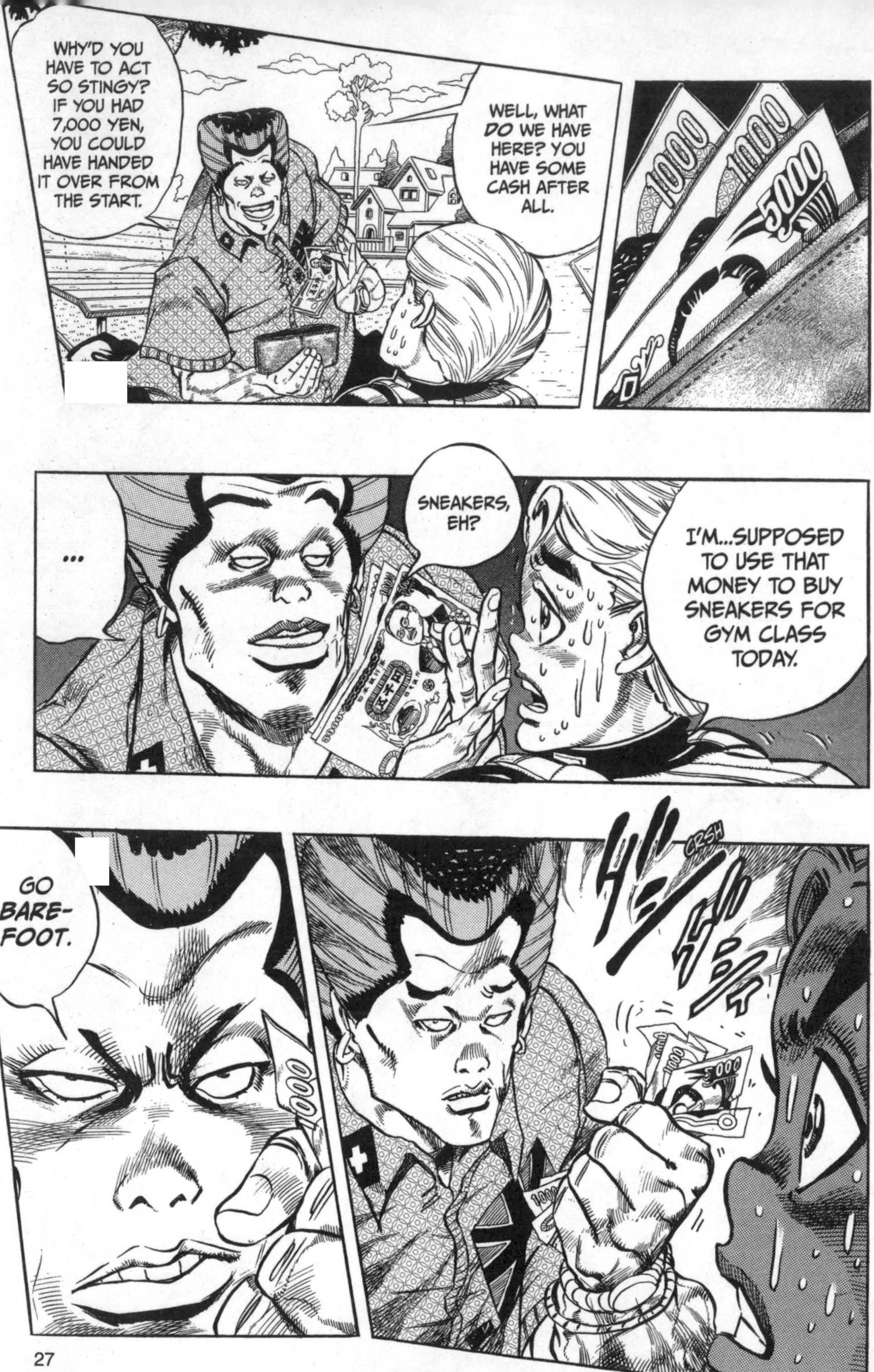
WELL, WHAT DO WE HAVE HERE? YOU HAVE SOME CASH AFTER ALL.
WHY'D YOU HAVE TO ACT SO STINGY? IF YOU HAD 7,000 YEN, YOU COULD HAVE HANDED IT OVER FROM THE START.
I'M...SUPPOSED TO USE THAT MONEY TO BUY SNEAKERS FOR GYM CLASS TODAY.
SNEAKERS, EH?
...
CRSH
GO BARE-FOOT.

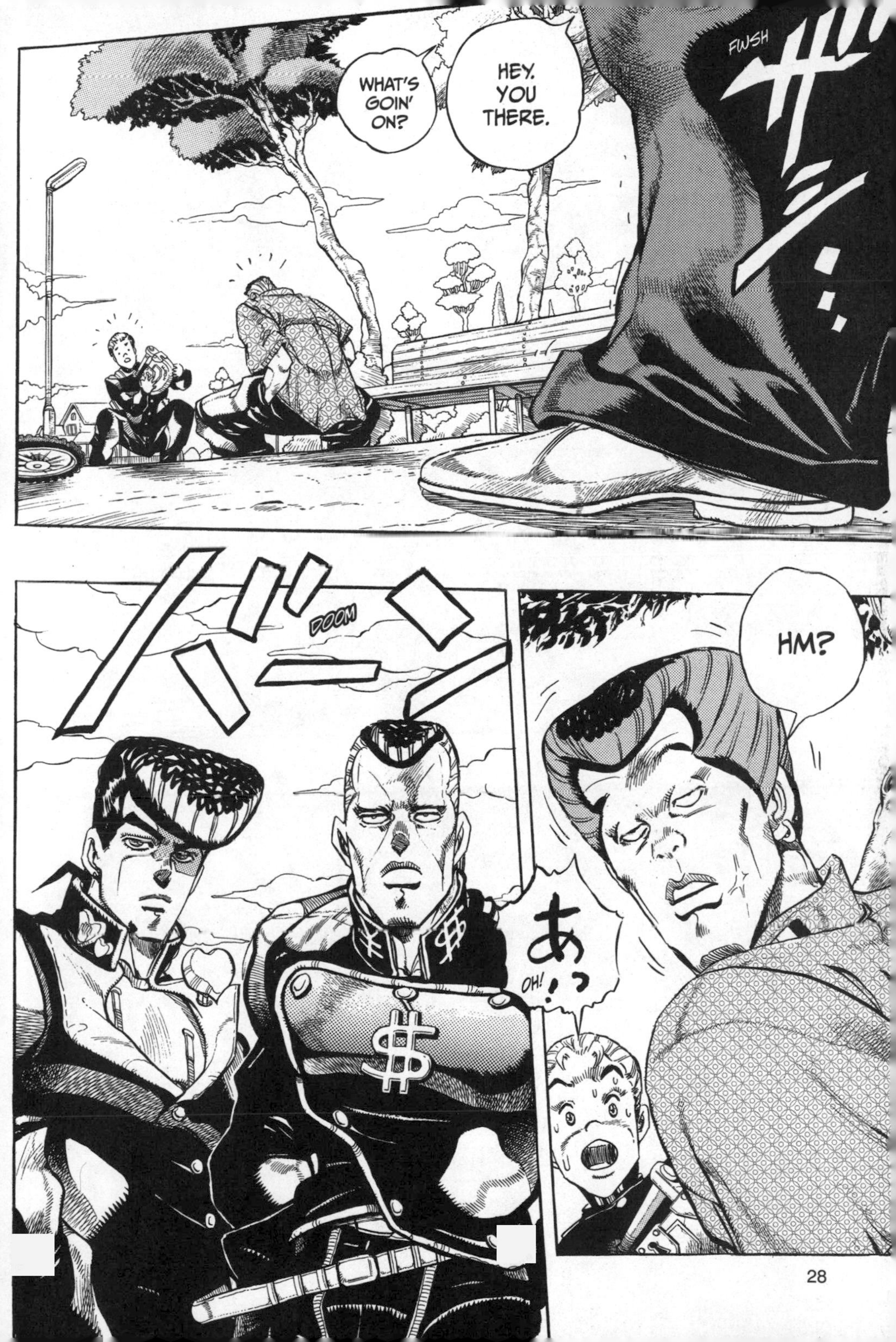
FWSH
HEY. YOU THERE.
WHAT'S GOIN' ON?
HM?
あっ
OH!
バーン
DOOM

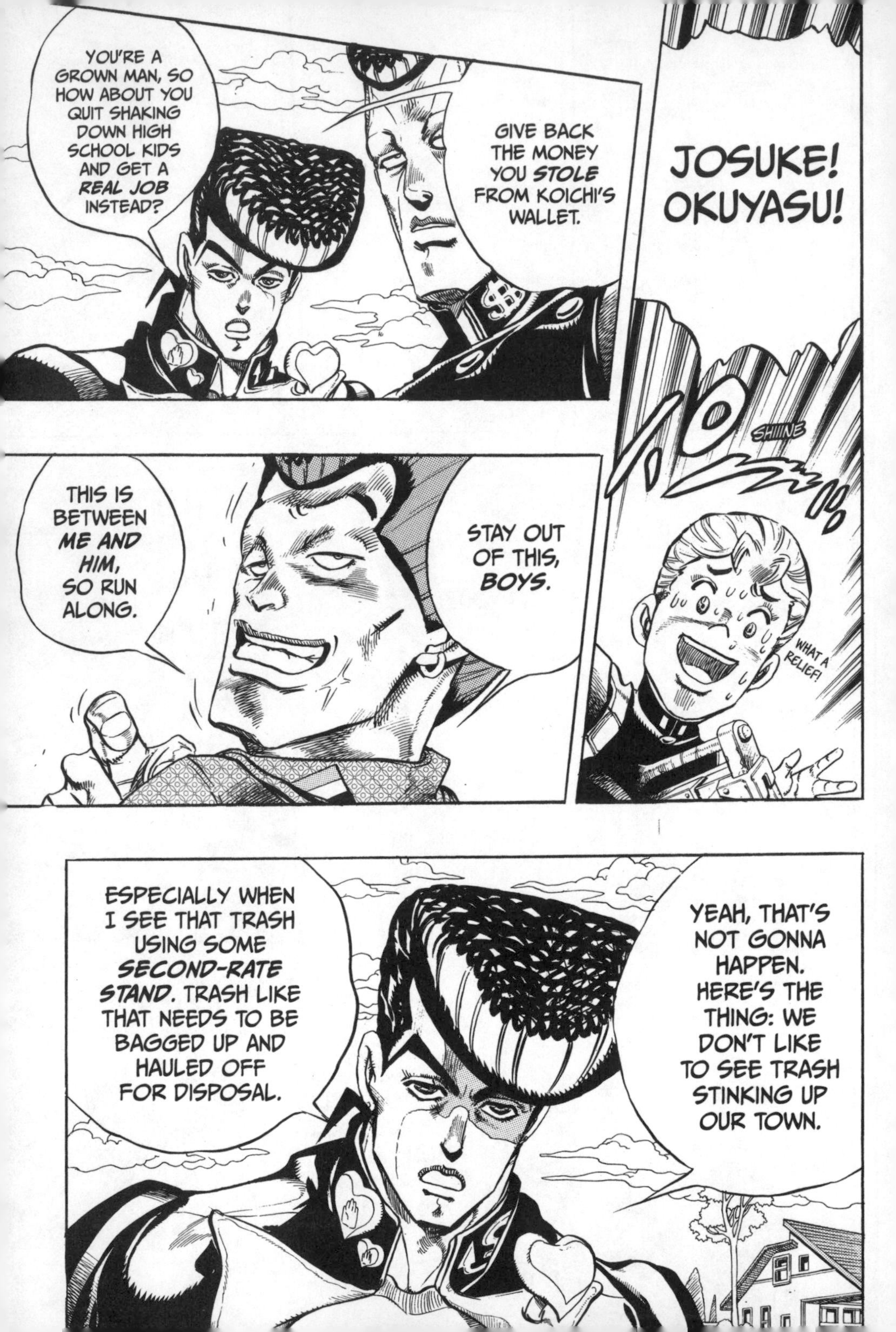
JOSUKE! OKUYASU!
SHIIINE
WHAT A RELIEF!
GIVE BACK THE MONEY YOU STOLE FROM KOICHI'S WALLET.
YOU'RE A GROWN MAN, SO HOW ABOUT YOU QUIT SHAKING DOWN HIGH SCHOOL KIDS AND GET A REAL JOB INSTEAD?
STAY OUT OF THIS, BOYS.
THIS IS BETWEEN ME AND HIM, SO RUN ALONG.
YEAH, THAT'S NOT GONNA HAPPEN. HERE'S THE THING: WE DON'T LIKE TO SEE TRASH STINKING UP OUR TOWN.
ESPECIALLY WHEN I SEE THAT TRASH USING SOME SECOND-RATE STAND. TRASH LIKE THAT NEEDS TO BE BAGGED UP AND HAULED OFF FOR DISPOSAL.

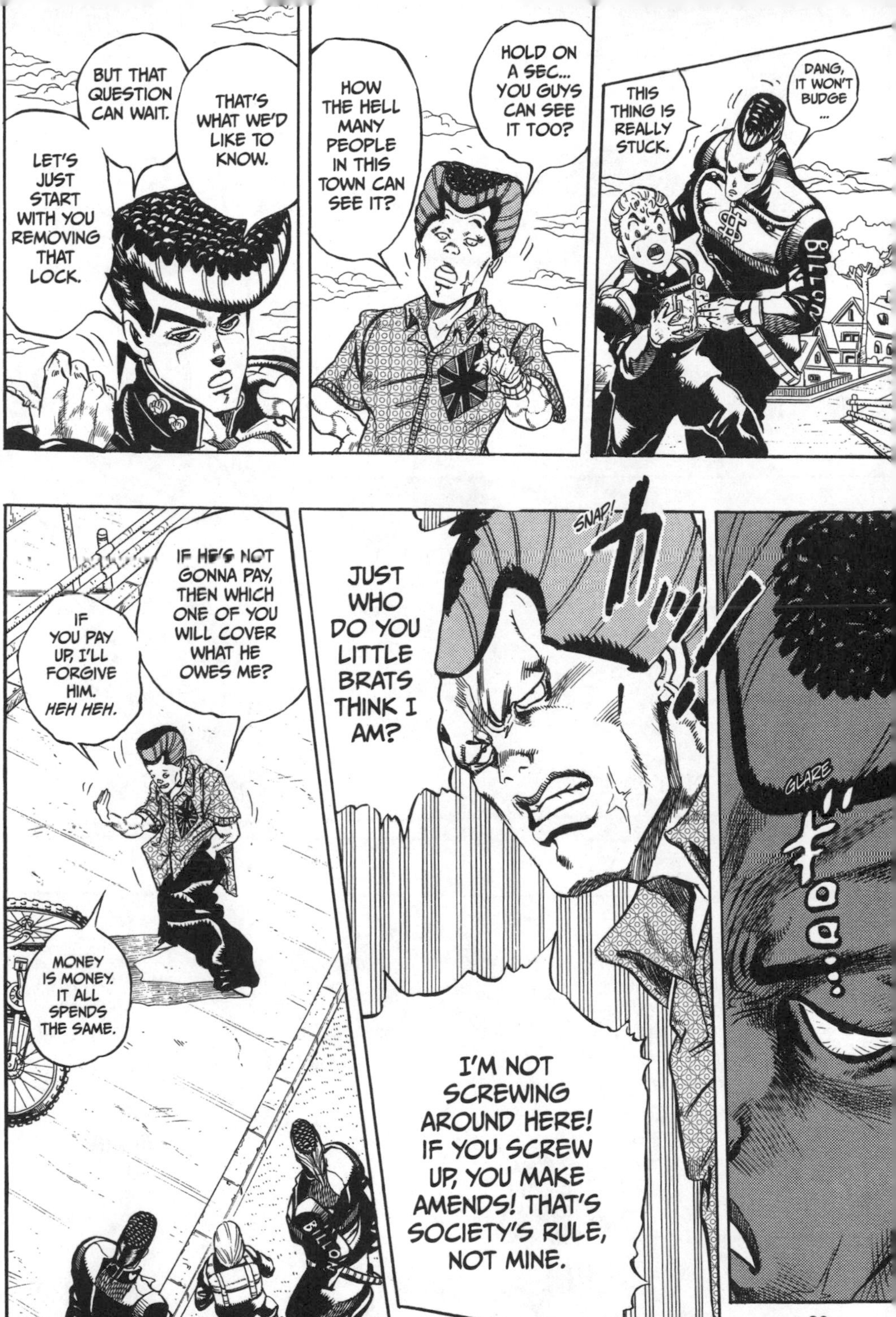
DANG, IT WON'T BUDGE ...
THIS THING IS REALLY STUCK.
HOLD ON A SEC... YOU GUYS CAN SEE IT TOO?
HOW THE HELL MANY PEOPLE IN THIS TOWN CAN SEE IT?
THAT'S WHAT WE'D LIKE TO KNOW.
BUT THAT QUESTION CAN WAIT.
LET'S JUST START WITH YOU REMOVING THAT LOCK.
GLARE
SNAP!
JUST WHO DO YOU LITTLE BRATS THINK I AM?
I'M NOT SCREWING AROUND HERE! IF YOU SCREW UP, YOU MAKE AMENDS! THAT'S SOCIETY'S RULE, NOT MINE.
IF HE'S NOT GONNA PAY, THEN WHICH ONE OF YOU WILL COVER WHAT HE OWES ME?
IF YOU PAY UP, I'LL FORGIVE HIM. *HEH HEH.*
MONEY IS MONEY. IT ALL SPENDS THE SAME.

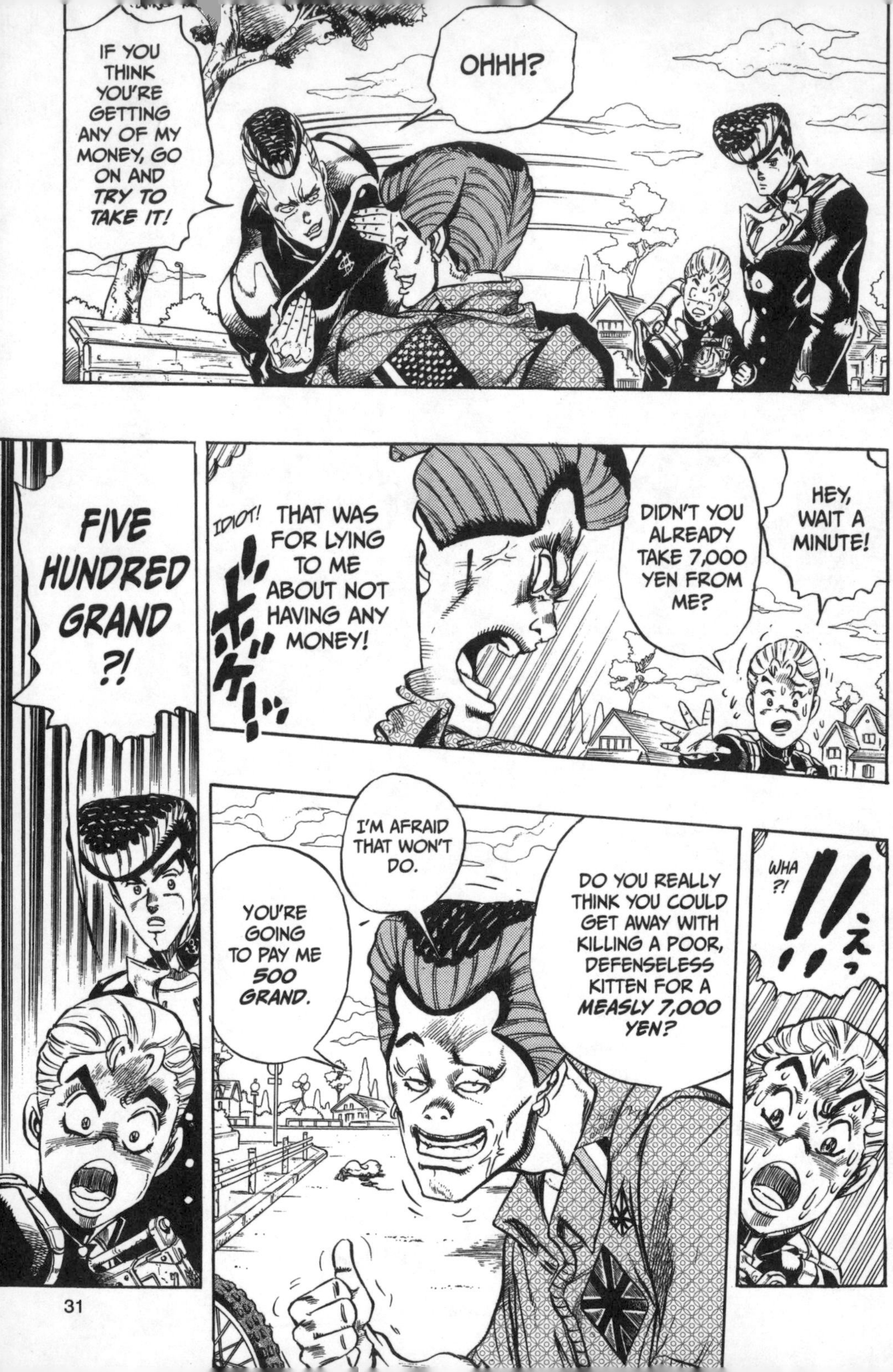
OHHH?
IF YOU THINK YOU'RE GETTING ANY OF MY MONEY, GO ON AND *TRY TO TAKE IT!*
HEY, WAIT A MINUTE!
DIDN'T YOU ALREADY TAKE 7,000 YEN FROM ME?
THAT WAS FOR LYING TO ME ABOUT NOT HAVING ANY MONEY!
IDIOT!
ボゲッ
WHA ?!
えっ
DO YOU REALLY THINK YOU COULD GET AWAY WITH KILLING A POOR, DEFENSELESS KITTEN FOR A *MEASLY* 7,000 YEN?
I'M AFRAID THAT WON'T DO.
YOU'RE GOING TO PAY ME *500 GRAND.*
FIVE HUNDRED GRAND ?!

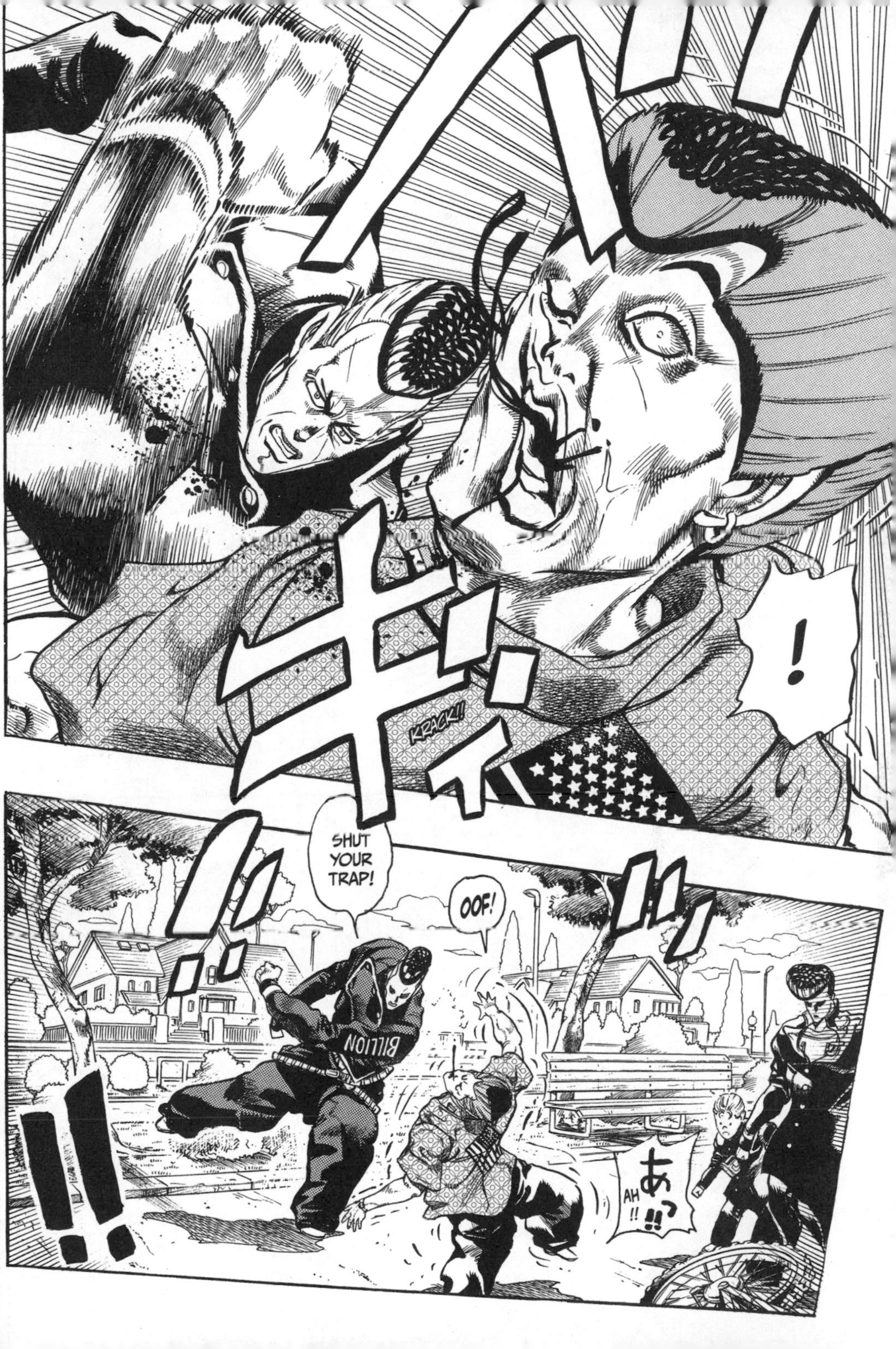
!
ギィ
KRACK!!
OOF!
SHUT YOUR TRAP!
あっ!!
AH!!
!!

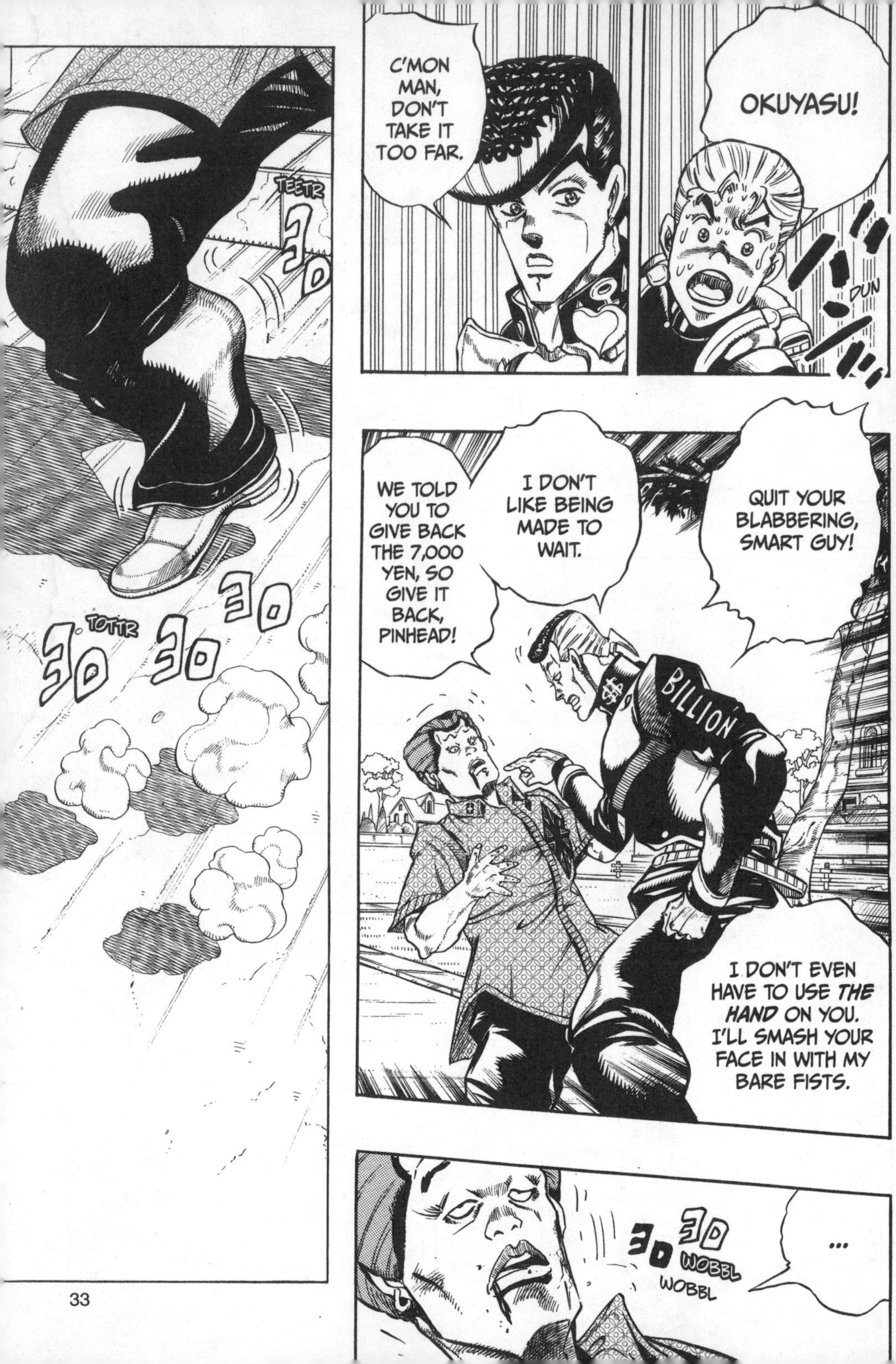
OKUYASU!
DUN
C'MON MAN, DON'T TAKE IT TOO FAR.
QUIT YOUR BLABBERING, SMART GUY!
I DON'T LIKE BEING MADE TO WAIT.
WE TOLD YOU TO GIVE BACK THE 7,000 YEN, SO GIVE IT BACK, PINHEAD!
BILLION
I DON'T EVEN HAVE TO USE *THE HAND* ON YOU. I'LL SMASH YOUR FACE IN WITH MY BARE FISTS.
...
WOBBL
WOBBL
TEETR
TOTTR

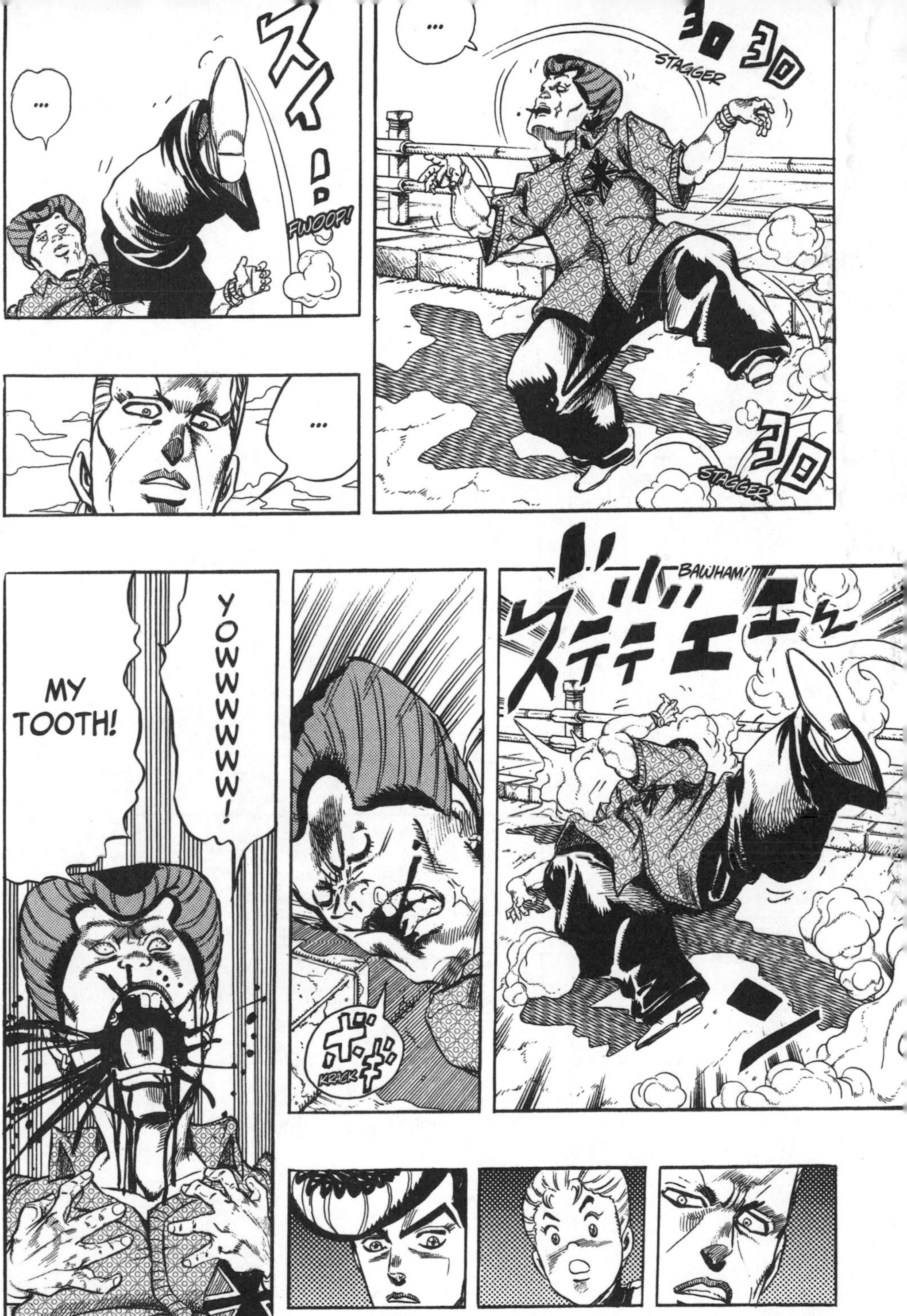
...
STAGGER
STAGGER
...
FWOOP!
...
BAWHAM!
KRACK
YOWWWWWWW!
MY TOOTH!

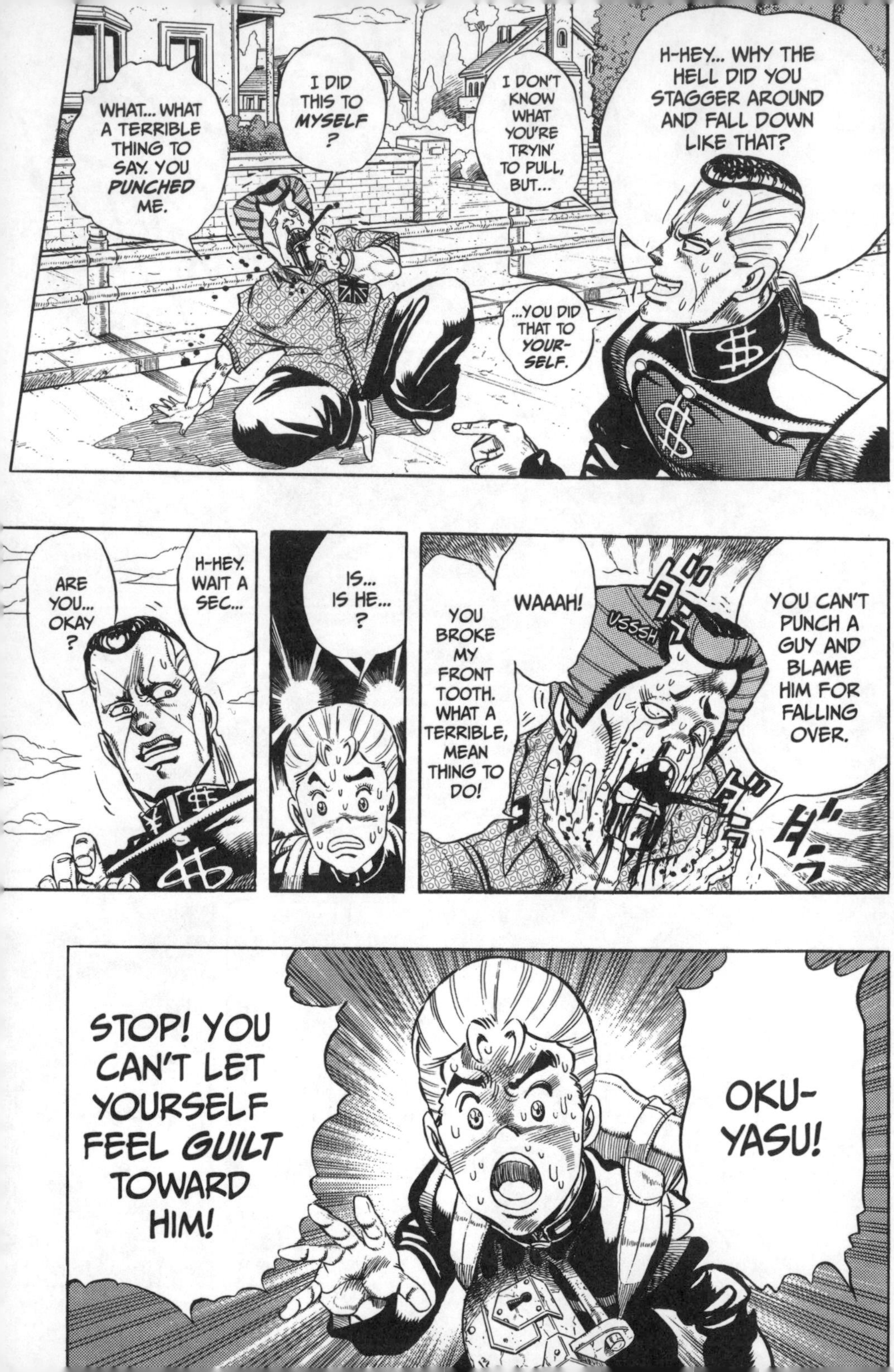
H-HEY... WHY THE HELL DID YOU STAGGER AROUND AND FALL DOWN LIKE THAT?
I DON'T KNOW WHAT YOU'RE TRYIN' TO PULL, BUT...
...YOU DID THAT TO YOURSELF.
I DID THIS TO MYSELF?
WHAT... WHAT A TERRIBLE THING TO SAY. YOU PUNCHED ME.
YOU CAN'T PUNCH A GUY AND BLAME HIM FOR FALLING OVER.
VSSSH
WAAAH!
YOU BROKE MY FRONT TOOTH. WHAT A TERRIBLE, MEAN THING TO DO!
IS... IS HE...?
H-HEY. WAIT A SEC...
ARE YOU... OKAY?
OKU-YASU!
STOP! YOU CAN'T LET YOURSELF FEEL GUILT TOWARD HIM!

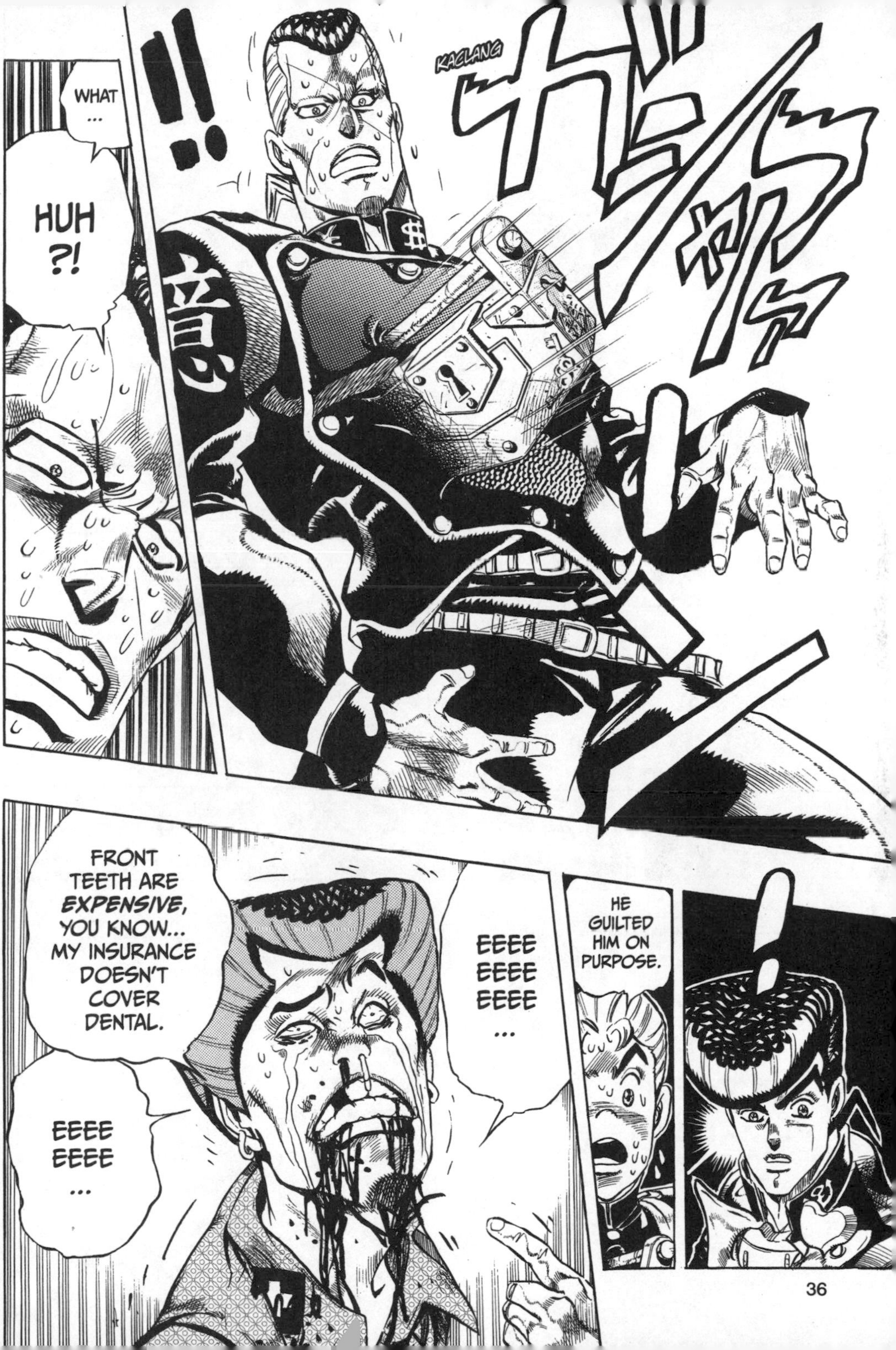
KACLANG
!!
WHAT ...
HUH ?!
!
HE GUILTED HIM ON PURPOSE.
FRONT TEETH ARE *EXPENSIVE*, YOU KNOW... MY INSURANCE DOESN'T COVER DENTAL.
EEEE EEEE EEEE ...
EEEE EEEE ...

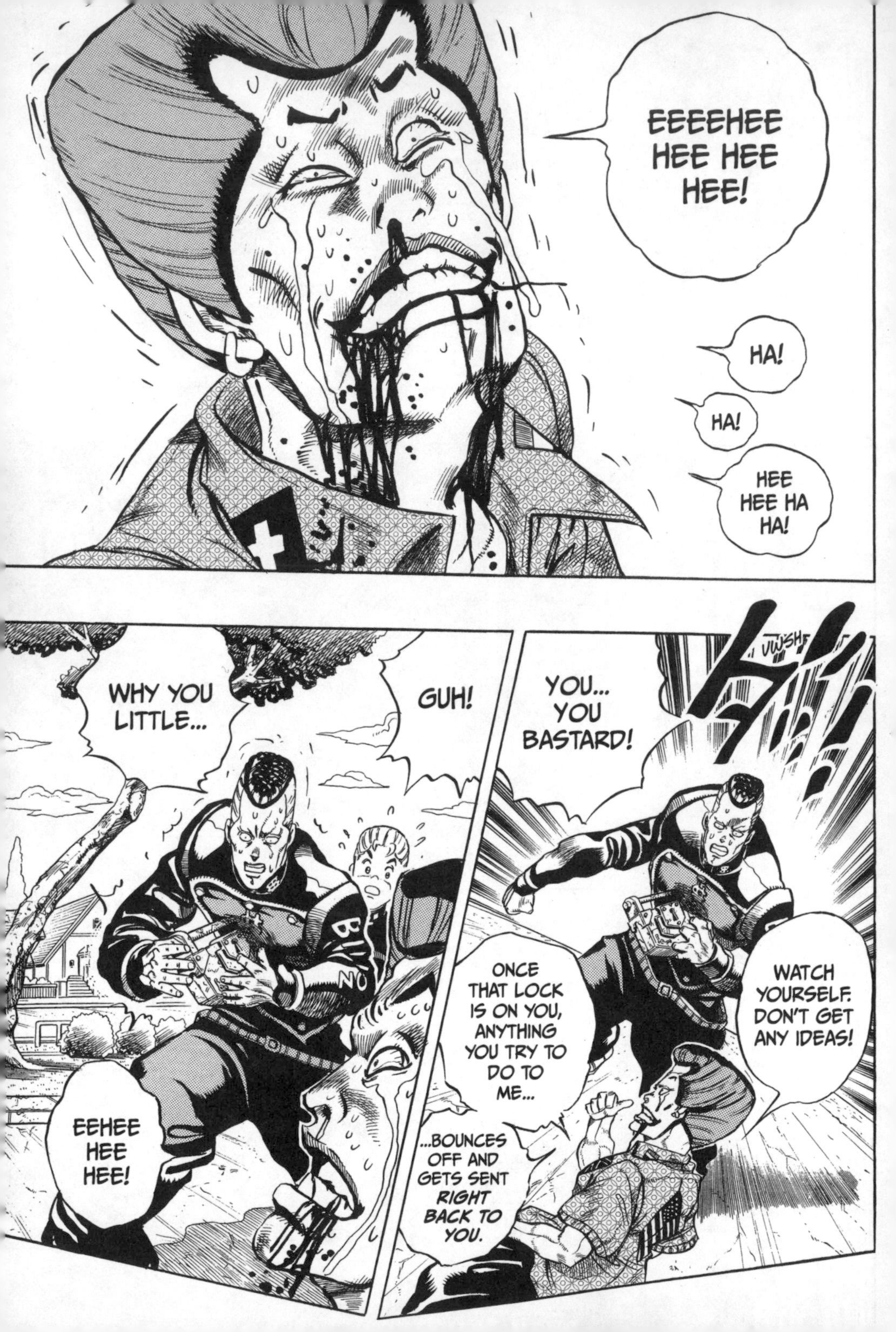
EEEEHEE HEE HEE HEE!
HA!
HA!
HEE HEE HA HA!
VWSH
YOU... YOU BASTARD!
WATCH YOURSELF. DON'T GET ANY IDEAS!
ONCE THAT LOCK IS ON YOU, ANYTHING YOU TRY TO DO TO ME...
...BOUNCES OFF AND GETS SENT *RIGHT* BACK TO YOU.
GUH!
WHY YOU LITTLE...
EEHEE HEE HEE!

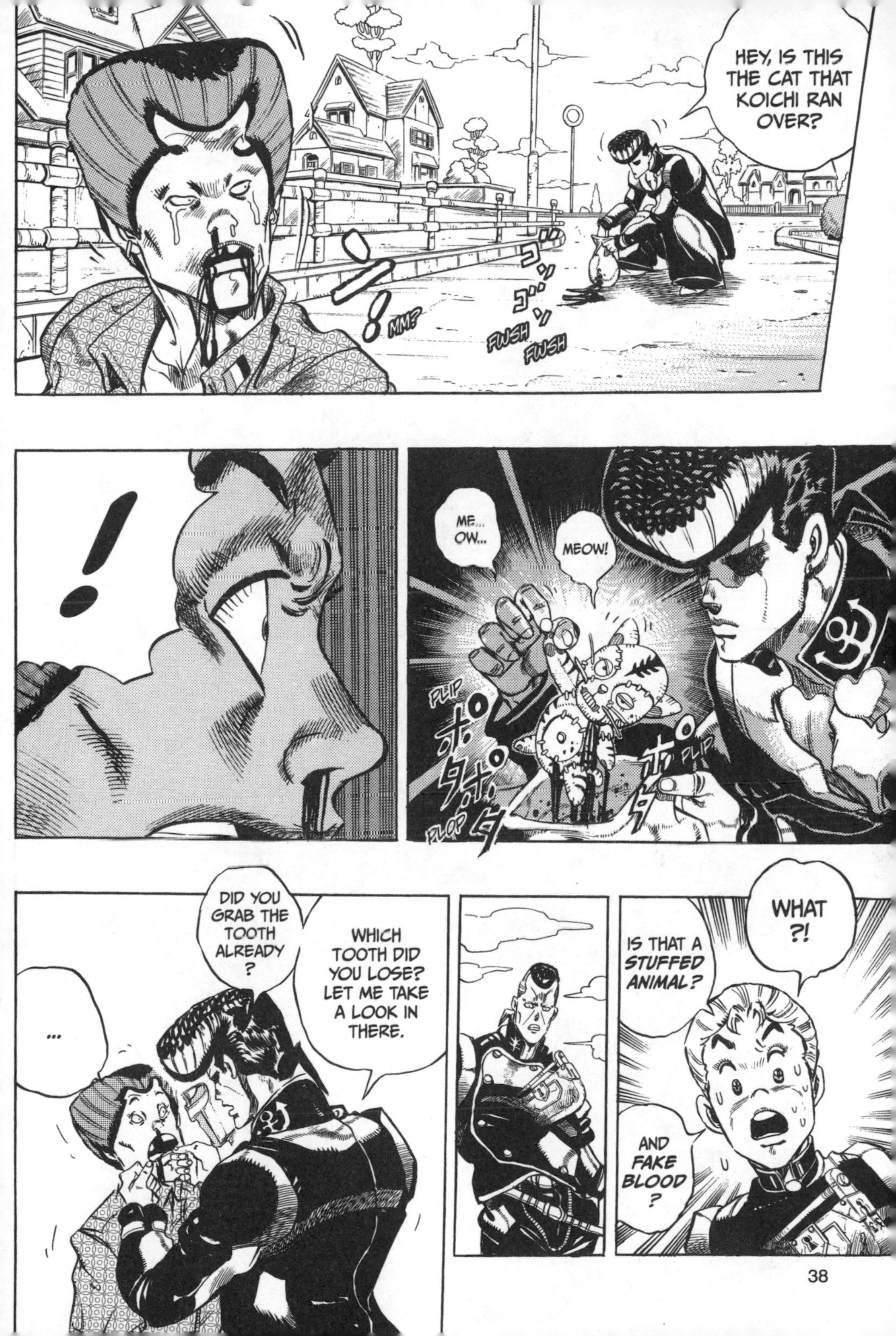
HEY, IS THIS THE CAT THAT KOICHI RAN OVER?
FWSH FWSH
MM?
ME... OW...
MEOW!
PLIP
PLIP
PLOP
!
WHAT ?!
IS THAT A STUFFED ANIMAL?
AND FAKE BLOOD ?
WHICH TOOTH DID YOU LOSE? LET ME TAKE A LOOK IN THERE.
DID YOU GRAB THE TOOTH ALREADY ?
...

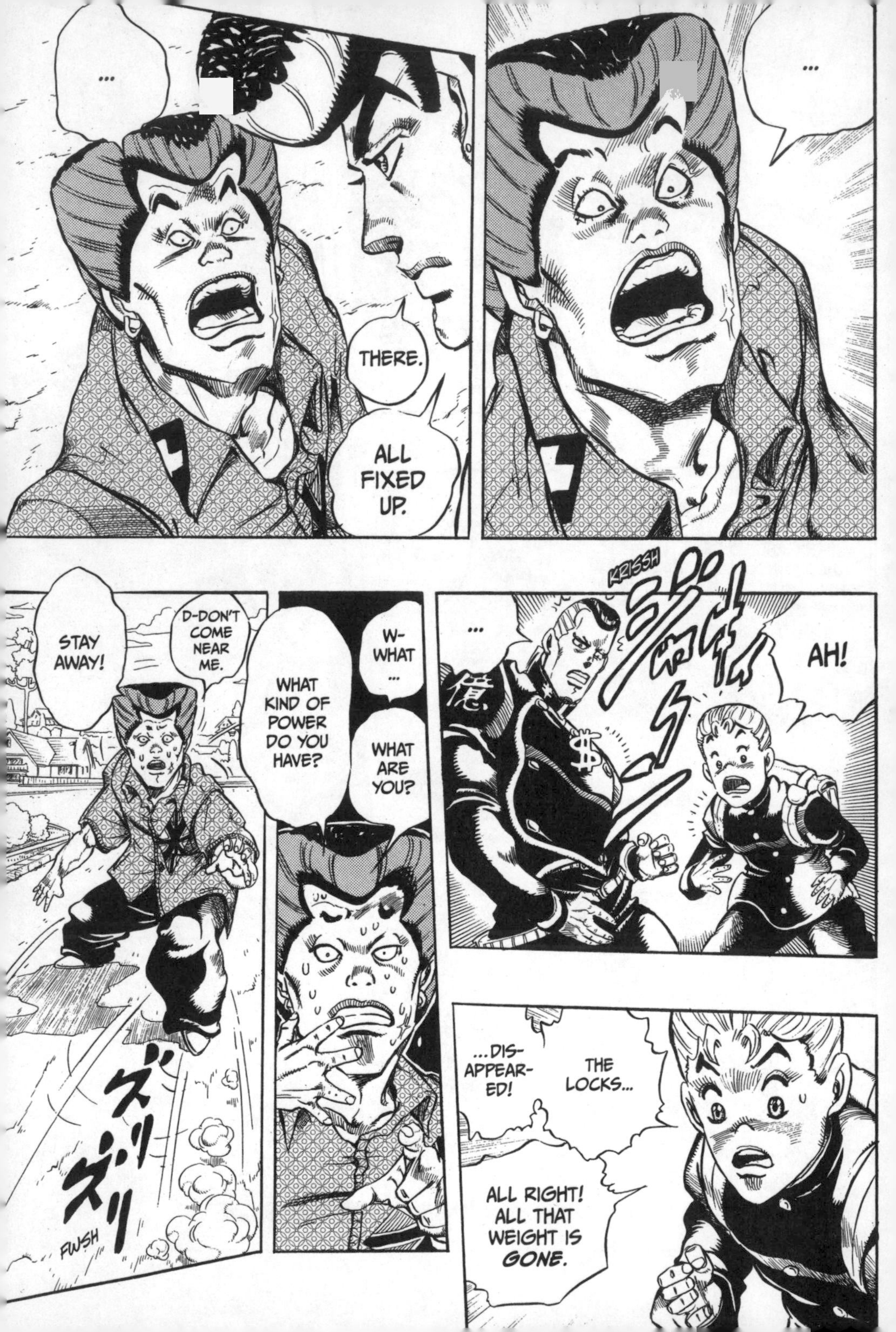
...
...
THERE.
ALL FIXED UP.
KRISSH
...
AH!
THE LOCKS...
...DIS-APPEARED!
ALL RIGHT! ALL THAT WEIGHT IS GONE.
W-WHAT...
WHAT ARE YOU?
WHAT KIND OF POWER DO YOU HAVE?
D-DON'T COME NEAR ME.
STAY AWAY!
FWSH

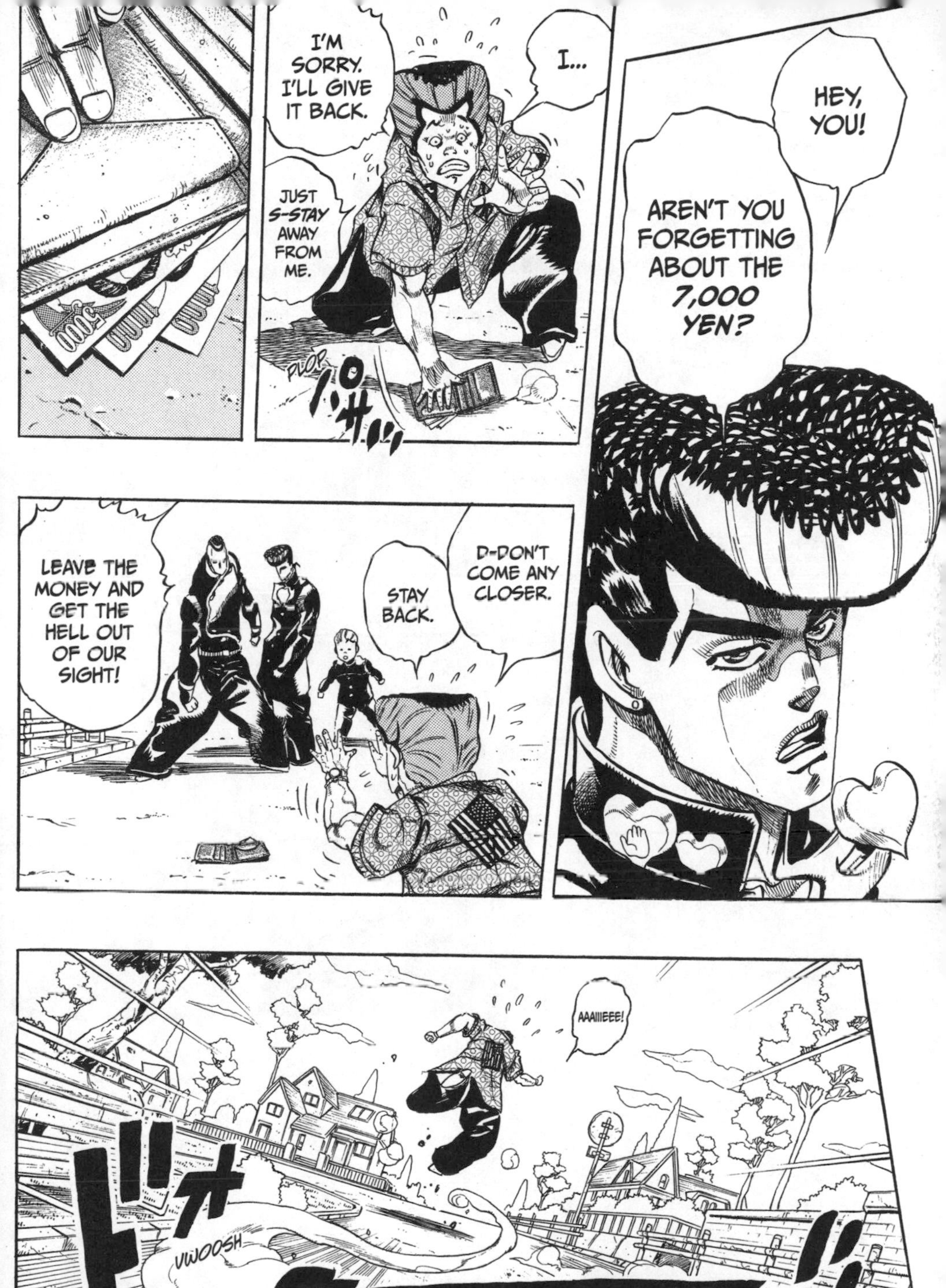
HEY, YOU!
AREN'T YOU FORGETTING ABOUT THE 7,000 YEN?
I...
I'M SORRY. I'LL GIVE IT BACK.
JUST S-STAY AWAY FROM ME.
PLOP
D-DON'T COME ANY CLOSER.
STAY BACK.
LEAVE THE MONEY AND GET THE HELL OUT OF OUR SIGHT!
AAIIIEEE!
VWOOSH

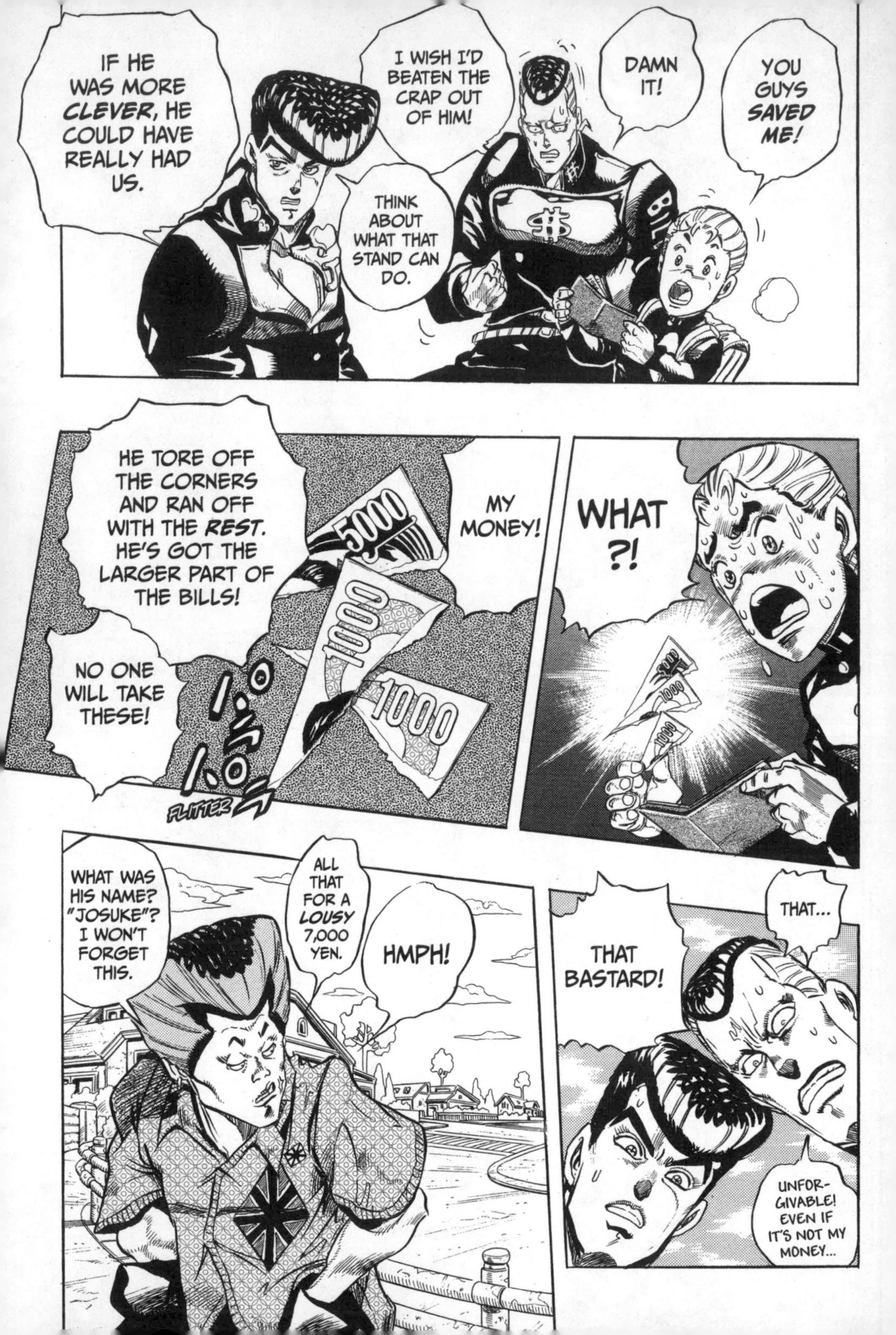
YOU GUYS SAVED ME!
DAMN IT!
I WISH I'D BEATEN THE CRAP OUT OF HIM!
IF HE WAS MORE CLEVER, HE COULD HAVE REALLY HAD US.
THINK ABOUT WHAT THAT STAND CAN DO.
WHAT ?!
MY MONEY!
HE TORE OFF THE CORNERS AND RAN OFF WITH THE REST. HE'S GOT THE LARGER PART OF THE BILLS!
NO ONE WILL TAKE THESE!
FLITTER
THAT...
THAT BASTARD!
UNFORGIVABLE! EVEN IF IT'S NOT MY MONEY...
HMPH!
ALL THAT FOR A LOUSY 7,000 YEN.
WHAT WAS HIS NAME? "JOSUKE"? I WON'T FORGET THIS.

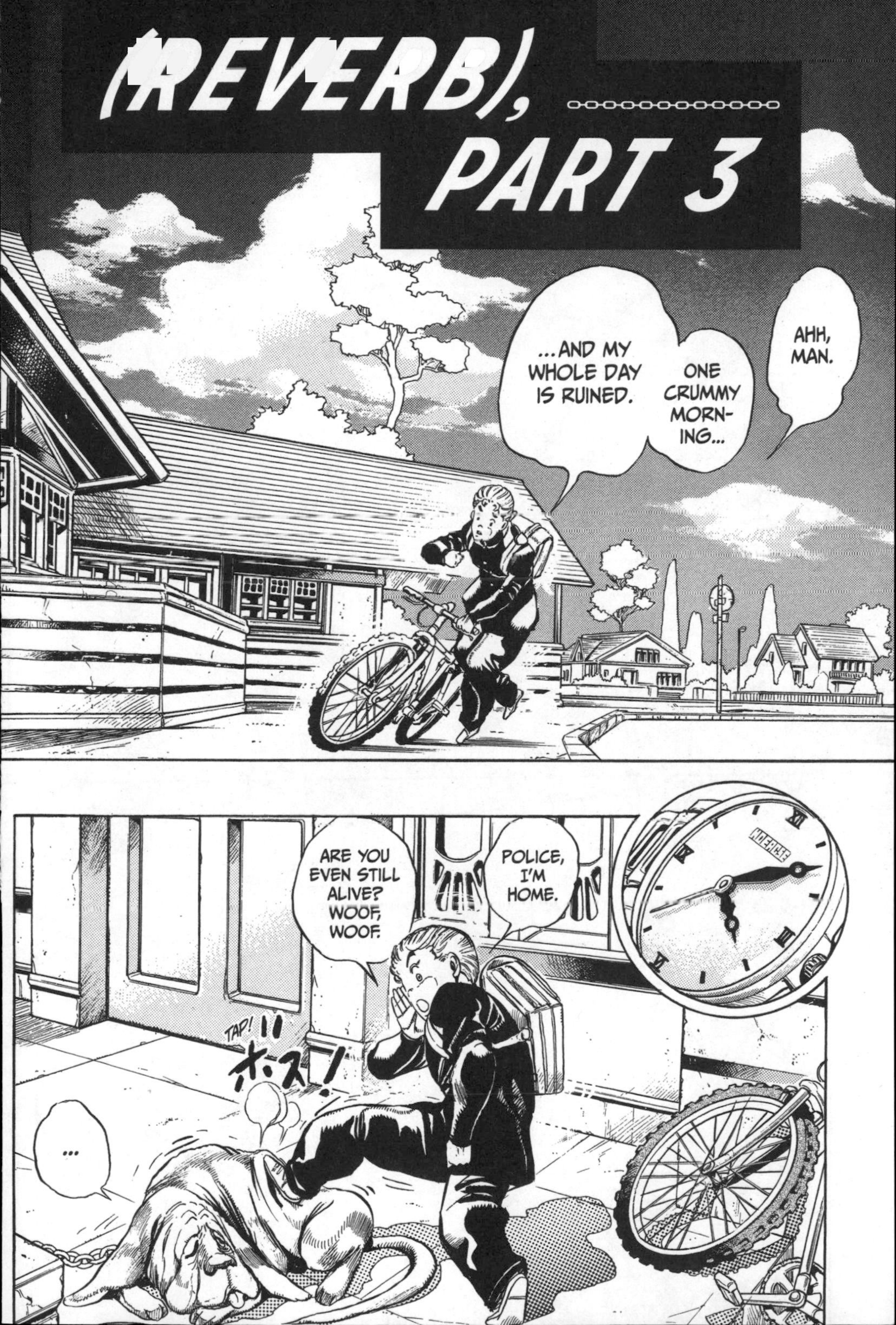
(REVERB), PART 3
AHH, MAN.
ONE CRUMMY MORNING...
...AND MY WHOLE DAY IS RUINED.
POLICE, I'M HOME.
ARE YOU EVEN STILL ALIVE? WOOF, WOOF.
TAP!!
...

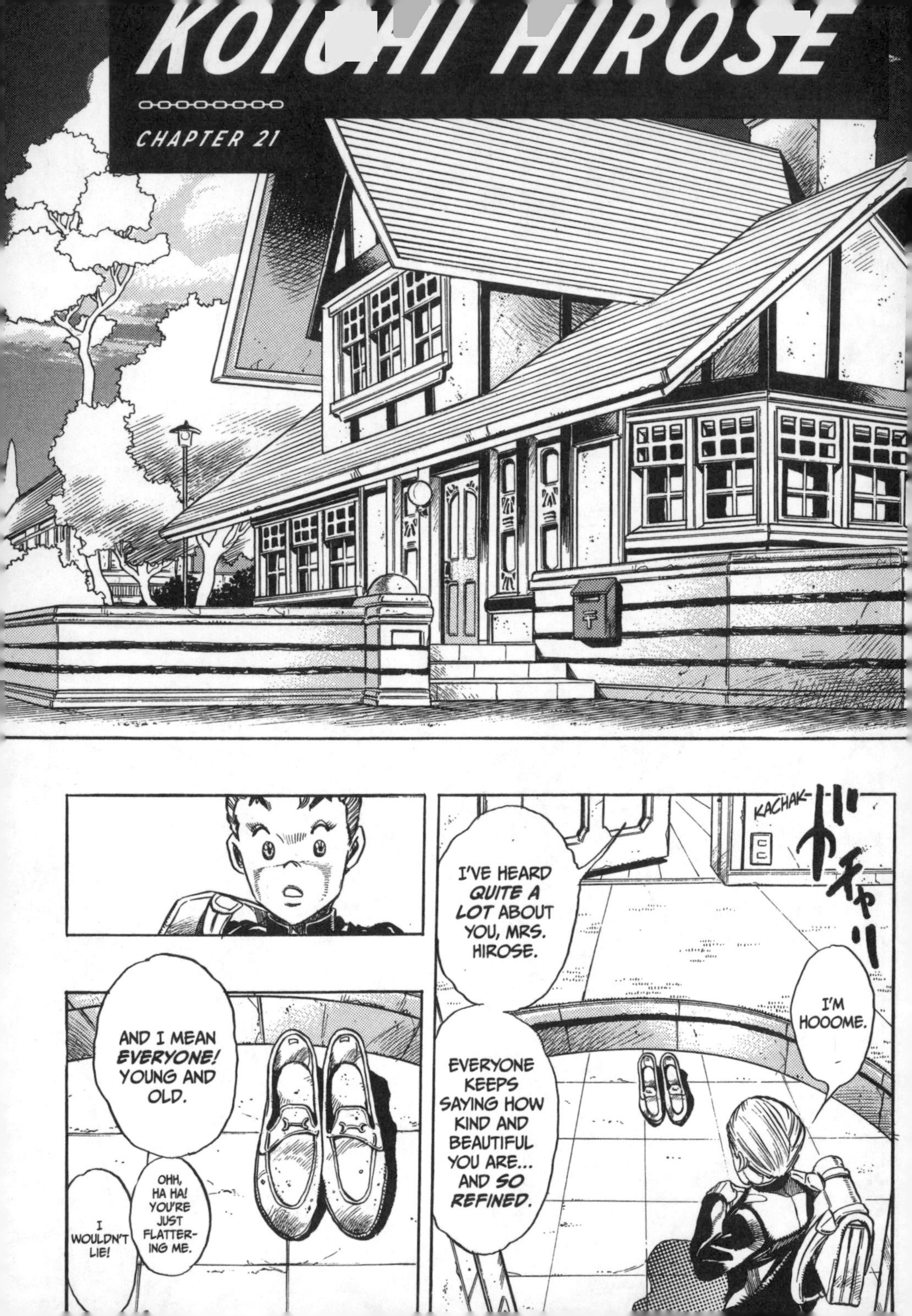
KOICHI HIROSE
CHAPTER 21
KACHAK
I'M HOOOME.
I'VE HEARD QUITE A LOT ABOUT YOU, MRS. HIROSE.
EVERYONE KEEPS SAYING HOW KIND AND BEAUTIFUL YOU ARE... AND SO REFINED.
AND I MEAN EVERYONE! YOUNG AND OLD.
OHH, HA HA! YOU'RE JUST FLATTERING ME.
I WOULDN'T LIE!

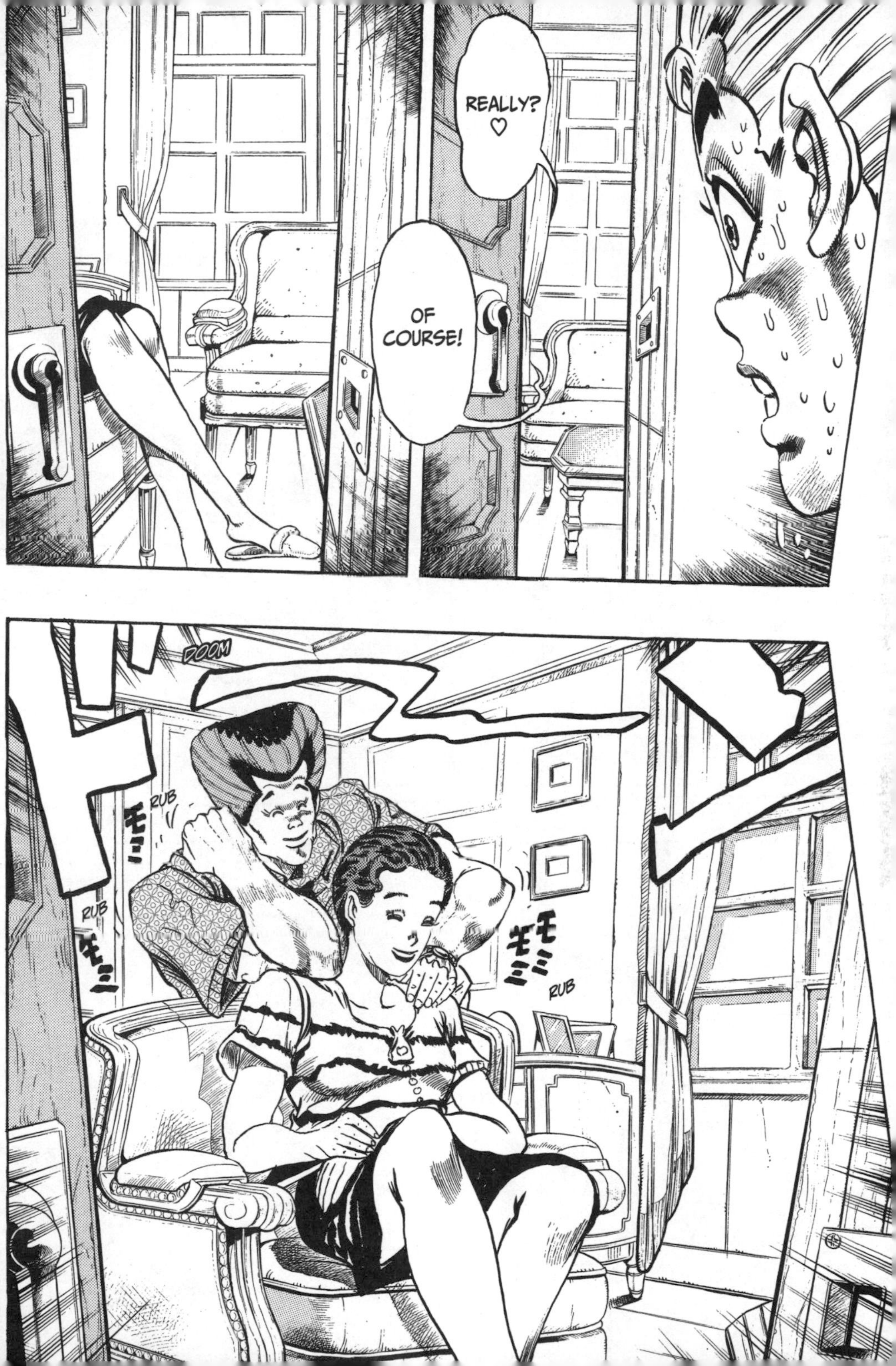
REALLY? ♡
OF COURSE!
DOOM
RUB
RUB
RUB

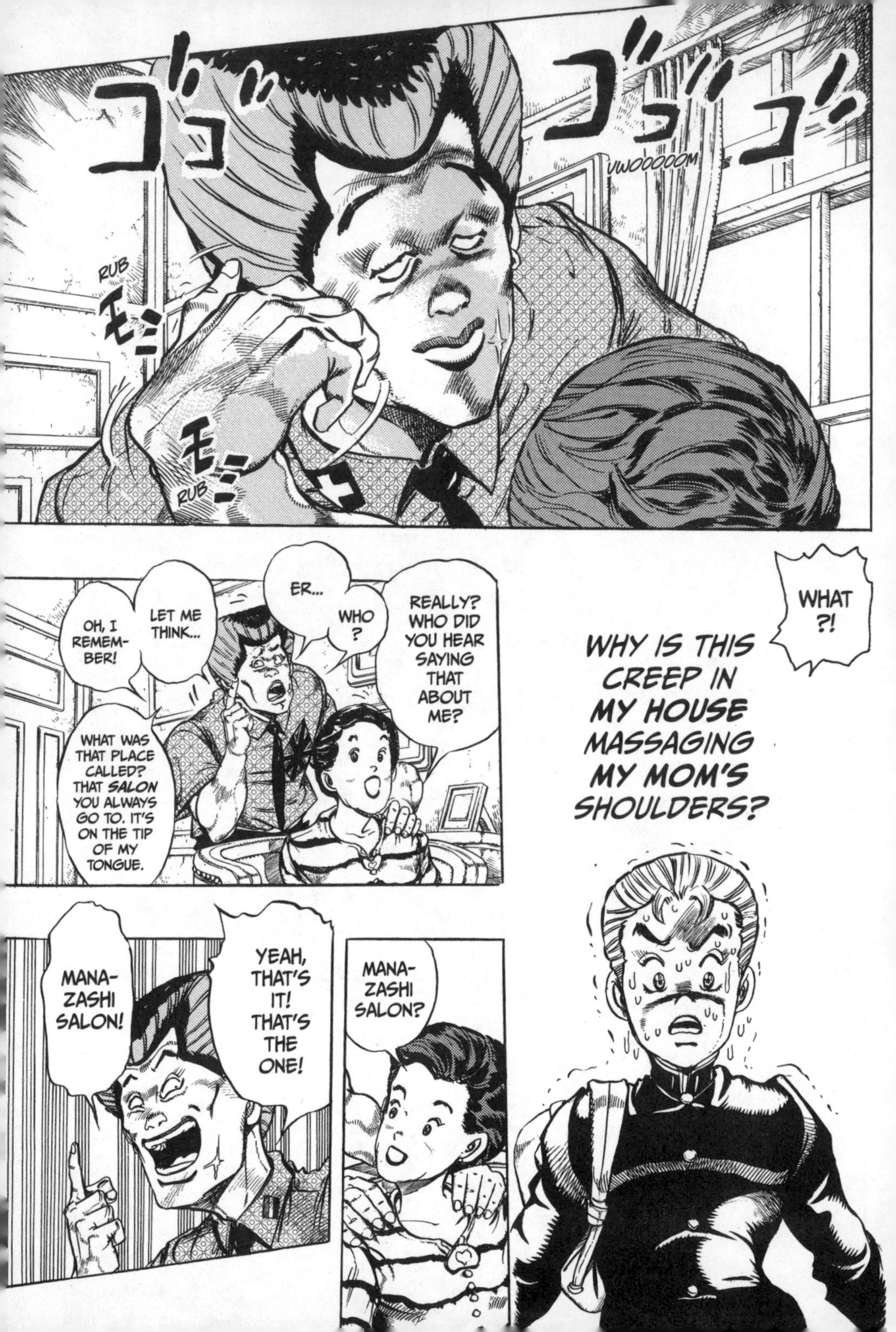

ゴゴゴゴ
VWOOOOOM
ゴゴ
RUB
モミ
RUB
モミ
WHAT ?!
WHY IS THIS CREEP IN MY HOUSE MASSAGING MY MOM'S SHOULDERS?
REALLY? WHO DID YOU HEAR SAYING THAT ABOUT ME?
ER...
WHO ?
LET ME THINK...
OH, I REMEMBER!
WHAT WAS THAT PLACE CALLED? THAT SALON YOU ALWAYS GO TO. IT'S ON THE TIP OF MY TONGUE.
MANA-ZASHI SALON?
YEAH, THAT'S IT! THAT'S THE ONE!
MANA-ZASHI SALON!

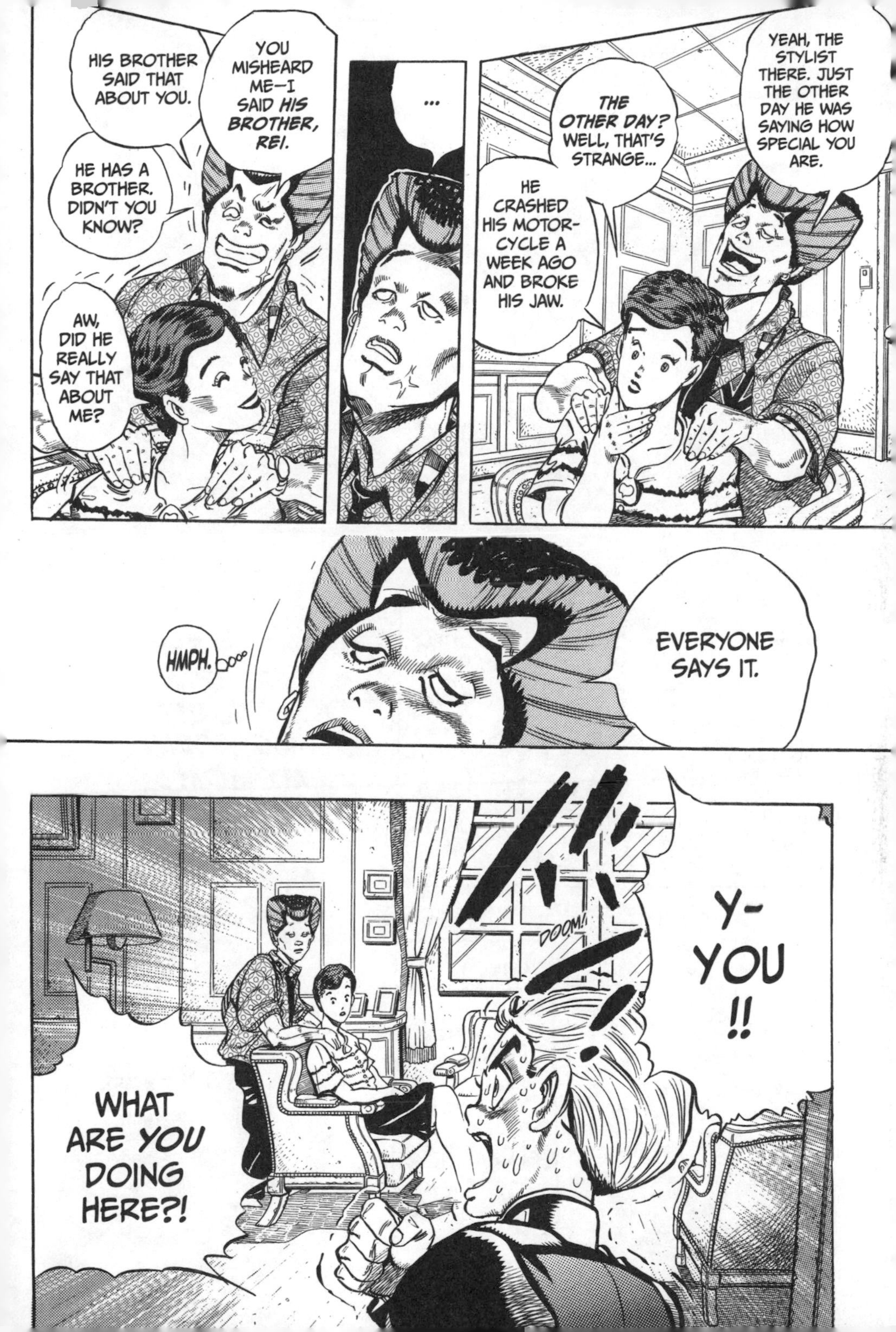
YEAH, THE STYLIST THERE. JUST THE OTHER DAY HE WAS SAYING HOW SPECIAL YOU ARE.
THE OTHER DAY? WELL, THAT'S STRANGE...
HE CRASHED HIS MOTORCYCLE A WEEK AGO AND BROKE HIS JAW.
...
YOU MISHEARD ME—I SAID HIS BROTHER, REI.
HIS BROTHER SAID THAT ABOUT YOU.
HE HAS A BROTHER. DIDN'T YOU KNOW?
AW, DID HE REALLY SAY THAT ABOUT ME?
EVERYONE SAYS IT.
HMPH.
Y-YOU!!
DOOM!
WHAT ARE YOU DOING HERE?!

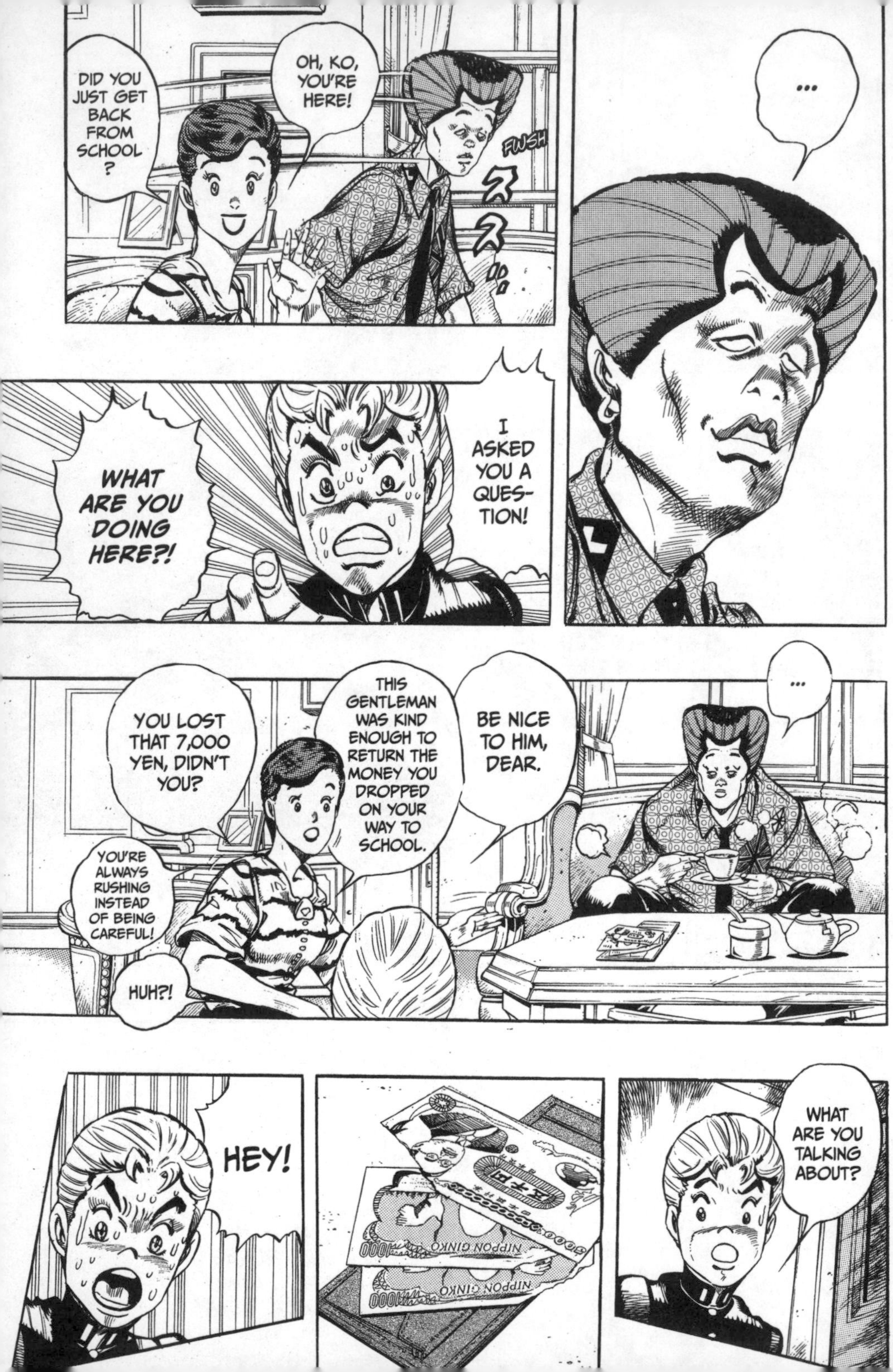

...
OH, KO, YOU'RE HERE!
DID YOU JUST GET BACK FROM SCHOOL?
FWSH
I ASKED YOU A QUES-TION!
WHAT ARE YOU DOING HERE?!
...
BE NICE TO HIM, DEAR.
THIS GENTLEMAN WAS KIND ENOUGH TO RETURN THE MONEY YOU DROPPED ON YOUR WAY TO SCHOOL.
YOU LOST THAT 7,000 YEN, DIDN'T YOU?
YOU'RE ALWAYS RUSHING INSTEAD OF BEING CAREFUL!
HUH?!
WHAT ARE YOU TALKING ABOUT?
NIPPON GINKO
NIPPON GINKO
HEY!

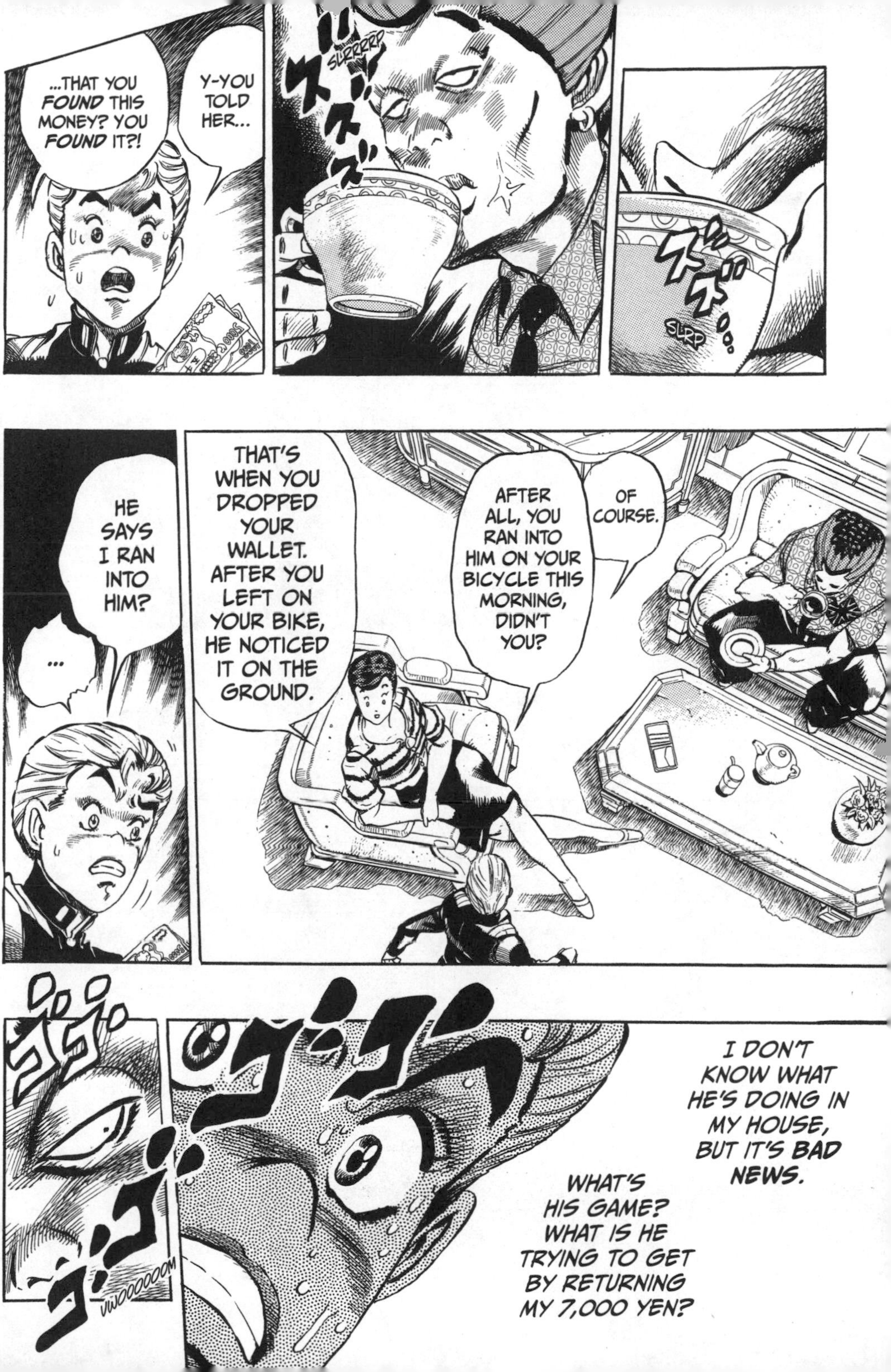
SLURP
SLURRRRP
Y-YOU TOLD HER...
...THAT YOU FOUND THIS MONEY? YOU FOUND IT?!
OF COURSE.
AFTER ALL, YOU RAN INTO HIM ON YOUR BICYCLE THIS MORNING, DIDN'T YOU?
THAT'S WHEN YOU DROPPED YOUR WALLET. AFTER YOU LEFT ON YOUR BIKE, HE NOTICED IT ON THE GROUND.
HE SAYS I RAN INTO HIM?
...
I DON'T KNOW WHAT HE'S DOING IN MY HOUSE, BUT IT'S BAD NEWS.
WHAT'S HIS GAME? WHAT IS HE TRYING TO GET BY RETURNING MY 7,000 YEN?
VWOOOOOOM

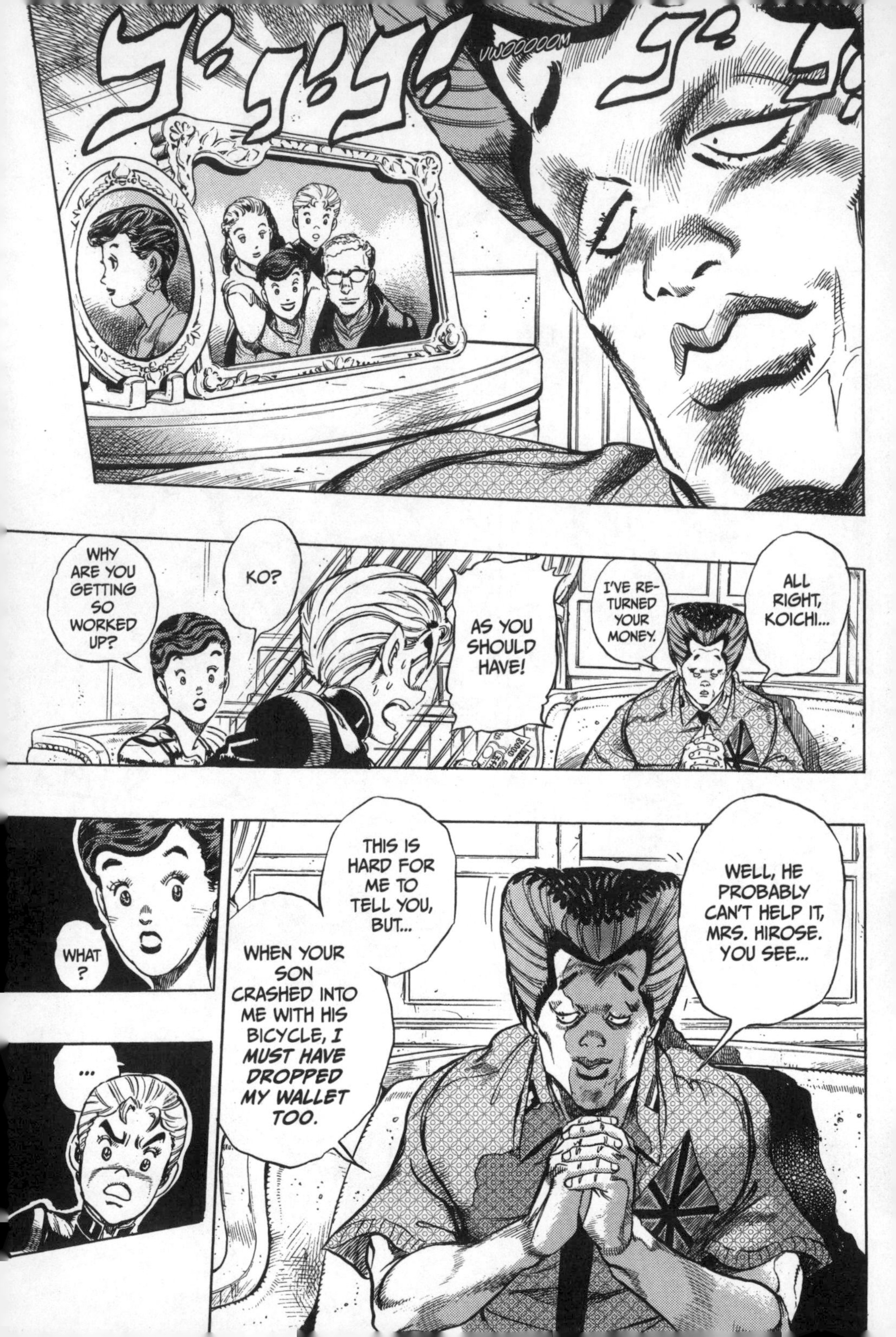
VWOOOOOM
ALL RIGHT, KOICHI...
I'VE RE-TURNED YOUR MONEY.
AS YOU SHOULD HAVE!
KO?
WHY ARE YOU GETTING SO WORKED UP?
WELL, HE PROBABLY CAN'T HELP IT, MRS. HIROSE. YOU SEE...
THIS IS HARD FOR ME TO TELL YOU, BUT...
WHEN YOUR SON CRASHED INTO ME WITH HIS BICYCLE, I *MUST HAVE DROPPED MY WALLET* TOO.
WHAT?
...

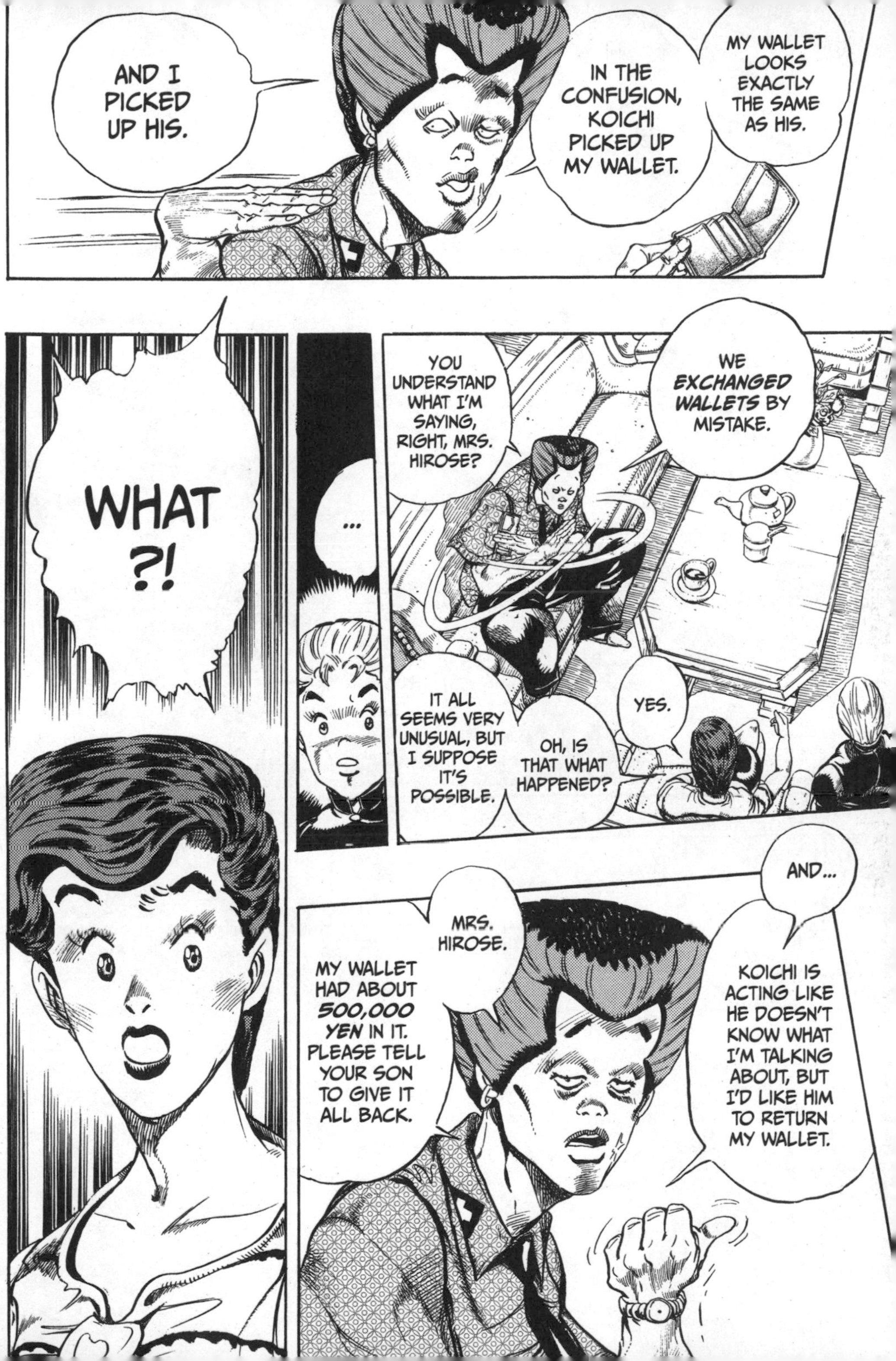
MY WALLET LOOKS EXACTLY THE SAME AS HIS.
IN THE CONFUSION, KOICHI PICKED UP MY WALLET.
AND I PICKED UP HIS.
WE *EXCHANGED WALLETS* BY MISTAKE.
YOU UNDERSTAND WHAT I'M SAYING, RIGHT, MRS. HIROSE?
YES.
OH, IS THAT WHAT HAPPENED?
IT ALL SEEMS VERY UNUSUAL, BUT I SUPPOSE IT'S POSSIBLE.
...
AND...
KOICHI IS ACTING LIKE HE DOESN'T KNOW WHAT I'M TALKING ABOUT, BUT I'D LIKE HIM TO RETURN MY WALLET.
MRS. HIROSE.
MY WALLET HAD ABOUT *500,000 YEN* IN IT. PLEASE TELL YOUR SON TO GIVE IT ALL BACK.
WHAT ?!

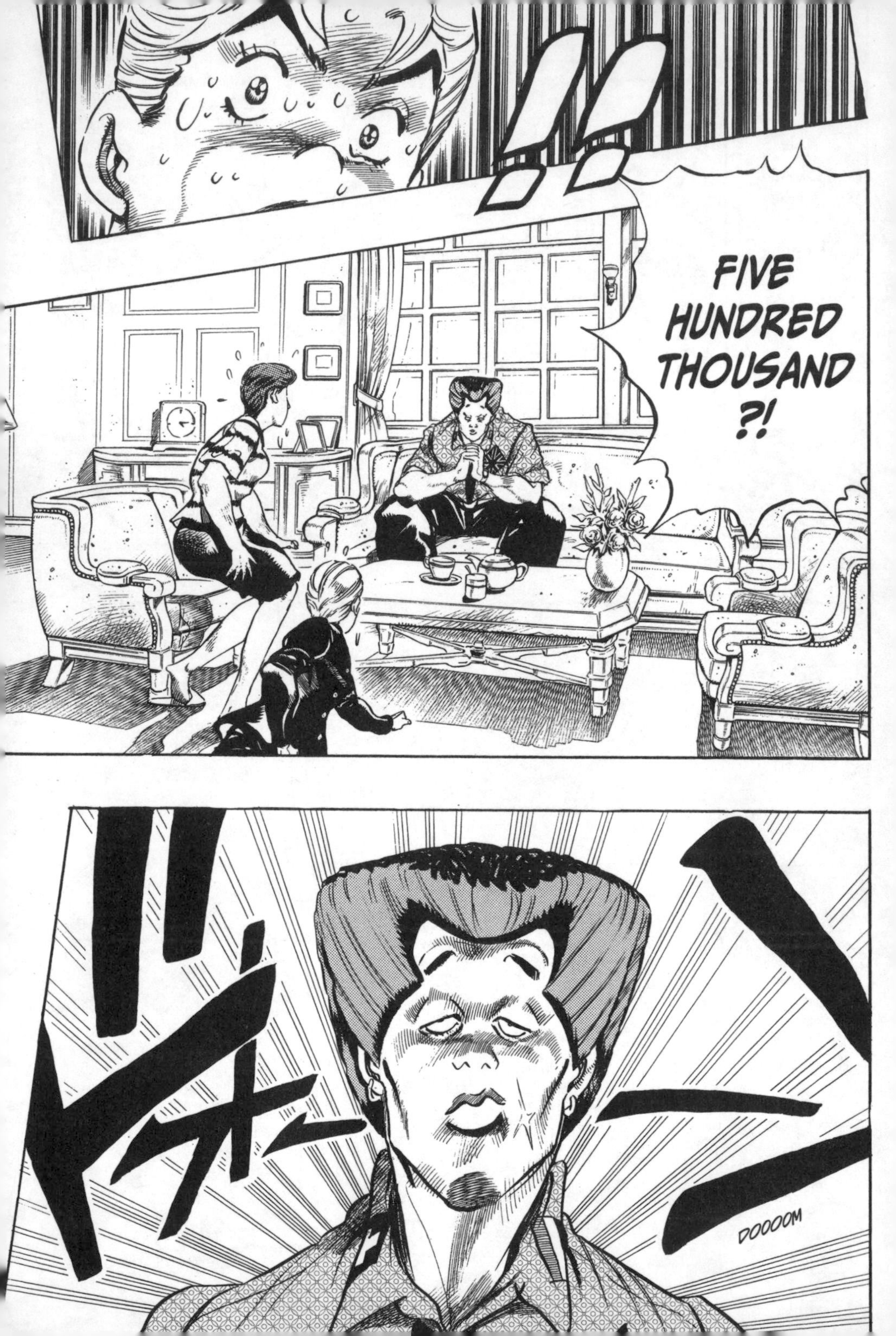
FIVE HUNDRED THOUSAND ?!
DOOOOM

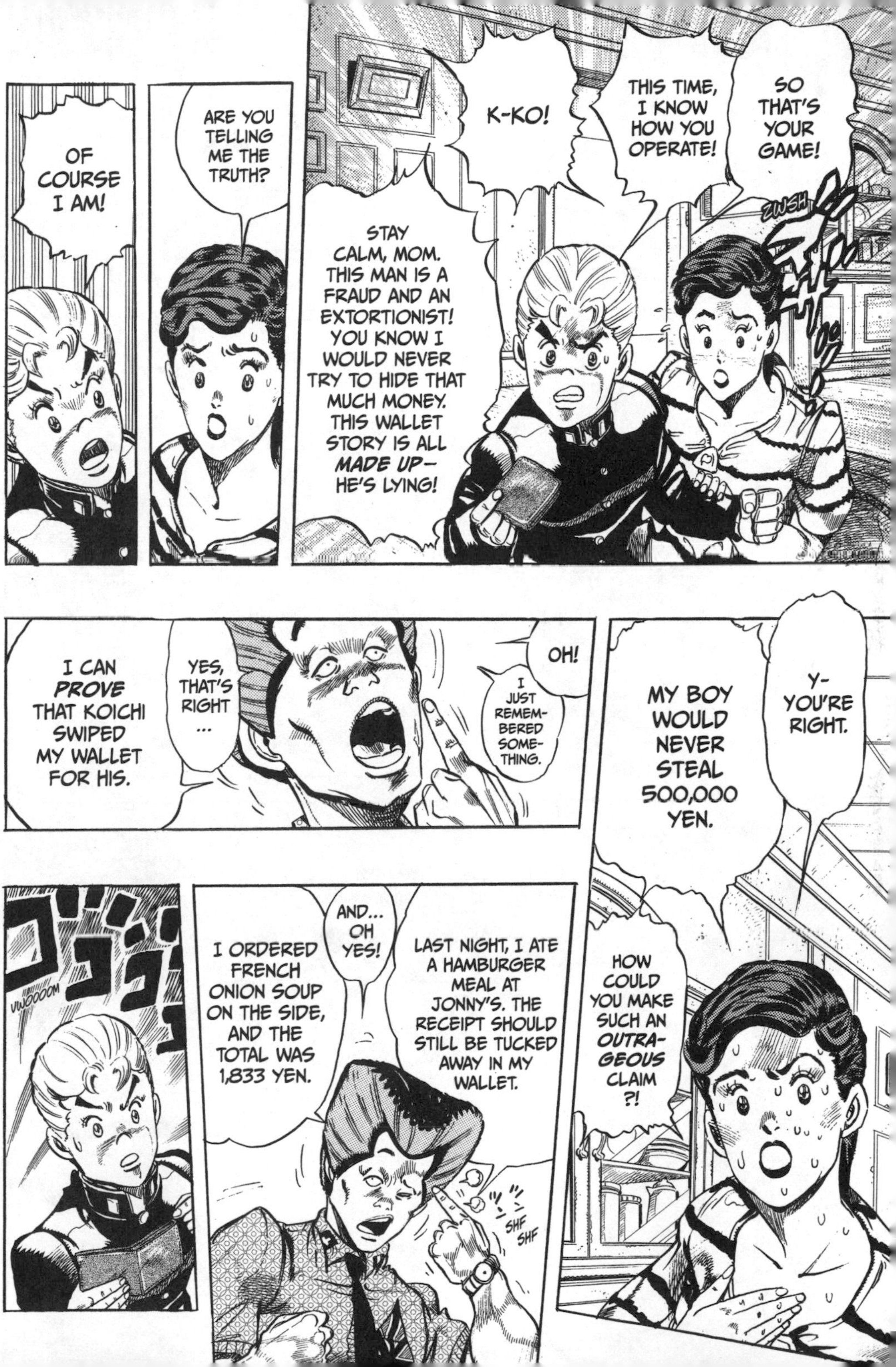
SO THAT'S YOUR GAME!
THIS TIME, I KNOW HOW YOU OPERATE!
K-KO!
ZWSH
STAY CALM, MOM. THIS MAN IS A FRAUD AND AN EXTORTIONIST! YOU KNOW I WOULD NEVER TRY TO HIDE THAT MUCH MONEY. THIS WALLET STORY IS ALL *MADE UP*— HE'S LYING!
ARE YOU TELLING ME THE TRUTH?
OF COURSE I AM!
Y- YOU'RE RIGHT.
MY BOY WOULD NEVER STEAL 500,000 YEN.
HOW COULD YOU MAKE SUCH AN *OUTRAGEOUS* CLAIM ?!
OH!
I JUST REMEMBERED SOMETHING.
YES, THAT'S RIGHT ...
I CAN *PROVE* THAT KOICHI SWIPED MY WALLET FOR HIS.
AND... OH YES!
LAST NIGHT, I ATE A HAMBURGER MEAL AT JONNY'S. THE RECEIPT SHOULD STILL BE TUCKED AWAY IN MY WALLET.
I ORDERED FRENCH ONION SOUP ON THE SIDE, AND THE TOTAL WAS 1,833 YEN.
SHF SHF
VWOOOOM

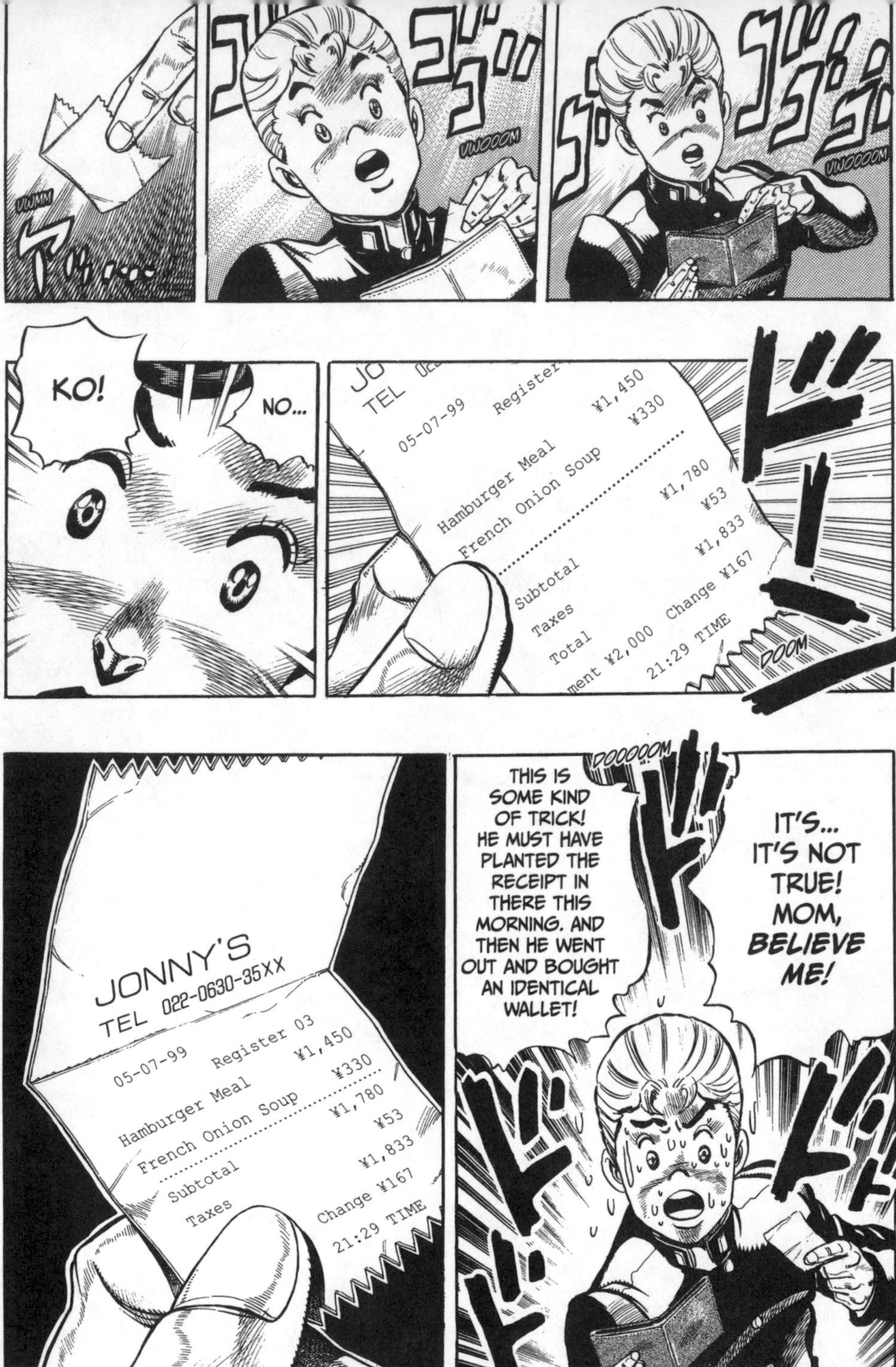
UWOOOOM
UWOOOM
VUMM
DOOM
05-07-99 Register
Hamburger Meal ¥1,450
French Onion Soup ¥330
¥1,780
¥53
¥1,833
Subtotal
Taxes
Total
Change ¥167
¥2,000
21:29 TIME
KO!
NO...
DOOOOOM
IT'S... IT'S NOT TRUE! MOM, *BELIEVE ME!*
THIS IS SOME KIND OF TRICK! HE MUST HAVE PLANTED THE RECEIPT IN THERE THIS MORNING. AND THEN HE WENT OUT AND BOUGHT AN IDENTICAL WALLET!
JONNY'S
TEL 022-0630-35XX
05-07-99 Register 03
Hamburger Meal ¥1,450
French Onion Soup ¥330
¥1,780
¥53
¥1,833
Subtotal
Taxes
Change ¥167
21:29 TIME

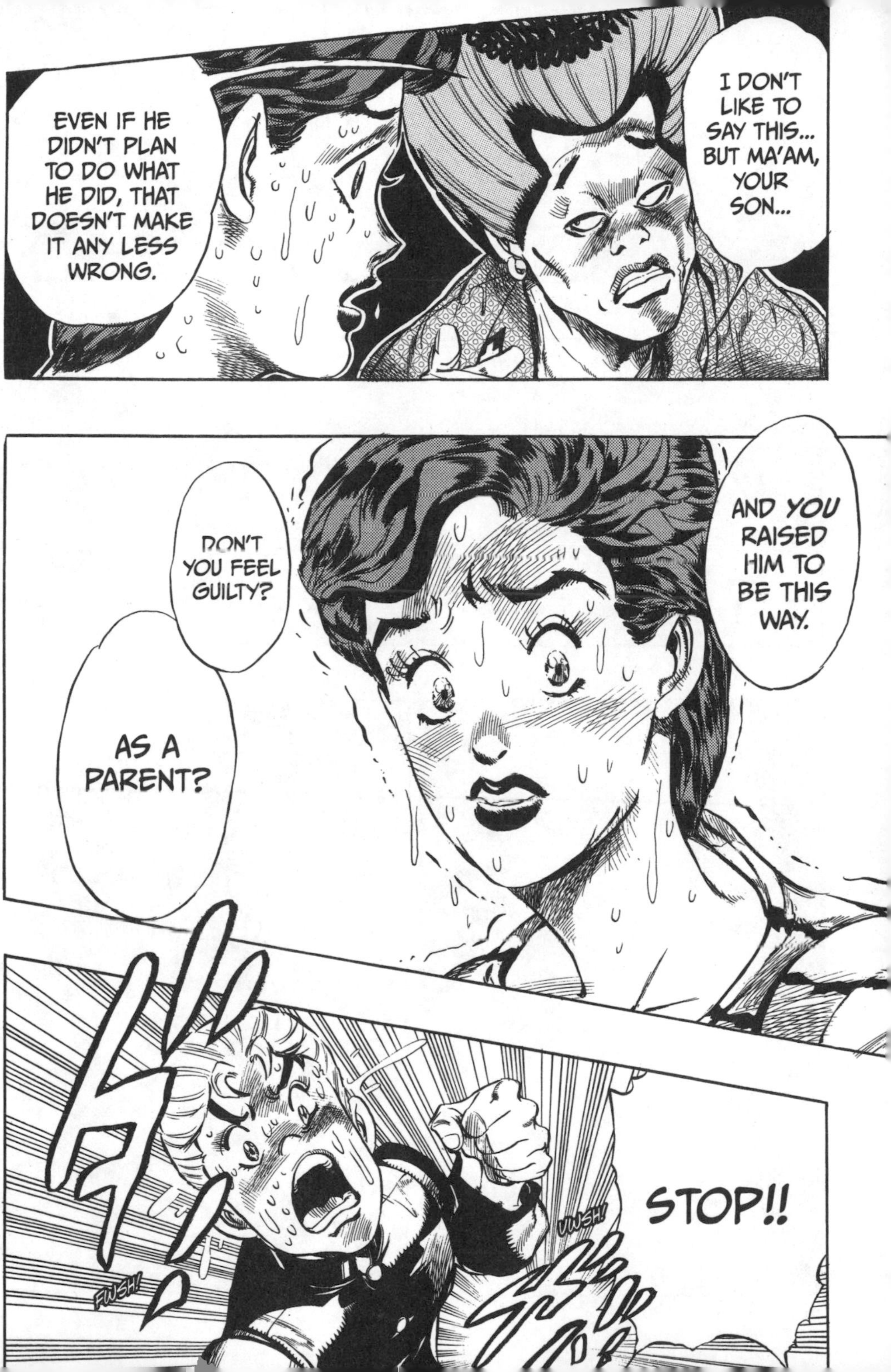
I DON'T LIKE TO SAY THIS... BUT MA'AM, YOUR SON...
EVEN IF HE DIDN'T PLAN TO DO WHAT HE DID, THAT DOESN'T MAKE IT ANY LESS WRONG.
AND *YOU* RAISED HIM TO BE THIS WAY.
DON'T YOU FEEL GUILTY?
AS A PARENT?
STOP!!
VWSH!
FWSH!

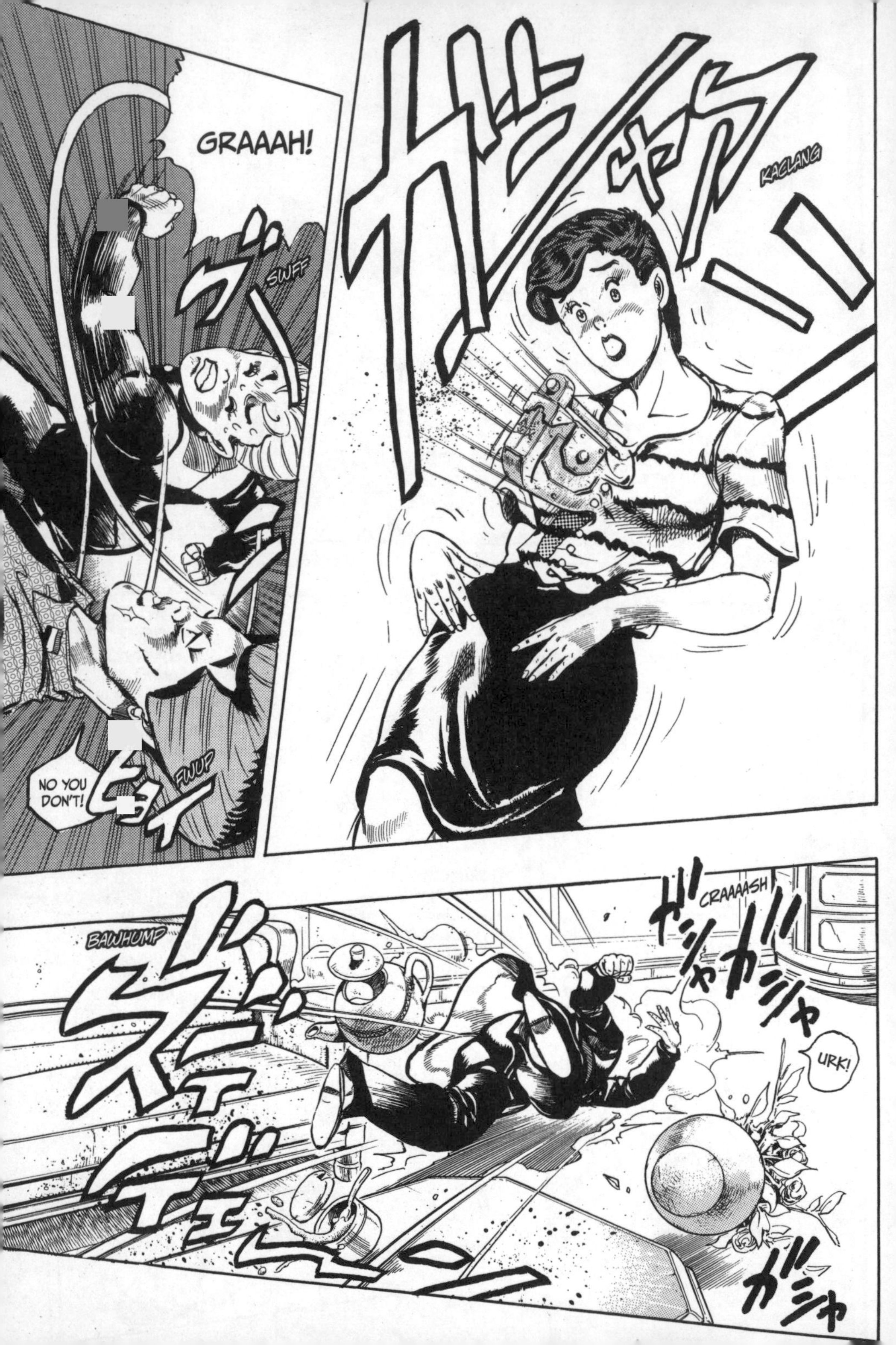
KACLANG
GRAAAH!
SWFF
NO YOU DON'T!
FWUP
CRAAAASH
URK!
BAWHUMP

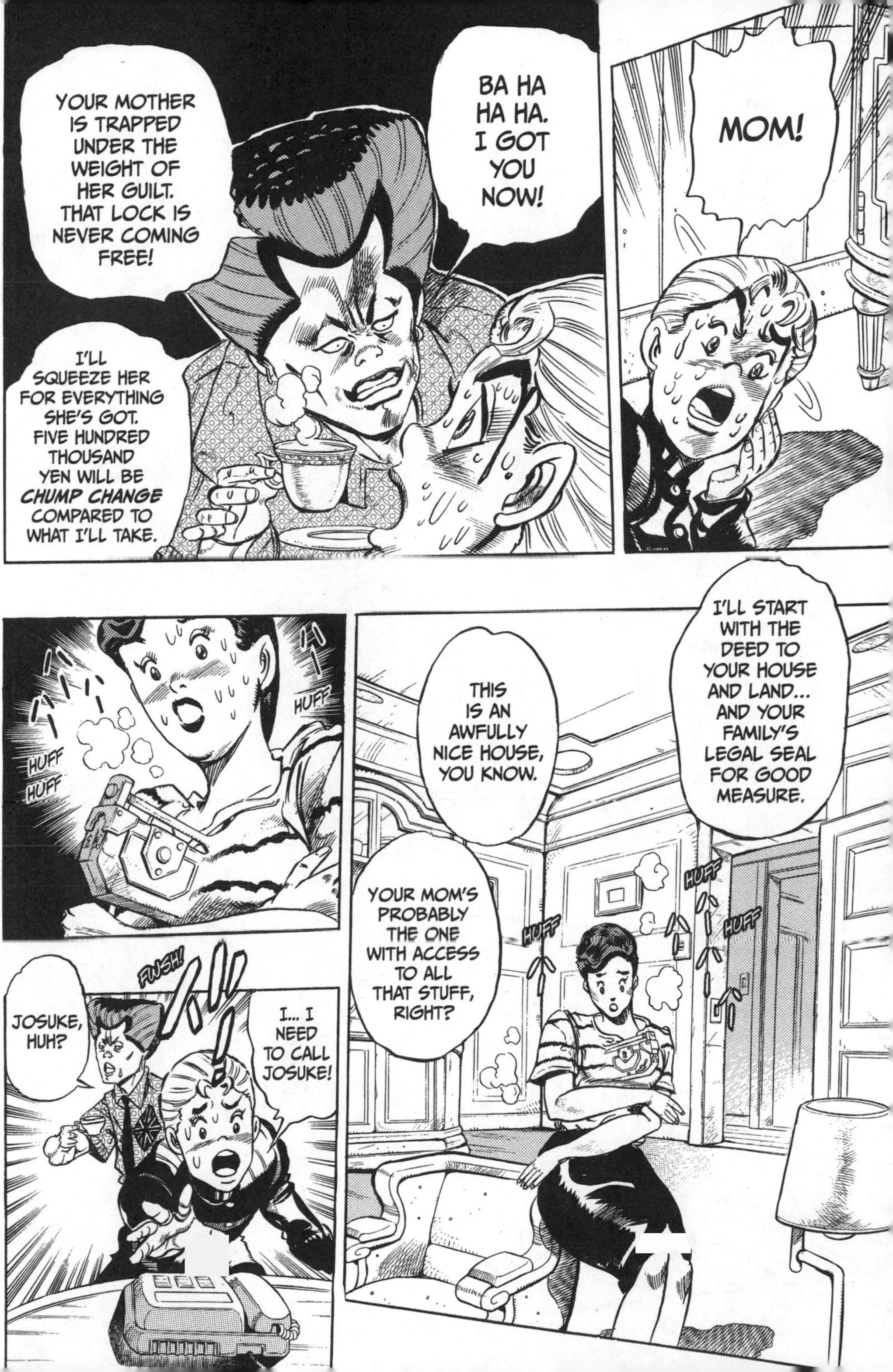
MOM!
BA HA HA HA. I GOT YOU NOW!
YOUR MOTHER IS TRAPPED UNDER THE WEIGHT OF HER GUILT. THAT LOCK IS NEVER COMING FREE!
I'LL SQUEEZE HER FOR EVERYTHING SHE'S GOT. FIVE HUNDRED THOUSAND YEN WILL BE *CHUMP CHANGE* COMPARED TO WHAT I'LL TAKE.
I'LL START WITH THE DEED TO YOUR HOUSE AND LAND... AND YOUR FAMILY'S LEGAL SEAL FOR GOOD MEASURE.
THIS IS AN AWFULLY NICE HOUSE, YOU KNOW.
HUFF
HUFF
YOUR MOM'S PROBABLY THE ONE WITH ACCESS TO ALL THAT STUFF, RIGHT?
HUFF
HUFF
HUFF
HUFF
I... I NEED TO CALL JOSUKE!
FWSH!
JOSUKE, HUH?

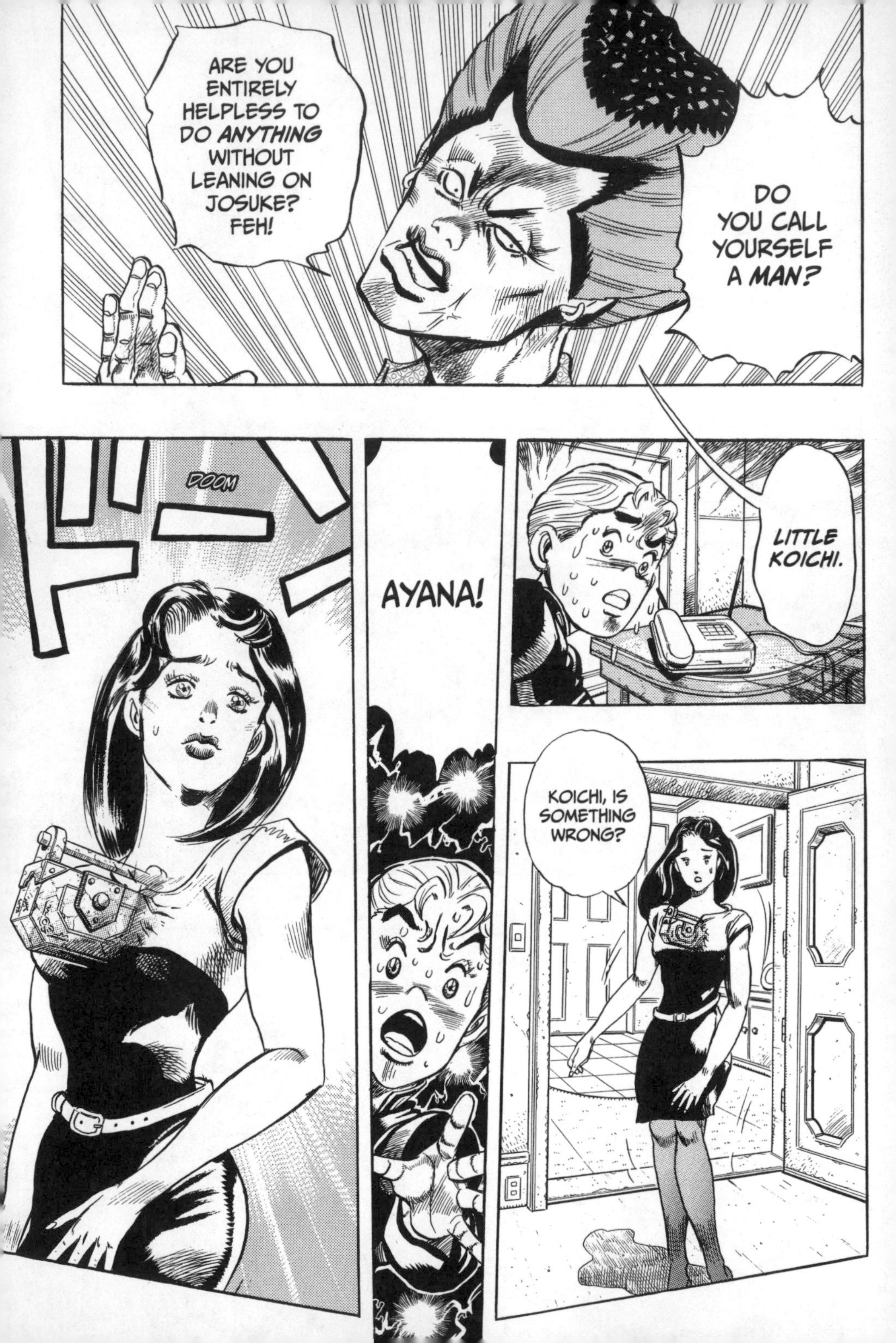
ARE YOU ENTIRELY HELPLESS TO DO ANYTHING WITHOUT LEANING ON JOSUKE? FEH!
DO YOU CALL YOURSELF A MAN?
LITTLE KOICHI.
KOICHI, IS SOMETHING WRONG?
AYANA!
DOOM

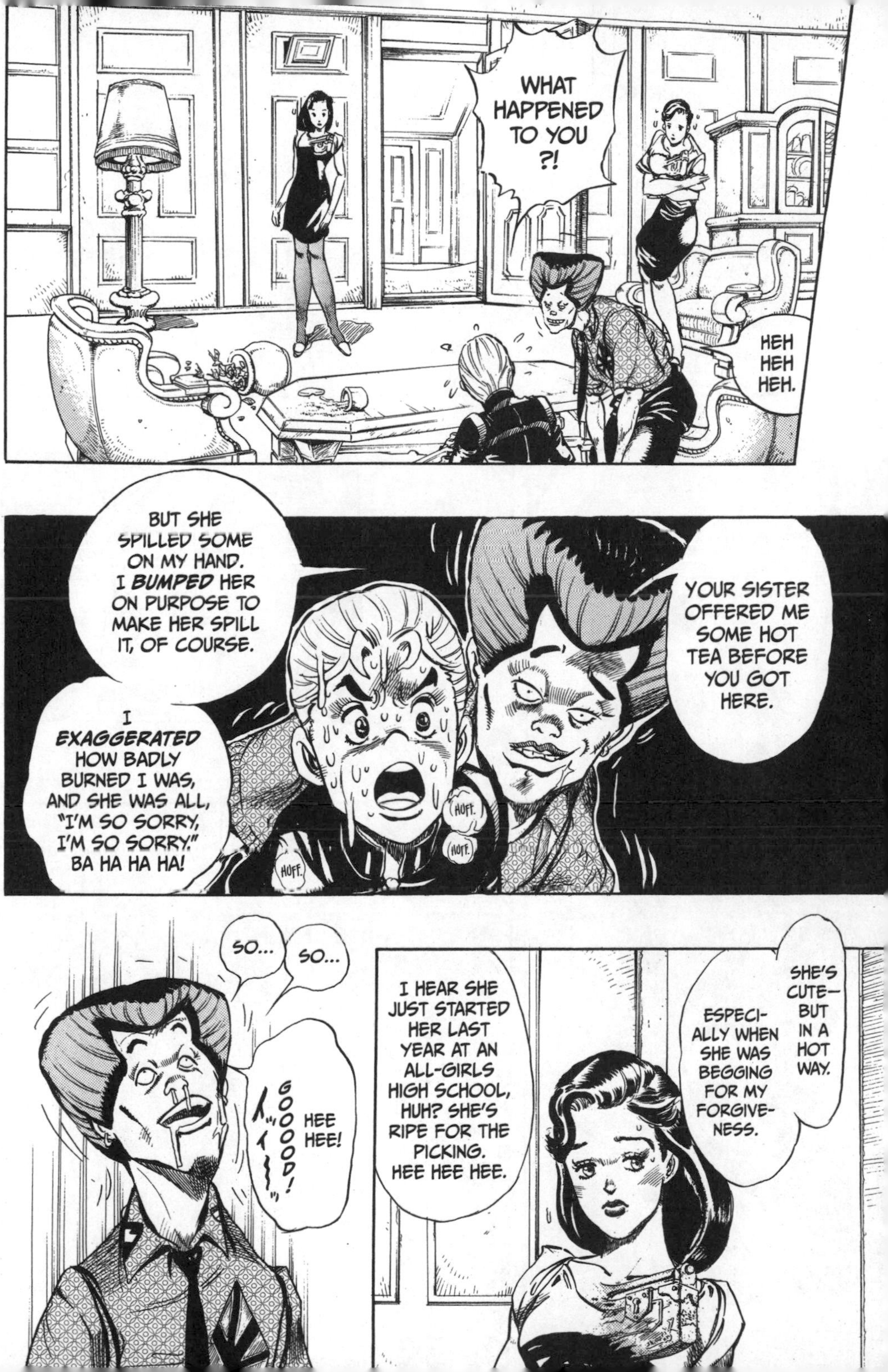
WHAT HAPPENED TO YOU ?!
HEH HEH HEH.
YOUR SISTER OFFERED ME SOME HOT TEA BEFORE YOU GOT HERE.
BUT SHE SPILLED SOME ON MY HAND. I BUMPED HER ON PURPOSE TO MAKE HER SPILL IT, OF COURSE.
I EXAGGERATED HOW BADLY BURNED I WAS, AND SHE WAS ALL, "I'M SO SORRY, I'M SO SORRY." BA HA HA HA!
HUFF.
HUFF.
HUFF.
SHE'S CUTE— BUT IN A HOT WAY.
ESPECIALLY WHEN SHE WAS BEGGING FOR MY FORGIVENESS.
I HEAR SHE JUST STARTED HER LAST YEAR AT AN ALL-GIRLS HIGH SCHOOL, HUH? SHE'S RIPE FOR THE PICKING. HEE HEE HEE.
SO...
SO...
HEE HEE!
GOOOOOD!

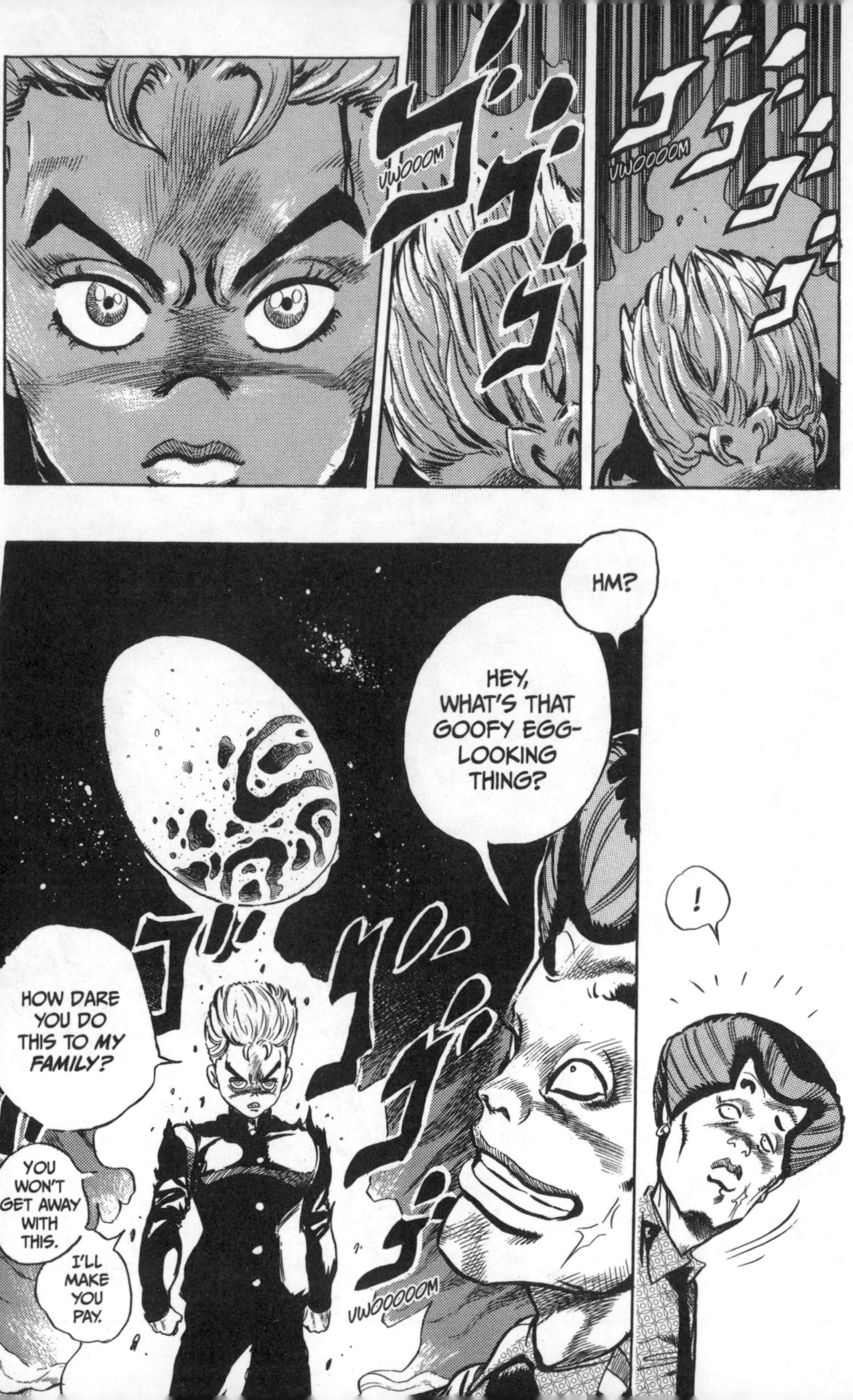
VWOOOOM
VWOOOM
HM?
HEY, WHAT'S THAT GOOFY EGG-LOOKING THING?
!
HOW DARE YOU DO THIS TO MY FAMILY?
YOU WON'T GET AWAY WITH THIS.
I'LL MAKE YOU PAY.
VWOOOOOM

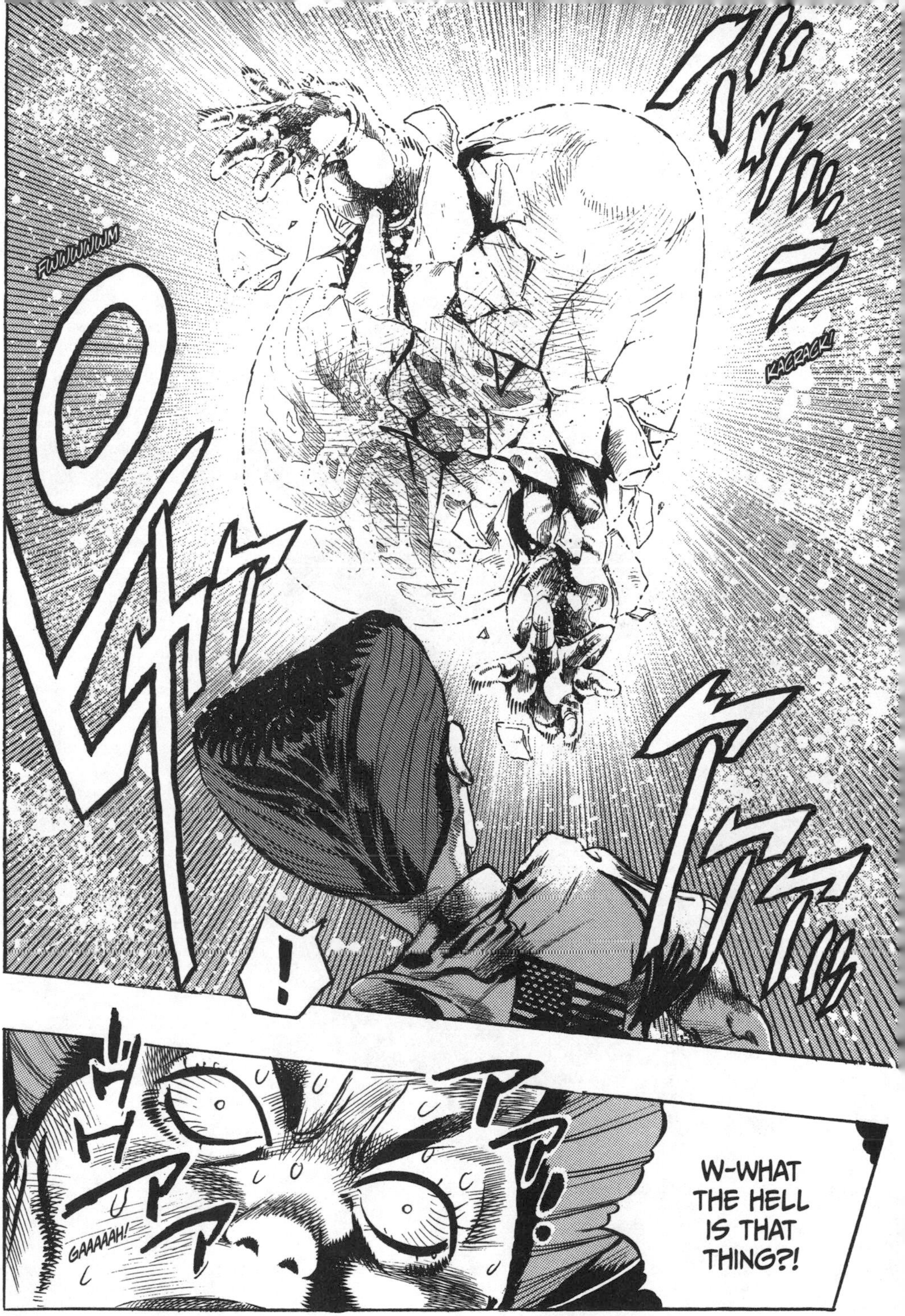
FWWWWWM
KACRACK!
!
W-WHAT THE HELL IS THAT THING?!
GAAAAAH!

CHAPTER 22

KOICHI HIROSE (REVERB), PART 4

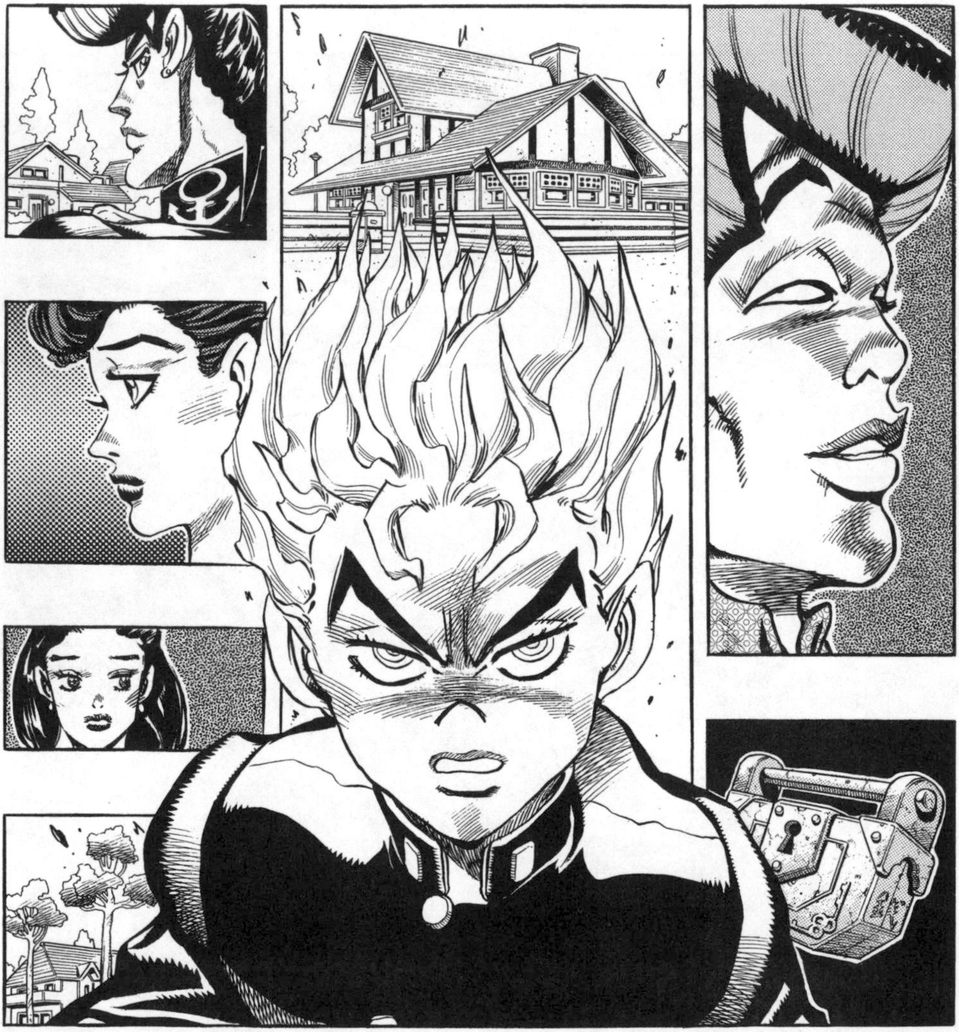

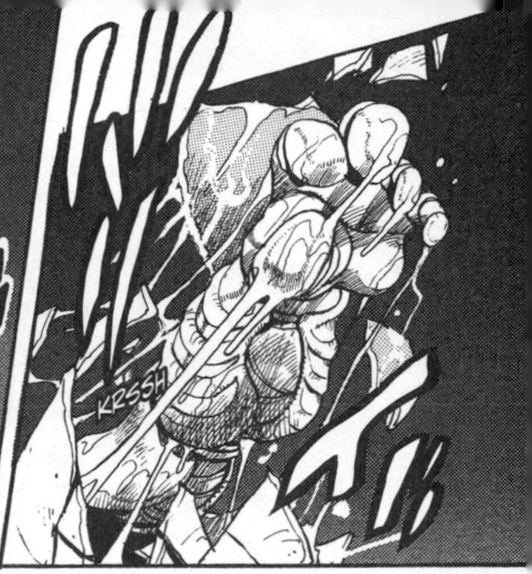
KRSSH
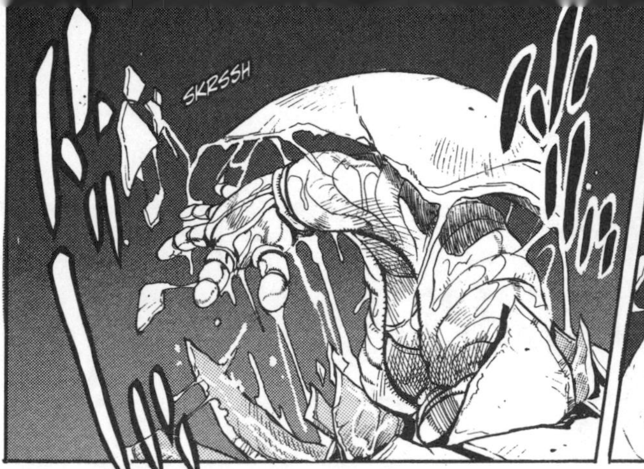
SKRSSH
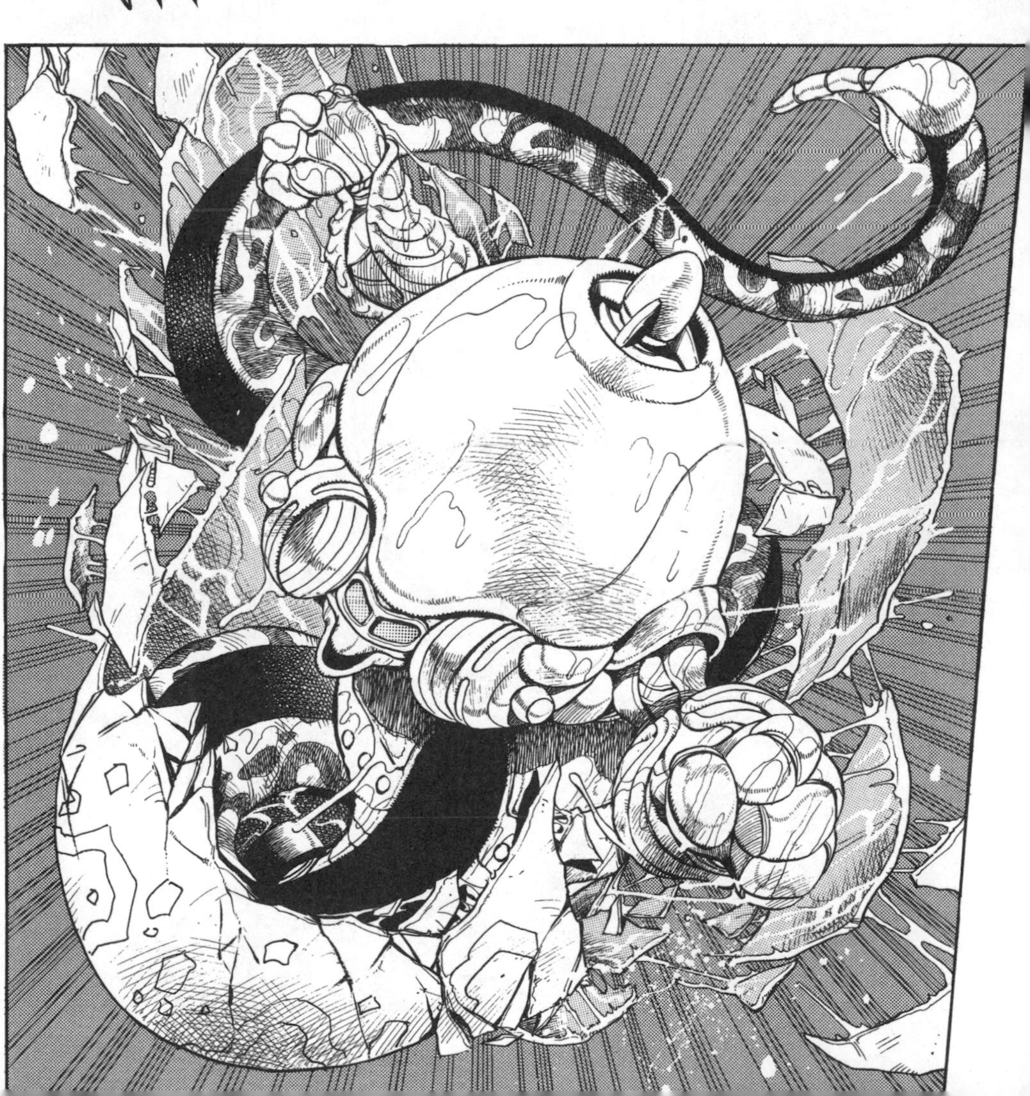

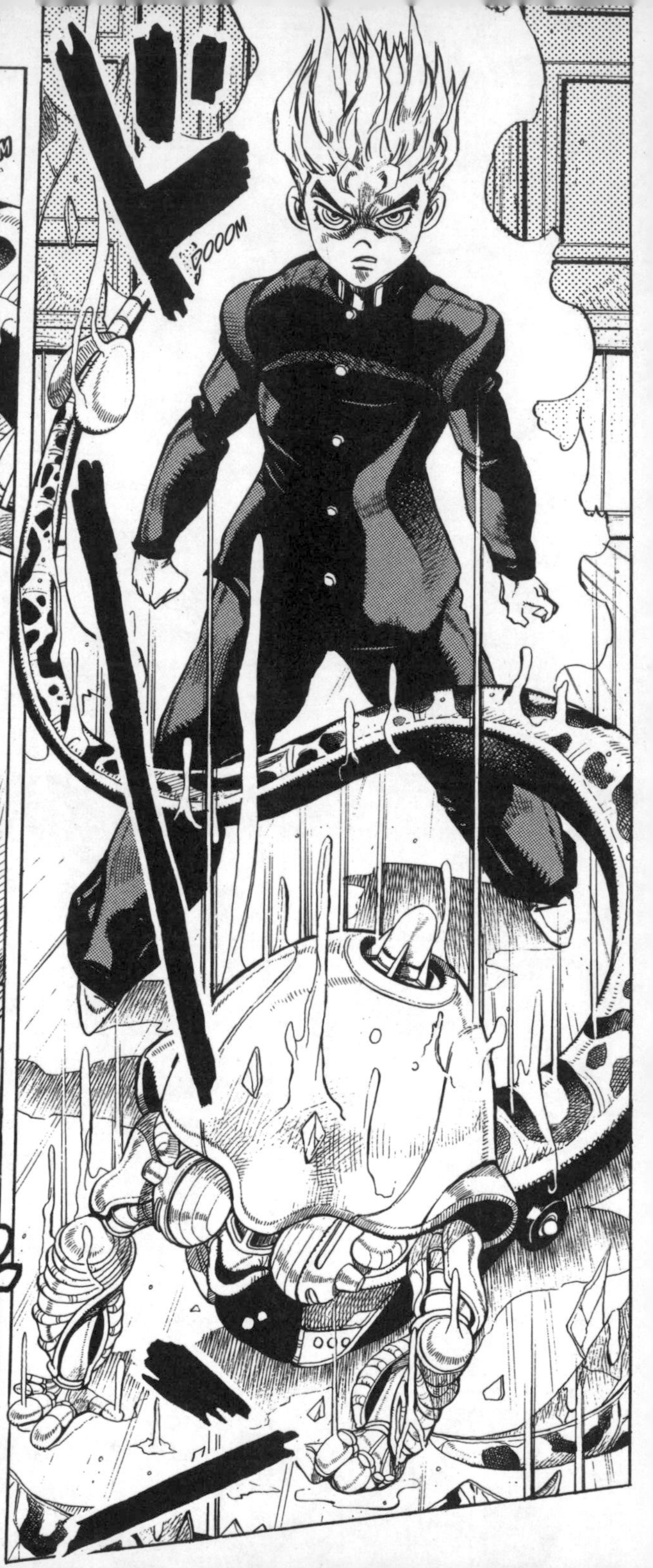
DOOOM
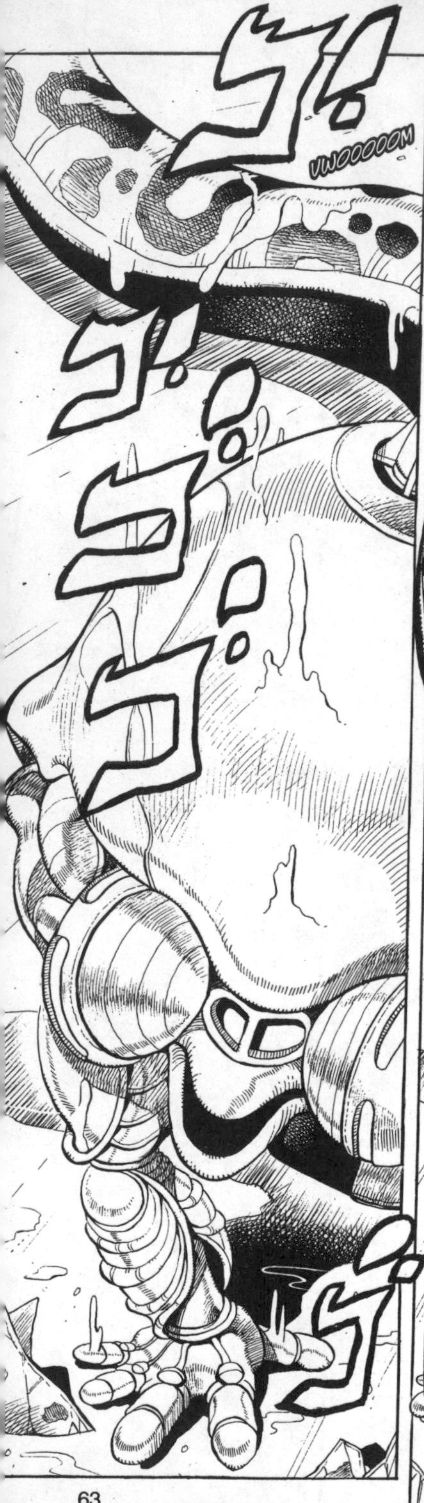
VWOOOOOM

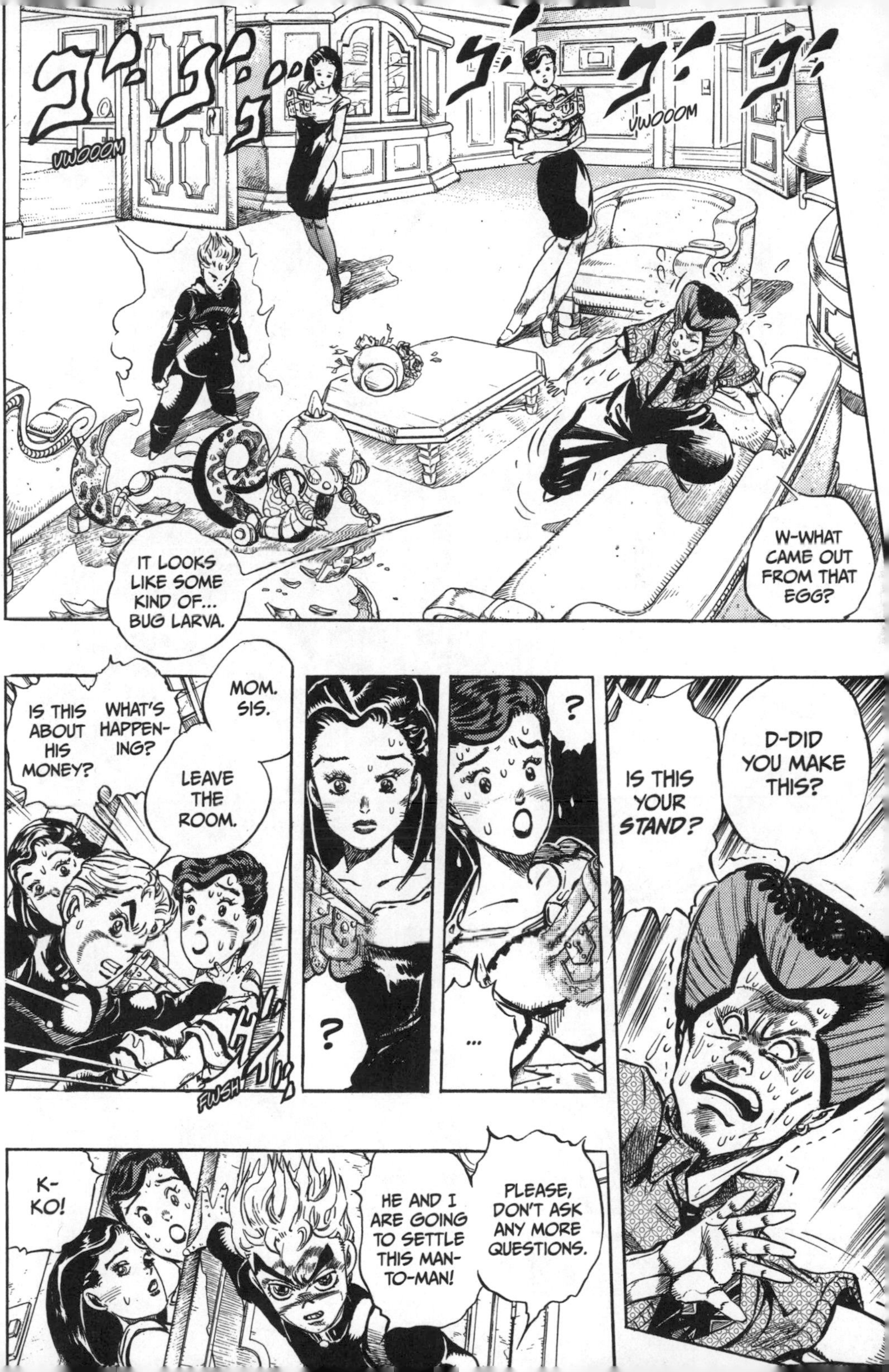
VWOOOM
VWOOOM
W-WHAT CAME OUT FROM THAT EGG?
IT LOOKS LIKE SOME KIND OF... BUG LARVA.
D-DID YOU MAKE THIS?
IS THIS YOUR STAND?
?
...
?
MOM. SIS.
LEAVE THE ROOM.
WHAT'S HAPPENING?
IS THIS ABOUT HIS MONEY?
FWSH
PLEASE, DON'T ASK ANY MORE QUESTIONS.
HE AND I ARE GOING TO SETTLE THIS MAN-TO-MAN!
K-KO!

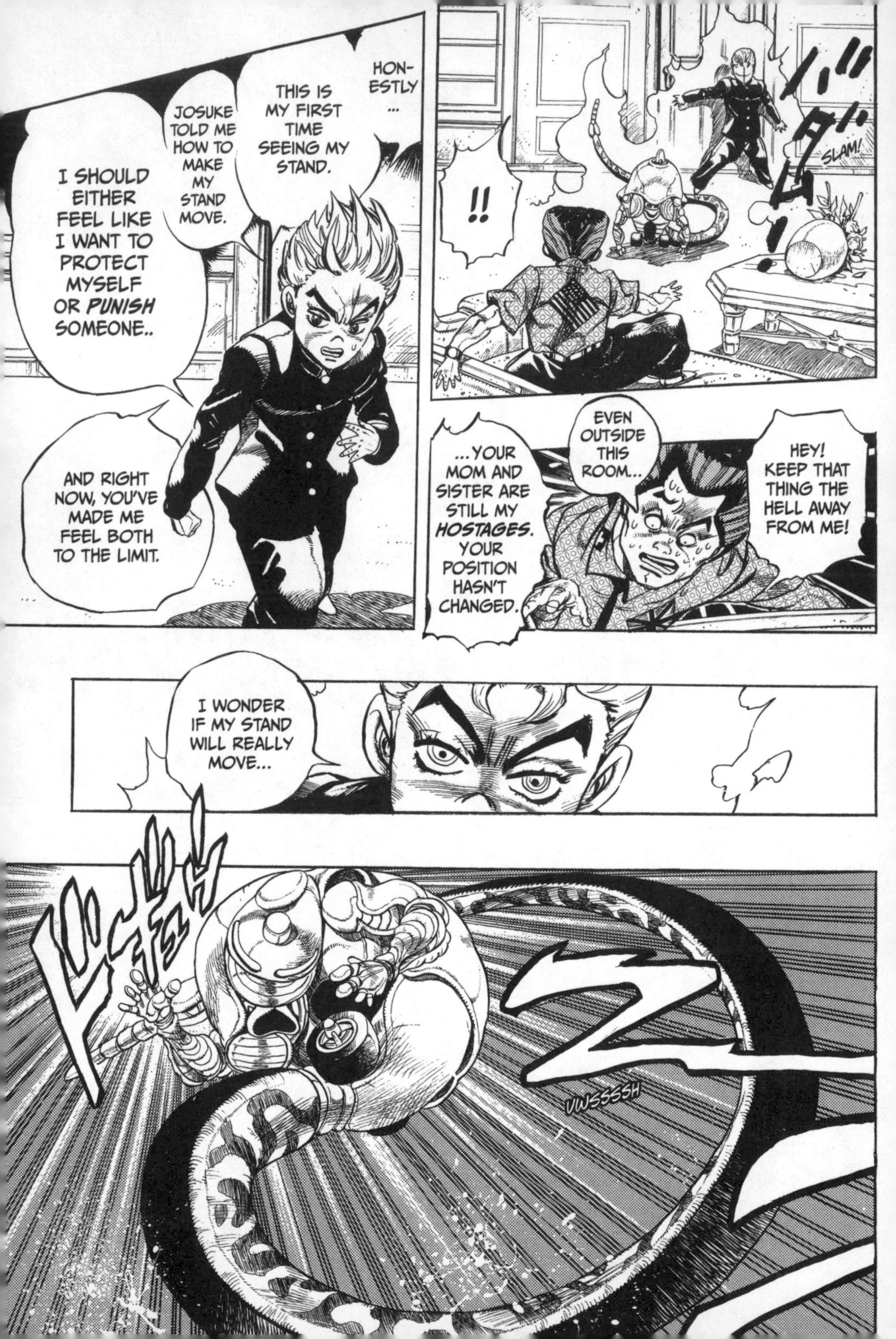

SLAM!
!!
HEY! KEEP THAT THING THE HELL AWAY FROM ME!
EVEN OUTSIDE THIS ROOM...
...YOUR MOM AND SISTER ARE STILL MY *HOSTAGES*. YOUR POSITION HASN'T CHANGED.
HONESTLY ...
THIS IS MY FIRST TIME SEEING MY STAND.
JOSUKE TOLD ME HOW TO MAKE MY STAND MOVE.
I SHOULD EITHER FEEL LIKE I WANT TO PROTECT MYSELF OR *PUNISH* SOMEONE..
AND RIGHT NOW, YOU'VE MADE ME FEEL BOTH TO THE LIMIT.
I WONDER IF MY STAND WILL REALLY MOVE...
VWSSSSH

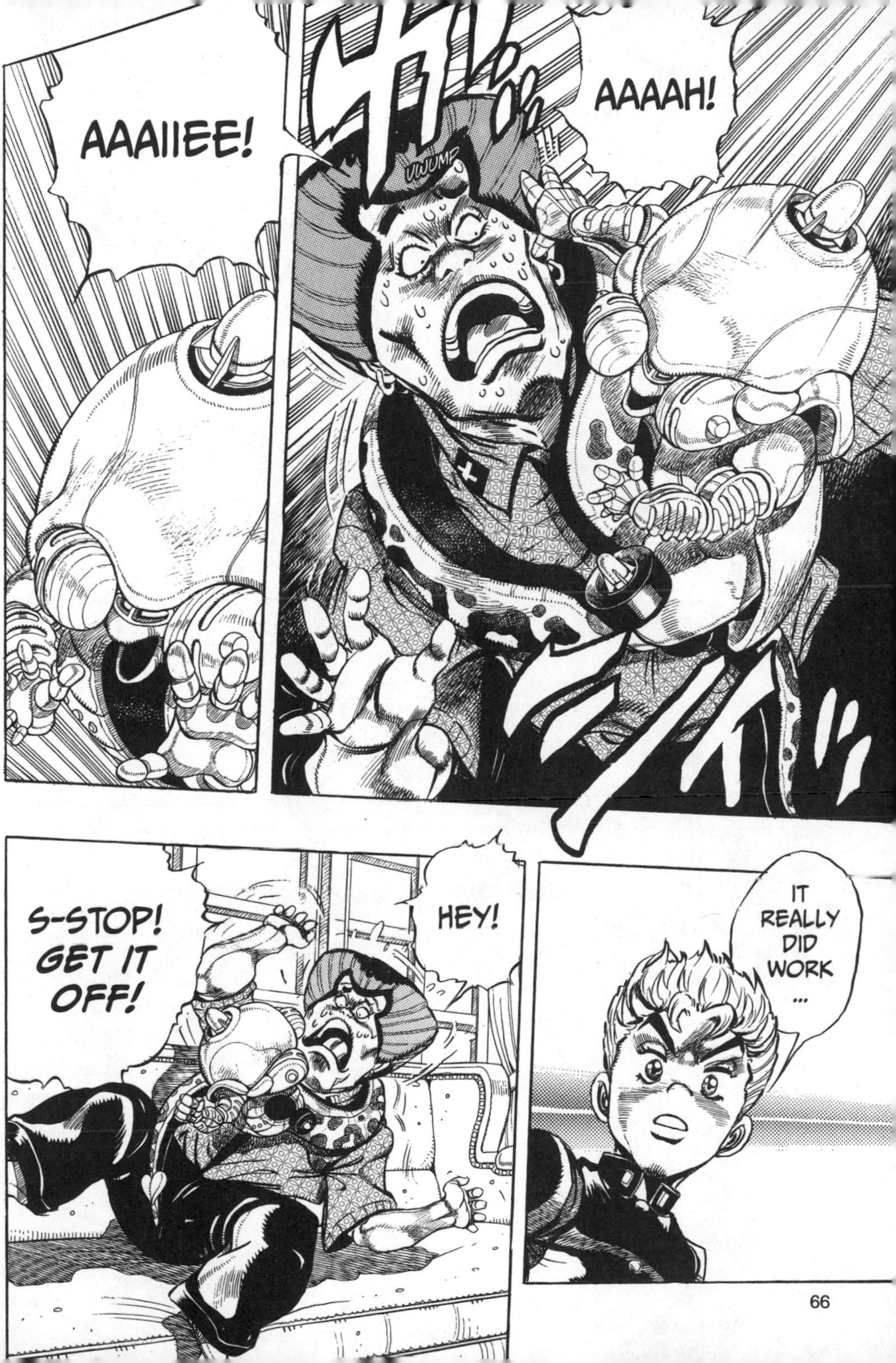
VWUMP
AAAAH!
AAAIIEE!
IT REALLY DID WORK ...
HEY!
S-STOP! GET IT OFF!

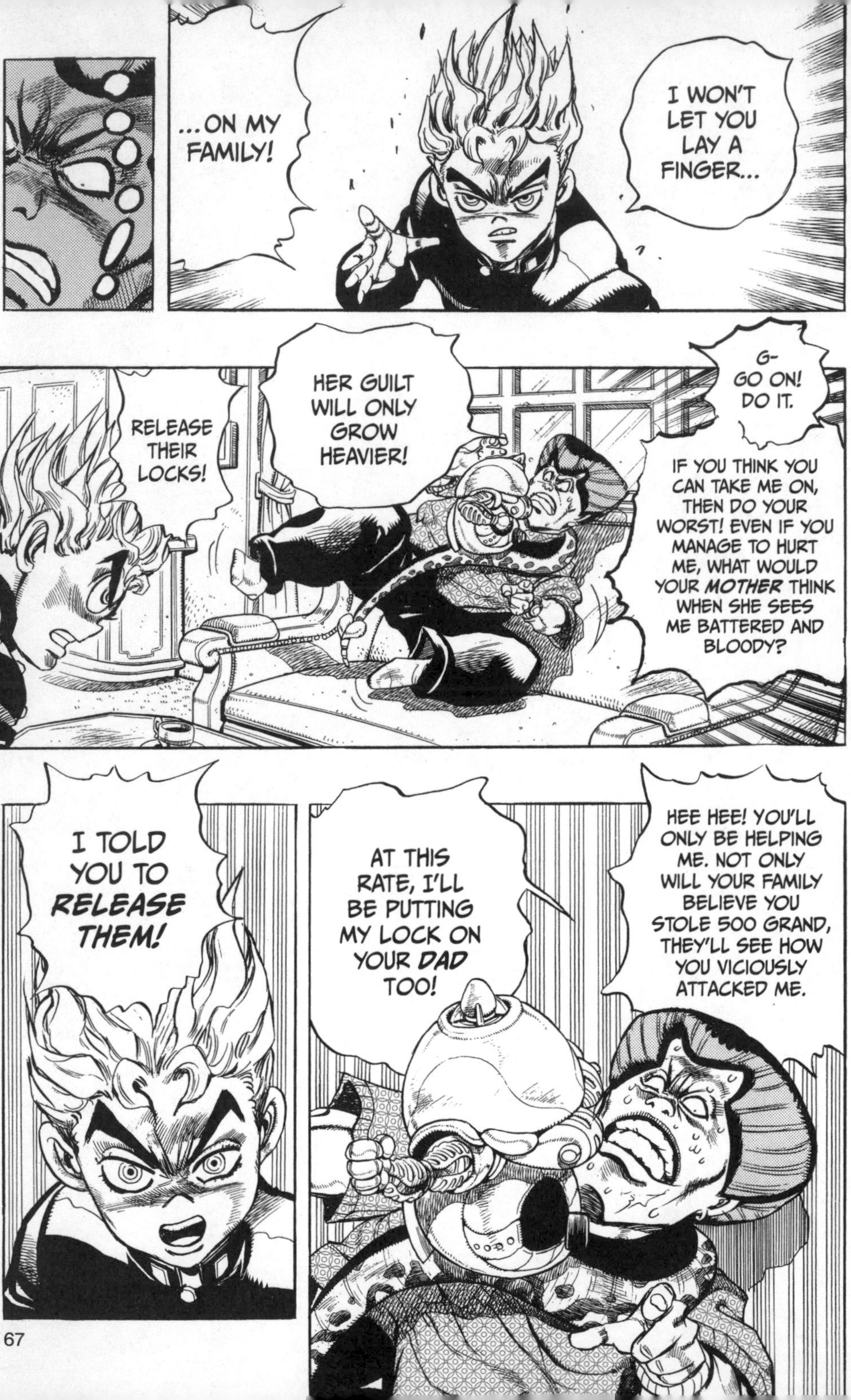
I WON'T LET YOU LAY A FINGER...
...ON MY FAMILY!
G- GO ON! DO IT.
IF YOU THINK YOU CAN TAKE ME ON, THEN DO YOUR WORST! EVEN IF YOU MANAGE TO HURT ME, WHAT WOULD YOUR *MOTHER* THINK WHEN SHE SEES ME BATTERED AND BLOODY?
HER GUILT WILL ONLY GROW HEAVIER!
RELEASE THEIR LOCKS!
HEE HEE! YOU'LL ONLY BE HELPING ME. NOT ONLY WILL YOUR FAMILY BELIEVE YOU STOLE 500 GRAND, THEY'LL SEE HOW YOU VICIOUSLY ATTACKED ME.
AT THIS RATE, I'LL BE PUTTING MY LOCK ON YOUR *DAD* TOO!
I TOLD YOU TO ***RELEASE THEM!***

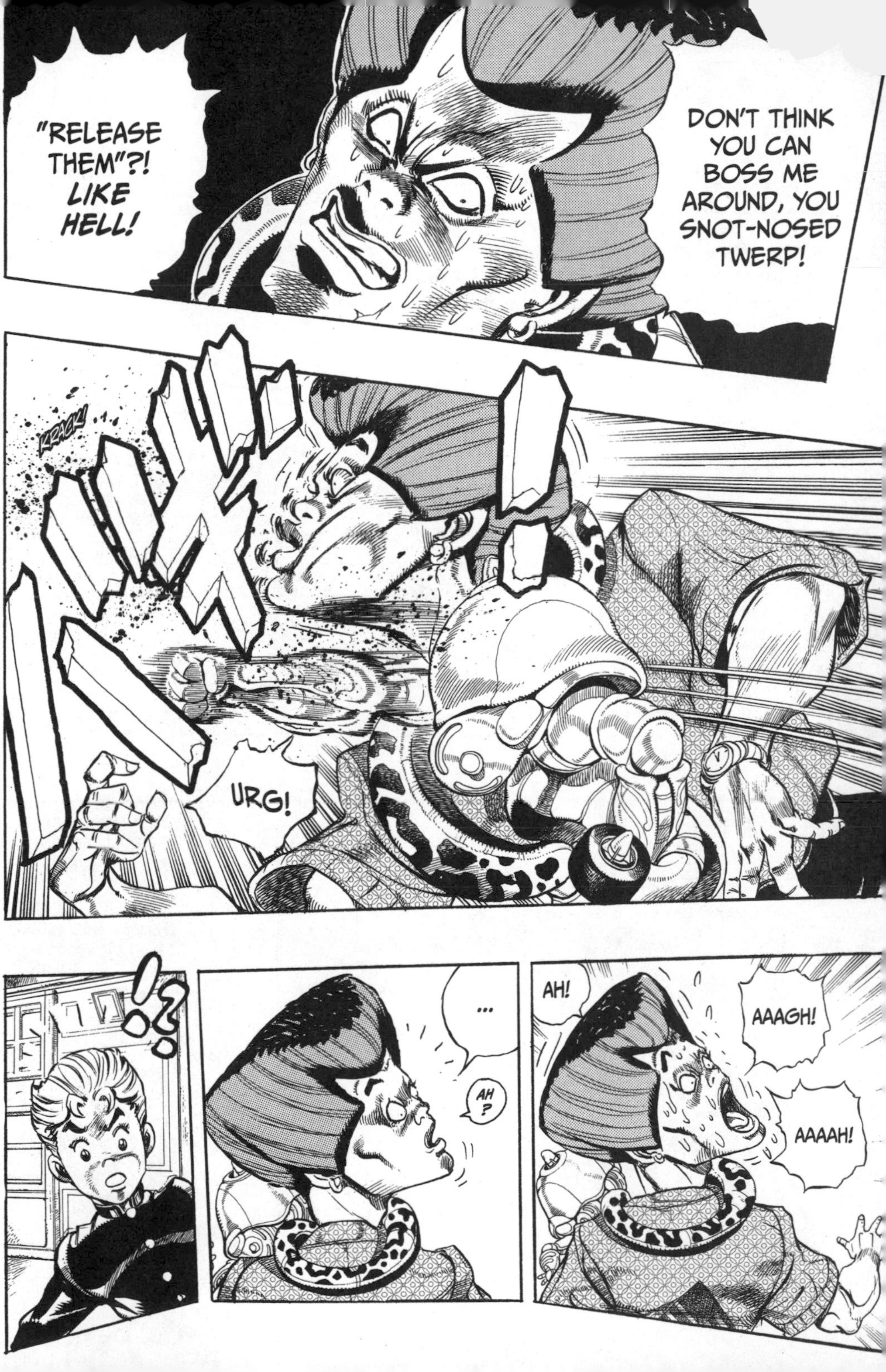
DON'T THINK YOU CAN BOSS ME AROUND, YOU SNOT-NOSED TWERP!
"RELEASE THEM"?! LIKE HELL!
KRACK!
URG!
AH!
AAAGH!
AAAAH!
...
AH?
!?

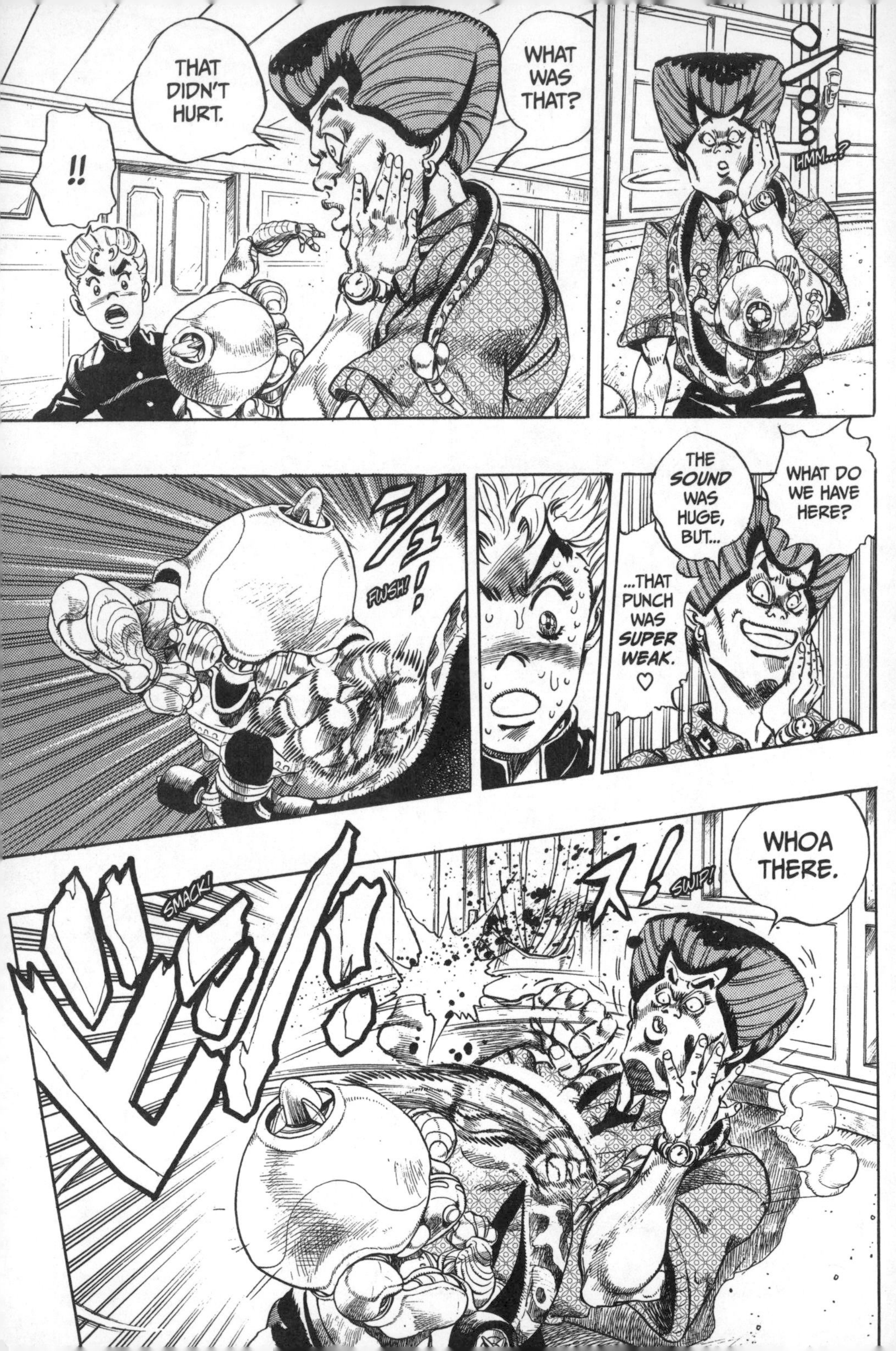
HMM...?
WHAT WAS THAT?
THAT DIDN'T HURT.
!!
WHAT DO WE HAVE HERE?
THE SOUND WAS HUGE, BUT...
...THAT PUNCH WAS SUPER WEAK. ♡
FWSH!
WHOA THERE.
SWIP!
SMACK!

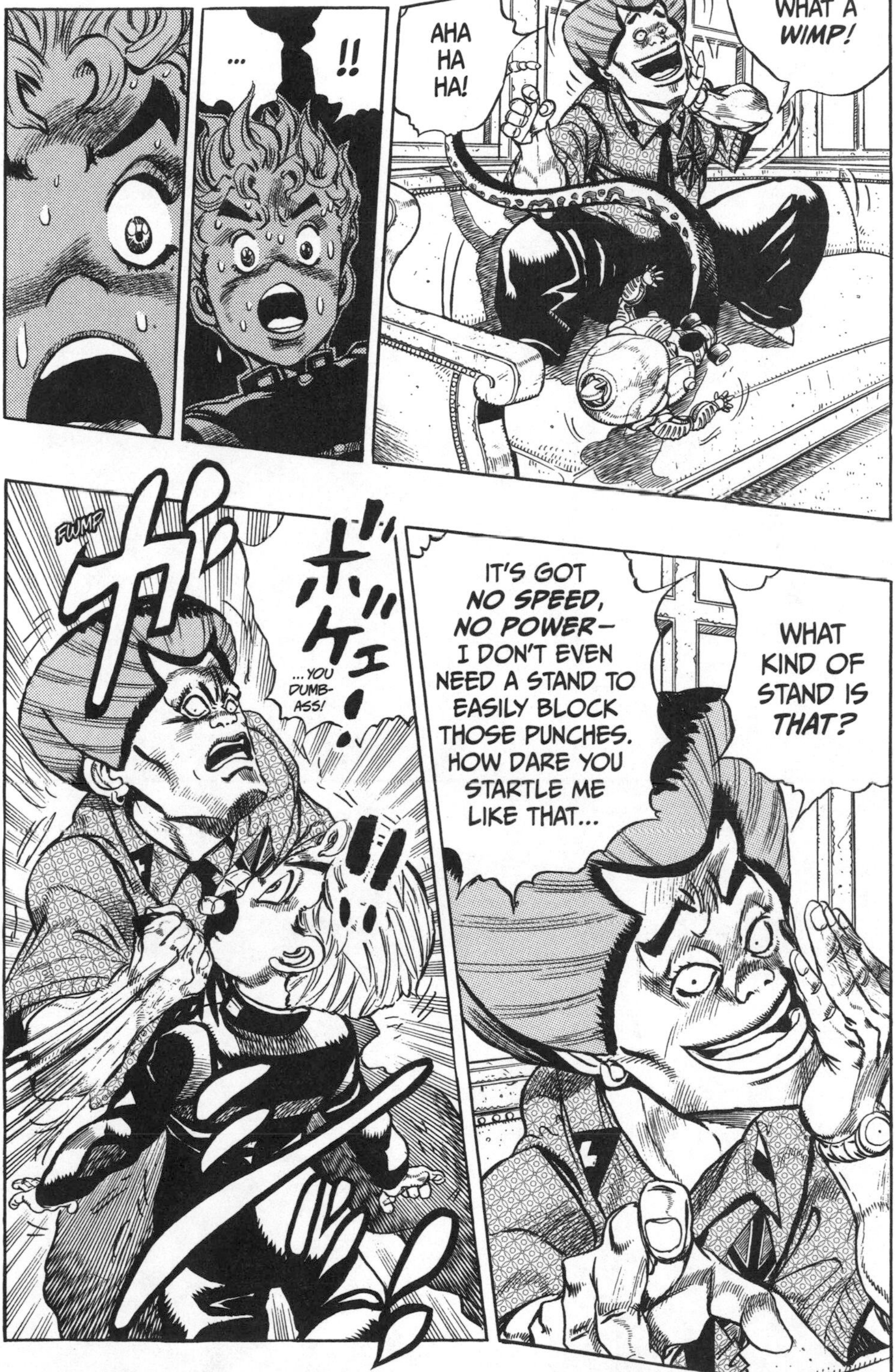
HO HO! WHAT A WIMP!
AHA HA HA!
...
!!
WHAT KIND OF STAND IS THAT?
IT'S GOT NO SPEED, NO POWER– I DON'T EVEN NEED A STAND TO EASILY BLOCK THOSE PUNCHES. HOW DARE YOU STARTLE ME LIKE THAT...
FWUMP
...YOU DUMB-ASS!

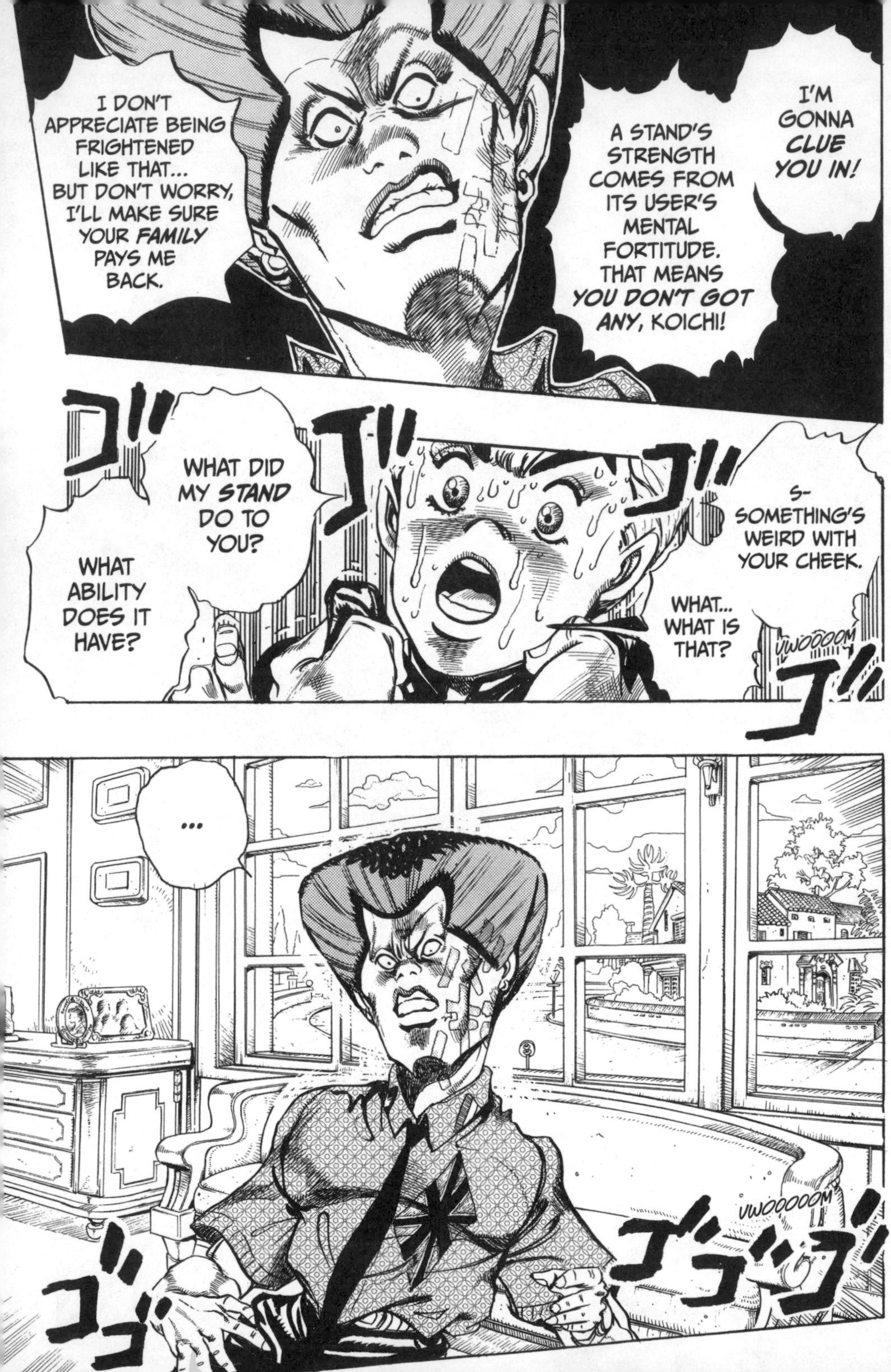
I'M GONNA CLUE YOU IN!
A STAND'S STRENGTH COMES FROM ITS USER'S MENTAL FORTITUDE. THAT MEANS YOU DON'T GOT ANY, KOICHI!
I DON'T APPRECIATE BEING FRIGHTENED LIKE THAT... BUT DON'T WORRY, I'LL MAKE SURE YOUR FAMILY PAYS ME BACK.
S-SOMETHING'S WEIRD WITH YOUR CHEEK.
WHAT... WHAT IS THAT?
VWOOOOM
WHAT DID MY STAND DO TO YOU?
WHAT ABILITY DOES IT HAVE?
...
VWOOOOOM

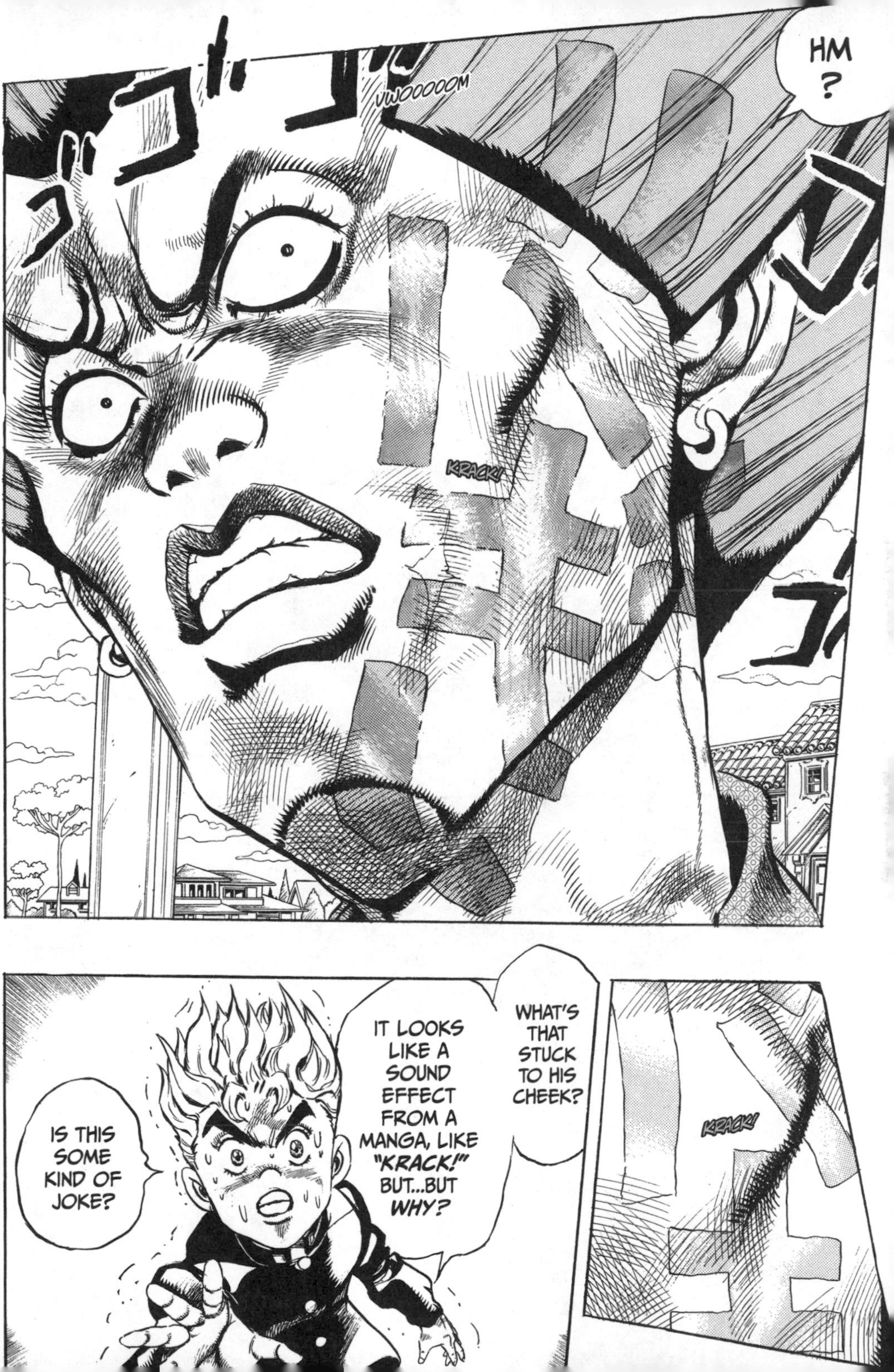
HM ?
VWOOOOOM
KRACK!
KRACK!
WHAT'S THAT STUCK TO HIS CHEEK?
IT LOOKS LIKE A SOUND EFFECT FROM A MANGA, LIKE "KRACK!" BUT...BUT WHY?
IS THIS SOME KIND OF JOKE?

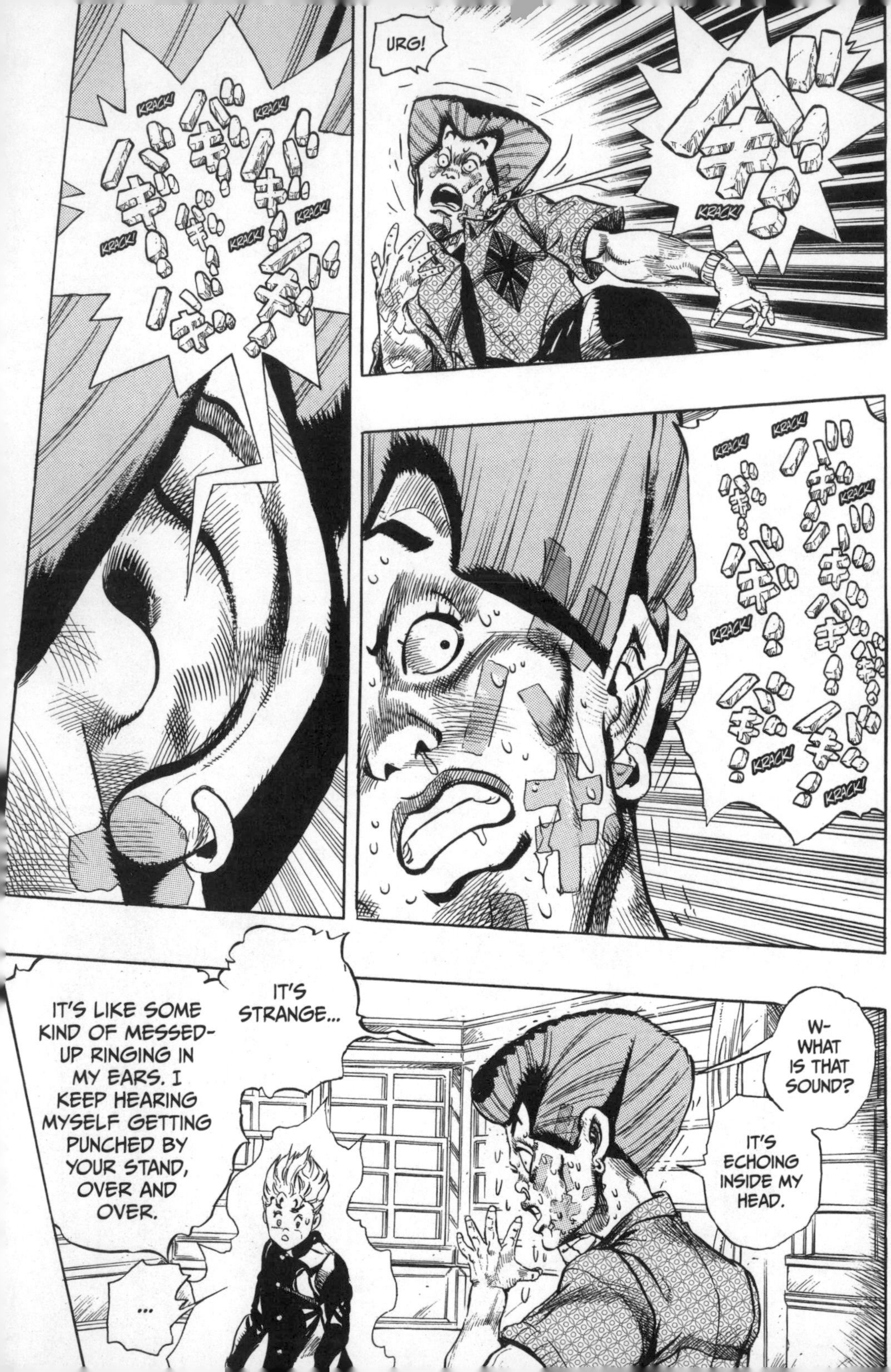
URG!
KRACK!
KRACK!
KRACK!
KRACK!
KRACK!
KRACK!
KRACK!
KRACK!
KRACK!
KRACK!
KRACK!
KRACK!
W-WHAT IS THAT SOUND?
IT'S ECHOING INSIDE MY HEAD.
IT'S STRANGE...
IT'S LIKE SOME KIND OF MESSED-UP RINGING IN MY EARS. I KEEP HEARING MYSELF GETTING PUNCHED BY YOUR STAND, OVER AND OVER.
...

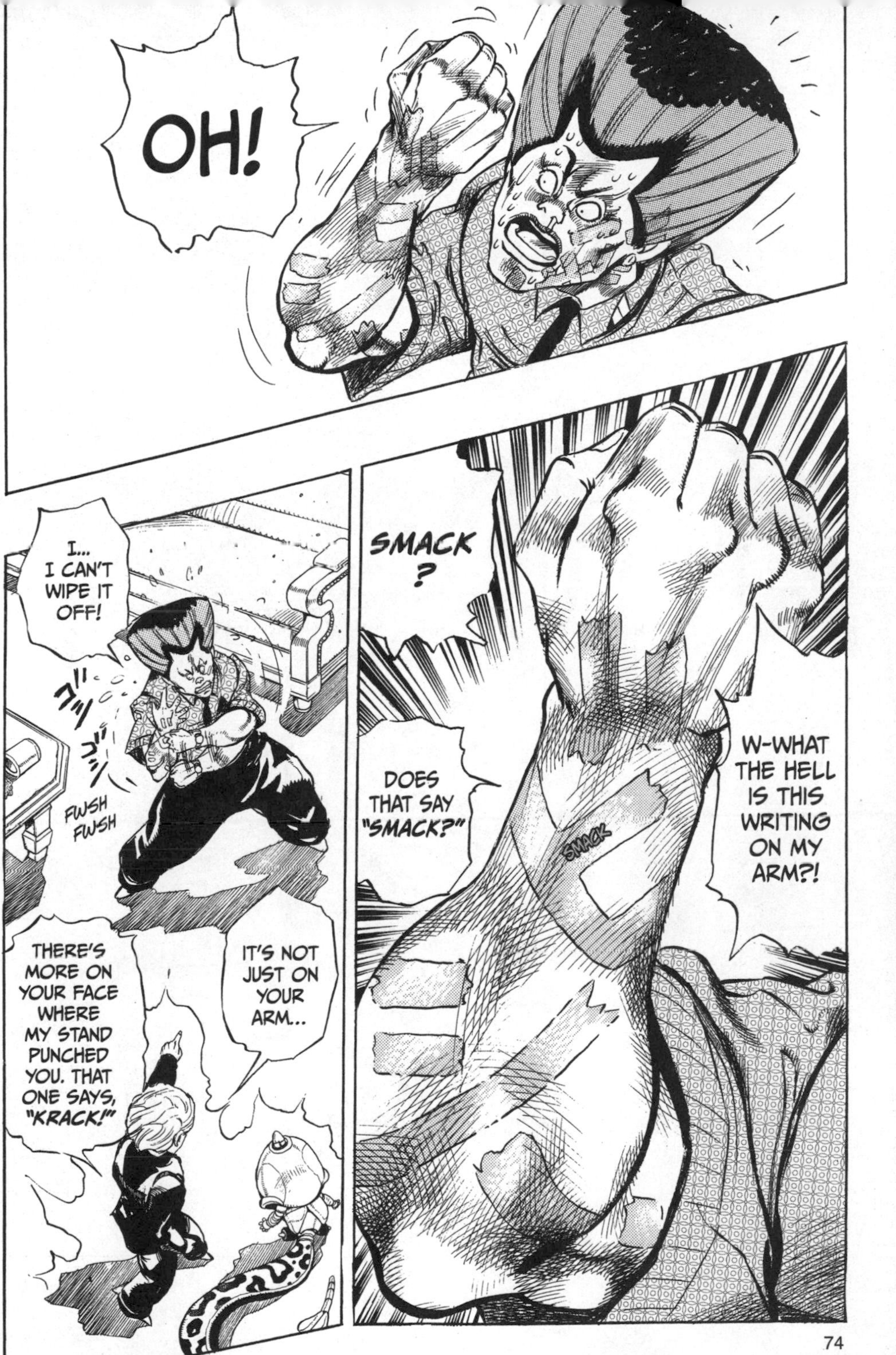
OH!
W-WHAT THE HELL IS THIS WRITING ON MY ARM?!
DOES THAT SAY "SMACK?"
SMACK ?
SMACK
I... I CAN'T WIPE IT OFF!
FWSH FWSH
IT'S NOT JUST ON YOUR ARM...
THERE'S MORE ON YOUR FACE WHERE MY STAND PUNCHED YOU. THAT ONE SAYS, "KRACK!"

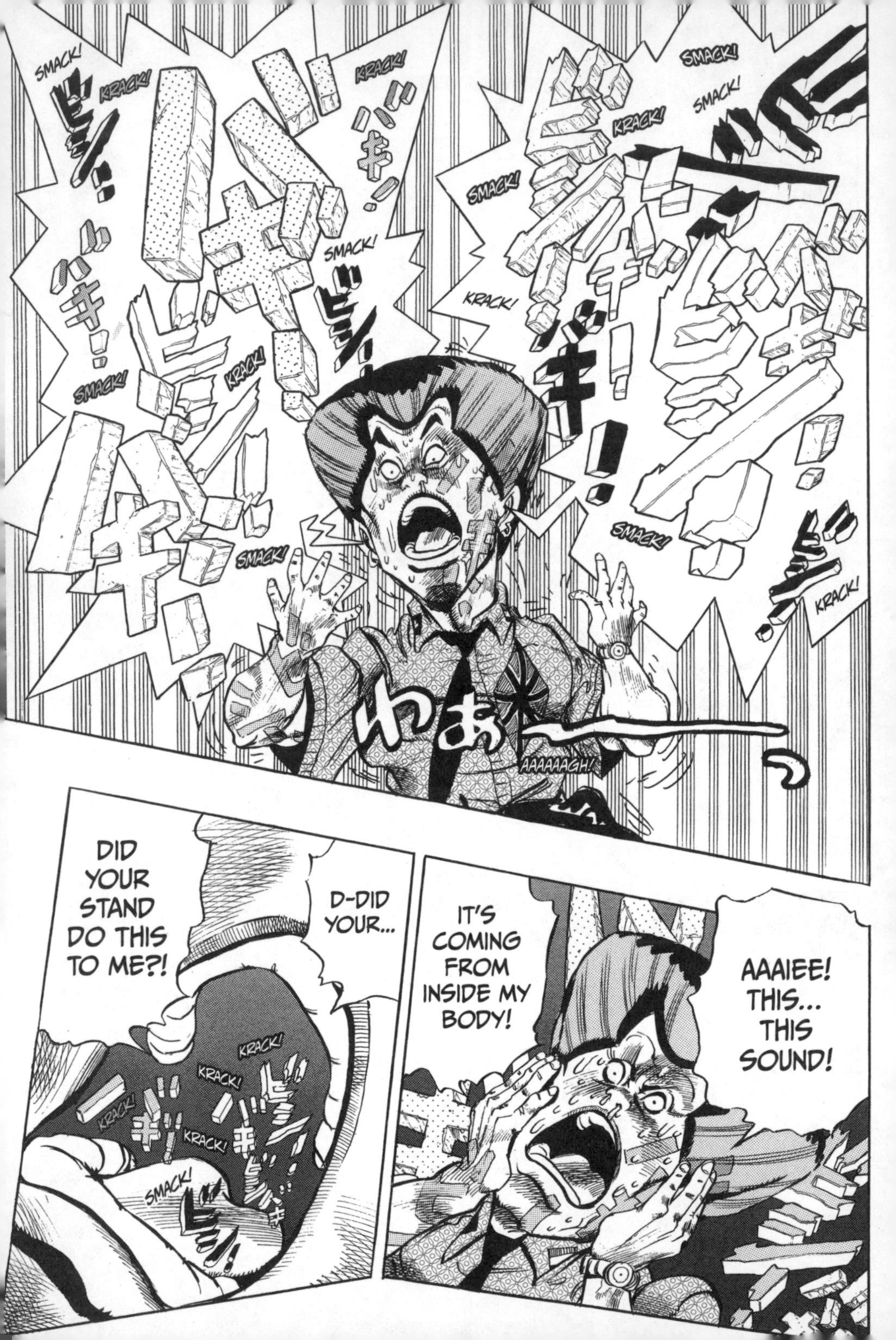
SMACK!
SMACK!
KRACK!
SMACK!
KRACK!
SMACK!
KRACK!
SMACK!
KRACK!
KRACK!
SMACK!
KRACK!
SMACK!
KRACK!
SMACK!
SMACK!
AAAAAAAGH!
AAAIEE! THIS... THIS SOUND!
IT'S COMING FROM INSIDE MY BODY!
D-DID YOUR...
DID YOUR STAND DO THIS TO ME?!
KRACK!
KRACK!
KRACK!
KRACK!
SMACK!

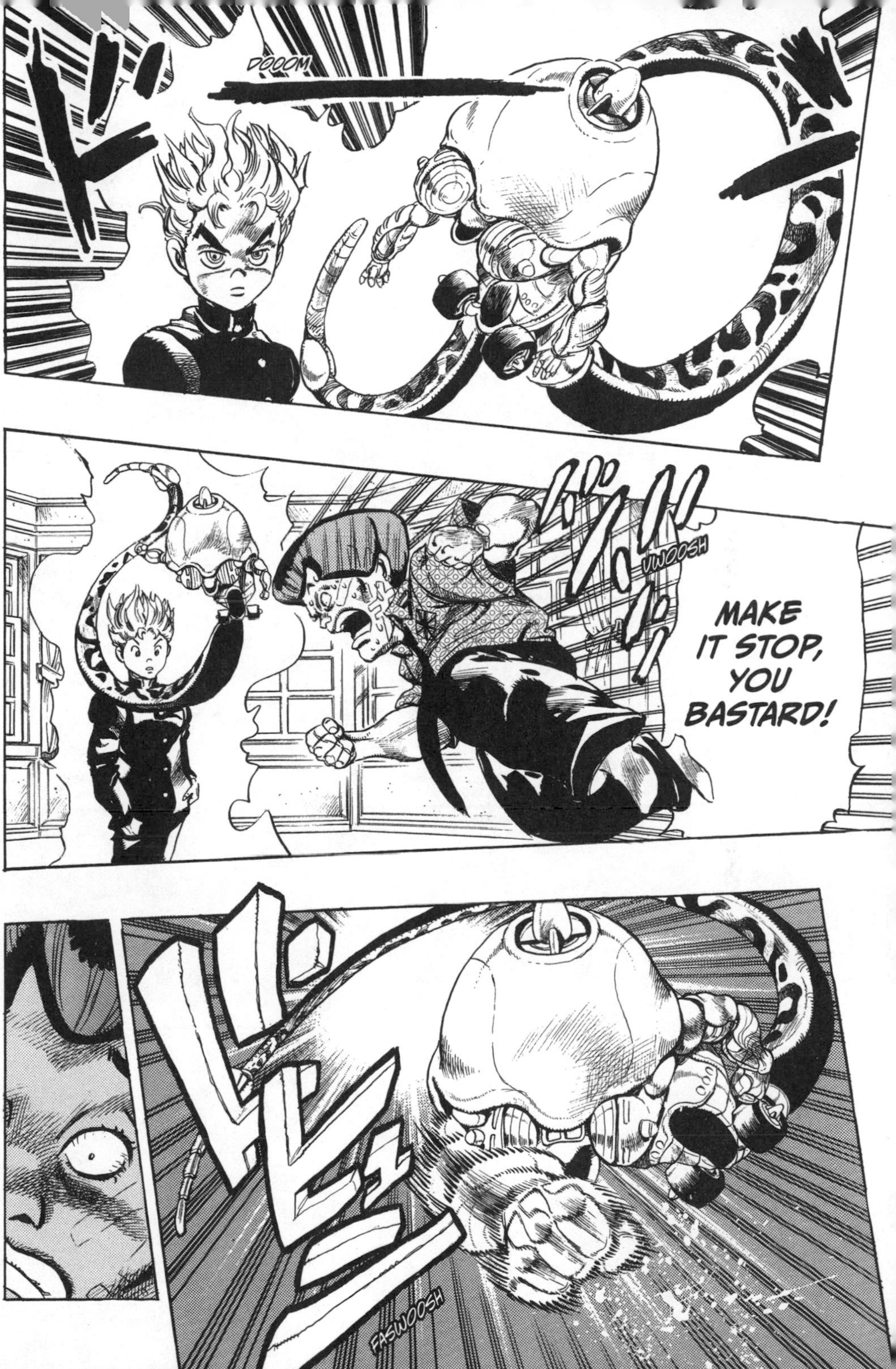
DOOOM
VWOOSH
MAKE IT STOP, YOU BASTARD!
FASWOOSH

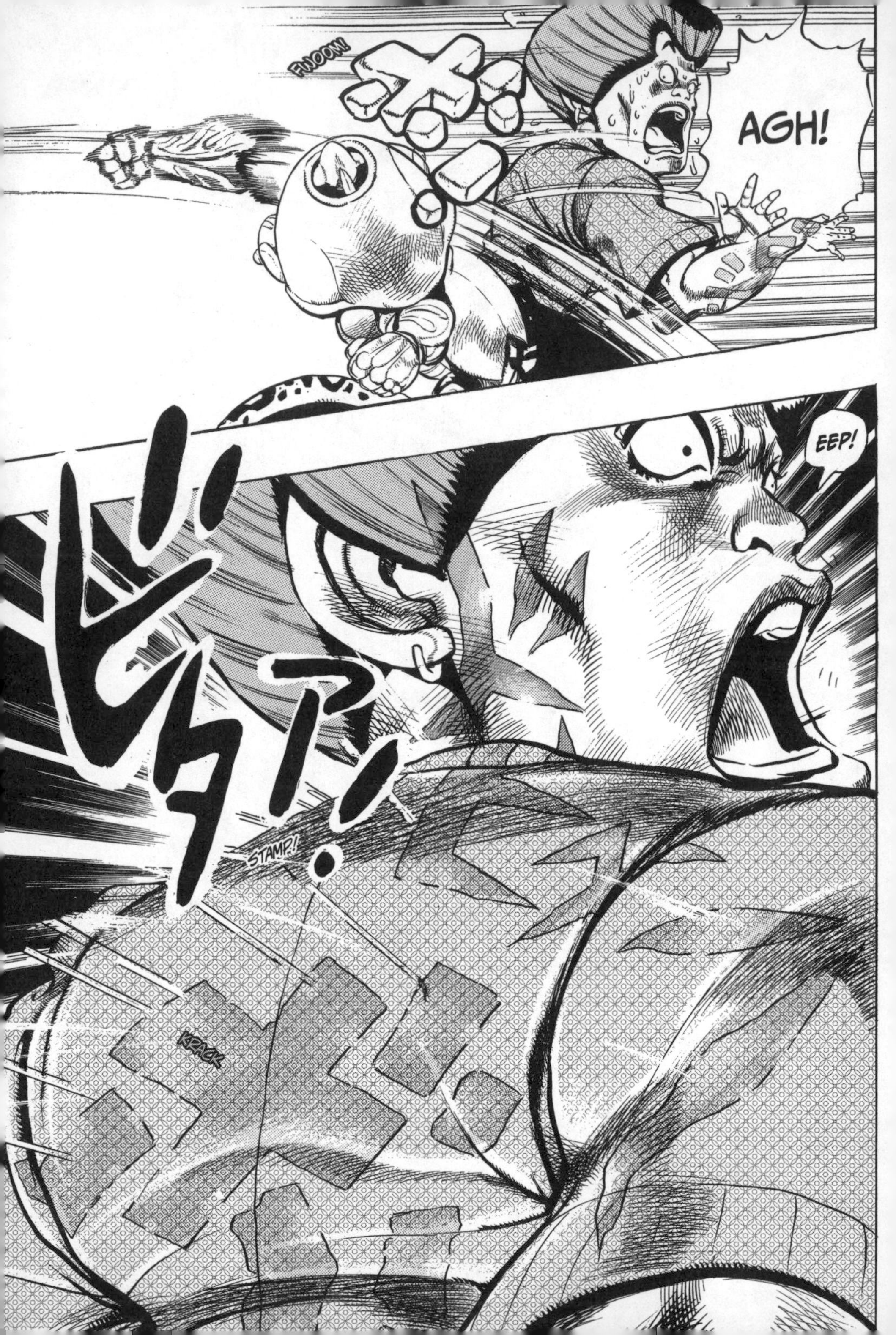
AGH!
FWOOM!
EEP!
STAMP!
KRACK

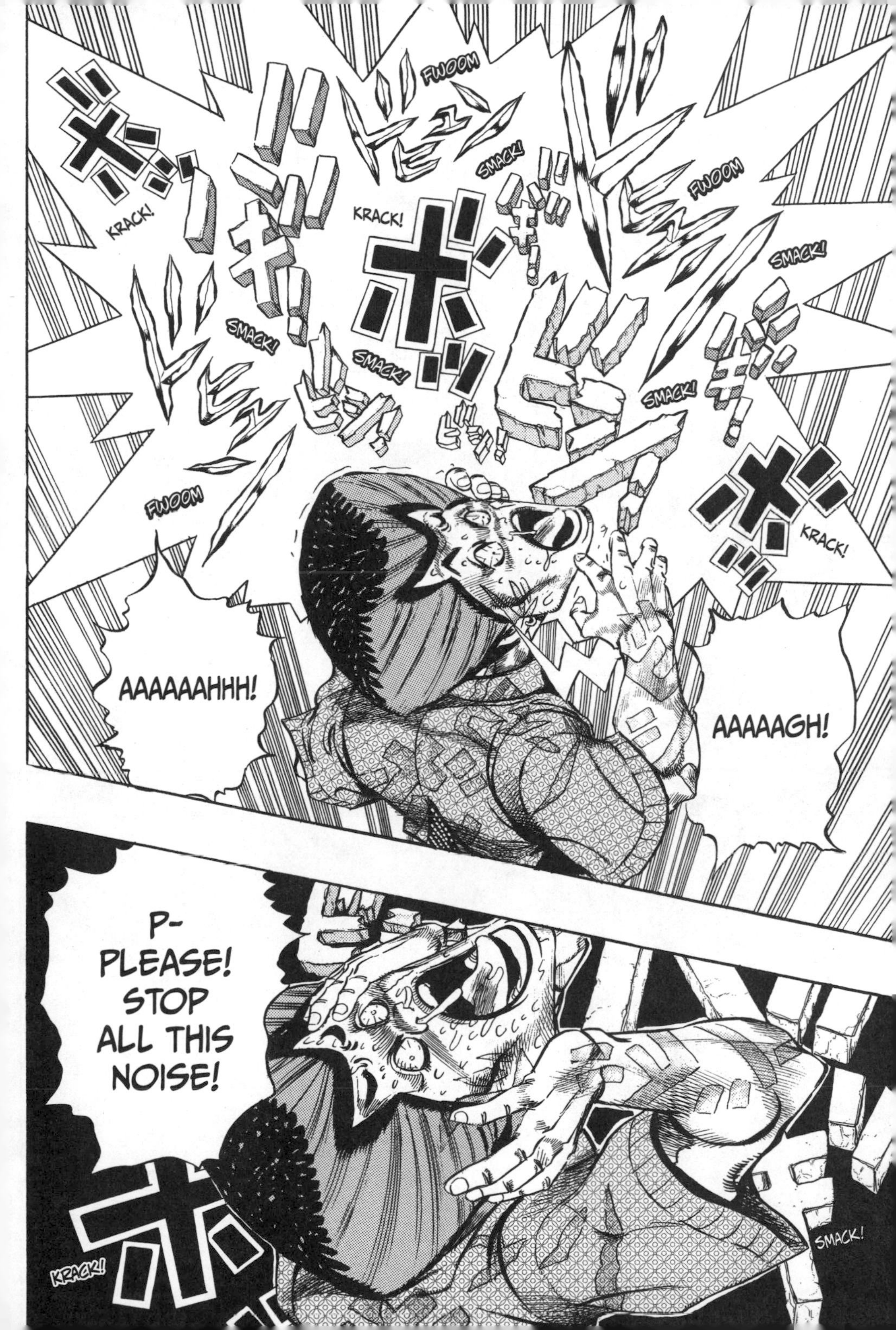

FWOOM
SMACK!
SMACK!
KRACK!
FWOOM
SMACK!
KRACK!
SMACK!
SMACK!
KRACK!
FWOOM
AAAAAGH!
AAAAAAHHH!
P-
PLEASE!
STOP
ALL THIS
NOISE!
SMACK!
KRACK!

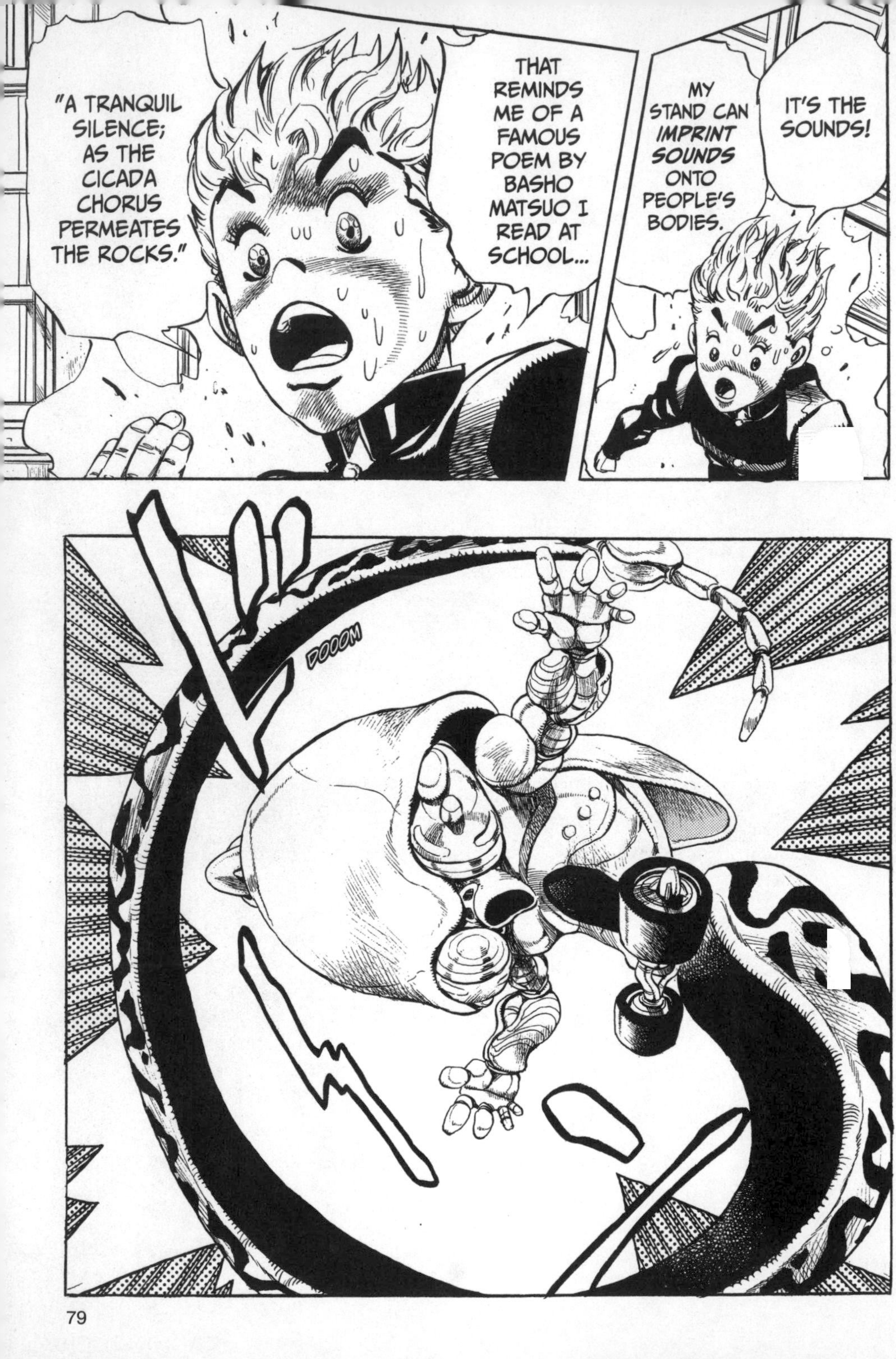
IT'S THE SOUNDS!
MY STAND CAN IMPRINT SOUNDS ONTO PEOPLE'S BODIES.
THAT REMINDS ME OF A FAMOUS POEM BY BASHO MATSUO I READ AT SCHOOL...
"A TRANQUIL SILENCE; AS THE CICADA CHORUS PERMEATES THE ROCKS."
DOOOM

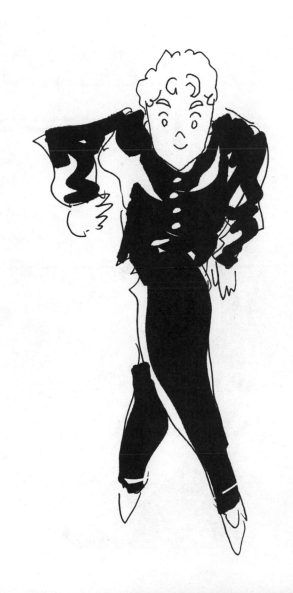

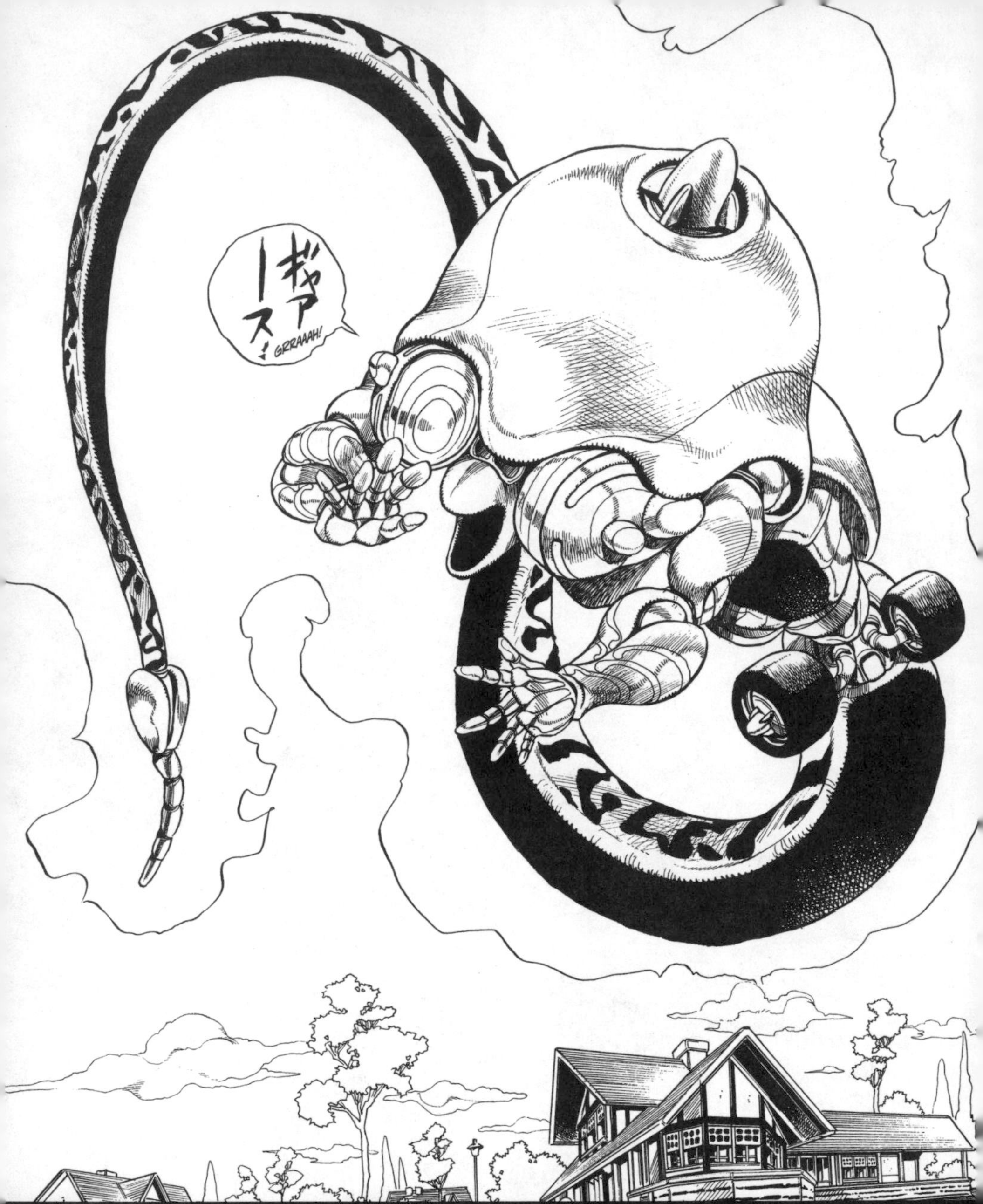
ギャアース!
GRRAAAH!

CHAPTER 23

KOICHI HIROSE (REVERB), PART 5

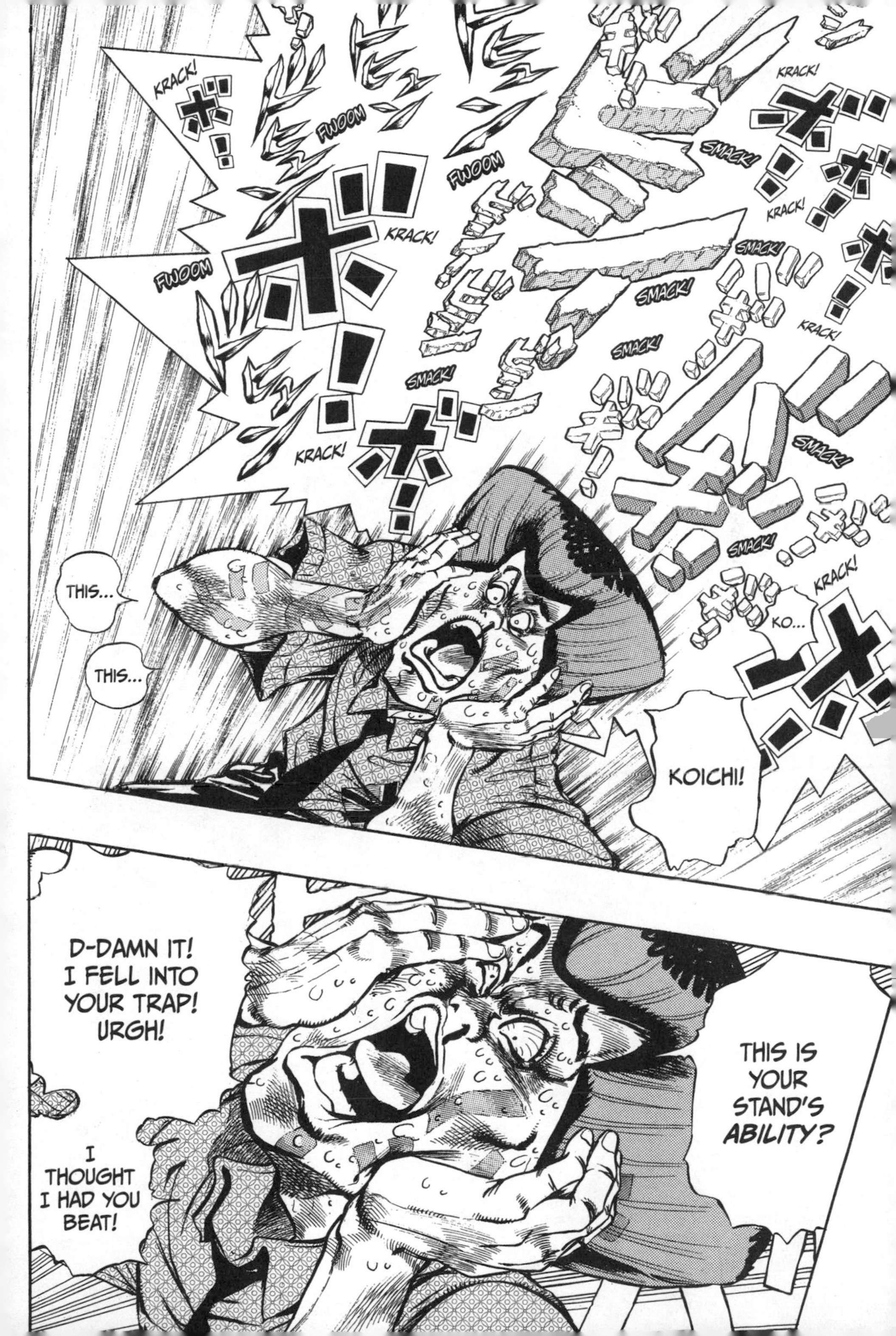
KRACK!
SMACK!
KRACK!
SMACK!
SMACK!
KRACK!
SMACK!
SMACK!
SMACK!
KRACK!
KO...
KOICHI!
FWOOM
FWOOM
KRACK!
KRACK!
FWOOM
SMACK!
KRACK!
THIS...
THIS...
THIS IS YOUR STAND'S ABILITY?
D-DAMN IT! I FELL INTO YOUR TRAP! URGH!
I THOUGHT I HAD YOU BEAT!

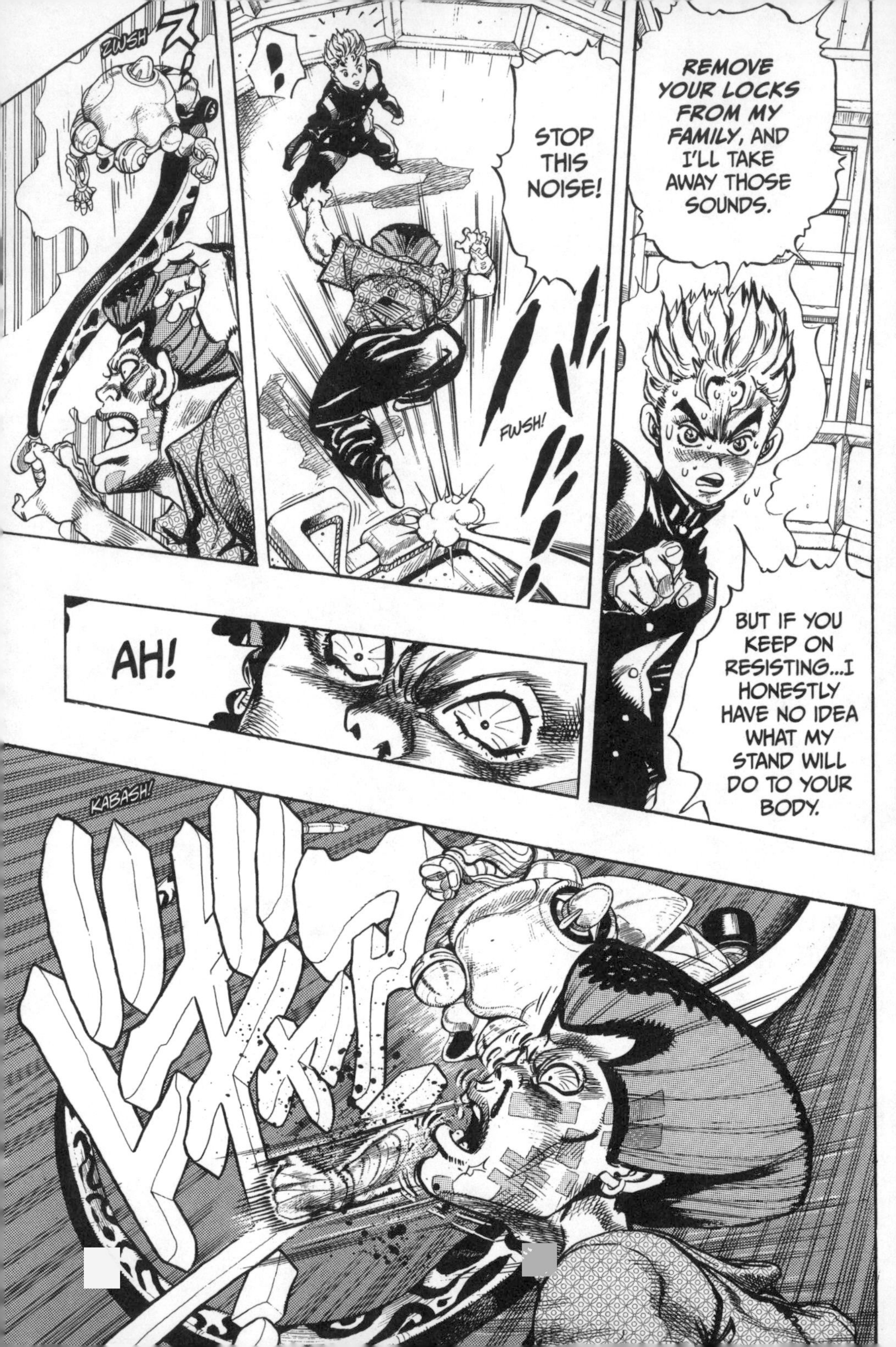
REMOVE YOUR LOCKS FROM MY FAMILY, AND I'LL TAKE AWAY THOSE SOUNDS.
BUT IF YOU KEEP ON RESISTING...I HONESTLY HAVE NO IDEA WHAT MY STAND WILL DO TO YOUR BODY.
STOP THIS NOISE!
FWSH!
ZWSH
AH!
KABASH!

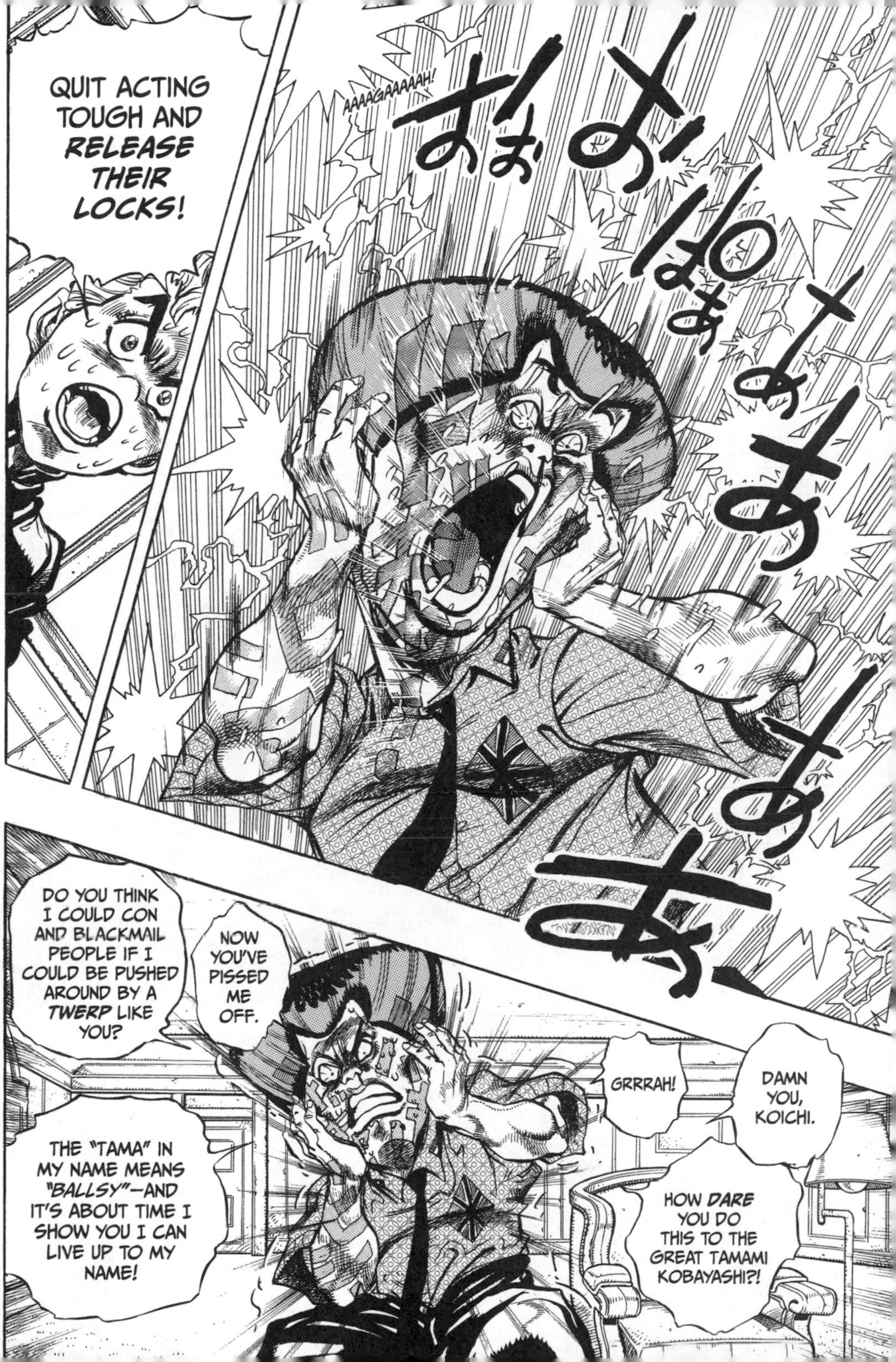
AAAAGAAAAAH!
QUIT ACTING TOUGH AND RELEASE THEIR LOCKS!
DAMN YOU, KOICHI.
GRRRAH!
HOW DARE YOU DO THIS TO THE GREAT TAMAMI KOBAYASHI?!
NOW YOU'VE PISSED ME OFF.
DO YOU THINK I COULD CON AND BLACKMAIL PEOPLE IF I COULD BE PUSHED AROUND BY A TWERP LIKE YOU?
THE "TAMA" IN MY NAME MEANS "BALLSY"—AND IT'S ABOUT TIME I SHOW YOU I CAN LIVE UP TO MY NAME!

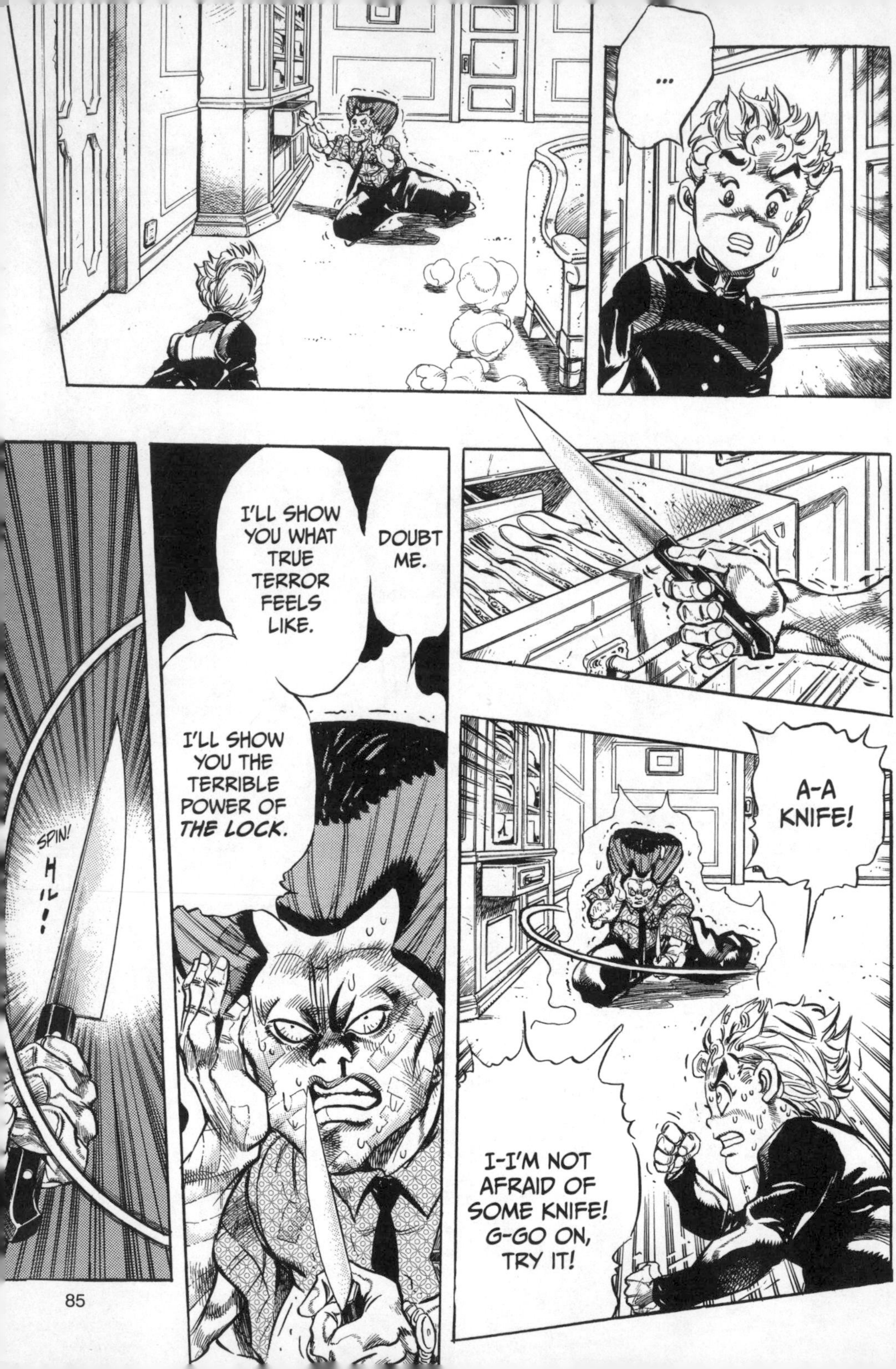
...
A-A KNIFE!
I-I'M NOT AFRAID OF SOME KNIFE! G-GO ON, TRY IT!
DOUBT ME.
I'LL SHOW YOU WHAT TRUE TERROR FEELS LIKE.
I'LL SHOW YOU THE TERRIBLE POWER OF *THE LOCK*.
SPIN!

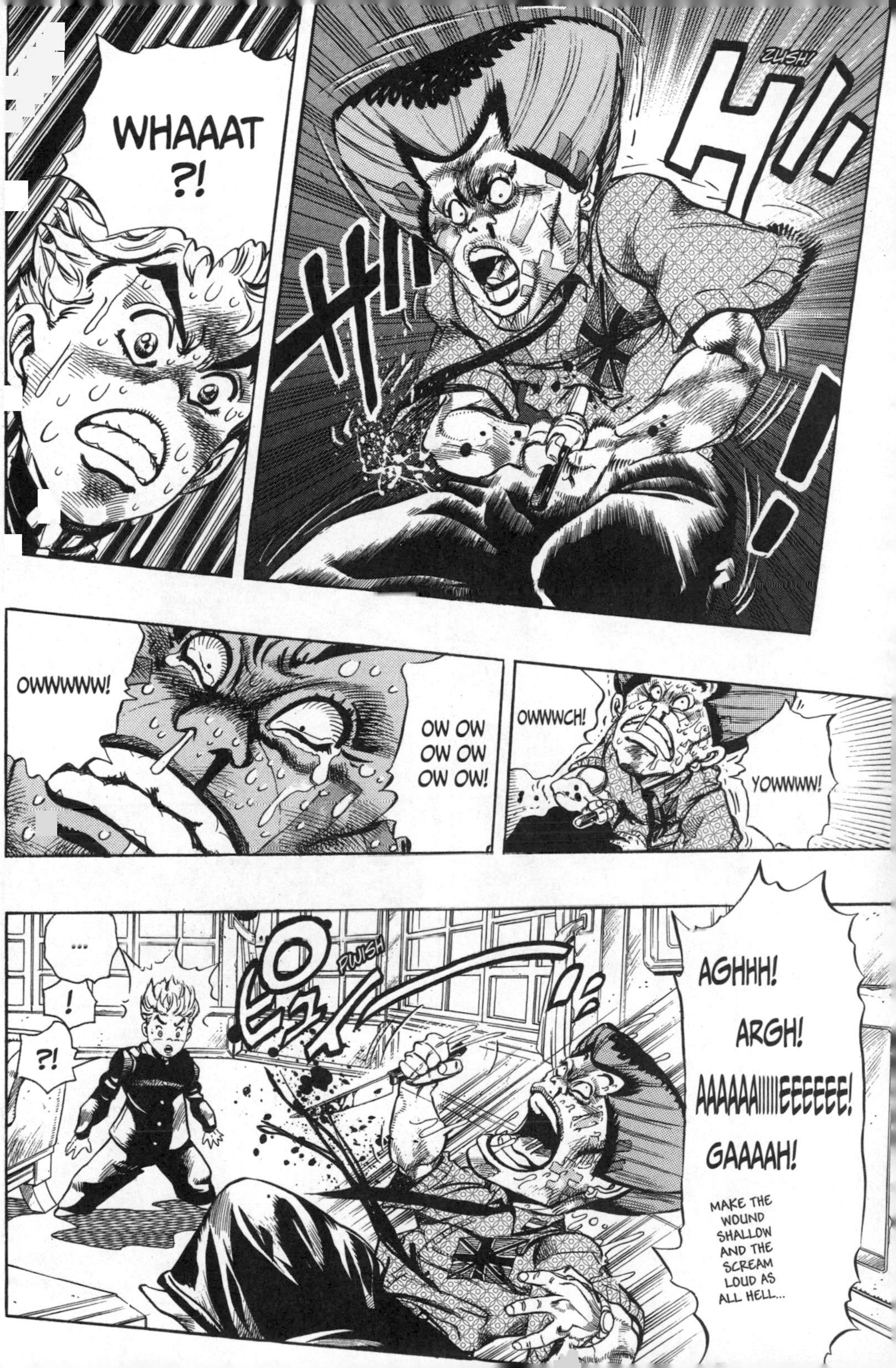
ZUSH!
WHAAAT ?!
OWWWCH!
YOWWWW!
OWWWWW!
OW OW OW OW OW OW!
AGHHH!
ARGH!
AAAAAAIIIIIEEEEEE!
GAAAAH!
MAKE THE WOUND SHALLOW AND THE SCREAM LOUD AS ALL HELL...
PWISH
...
!
?!

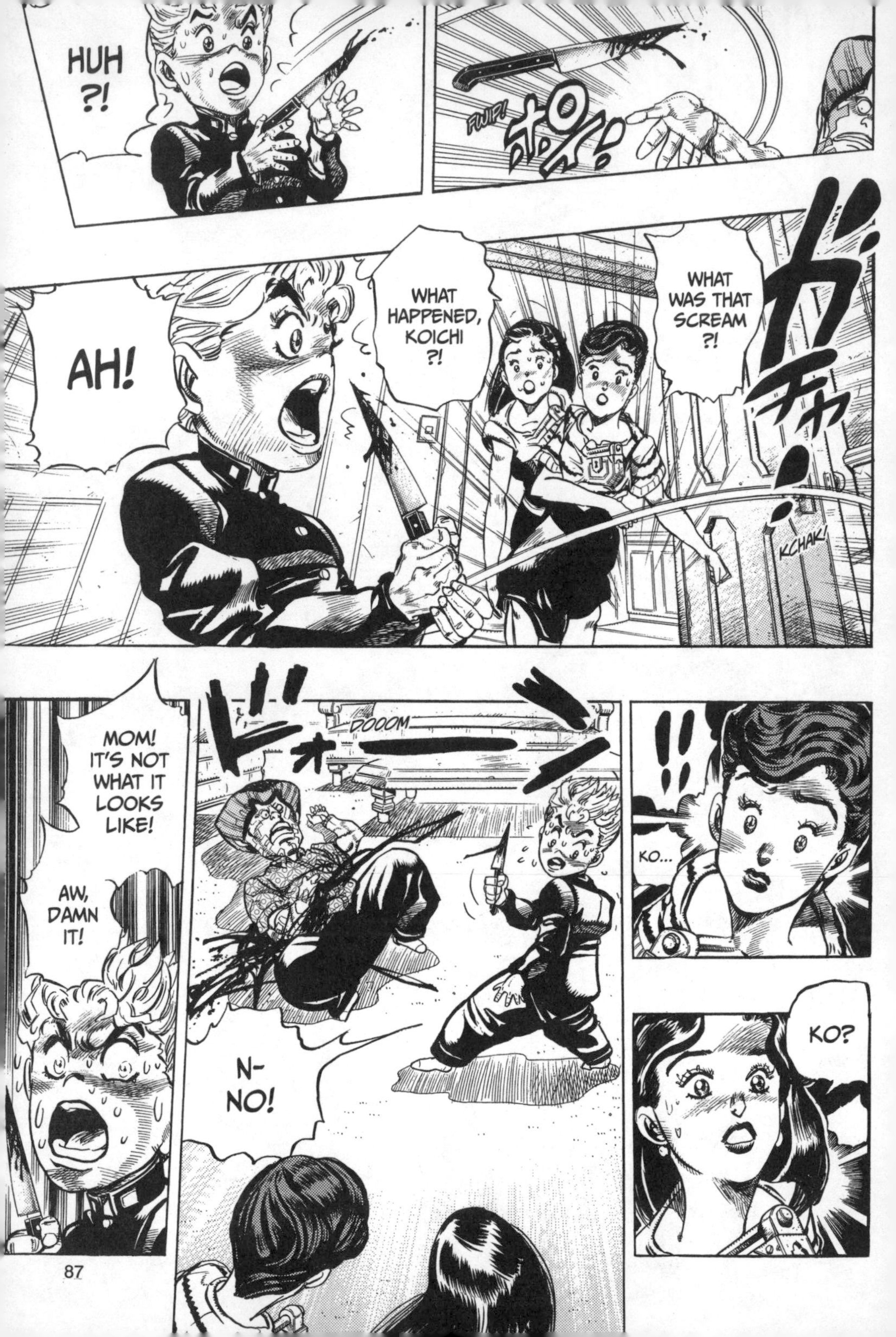
FWIP!
HUH ?!
KCHAK!
WHAT WAS THAT SCREAM ?!
WHAT HAPPENED, KOICHI ?!
AH!
!!
KO...
KO?
DOOOM
N-NO!
MOM! IT'S NOT WHAT IT LOOKS LIKE!
AW, DAMN IT!

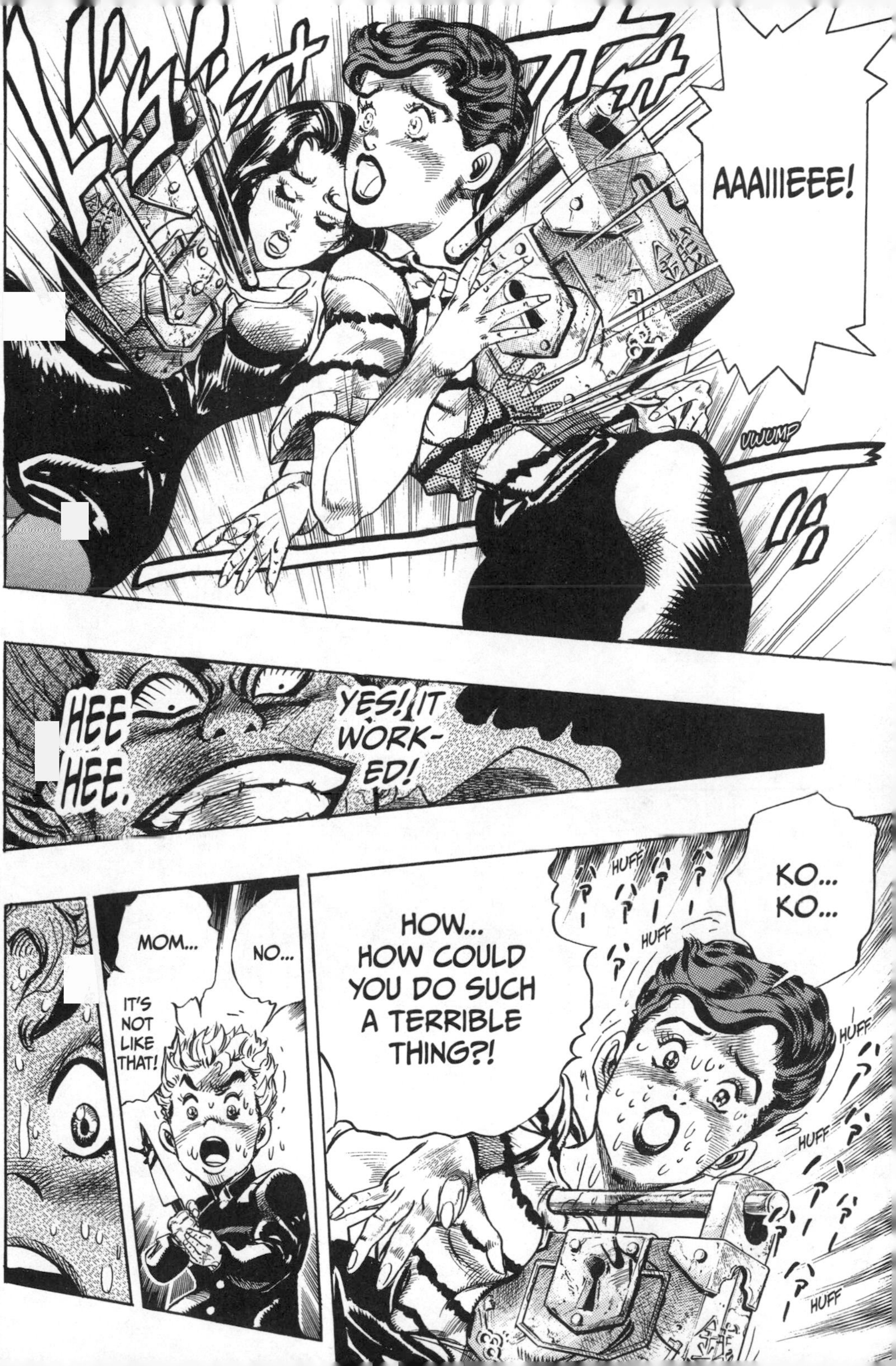
AAAIIIEEE!
VWUMP
YES! IT WORK-ED!
HEE HEE.
KO... KO...
HUFF
HUFF
HOW... HOW COULD YOU DO SUCH A TERRIBLE THING?!
HUFF
HUFF
HUFF
NO...
MOM...
IT'S NOT LIKE THAT!

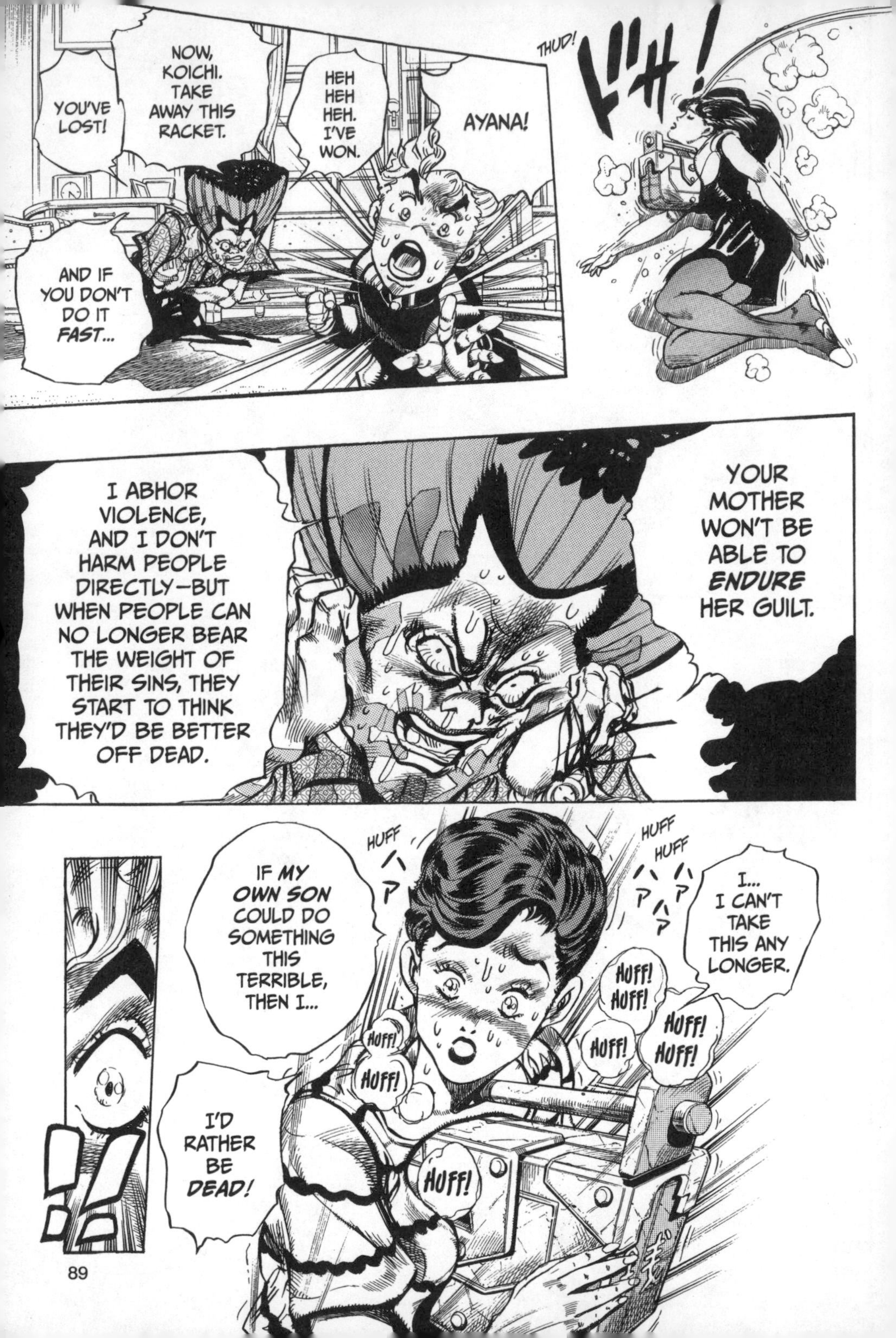
THUD!
AYANA!
HEH HEH HEH. I'VE WON.
NOW, KOICHI. TAKE AWAY THIS RACKET.
YOU'VE LOST!
AND IF YOU DON'T DO IT *FAST*...
YOUR MOTHER WON'T BE ABLE TO *ENDURE* HER GUILT.
I ABHOR VIOLENCE, AND I DON'T HARM PEOPLE DIRECTLY—BUT WHEN PEOPLE CAN NO LONGER BEAR THE WEIGHT OF THEIR SINS, THEY START TO THINK THEY'D BE BETTER OFF DEAD.
HUFF HUFF
I... I CAN'T TAKE THIS ANY LONGER.
HUFF! HUFF!
HUFF! HUFF!
HUFF!
HUFF
IF *MY OWN SON* COULD DO SOMETHING THIS TERRIBLE, THEN I...
HUFF!
HUFF!
HUFF!
I'D RATHER BE *DEAD*!

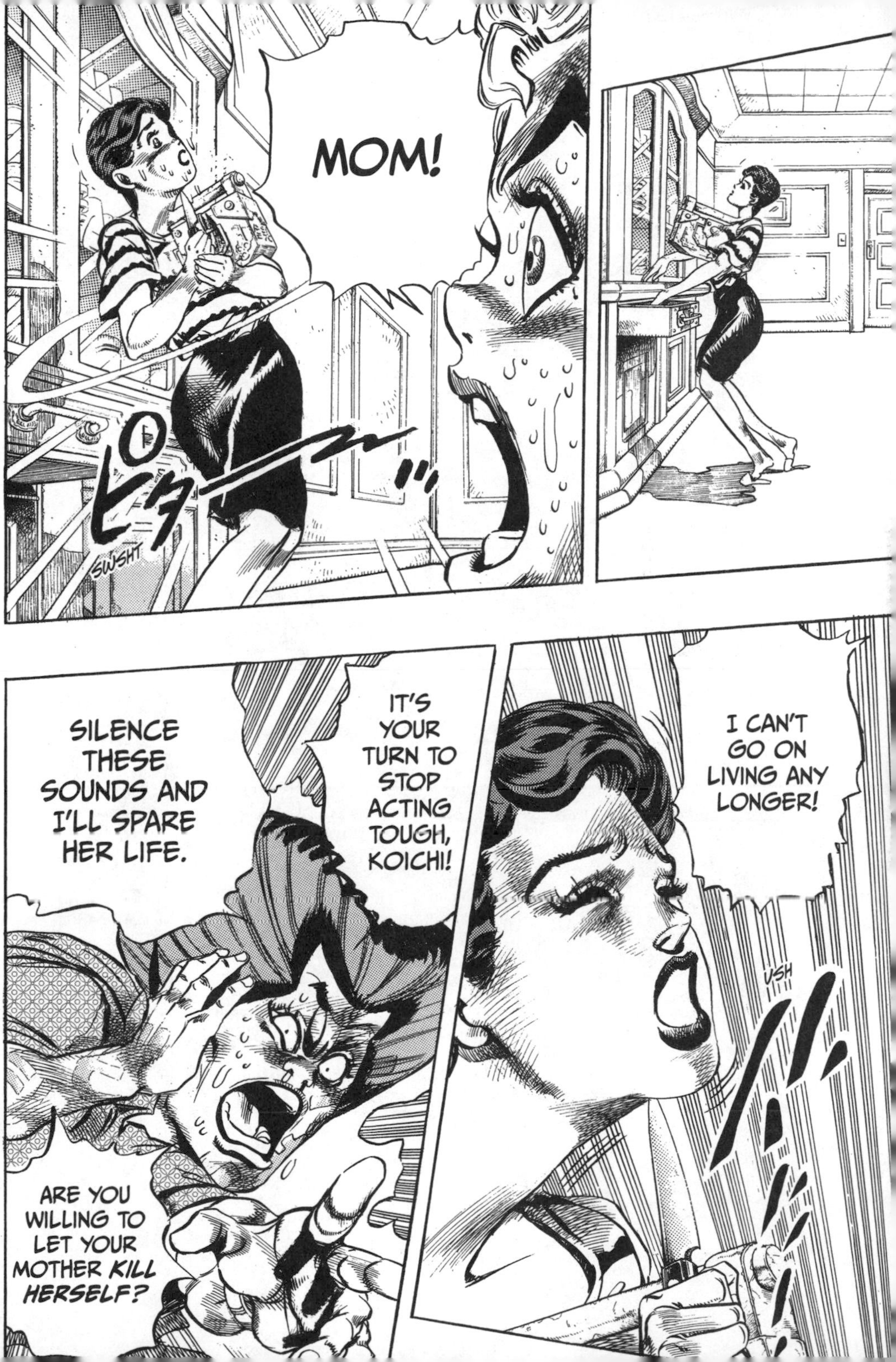
MOM!
SWSHT
I CAN'T GO ON LIVING ANY LONGER!
USH
IT'S YOUR TURN TO STOP ACTING TOUGH, KOICHI!
SILENCE THESE SOUNDS AND I'LL SPARE HER LIFE.
ARE YOU WILLING TO LET YOUR MOTHER *KILL HERSELF*?

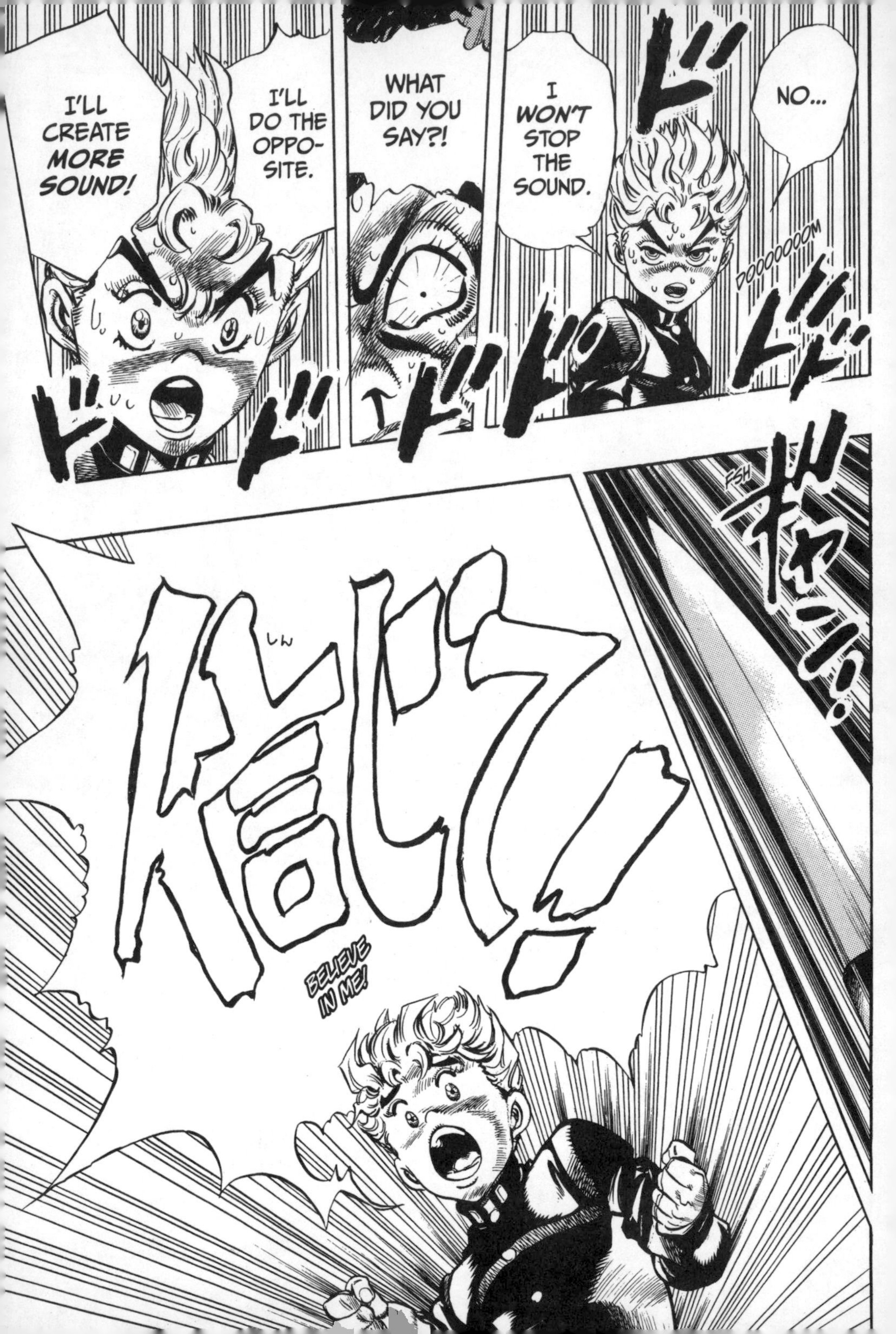
NO...
I WON'T STOP THE SOUND.
DOOOOOOOOM
WHAT DID YOU SAY?!
I'LL DO THE OPPO-SITE.
I'LL CREATE MORE SOUND!
FSH
信じて!
BELIEVE IN ME!

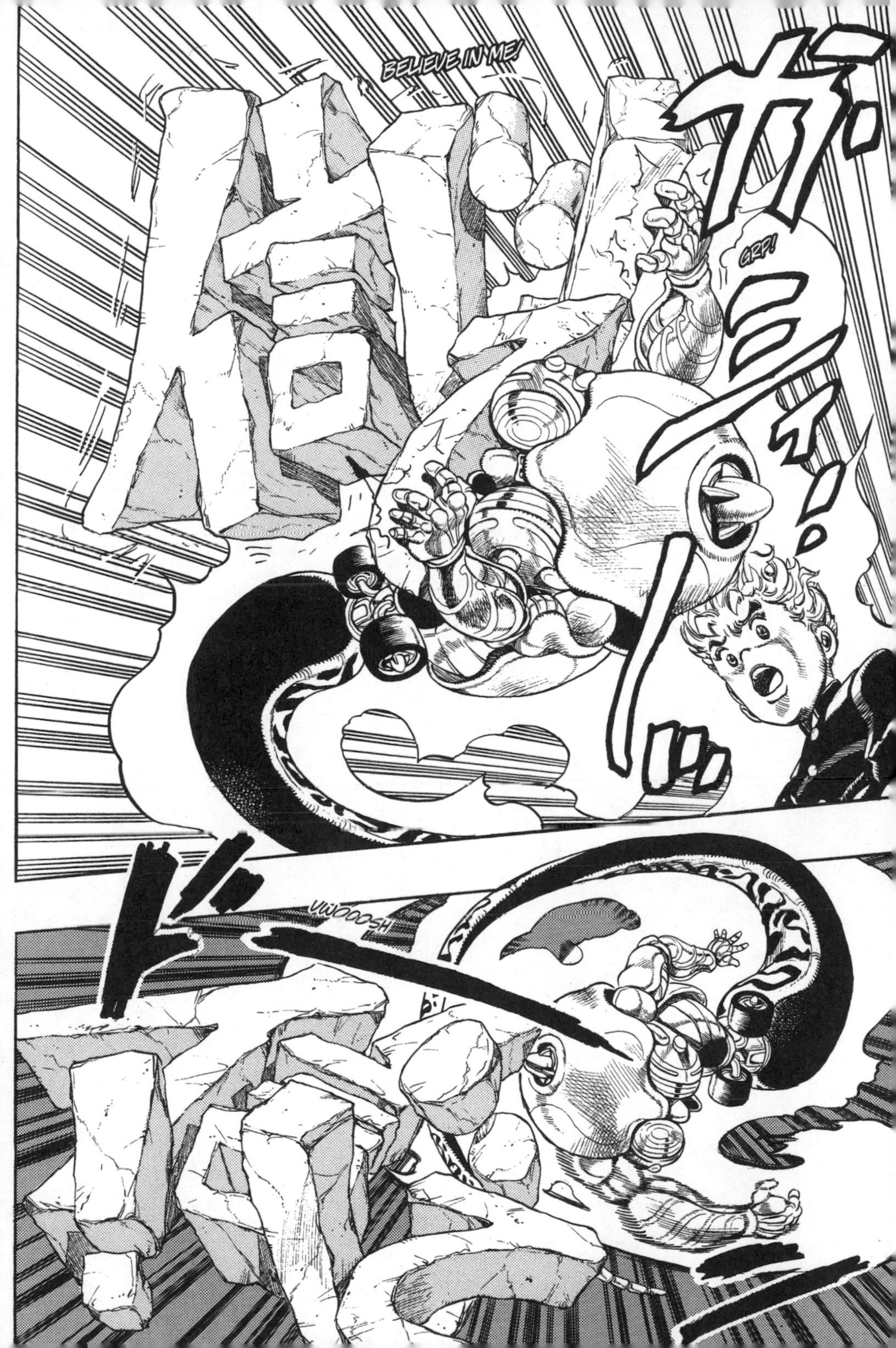
BELIEVE IN ME!
GRP!
VWOOOSH

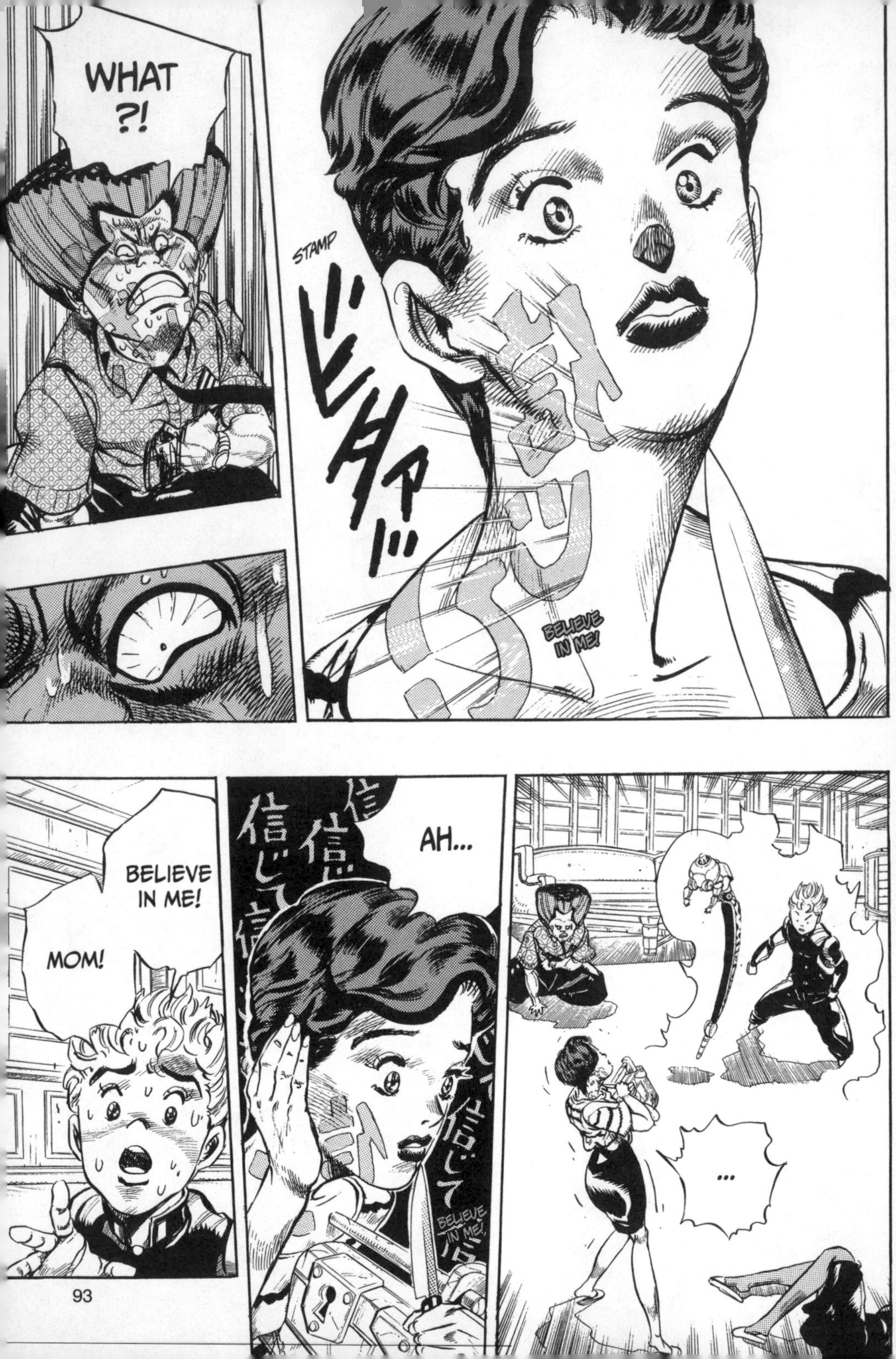
STAMP
BELIEVE IN ME!
WHAT ?!
...
AH...
信じて
BELIEVE IN ME!
BELIEVE IN ME!
MOM!

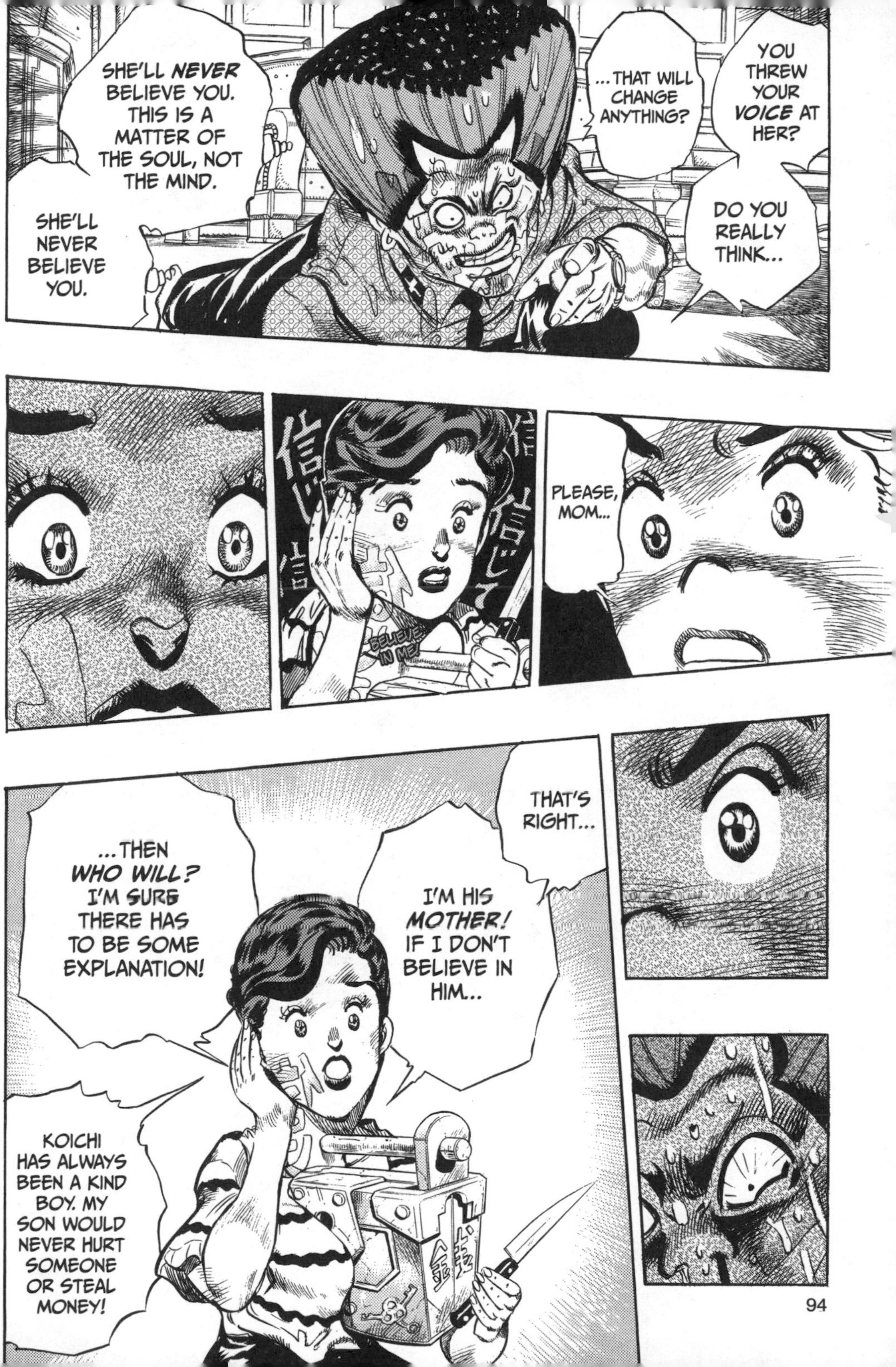
YOU THREW YOUR *VOICE* AT HER?
DO YOU REALLY THINK...
...THAT WILL CHANGE ANYTHING?
SHE'LL *NEVER* BELIEVE YOU. THIS IS A MATTER OF THE SOUL, NOT THE MIND.
SHE'LL NEVER BELIEVE YOU.
PLEASE, MOM...
BELIEVE IN ME!
THAT'S RIGHT...
I'M HIS *MOTHER!* IF I DON'T BELIEVE IN HIM...
...THEN *WHO WILL?* I'M SURE THERE HAS TO BE SOME EXPLANATION!
KOICHI HAS ALWAYS BEEN A KIND BOY. MY SON WOULD NEVER HURT SOMEONE OR STEAL MONEY!

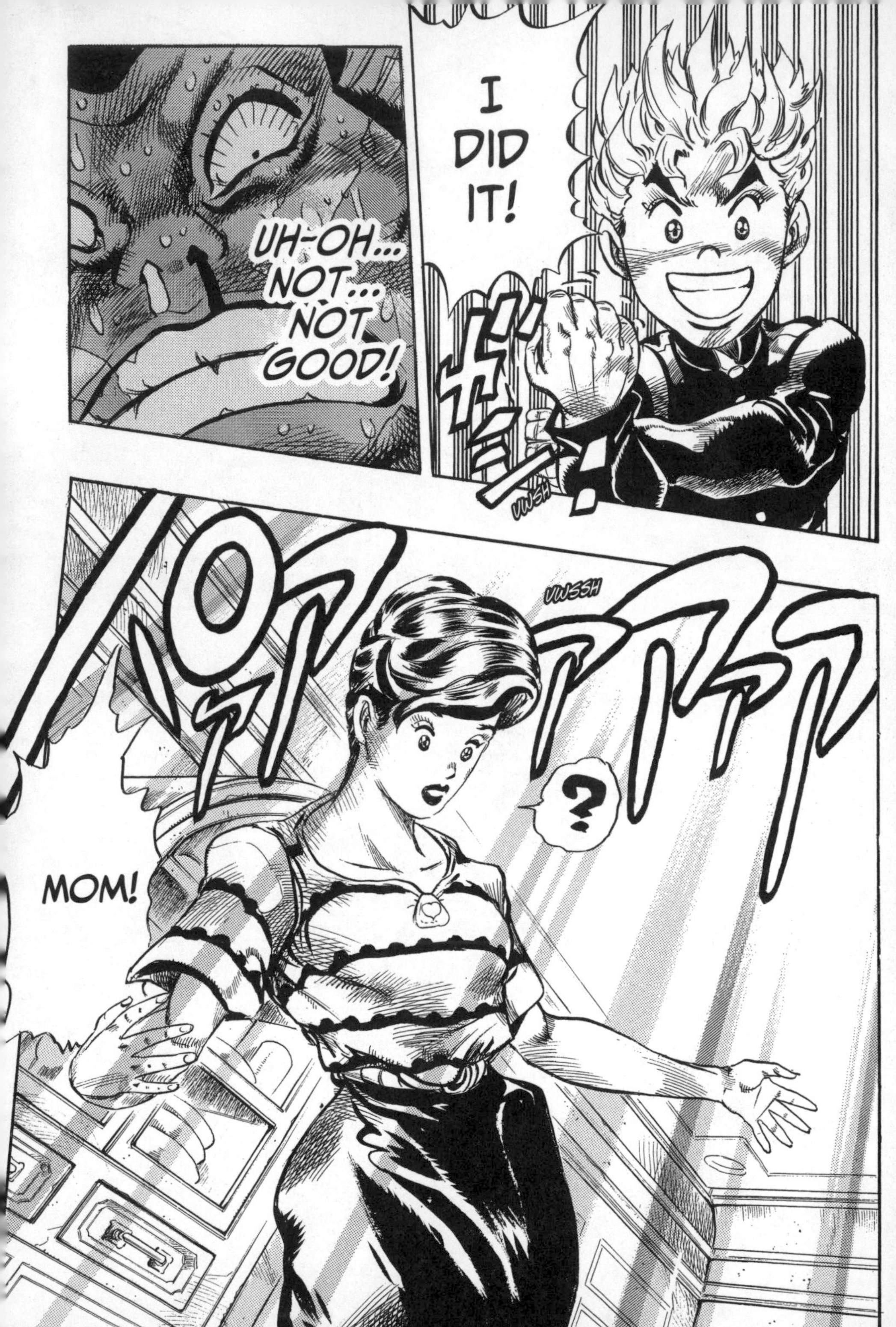
I DID IT!
VWSH
UH-OH... NOT... NOT GOOD!
VWSSH
?
MOM!

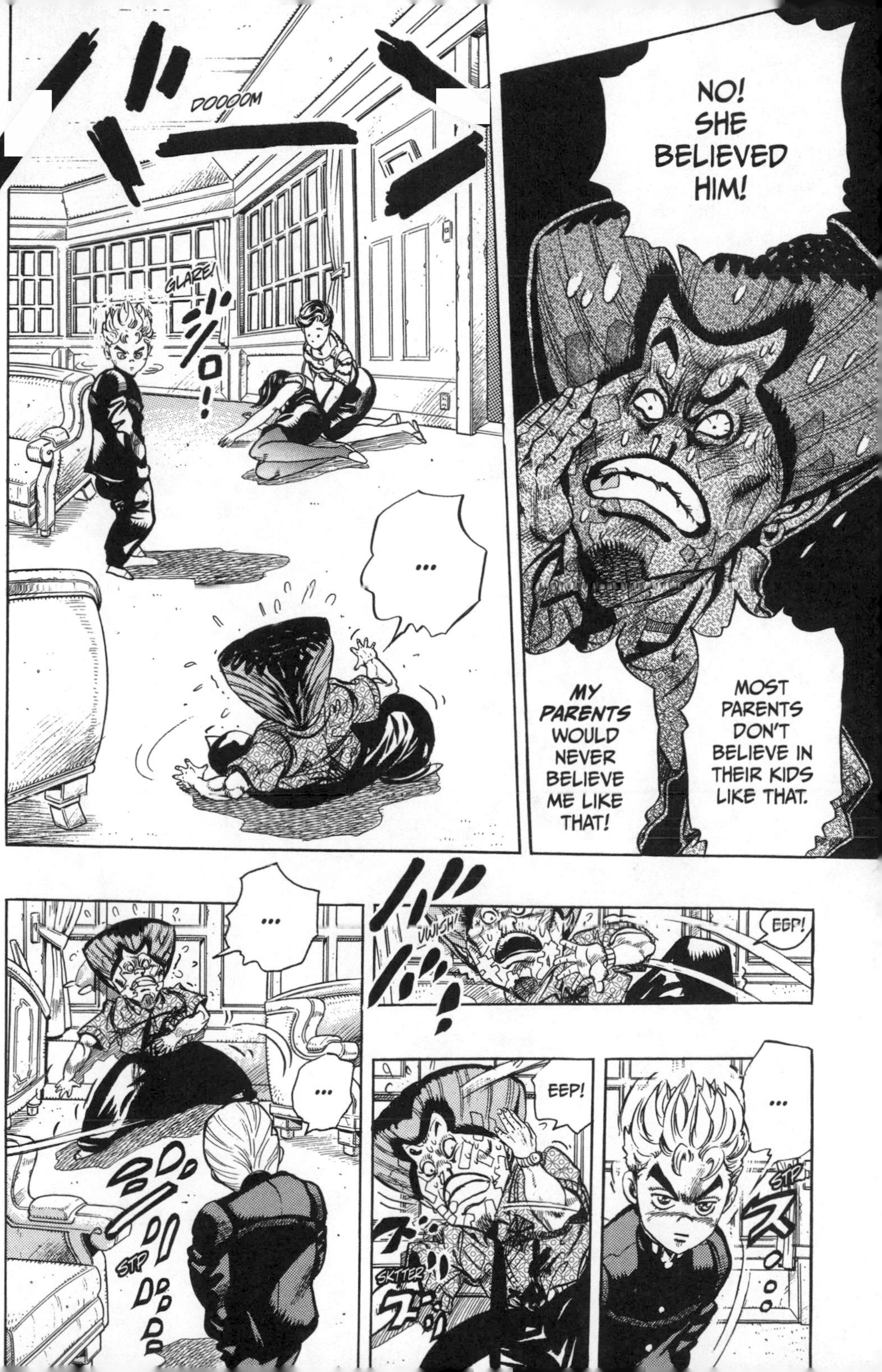
NO! SHE BELIEVED HIM!
MOST PARENTS DON'T BELIEVE IN THEIR KIDS LIKE THAT.
MY PARENTS WOULD NEVER BELIEVE ME LIKE THAT!
DOOOOM
GLARE!
...
EEP!
VWISH!
...
STIP
EEP!
SKTTER
...
...
STIP

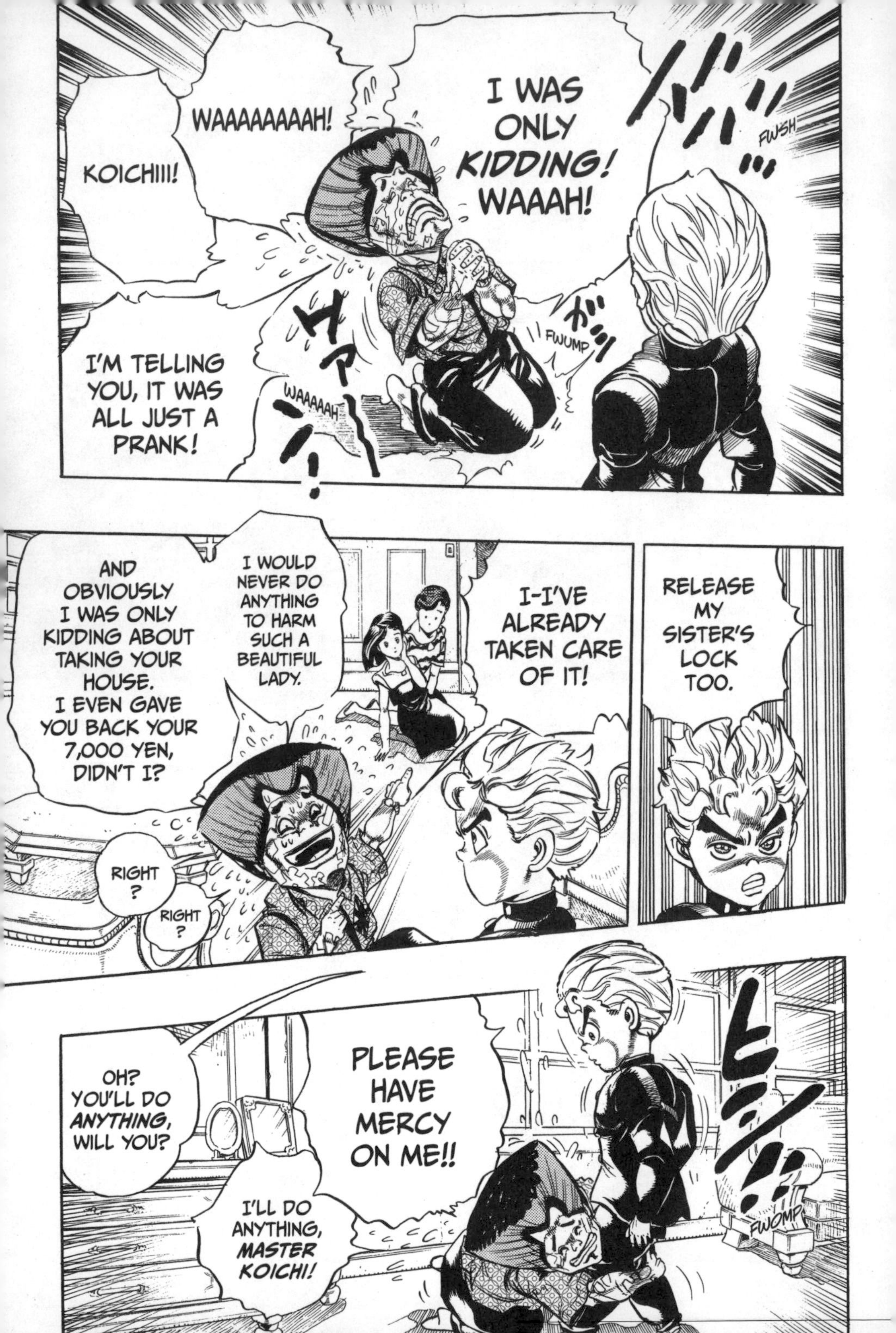
FWSH
I WAS ONLY KIDDING! WAAAH!
WAAAAAAAAAH!
KOICHIII!
FWUMP
I'M TELLING YOU, IT WAS ALL JUST A PRANK!
WAAAAAH
RELEASE MY SISTER'S LOCK TOO.
I-I'VE ALREADY TAKEN CARE OF IT!
I WOULD NEVER DO ANYTHING TO HARM SUCH A BEAUTIFUL LADY.
AND OBVIOUSLY I WAS ONLY KIDDING ABOUT TAKING YOUR HOUSE. I EVEN GAVE YOU BACK YOUR 7,000 YEN, DIDN'T I?
RIGHT?
RIGHT?
FWOMP
PLEASE HAVE MERCY ON ME!!
I'LL DO ANYTHING, MASTER KOICHI!
OH? YOU'LL DO ANYTHING, WILL YOU?

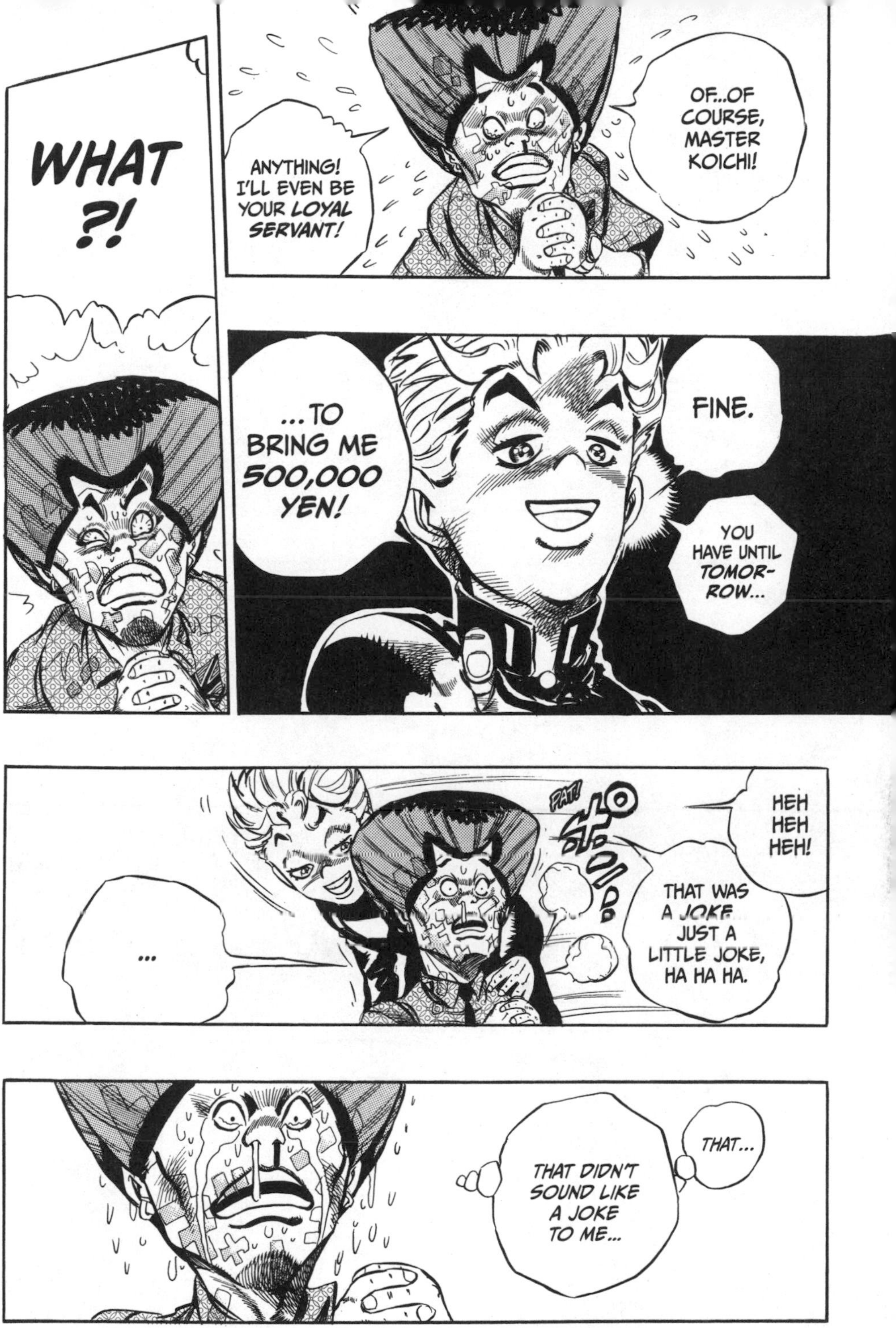

OF...OF COURSE, MASTER KOICHI!
ANYTHING! I'LL EVEN BE YOUR LOYAL SERVANT!
FINE.
YOU HAVE UNTIL TOMORROW...
...TO BRING ME 500,000 YEN!
WHAT ?!
HEH HEH HEH!
THAT WAS A JOKE... JUST A LITTLE JOKE, HA HA HA.
PAT!
...
THAT...
THAT DIDN'T SOUND LIKE A JOKE TO ME...

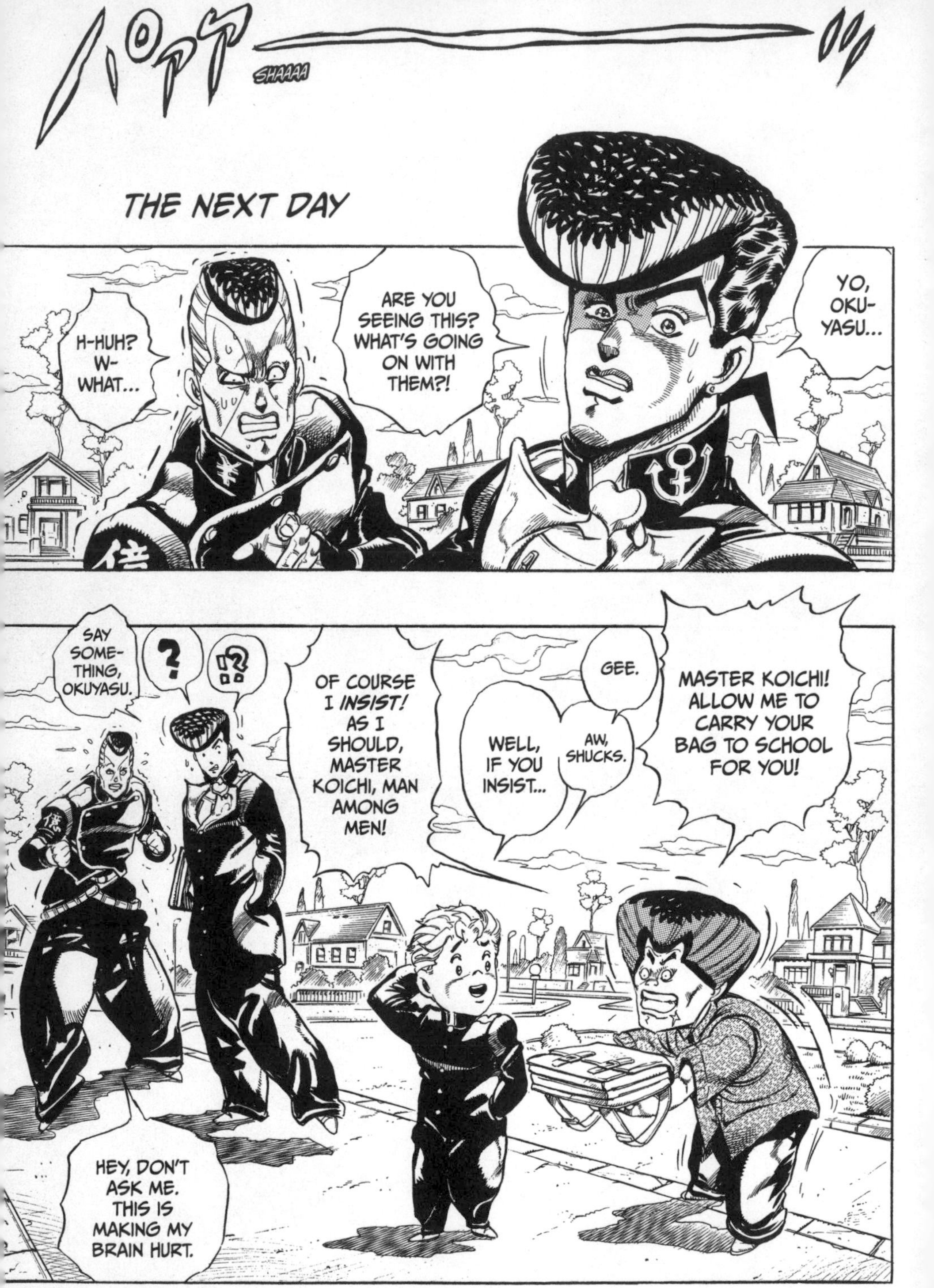
SHAAAA
THE NEXT DAY
YO, OKU-YASU...
ARE YOU SEEING THIS? WHAT'S GOING ON WITH THEM?!
H-HUH? W-WHAT...
MASTER KOICHI! ALLOW ME TO CARRY YOUR BAG TO SCHOOL FOR YOU!
GEE.
AW, SHUCKS.
WELL, IF YOU INSIST...
OF COURSE I *INSIST!* AS I SHOULD, MASTER KOICHI, MAN AMONG MEN!
!?
?
SAY SOME-THING, OKUYASU.
HEY, DON'T ASK ME. THIS IS MAKING MY BRAIN HURT.

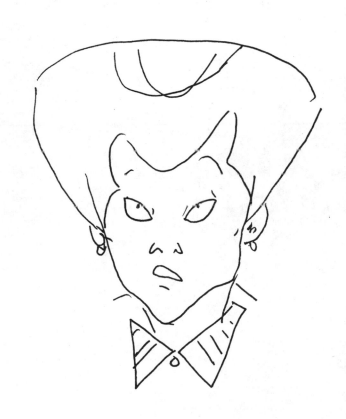

TOSHIKAZU HAZAMADA (SHOW OFF), PART 1

CHAPTER 24

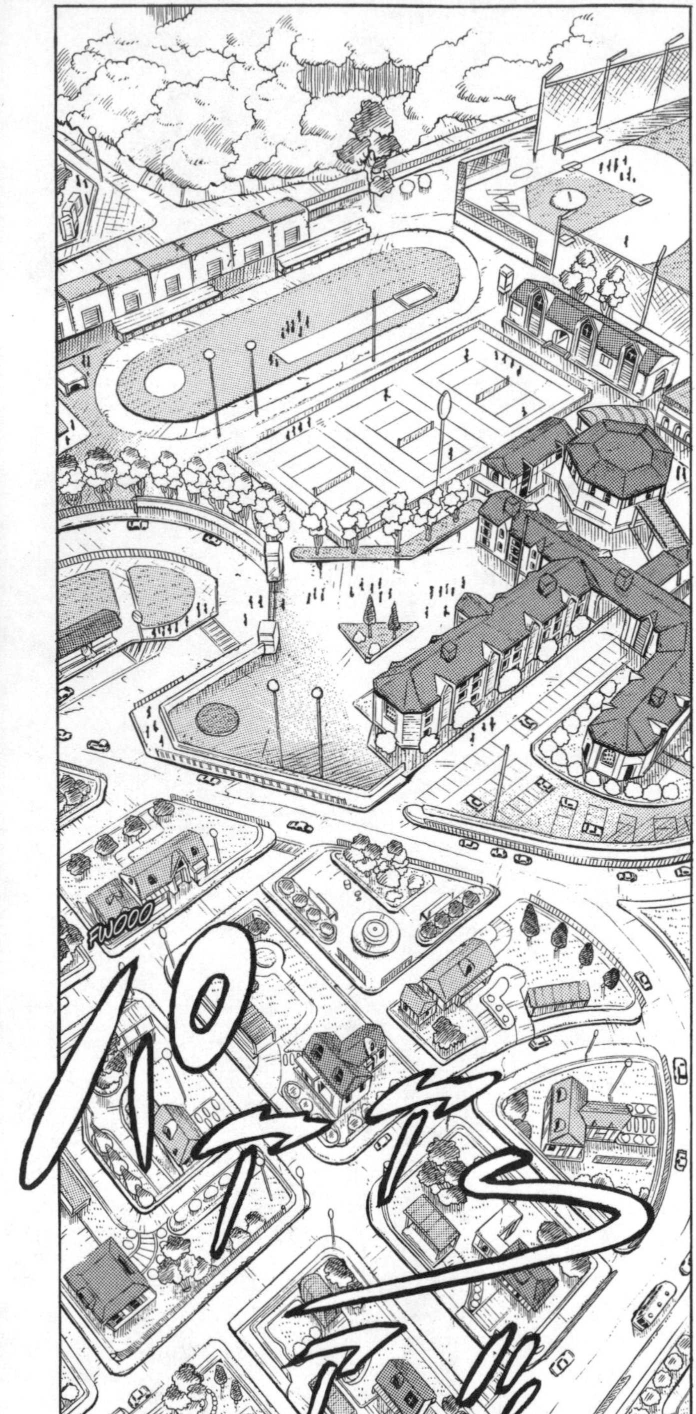
FWOOO

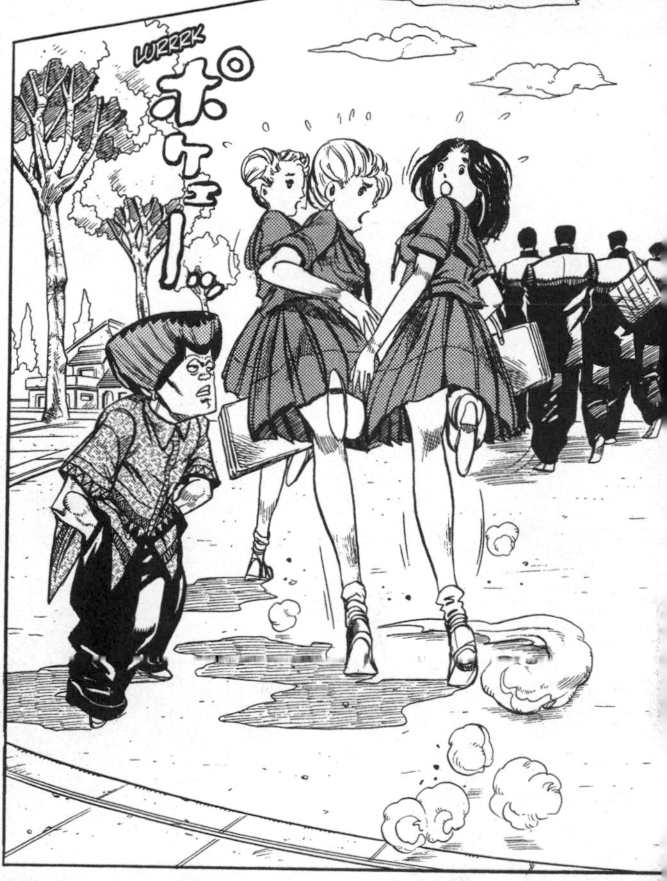
LURRRK
ポケェー
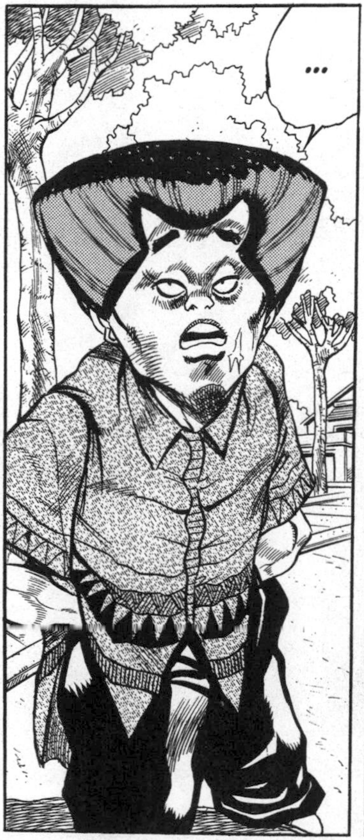
...
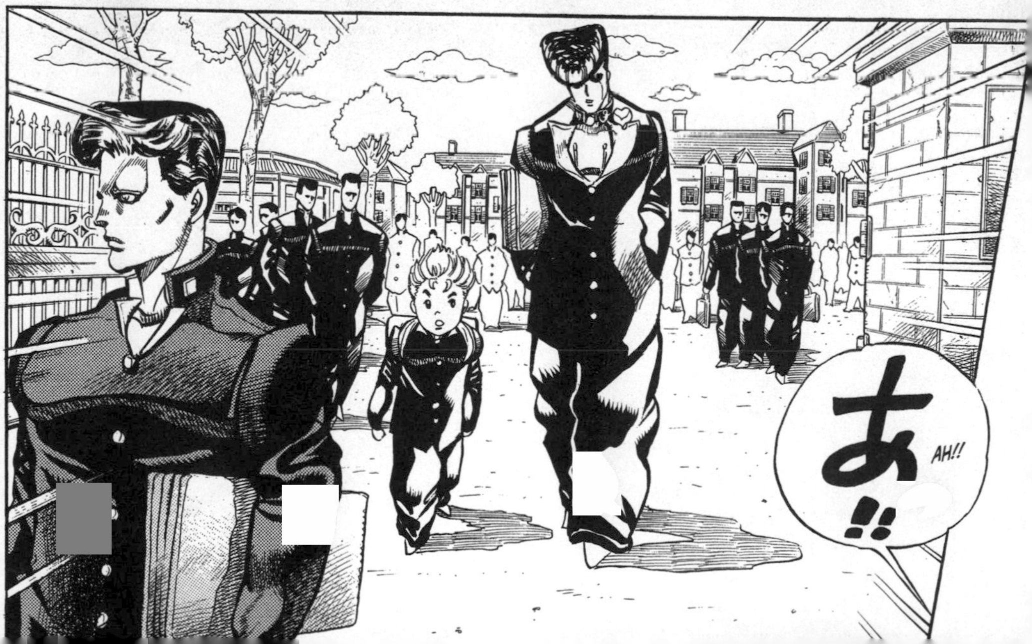
あ!!
AH!!

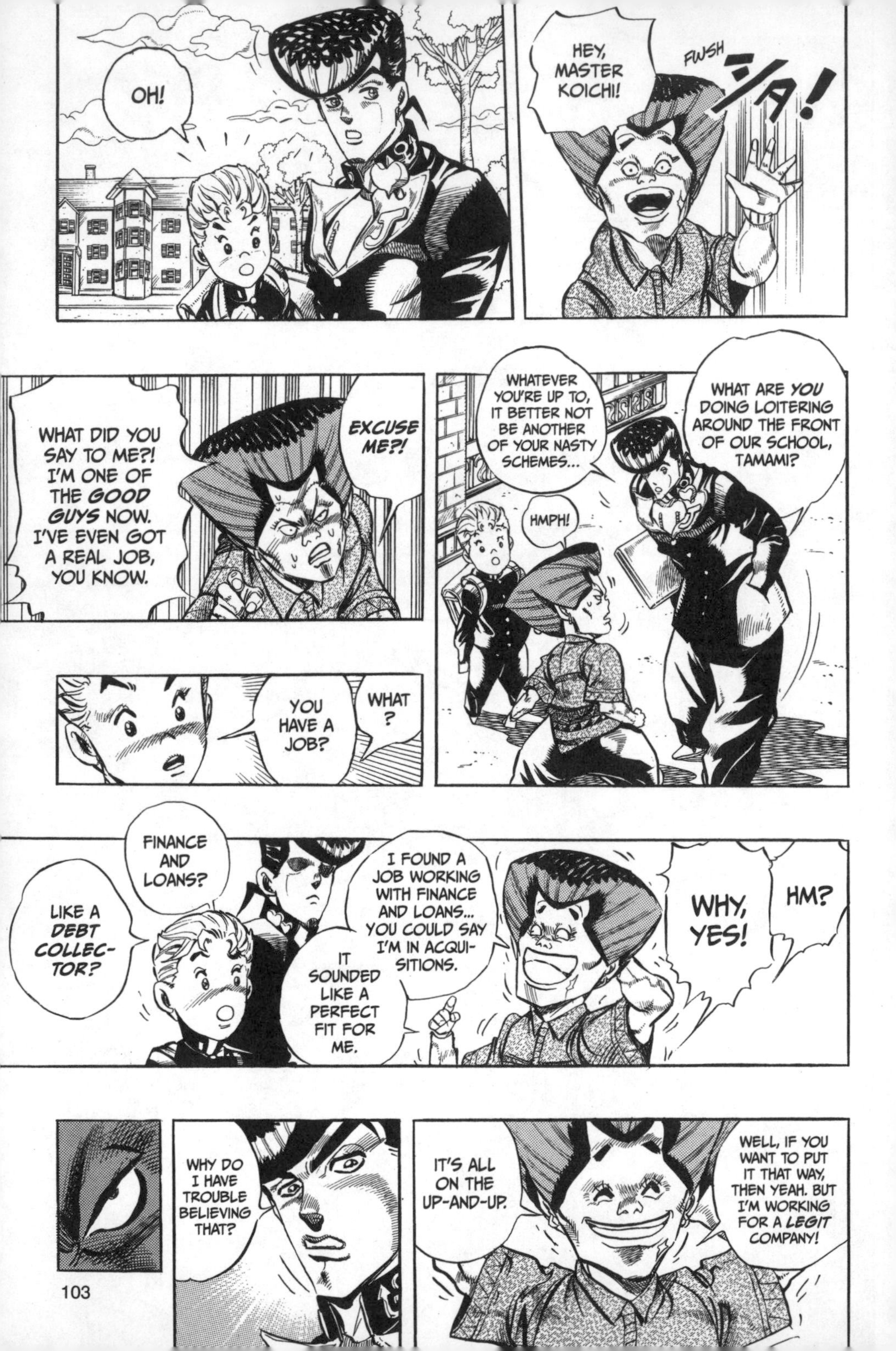
HEY, MASTER KOICHI!
FWSH
シャ!
OH!
WHAT ARE *YOU* DOING LOITERING AROUND THE FRONT OF OUR SCHOOL, TAMAMI?
WHATEVER YOU'RE UP TO, IT BETTER NOT BE ANOTHER OF YOUR NASTY SCHEMES...
HMPH!
EXCUSE ME?!
WHAT DID YOU SAY TO ME?! I'M ONE OF THE *GOOD GUYS* NOW. I'VE EVEN GOT A REAL JOB, YOU KNOW.
WHAT?
YOU HAVE A JOB?
HM?
WHY, YES!
I FOUND A JOB WORKING WITH FINANCE AND LOANS... YOU COULD SAY I'M IN ACQUISITIONS.
IT SOUNDED LIKE A PERFECT FIT FOR ME.
FINANCE AND LOANS?
LIKE A *DEBT COLLECTOR?*
WELL, IF YOU WANT TO PUT IT THAT WAY, THEN YEAH. BUT I'M WORKING FOR A *LEGIT* COMPANY!
IT'S ALL ON THE UP-AND-UP.
WHY DO I HAVE TROUBLE BELIEVING THAT?

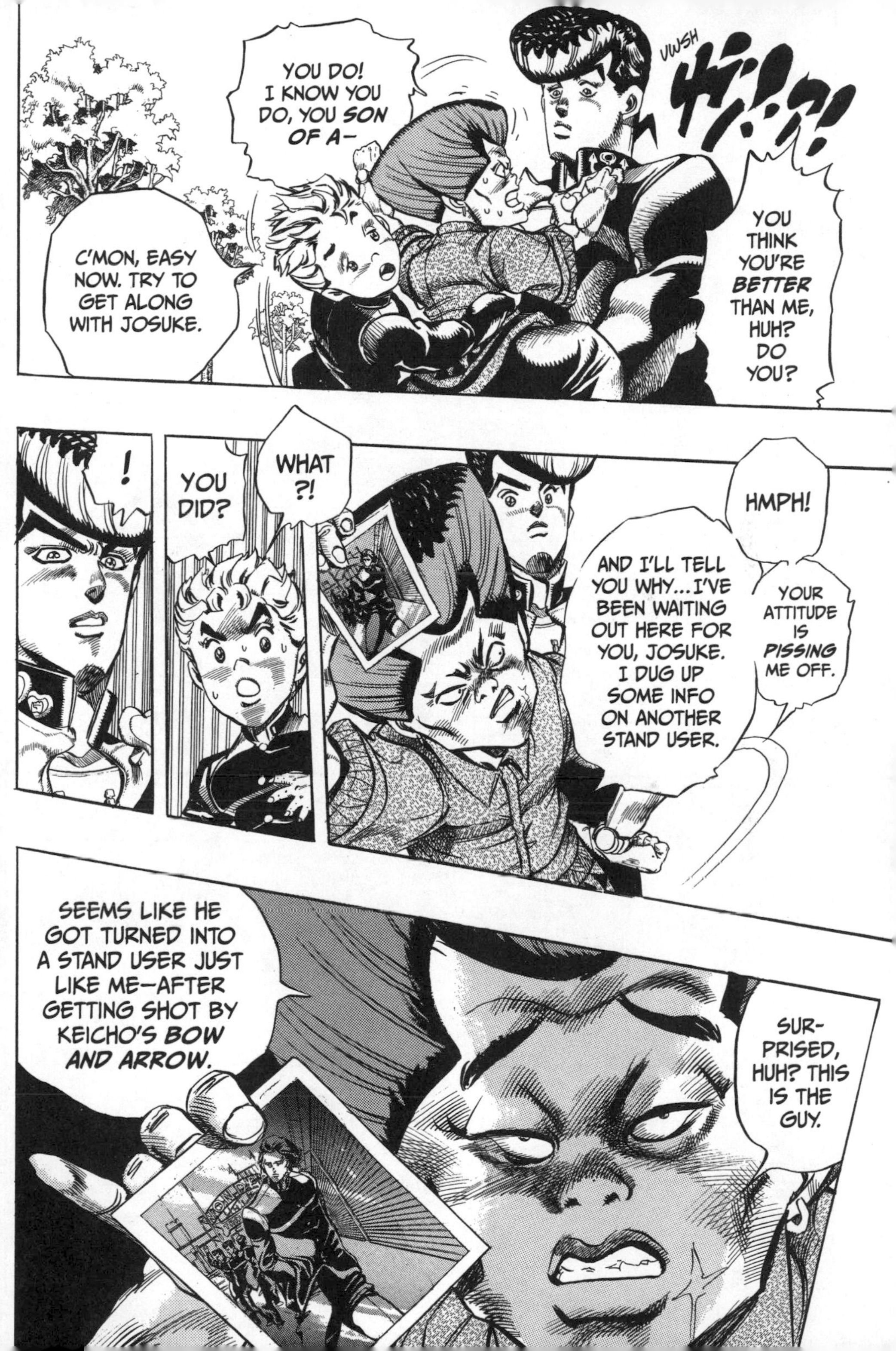
VWSH
YOU THINK YOU'RE BETTER THAN ME, HUH? DO YOU?
YOU DO! I KNOW YOU DO, YOU SON OF A–
C'MON, EASY NOW. TRY TO GET ALONG WITH JOSUKE.
HMPH!
YOUR ATTITUDE IS PISSING ME OFF.
AND I'LL TELL YOU WHY... I'VE BEEN WAITING OUT HERE FOR YOU, JOSUKE. I DUG UP SOME INFO ON ANOTHER STAND USER.
WHAT?!
YOU DID?
!
SUR-PRISED, HUH? THIS IS THE GUY.
SEEMS LIKE HE GOT TURNED INTO A STAND USER JUST LIKE ME—AFTER GETTING SHOT BY KEICHO'S BOW AND ARROW.

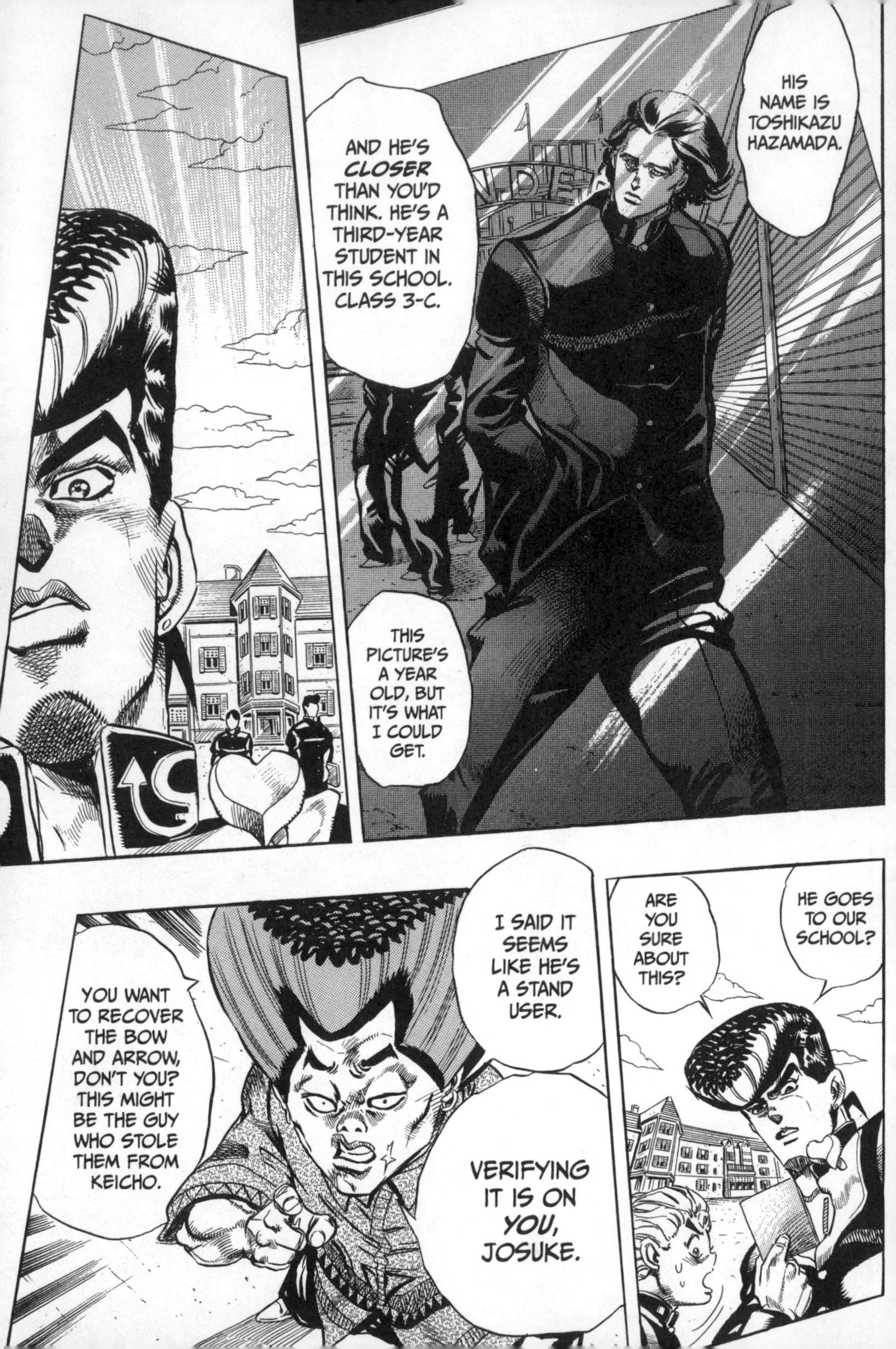
HIS NAME IS TOSHIKAZU HAZAMADA.
AND HE'S CLOSER THAN YOU'D THINK. HE'S A THIRD-YEAR STUDENT IN THIS SCHOOL. CLASS 3-C.
THIS PICTURE'S A YEAR OLD, BUT IT'S WHAT I COULD GET.
HE GOES TO OUR SCHOOL?
ARE YOU SURE ABOUT THIS?
I SAID IT SEEMS LIKE HE'S A STAND USER.
YOU WANT TO RECOVER THE BOW AND ARROW, DON'T YOU? THIS MIGHT BE THE GUY WHO STOLE THEM FROM KEICHO.
VERIFYING IT IS ON YOU, JOSUKE.

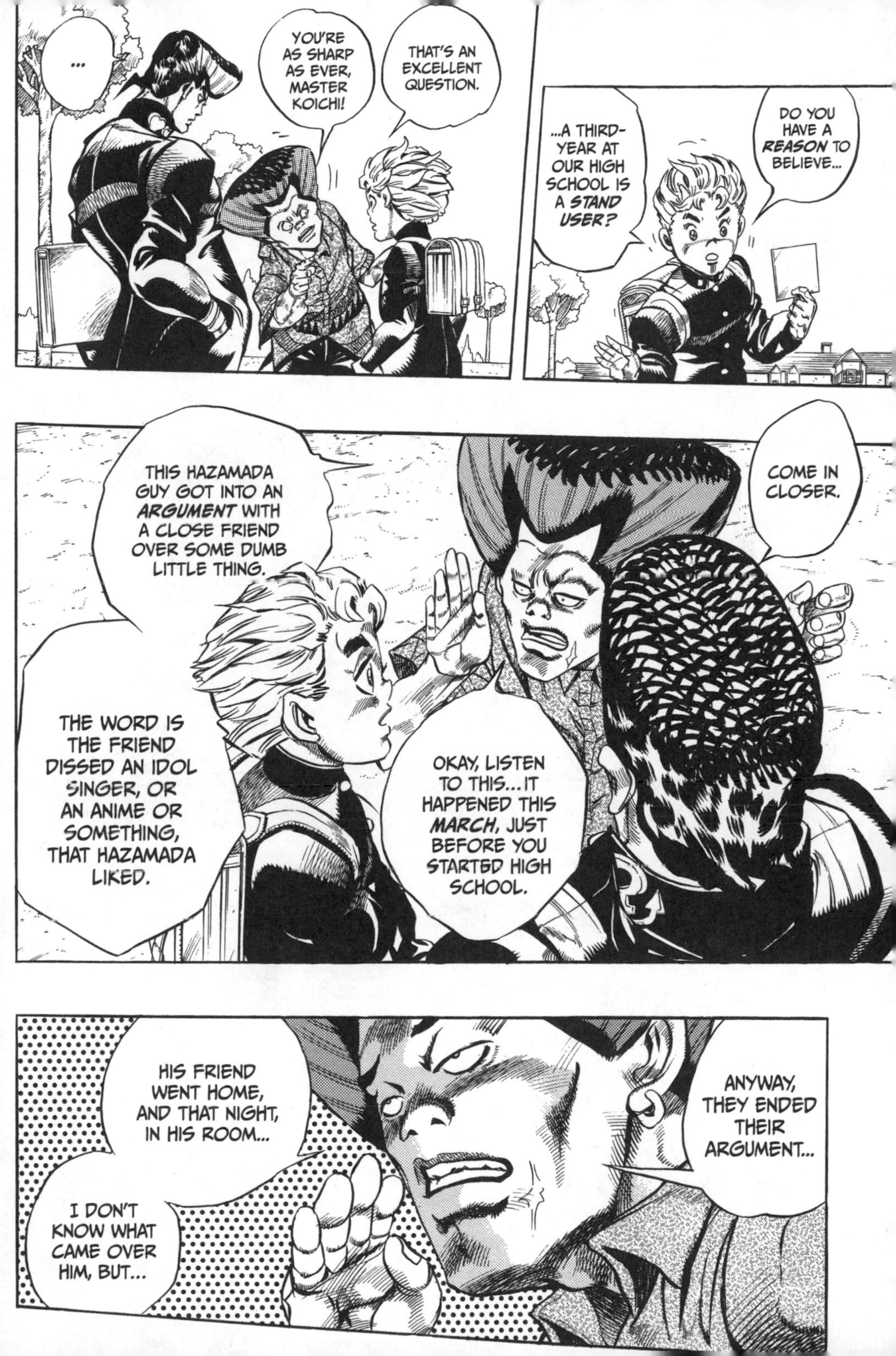
DO YOU HAVE A REASON TO BELIEVE...
...A THIRD-YEAR AT OUR HIGH SCHOOL IS A STAND USER?
THAT'S AN EXCELLENT QUESTION.
YOU'RE AS SHARP AS EVER, MASTER KOICHI!
...
COME IN CLOSER.
OKAY, LISTEN TO THIS...IT HAPPENED THIS MARCH, JUST BEFORE YOU STARTED HIGH SCHOOL.
THIS HAZAMADA GUY GOT INTO AN ARGUMENT WITH A CLOSE FRIEND OVER SOME DUMB LITTLE THING.
THE WORD IS THE FRIEND DISSED AN IDOL SINGER, OR AN ANIME OR SOMETHING, THAT HAZAMADA LIKED.
ANYWAY, THEY ENDED THEIR ARGUMENT...
HIS FRIEND WENT HOME, AND THAT NIGHT, IN HIS ROOM...
I DON'T KNOW WHAT CAME OVER HIM, BUT...

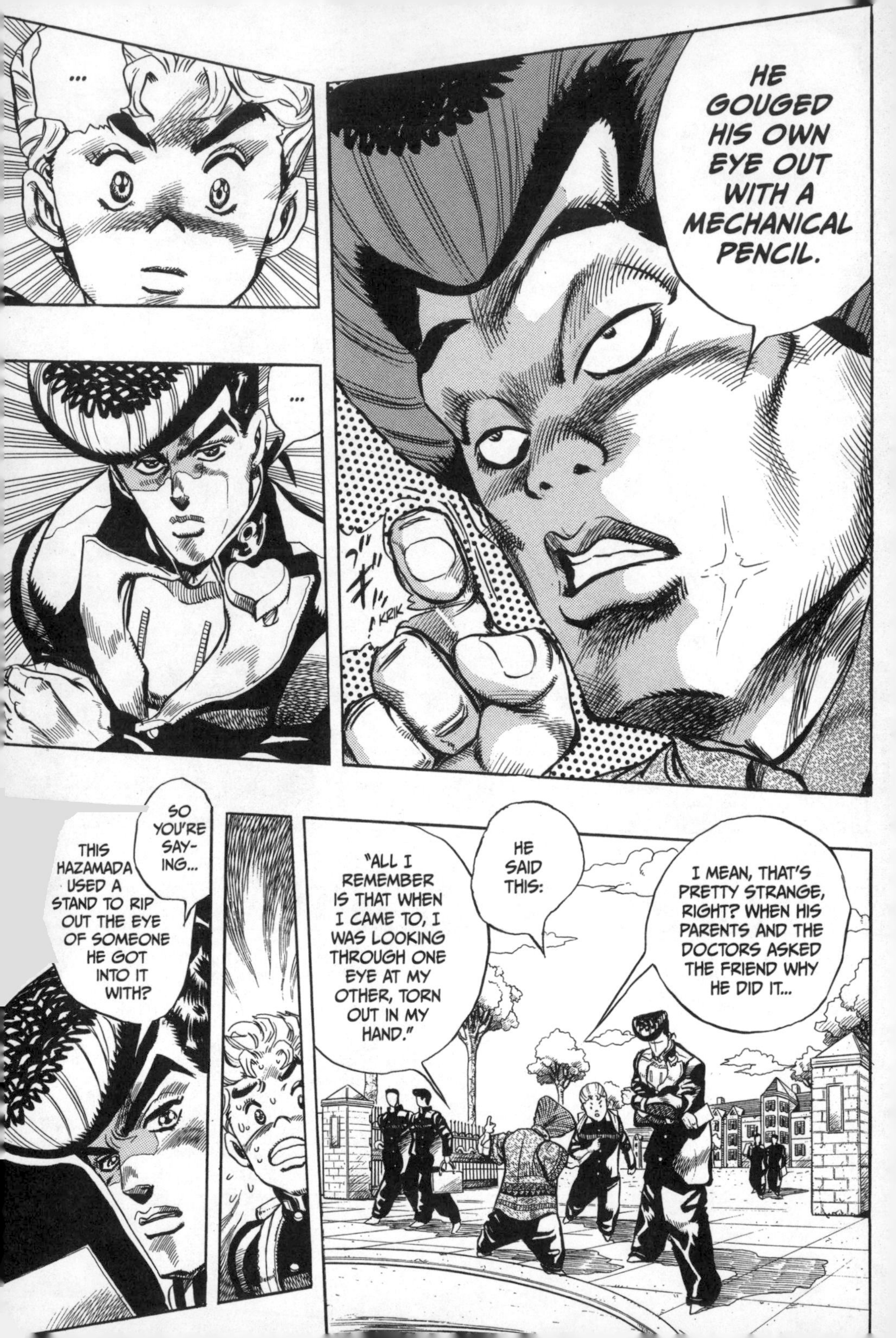
HE GOUGED HIS OWN EYE OUT WITH A MECHANICAL PENCIL.
KRIK
...
...
I MEAN, THAT'S PRETTY STRANGE, RIGHT? WHEN HIS PARENTS AND THE DOCTORS ASKED THE FRIEND WHY HE DID IT...
HE SAID THIS:
"ALL I REMEMBER IS THAT WHEN I CAME TO, I WAS LOOKING THROUGH ONE EYE AT MY OTHER, TORN OUT IN MY HAND."
SO YOU'RE SAYING...
THIS HAZAMADA USED A STAND TO RIP OUT THE EYE OF SOMEONE HE GOT INTO IT WITH?

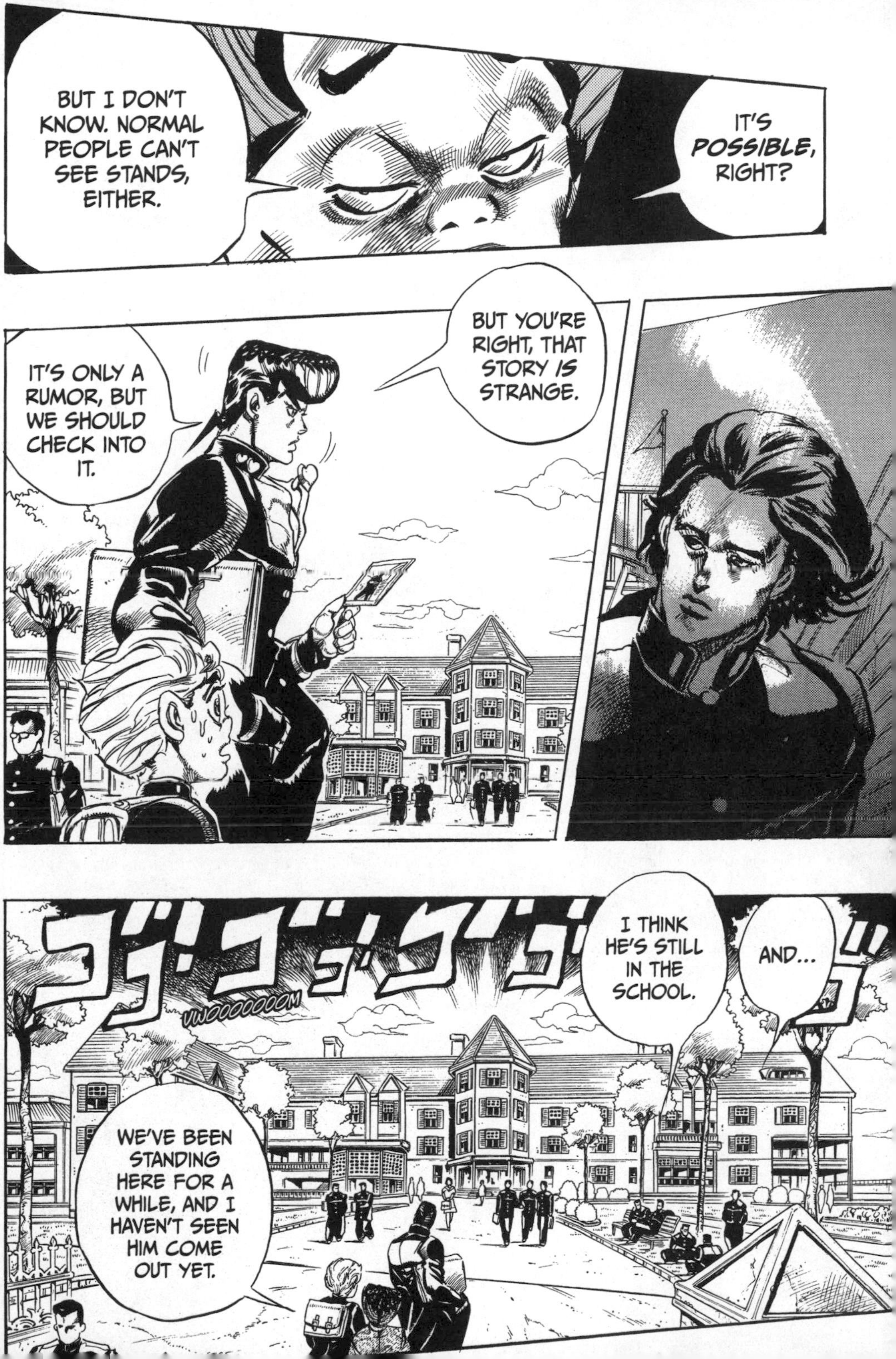
IT'S POSSIBLE, RIGHT?
BUT I DON'T KNOW. NORMAL PEOPLE CAN'T SEE STANDS, EITHER.
BUT YOU'RE RIGHT, THAT STORY IS STRANGE.
IT'S ONLY A RUMOR, BUT WE SHOULD CHECK INTO IT.
AND...
I THINK HE'S STILL IN THE SCHOOL.
ゴゴゴゴゴ
VWOOOOOOOM
WE'VE BEEN STANDING HERE FOR A WHILE, AND I HAVEN'T SEEN HIM COME OUT YET.

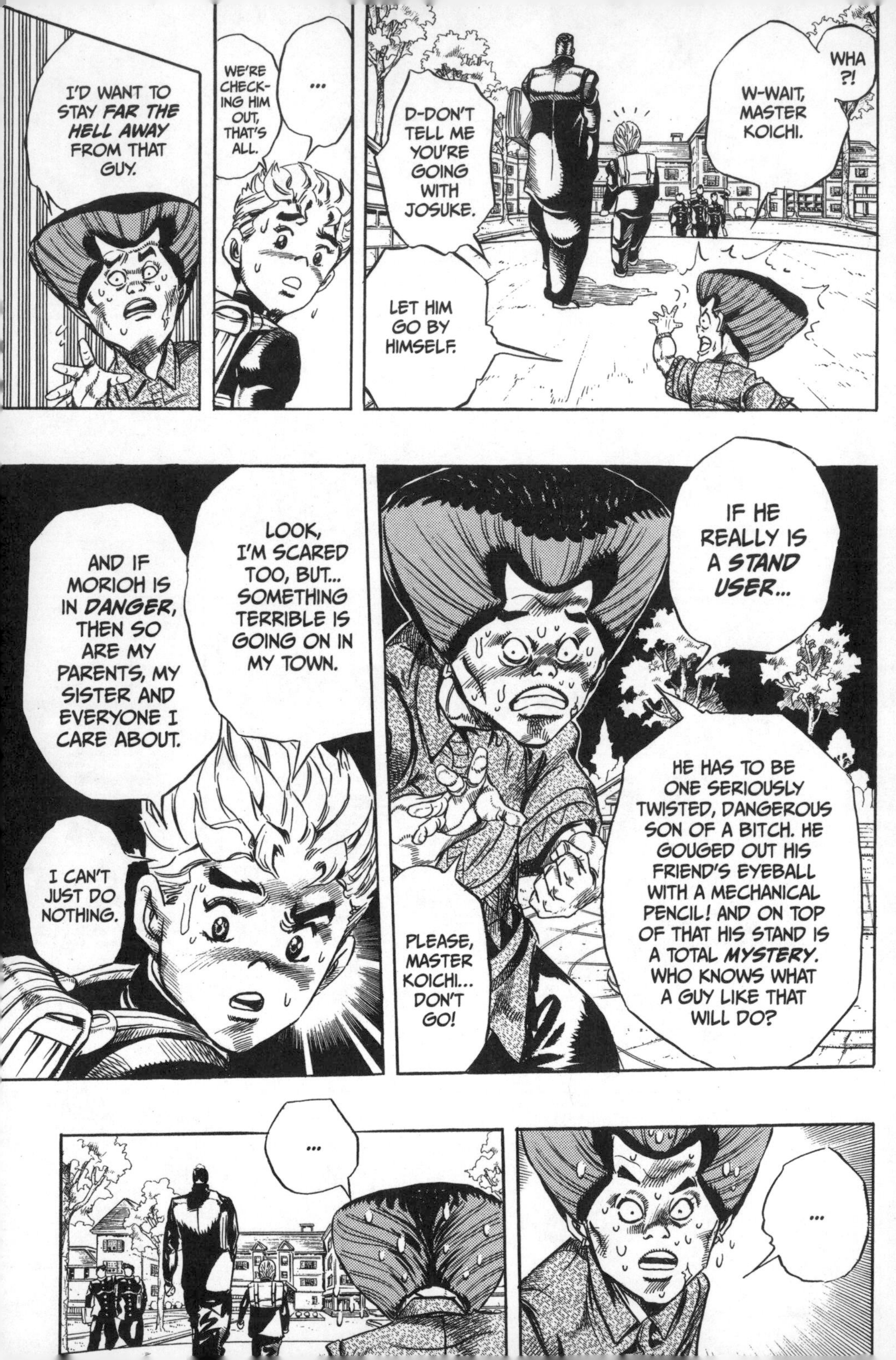
WHA ?!
W-WAIT, MASTER KOICHI.
D-DON'T TELL ME YOU'RE GOING WITH JOSUKE.
LET HIM GO BY HIMSELF.
...
WE'RE CHECKING HIM OUT, THAT'S ALL.
I'D WANT TO STAY FAR THE HELL AWAY FROM THAT GUY.
IF HE REALLY IS A STAND USER...
HE HAS TO BE ONE SERIOUSLY TWISTED, DANGEROUS SON OF A BITCH. HE GOUGED OUT HIS FRIEND'S EYEBALL WITH A MECHANICAL PENCIL! AND ON TOP OF THAT HIS STAND IS A TOTAL MYSTERY. WHO KNOWS WHAT A GUY LIKE THAT WILL DO?
PLEASE, MASTER KOICHI... DON'T GO!
LOOK, I'M SCARED TOO, BUT... SOMETHING TERRIBLE IS GOING ON IN MY TOWN.
AND IF MORIOH IS IN DANGER, THEN SO ARE MY PARENTS, MY SISTER AND EVERYONE I CARE ABOUT.
I CAN'T JUST DO NOTHING.
...
...

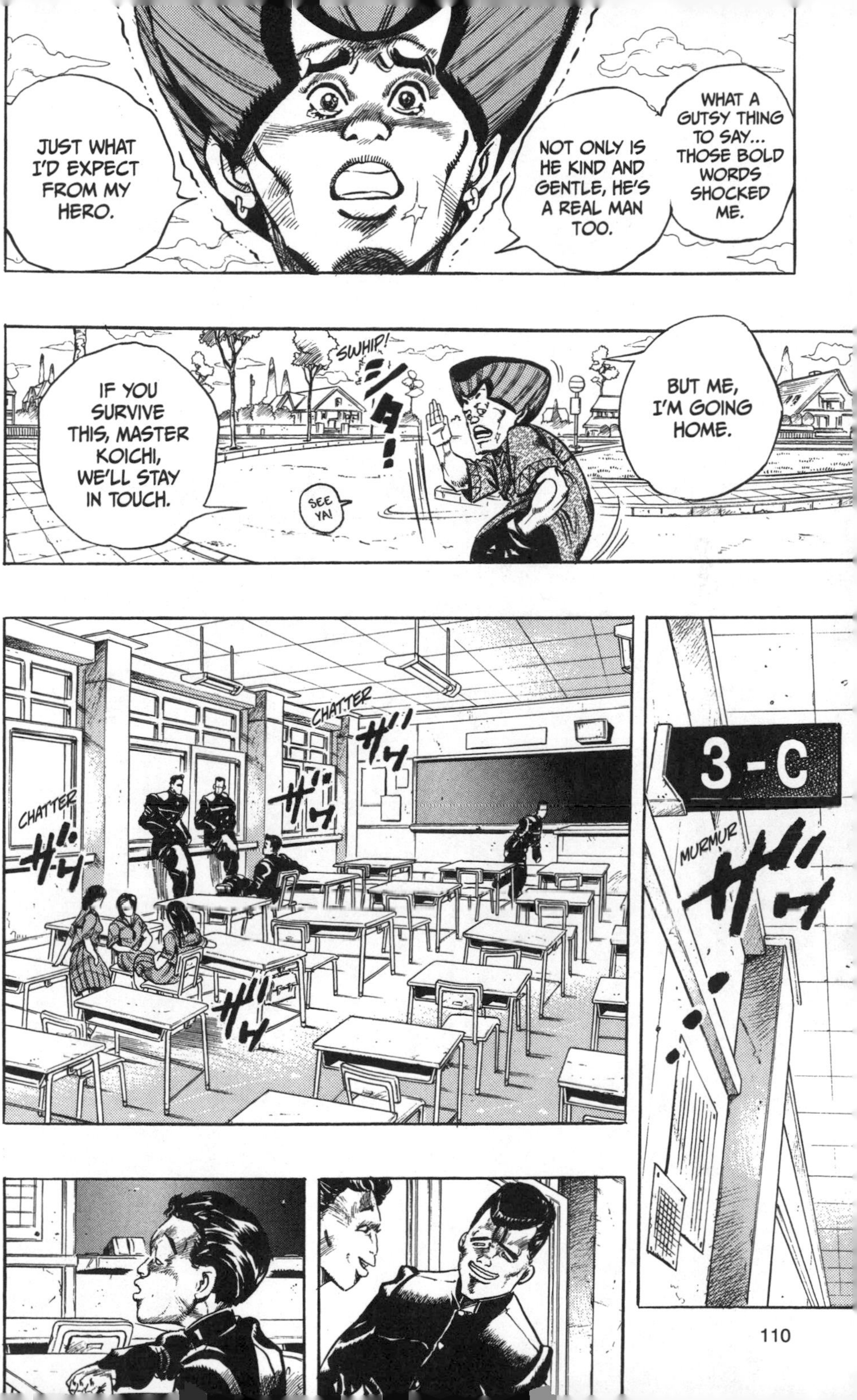
WHAT A GUTSY THING TO SAY... THOSE BOLD WORDS SHOCKED ME.
NOT ONLY IS HE KIND AND GENTLE, HE'S A REAL MAN TOO.
JUST WHAT I'D EXPECT FROM MY HERO.
BUT ME, I'M GOING HOME.
SWHIP!
SEE YA!
IF YOU SURVIVE THIS, MASTER KOICHI, WE'LL STAY IN TOUCH.
3-C
MURMUR
CHATTER
CHATTER

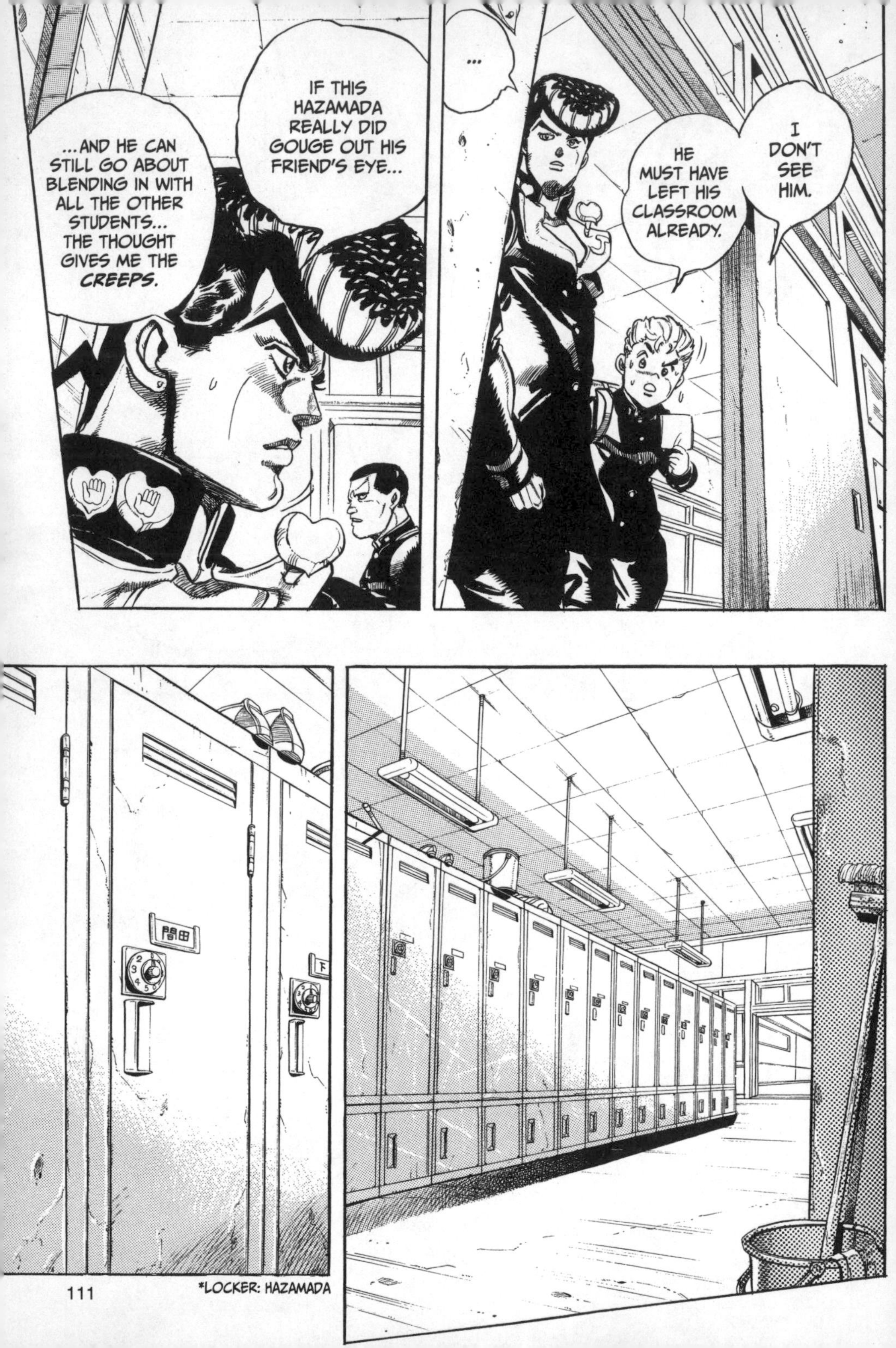

I DON'T SEE HIM.
HE MUST HAVE LEFT HIS CLASSROOM ALREADY.
...
IF THIS HAZAMADA REALLY DID GOUGE OUT HIS FRIEND'S EYE...
...AND HE CAN STILL GO ABOUT BLENDING IN WITH ALL THE OTHER STUDENTS... THE THOUGHT GIVES ME THE *CREEPS*.
間田

*LOCKER: HAZAMADA

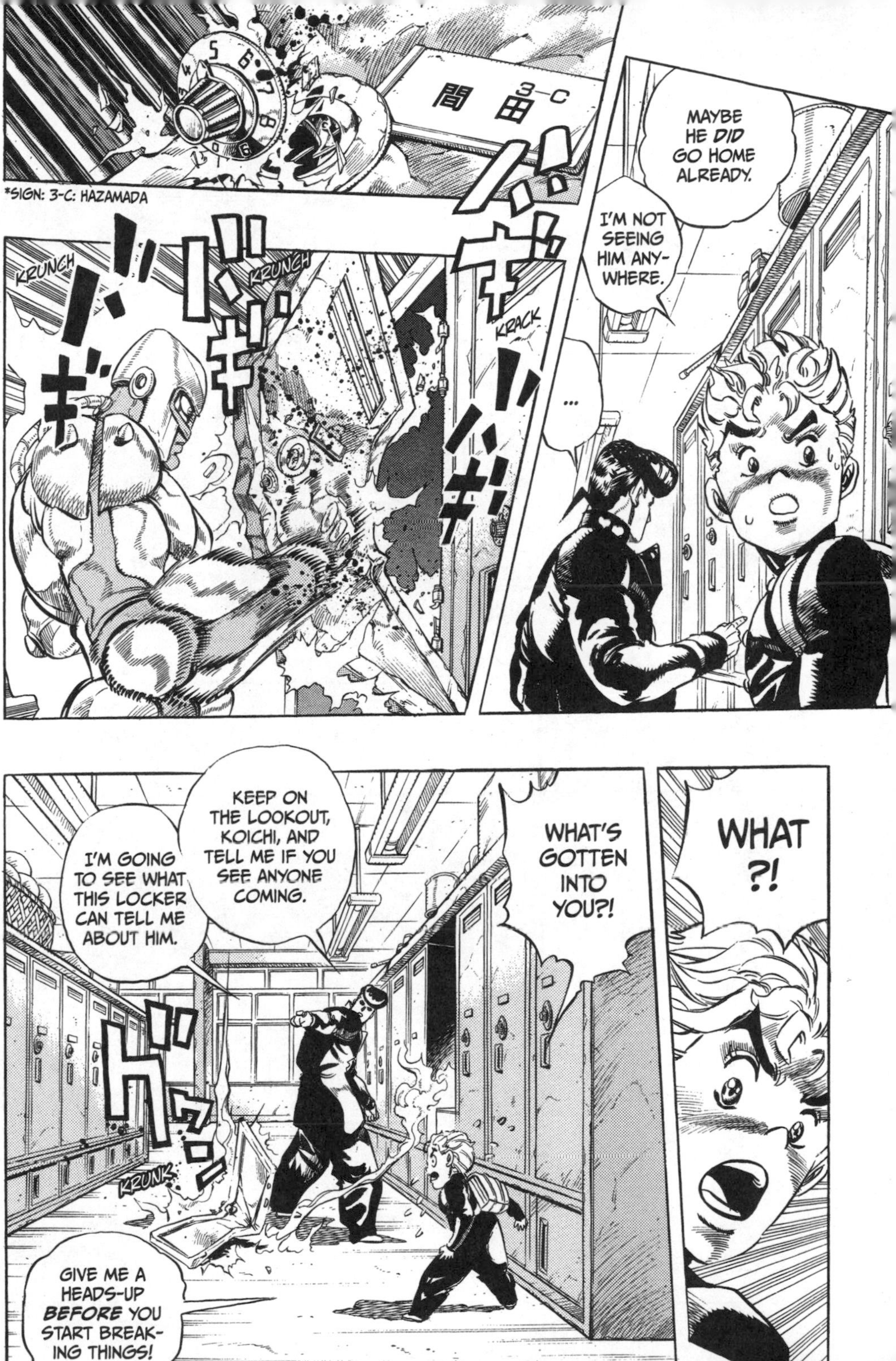
MAYBE HE DID GO HOME ALREADY.
I'M NOT SEEING HIM ANY-WHERE.
...
間田 3-C
*SIGN: 3-C: HAZAMADA
KRUNCH
KRUNCH
KRACK
WHAT ?!
WHAT'S GOTTEN INTO YOU?!
KEEP ON THE LOOKOUT, KOICHI, AND TELL ME IF YOU SEE ANYONE COMING.
I'M GOING TO SEE WHAT THIS LOCKER CAN TELL ME ABOUT HIM.
KRUNK
GIVE ME A HEADS-UP BEFORE YOU START BREAK-ING THINGS!

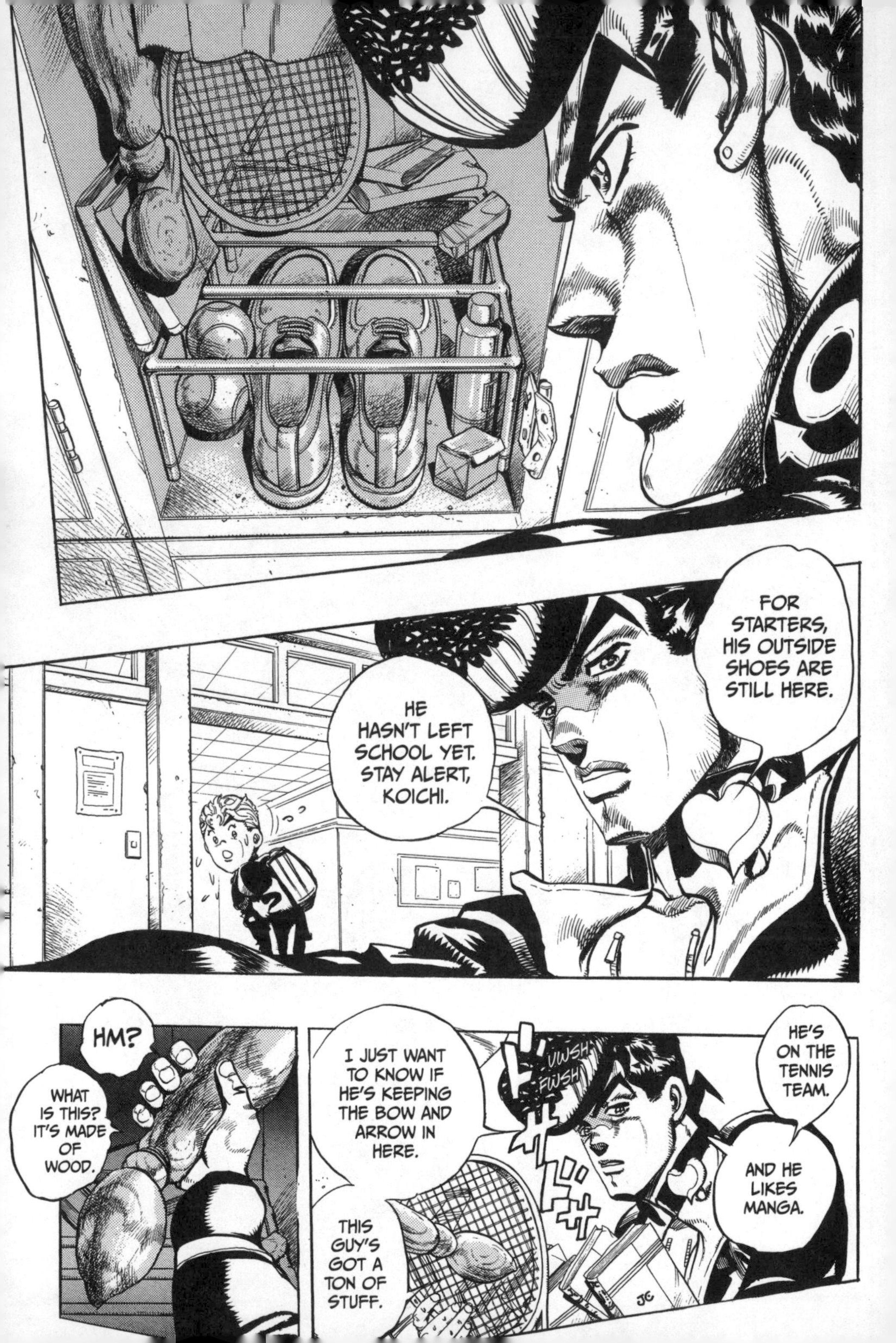
FOR STARTERS, HIS OUTSIDE SHOES ARE STILL HERE.
HE HASN'T LEFT SCHOOL YET. STAY ALERT, KOICHI.
HE'S ON THE TENNIS TEAM.
AND HE LIKES MANGA.
VWSH
FWSH
I JUST WANT TO KNOW IF HE'S KEEPING THE BOW AND ARROW IN HERE.
THIS GUY'S GOT A TON OF STUFF.
HM?
WHAT IS THIS? IT'S MADE OF WOOD.

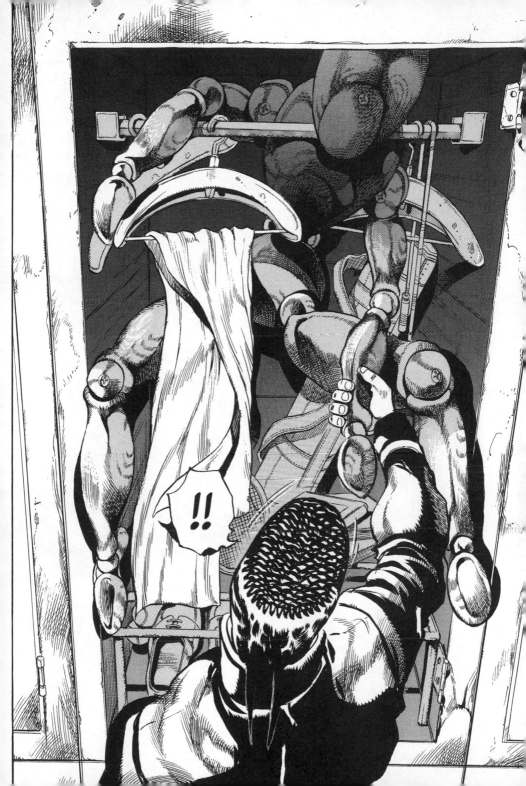

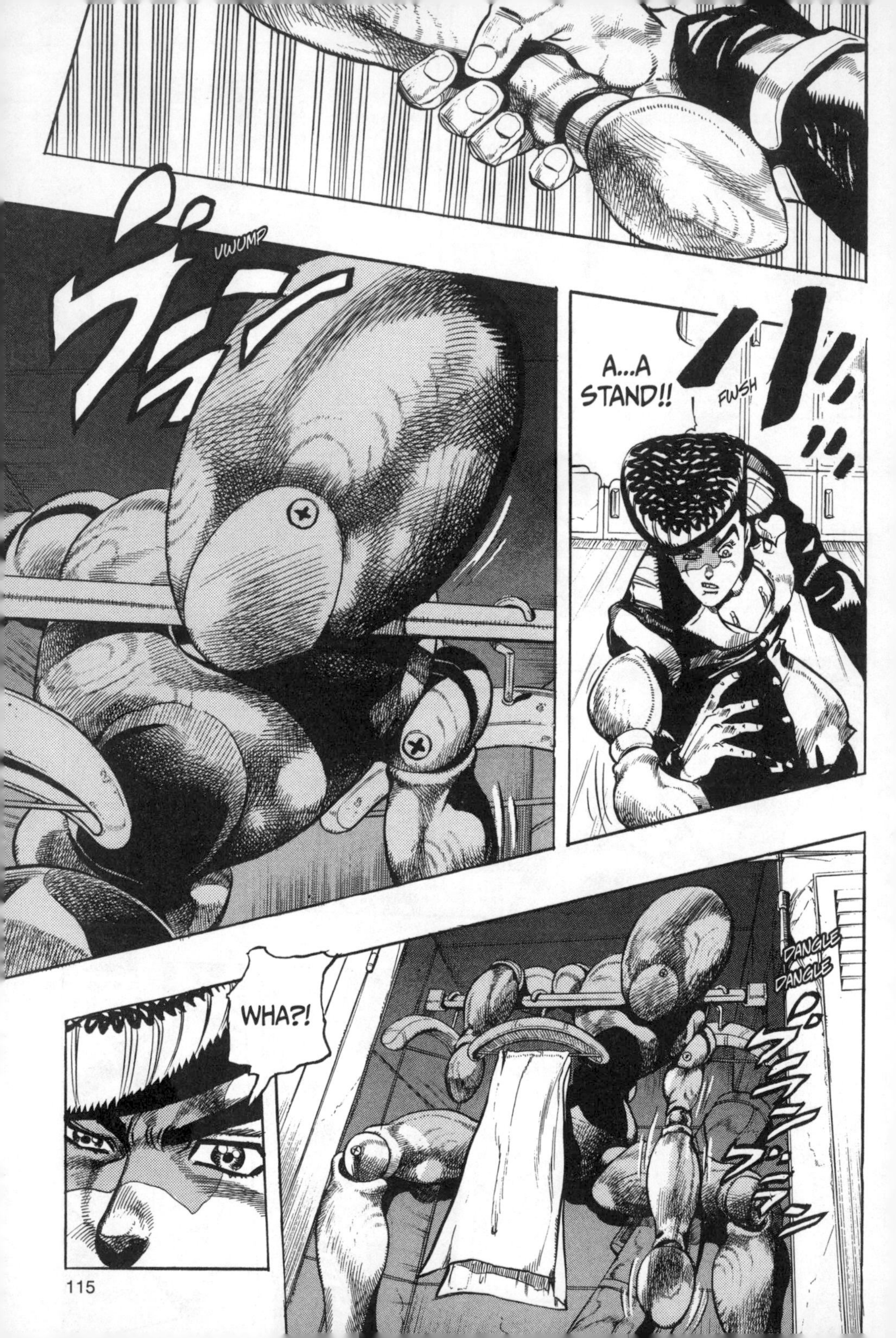
A...A STAND!!
FWSH
VWUMP
DANGLE
DANGLE
WHA?!

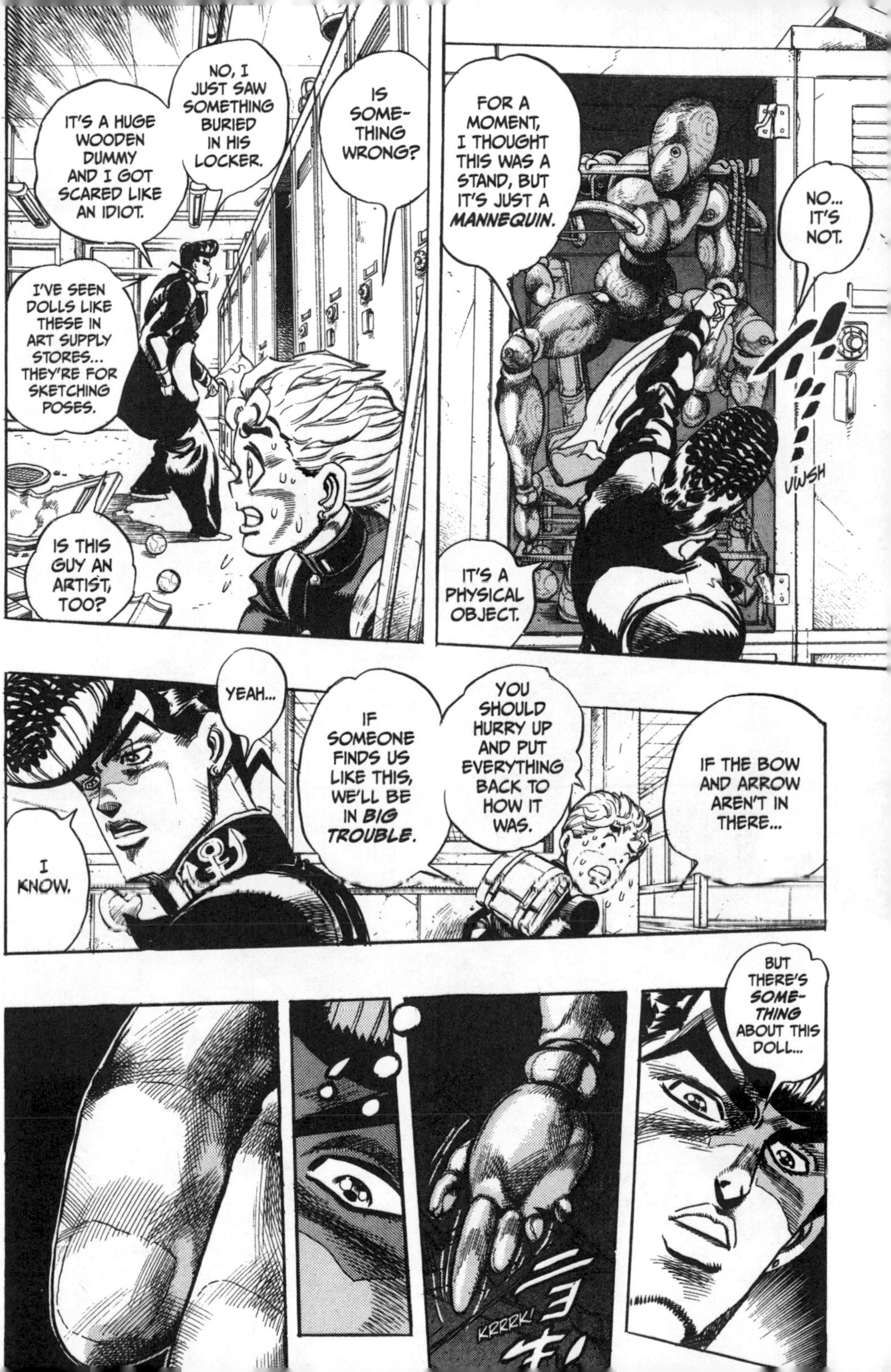
FOR A MOMENT, I THOUGHT THIS WAS A STAND, BUT IT'S JUST A *MANNEQUIN*.
NO... IT'S NOT.
VWSH
IT'S A PHYSICAL OBJECT.
IS SOME-THING WRONG?
NO, I JUST SAW SOMETHING BURIED IN HIS LOCKER.
IT'S A HUGE WOODEN DUMMY AND I GOT SCARED LIKE AN IDIOT.
I'VE SEEN DOLLS LIKE THESE IN ART SUPPLY STORES... THEY'RE FOR SKETCHING POSES.
IS THIS GUY AN ARTIST, TOO?
IF THE BOW AND ARROW AREN'T IN THERE...
YOU SHOULD HURRY UP AND PUT EVERYTHING BACK TO HOW IT WAS.
IF SOMEONE FINDS US LIKE THIS, WE'LL BE IN *BIG TROUBLE*.
YEAH...
I KNOW.
BUT THERE'S *SOME-THING* ABOUT THIS DOLL...
KRRRK!

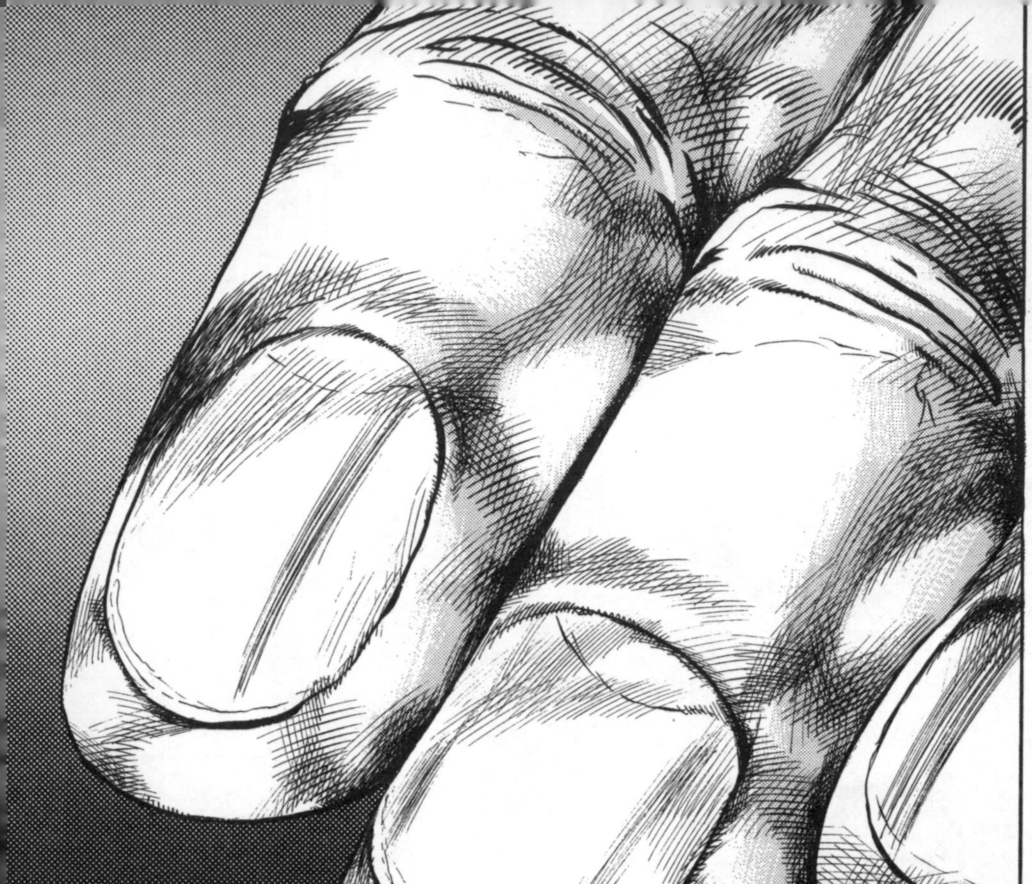

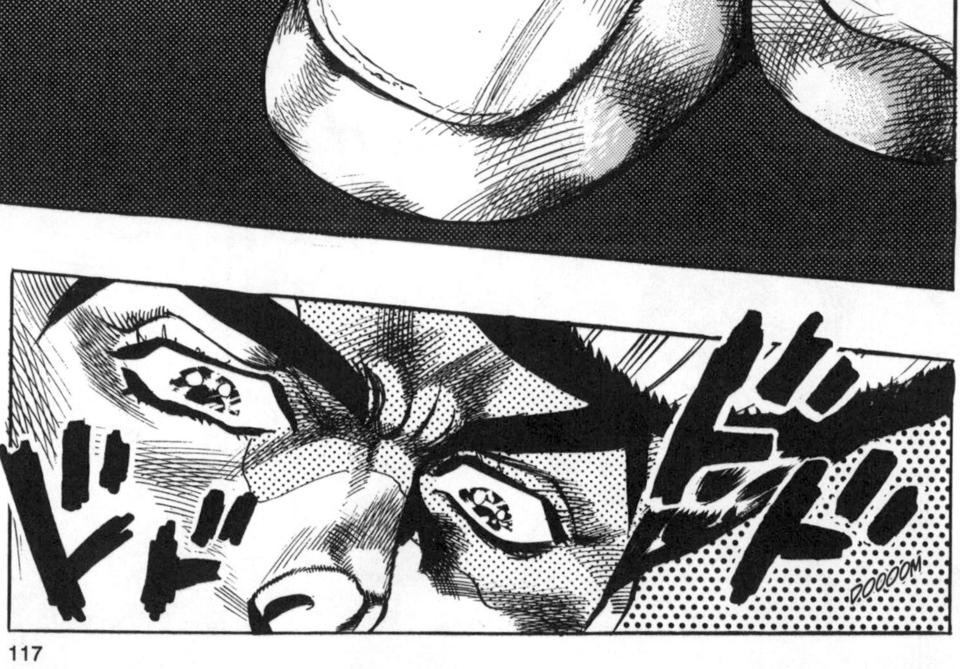
DOOOOM

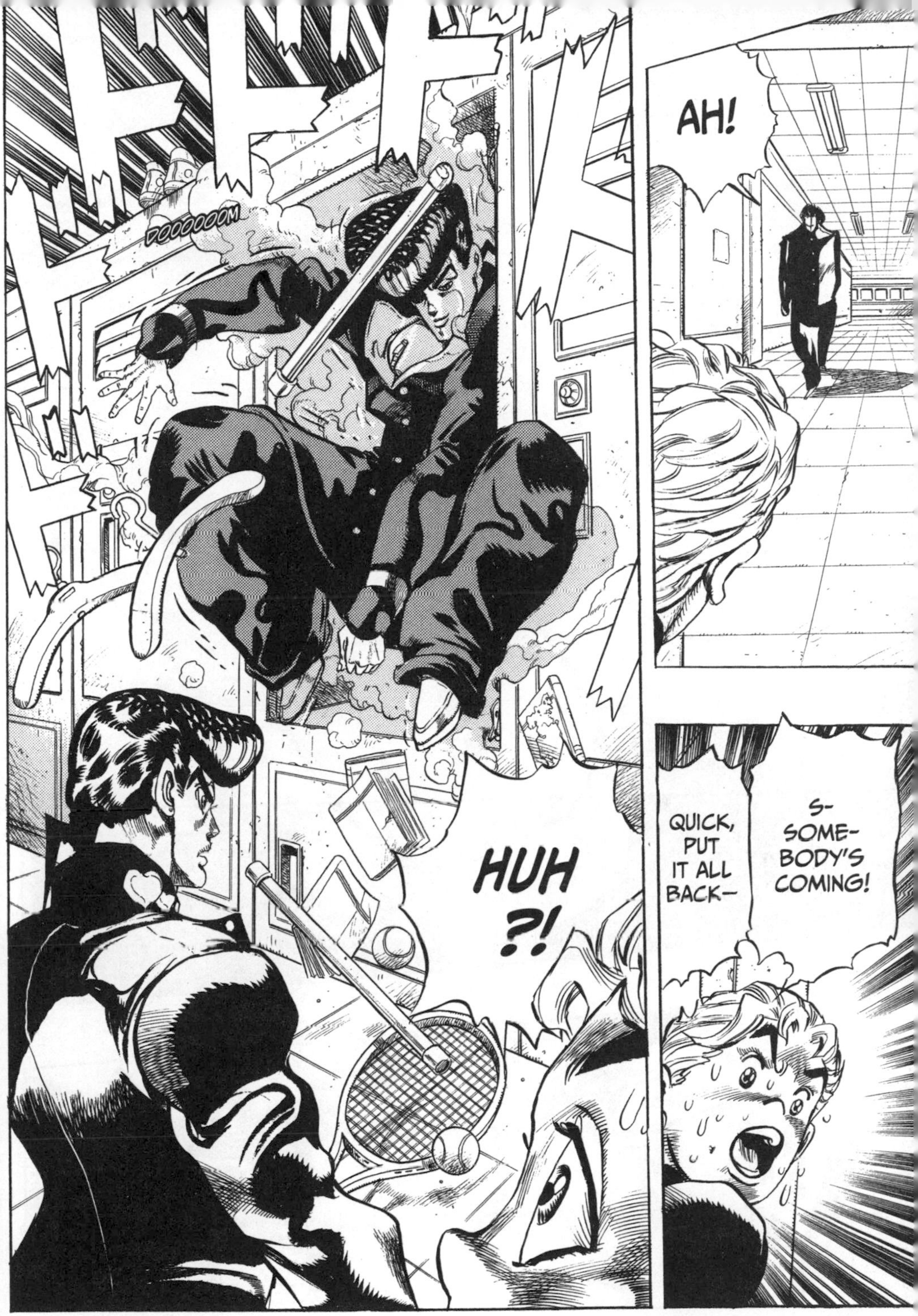
AH!
S-
SOME-
BODY'S
COMING!
QUICK,
PUT
IT ALL
BACK—
DOOOOOOM
HUH
?!

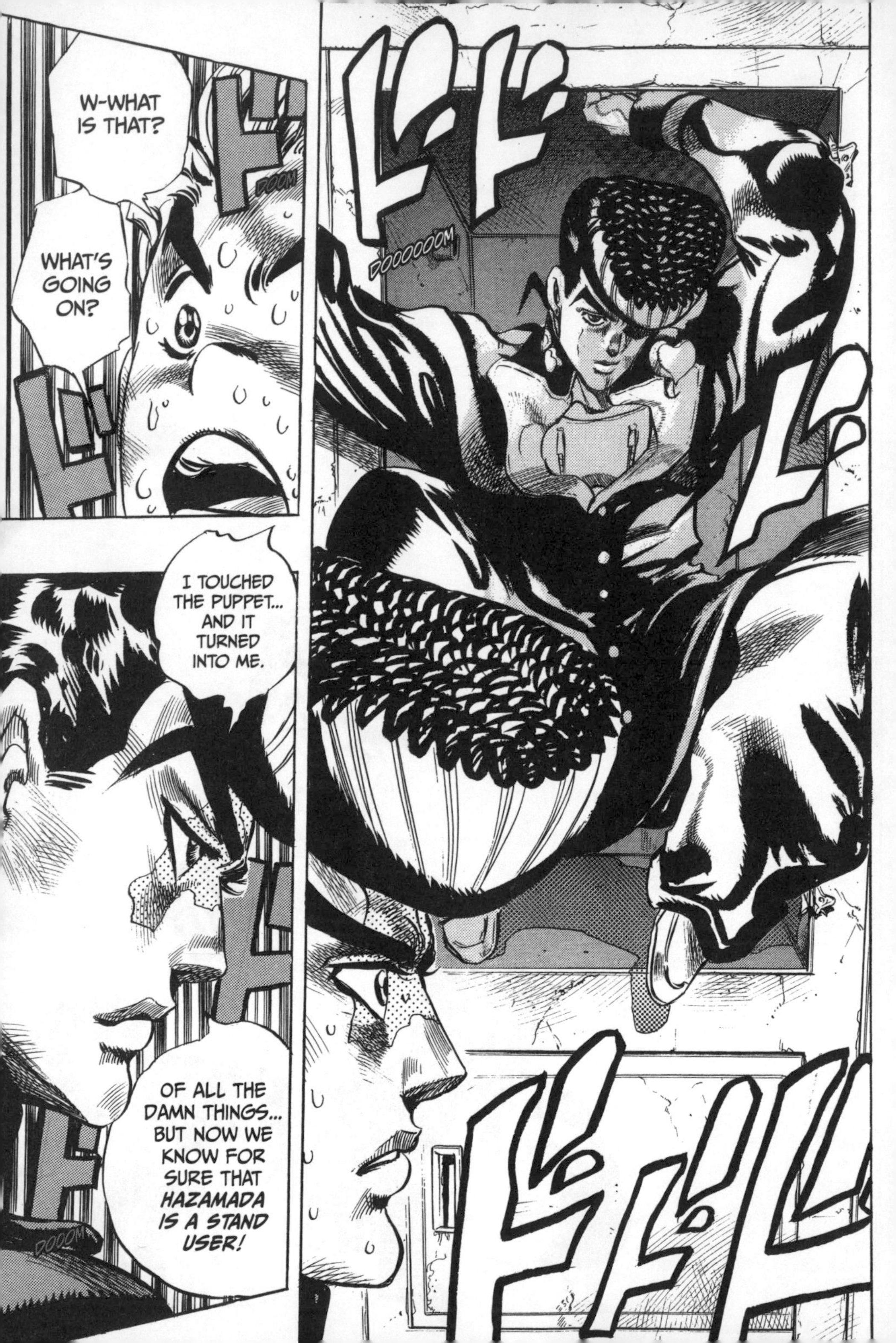
DOOOOOOM
W-WHAT IS THAT?
DOOM
WHAT'S GOING ON?
I TOUCHED THE PUPPET... AND IT TURNED INTO ME.
OF ALL THE DAMN THINGS... BUT NOW WE KNOW FOR SURE THAT *HAZAMADA* IS A STAND USER!
DOOOM

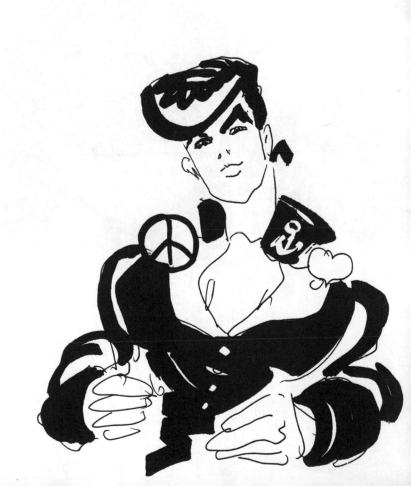

CHAPTER 25 ★ TOSHIKAZU HAZAMADA (SHOW OFF), PART 2

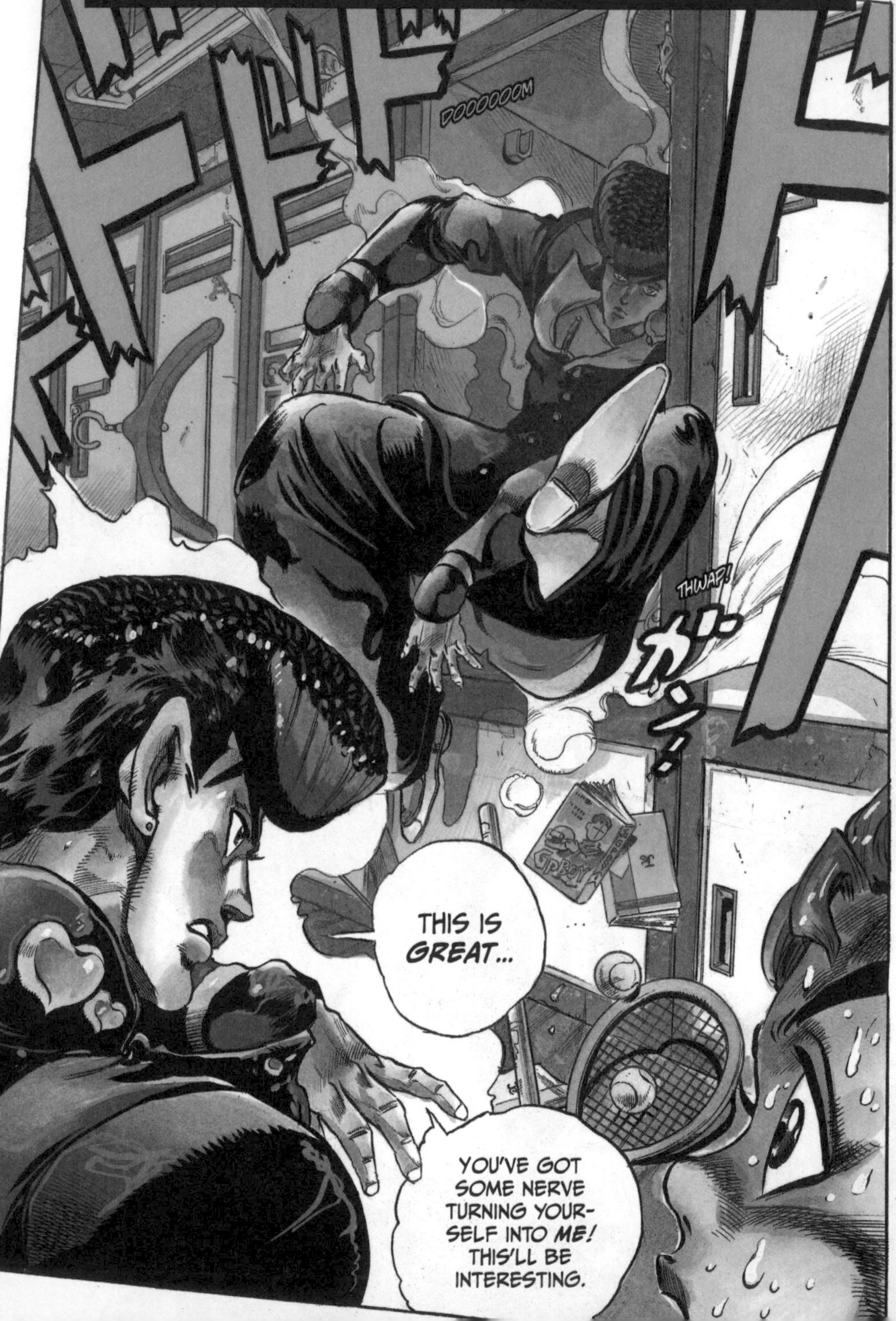

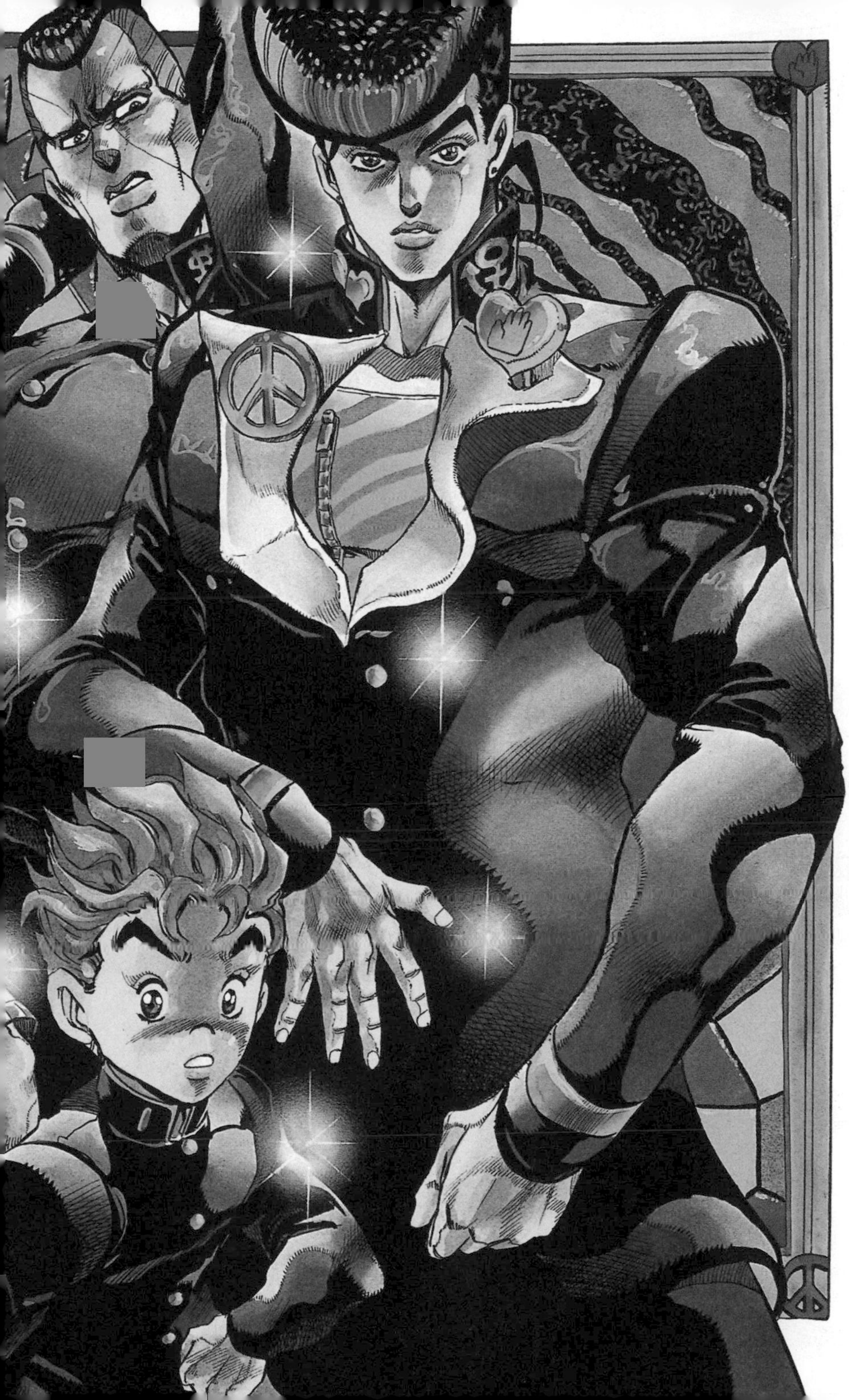

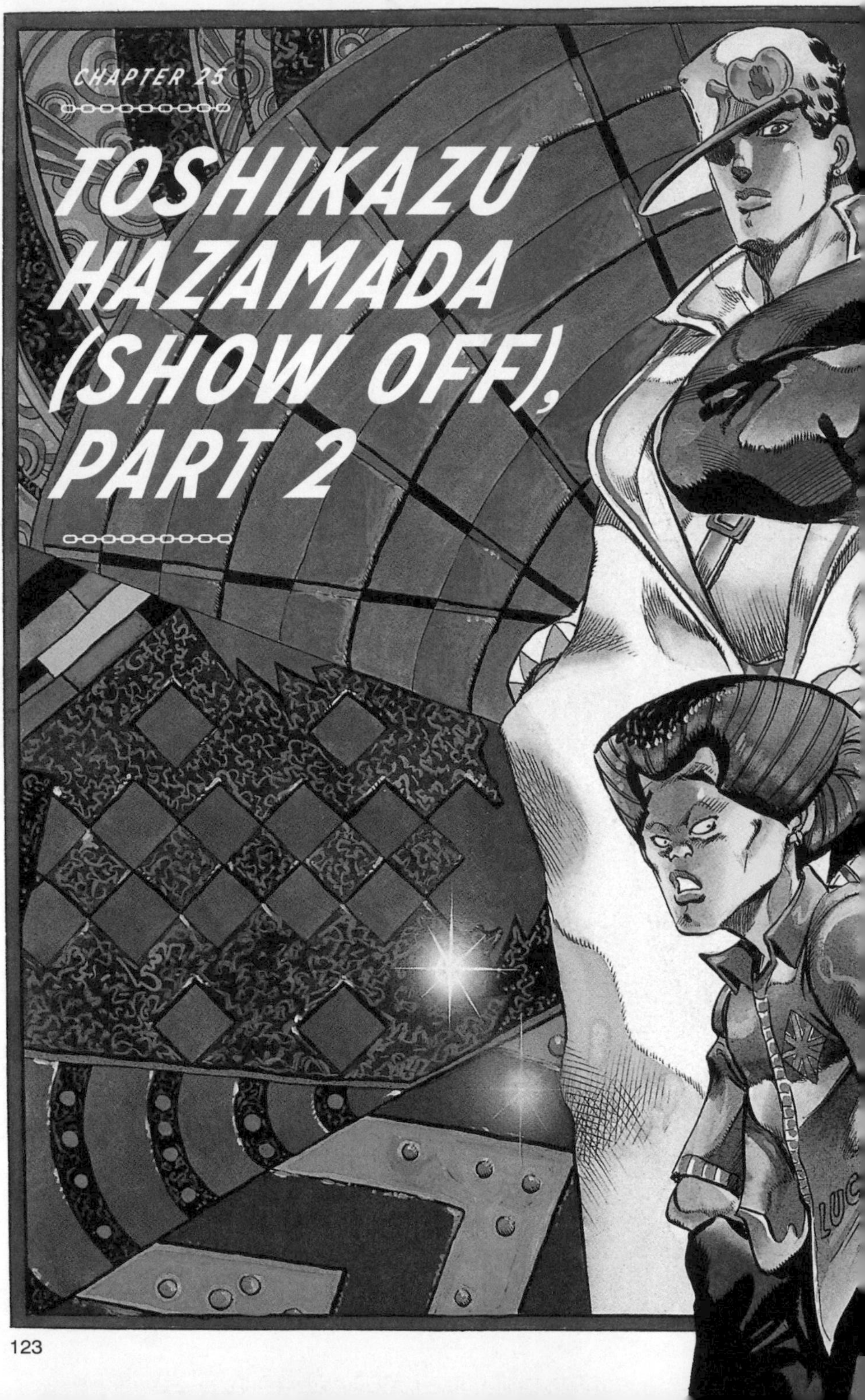
CHAPTER 25
TOSHIKAZU HAZAMADA (SHOW OFF), PART 2

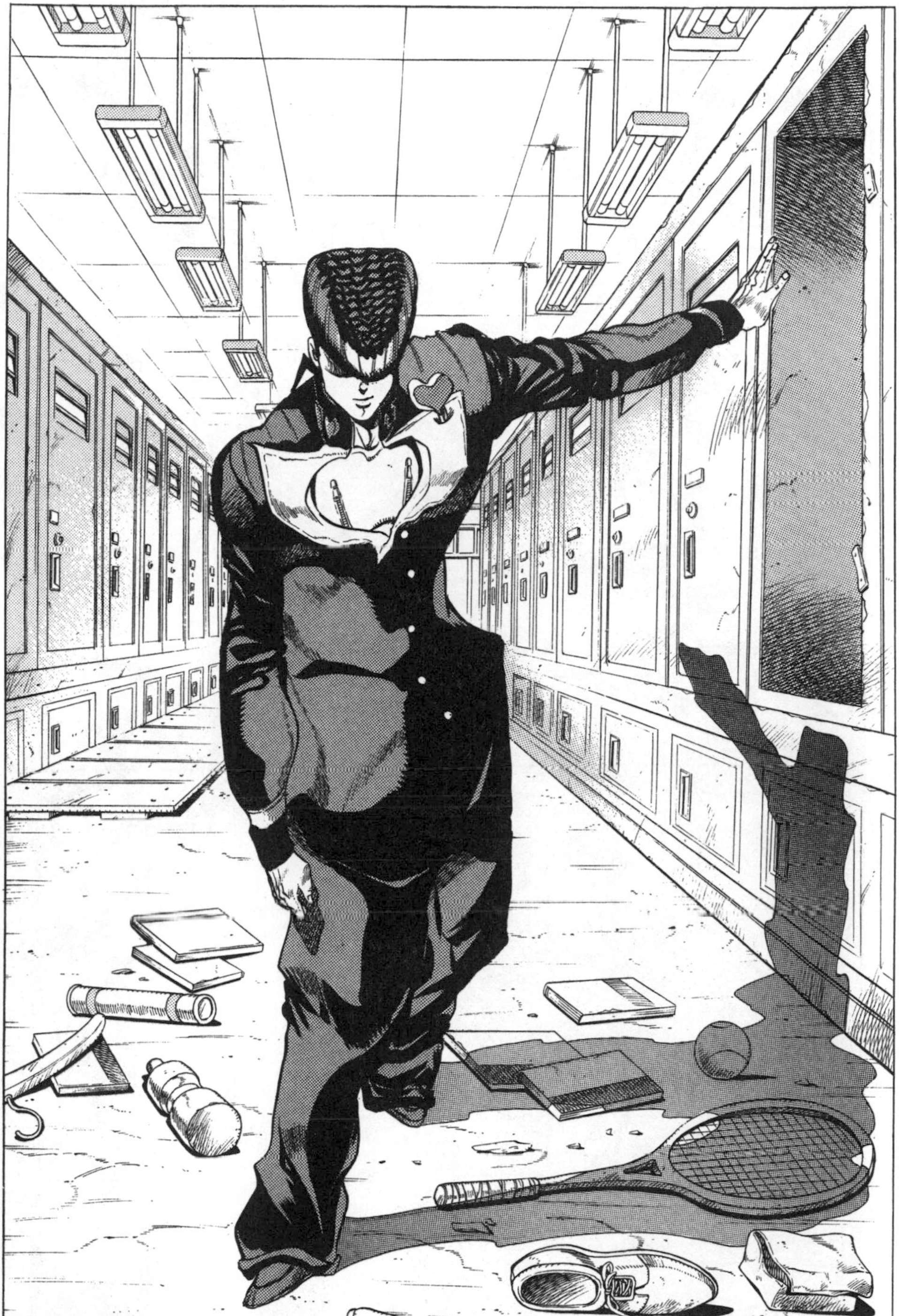

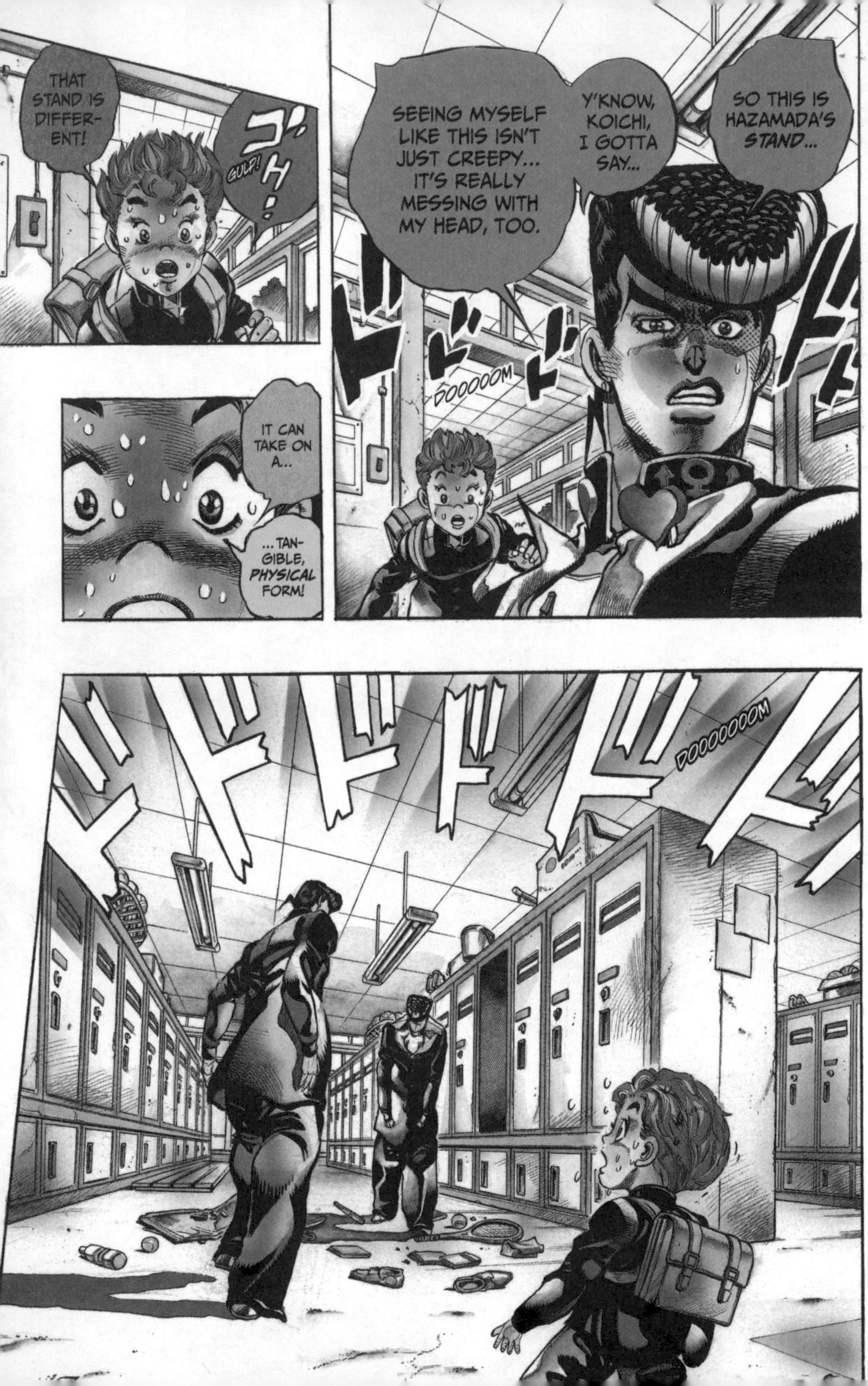
SO THIS IS HAZAMADA'S *STAND*...
Y'KNOW, KOICHI, I GOTTA SAY...
SEEING MYSELF LIKE THIS ISN'T JUST CREEPY... IT'S REALLY MESSING WITH MY HEAD, TOO.
DOOOOOM
GULP!
THAT STAND IS DIFFER-ENT!
IT CAN TAKE ON A...
...TAN-GIBLE, *PHYSICAL* FORM!
DOOOOOOOM

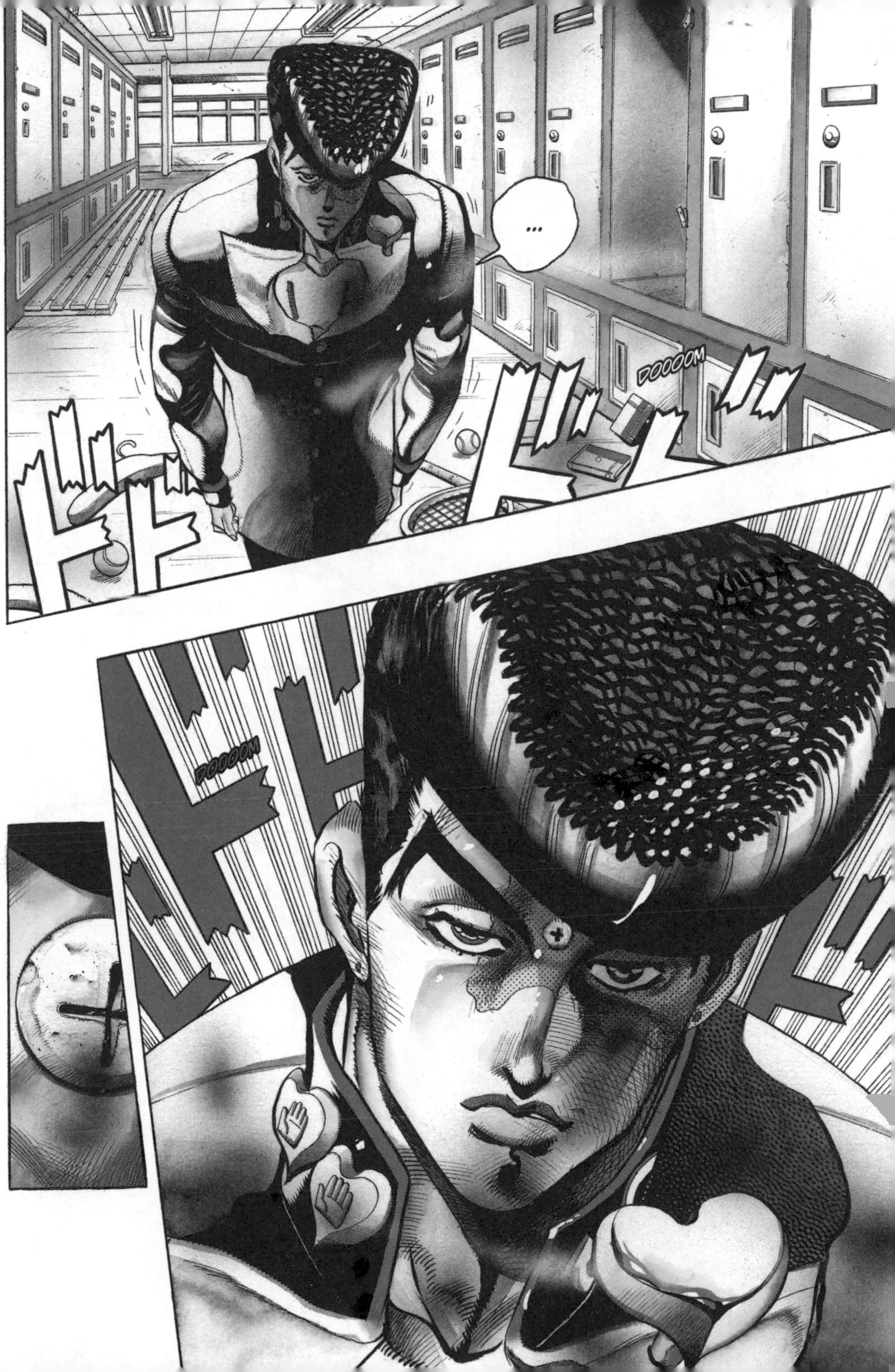
...
DOOOOM
DOOOOM

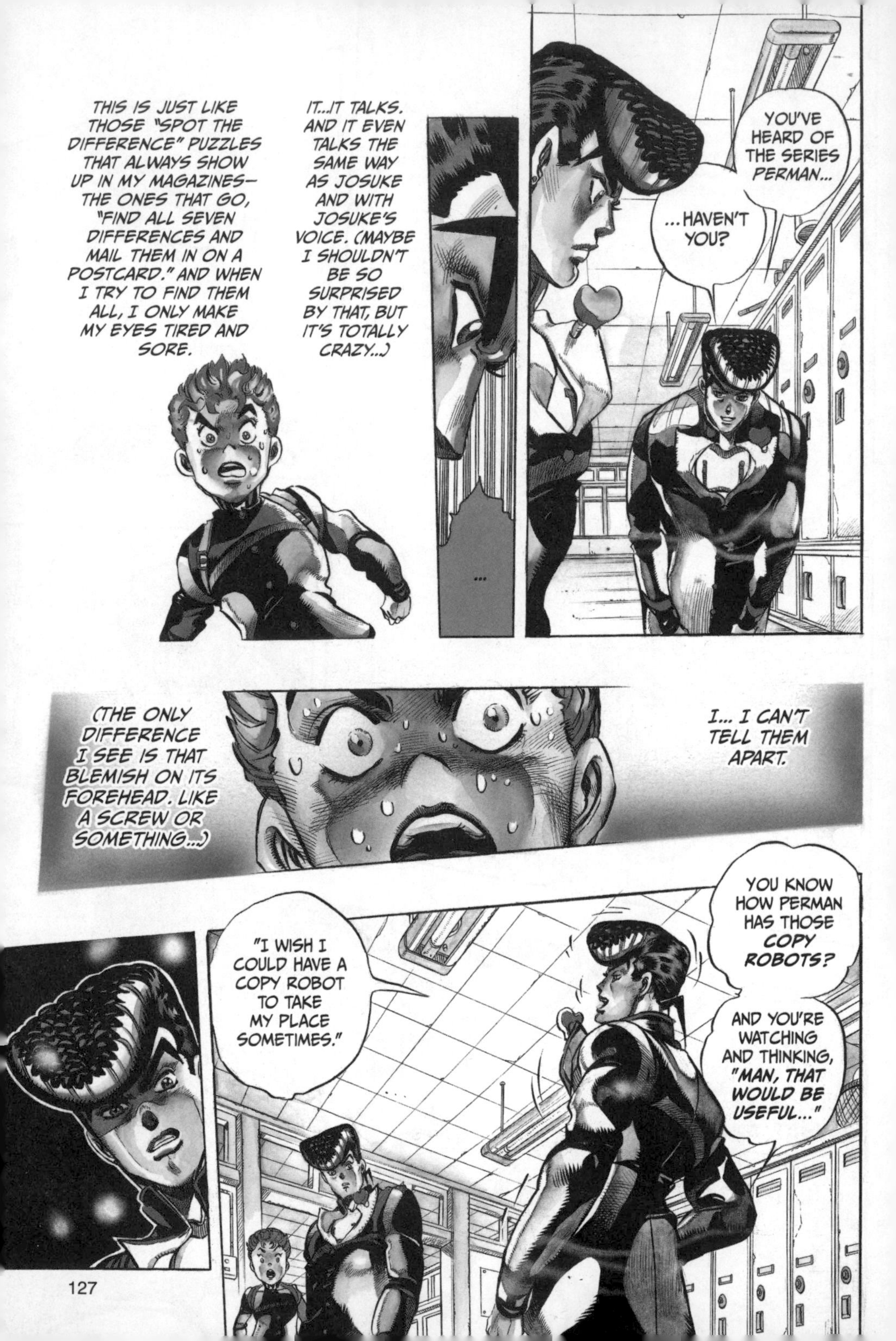
YOU'VE HEARD OF THE SERIES PERMAN...
...HAVEN'T YOU?
IT...IT TALKS. AND IT EVEN TALKS THE SAME WAY AS JOSUKE AND WITH JOSUKE'S VOICE. (MAYBE I SHOULDN'T BE SO SURPRISED BY THAT, BUT IT'S TOTALLY CRAZY...)
...
THIS IS JUST LIKE THOSE "SPOT THE DIFFERENCE" PUZZLES THAT ALWAYS SHOW UP IN MY MAGAZINES— THE ONES THAT GO, "FIND ALL SEVEN DIFFERENCES AND MAIL THEM IN ON A POSTCARD." AND WHEN I TRY TO FIND THEM ALL, I ONLY MAKE MY EYES TIRED AND SORE.
I... I CAN'T TELL THEM APART.
(THE ONLY DIFFERENCE I SEE IS THAT BLEMISH ON ITS FOREHEAD. LIKE A SCREW OR SOMETHING...)
YOU KNOW HOW PERMAN HAS THOSE COPY ROBOTS?
AND YOU'RE WATCHING AND THINKING, "MAN, THAT WOULD BE USEFUL..."
"I WISH I COULD HAVE A COPY ROBOT TO TAKE MY PLACE SOMETIMES."

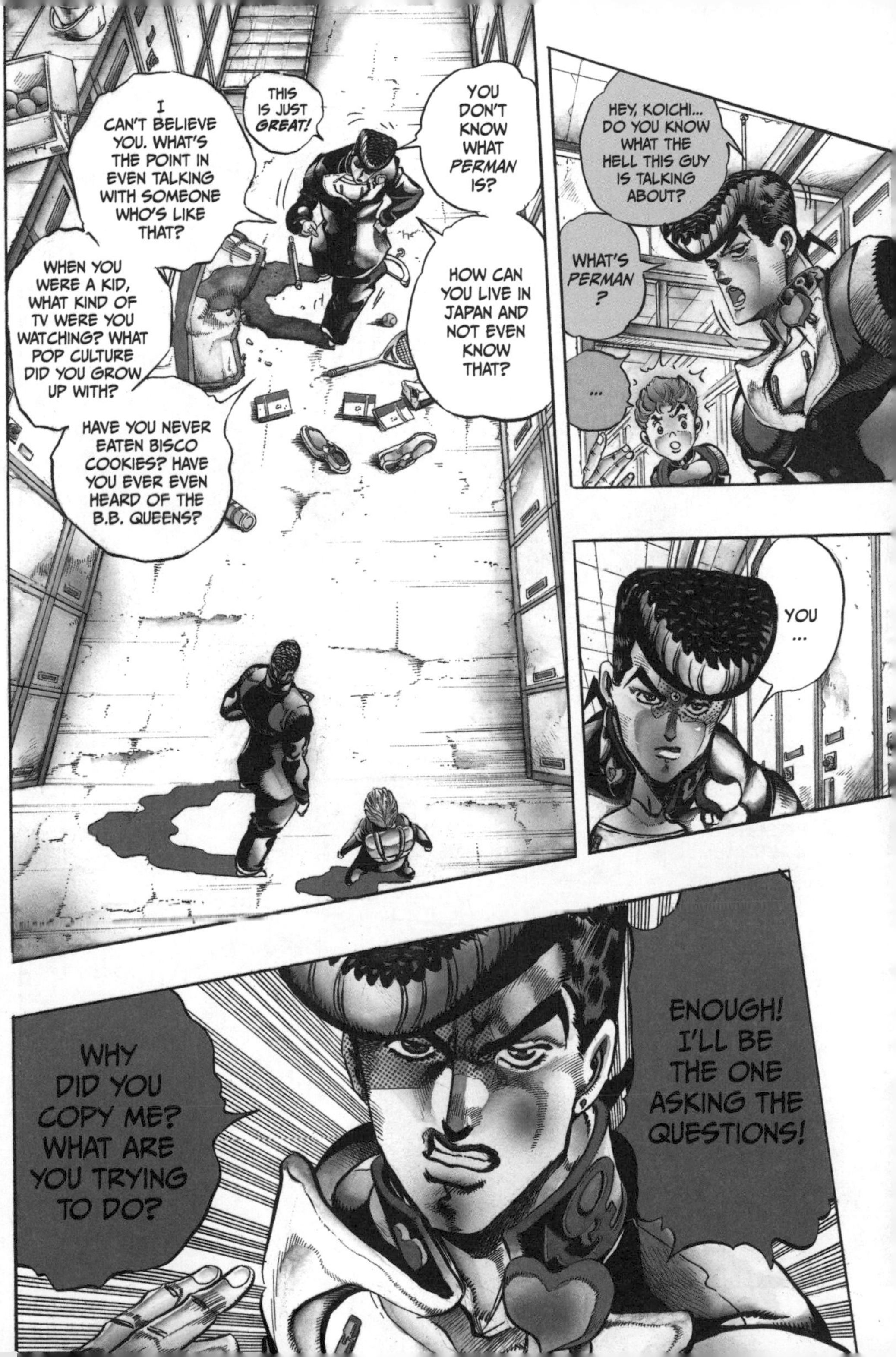
HEY, KOICHI... DO YOU KNOW WHAT THE HELL THIS GUY IS TALKING ABOUT?
WHAT'S *PERMAN*?
...
YOU ...
YOU DON'T KNOW WHAT *PERMAN* IS?
HOW CAN YOU LIVE IN JAPAN AND NOT EVEN KNOW THAT?
THIS IS JUST *GREAT!*
I CAN'T BELIEVE YOU. WHAT'S THE POINT IN EVEN TALKING WITH SOMEONE WHO'S LIKE THAT?
WHEN YOU WERE A KID, WHAT KIND OF TV WERE YOU WATCHING? WHAT POP CULTURE DID YOU GROW UP WITH?
HAVE YOU NEVER EATEN BISCO COOKIES? HAVE YOU EVER EVEN HEARD OF THE B.B. QUEENS?
ENOUGH! I'LL BE THE ONE ASKING THE QUESTIONS!
WHY DID YOU COPY ME? WHAT ARE YOU TRYING TO DO?

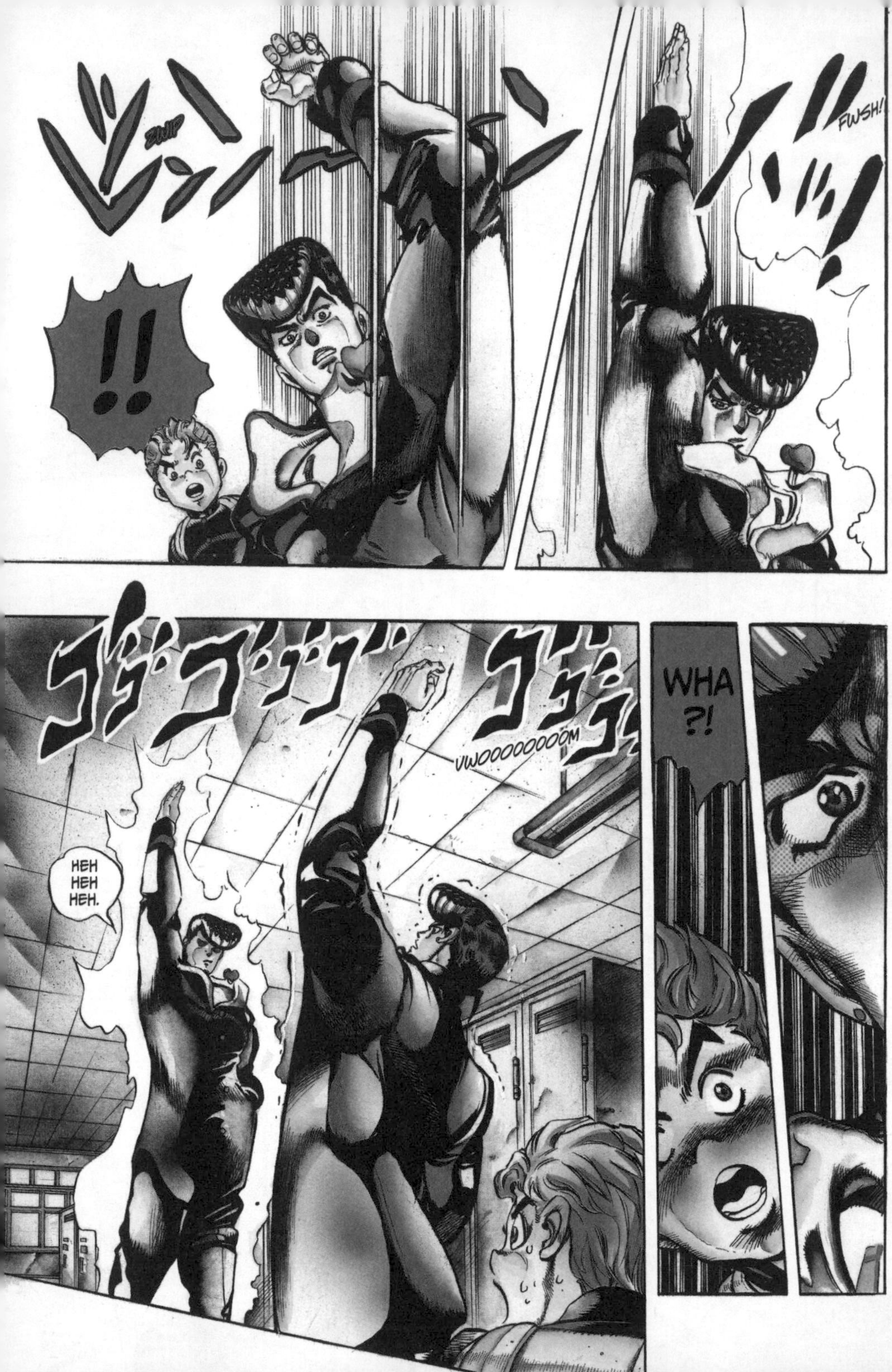
FWSH!
ZWIP
!!
WHA ?!
VWOOOOOOOOM
HEH HEH HEH.

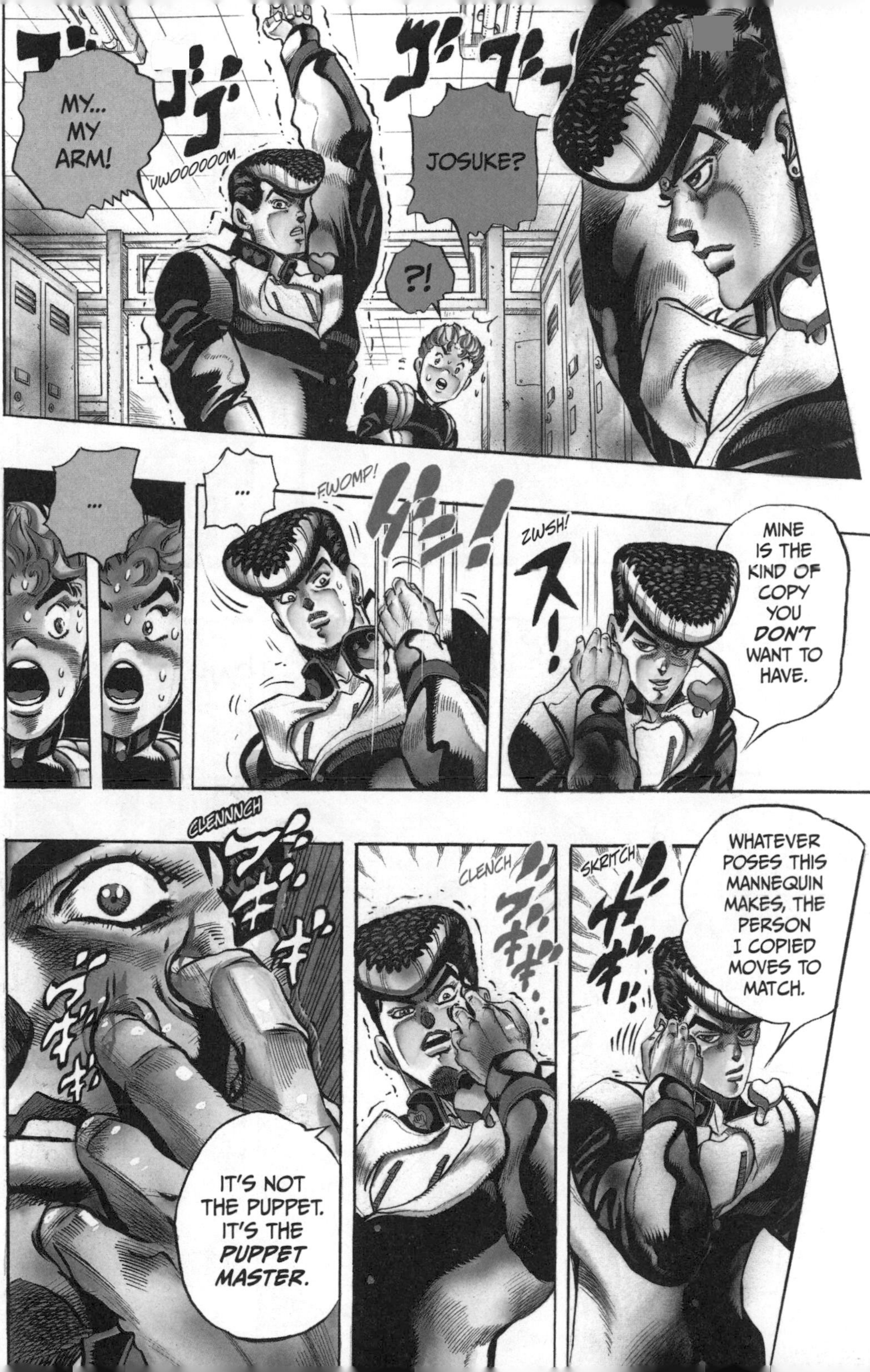
MY... MY ARM!
VWOOOOOOM
JOSUKE?
?!
ZWSH!
MINE IS THE KIND OF COPY YOU *DON'T* WANT TO HAVE.
FWOMP!
...
...
SKRITCH
WHATEVER POSES THIS MANNEQUIN MAKES, THE PERSON I COPIED MOVES TO MATCH.
CLENCH
CLENNNCH
IT'S NOT THE PUPPET. IT'S THE *PUPPET MASTER*.

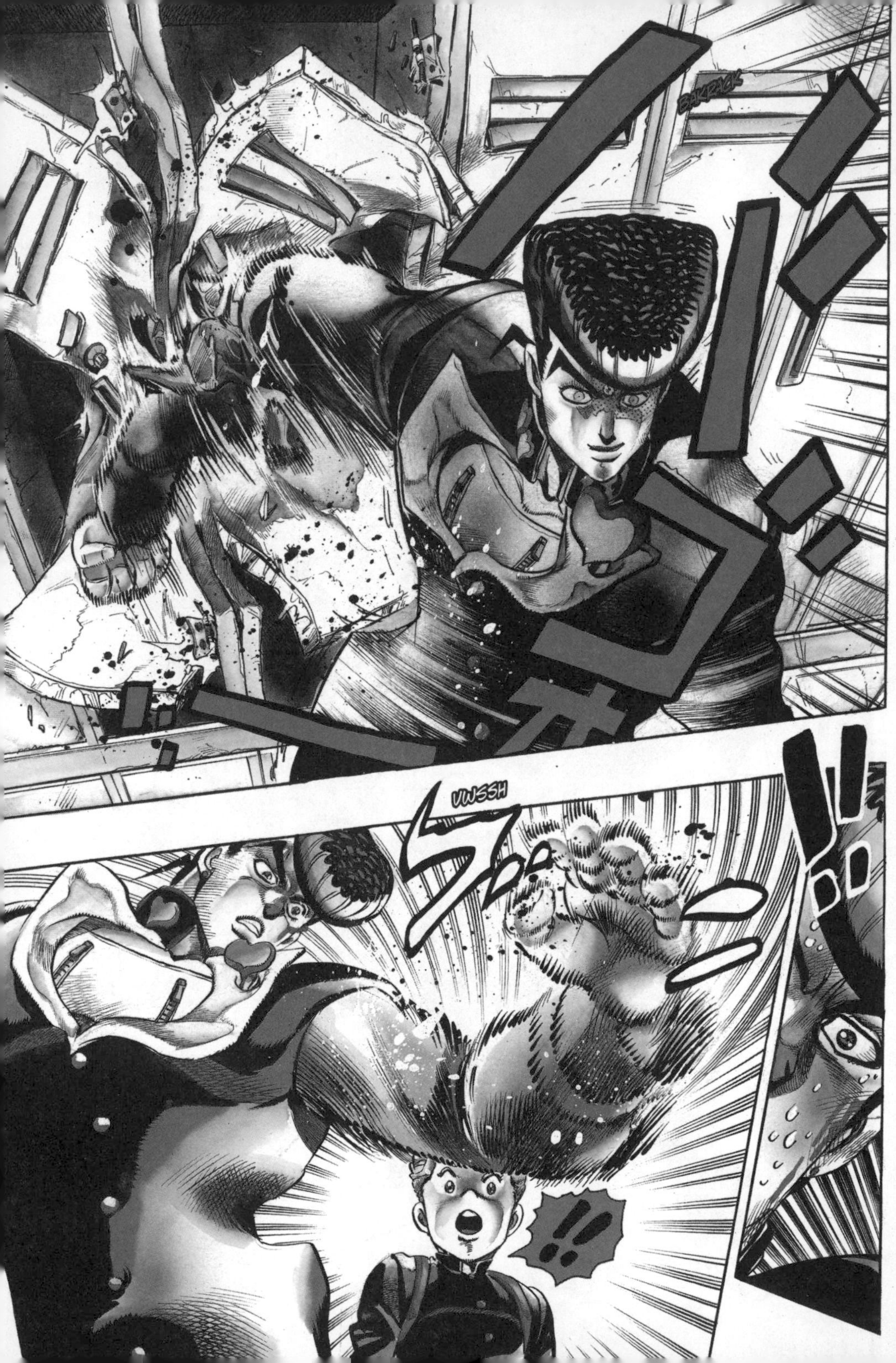
BAKRACK
VWSSH
!!

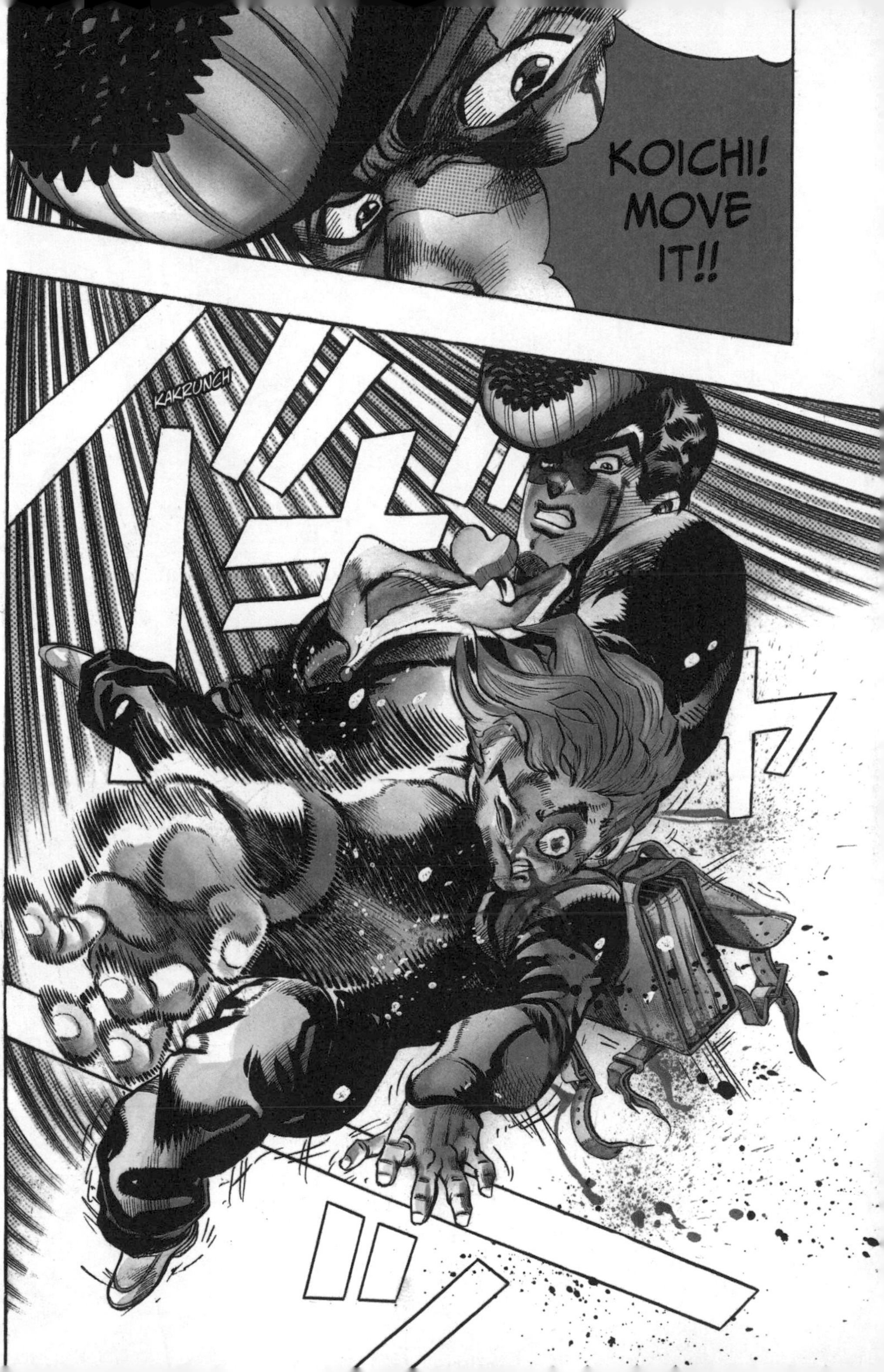
KOICHI! MOVE IT!!
KAKRUNCH

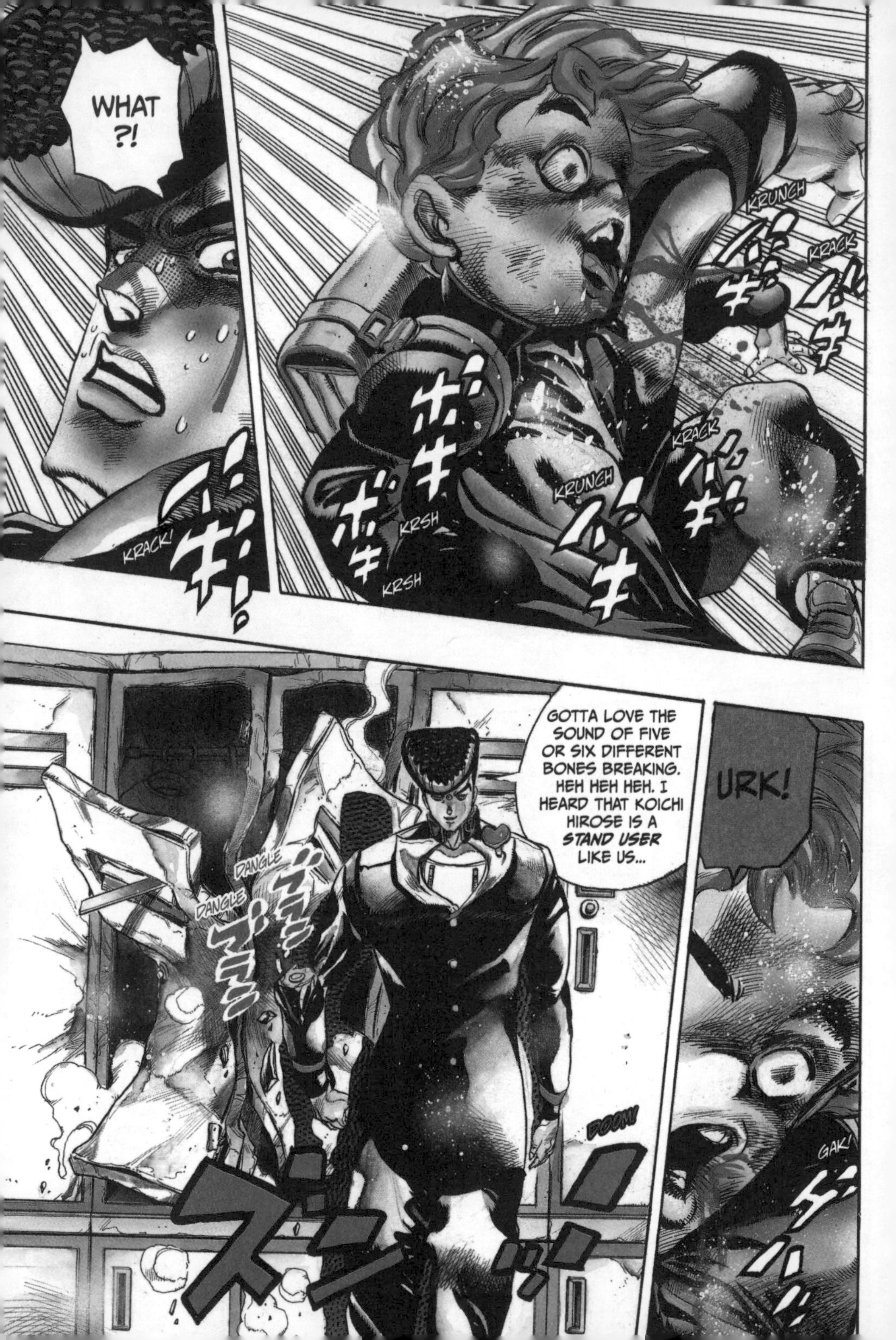
KRUNCH
KRACK
KRACK
KRUNCH
KRSH
KRSH
WHAT ?!
KRACK!
URK!
GAK!
GOTTA LOVE THE SOUND OF FIVE OR SIX DIFFERENT BONES BREAKING. HEH HEH HEH. I HEARD THAT KOICHI HIROSE IS A *STAND USER* LIKE US...
DANGLE
DANGLE
DOOM!

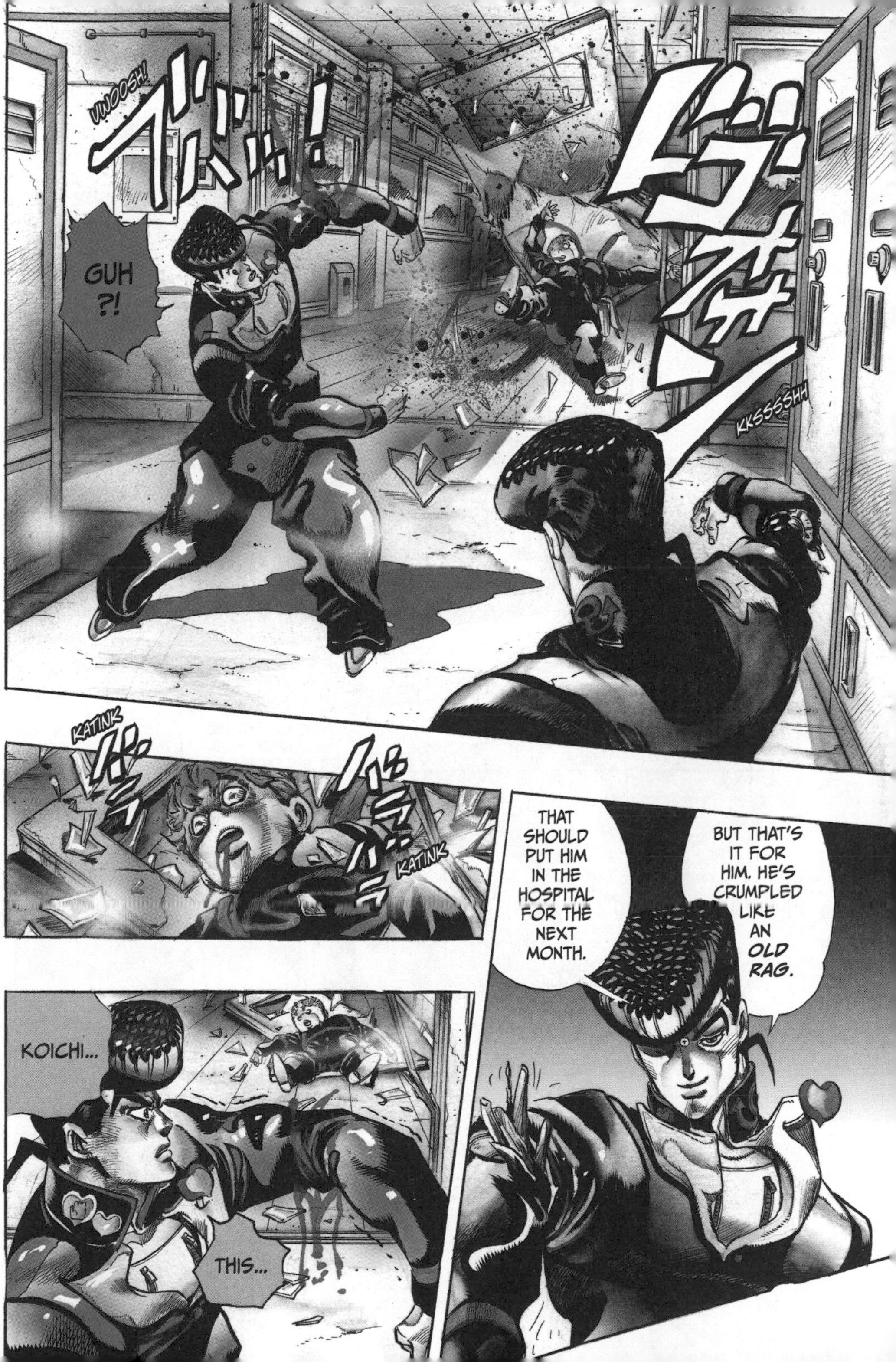
UWOOSH!
GUH ?!
KKSSSSHH
BUT THAT'S IT FOR HIM. HE'S CRUMPLED LIKE AN OLD RAG.
THAT SHOULD PUT HIM IN THE HOSPITAL FOR THE NEXT MONTH.
KATINK
KATINK
KOICHI...
THIS...

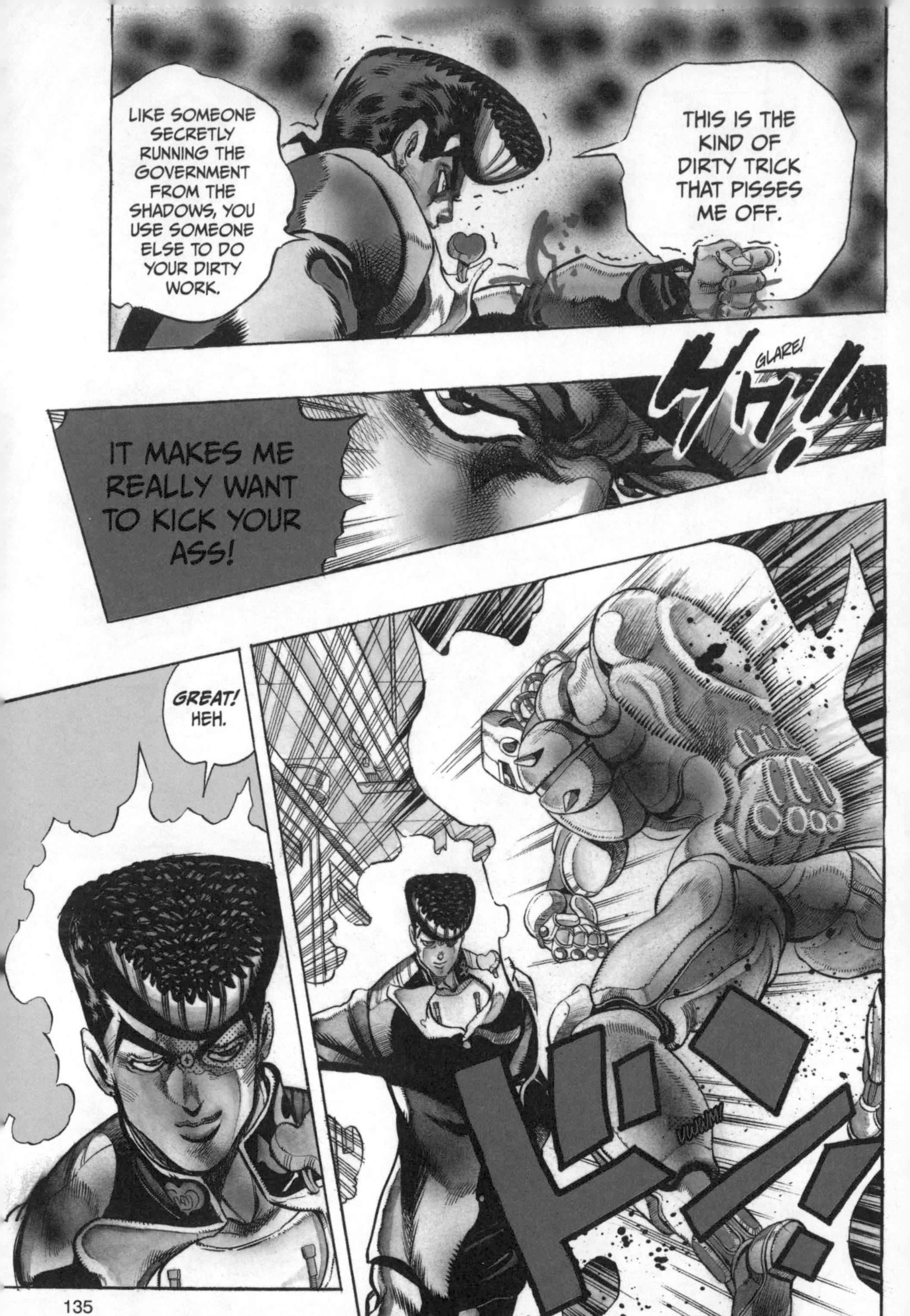
THIS IS THE KIND OF DIRTY TRICK THAT PISSES ME OFF.
LIKE SOMEONE SECRETLY RUNNING THE GOVERNMENT FROM THE SHADOWS, YOU USE SOMEONE ELSE TO DO YOUR DIRTY WORK.
GLARE!
IT MAKES ME REALLY WANT TO KICK YOUR ASS!
GREAT! HEH.

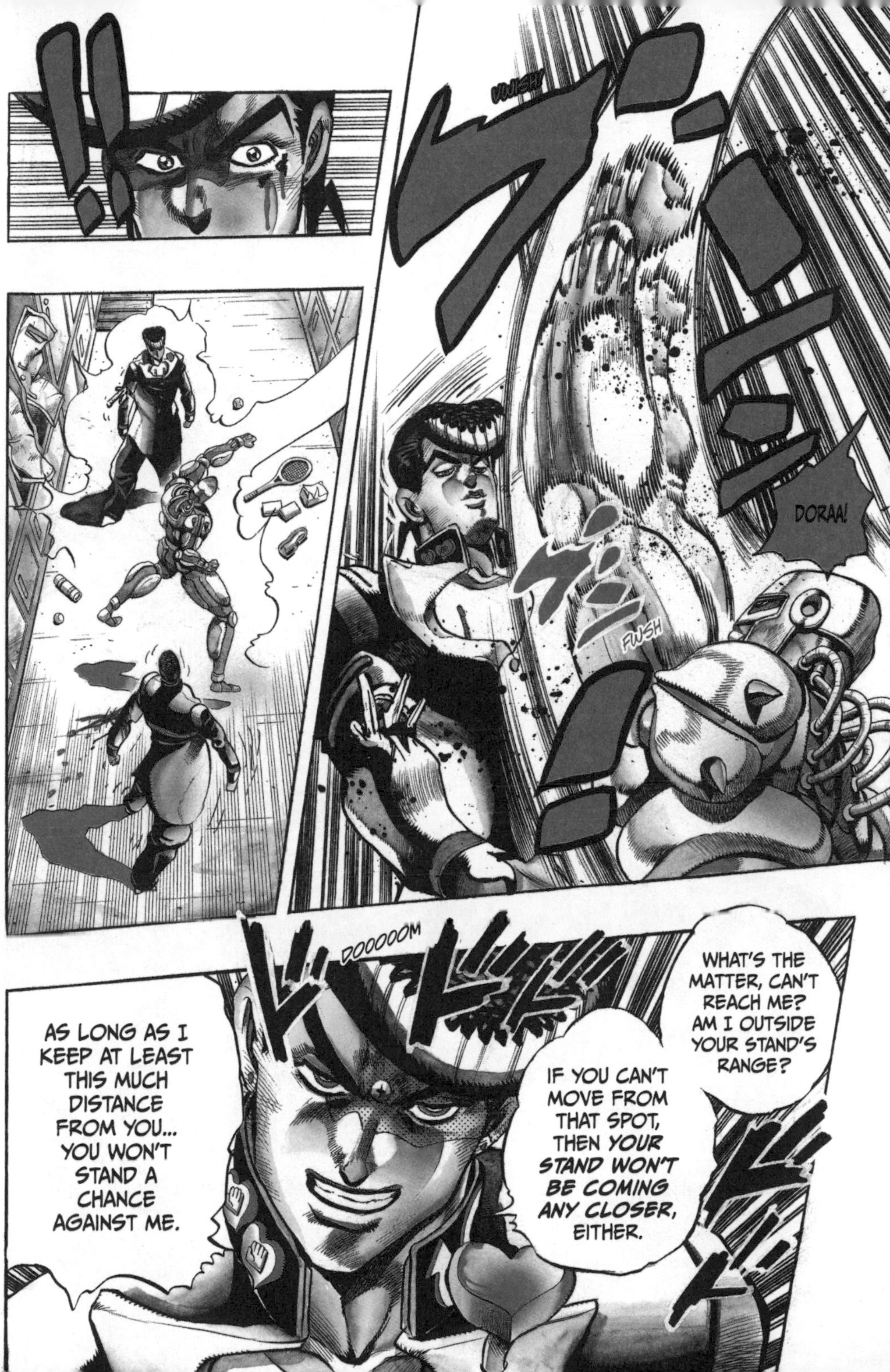
VWISH
DORAA!
FWSH
DOOOOOM
WHAT'S THE MATTER, CAN'T REACH ME? AM I OUTSIDE YOUR STAND'S RANGE?
IF YOU CAN'T MOVE FROM THAT SPOT, THEN *YOUR STAND WON'T BE COMING ANY CLOSER,* EITHER.
AS LONG AS I KEEP AT LEAST THIS MUCH DISTANCE FROM YOU... YOU WON'T STAND A CHANCE AGAINST ME.

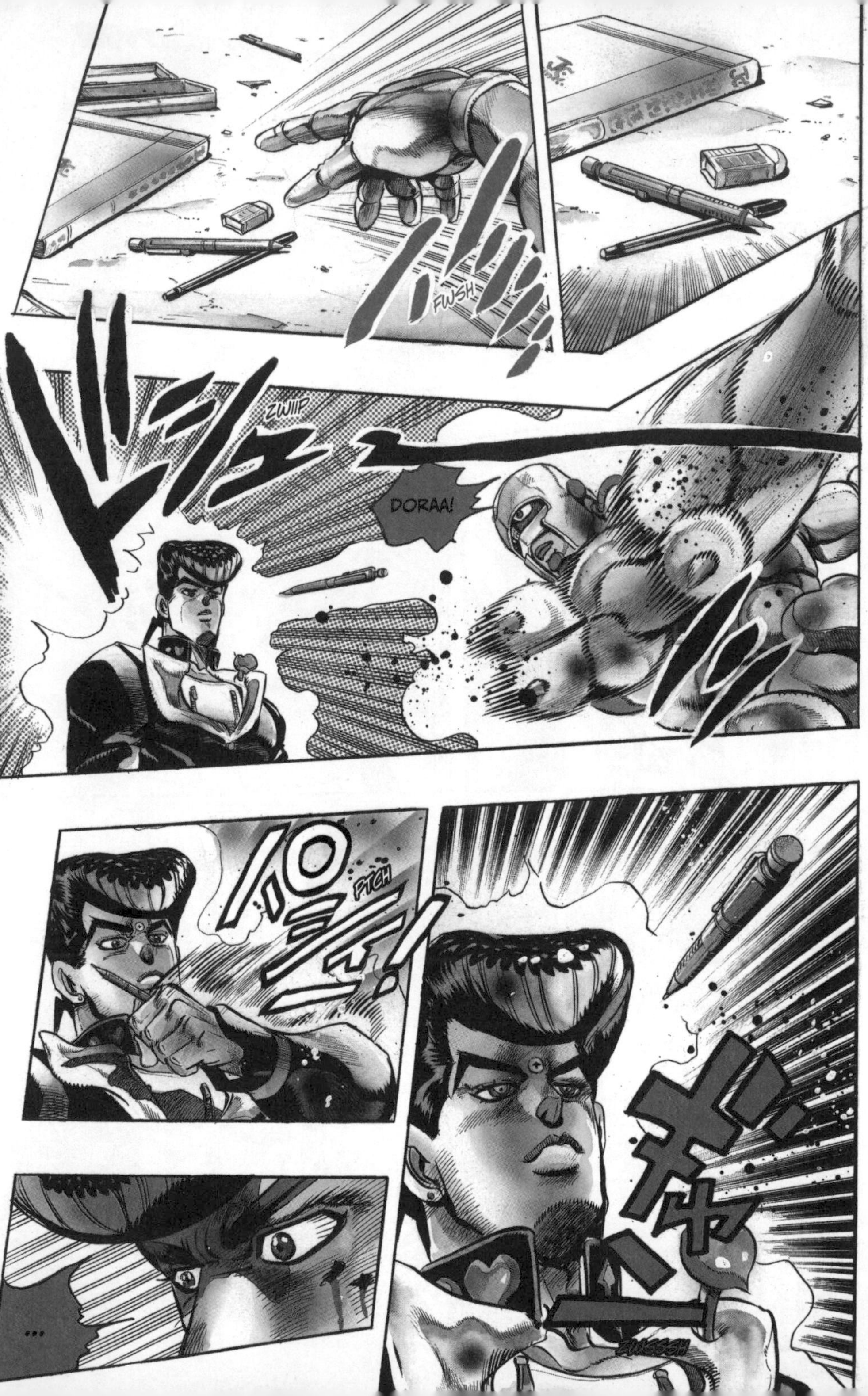
FWSH
ZWIIP
DORAA!
ZWSSSH
PITCH
...

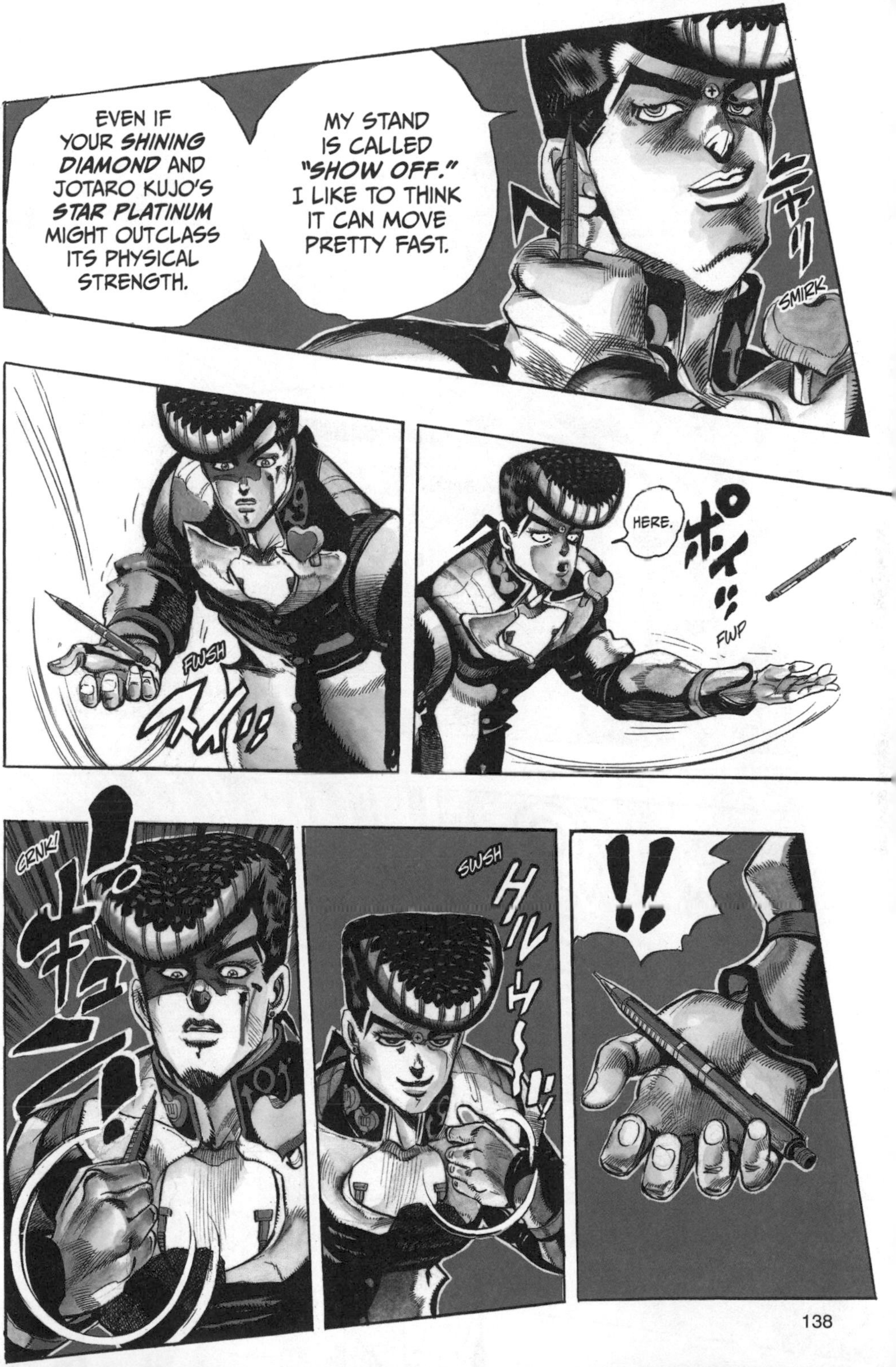
MY STAND IS CALLED "SHOW OFF." I LIKE TO THINK IT CAN MOVE PRETTY FAST.
EVEN IF YOUR SHINING DIAMOND AND JOTARO KUJO'S STAR PLATINUM MIGHT OUTCLASS ITS PHYSICAL STRENGTH.
SMIRK
HERE.
FWP
FWSH
!!
SWSH
GRNK!

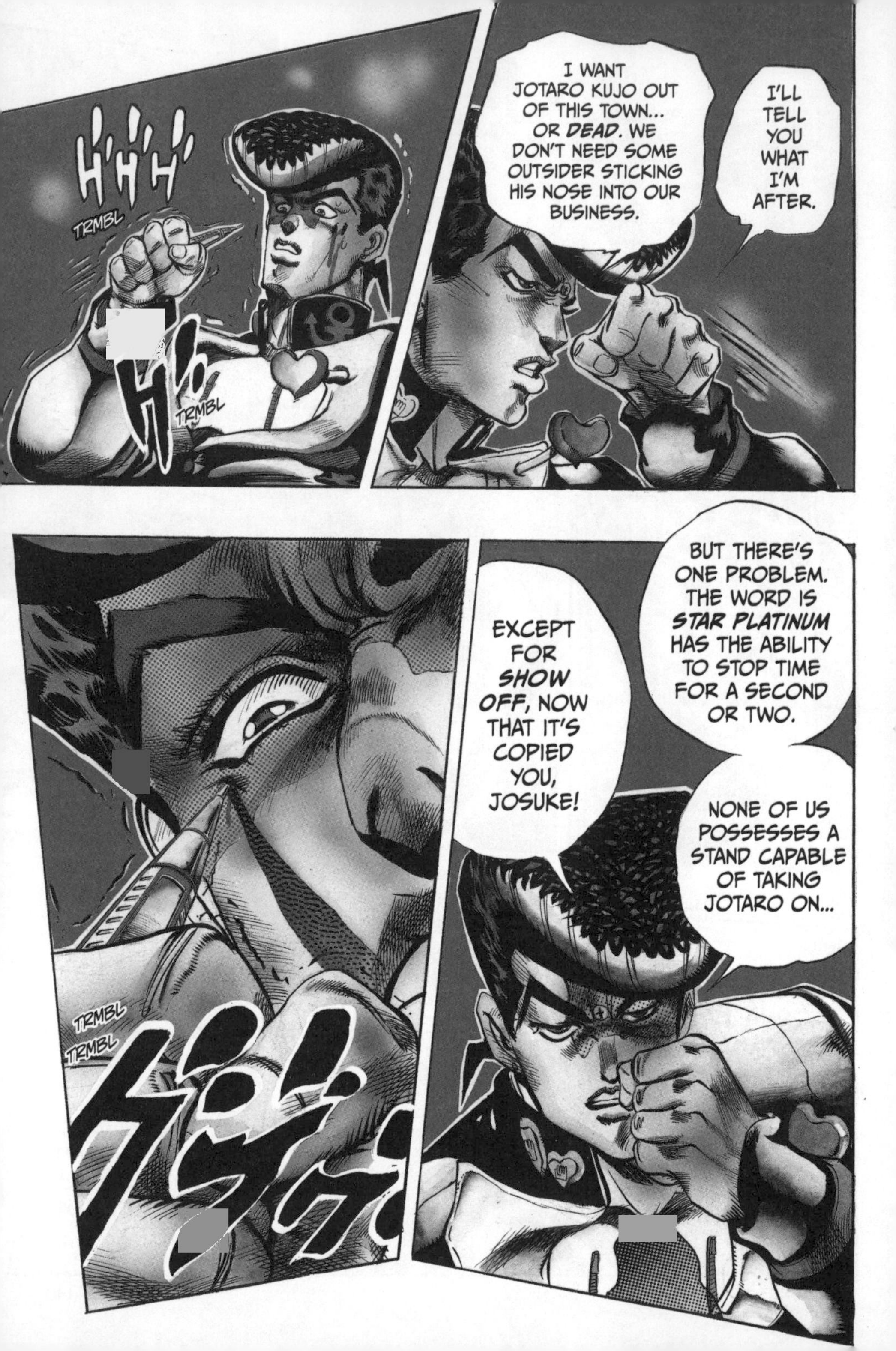
I'LL TELL YOU WHAT I'M AFTER.
I WANT JOTARO KUJO OUT OF THIS TOWN... OR *DEAD*. WE DON'T NEED SOME OUTSIDER STICKING HIS NOSE INTO OUR BUSINESS.
TRMBL
TRMBL
BUT THERE'S ONE PROBLEM. THE WORD IS *STAR PLATINUM* HAS THE ABILITY TO STOP TIME FOR A SECOND OR TWO.
NONE OF US POSSESSES A STAND CAPABLE OF TAKING JOTARO ON...
EXCEPT FOR *SHOW OFF*, NOW THAT IT'S COPIED YOU, JOSUKE!
TRMBL
TRMBL

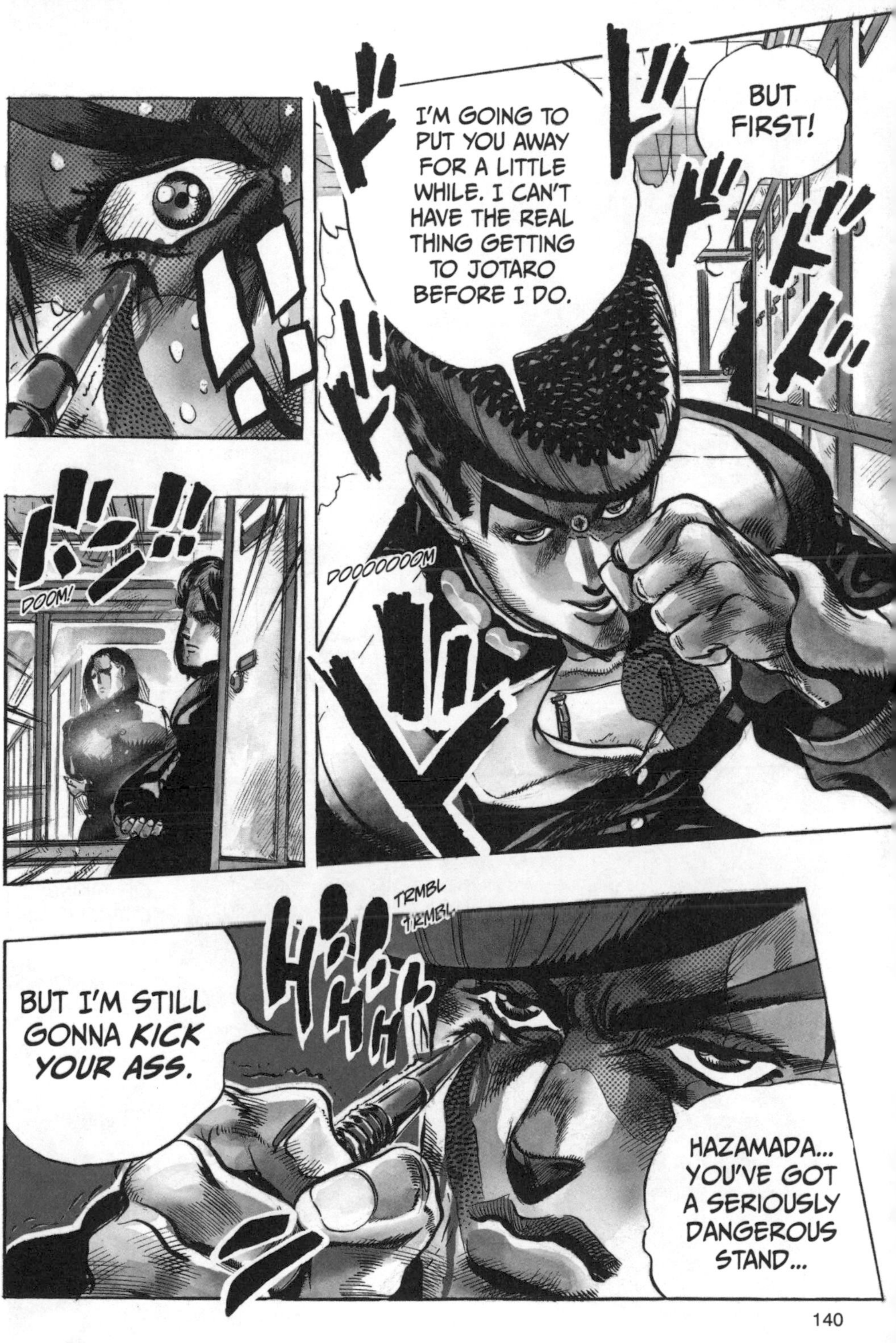
BUT FIRST!
I'M GOING TO PUT YOU AWAY FOR A LITTLE WHILE. I CAN'T HAVE THE REAL THING GETTING TO JOTARO BEFORE I DO.
DOOOOOOOM
DOOM!
TRMBL TRMBL
HAZAMADA... YOU'VE GOT A SERIOUSLY DANGEROUS STAND...
BUT I'M STILL GONNA *KICK YOUR ASS.*

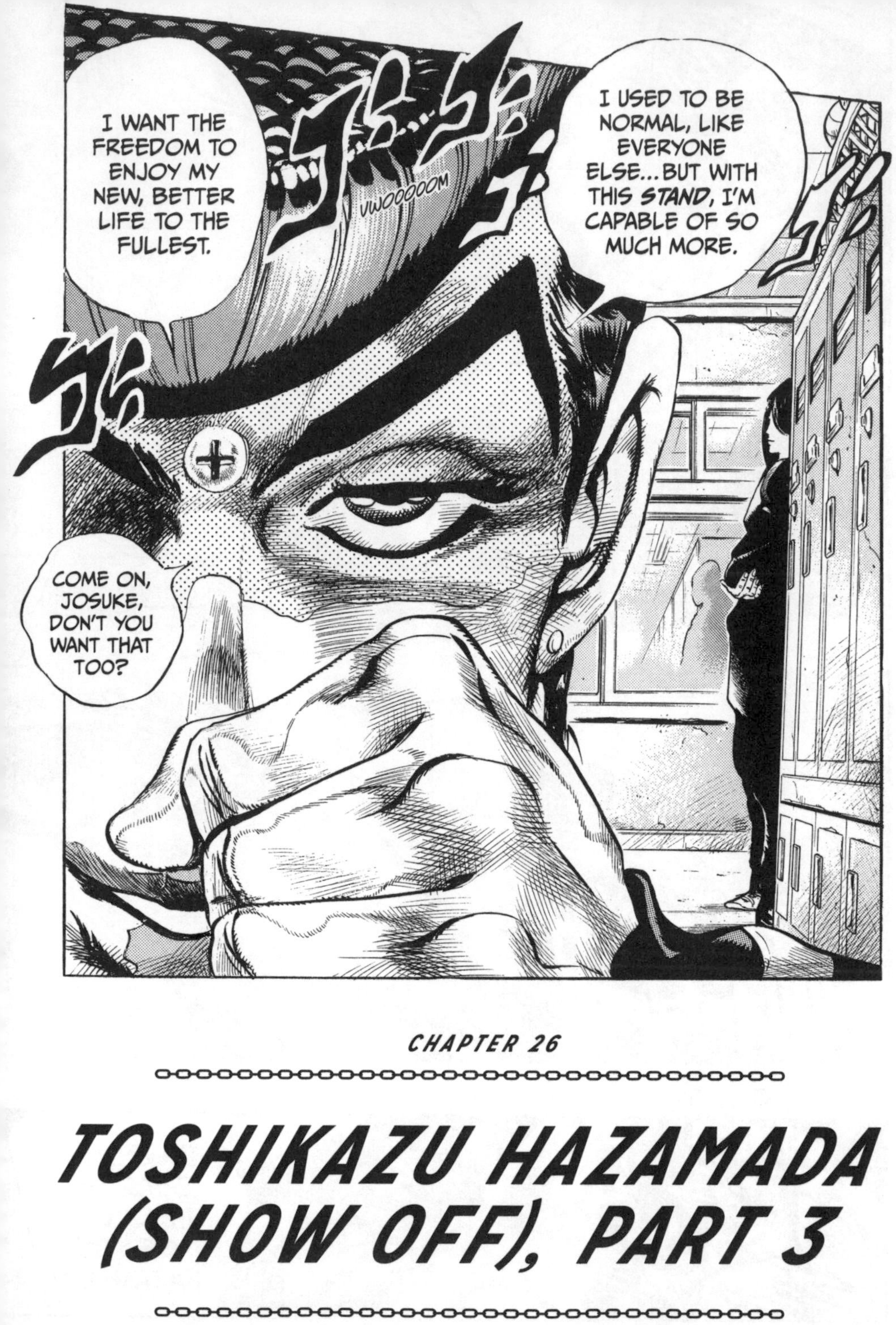
I USED TO BE NORMAL, LIKE EVERYONE ELSE... BUT WITH THIS *STAND*, I'M CAPABLE OF SO MUCH MORE.
VWOOOOOM
I WANT THE FREEDOM TO ENJOY MY NEW, BETTER LIFE TO THE FULLEST.
COME ON, JOSUKE, DON'T YOU WANT THAT TOO?

CHAPTER 26

TOSHIKAZU HAZAMADA (SHOW OFF), PART 3

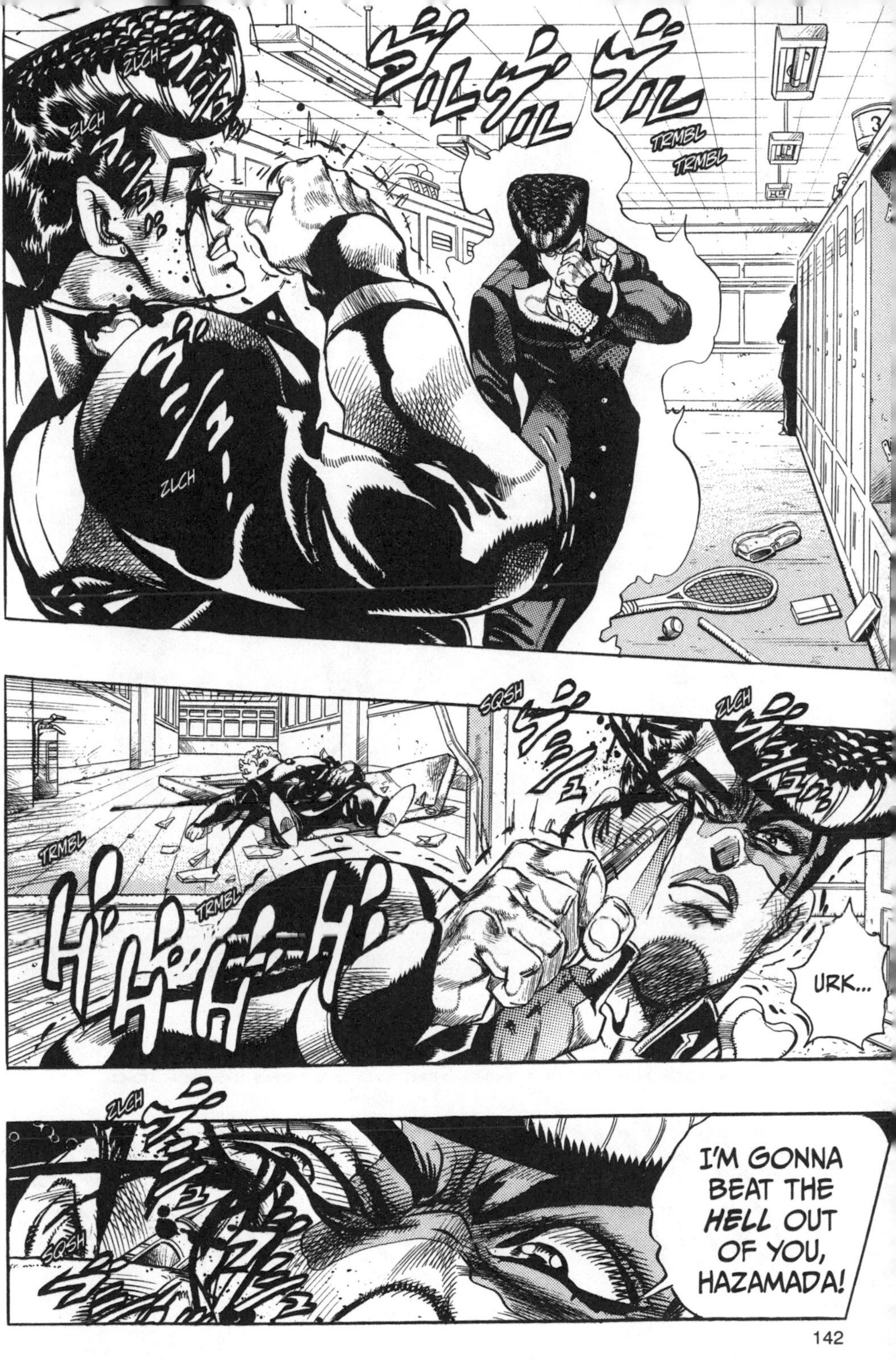

TRMBL
TRMBL
ZLCH
ZLCH
ZLCH
URK...
ZLCH
SQSH
TRMBL
TRMBL
I'M GONNA BEAT THE HELL OUT OF YOU, HAZAMADA!
ZLCH
SQSH

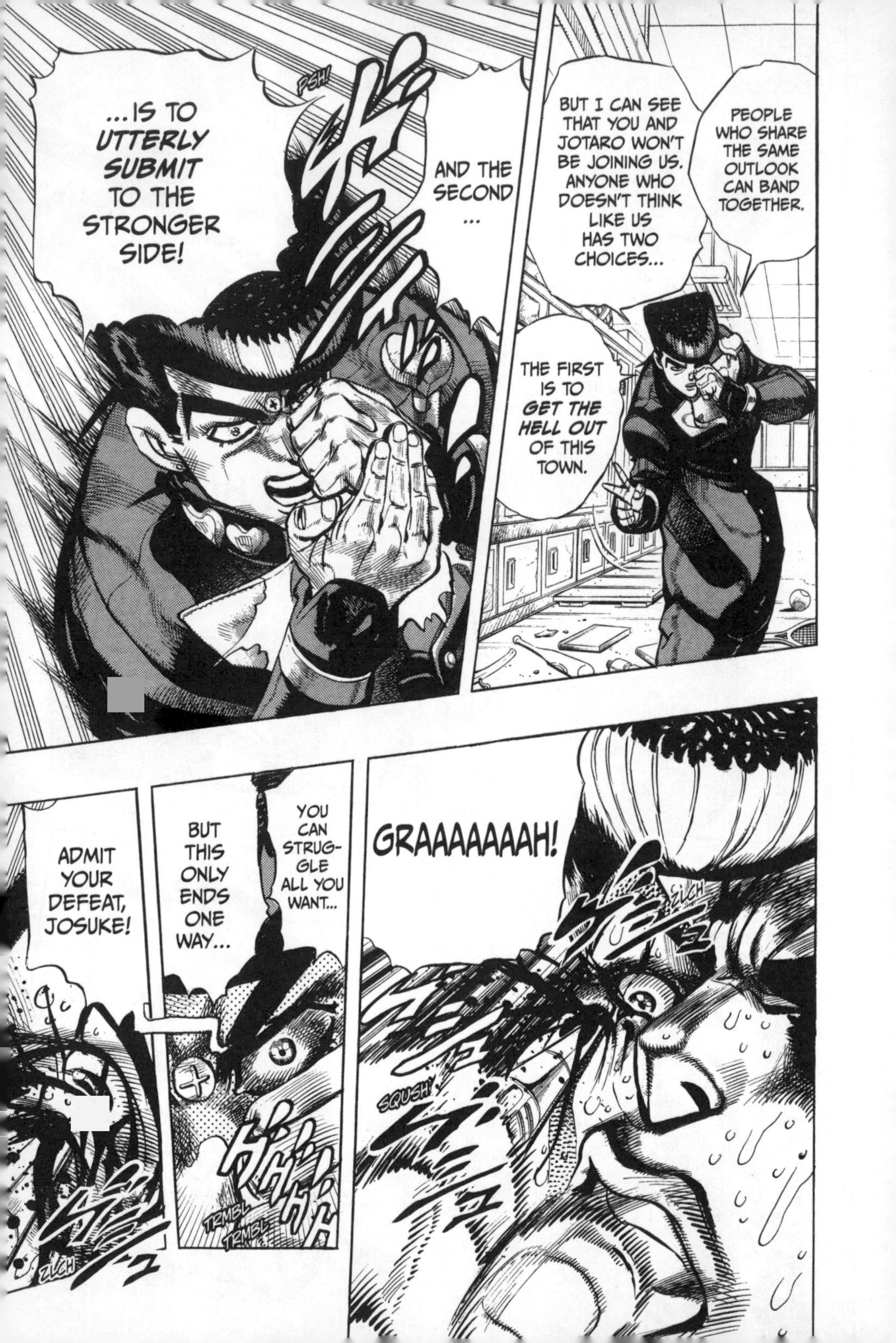
PEOPLE WHO SHARE THE SAME OUTLOOK CAN BAND TOGETHER.
BUT I CAN SEE THAT YOU AND JOTARO WON'T BE JOINING US. ANYONE WHO DOESN'T THINK LIKE US HAS TWO CHOICES...
THE FIRST IS TO *GET THE HELL OUT* OF THIS TOWN.
AND THE SECOND ...
PSH!
...IS TO *UTTERLY SUBMIT* TO THE STRONGER SIDE!
GRAAAAAAAH!
ZLCH
SQUSH!
YOU CAN STRUG-GLE ALL YOU WANT...
BUT THIS ONLY ENDS ONE WAY...
TRMBL TRMBL
ADMIT YOUR DEFEAT, JOSUKE!
ZLCH

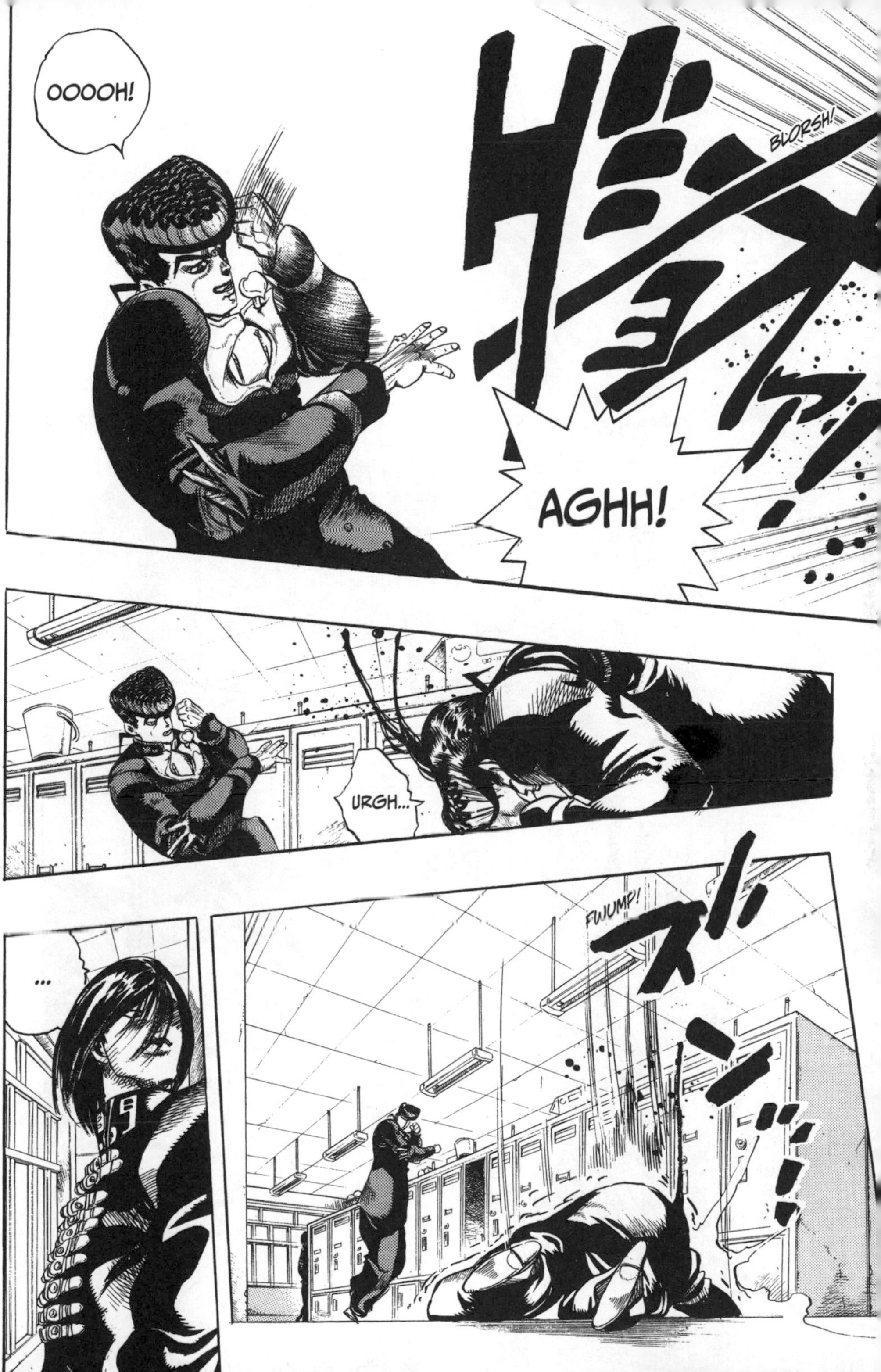

BLORSH!
OOOOH!
AGHH!
URGH...
FWUMP!
...

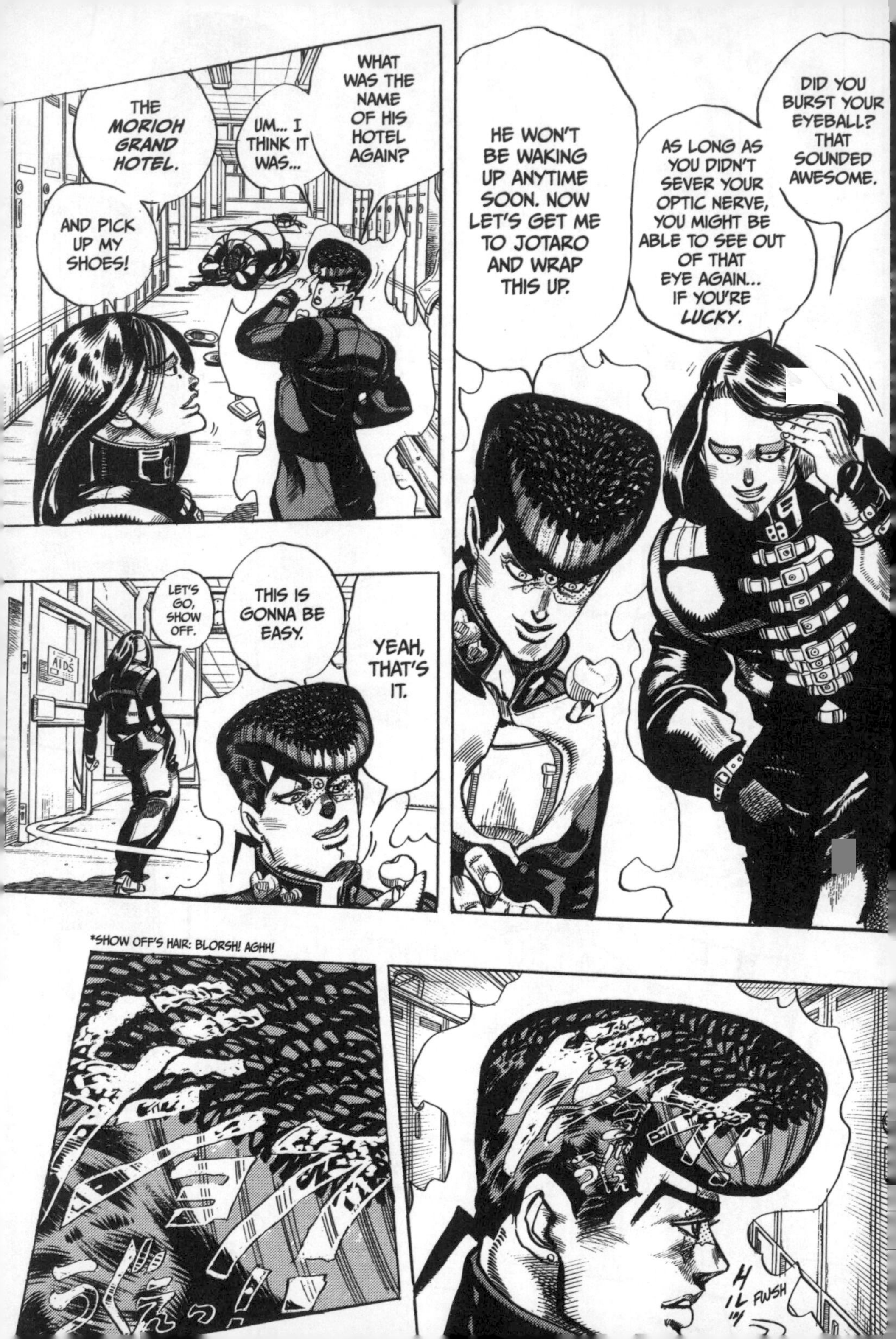
DID YOU BURST YOUR EYEBALL? THAT SOUNDED AWESOME.
AS LONG AS YOU DIDN'T SEVER YOUR OPTIC NERVE, YOU MIGHT BE ABLE TO SEE OUT OF THAT EYE AGAIN... IF YOU'RE *LUCKY*.
HE WON'T BE WAKING UP ANYTIME SOON. NOW LET'S GET ME TO JOTARO AND WRAP THIS UP.
WHAT WAS THE NAME OF HIS HOTEL AGAIN?
UM... I THINK IT WAS...
THE *MORIOH GRAND HOTEL.*
AND PICK UP MY SHOES!
YEAH, THAT'S IT.
THIS IS GONNA BE EASY.
LET'S GO, SHOW OFF.
AIDS
FWSH

*SHOW OFF'S HAIR: BLORSH! AGHH!

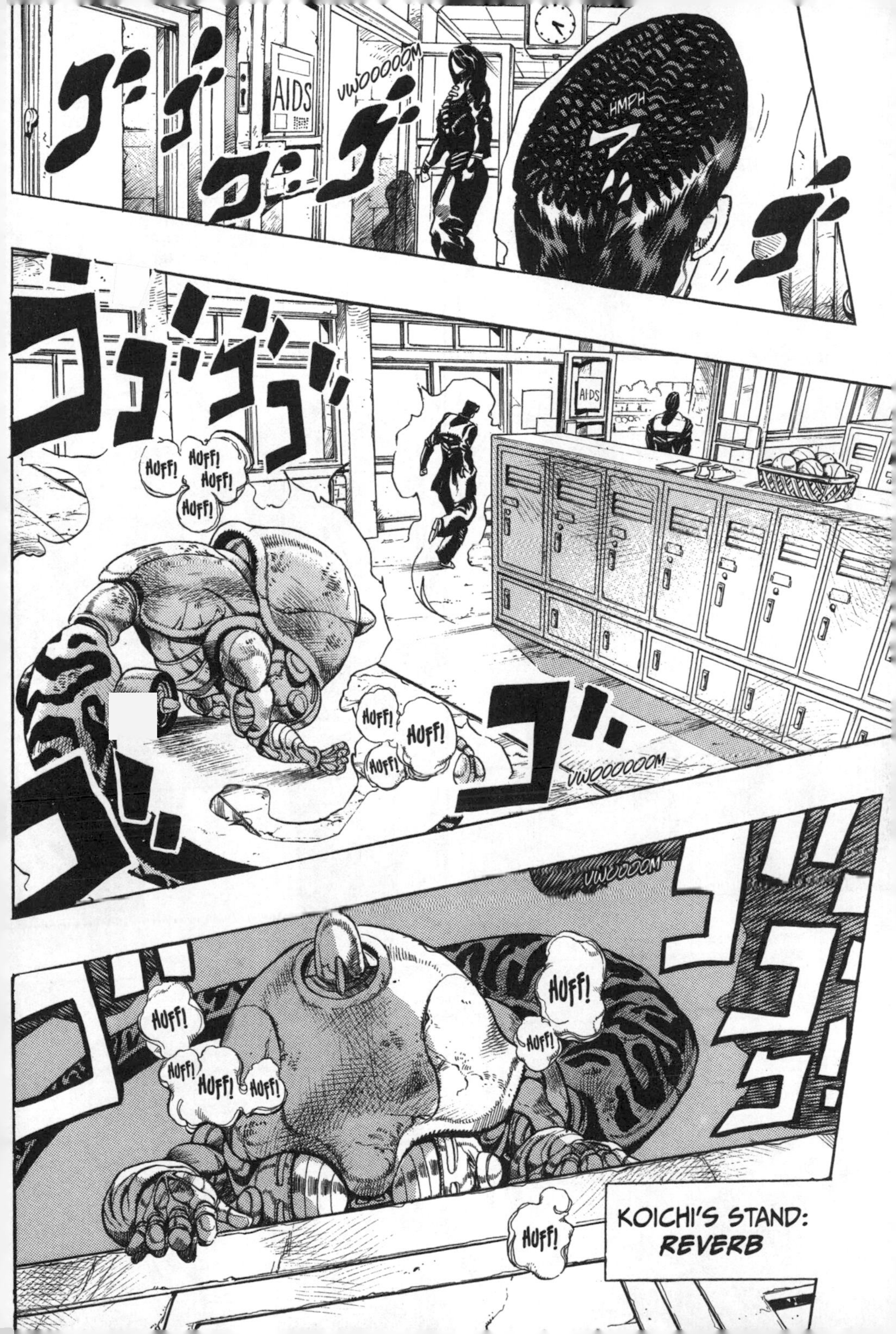
HMPH
VWOOOOOM
VWOOOOOOM
HUFF!
HUFF!
HUFF!
HUFF!
HUFF! HUFF!
HUFF!
VWOOOOOM
HUFF!
HUFF!
HUFF!
HUFF!
HUFF!
HUFF!
KOICHI'S STAND:
REVERB

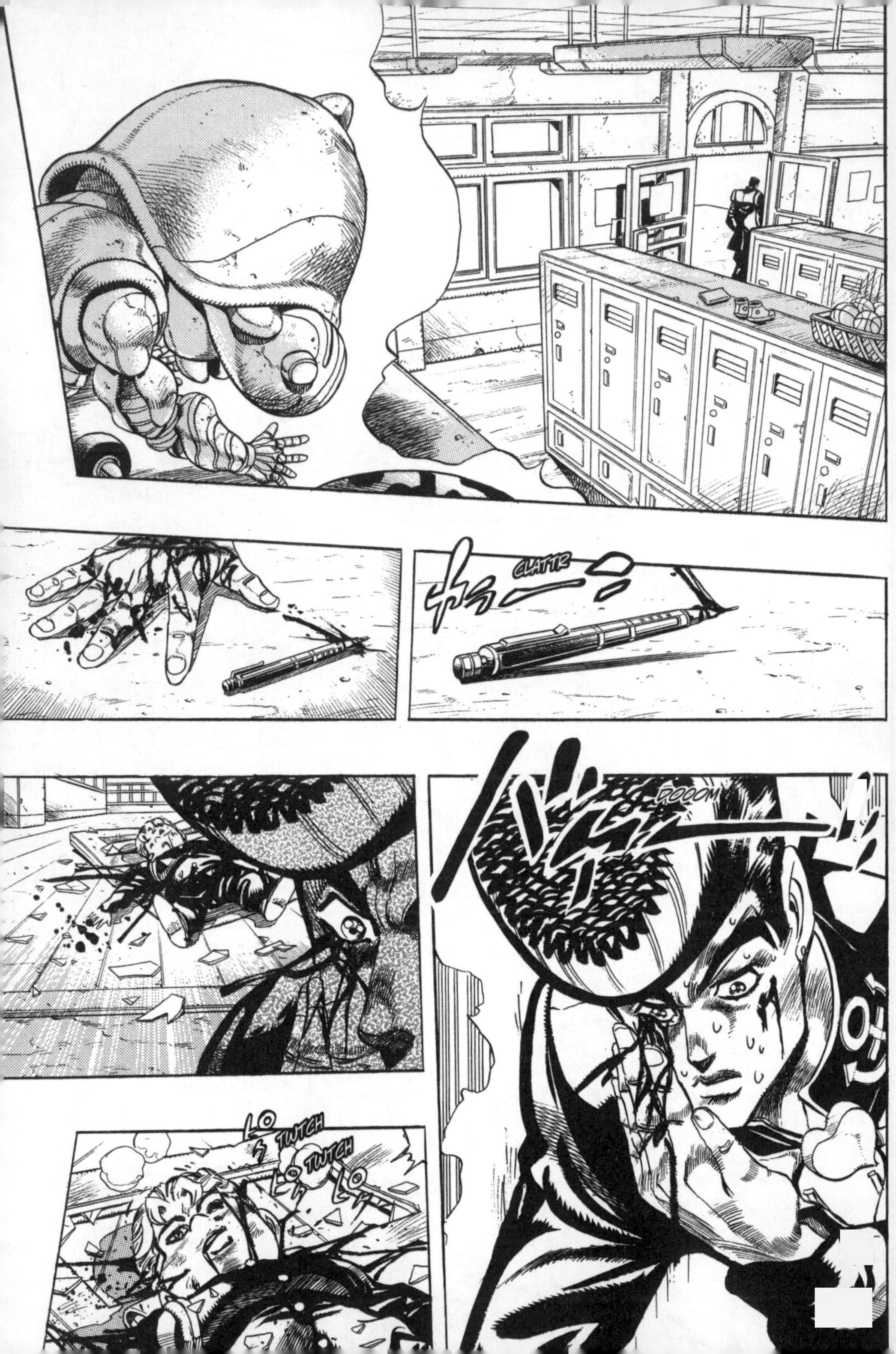
CLATTR
DOOOM
TWITCH
TWITCH

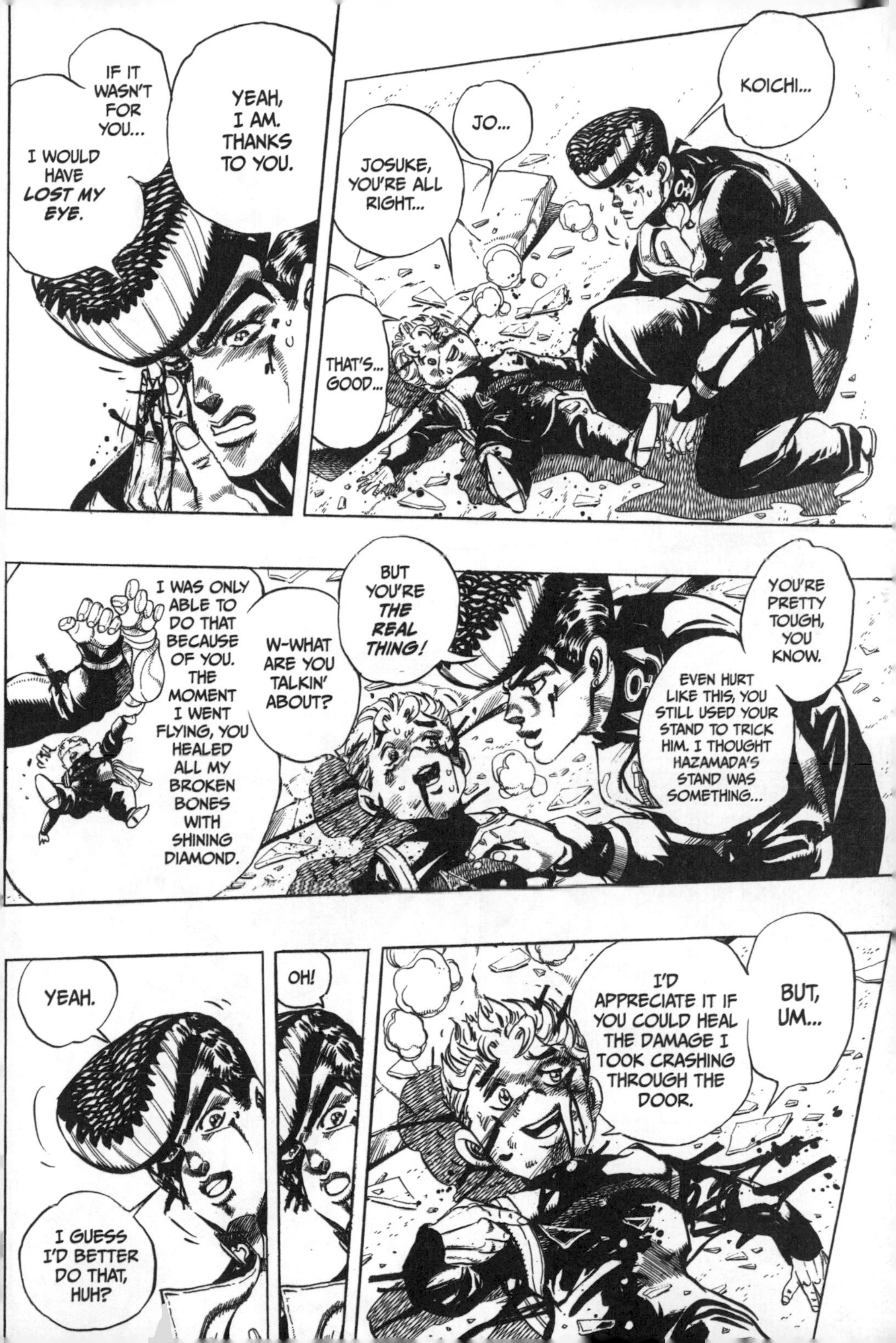

KOICHI...
JO...
JOSUKE, YOU'RE ALL RIGHT...
THAT'S... GOOD...
YEAH, I AM. THANKS TO YOU.
IF IT WASN'T FOR YOU...
I WOULD HAVE *LOST MY EYE.*
YOU'RE PRETTY TOUGH, YOU KNOW.
EVEN HURT LIKE THIS, YOU STILL USED YOUR STAND TO TRICK HIM. I THOUGHT HAZAMADA'S STAND WAS SOMETHING...
BUT YOU'RE *THE REAL THING!*
W-WHAT ARE YOU TALKIN' ABOUT?
I WAS ONLY ABLE TO DO THAT BECAUSE OF YOU. THE MOMENT I WENT FLYING, YOU HEALED ALL MY BROKEN BONES WITH SHINING DIAMOND.
BUT, UM...
I'D APPRECIATE IT IF YOU COULD HEAL THE DAMAGE I TOOK CRASHING THROUGH THE DOOR.
OH!
YEAH.
I GUESS I'D BETTER DO THAT, HUH?

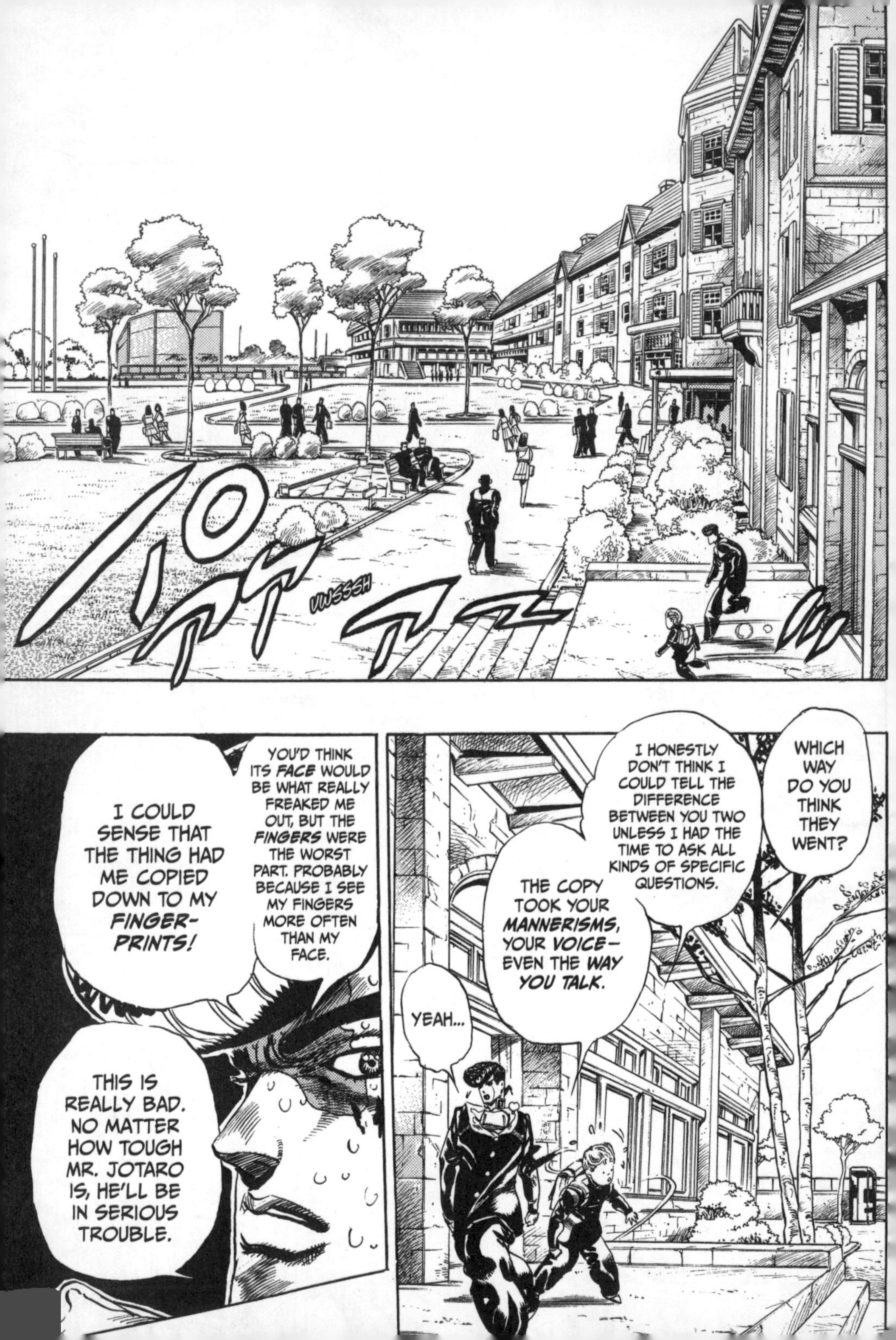
VWSSSH
WHICH WAY DO YOU THINK THEY WENT?
I HONESTLY DON'T THINK I COULD TELL THE DIFFERENCE BETWEEN YOU TWO UNLESS I HAD THE TIME TO ASK ALL KINDS OF SPECIFIC QUESTIONS.
THE COPY TOOK YOUR *MANNERISMS*, YOUR *VOICE*— EVEN THE *WAY YOU TALK*.
YEAH...
YOU'D THINK ITS *FACE* WOULD BE WHAT REALLY FREAKED ME OUT, BUT THE *FINGERS* WERE THE WORST PART. PROBABLY BECAUSE I SEE MY FINGERS MORE OFTEN THAN MY FACE.
I COULD SENSE THAT THE THING HAD ME COPIED DOWN TO MY *FINGER-PRINTS!*
THIS IS REALLY BAD. NO MATTER HOW TOUGH MR. JOTARO IS, HE'LL BE IN SERIOUS TROUBLE.

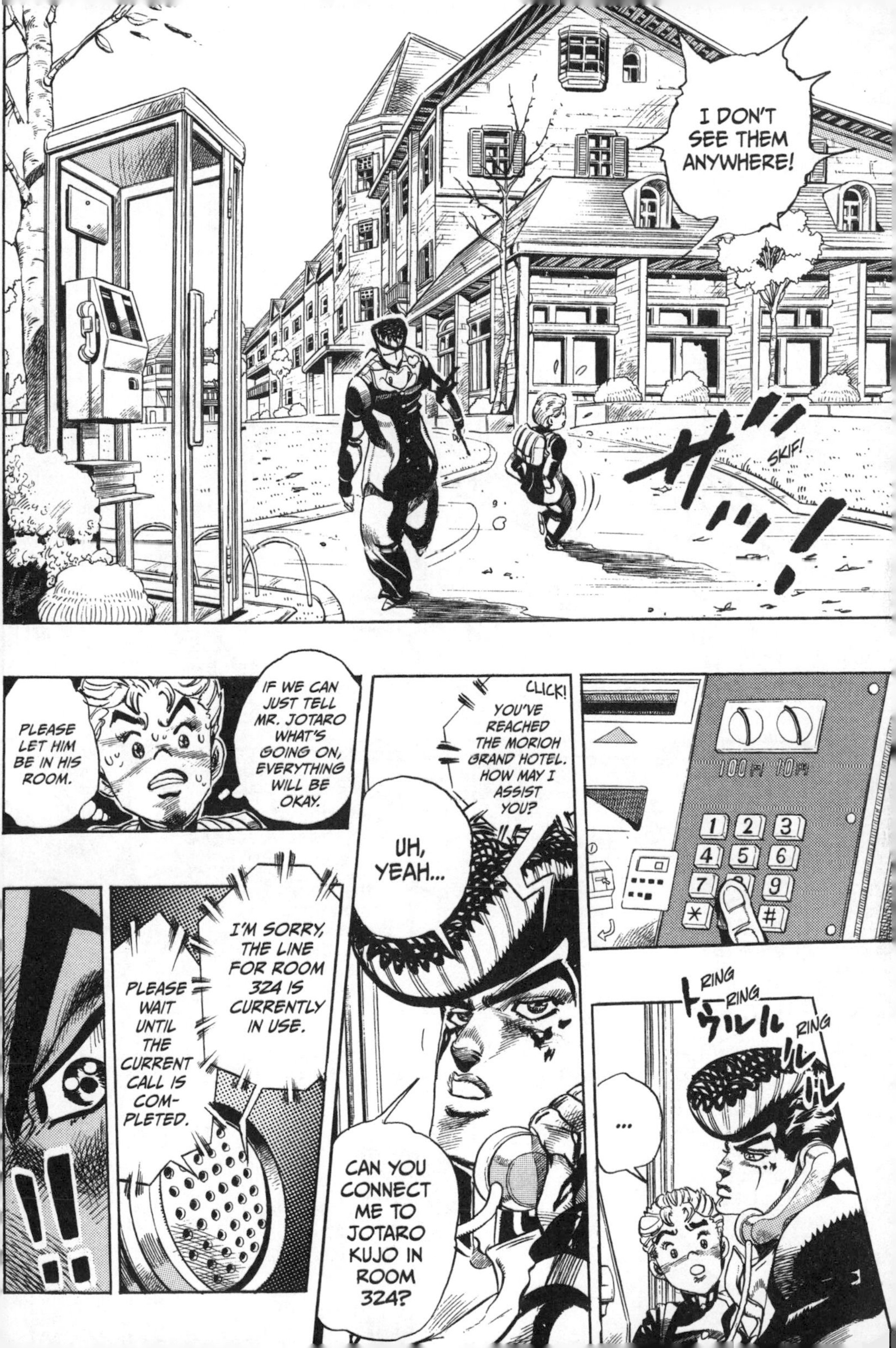
I DON'T SEE THEM ANYWHERE!
ザッ!
SKIF!
100円 10円
トゥルルル
RING
RING
RING
...
CLICK!
YOU'VE REACHED THE MORIOH GRAND HOTEL. HOW MAY I ASSIST YOU?
UH, YEAH...
CAN YOU CONNECT ME TO JOTARO KUJO IN ROOM 324?
IF WE CAN JUST TELL MR. JOTARO WHAT'S GOING ON, EVERYTHING WILL BE OKAY.
PLEASE LET HIM BE IN HIS ROOM.
I'M SORRY, THE LINE FOR ROOM 324 IS CURRENTLY IN USE.
PLEASE WAIT UNTIL THE CURRENT CALL IS COMPLETED.
!!

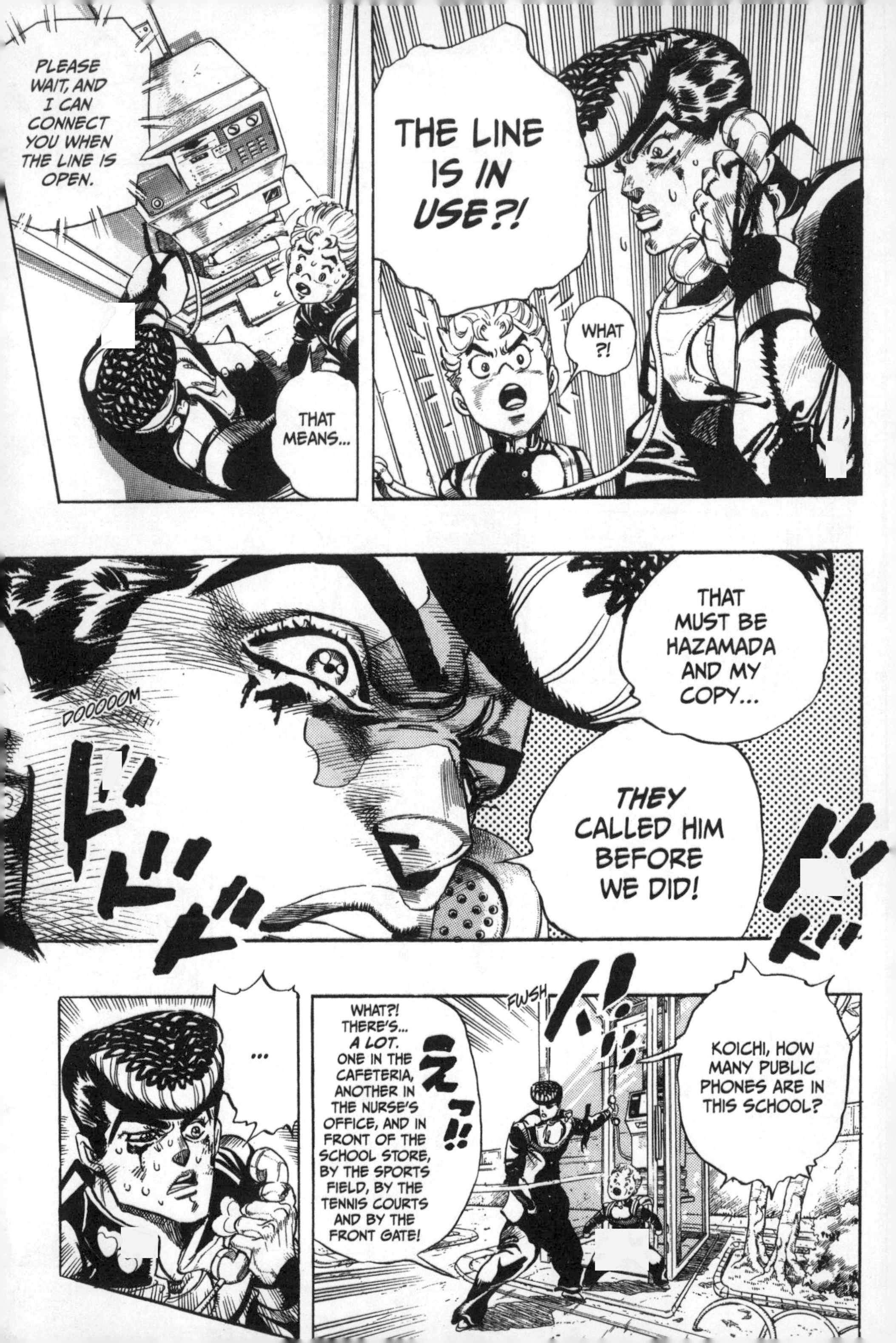
THE LINE IS IN USE?!
WHAT ?!
PLEASE WAIT, AND I CAN CONNECT YOU WHEN THE LINE IS OPEN.
THAT MEANS...
THAT MUST BE HAZAMADA AND MY COPY...
THEY CALLED HIM BEFORE WE DID!
DOOOOOM
KOICHI, HOW MANY PUBLIC PHONES ARE IN THIS SCHOOL?
FWSH
えっ!!
WHAT?! THERE'S... A LOT. ONE IN THE CAFETERIA, ANOTHER IN THE NURSE'S OFFICE, AND IN FRONT OF THE SCHOOL STORE, BY THE SPORTS FIELD, BY THE TENNIS COURTS AND BY THE FRONT GATE!
...

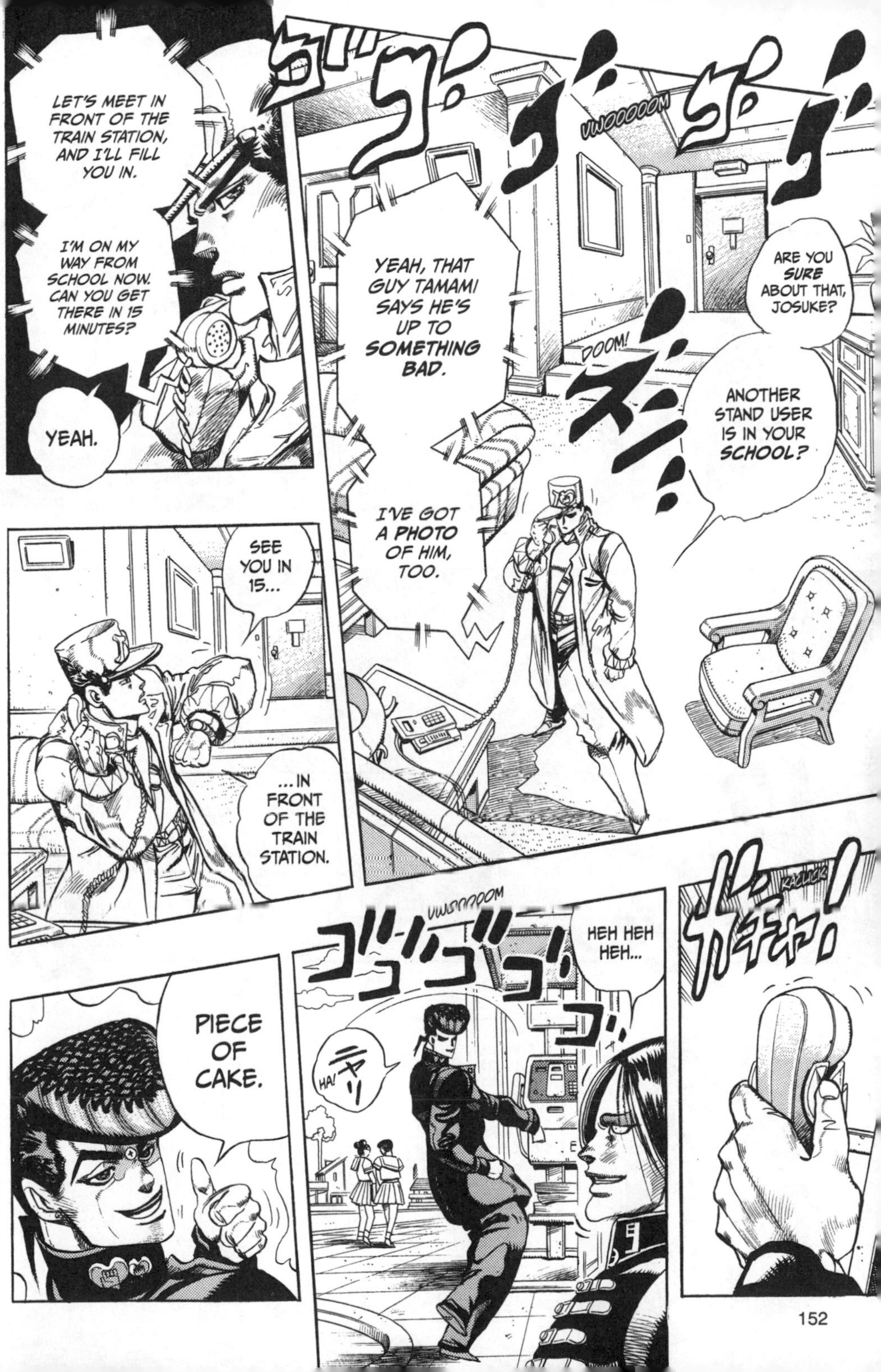
VWOOOOOM
ARE YOU SURE ABOUT THAT, JOSUKE?
ANOTHER STAND USER IS IN YOUR SCHOOL?
DOOM!
YEAH, THAT GUY TAMAMI SAYS HE'S UP TO SOMETHING BAD.
I'VE GOT A PHOTO OF HIM, TOO.
LET'S MEET IN FRONT OF THE TRAIN STATION, AND I'LL FILL YOU IN.
I'M ON MY WAY FROM SCHOOL NOW. CAN YOU GET THERE IN 15 MINUTES?
YEAH.
SEE YOU IN 15...
...IN FRONT OF THE TRAIN STATION.
KALICK
ガチャ!
HEH HEH HEH...
VWOOOOOM
ニヤリ
HA!
PIECE OF CAKE.

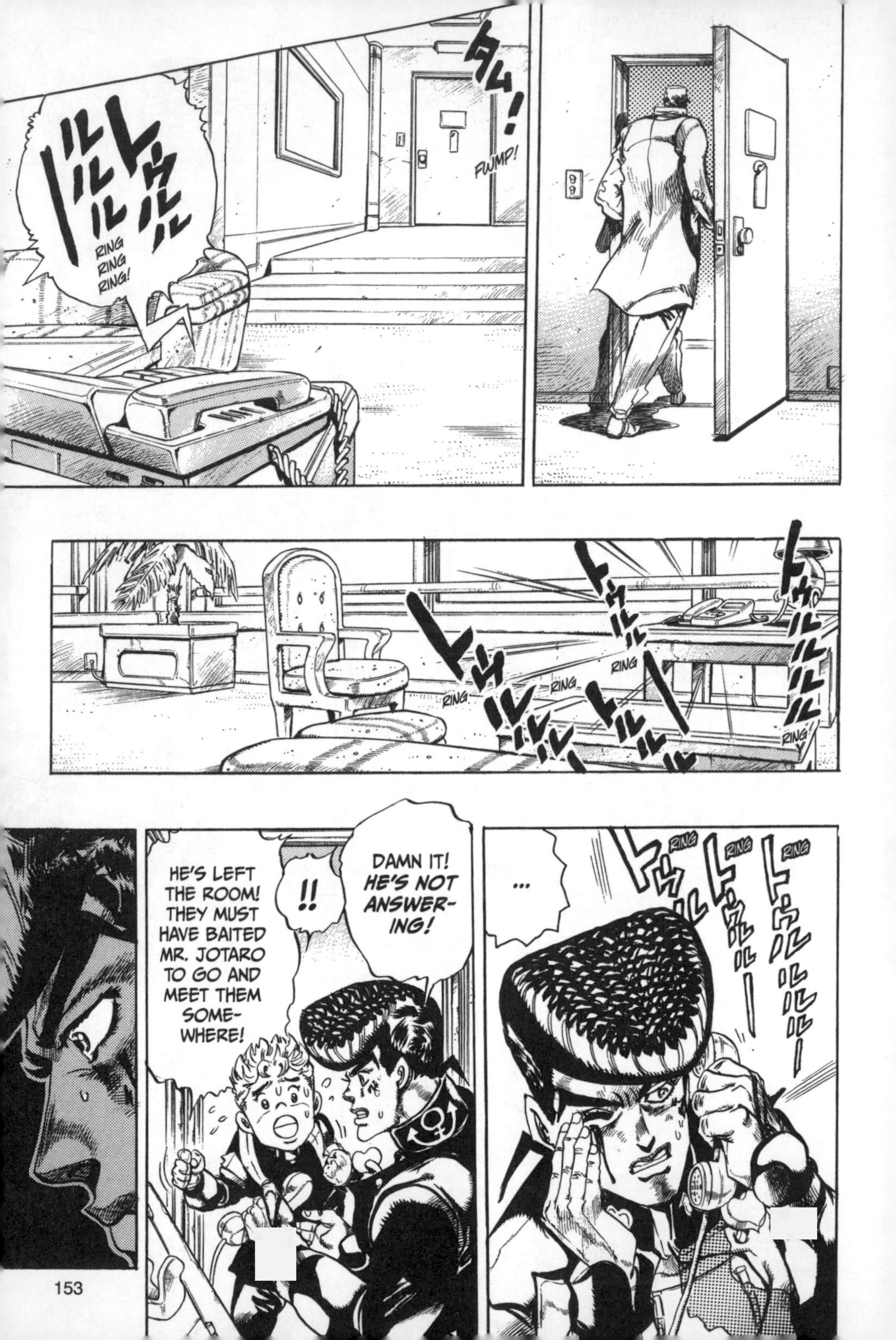

タム!
FWUMP!
RING RING RING!
RING
RING
RING
RING
RING RING RING
...
DAMN IT! HE'S NOT ANSWERING!
!!
HE'S LEFT THE ROOM! THEY MUST HAVE BAITED MR. JOTARO TO GO AND MEET THEM SOMEWHERE!

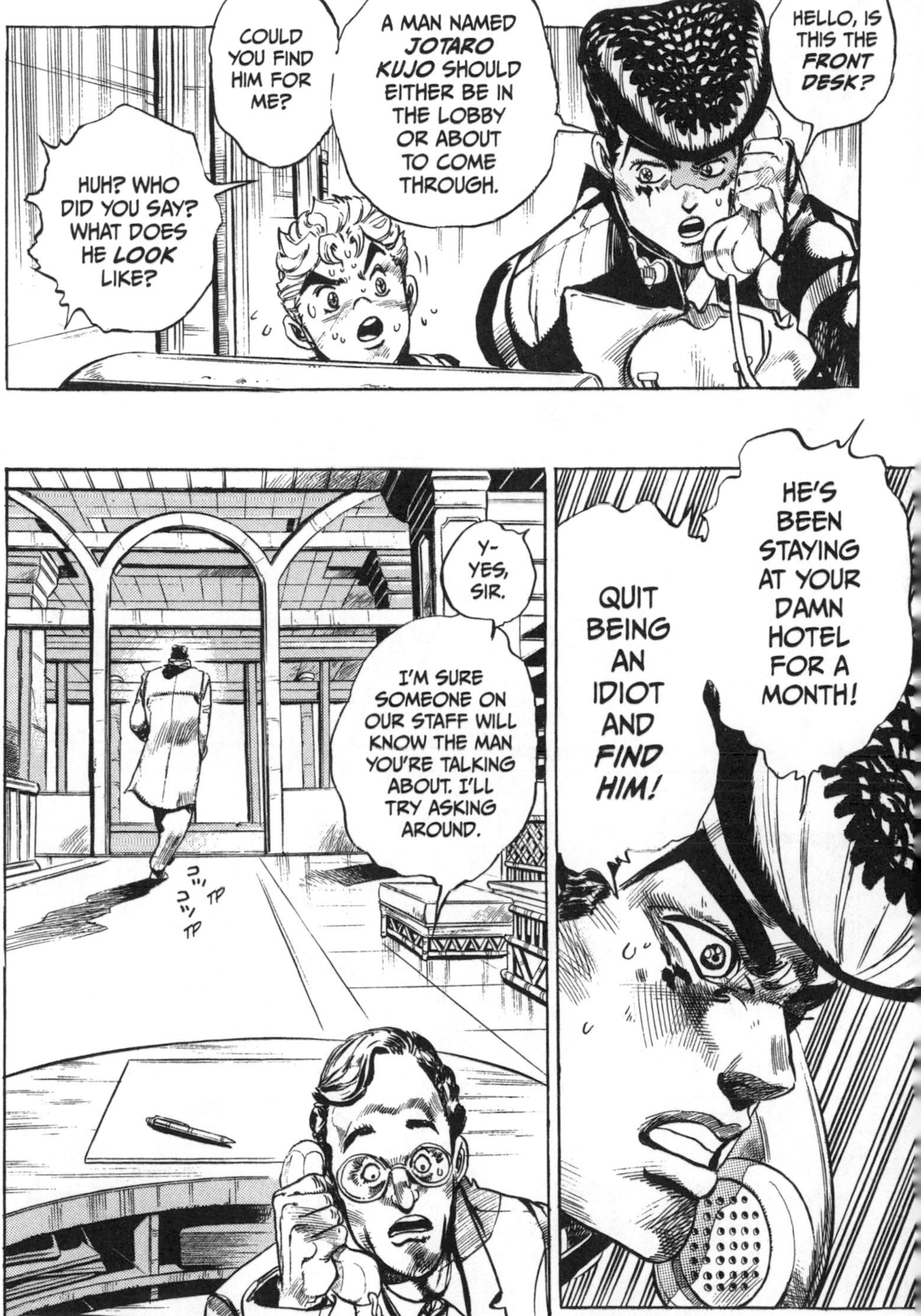
HELLO, IS THIS THE *FRONT DESK?*
A MAN NAMED *JOTARO KUJO* SHOULD EITHER BE IN THE LOBBY OR ABOUT TO COME THROUGH.
COULD YOU FIND HIM FOR ME?
HUH? WHO DID YOU SAY? WHAT DOES HE *LOOK* LIKE?
HE'S BEEN STAYING AT YOUR DAMN HOTEL FOR A MONTH!
QUIT BEING AN IDIOT AND *FIND HIM!*
Y-YES, SIR.
I'M SURE SOMEONE ON OUR STAFF WILL KNOW THE MAN YOU'RE TALKING ABOUT. I'LL TRY ASKING AROUND.
TP
TP

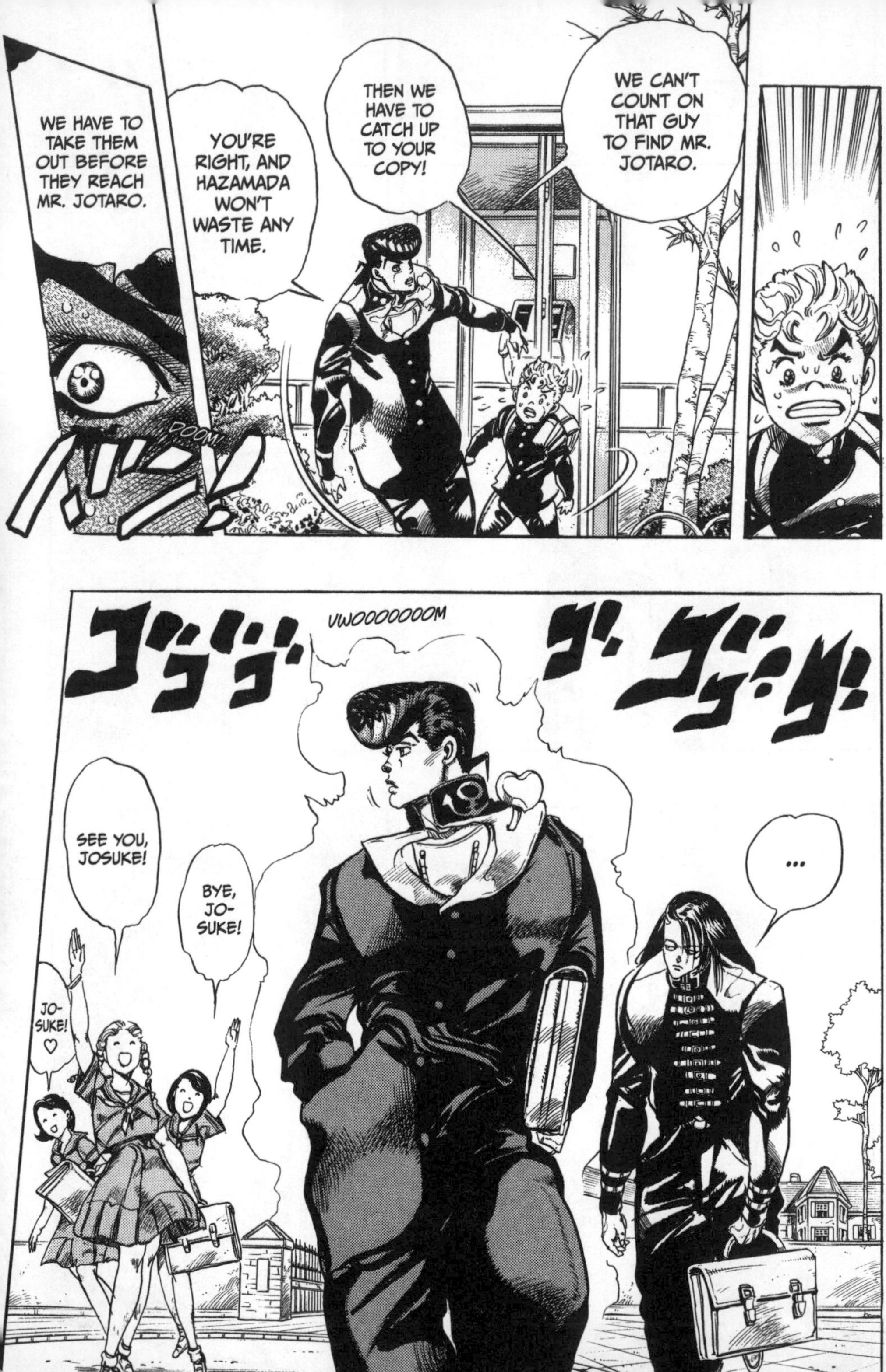
WE CAN'T COUNT ON THAT GUY TO FIND MR. JOTARO.
THEN WE HAVE TO CATCH UP TO YOUR COPY!
YOU'RE RIGHT, AND HAZAMADA WON'T WASTE ANY TIME.
WE HAVE TO TAKE THEM OUT BEFORE THEY REACH MR. JOTARO.
DOOM!
VWOOOOOOOM
...
BYE, JO-SUKE!
SEE YOU, JOSUKE!
JO-SUKE! ♡

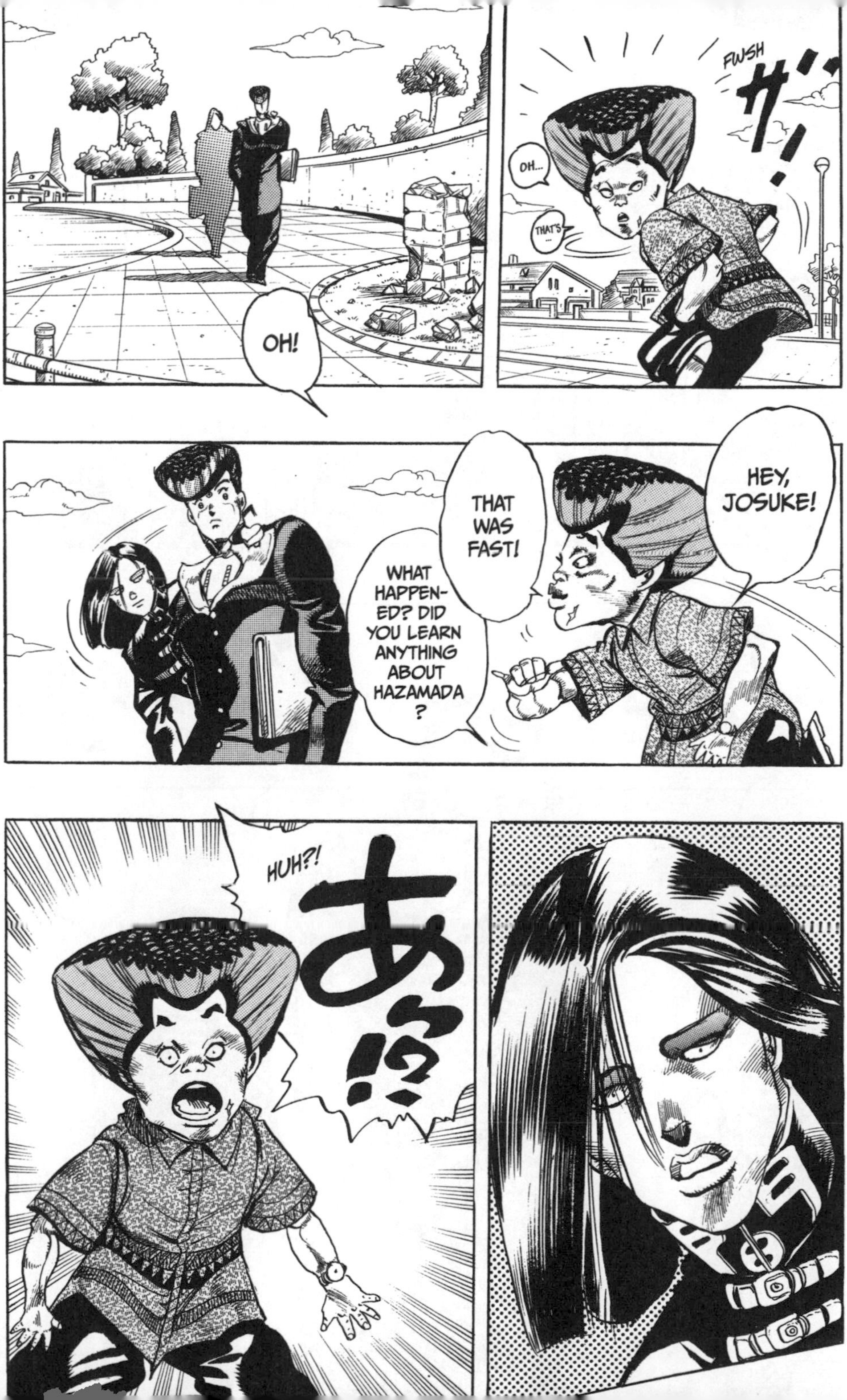
FWSH
OH...
THAT'S ...
OH!
HEY, JOSUKE!
THAT WAS FAST!
WHAT HAPPEN-ED? DID YOU LEARN ANYTHING ABOUT HAZAMADA ?
HUH?!

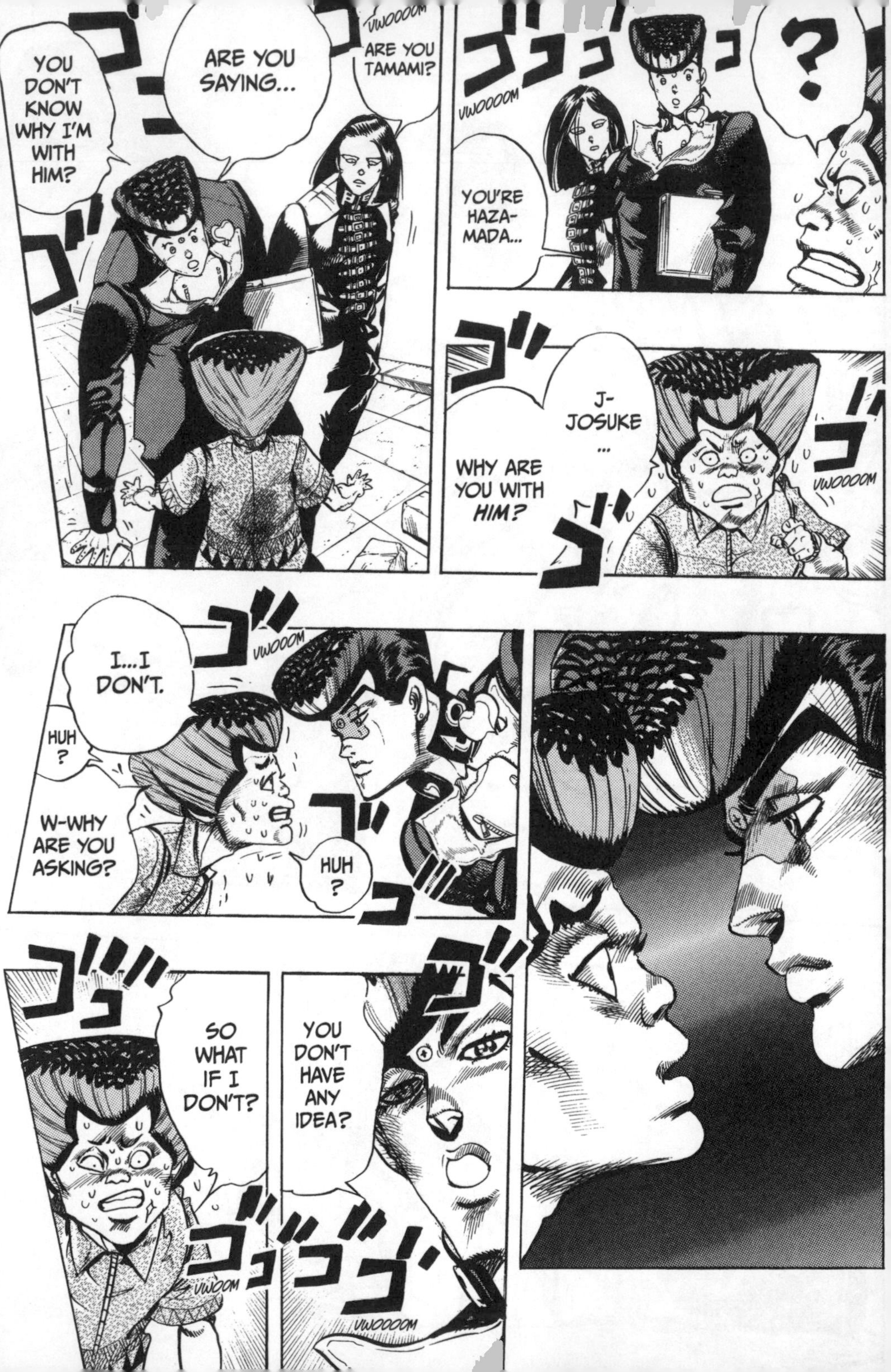
VWOOOOM
?
YOU'RE HAZAMADA...
J-JOSUKE...
WHY ARE YOU WITH HIM?
VWOOOOM
VWOOOOM
ARE YOU TAMAMI?
ARE YOU SAYING...
YOU DON'T KNOW WHY I'M WITH HIM?
VWOOOM
I...I DON'T.
HUH?
W-WHY ARE YOU ASKING?
HUH?
YOU DON'T HAVE ANY IDEA?
VWOOOOM
SO WHAT IF I DON'T?
VWOOM

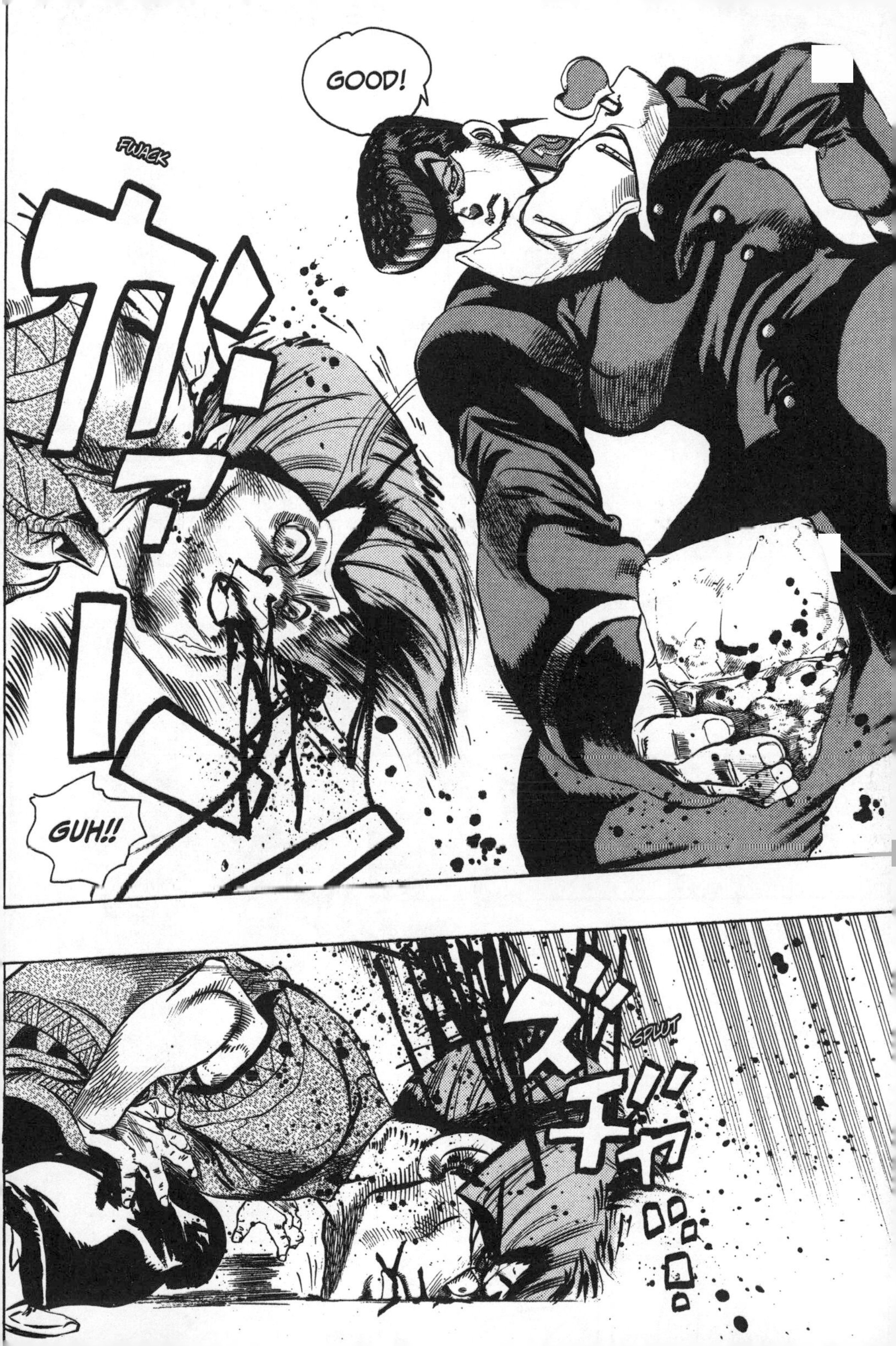
GOOD!
FWACK
GUH!!
SPLUT

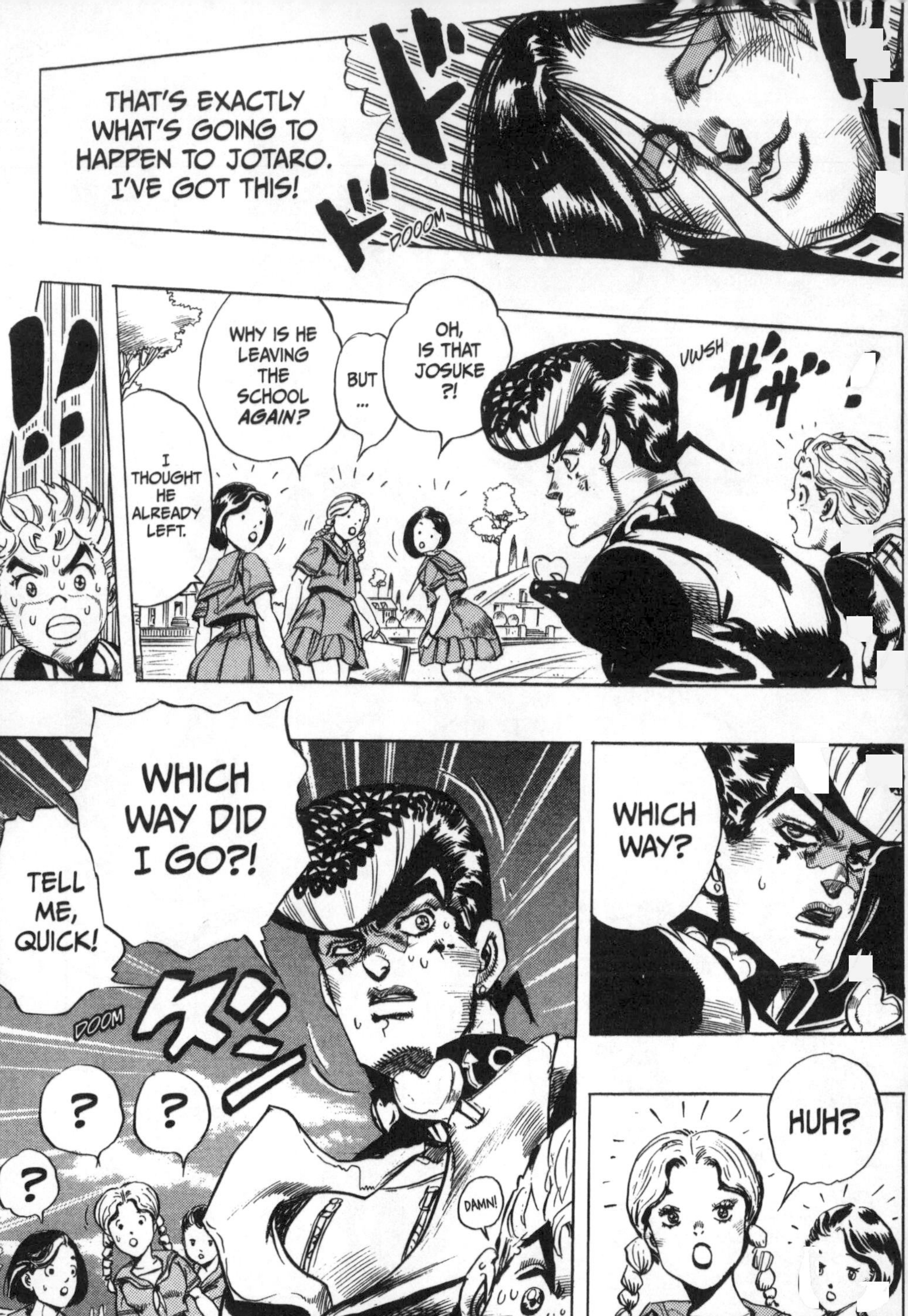
THAT'S EXACTLY WHAT'S GOING TO HAPPEN TO JOTARO. I'VE GOT THIS!
DOOOM
VUWSH
OH, IS THAT JOSUKE?!
BUT ...
WHY IS HE LEAVING THE SCHOOL AGAIN?
I THOUGHT HE ALREADY LEFT.
WHICH WAY?
HUH?
WHICH WAY DID I GO?!
TELL ME, QUICK!
DOOM
?
?
?
DAMN!

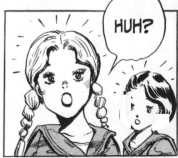

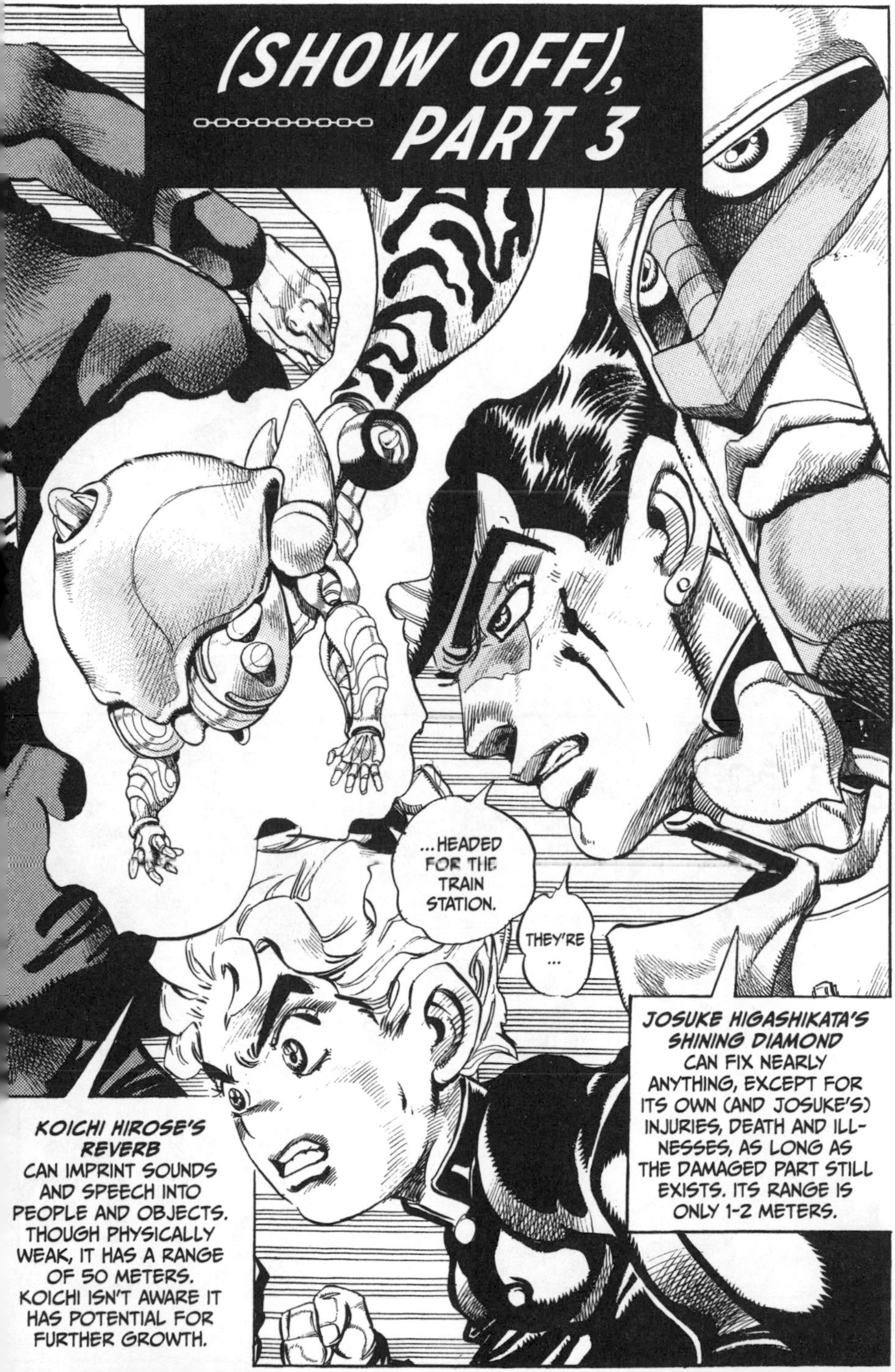
(SHOW OFF), PART 3
THEY'RE ...
...HEADED FOR THE TRAIN STATION.
JOSUKE HIGASHIKATA'S SHINING DIAMOND CAN FIX NEARLY ANYTHING, EXCEPT FOR ITS OWN (AND JOSUKE'S) INJURIES, DEATH AND ILLNESSES, AS LONG AS THE DAMAGED PART STILL EXISTS. ITS RANGE IS ONLY 1-2 METERS.
KOICHI HIROSE'S REVERB CAN IMPRINT SOUNDS AND SPEECH INTO PEOPLE AND OBJECTS. THOUGH PHYSICALLY WEAK, IT HAS A RANGE OF 50 METERS. KOICHI ISN'T AWARE IT HAS POTENTIAL FOR FURTHER GROWTH.

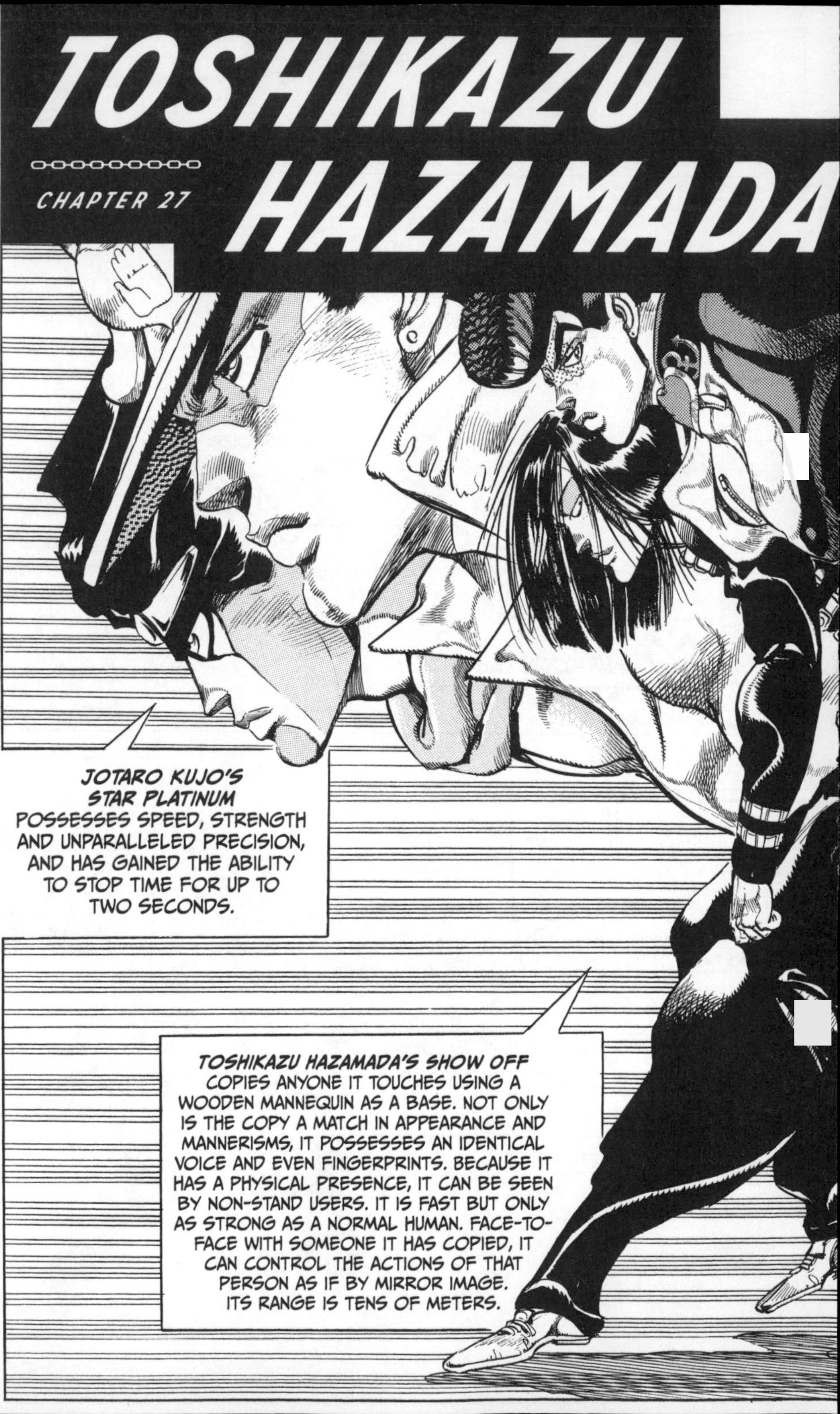
TOSHIKAZU HAZAMADA
CHAPTER 27
JOTARO KUJO'S STAR PLATINUM POSSESSES SPEED, STRENGTH AND UNPARALLELED PRECISION, AND HAS GAINED THE ABILITY TO STOP TIME FOR UP TO TWO SECONDS.
TOSHIKAZU HAZAMADA'S SHOW OFF COPIES ANYONE IT TOUCHES USING A WOODEN MANNEQUIN AS A BASE. NOT ONLY IS THE COPY A MATCH IN APPEARANCE AND MANNERISMS, IT POSSESSES AN IDENTICAL VOICE AND EVEN FINGERPRINTS. BECAUSE IT HAS A PHYSICAL PRESENCE, IT CAN BE SEEN BY NON-STAND USERS. IT IS FAST BUT ONLY AS STRONG AS A NORMAL HUMAN. FACE-TO-FACE WITH SOMEONE IT HAS COPIED, IT CAN CONTROL THE ACTIONS OF THAT PERSON AS IF BY MIRROR IMAGE. ITS RANGE IS TENS OF METERS.

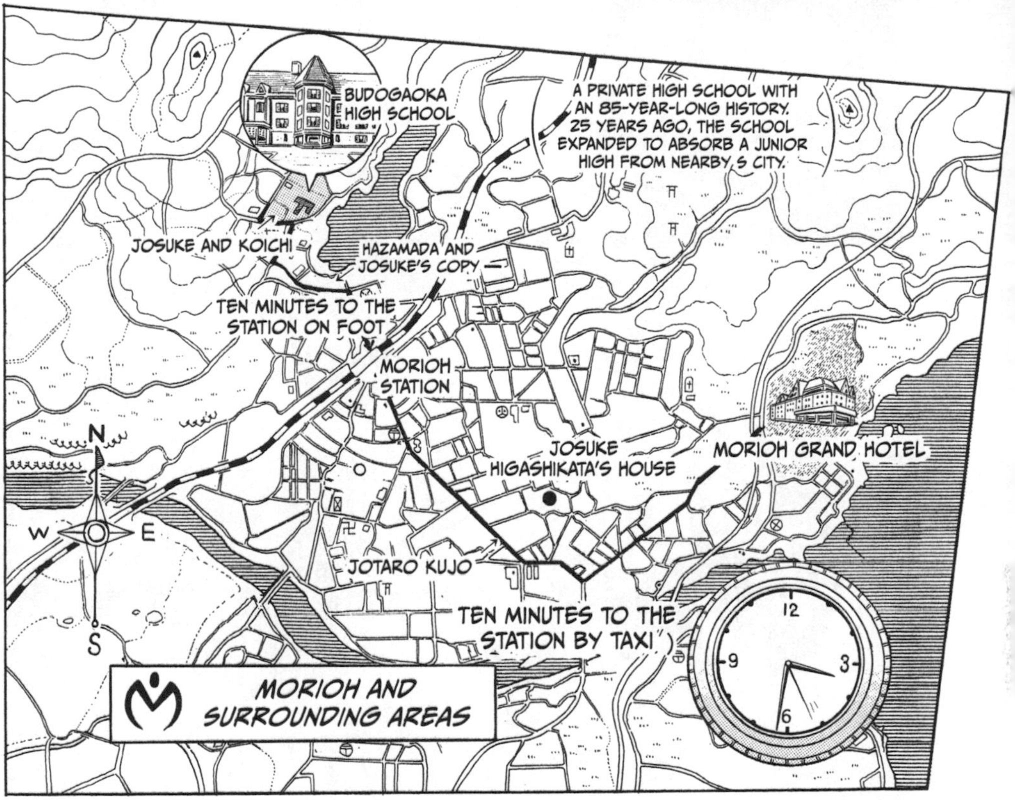
A PRIVATE HIGH SCHOOL WITH AN 85-YEAR-LONG HISTORY. 25 YEARS AGO, THE SCHOOL EXPANDED TO ABSORB A JUNIOR HIGH FROM NEARBY S CITY.
BUDOGAOKA HIGH SCHOOL
HAZAMADA AND JOSUKE'S COPY
JOSUKE AND KOICHI
TEN MINUTES TO THE STATION ON FOOT
MORIOH STATION
MORIOH GRAND HOTEL
JOSUKE HIGASHIKATA'S HOUSE
N
W
E
S
JOTARO KUJO
TEN MINUTES TO THE STATION BY TAXI
12
9
3
6
MORIOH AND SURROUNDING AREAS

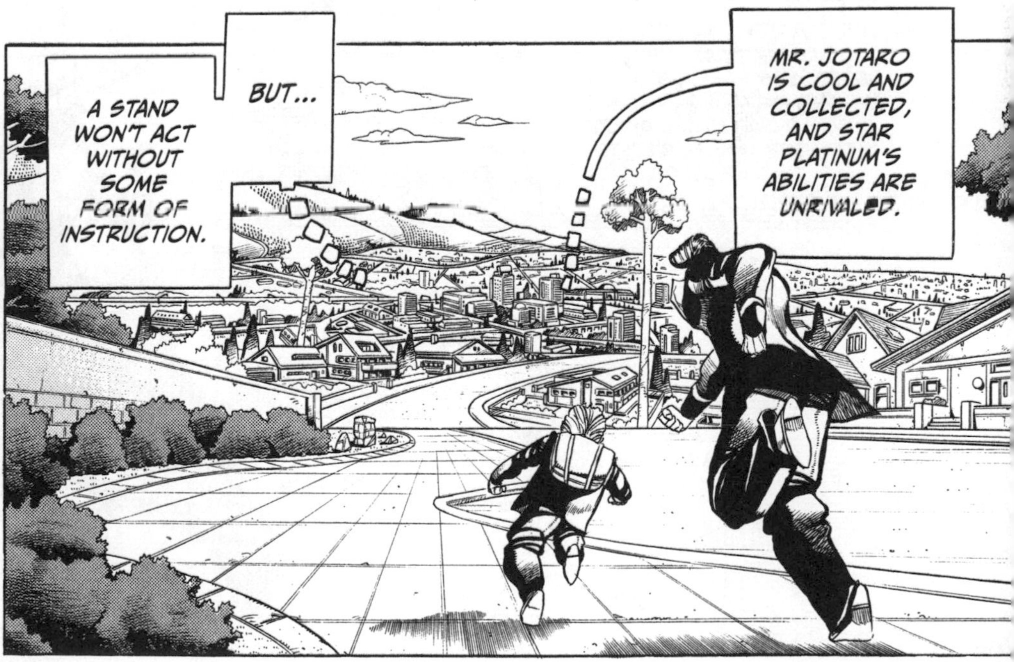
MR. JOTARO IS COOL AND COLLECTED, AND STAR PLATINUM'S ABILITIES ARE UNRIVALED.
BUT...
A STAND WON'T ACT WITHOUT SOME FORM OF INSTRUCTION.

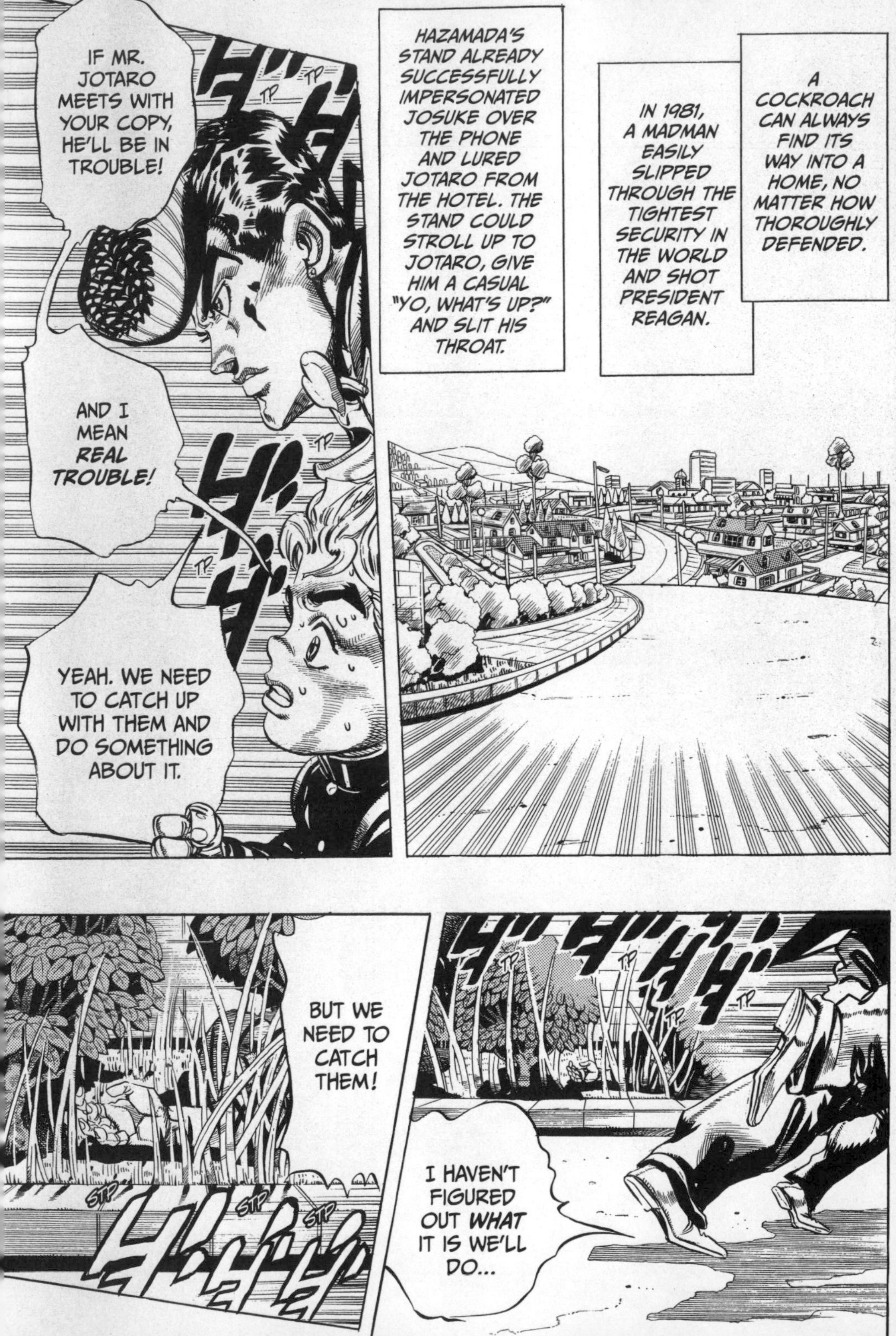
A COCKROACH CAN ALWAYS FIND ITS WAY INTO A HOME, NO MATTER HOW THOROUGHLY DEFENDED.
IN 1981, A MADMAN EASILY SLIPPED THROUGH THE TIGHTEST SECURITY IN THE WORLD AND SHOT PRESIDENT REAGAN.
HAZAMADA'S STAND ALREADY SUCCESSFULLY IMPERSONATED JOSUKE OVER THE PHONE AND LURED JOTARO FROM THE HOTEL. THE STAND COULD STROLL UP TO JOTARO, GIVE HIM A CASUAL "YO, WHAT'S UP?" AND SLIT HIS THROAT.
IF MR. JOTARO MEETS WITH YOUR COPY, HE'LL BE IN TROUBLE!
AND I MEAN REAL TROUBLE!
YEAH. WE NEED TO CATCH UP WITH THEM AND DO SOMETHING ABOUT IT.
I HAVEN'T FIGURED OUT WHAT IT IS WE'LL DO...
BUT WE NEED TO CATCH THEM!

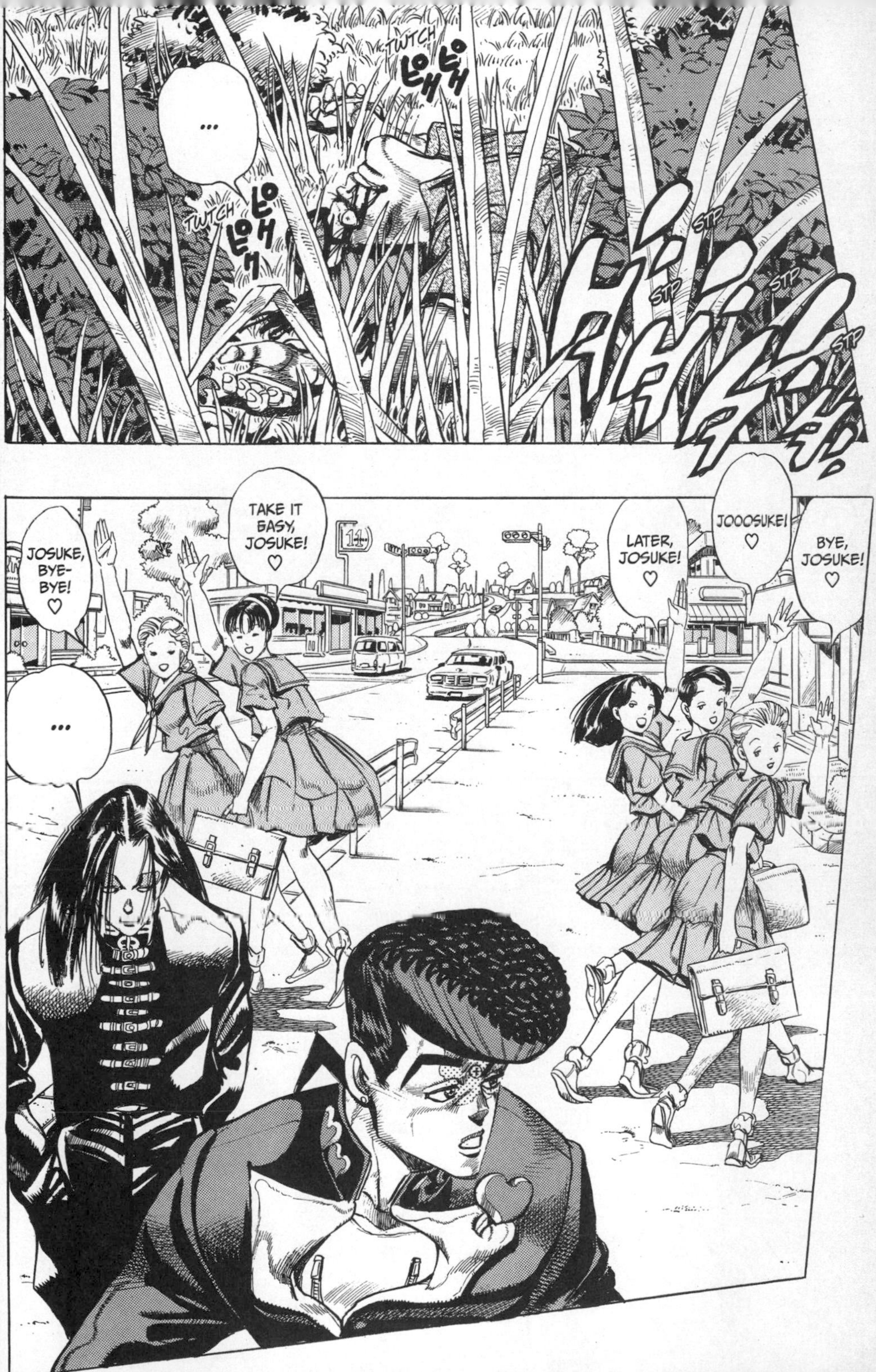
STP STP STP STP STP
TWTCH
...
TWTCH
BYE, JOSUKE! ♡
JOOOSUKE! ♡
LATER, JOSUKE! ♡
TAKE IT EASY, JOSUKE! ♡
JOSUKE, BYE-BYE! ♡
...

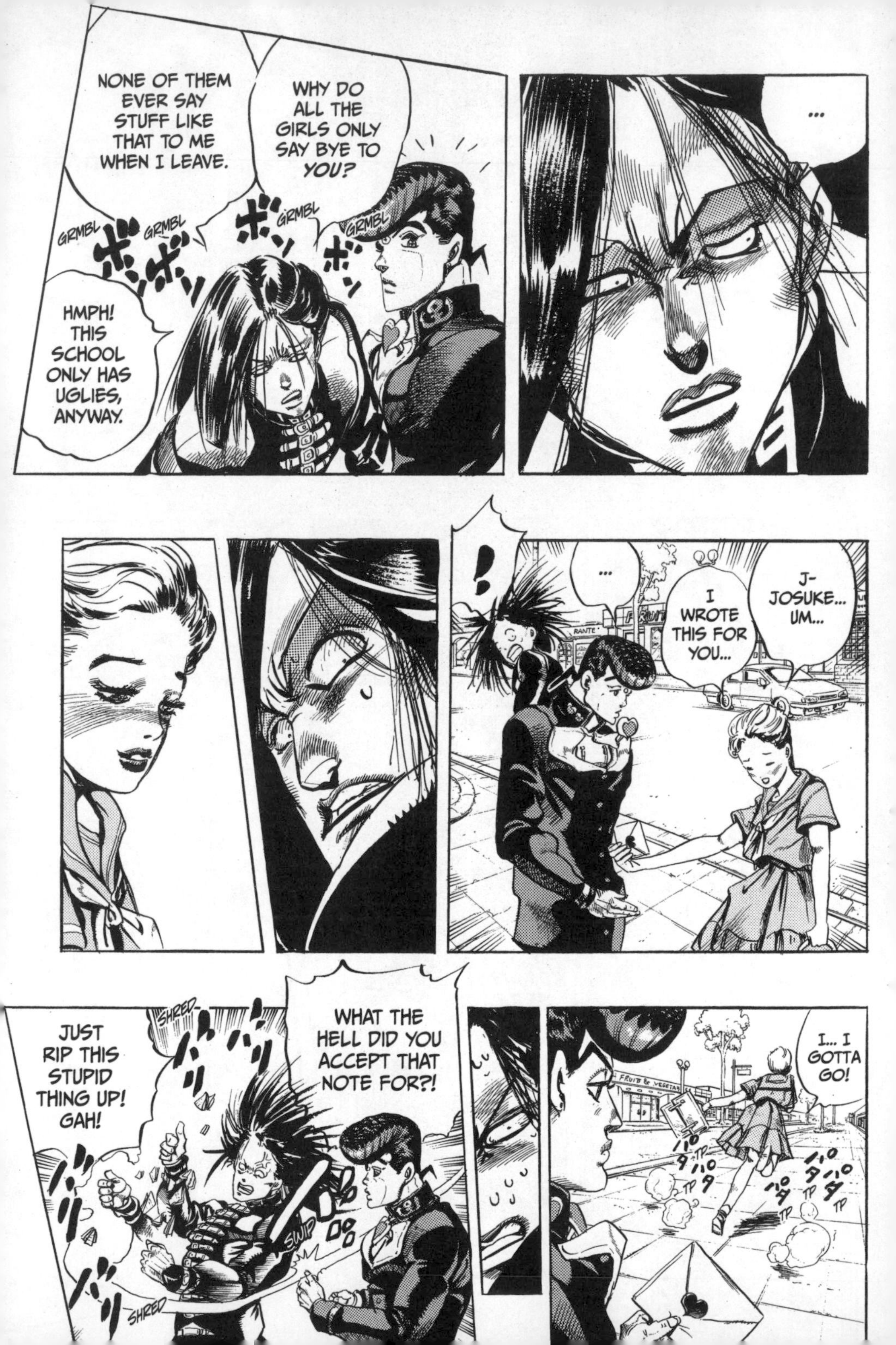
...
WHY DO ALL THE GIRLS ONLY SAY BYE TO YOU?
NONE OF THEM EVER SAY STUFF LIKE THAT TO ME WHEN I LEAVE.
GRMBL
GRMBL
GRMBL
GRMBL
HMPH! THIS SCHOOL ONLY HAS UGLIES, ANYWAY.
J- JOSUKE... UM...
I WROTE THIS FOR YOU...
...
!
RANTE
I... I GOTTA GO!
TP
TP
TP
TP
WHAT THE HELL DID YOU ACCEPT THAT NOTE FOR?!
SHRED
JUST RIP THIS STUPID THING UP! GAH!
SWIP
SHRED

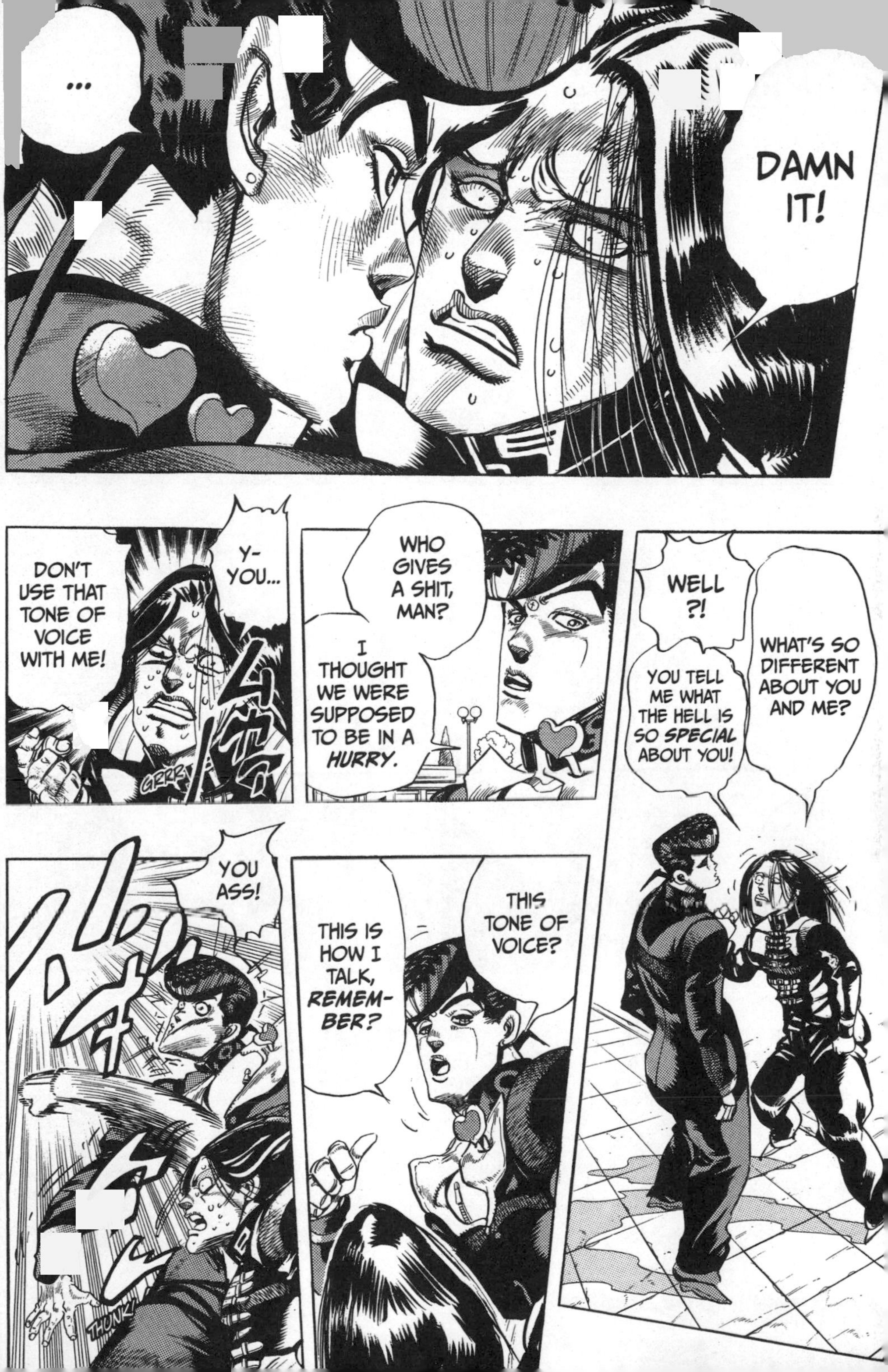
DAMN IT!
...
WELL?!
WHAT'S SO DIFFERENT ABOUT YOU AND ME?
YOU TELL ME WHAT THE HELL IS SO *SPECIAL* ABOUT YOU!
WHO GIVES A SHIT, MAN?
I THOUGHT WE WERE SUPPOSED TO BE IN A *HURRY*.
Y-YOU...
DON'T USE THAT TONE OF VOICE WITH ME!
GRRR
THIS TONE OF VOICE?
THIS IS HOW I TALK, *REMEMBER?*
YOU ASS!
THUNK!

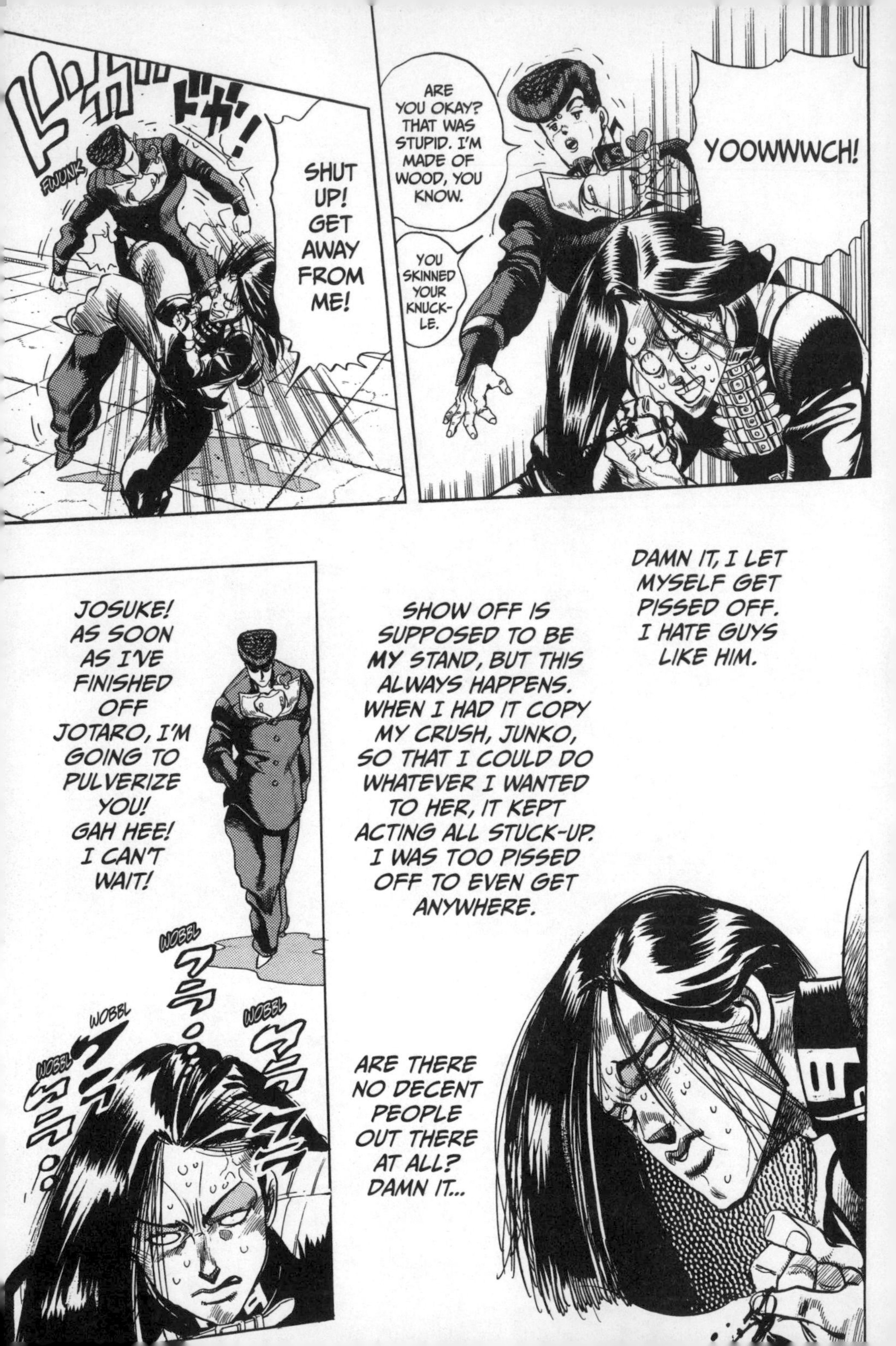
YOOWWWCH!
ARE YOU OKAY? THAT WAS STUPID. I'M MADE OF WOOD, YOU KNOW.
YOU SKINNED YOUR KNUCK-LE.
SHUT UP! GET AWAY FROM ME!
FWUNK
DAMN IT, I LET MYSELF GET PISSED OFF. I HATE GUYS LIKE HIM.
SHOW OFF IS SUPPOSED TO BE MY STAND, BUT THIS ALWAYS HAPPENS. WHEN I HAD IT COPY MY CRUSH, JUNKO, SO THAT I COULD DO WHATEVER I WANTED TO HER, IT KEPT ACTING ALL STUCK-UP. I WAS TOO PISSED OFF TO EVEN GET ANYWHERE.
ARE THERE NO DECENT PEOPLE OUT THERE AT ALL? DAMN IT...
JOSUKE! AS SOON AS I'VE FINISHED OFF JOTARO, I'M GOING TO PULVERIZE YOU! GAH HEE! I CAN'T WAIT!
WOBBL
WOBBL
WOBBL
WOBBL

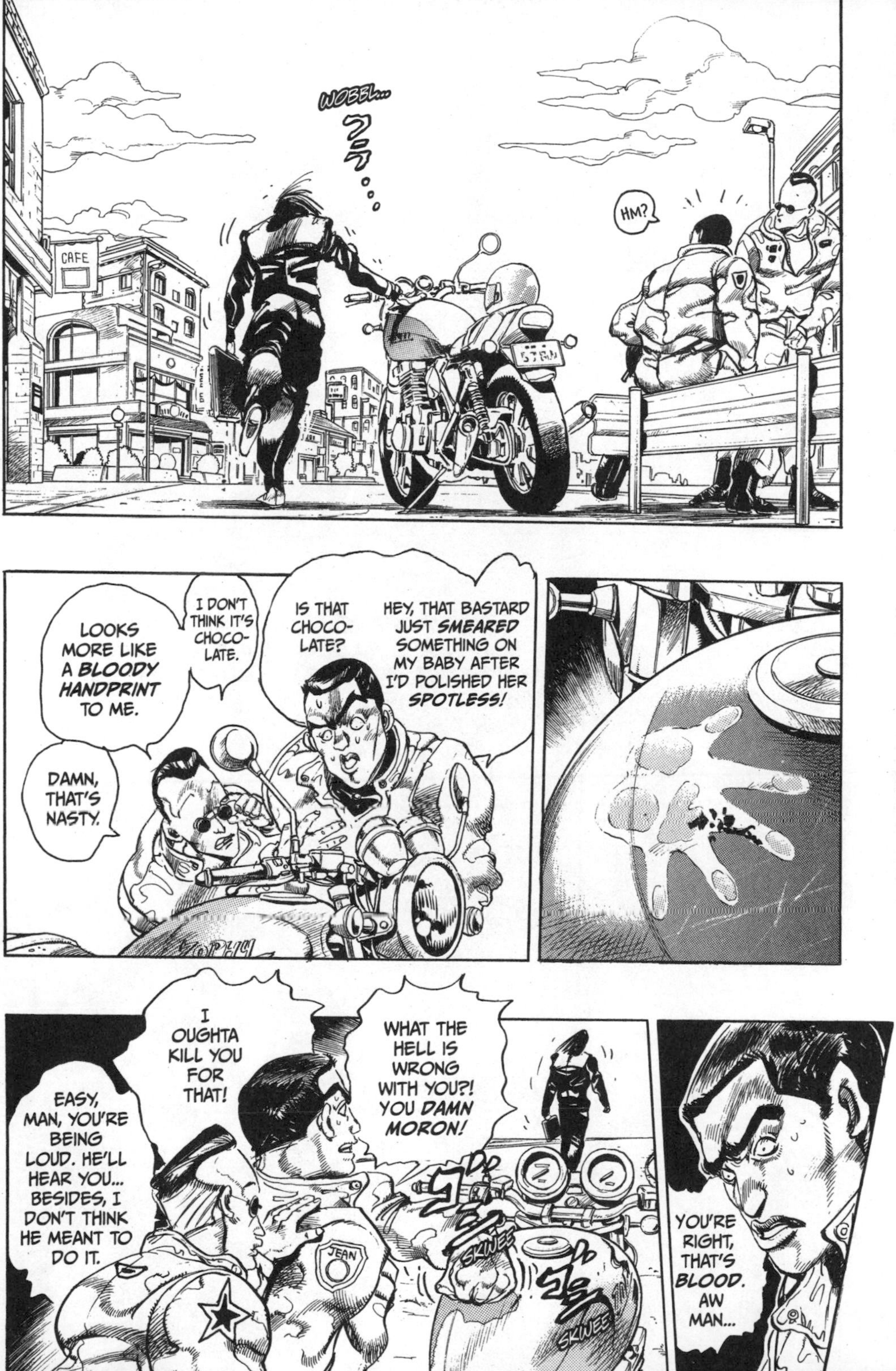

WOBBL...
HM?
CAFE
HEY, THAT BASTARD JUST SMEARED SOMETHING ON MY BABY AFTER I'D POLISHED HER SPOTLESS!
IS THAT CHOCOLATE?
I DON'T THINK IT'S CHOCOLATE.
LOOKS MORE LIKE A BLOODY HANDPRINT TO ME.
DAMN, THAT'S NASTY.
YOU'RE RIGHT, THAT'S BLOOD. AW MAN...
WHAT THE HELL IS WRONG WITH YOU?! YOU DAMN MORON!
I OUGHTA KILL YOU FOR THAT!
EASY, MAN, YOU'RE BEING LOUD. HE'LL HEAR YOU... BESIDES, I DON'T THINK HE MEANT TO DO IT.
JEAN

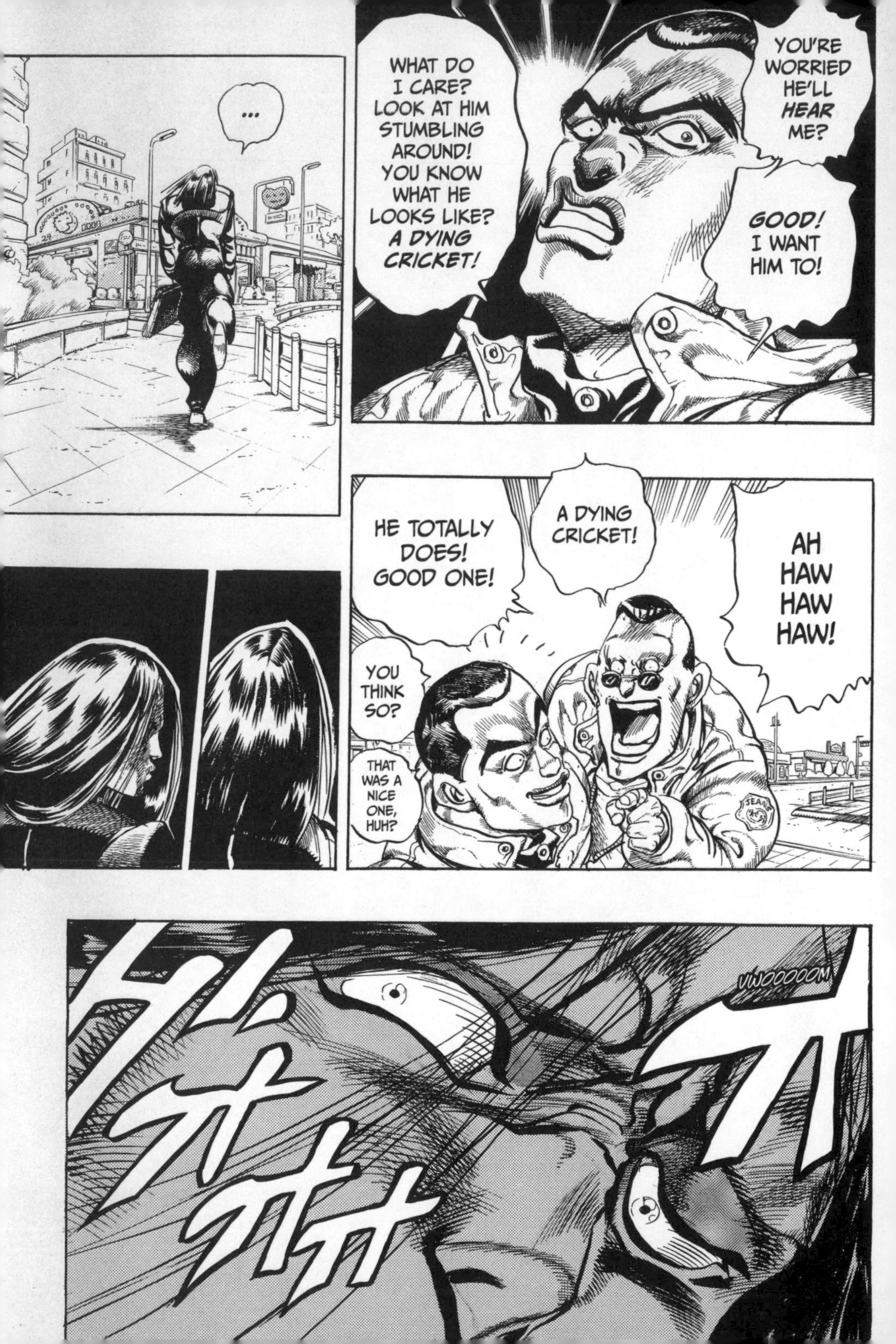
YOU'RE WORRIED HE'LL HEAR ME?
GOOD! I WANT HIM TO!
WHAT DO I CARE? LOOK AT HIM STUMBLING AROUND! YOU KNOW WHAT HE LOOKS LIKE? A DYING CRICKET!
...
AH HAW HAW HAW!
A DYING CRICKET!
HE TOTALLY DOES! GOOD ONE!
YOU THINK SO?
THAT WAS A NICE ONE, HUH?
VWOOOOOM

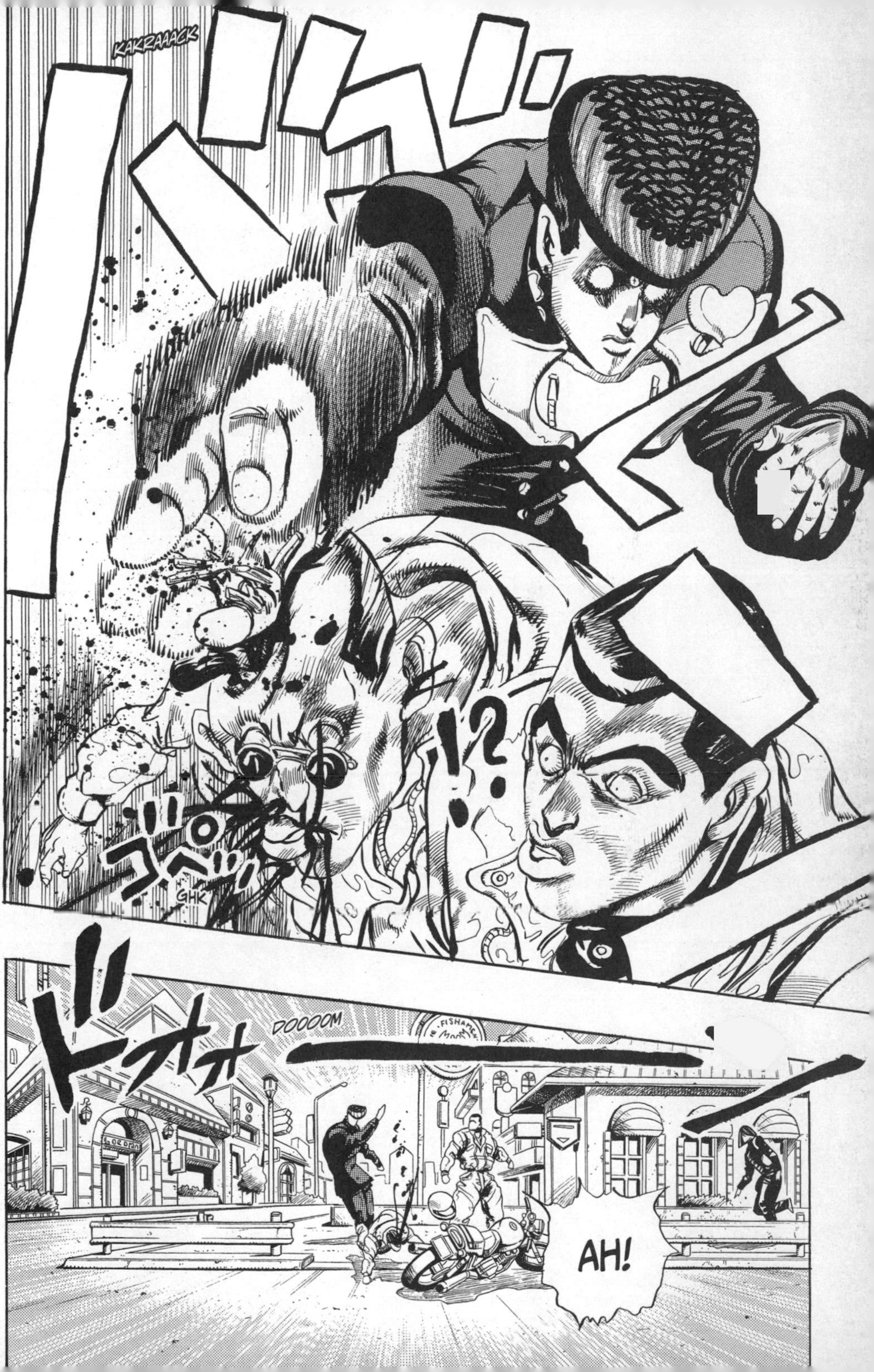
KAKRAAACK
!?
GHK
DOOOOM
AH!

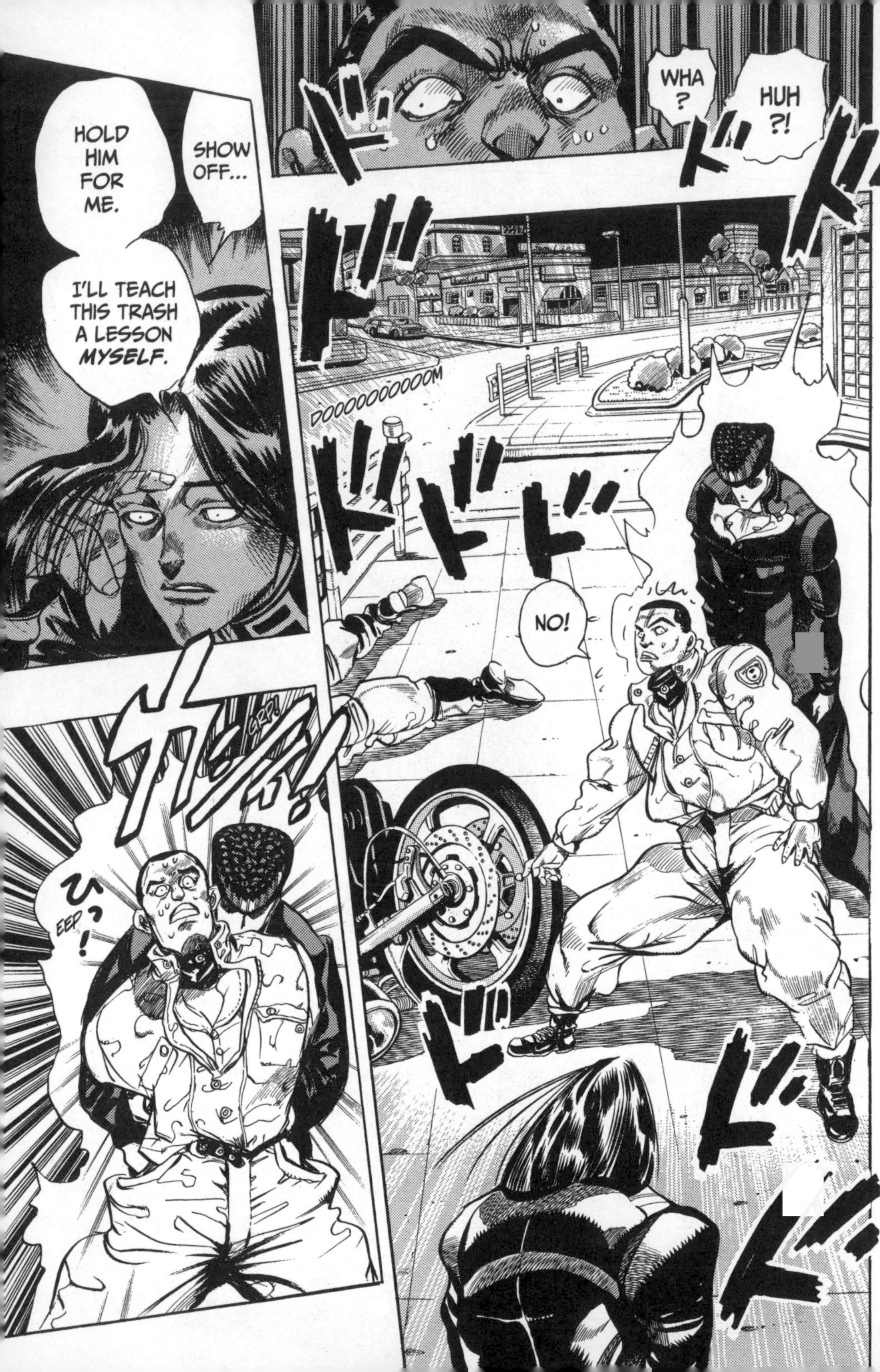
HUH ?!
WHA ?
SHOW OFF...
HOLD HIM FOR ME.
I'LL TEACH THIS TRASH A LESSON *MYSELF*.
DOOOOOOOOOOM
NO!
GRIP
ひっ
EEP!

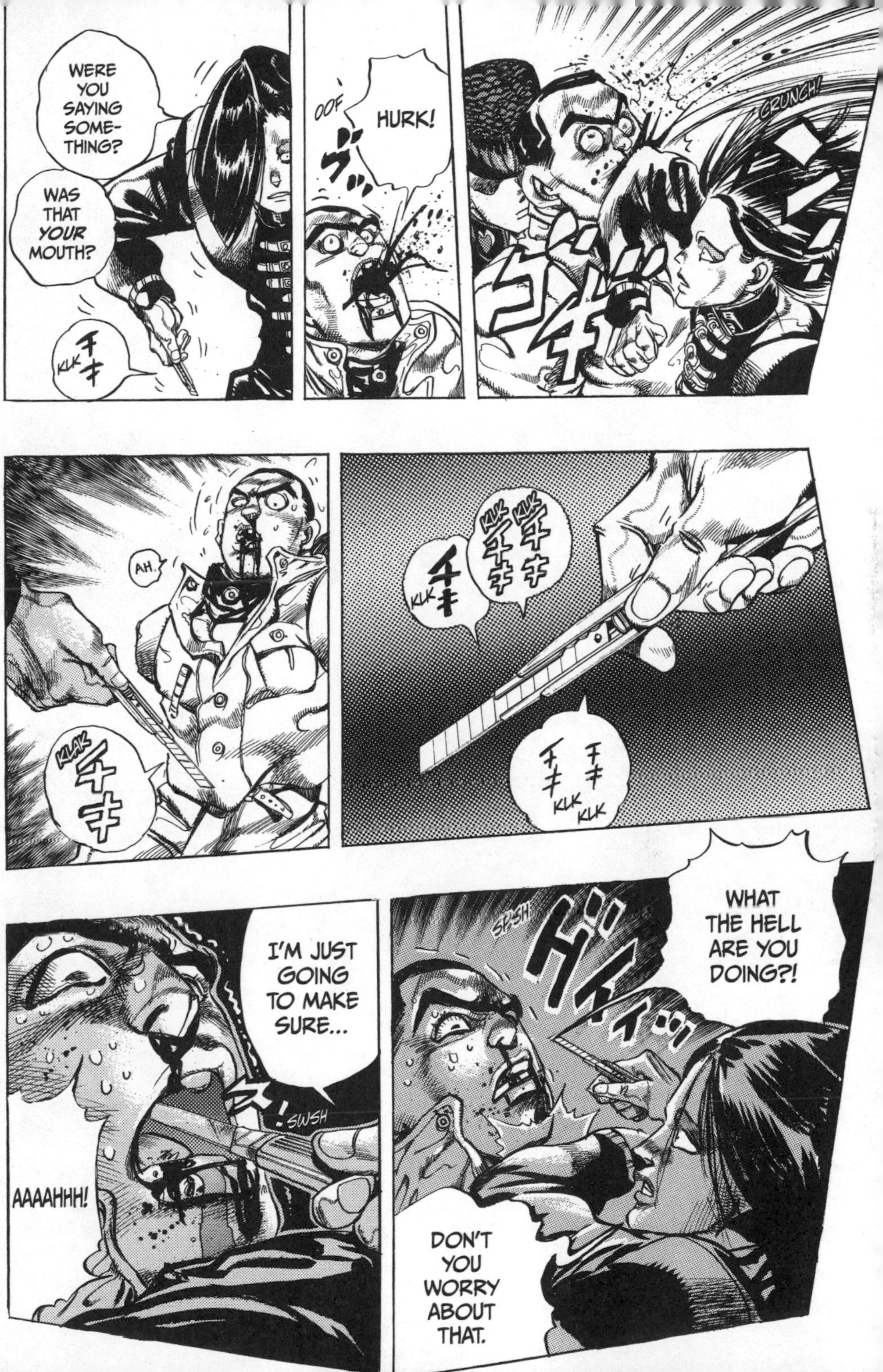
CRUNCH!
OOF
HURK!
WERE YOU SAYING SOME-THING?
WAS THAT *YOUR* MOUTH?
KLK
KLK KLK
KLK
KLK KLK
AH.
KLAK
WHAT THE HELL ARE YOU DOING?!
DON'T YOU WORRY ABOUT THAT.
I'M JUST GOING TO MAKE SURE...
SWSH
AAAAHHH!

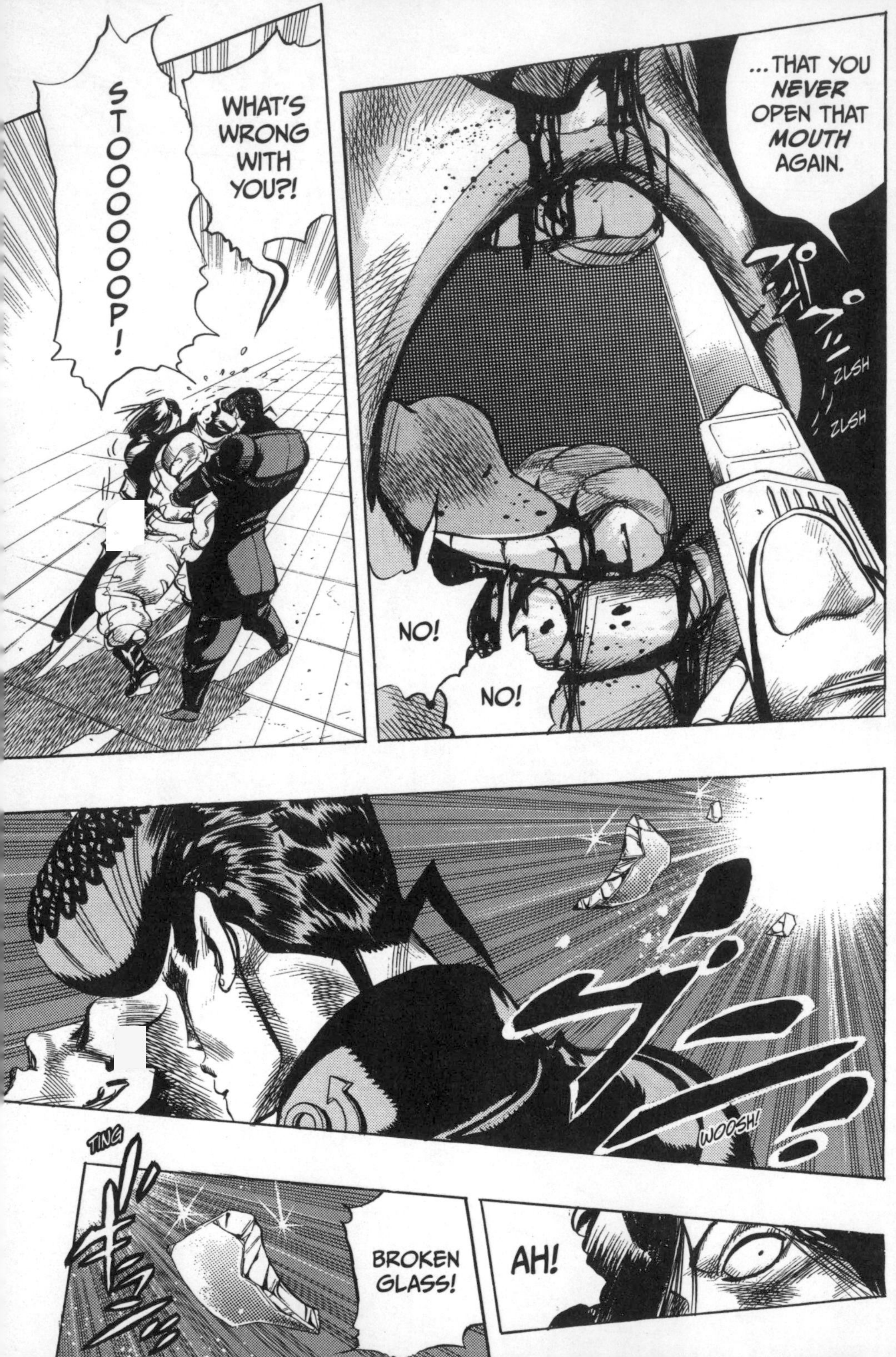
...THAT YOU NEVER OPEN THAT MOUTH AGAIN.
ZLSH
ZLSH
NO!
NO!
WHAT'S WRONG WITH YOU?!
STOOOOOOOP!
WOOSH!
AH!
TING
BROKEN GLASS!

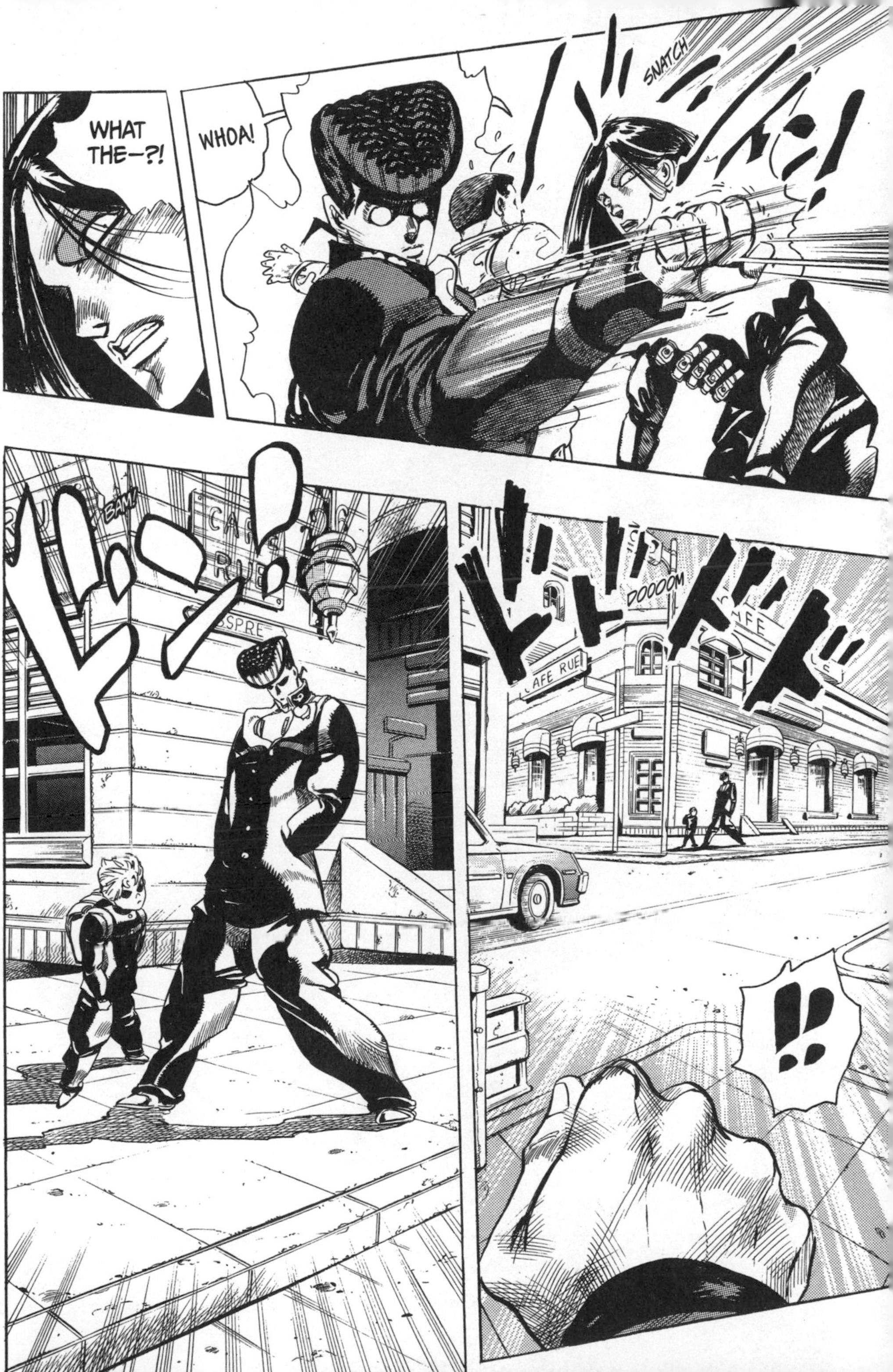
SNATCH
WHOA!
WHAT THE—?!
DOOOOM
CAFE RUE
!!
BAM!

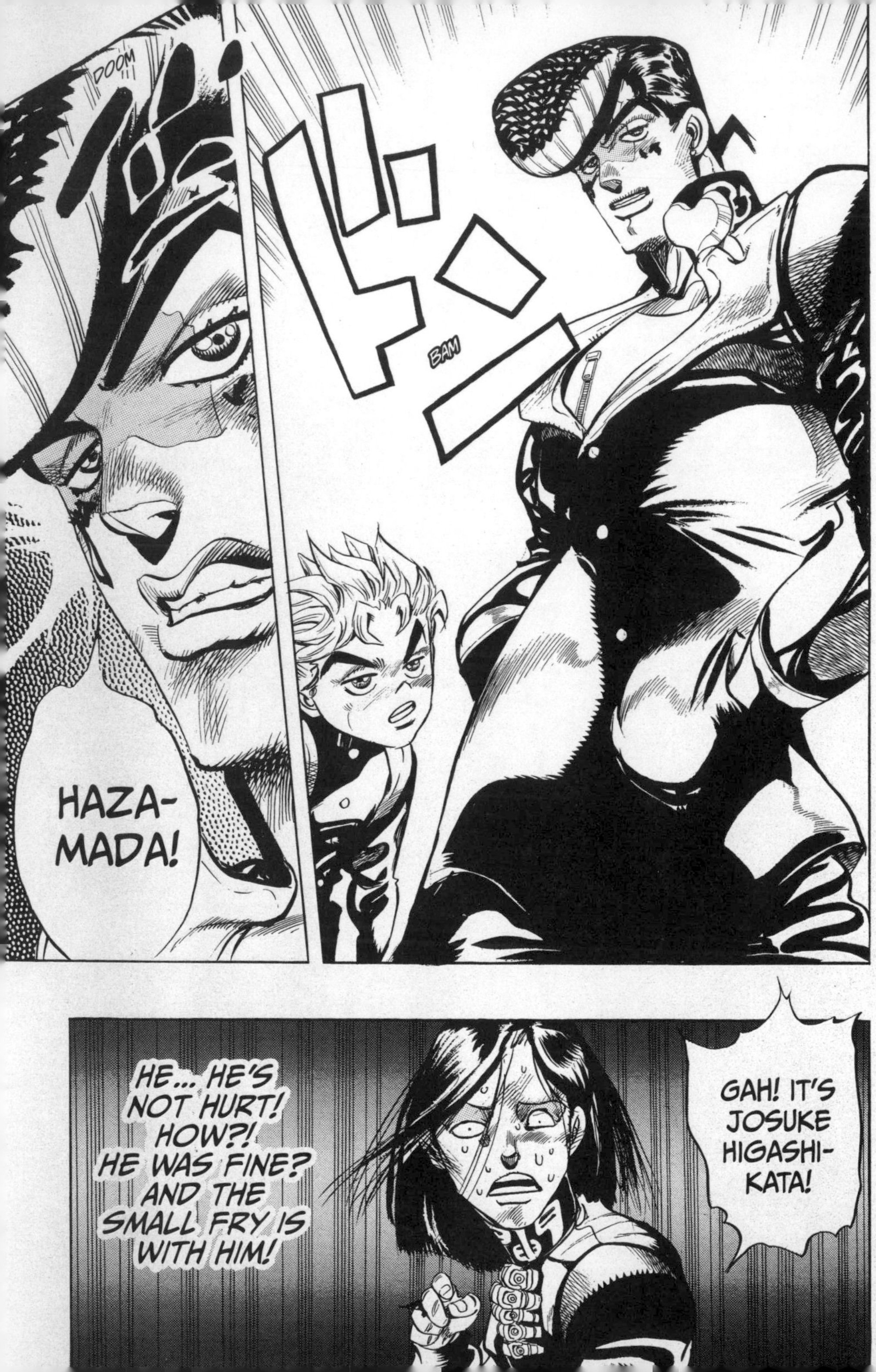
BAM
DOOM
HAZA-
MADA!
GAH! IT'S
JOSUKE
HIGASHI-
KATA!
HE... HE'S
NOT HURT!
HOW?!
HE WAS FINE?
AND THE
SMALL FRY IS
WITH HIM!

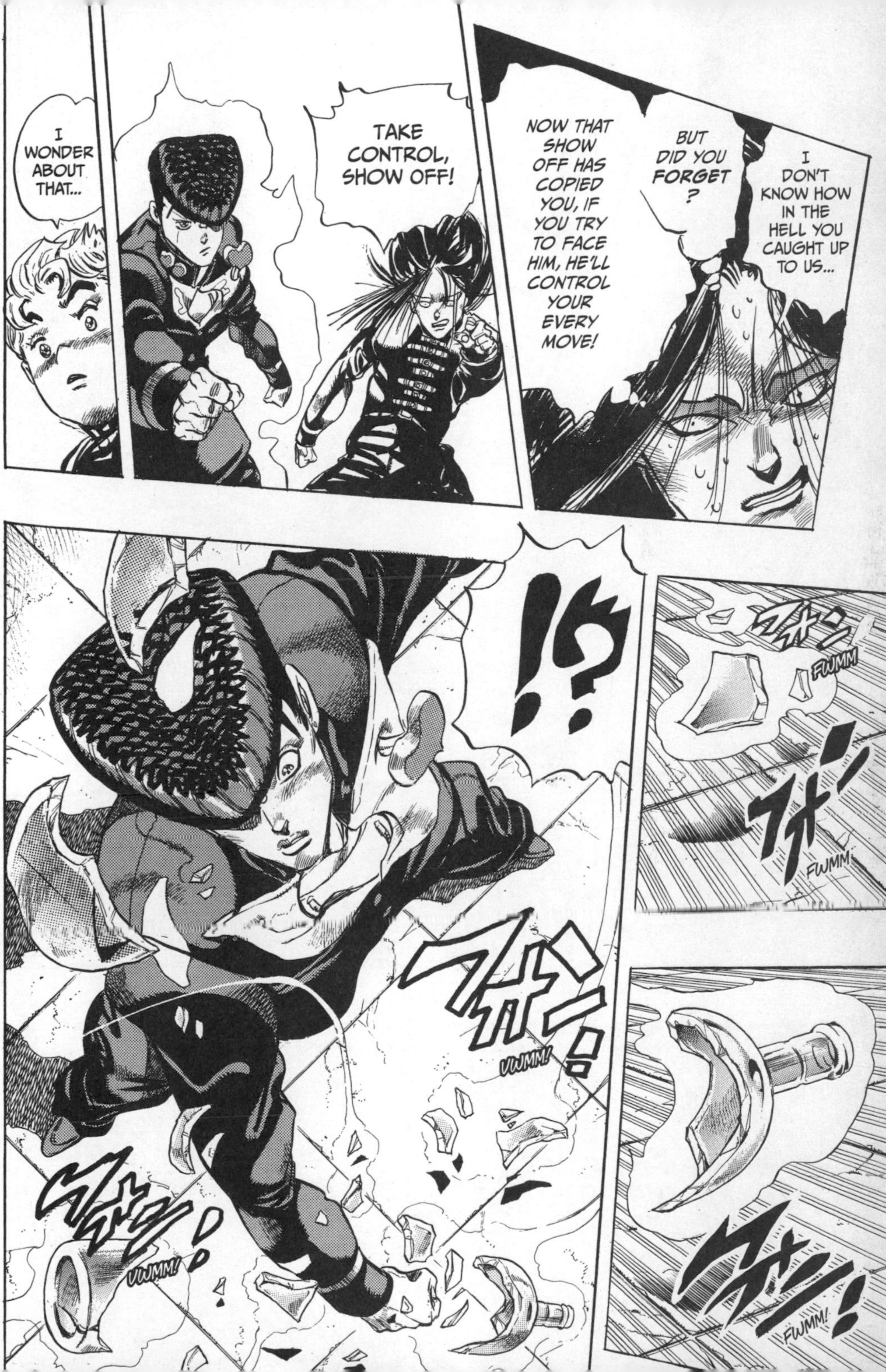
I DON'T KNOW HOW IN THE HELL YOU CAUGHT UP TO US...
BUT DID YOU FORGET?
NOW THAT SHOW OFF HAS COPIED YOU, IF YOU TRY TO FACE HIM, HE'LL CONTROL YOUR EVERY MOVE!
TAKE CONTROL, SHOW OFF!
I WONDER ABOUT THAT...
FWUMM
FWUMM
FWUMM!
!?
VWMM!
VWMM!

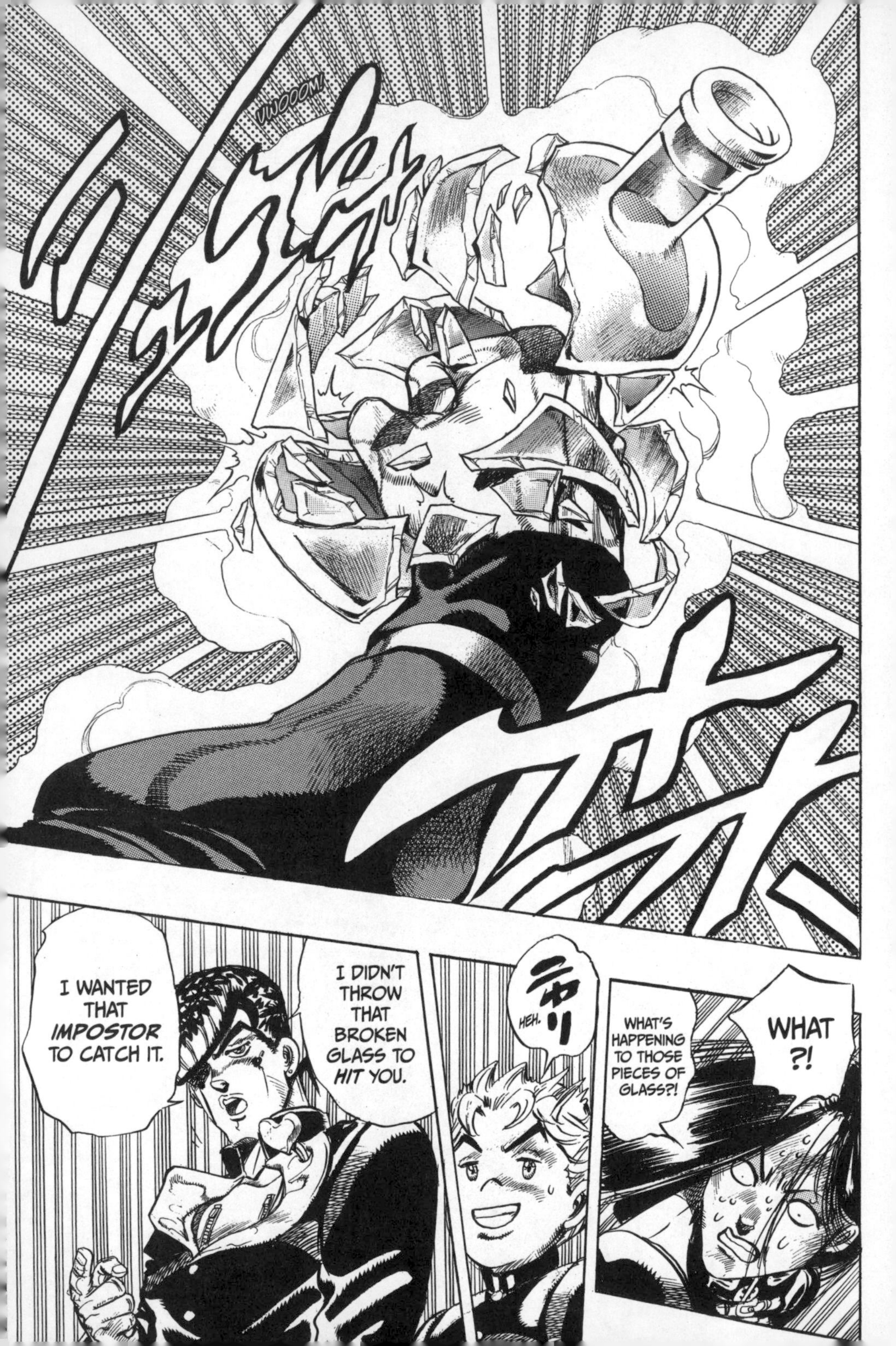
VWOOOM!
WHAT ?!
WHAT'S HAPPENING TO THOSE PIECES OF GLASS?!
ニヤリ
HEH.
I DIDN'T THROW THAT BROKEN GLASS TO *HIT* YOU.
I WANTED THAT *IMPOSTOR* TO CATCH IT.

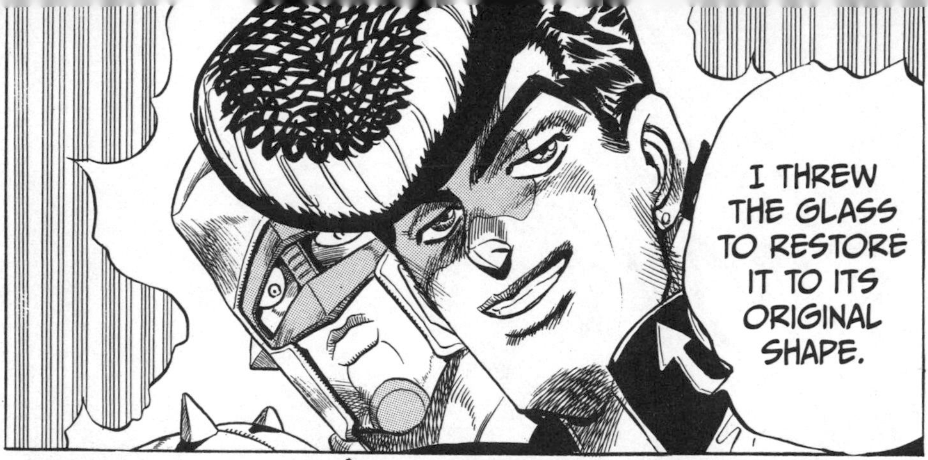
I THREW THE GLASS TO RESTORE IT TO ITS ORIGINAL SHAPE.
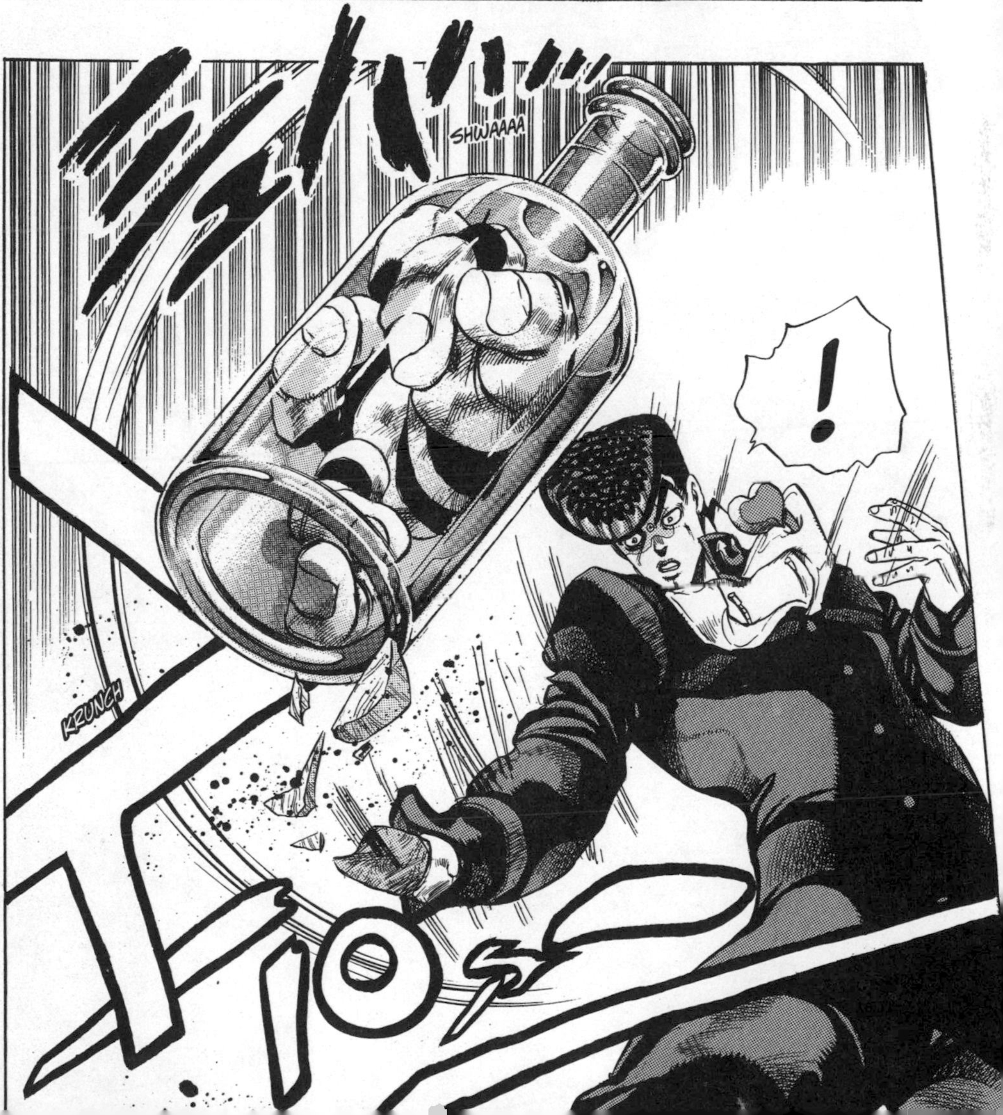
SHWAAAA
!
KRUNCH

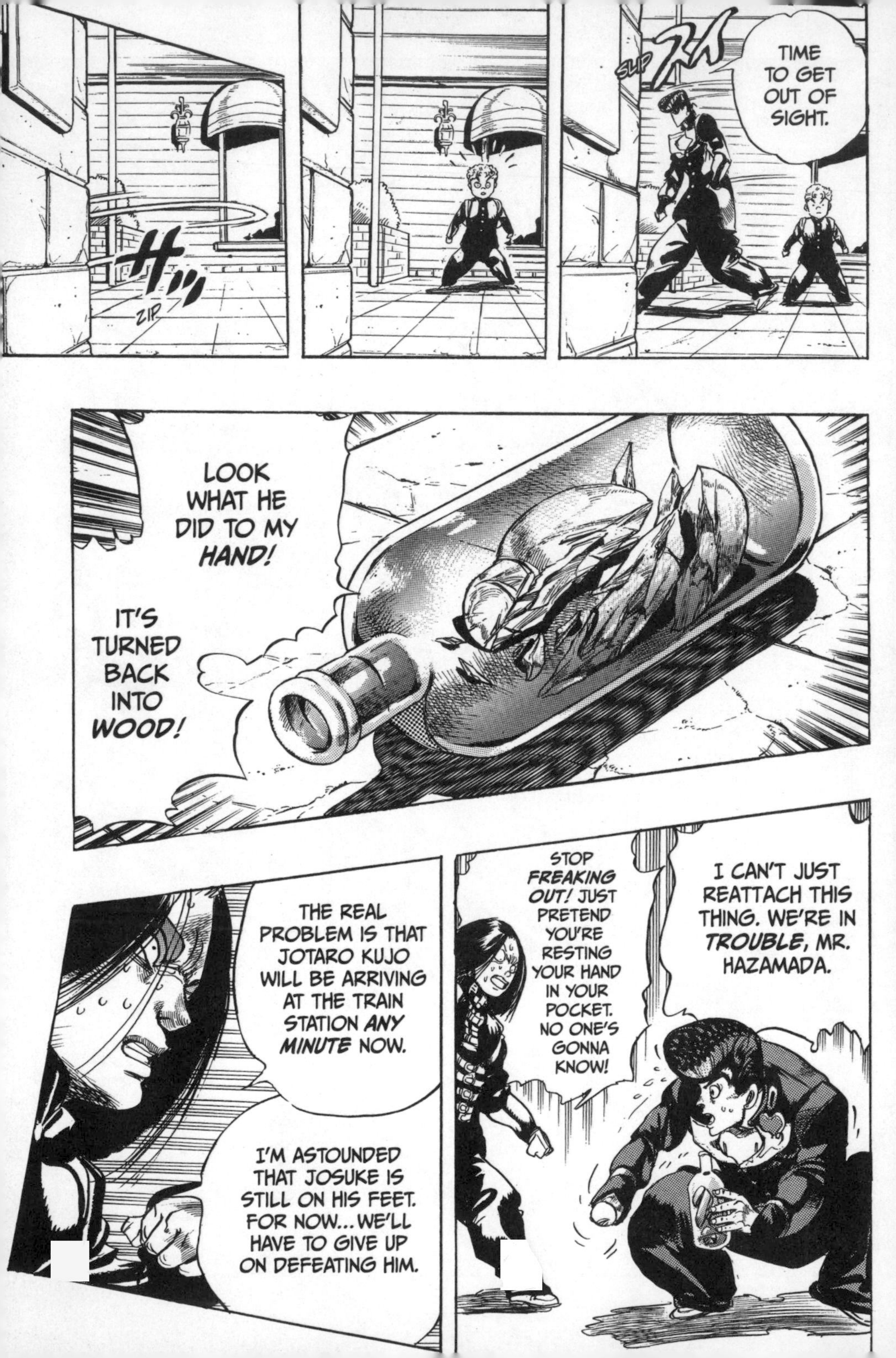
SLIP
TIME TO GET OUT OF SIGHT.
ZIP
LOOK WHAT HE DID TO MY HAND!
IT'S TURNED BACK INTO WOOD!
I CAN'T JUST REATTACH THIS THING. WE'RE IN TROUBLE, MR. HAZAMADA.
STOP FREAKING OUT! JUST PRETEND YOU'RE RESTING YOUR HAND IN YOUR POCKET. NO ONE'S GONNA KNOW!
THE REAL PROBLEM IS THAT JOTARO KUJO WILL BE ARRIVING AT THE TRAIN STATION ANY MINUTE NOW.
I'M ASTOUNDED THAT JOSUKE IS STILL ON HIS FEET. FOR NOW... WE'LL HAVE TO GIVE UP ON DEFEATING HIM.

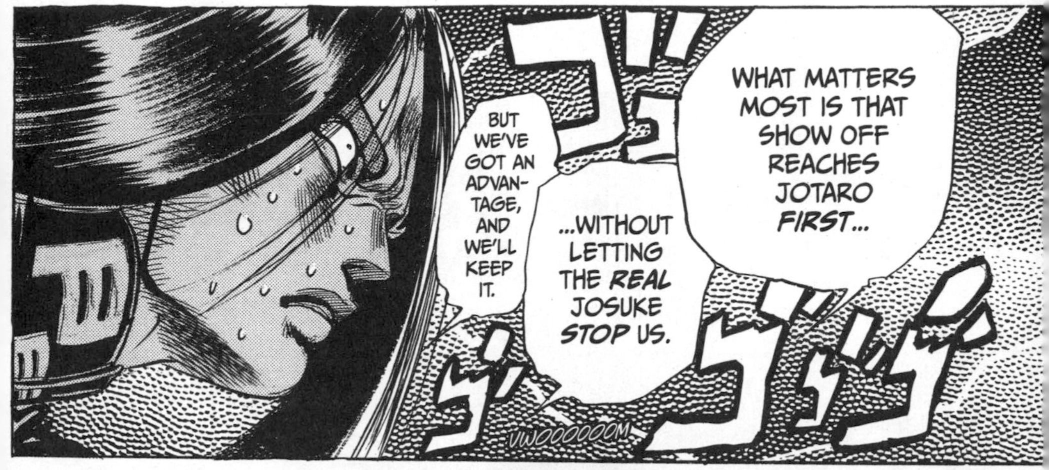
WHAT MATTERS MOST IS THAT SHOW OFF REACHES JOTARO *FIRST*...
...WITHOUT LETTING THE *REAL* JOSUKE *STOP* US.
BUT WE'VE GOT AN ADVAN-TAGE, AND WE'LL KEEP IT.
VWOOOOOOM

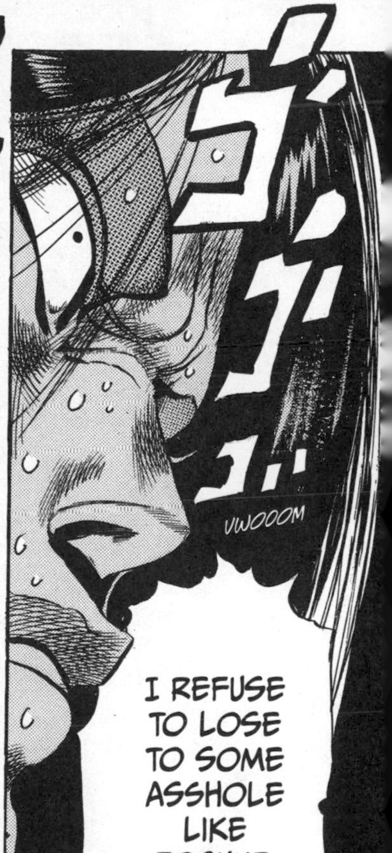
VWOOOM
I REFUSE TO LOSE TO SOME ASSHOLE LIKE JOSUKE.

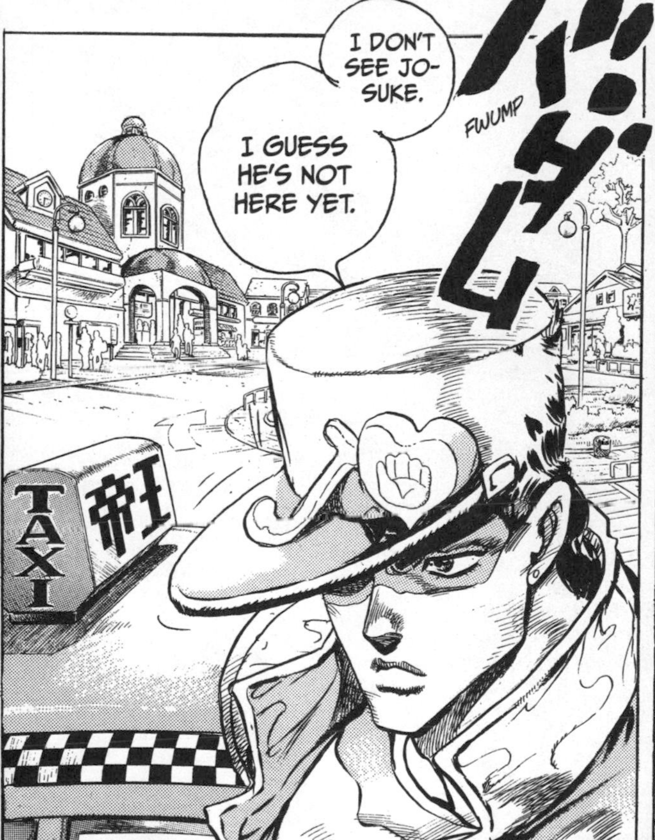
I DON'T SEE JO-SUKE.
I GUESS HE'S NOT HERE YET.
FWUMP
TAXI

*TAXI'S SIGN: IMPERIAL

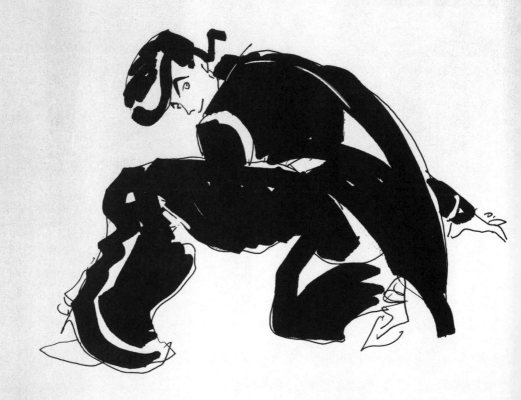

CHAPTER 28

TOSHIKAZU HAZAMADA (SHOW OFF), PART 5

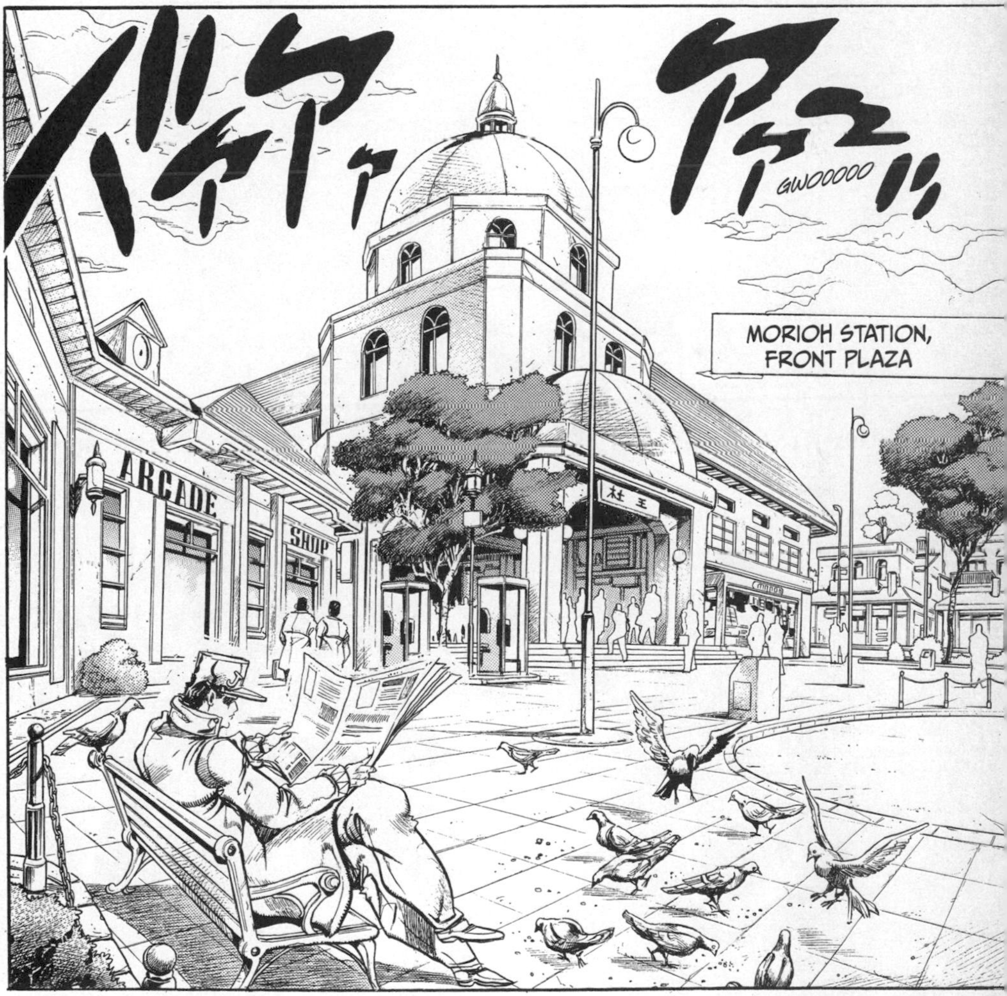
GWOOOOO
MORIOH STATION, FRONT PLAZA
ARCADE
SHOP

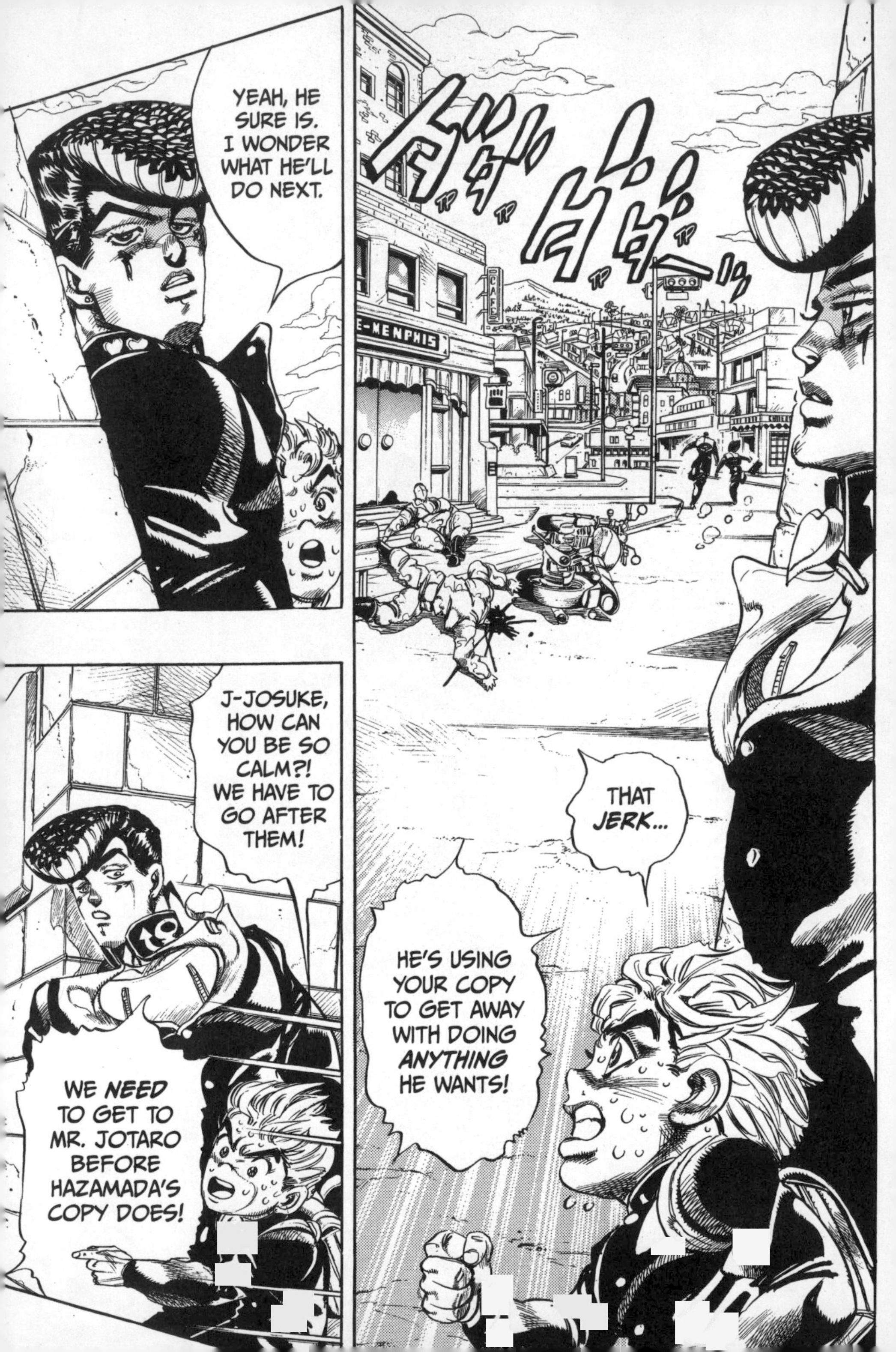

TP TP TP TP TP
THAT *JERK*...
HE'S USING YOUR COPY TO GET AWAY WITH DOING *ANYTHING* HE WANTS!
YEAH, HE SURE IS. I WONDER WHAT HE'LL DO NEXT.
J-JOSUKE, HOW CAN YOU BE SO CALM?! WE HAVE TO GO AFTER THEM!
WE *NEED* TO GET TO MR. JOTARO BEFORE HAZAMADA'S COPY DOES!

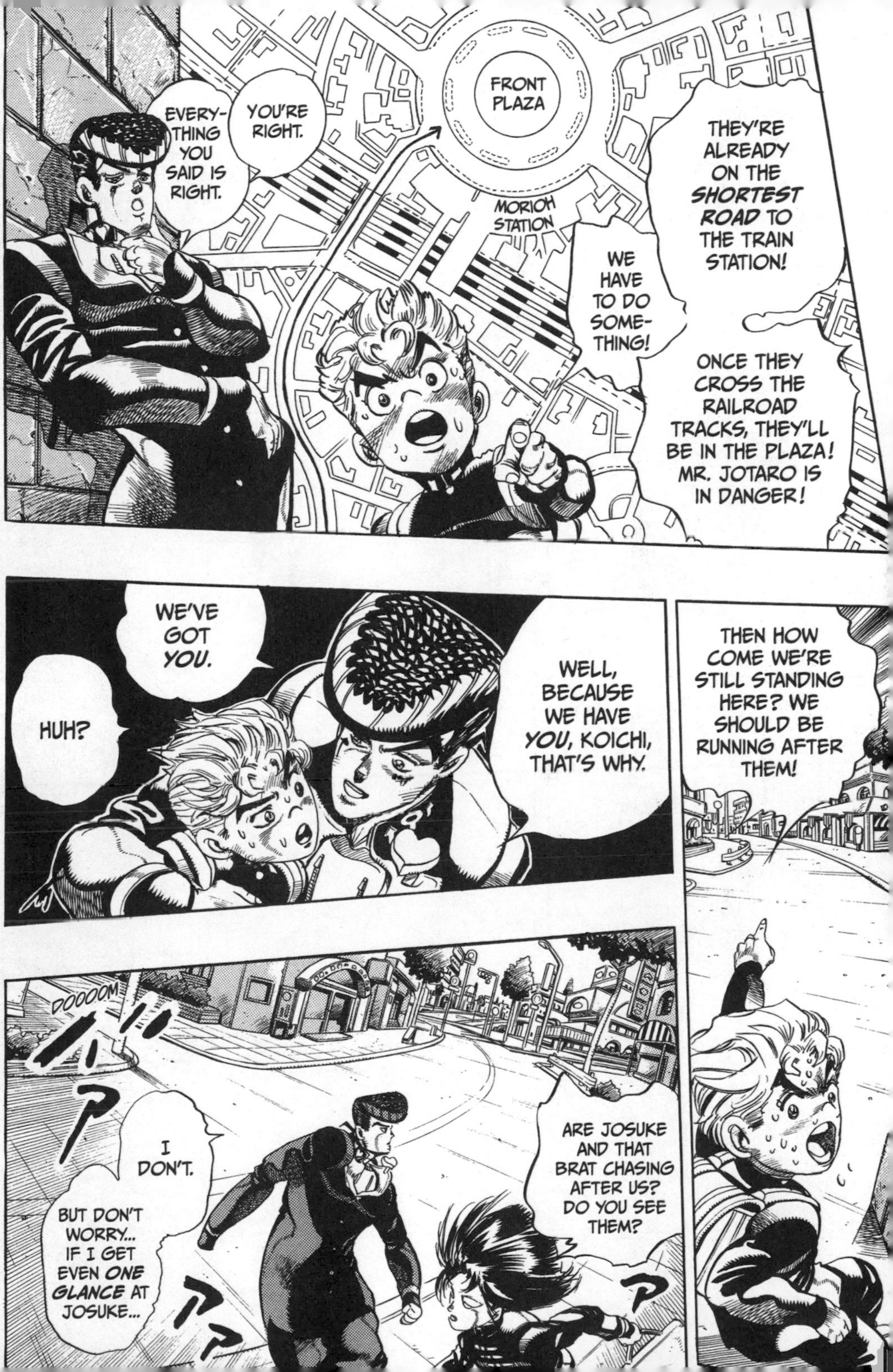
THEY'RE ALREADY ON THE SHORTEST ROAD TO THE TRAIN STATION!
ONCE THEY CROSS THE RAILROAD TRACKS, THEY'LL BE IN THE PLAZA! MR. JOTARO IS IN DANGER!
FRONT PLAZA
MORIOH STATION
WE HAVE TO DO SOME-THING!
YOU'RE RIGHT.
EVERY-THING YOU SAID IS RIGHT.
THEN HOW COME WE'RE STILL STANDING HERE? WE SHOULD BE RUNNING AFTER THEM!
WELL, BECAUSE WE HAVE YOU, KOICHI, THAT'S WHY.
WE'VE GOT YOU.
HUH?
ARE JOSUKE AND THAT BRAT CHASING AFTER US? DO YOU SEE THEM?
I DON'T.
BUT DON'T WORRY... IF I GET EVEN ONE GLANCE AT JOSUKE...
DOOOOM

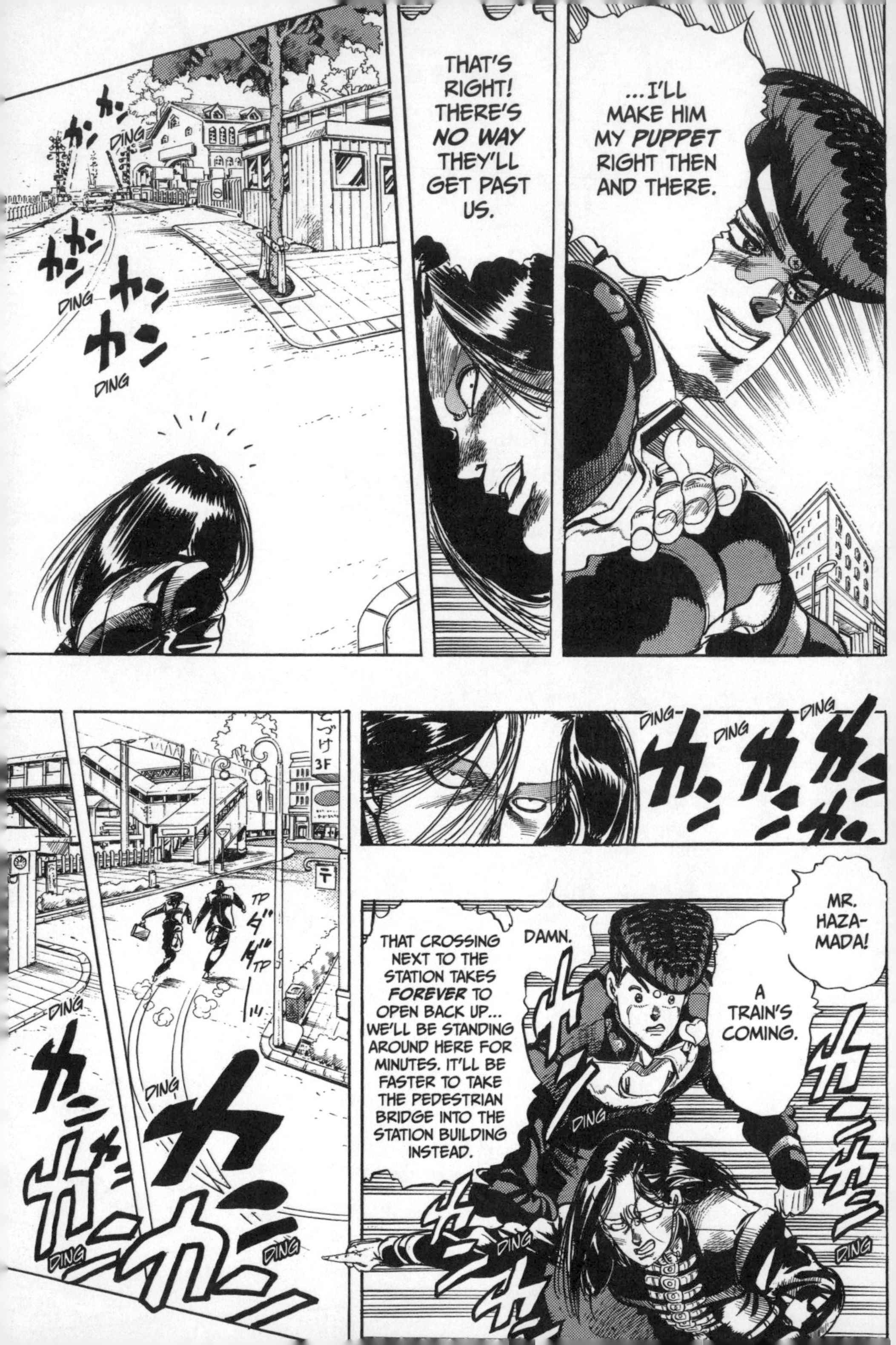
...I'LL MAKE HIM MY *PUPPET* RIGHT THEN AND THERE.
THAT'S RIGHT! THERE'S *NO WAY* THEY'LL GET PAST US.
DING
DING
DING
DING
DING-
DING
DING
MR. HAZAMADA!
A TRAIN'S COMING.
DAMN.
THAT CROSSING NEXT TO THE STATION TAKES *FOREVER* TO OPEN BACK UP... WE'LL BE STANDING AROUND HERE FOR MINUTES. IT'LL BE FASTER TO TAKE THE PEDESTRIAN BRIDGE INTO THE STATION BUILDING INSTEAD.
DING
DING
DING
DING
3F
TP
TP
DING
DING
DING
DING

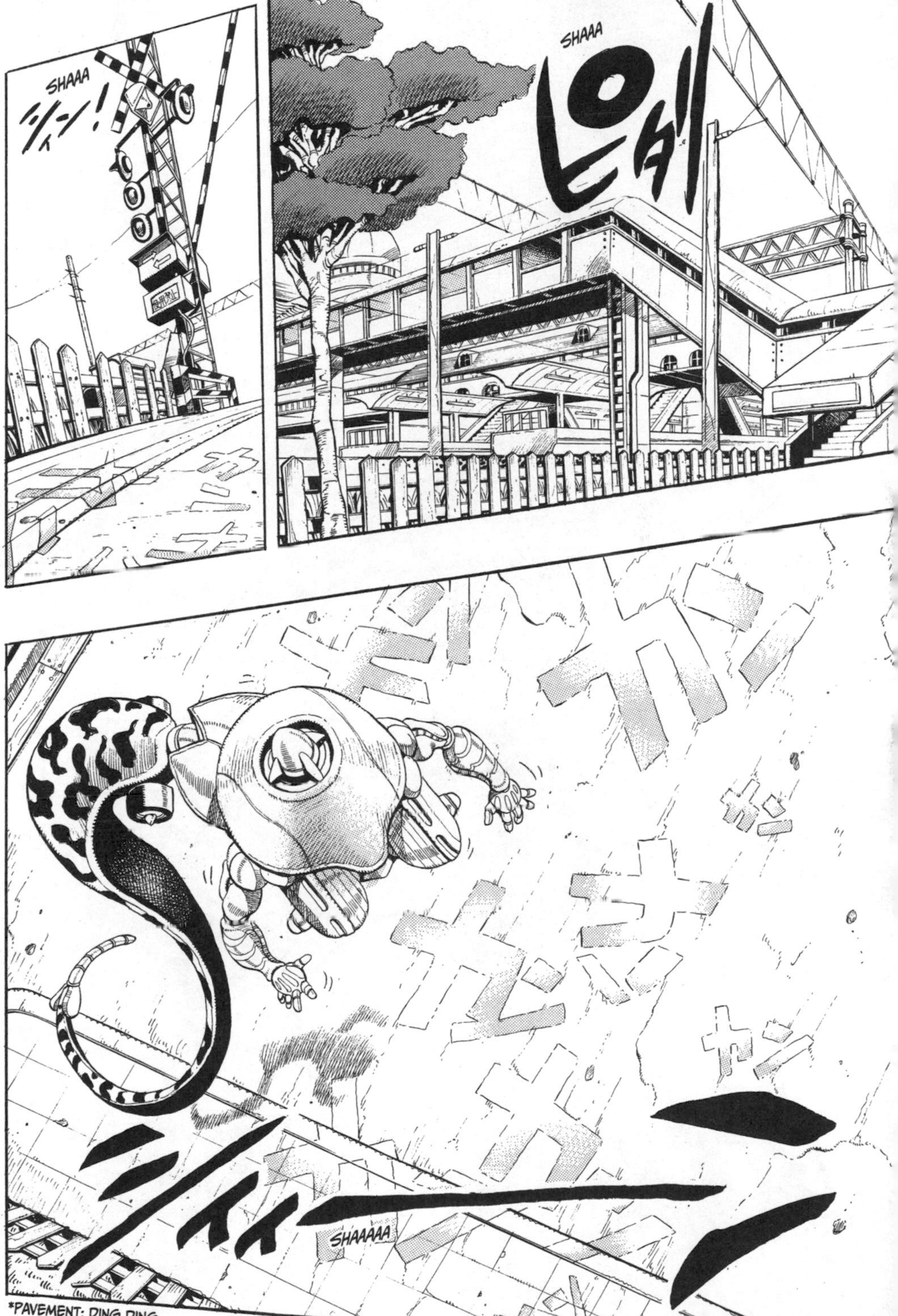

SHAAA
SHAAA
SHAAAAA

*PAVEMENT: DING DING

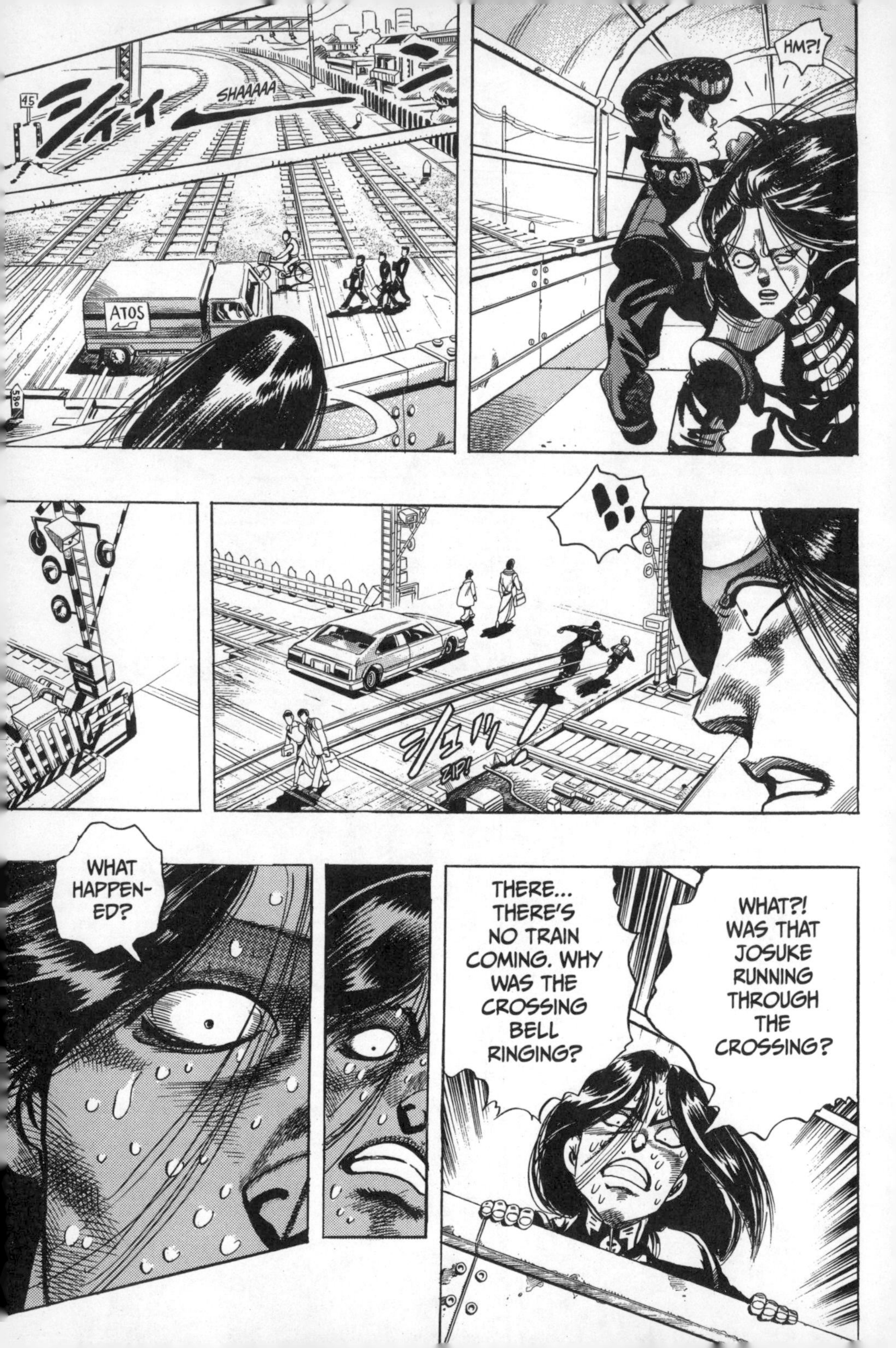
HM?!
シィィー
SHAAAAA
ATOS
!!
シュバ
ZIP!
WHAT?! WAS THAT JOSUKE RUNNING THROUGH THE CROSSING?
THERE... THERE'S NO TRAIN COMING. WHY WAS THE CROSSING BELL RINGING?
WHAT HAPPEN-ED?

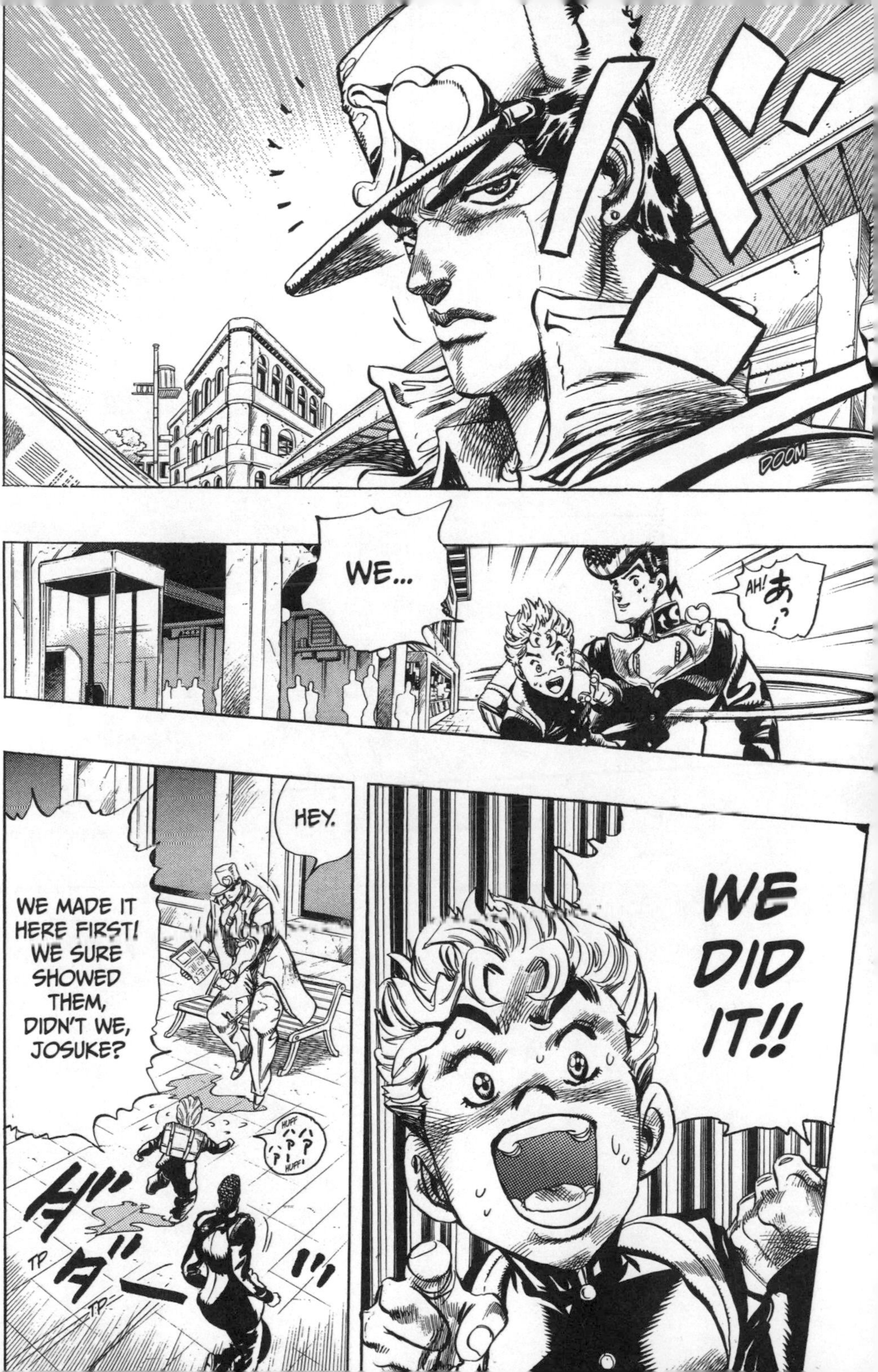
DOOM
WE...
AH! あっ!
WE DID IT!!
HEY.
WE MADE IT HERE FIRST! WE SURE SHOWED THEM, DIDN'T WE, JOSUKE?
HUFF ハァ ハァ HUFF
TP
TP

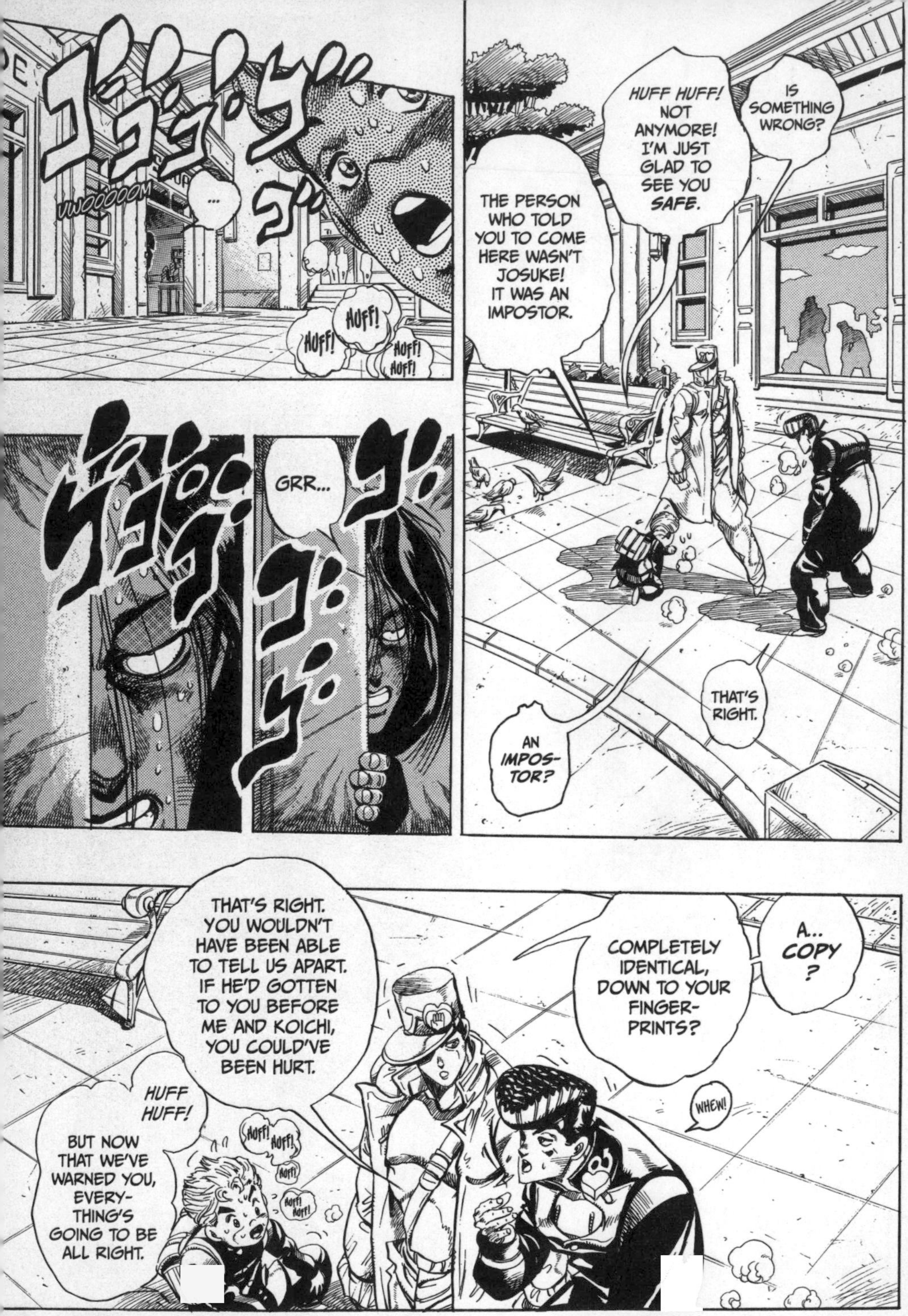
IS SOMETHING WRONG?
HUFF HUFF! NOT ANYMORE! I'M JUST GLAD TO SEE YOU *SAFE*.
THE PERSON WHO TOLD YOU TO COME HERE WASN'T JOSUKE! IT WAS AN IMPOSTOR.
THAT'S RIGHT.
AN *IMPOSTOR?*
VWOOOOOOM
...
HUFF!
HUFF!
HUFF! HUFF!
GRR...
A... *COPY*?
COMPLETELY IDENTICAL, DOWN TO YOUR FINGER-PRINTS?
WHEW!
THAT'S RIGHT. YOU WOULDN'T HAVE BEEN ABLE TO TELL US APART. IF HE'D GOTTEN TO YOU BEFORE ME AND KOICHI, YOU COULD'VE BEEN HURT.
HUFF! HUFF! HUFF!
HUFF! HUFF!
HUFF HUFF!
BUT NOW THAT WE'VE WARNED YOU, EVERYTHING'S GOING TO BE ALL RIGHT.

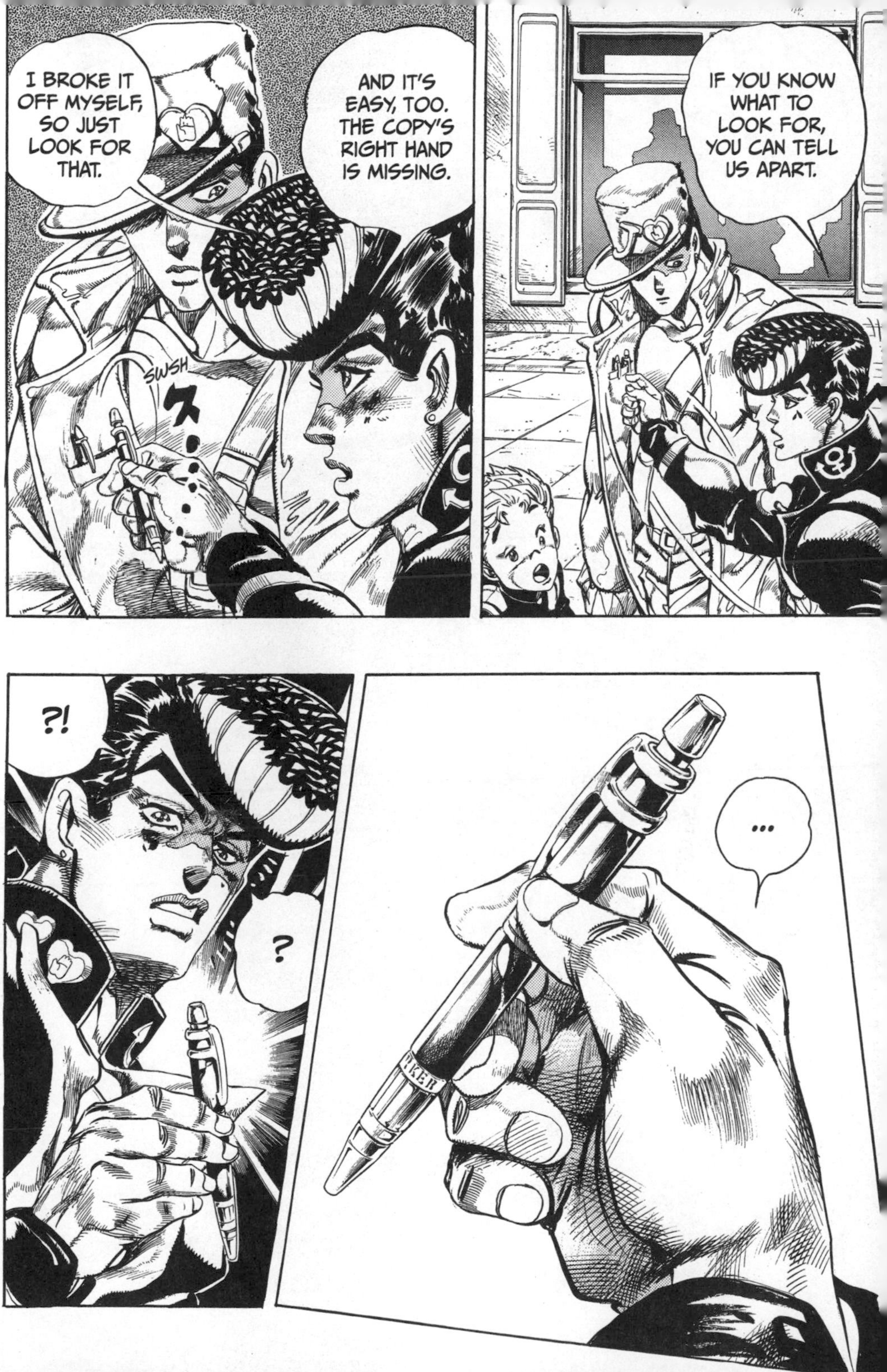
IF YOU KNOW WHAT TO LOOK FOR, YOU CAN TELL US APART.
AND IT'S EASY, TOO. THE COPY'S RIGHT HAND IS MISSING.
I BROKE IT OFF MYSELF, SO JUST LOOK FOR THAT.
SWSH
...
?!
?

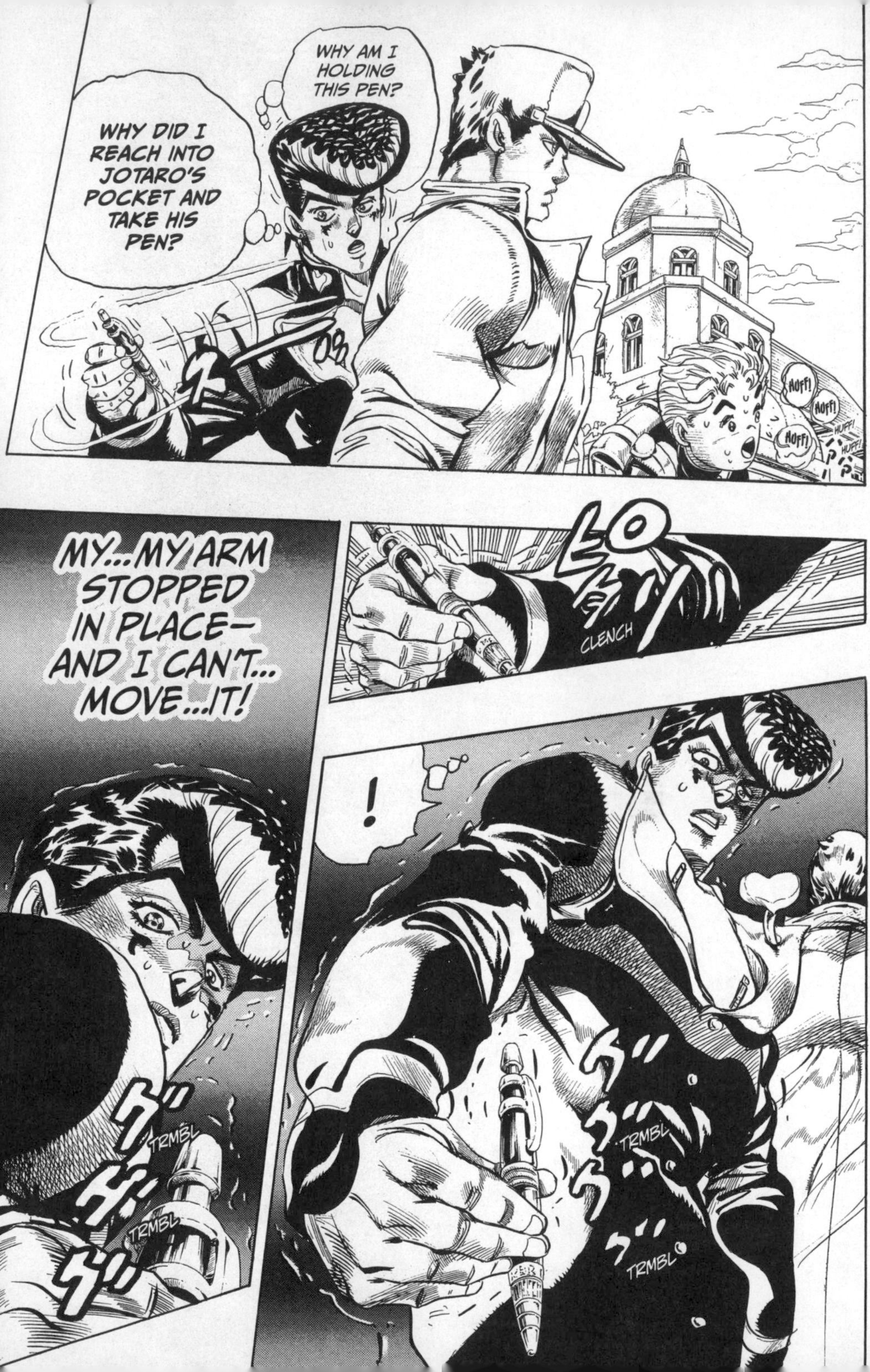
WHY AM I HOLDING THIS PEN?
WHY DID I REACH INTO JOTARO'S POCKET AND TAKE HIS PEN?
HUFF!
HUFF!
HUFF!
HUFF!
HUFF!
CLENCH
!
TRMBL
TRMBL
MY...MY ARM STOPPED IN PLACE— AND I CAN'T... MOVE...IT!
TRMBL
TRMBL

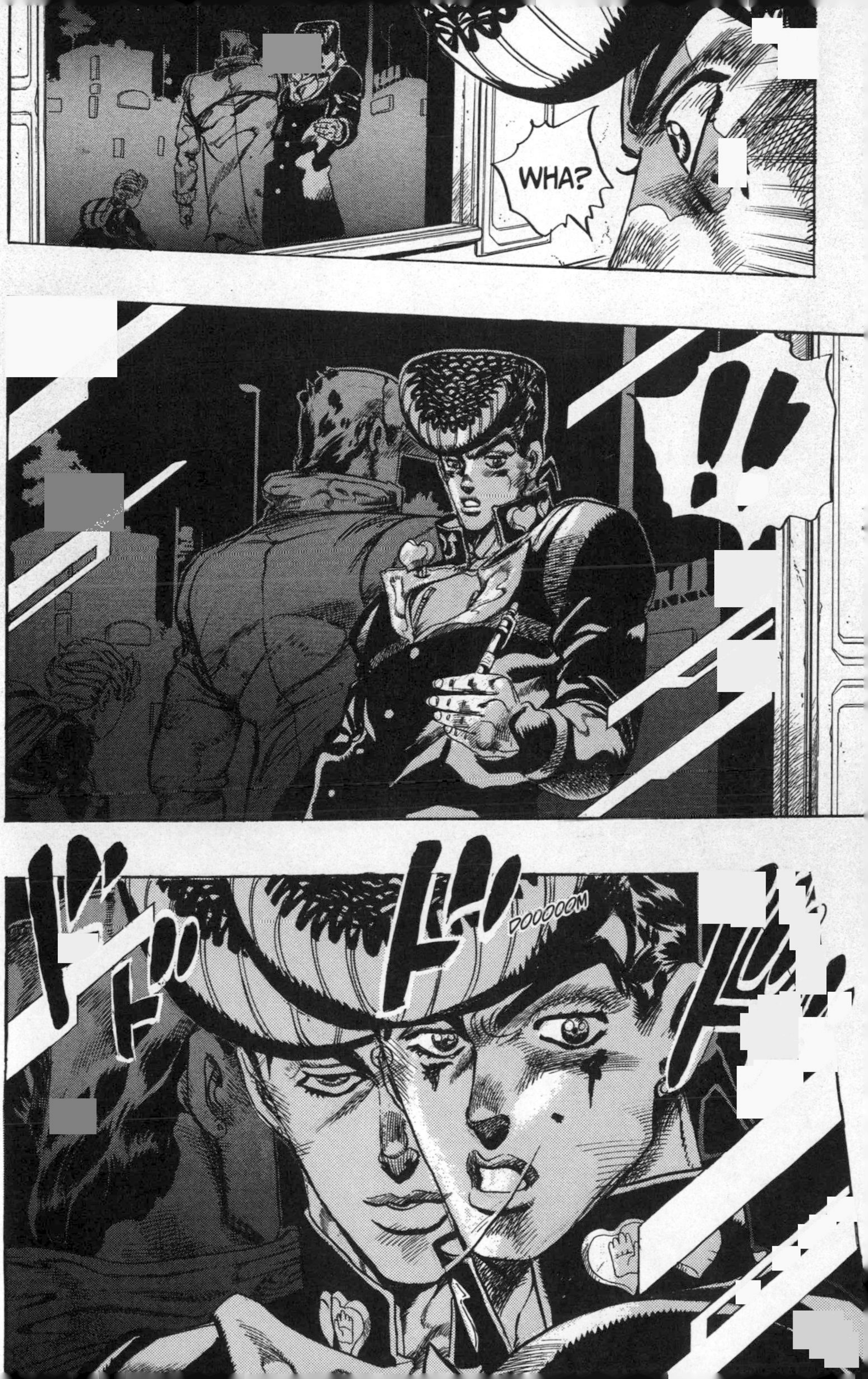
WHA?
!!
DOOOOOM

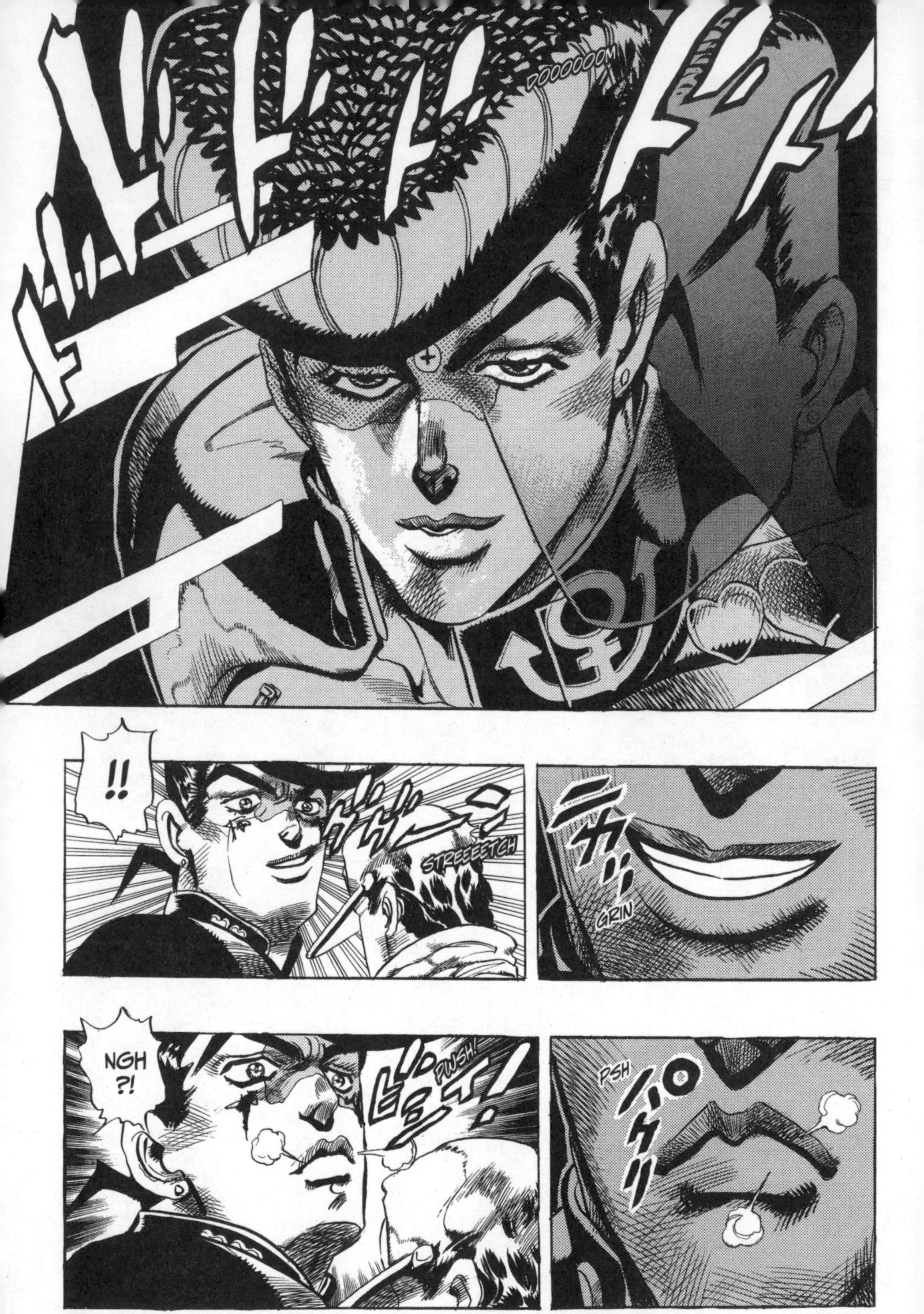
DOOOOOOOM
GRIN
!!
STREEEETCH
PSH
NGH ?!
PWSH!

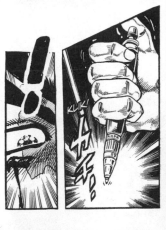

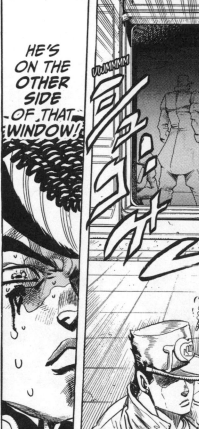

HE'S ON THE OTHER SIDE OF THAT WINDOW!

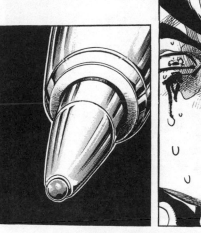

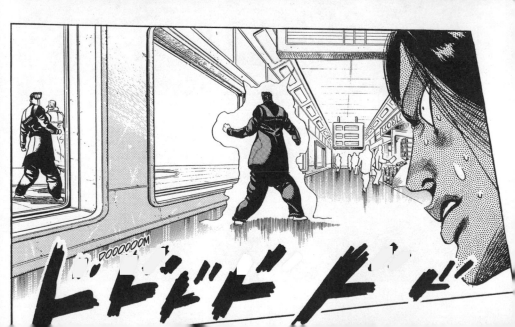

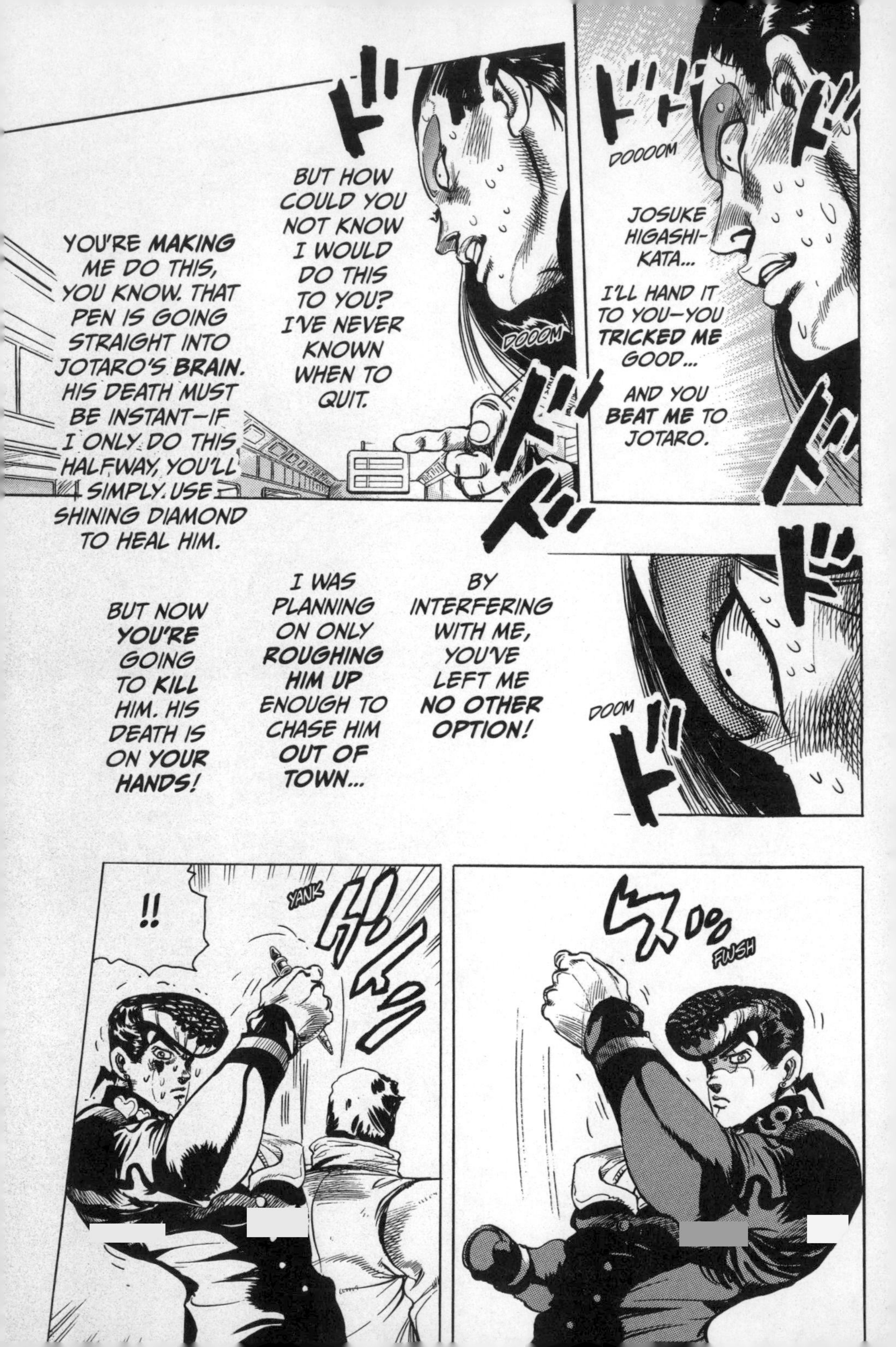
DOOOOM
JOSUKE HIGASHI-KATA...
I'LL HAND IT TO YOU—YOU TRICKED ME GOOD...
AND YOU BEAT ME TO JOTARO.
BUT HOW COULD YOU NOT KNOW I WOULD DO THIS TO YOU? I'VE NEVER KNOWN WHEN TO QUIT.
YOU'RE MAKING ME DO THIS, YOU KNOW. THAT PEN IS GOING STRAIGHT INTO JOTARO'S BRAIN. HIS DEATH MUST BE INSTANT—IF I ONLY DO THIS HALFWAY, YOU'LL SIMPLY USE SHINING DIAMOND TO HEAL HIM.
DOOOM
DOOM
BY INTERFERING WITH ME, YOU'VE LEFT ME NO OTHER OPTION!
I WAS PLANNING ON ONLY ROUGHING HIM UP ENOUGH TO CHASE HIM OUT OF TOWN...
BUT NOW YOU'RE GOING TO KILL HIM. HIS DEATH IS ON YOUR HANDS!
FWSH
YANK
!!

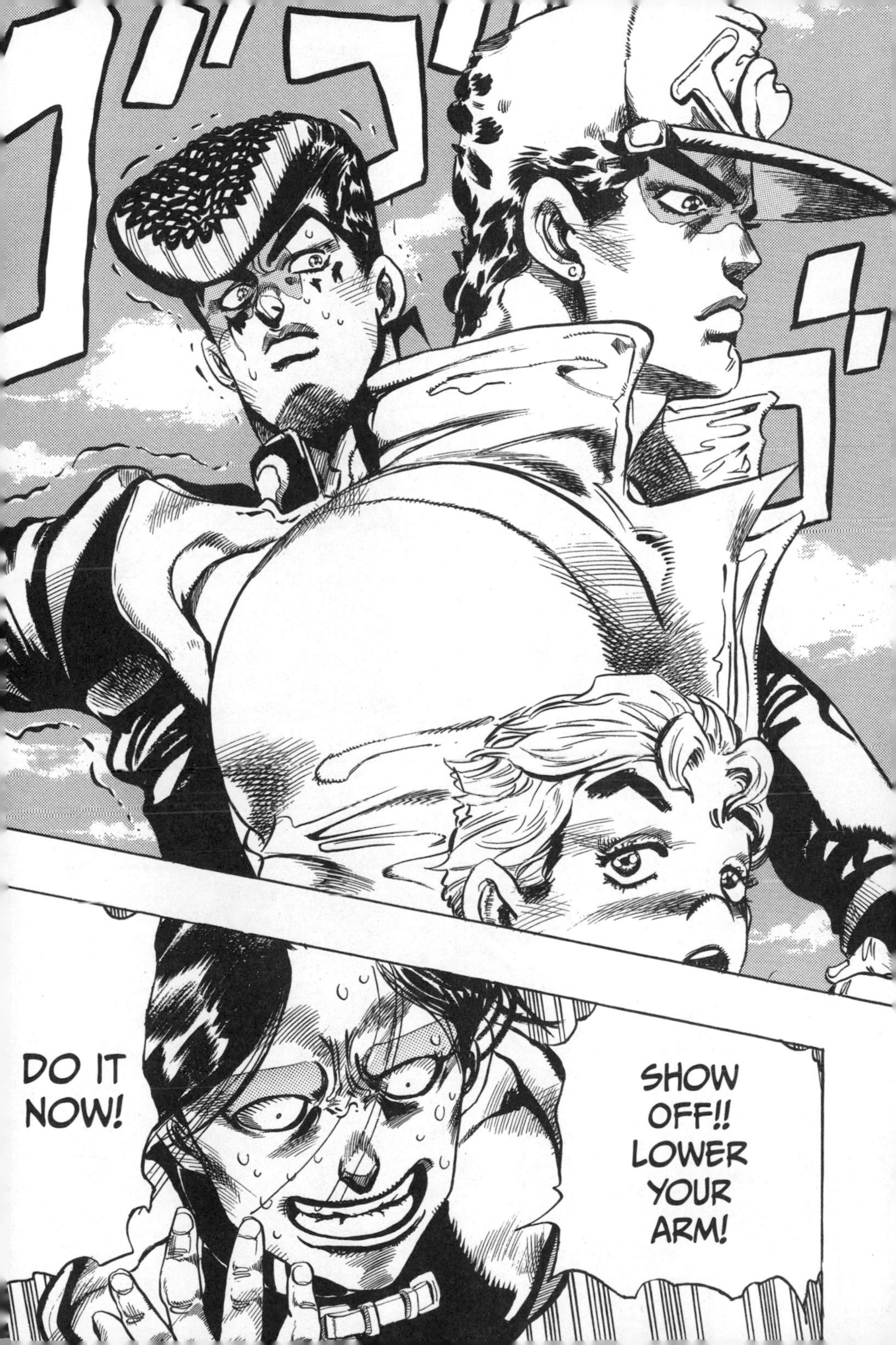
SHOW OFF!! LOWER YOUR ARM!
DO IT NOW!

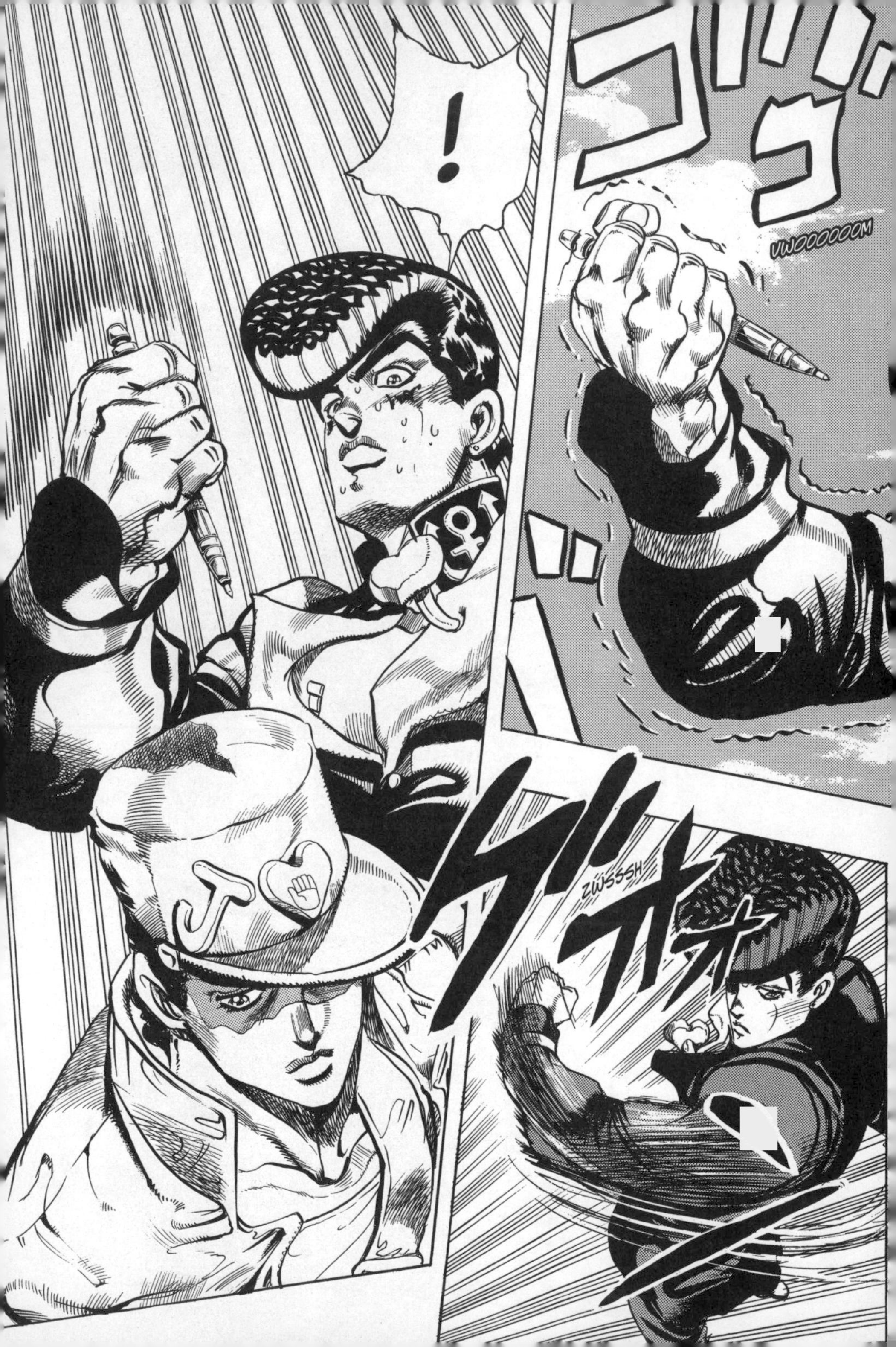
VWOOOOOOOM
ZWSSSH
!

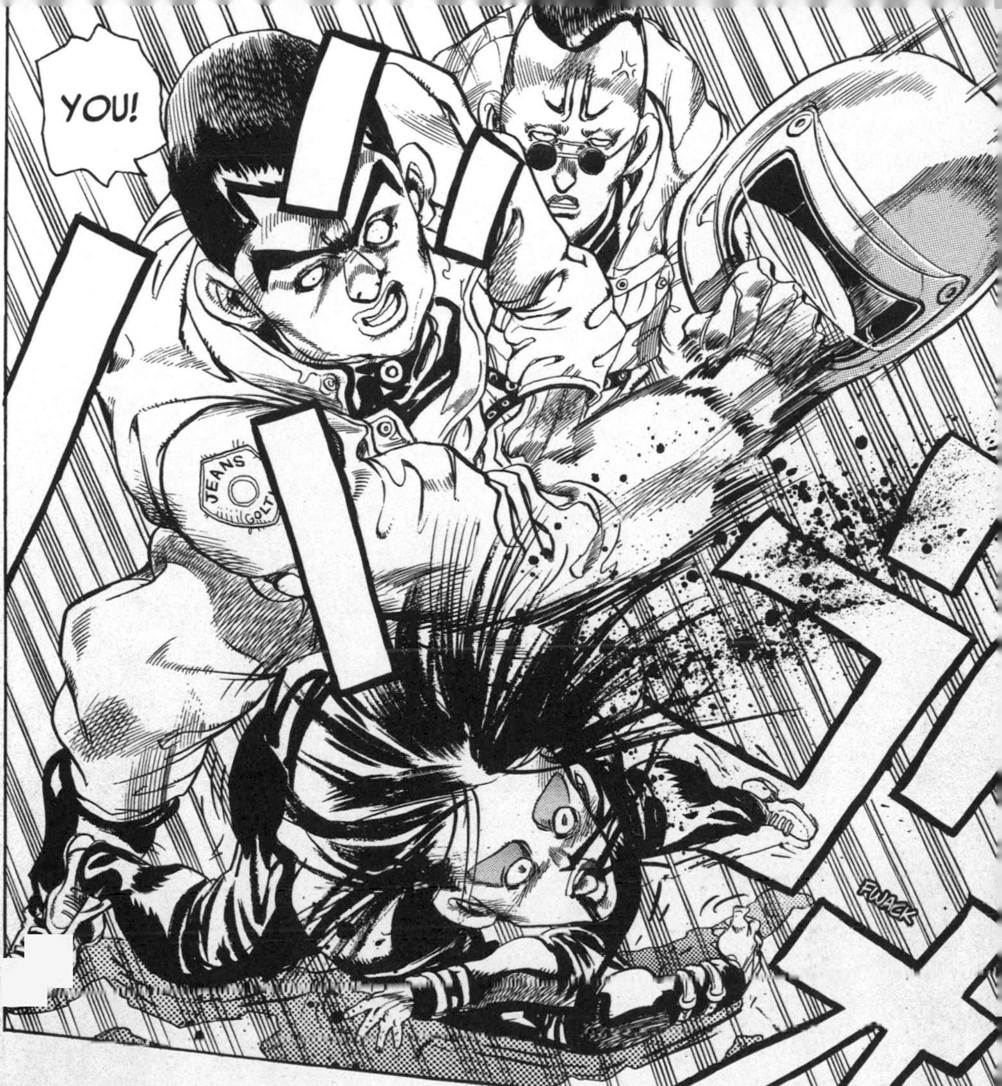
YOU!
FWACK
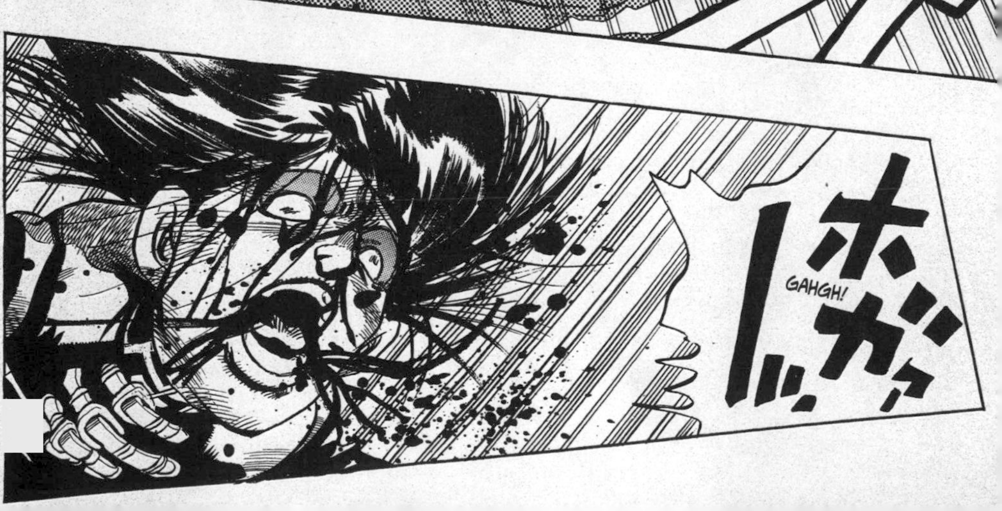
ホガァーッ
GAHGH!

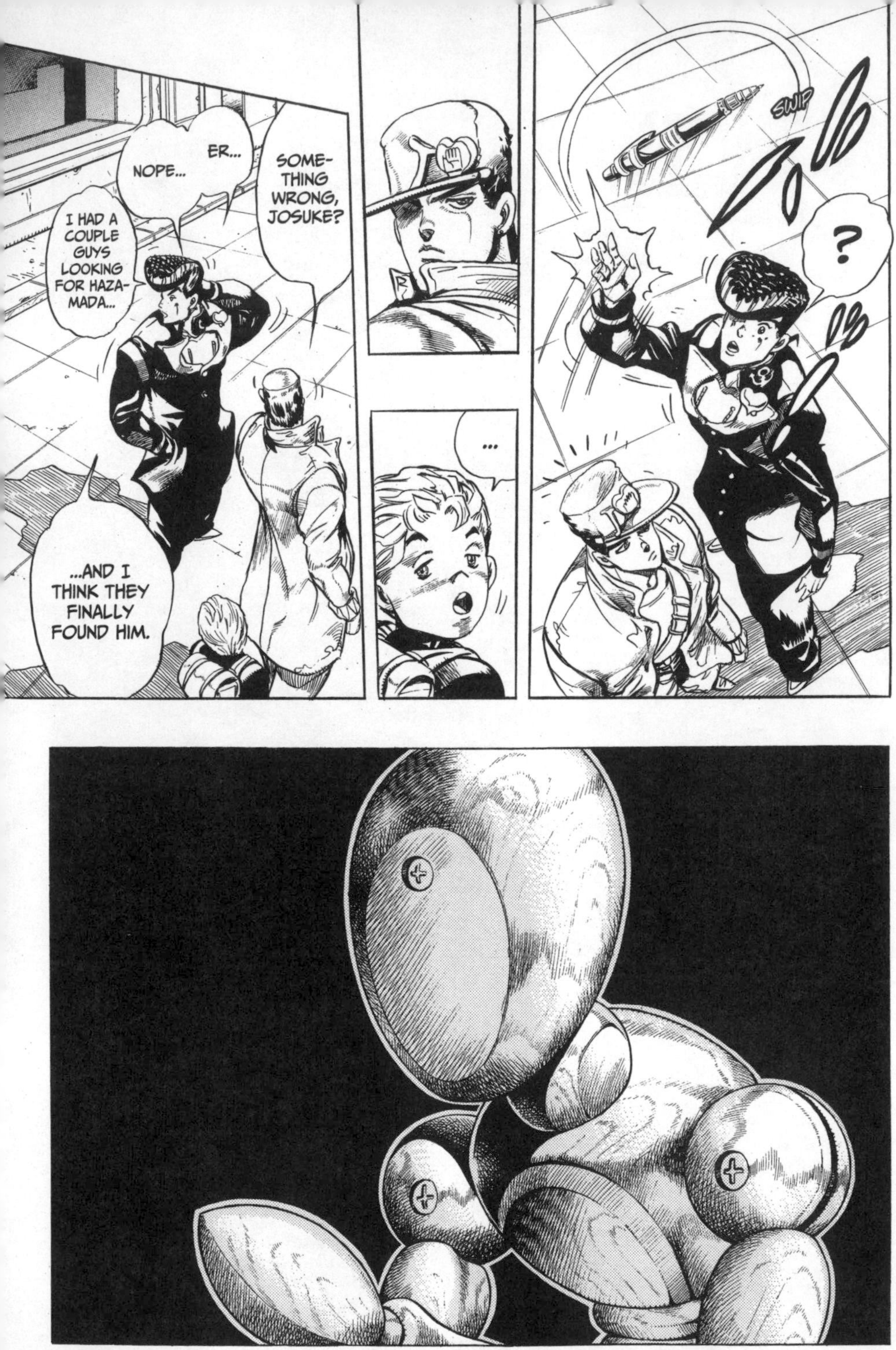
SWIP
?
SOMETHING WRONG, JOSUKE?
...
ER... NOPE...
I HAD A COUPLE GUYS LOOKING FOR HAZAMADA...
...AND I THINK THEY FINALLY FOUND HIM.

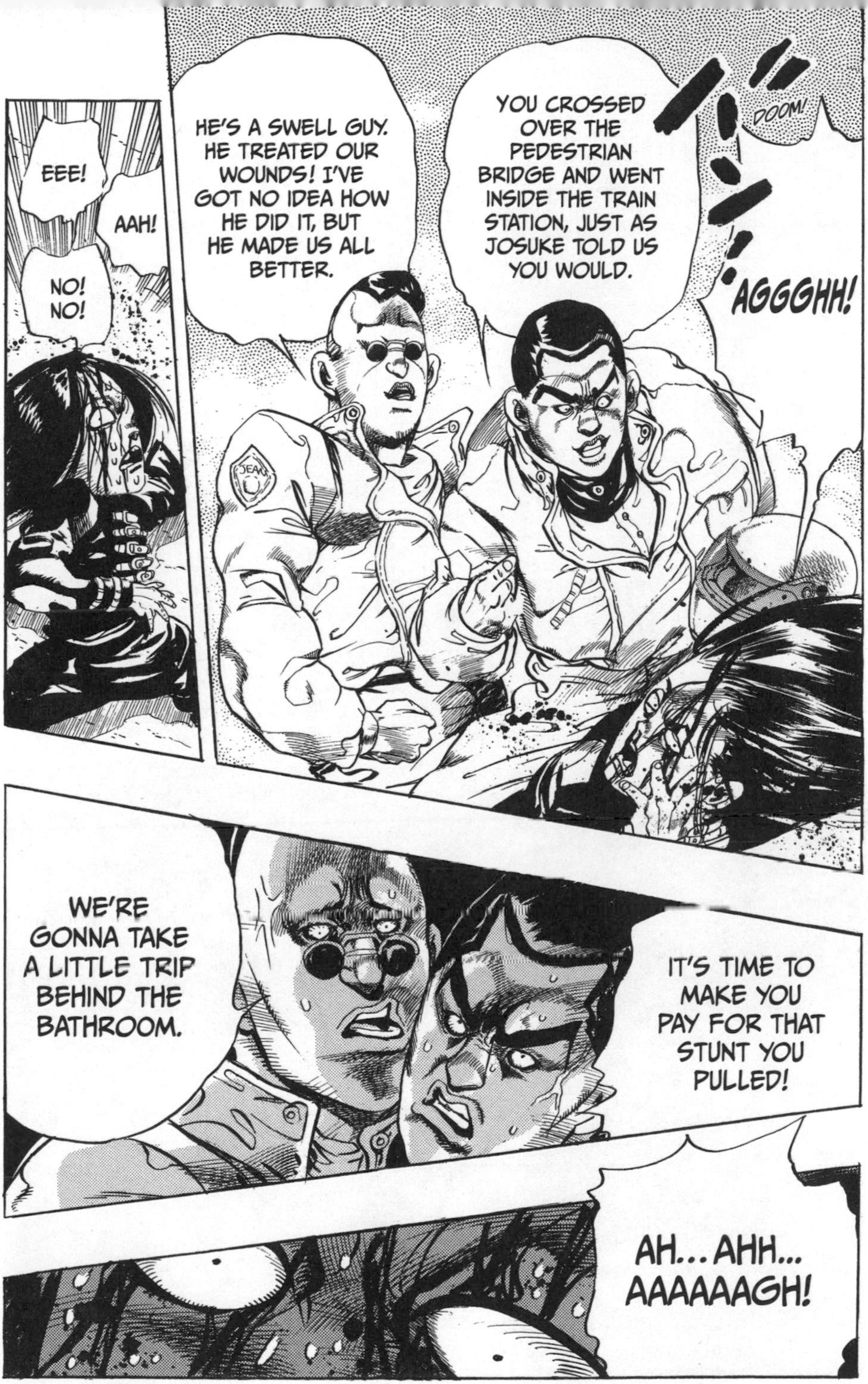
DOOM!
AGGGHH!
YOU CROSSED OVER THE PEDESTRIAN BRIDGE AND WENT INSIDE THE TRAIN STATION, JUST AS JOSUKE TOLD US YOU WOULD.
HE'S A SWELL GUY. HE TREATED OUR WOUNDS! I'VE GOT NO IDEA HOW HE DID IT, BUT HE MADE US ALL BETTER.
EEE!
AAH!
NO! NO!
IT'S TIME TO MAKE YOU PAY FOR THAT STUNT YOU PULLED!
WE'RE GONNA TAKE A LITTLE TRIP BEHIND THE BATHROOM.
AH... AHH... AAAAAAGH!

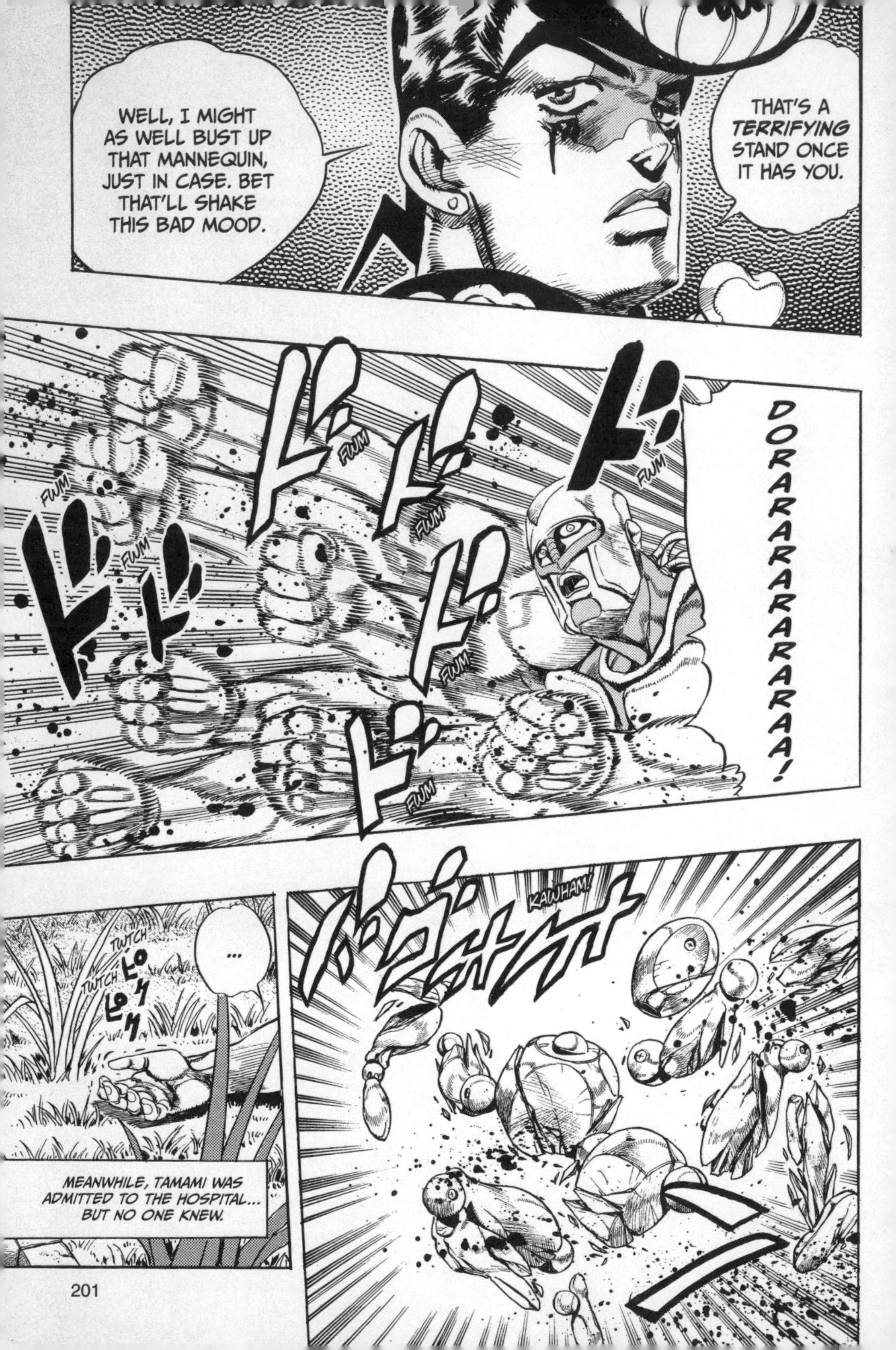
THAT'S A *TERRIFYING* STAND ONCE IT HAS YOU.
WELL, I MIGHT AS WELL BUST UP THAT MANNEQUIN, JUST IN CASE. BET THAT'LL SHAKE THIS BAD MOOD.
DORARARARARARARAA!
FWUM
FWUM
FWUM
FWUM
FWUM
FWUM
FWUM
FWUM
KAWHAM!
...
TWITCH
TWITCH
MEANWHILE, TAMAMI WAS ADMITTED TO THE HOSPITAL... BUT NO ONE KNEW.

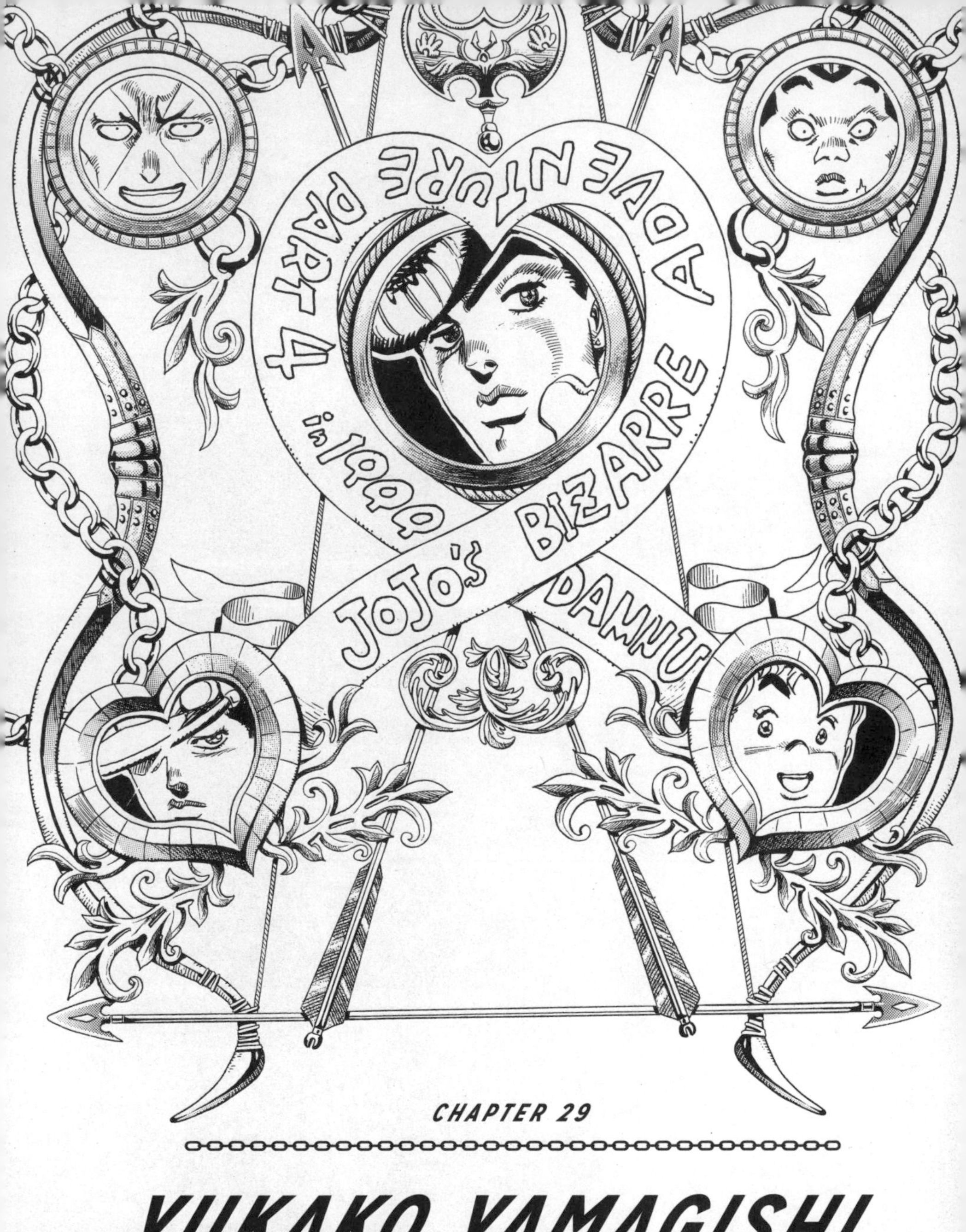
JOJO'S BIZARRE ADVENTURE
PART 4
in 1999

CHAPTER 29

YUKAKO YAMAGISHI FALLS IN LOVE, PART 1

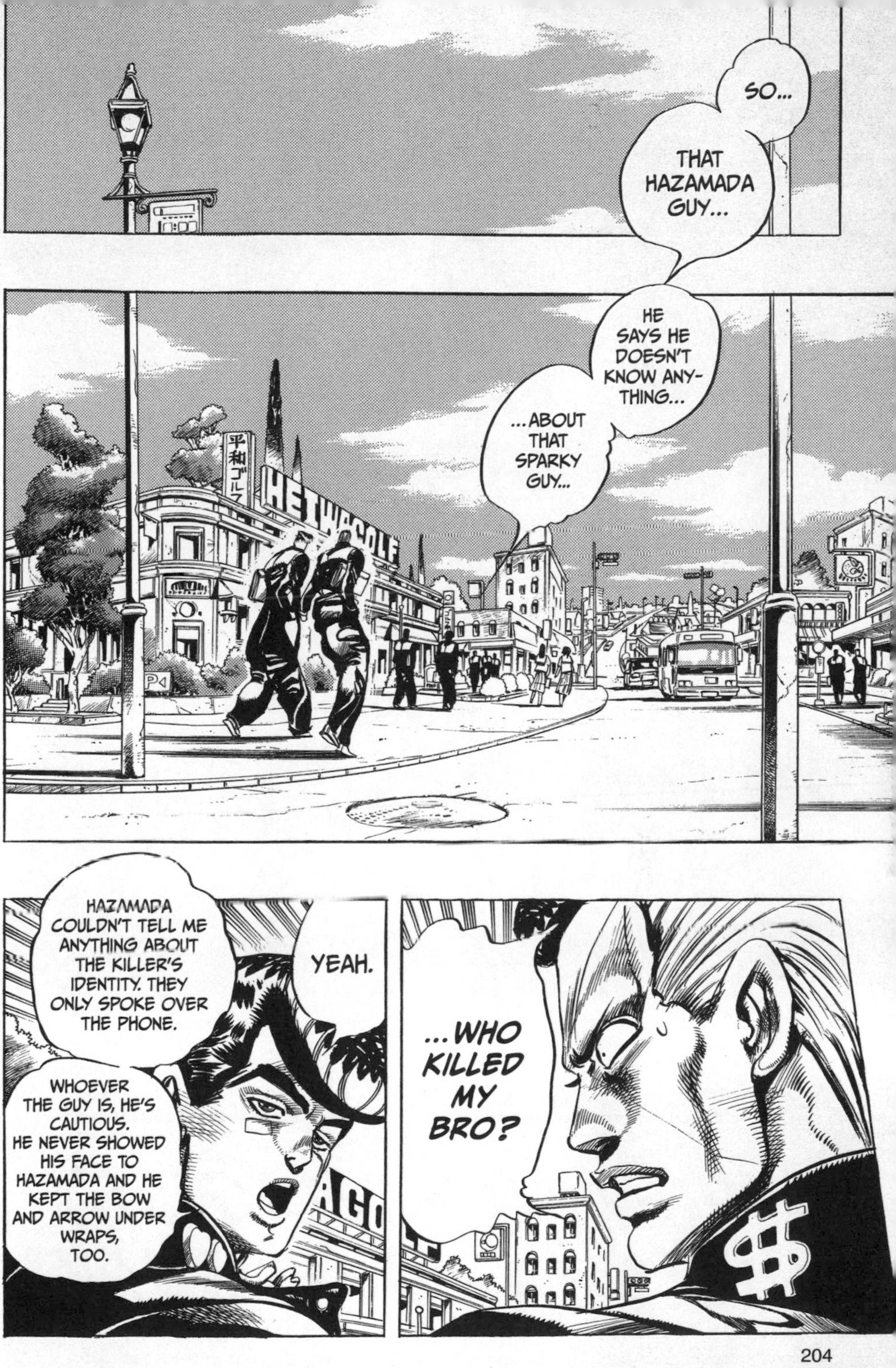

SO...
THAT HAZAMADA GUY...
HE SAYS HE DOESN'T KNOW ANY-THING...
...ABOUT THAT SPARKY GUY...
平和ゴルフ
HEIWAGOLF
...WHO KILLED MY BRO?
YEAH.
HAZAMADA COULDN'T TELL ME ANYTHING ABOUT THE KILLER'S IDENTITY. THEY ONLY SPOKE OVER THE PHONE.
WHOEVER THE GUY IS, HE'S CAUTIOUS. HE NEVER SHOWED HIS FACE TO HAZAMADA AND HE KEPT THE BOW AND ARROW UNDER WRAPS, TOO.

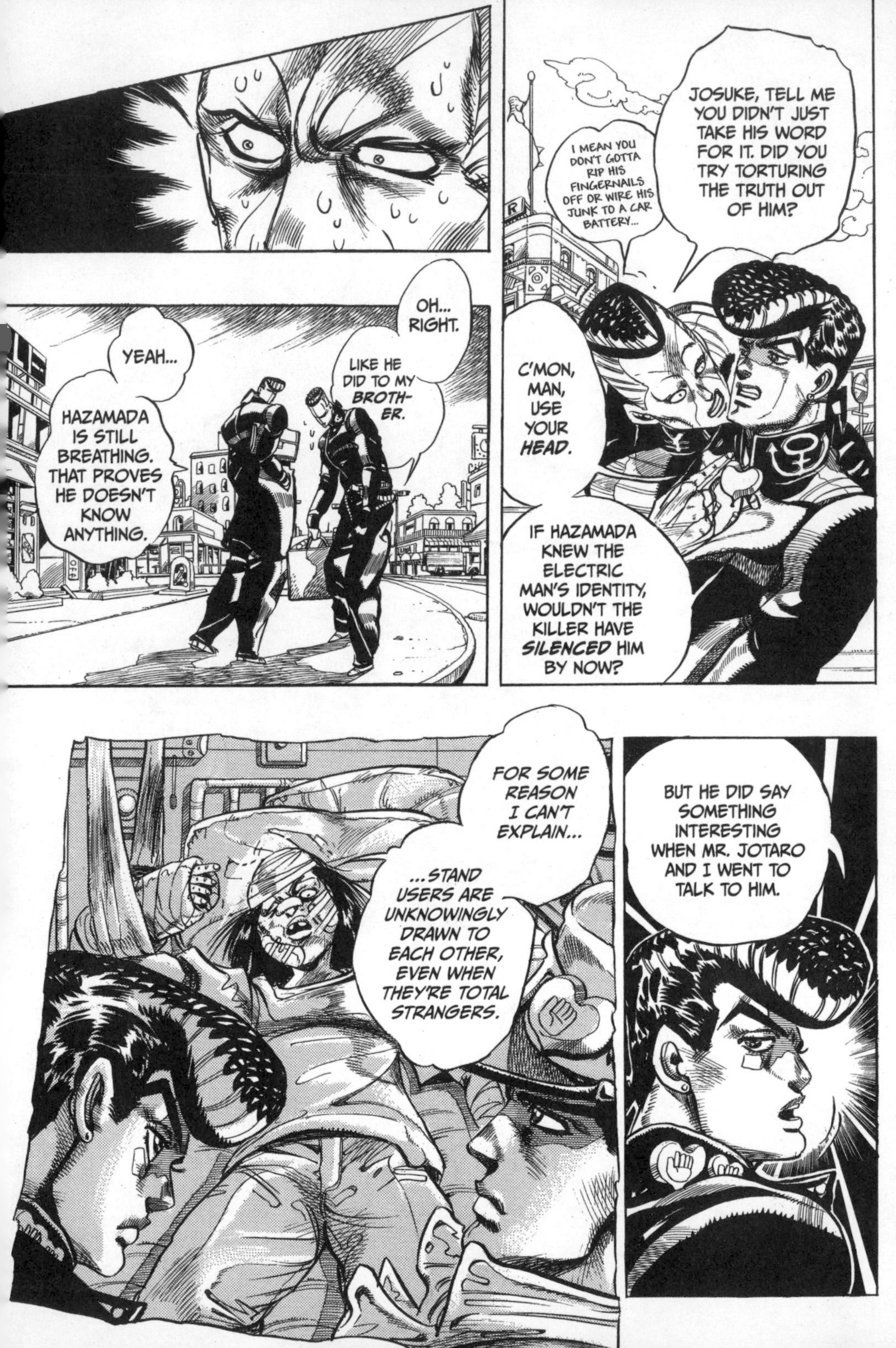
JOSUKE, TELL ME YOU DIDN'T JUST TAKE HIS WORD FOR IT. DID YOU TRY TORTURING THE TRUTH OUT OF HIM?
I MEAN YOU DON'T GOTTA RIP HIS FINGERNAILS OFF OR WIRE HIS JUNK TO A CAR BATTERY...
C'MON, MAN, USE YOUR HEAD.
IF HAZAMADA KNEW THE ELECTRIC MAN'S IDENTITY, WOULDN'T THE KILLER HAVE SILENCED HIM BY NOW?
OH... RIGHT.
LIKE HE DID TO MY BROTHER.
YEAH...
HAZAMADA IS STILL BREATHING. THAT PROVES HE DOESN'T KNOW ANYTHING.
BUT HE DID SAY SOMETHING INTERESTING WHEN MR. JOTARO AND I WENT TO TALK TO HIM.
FOR SOME REASON I CAN'T EXPLAIN...
...STAND USERS ARE UNKNOWINGLY DRAWN TO EACH OTHER, EVEN WHEN THEY'RE TOTAL STRANGERS.

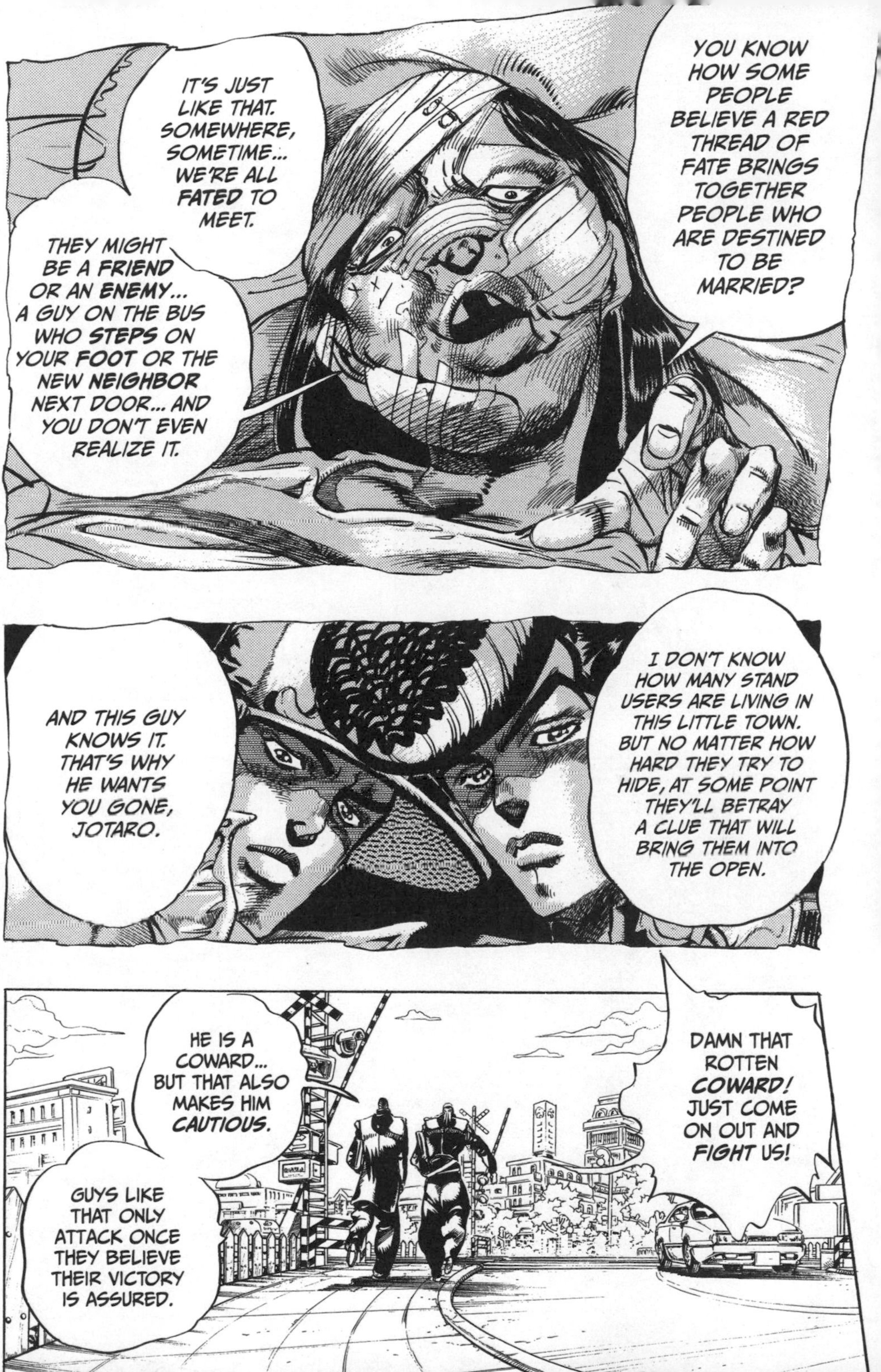
YOU KNOW HOW SOME PEOPLE BELIEVE A RED THREAD OF FATE BRINGS TOGETHER PEOPLE WHO ARE DESTINED TO BE MARRIED?
IT'S JUST LIKE THAT. SOMEWHERE, SOMETIME... WE'RE ALL FATED TO MEET.
THEY MIGHT BE A FRIEND OR AN ENEMY... A GUY ON THE BUS WHO STEPS ON YOUR FOOT OR THE NEW NEIGHBOR NEXT DOOR... AND YOU DON'T EVEN REALIZE IT.
I DON'T KNOW HOW MANY STAND USERS ARE LIVING IN THIS LITTLE TOWN. BUT NO MATTER HOW HARD THEY TRY TO HIDE, AT SOME POINT THEY'LL BETRAY A CLUE THAT WILL BRING THEM INTO THE OPEN.
AND THIS GUY KNOWS IT. THAT'S WHY HE WANTS YOU GONE, JOTARO.
DAMN THAT ROTTEN COWARD! JUST COME ON OUT AND FIGHT US!
HE IS A COWARD... BUT THAT ALSO MAKES HIM CAUTIOUS.
GUYS LIKE THAT ONLY ATTACK ONCE THEY BELIEVE THEIR VICTORY IS ASSURED.

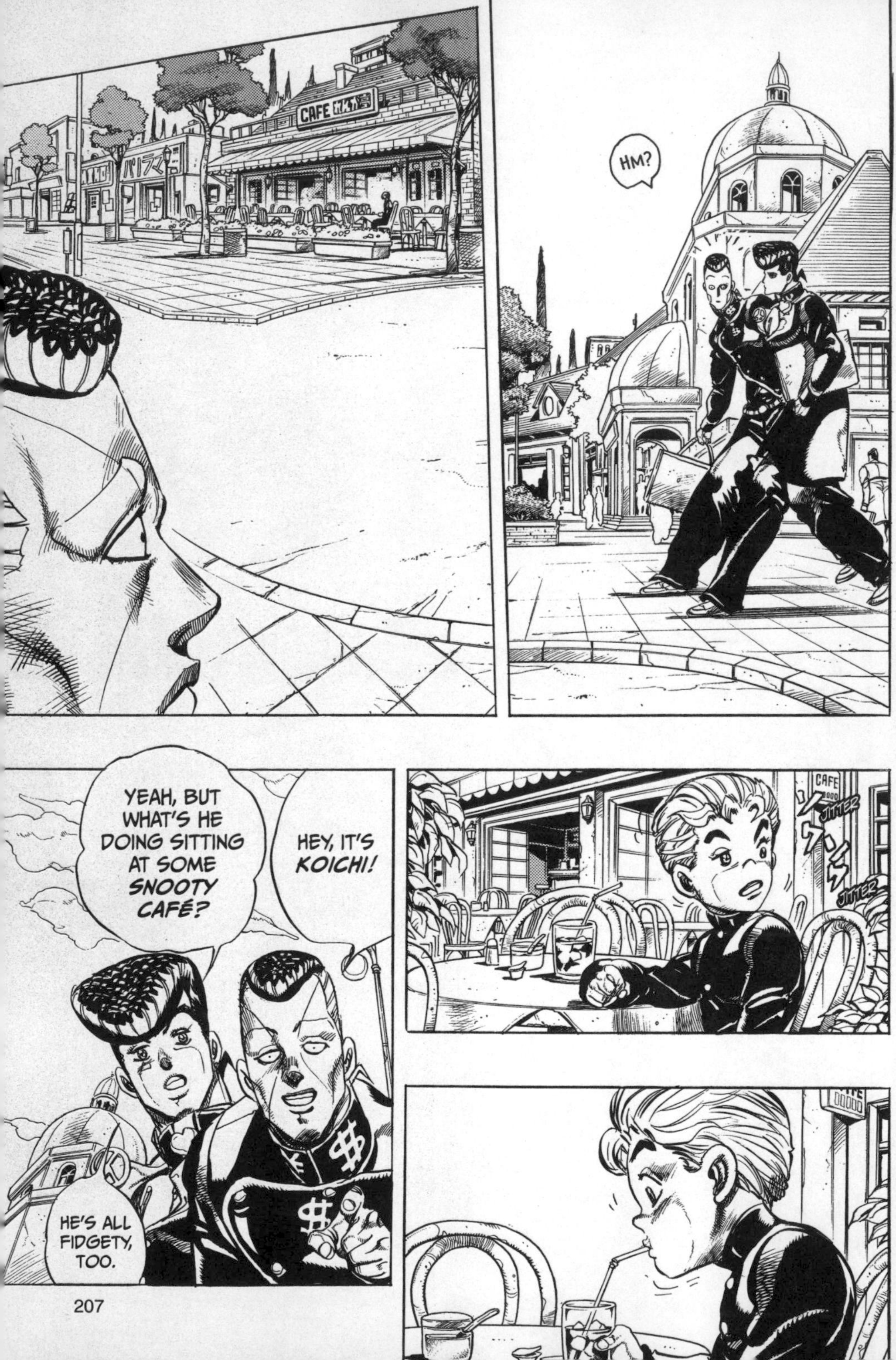
HM?
CAFE
JITTER
JITTER
HEY, IT'S *KOICHI!*
YEAH, BUT WHAT'S HE DOING SITTING AT SOME *SNOOTY CAFÉ?*
HE'S ALL FIDGETY, TOO.

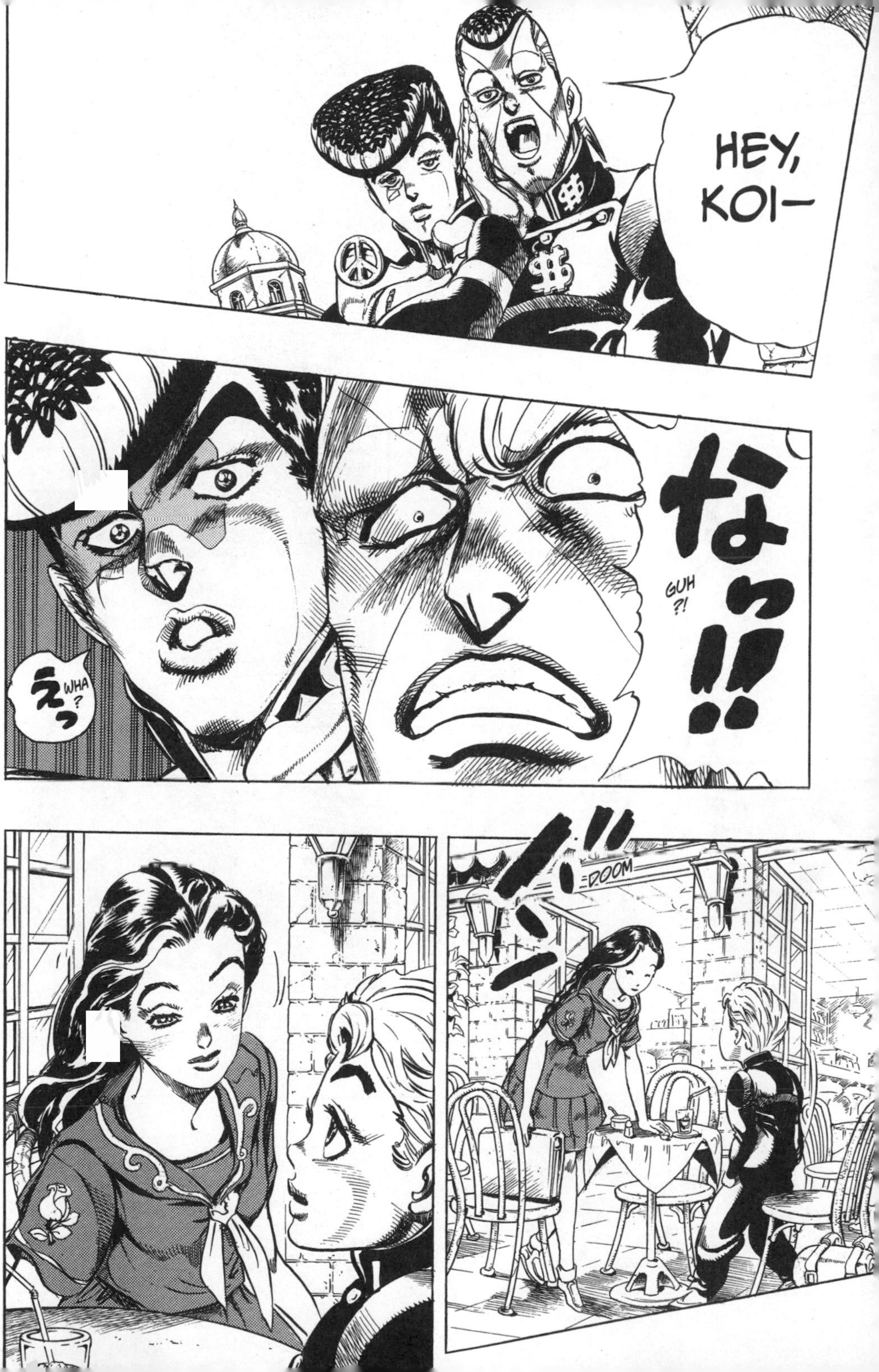

HEY, KOI—
なっ!!
GUH ?!
えっ
WHA ?
DOOM

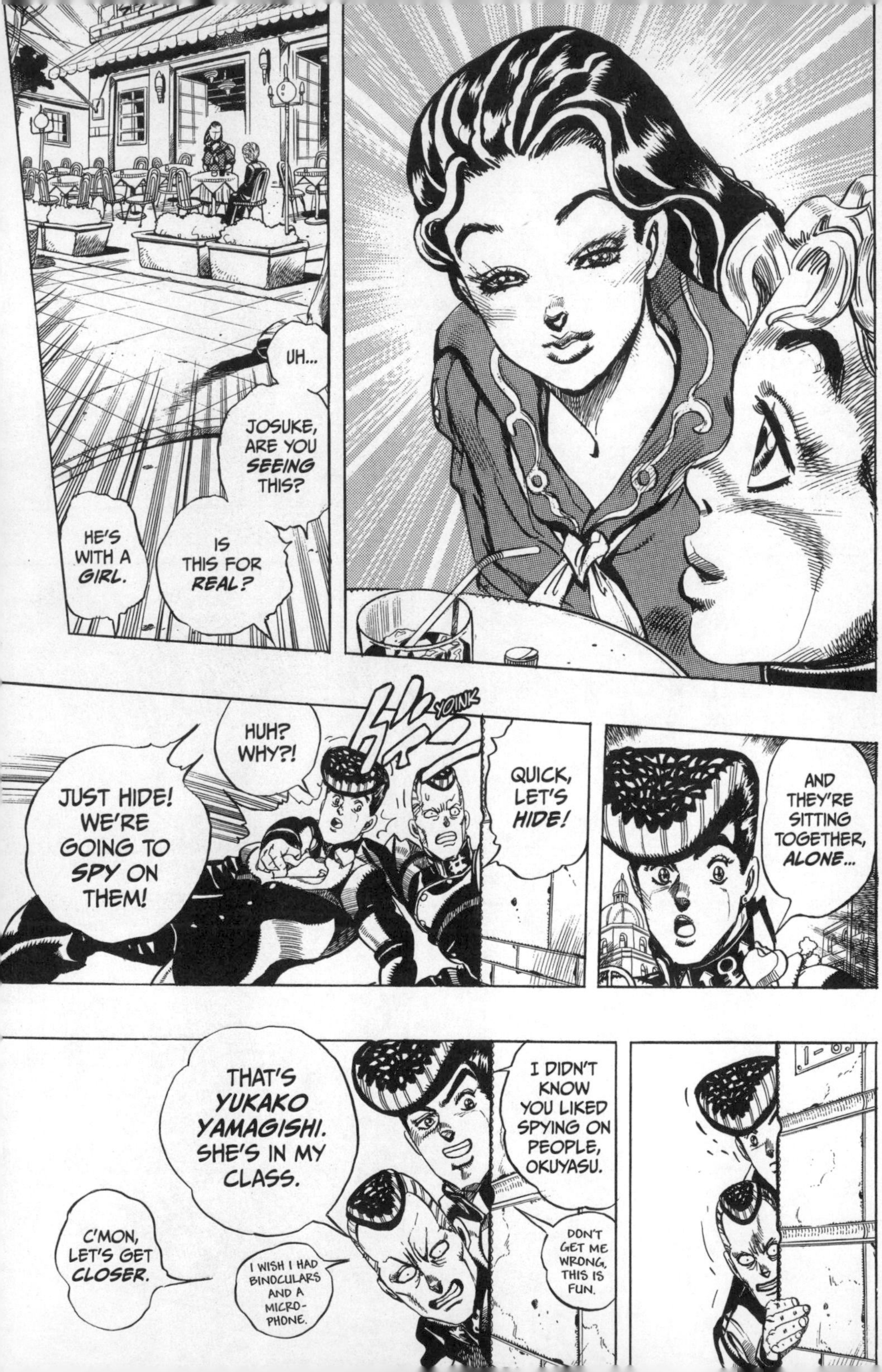
UH...
JOSUKE, ARE YOU SEEING THIS?
IS THIS FOR REAL?
HE'S WITH A GIRL.
AND THEY'RE SITTING TOGETHER, ALONE...
QUICK, LET'S HIDE!
YOINK
HUH? WHY?!
JUST HIDE! WE'RE GOING TO SPY ON THEM!
I DIDN'T KNOW YOU LIKED SPYING ON PEOPLE, OKUYASU.
THAT'S YUKAKO YAMAGISHI. SHE'S IN MY CLASS.
DON'T GET ME WRONG, THIS IS FUN.
I WISH I HAD BINOCULARS AND A MICRO-PHONE.
C'MON, LET'S GET CLOSER.

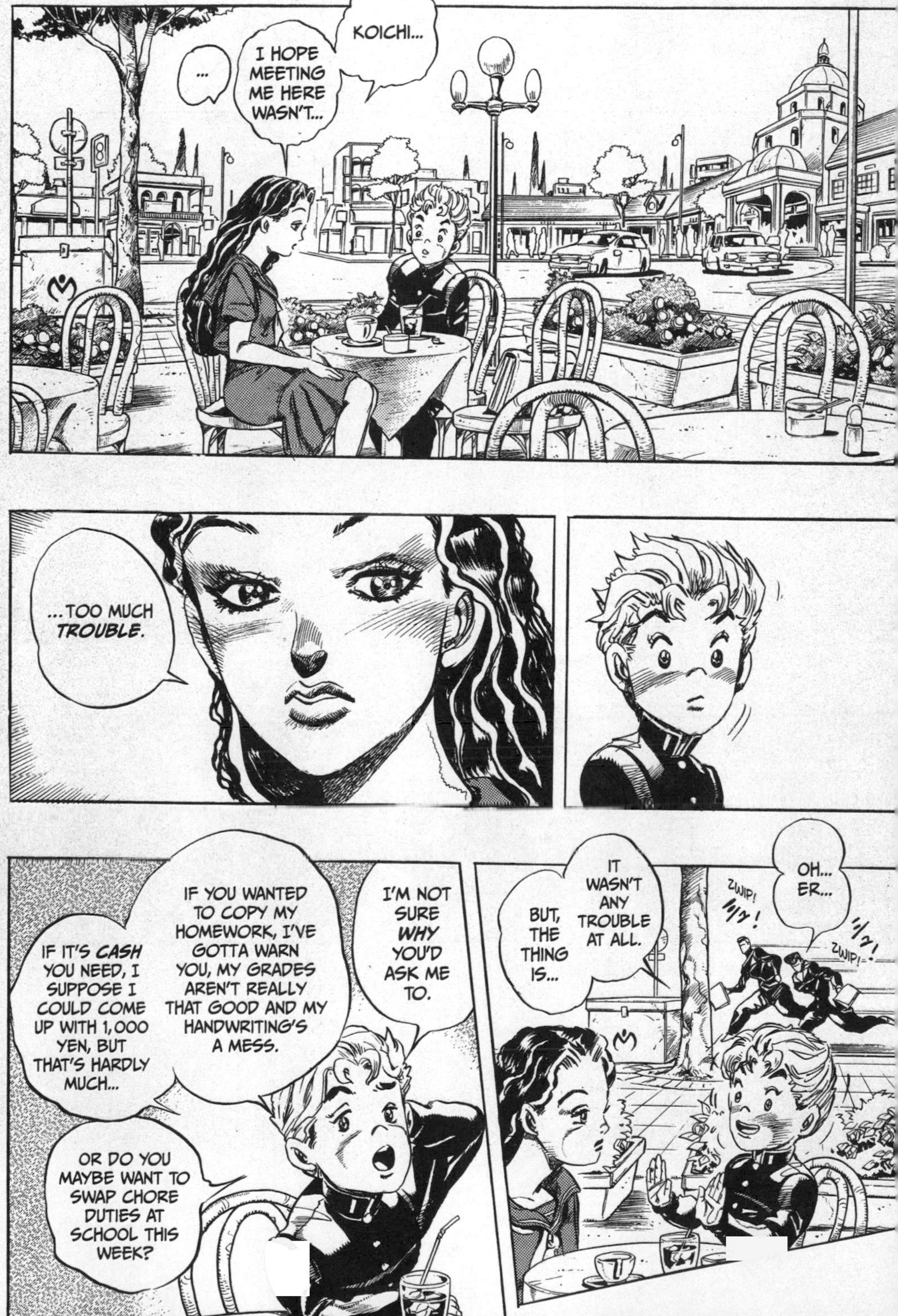
KOICHI...
I HOPE MEETING ME HERE WASN'T...
...
...TOO MUCH TROUBLE.
OH... ER...
ZWIP!
ZWIP!
IT WASN'T ANY TROUBLE AT ALL.
BUT, THE THING IS...
I'M NOT SURE WHY YOU'D ASK ME TO.
IF YOU WANTED TO COPY MY HOMEWORK, I'VE GOTTA WARN YOU, MY GRADES AREN'T REALLY THAT GOOD AND MY HANDWRITING'S A MESS.
IF IT'S CASH YOU NEED, I SUPPOSE I COULD COME UP WITH 1,000 YEN, BUT THAT'S HARDLY MUCH...
OR DO YOU MAYBE WANT TO SWAP CHORE DUTIES AT SCHOOL THIS WEEK?

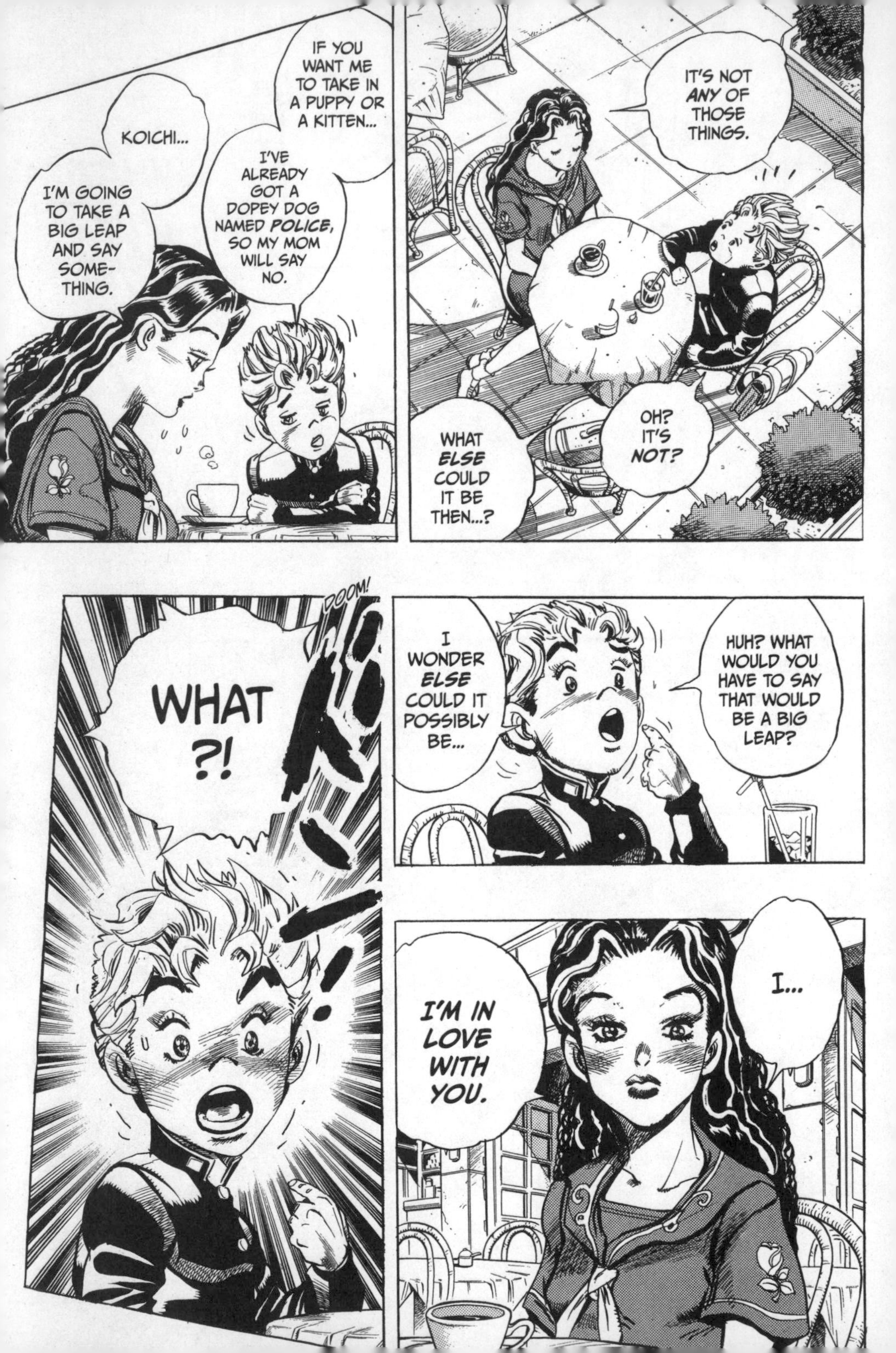
KOICHI...
I'M GOING TO TAKE A BIG LEAP AND SAY SOMETHING.
IF YOU WANT ME TO TAKE IN A PUPPY OR A KITTEN...
I'VE ALREADY GOT A DOPEY DOG NAMED POLICE, SO MY MOM WILL SAY NO.
IT'S NOT ANY OF THOSE THINGS.
OH? IT'S NOT?
WHAT ELSE COULD IT BE THEN...?
I WONDER ELSE COULD IT POSSIBLY BE...
HUH? WHAT WOULD YOU HAVE TO SAY THAT WOULD BE A BIG LEAP?
I...
I'M IN LOVE WITH YOU.
DOOM!
WHAT ?!

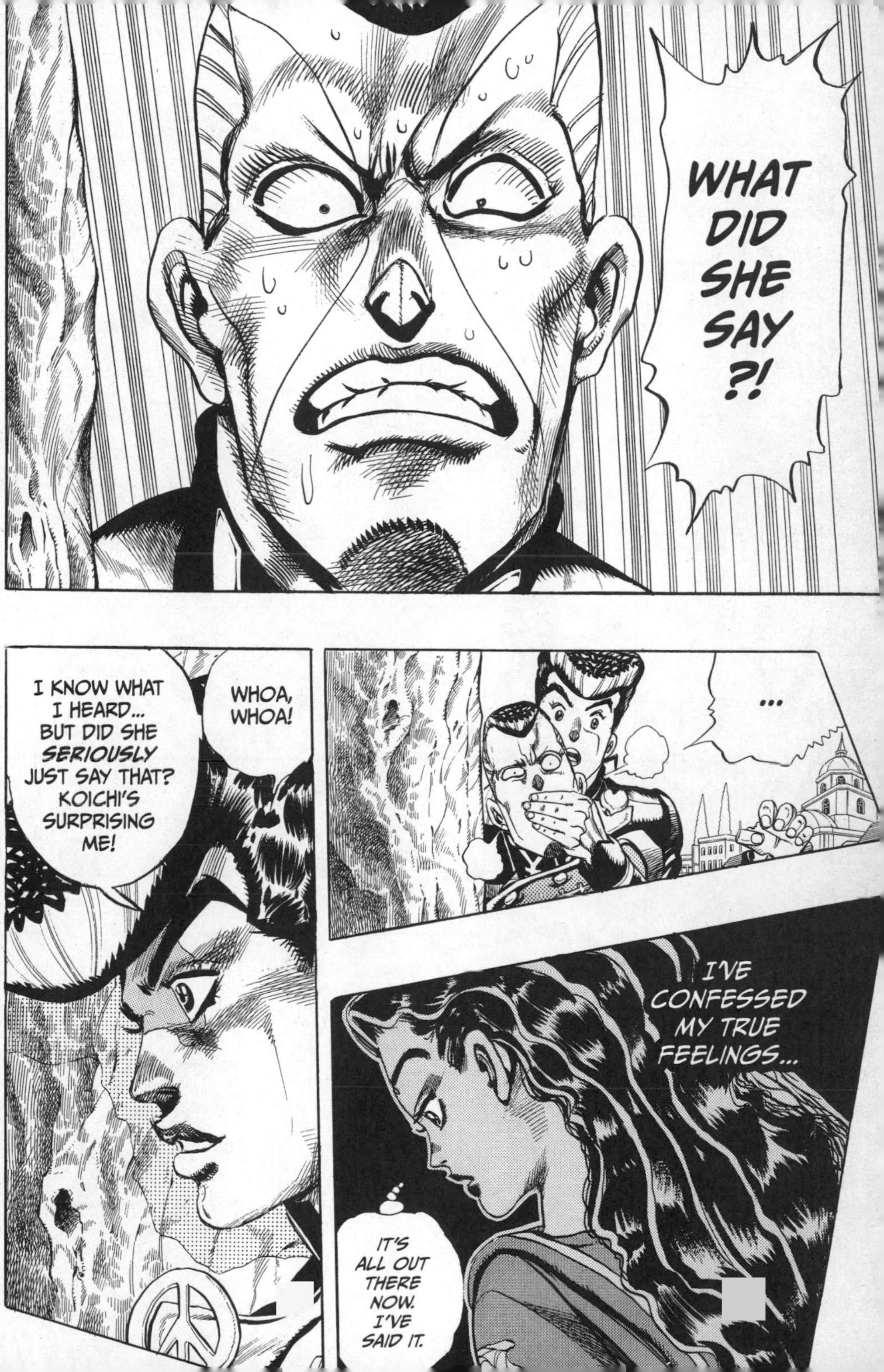
WHAT DID SHE SAY ?!
...
I'VE CONFESSED MY TRUE FEELINGS...
IT'S ALL OUT THERE NOW. I'VE SAID IT.
WHOA, WHOA!
I KNOW WHAT I HEARD... BUT DID SHE SERIOUSLY JUST SAY THAT? KOICHI'S SURPRISING ME!

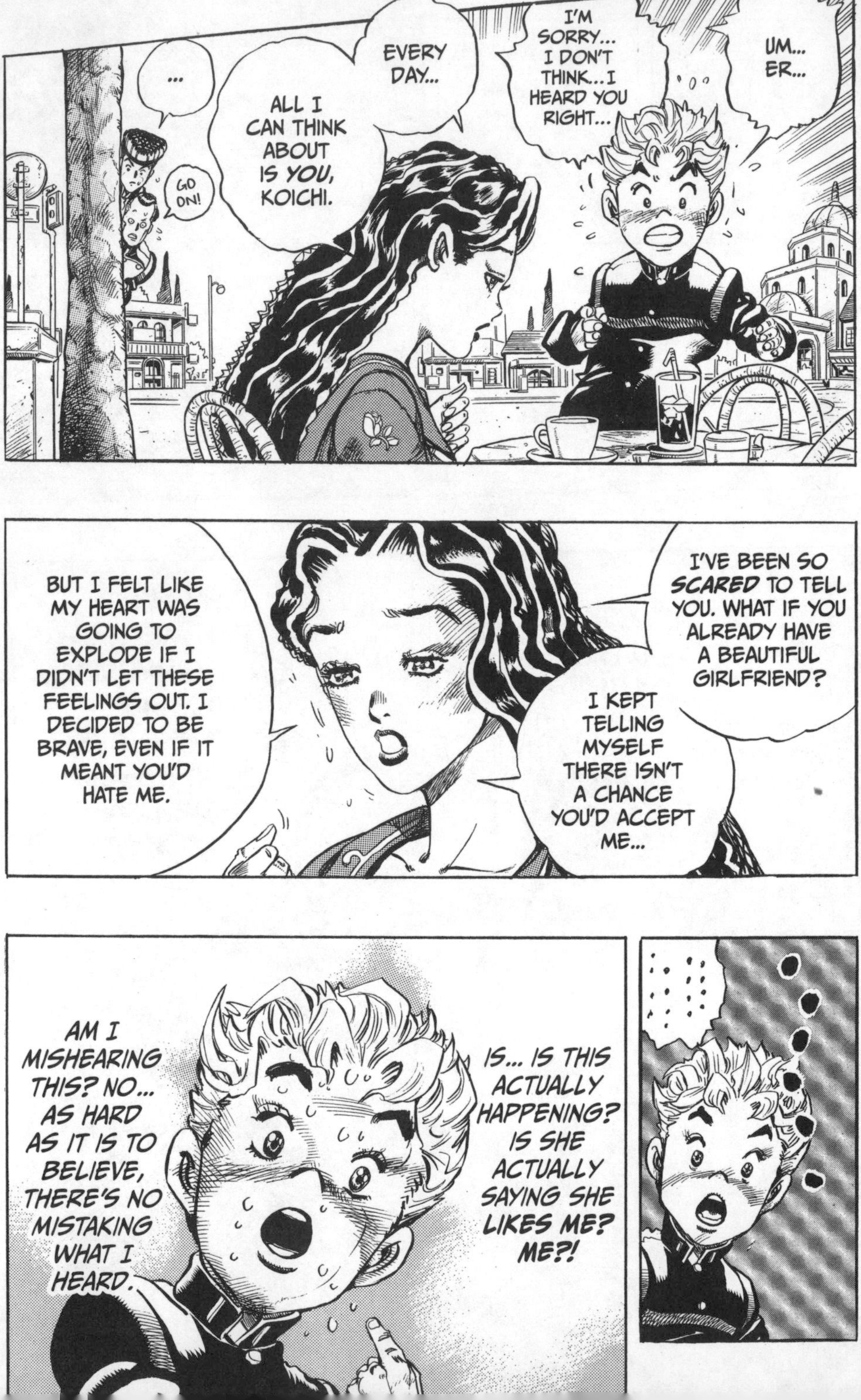
UM... ER...
I'M SORRY... I DON'T THINK...I HEARD YOU RIGHT...
EVERY DAY...
ALL I CAN THINK ABOUT IS *YOU*, KOICHI.
GO ON!
...
I'VE BEEN SO *SCARED* TO TELL YOU. WHAT IF YOU ALREADY HAVE A BEAUTIFUL GIRLFRIEND?
I KEPT TELLING MYSELF THERE ISN'T A CHANCE YOU'D ACCEPT ME...
BUT I FELT LIKE MY HEART WAS GOING TO EXPLODE IF I DIDN'T LET THESE FEELINGS OUT. I DECIDED TO BE BRAVE, EVEN IF IT MEANT YOU'D HATE ME.
IS... IS THIS ACTUALLY HAPPENING? IS SHE ACTUALLY SAYING SHE LIKES ME? ME?!
AM I MISHEARING THIS? NO... AS HARD AS IT IS TO BELIEVE, THERE'S NO MISTAKING WHAT I HEARD.

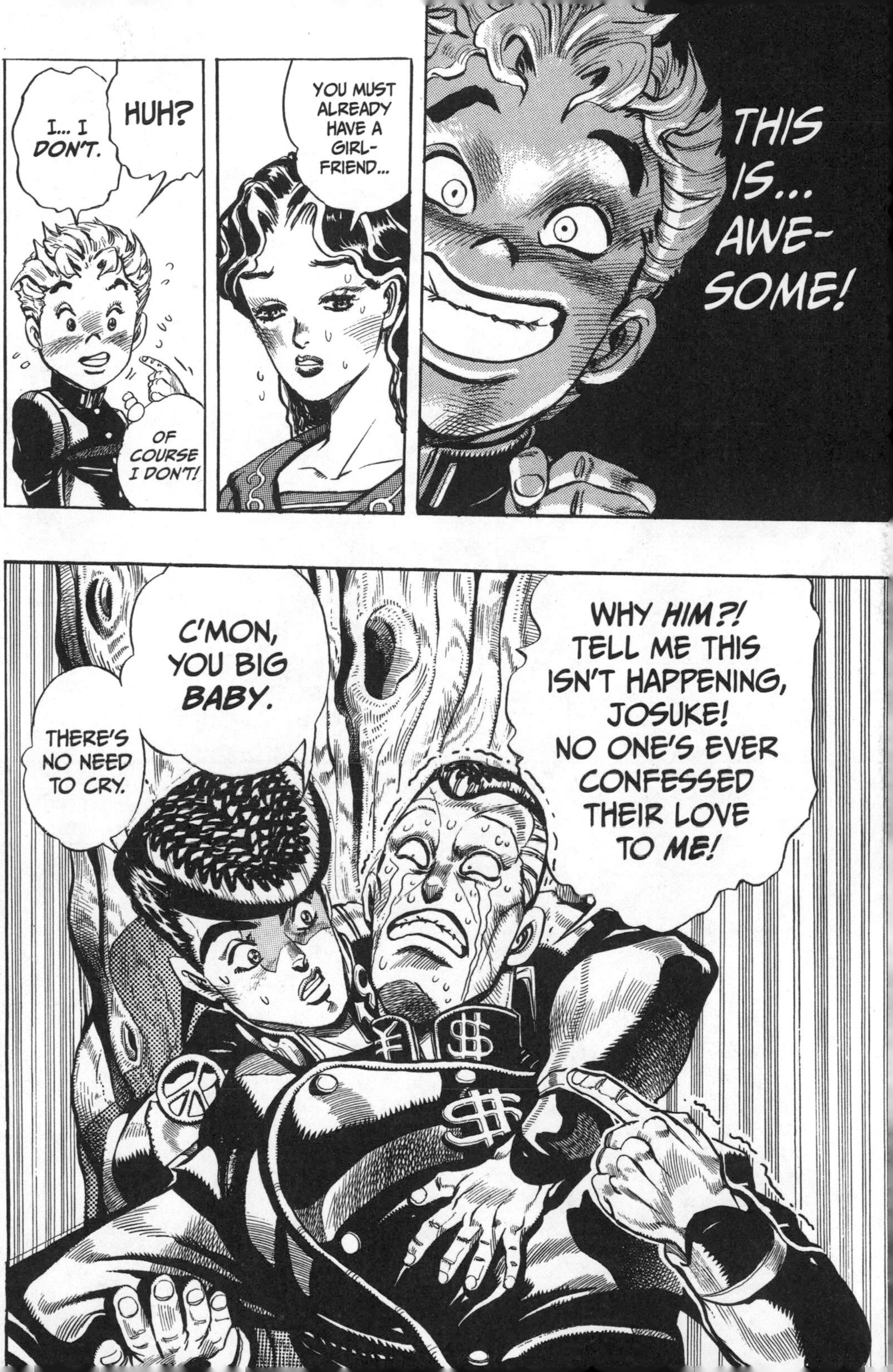
THIS IS... AWESOME!
YOU MUST ALREADY HAVE A GIRL-FRIEND...
HUH?
I... I DON'T.
OF COURSE I DON'T!
WHY HIM?! TELL ME THIS ISN'T HAPPENING, JOSUKE! NO ONE'S EVER CONFESSED THEIR LOVE TO ME!
C'MON, YOU BIG BABY.
THERE'S NO NEED TO CRY.

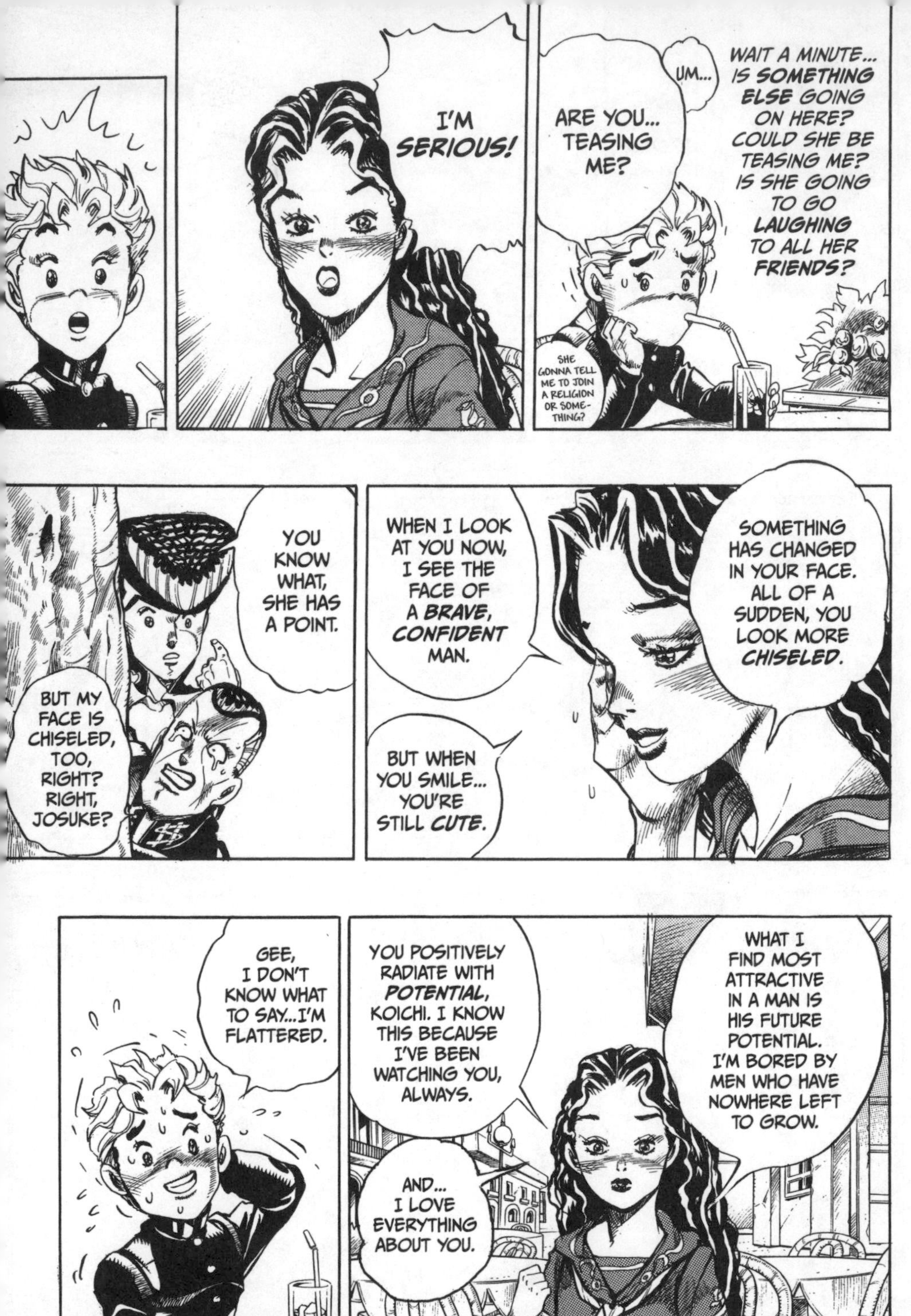
UM...
ARE YOU... TEASING ME?
WAIT A MINUTE... IS SOMETHING ELSE GOING ON HERE? COULD SHE BE TEASING ME? IS SHE GOING TO GO LAUGHING TO ALL HER FRIENDS?
SHE GONNA TELL ME TO JOIN A RELIGION OR SOMETHING?
I'M SERIOUS!
SOMETHING HAS CHANGED IN YOUR FACE. ALL OF A SUDDEN, YOU LOOK MORE CHISELED.
WHEN I LOOK AT YOU NOW, I SEE THE FACE OF A BRAVE, CONFIDENT MAN.
BUT WHEN YOU SMILE... YOU'RE STILL CUTE.
YOU KNOW WHAT, SHE HAS A POINT.
BUT MY FACE IS CHISELED, TOO, RIGHT? RIGHT, JOSUKE?
WHAT I FIND MOST ATTRACTIVE IN A MAN IS HIS FUTURE POTENTIAL. I'M BORED BY MEN WHO HAVE NOWHERE LEFT TO GROW.
YOU POSITIVELY RADIATE WITH POTENTIAL, KOICHI. I KNOW THIS BECAUSE I'VE BEEN WATCHING YOU, ALWAYS.
AND... I LOVE EVERYTHING ABOUT YOU.
GEE, I DON'T KNOW WHAT TO SAY...I'M FLATTERED.

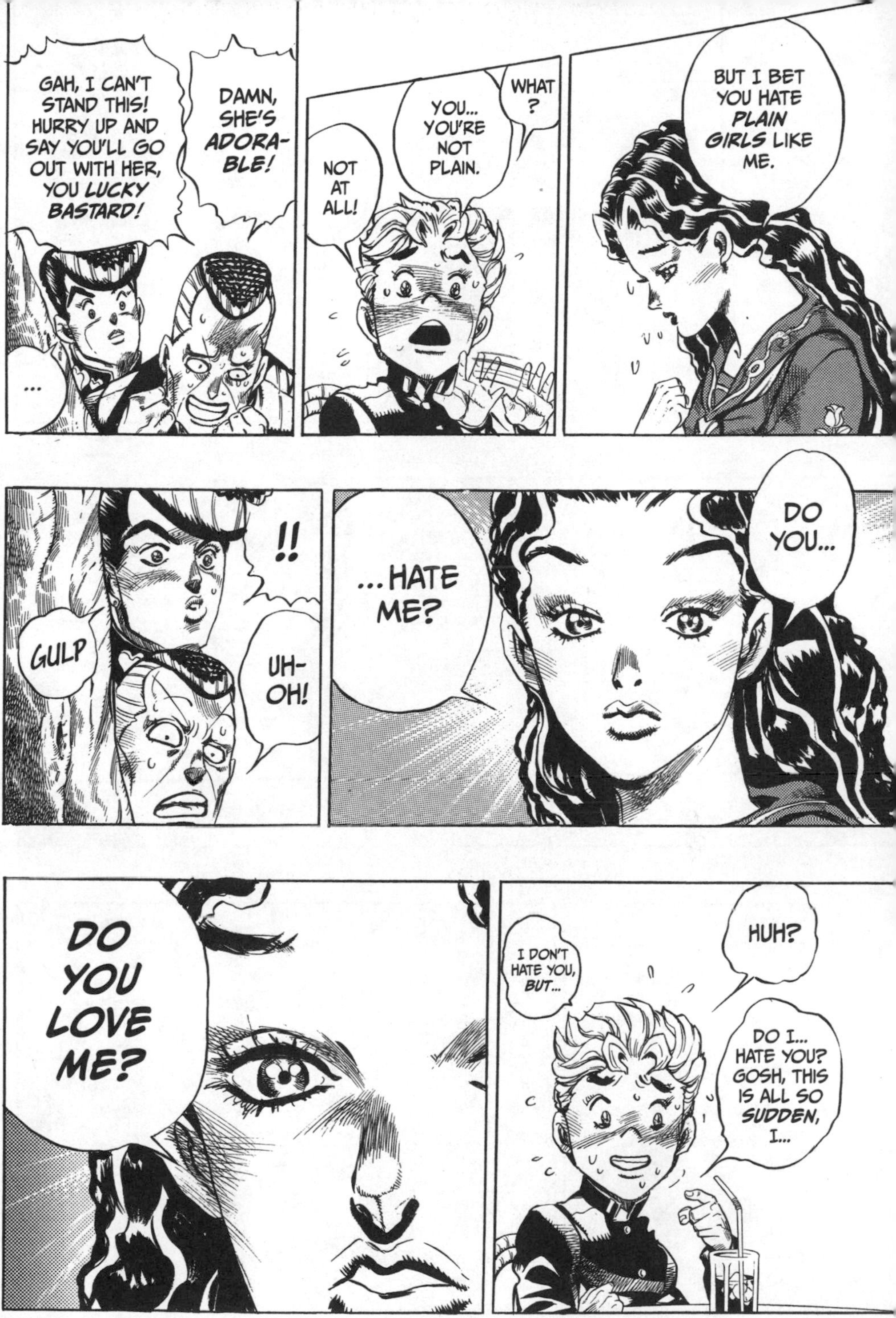
BUT I BET YOU HATE PLAIN GIRLS LIKE ME.
WHAT?
YOU... YOU'RE NOT PLAIN.
NOT AT ALL!
DAMN, SHE'S ADORABLE!
GAH, I CAN'T STAND THIS! HURRY UP AND SAY YOU'LL GO OUT WITH HER, YOU LUCKY BASTARD!
...
DO YOU...
...HATE ME?
!!
UH-OH!
GULP
HUH?
DO I... HATE YOU? GOSH, THIS IS ALL SO SUDDEN, I...
I DON'T HATE YOU, BUT...
DO YOU LOVE ME?

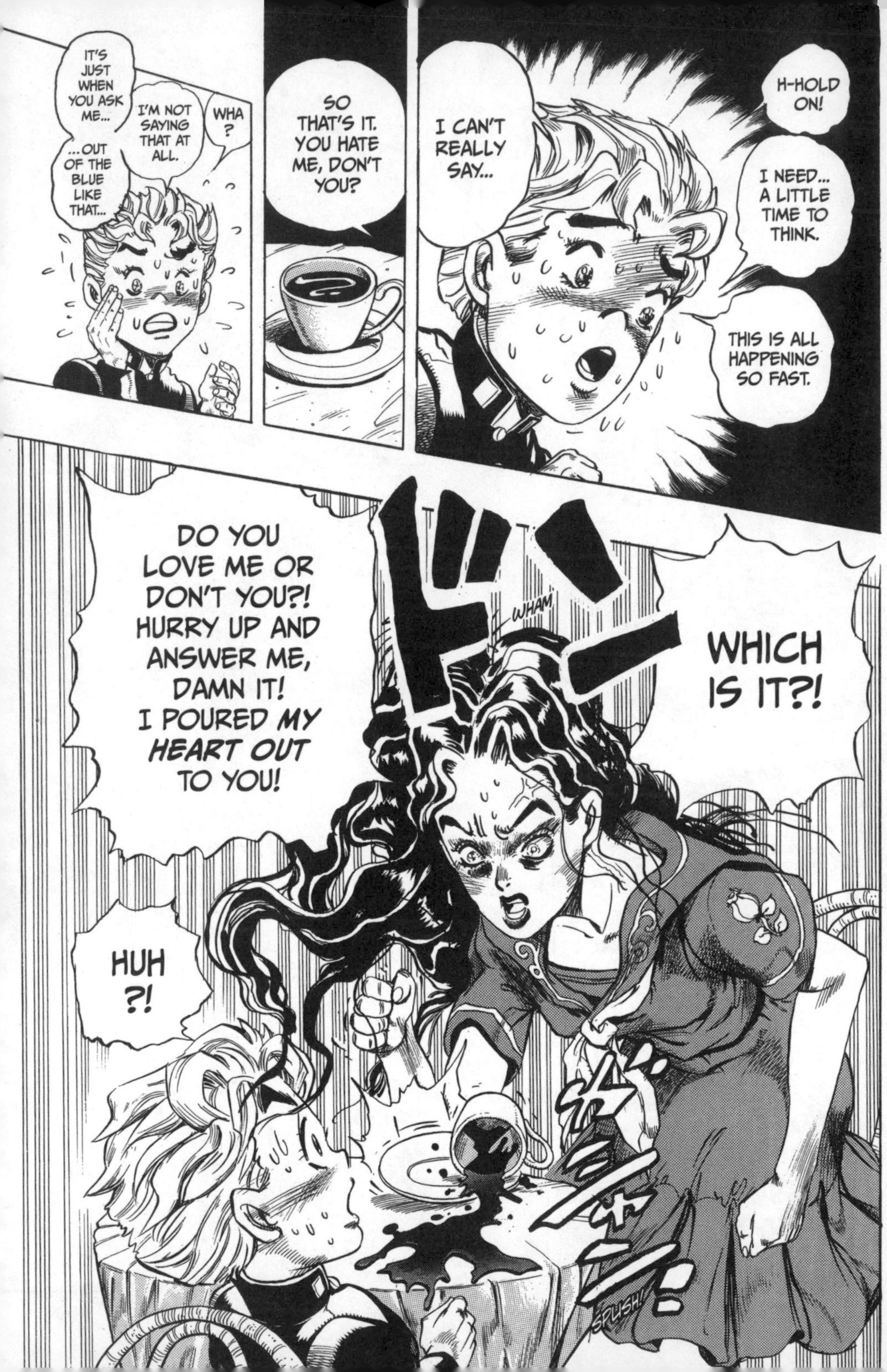
H-HOLD ON!
I NEED... A LITTLE TIME TO THINK.
THIS IS ALL HAPPENING SO FAST.
I CAN'T REALLY SAY...
SO THAT'S IT. YOU HATE ME, DON'T YOU?
WHA?
I'M NOT SAYING THAT AT ALL.
IT'S JUST WHEN YOU ASK ME...
...OUT OF THE BLUE LIKE THAT...
WHICH IS IT?!
WHAM
DO YOU LOVE ME OR DON'T YOU?! HURRY UP AND ANSWER ME, DAMN IT! I POURED *MY HEART OUT* TO YOU!
HUH?!
SPLISH!

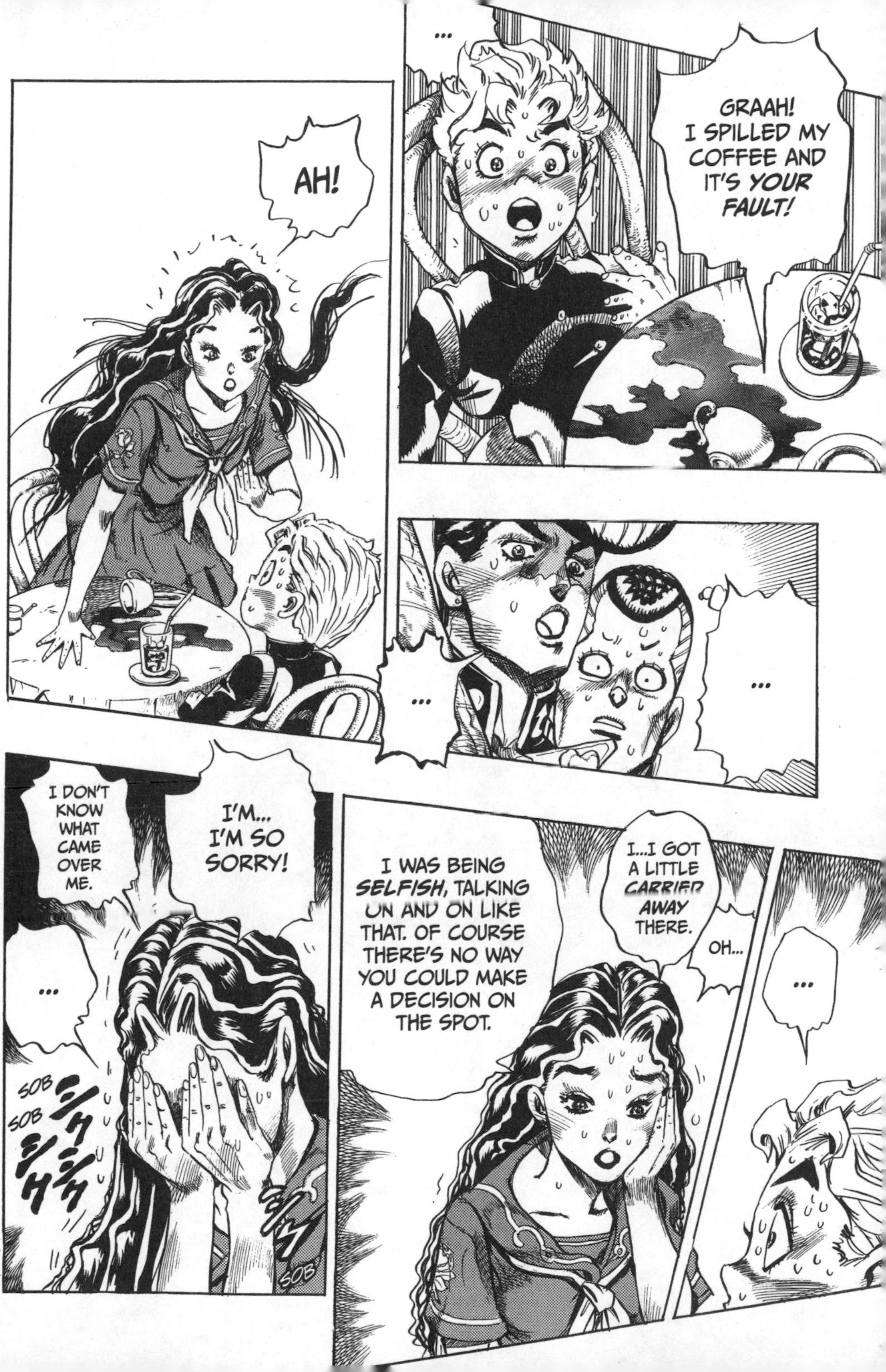

...
GRAAH! I SPILLED MY COFFEE AND IT'S *YOUR FAULT!*
...
...
AH!
...
I...I GOT A LITTLE *CARRIED AWAY* THERE.
OH...
I WAS BEING *SELFISH*, TALKING ON AND ON LIKE THAT. OF COURSE THERE'S NO WAY YOU COULD MAKE A DECISION ON THE SPOT.
I'M... I'M SO SORRY!
I DON'T KNOW WHAT CAME OVER ME.
...
SOB SOB
SOB

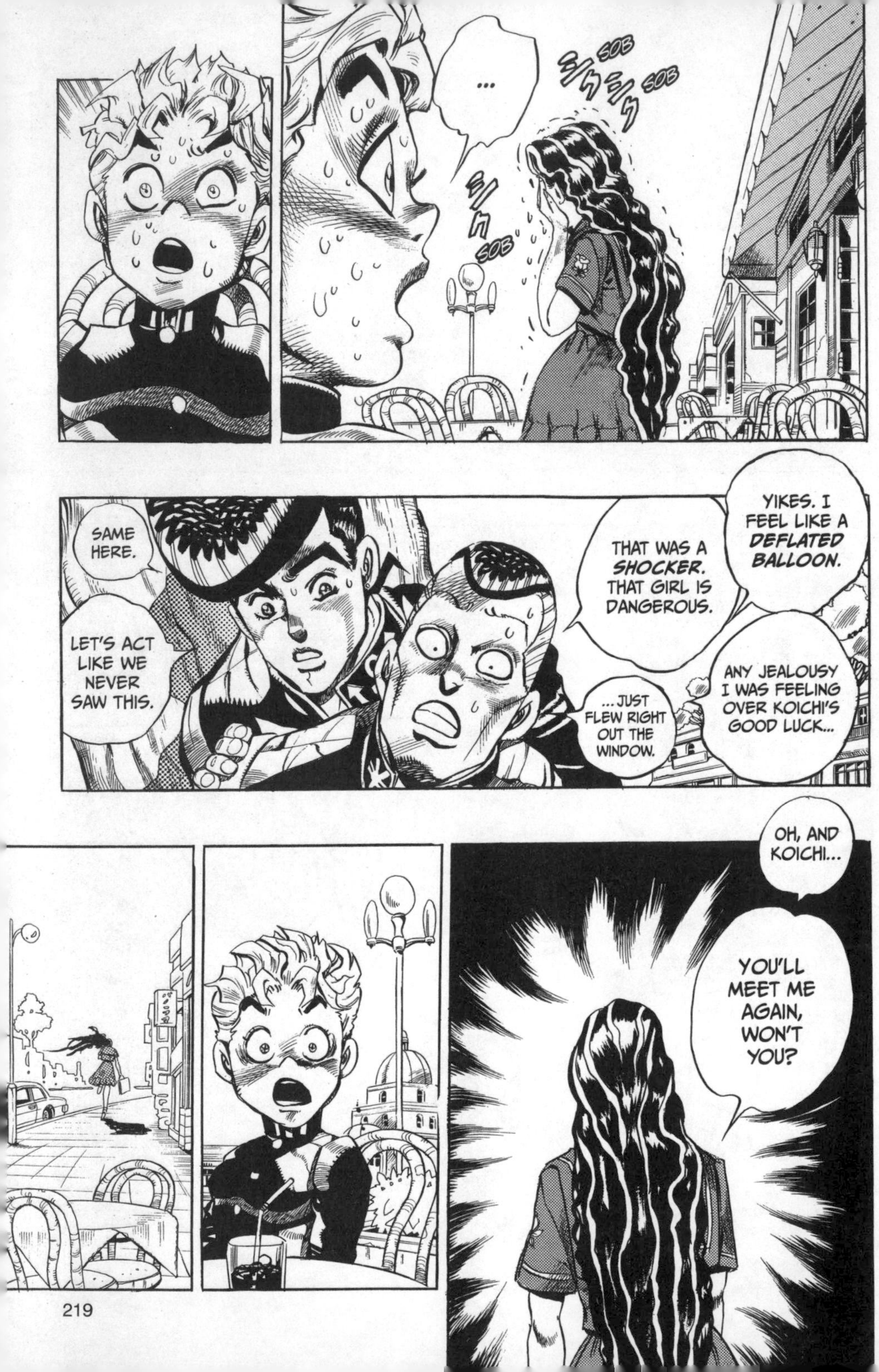
SOB
SOB
...
SOB
YIKES. I FEEL LIKE A *DEFLATED BALLOON.*
THAT WAS A *SHOCKER.* THAT GIRL IS DANGEROUS.
ANY JEALOUSY I WAS FEELING OVER KOICHI'S GOOD LUCK...
...JUST FLEW RIGHT OUT THE WINDOW.
SAME HERE.
LET'S ACT LIKE WE NEVER SAW THIS.
OH, AND KOICHI...
YOU'LL MEET ME AGAIN, WON'T YOU?

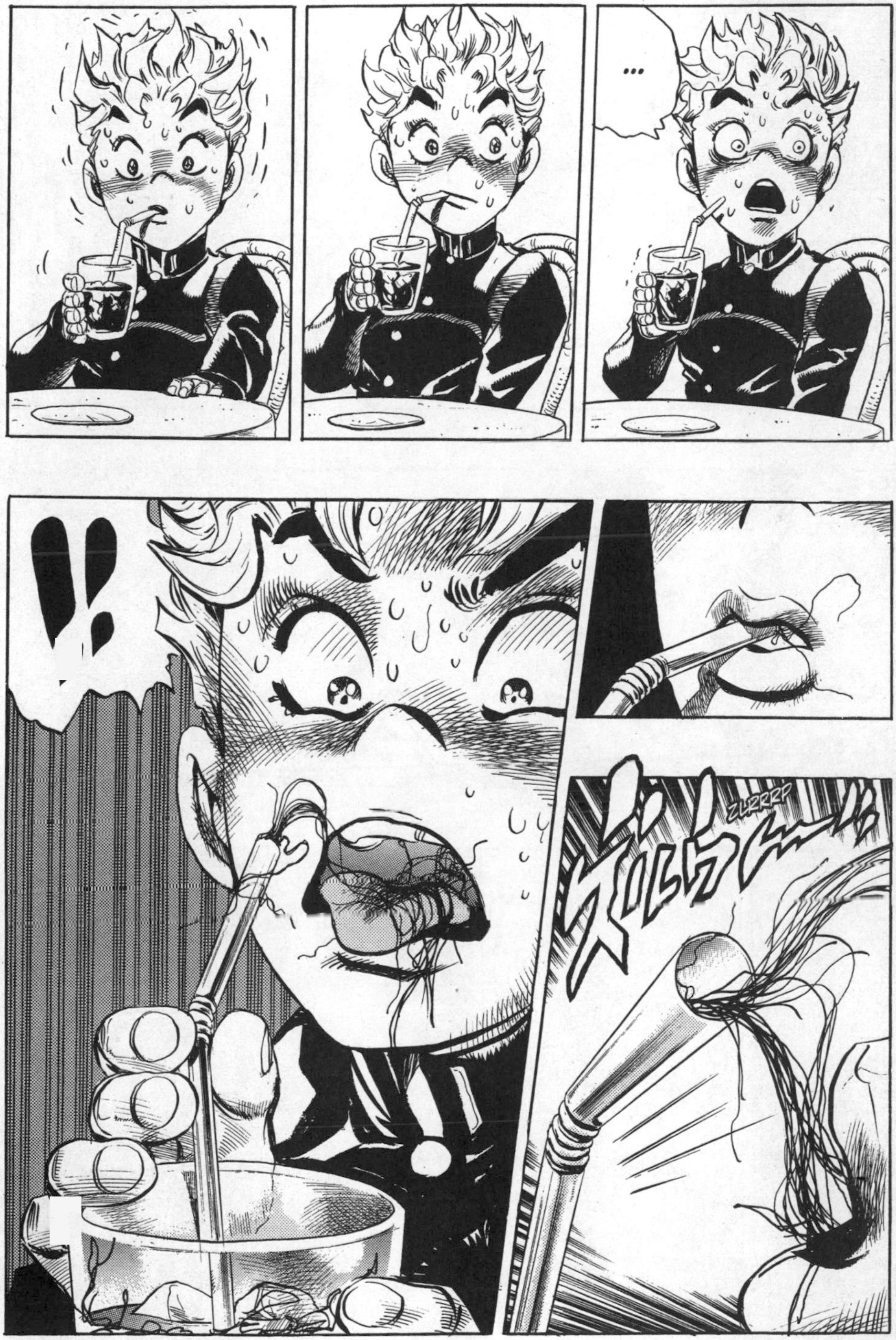
...
ZLRRRP
!!

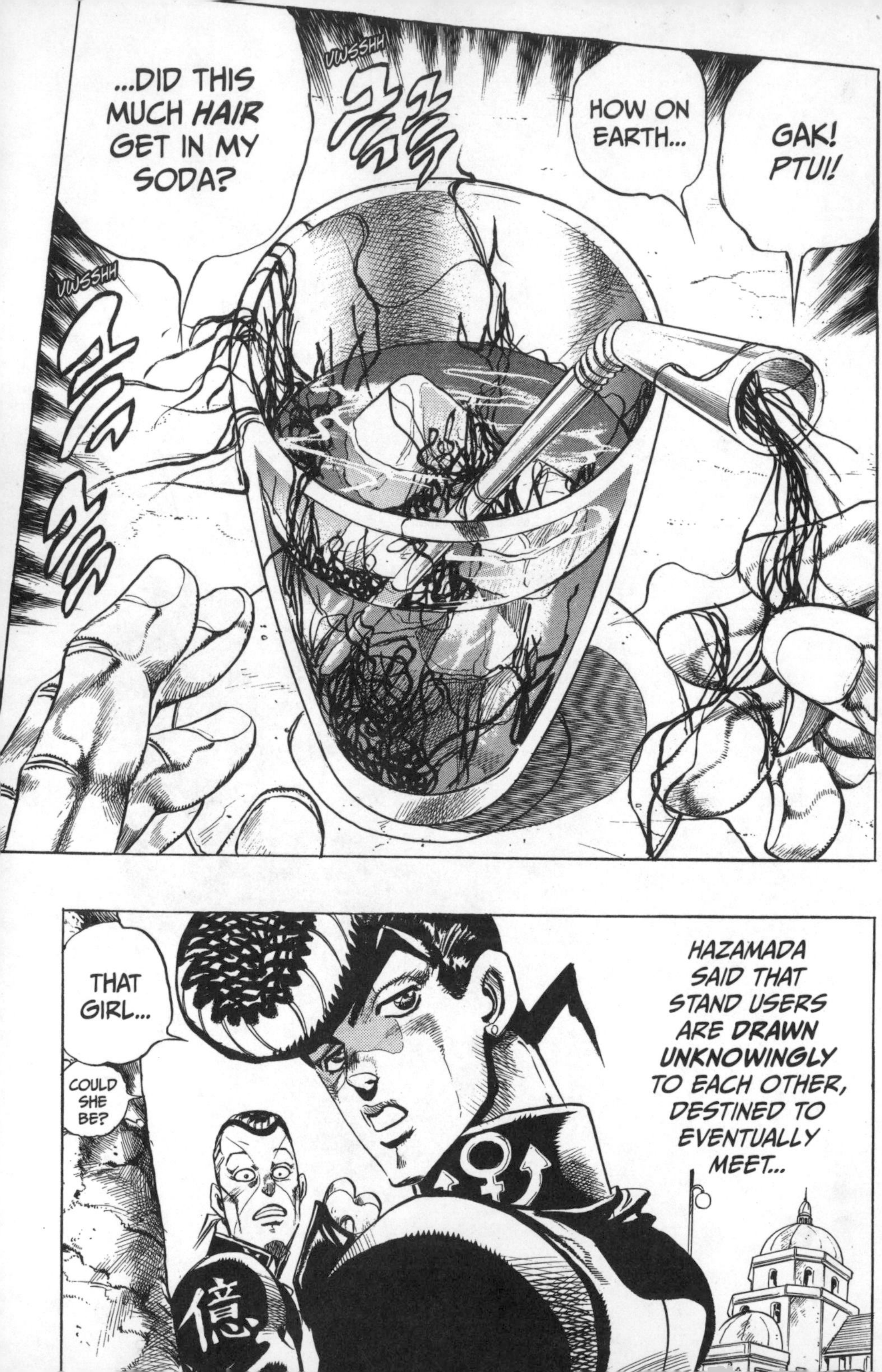
GAK! PTUI!
HOW ON EARTH...
VWSSHH
...DID THIS MUCH HAIR GET IN MY SODA?
VWSSHH
HAZAMADA SAID THAT STAND USERS ARE DRAWN UNKNOWINGLY TO EACH OTHER, DESTINED TO EVENTUALLY MEET...
THAT GIRL...
COULD SHE BE?

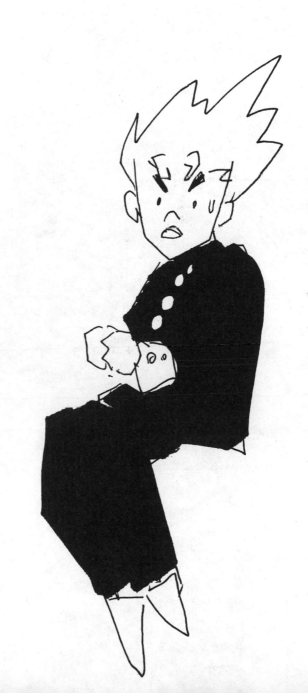

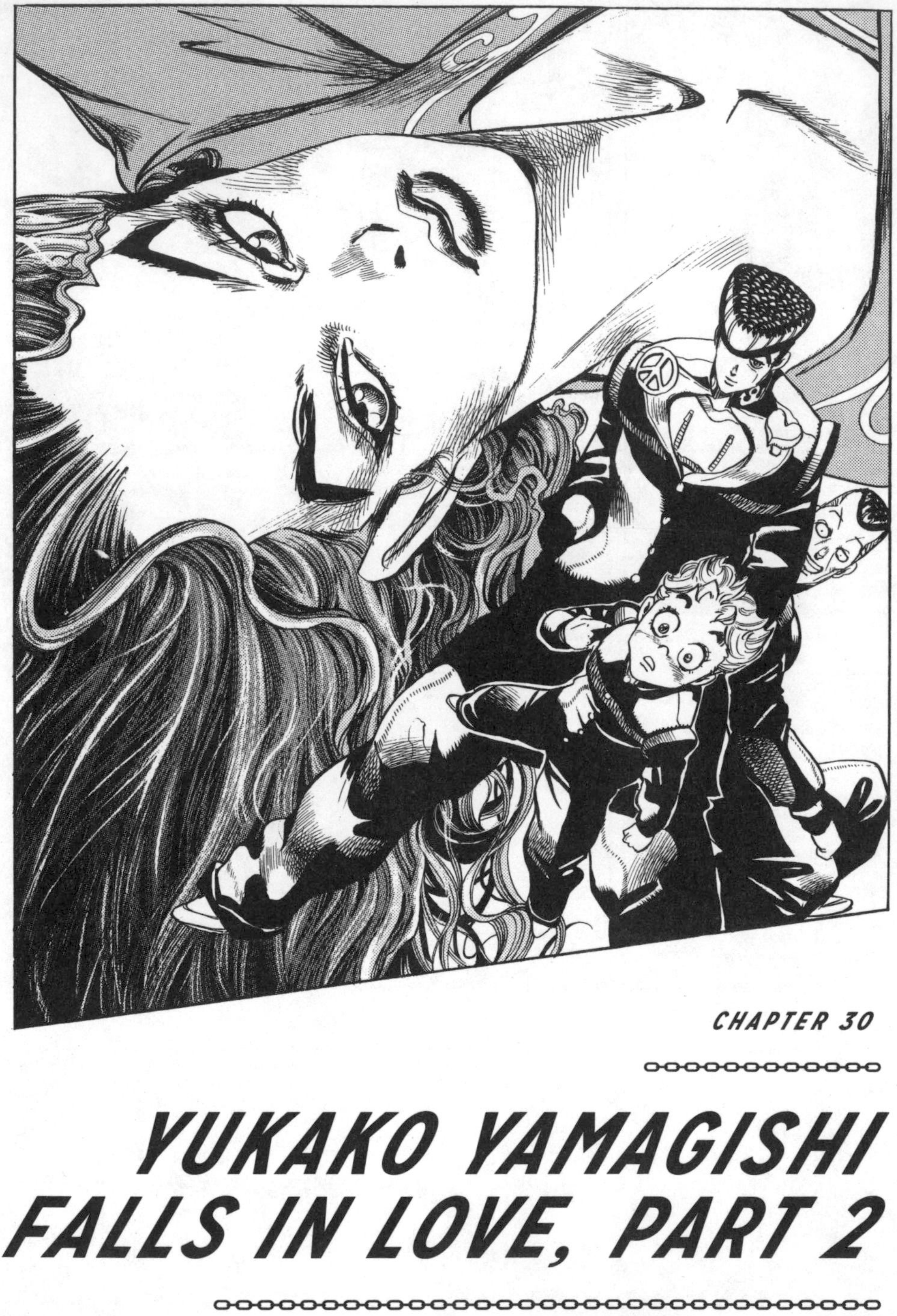

CHAPTER 30

YUKAKO YAMAGISHI FALLS IN LOVE, PART 2

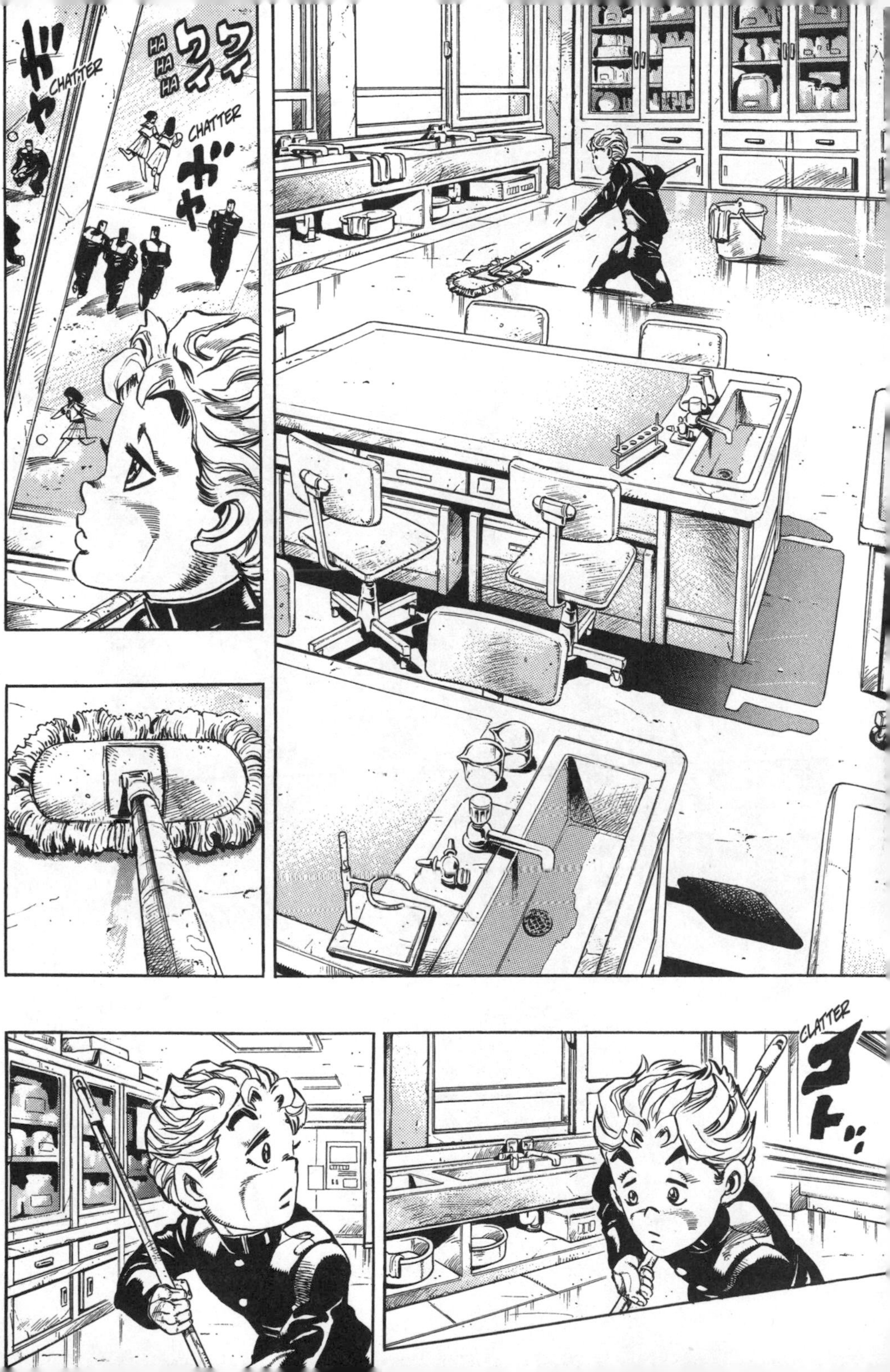
ガヤ
CHATTER
HA HA HA
CHATTER
ガヤ
CLATTER
ゴトッ

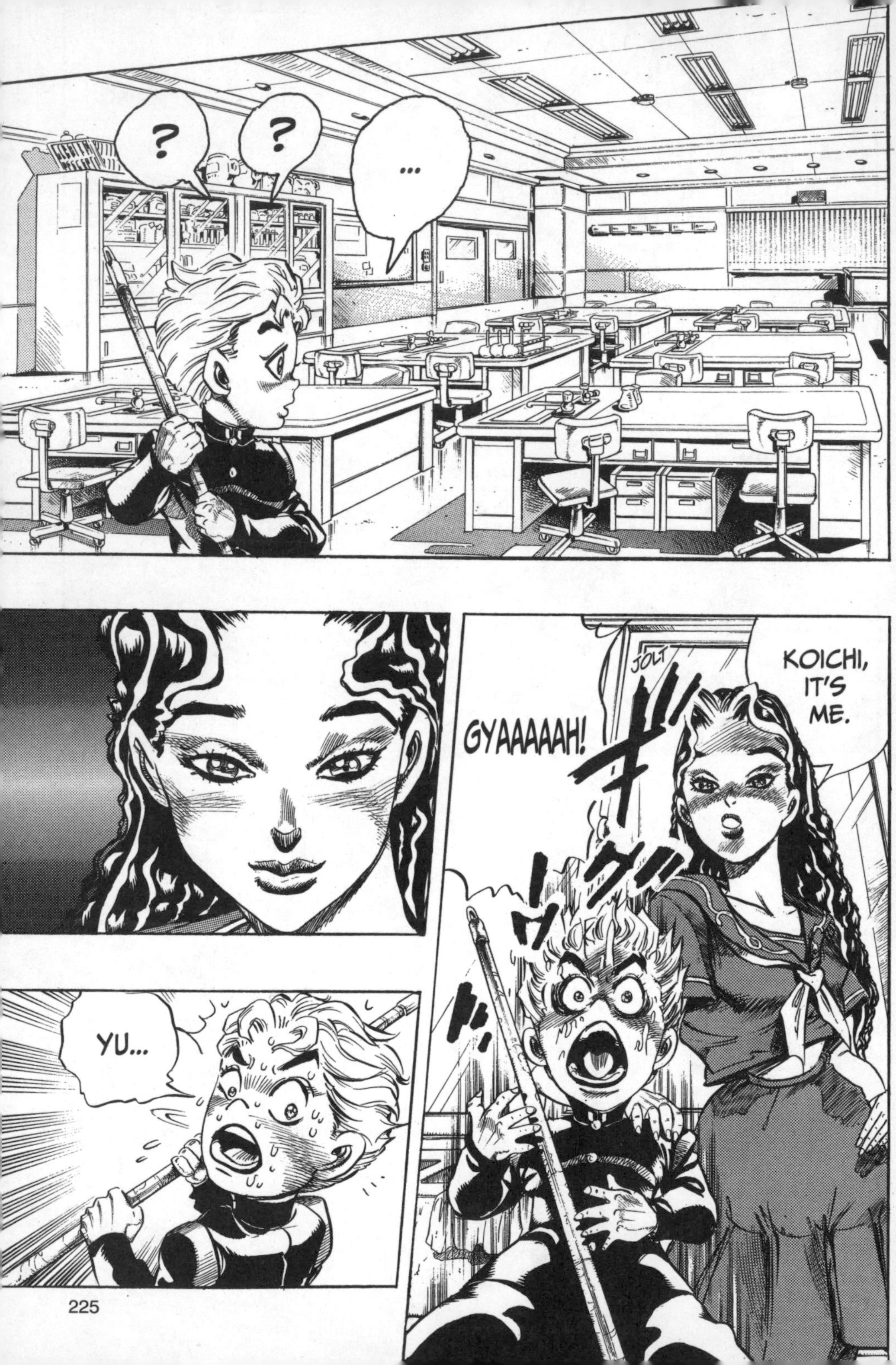
...
?
?
KOICHI, IT'S ME.
JOLT
GYAAAAAH!
YU...

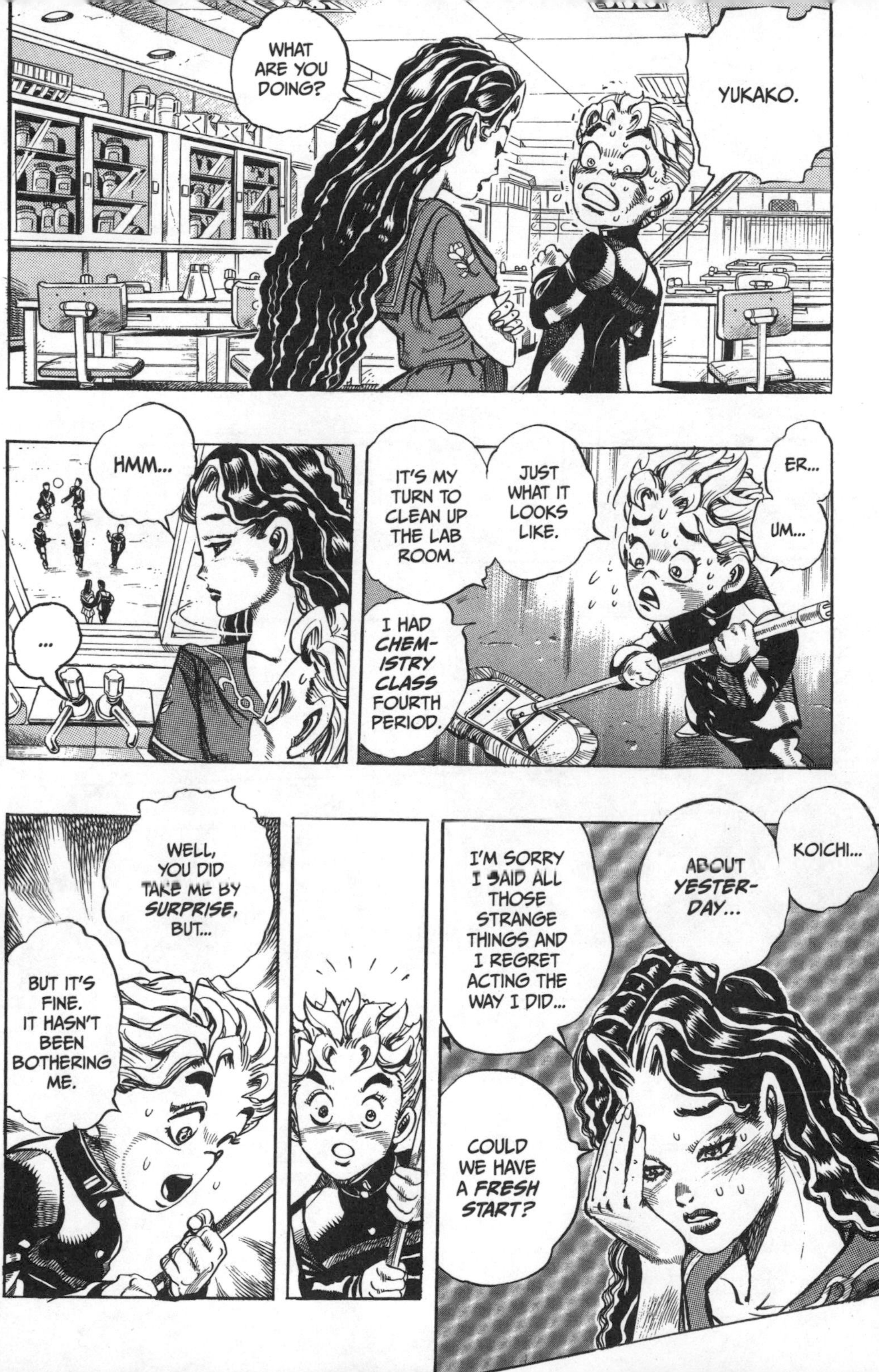
YUKAKO.
WHAT ARE YOU DOING?
ER...
UM...
JUST WHAT IT LOOKS LIKE.
IT'S MY TURN TO CLEAN UP THE LAB ROOM.
I HAD *CHEMISTRY CLASS* FOURTH PERIOD.
HMM...
...
KOICHI...
ABOUT *YESTERDAY*...
I'M SORRY I SAID ALL THOSE STRANGE THINGS AND I REGRET ACTING THE WAY I DID...
COULD WE HAVE A *FRESH START?*
WELL, YOU DID TAKE ME BY *SURPRISE*, BUT...
BUT IT'S FINE. IT HASN'T BEEN BOTHERING ME.

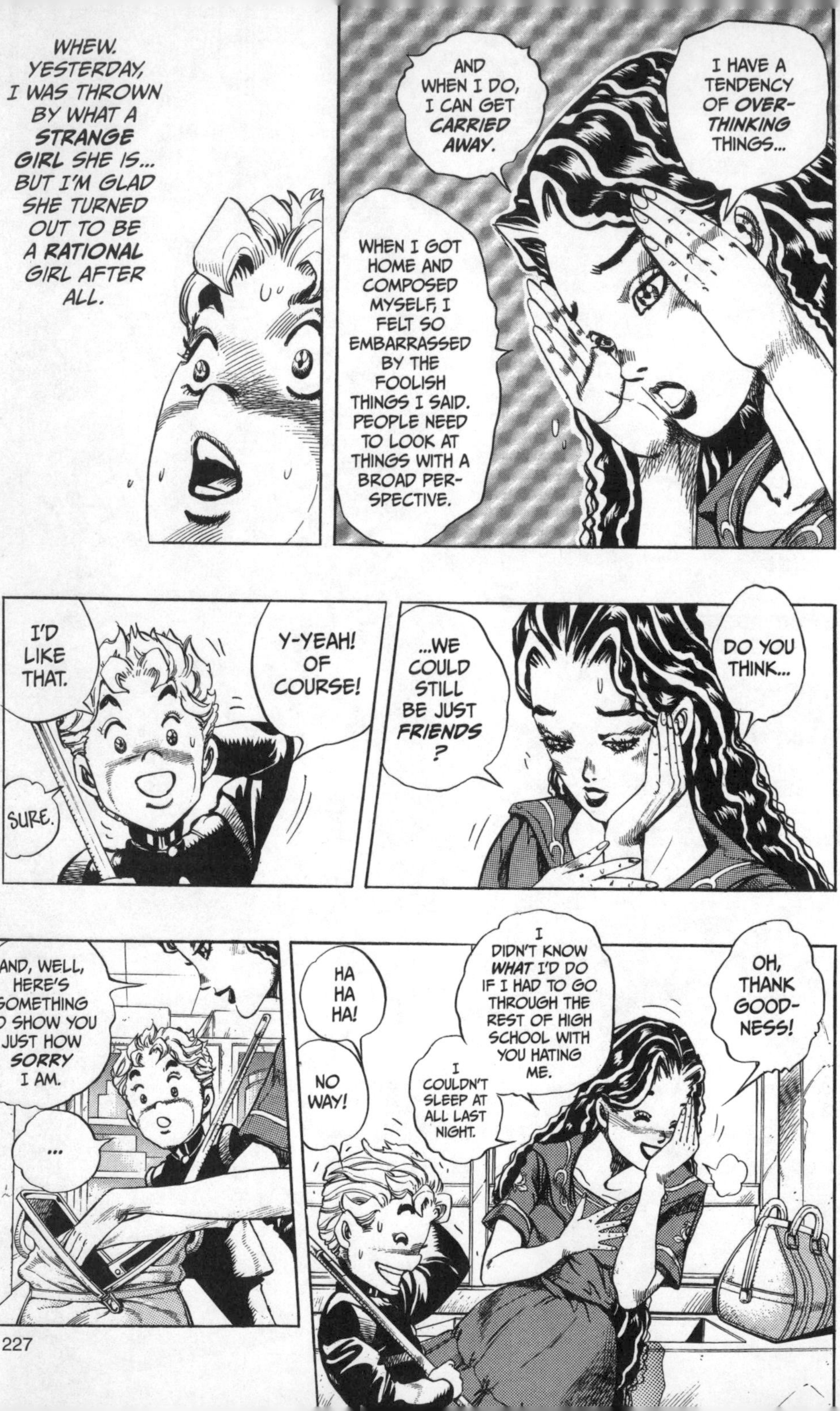
I HAVE A TENDENCY OF OVER-THINKING THINGS...
AND WHEN I DO, I CAN GET CARRIED AWAY.
WHEN I GOT HOME AND COMPOSED MYSELF, I FELT SO EMBARRASSED BY THE FOOLISH THINGS I SAID. PEOPLE NEED TO LOOK AT THINGS WITH A BROAD PER-SPECTIVE.
WHEW. YESTERDAY, I WAS THROWN BY WHAT A STRANGE GIRL SHE IS... BUT I'M GLAD SHE TURNED OUT TO BE A RATIONAL GIRL AFTER ALL.
DO YOU THINK...
...WE COULD STILL BE JUST FRIENDS?
Y-YEAH! OF COURSE!
I'D LIKE THAT.
SURE.
OH, THANK GOOD-NESS!
I DIDN'T KNOW WHAT I'D DO IF I HAD TO GO THROUGH THE REST OF HIGH SCHOOL WITH YOU HATING ME.
I COULDN'T SLEEP AT ALL LAST NIGHT.
HA HA HA!
NO WAY!
AND, WELL, HERE'S SOMETHING TO SHOW YOU JUST HOW SORRY I AM.
...

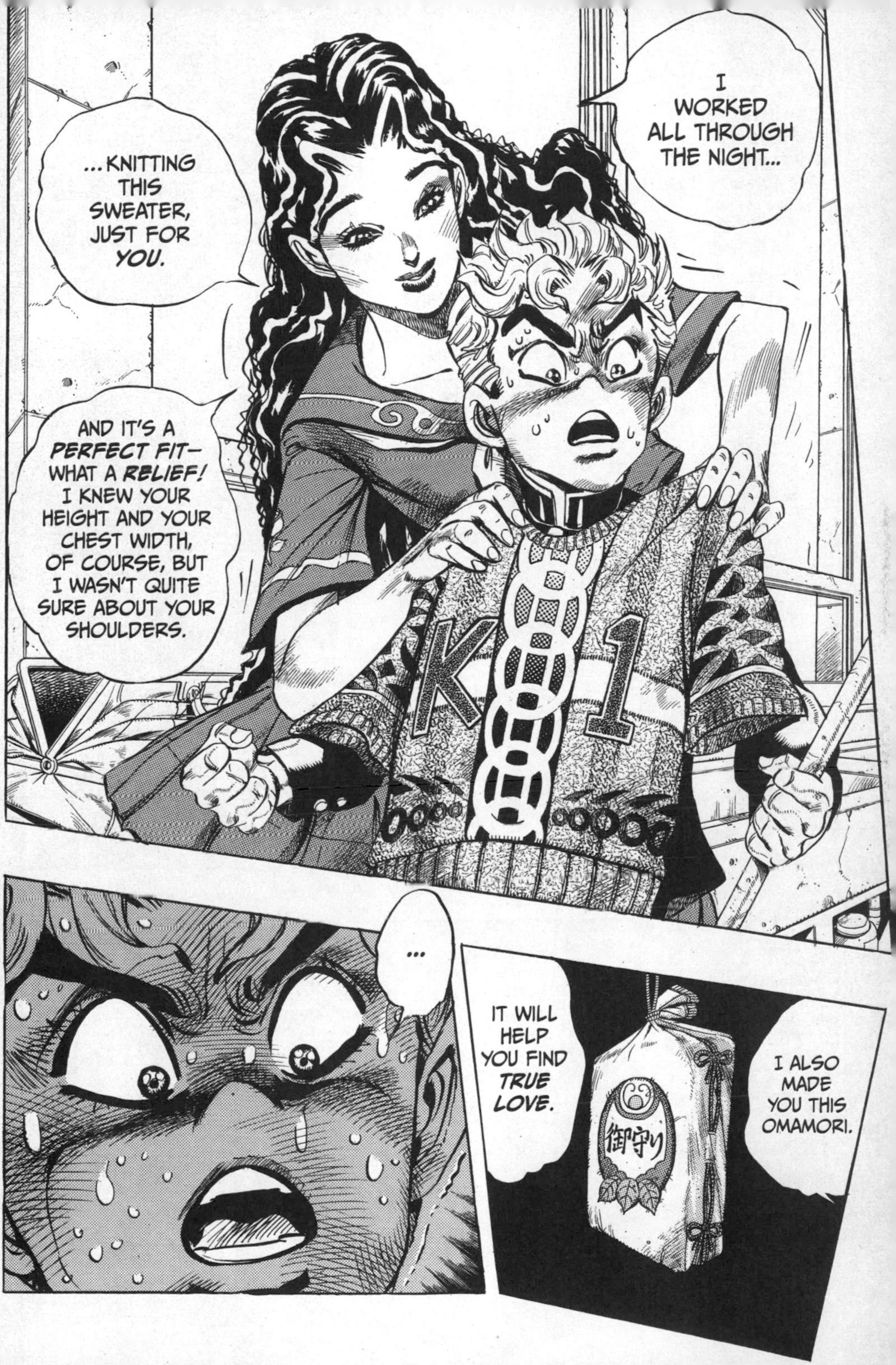

I WORKED ALL THROUGH THE NIGHT...
...KNITTING THIS SWEATER, JUST FOR *YOU*.
AND IT'S A *PERFECT FIT*— WHAT A *RELIEF!* I KNEW YOUR HEIGHT AND YOUR CHEST WIDTH, OF COURSE, BUT I WASN'T QUITE SURE ABOUT YOUR SHOULDERS.
I ALSO MADE YOU THIS OMAMORI.
IT WILL HELP YOU FIND *TRUE LOVE*.
御守り
...

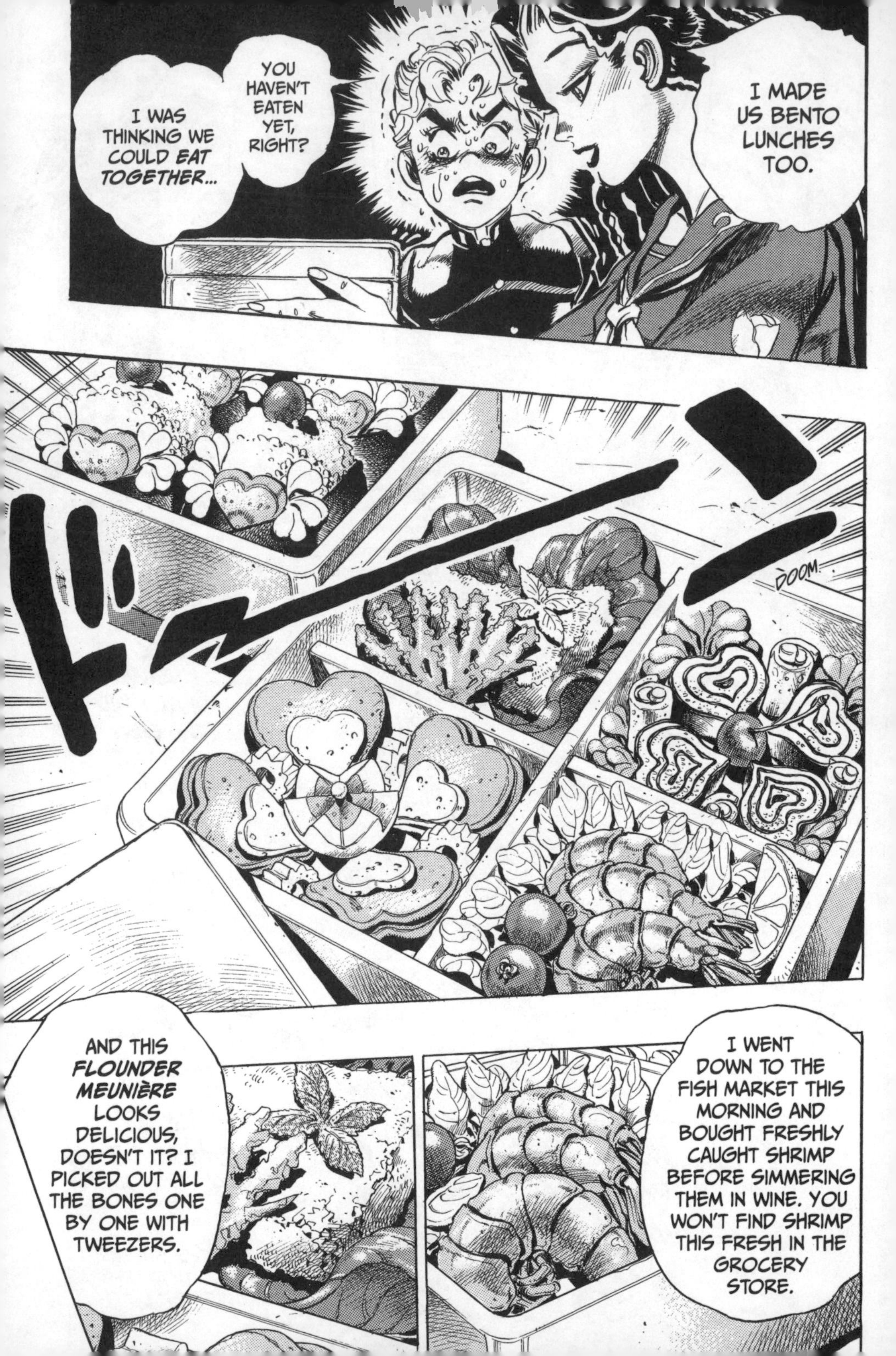
I MADE US BENTO LUNCHES TOO.
YOU HAVEN'T EATEN YET, RIGHT?
I WAS THINKING WE COULD EAT TOGETHER...
DOOM
I WENT DOWN TO THE FISH MARKET THIS MORNING AND BOUGHT FRESHLY CAUGHT SHRIMP BEFORE SIMMERING THEM IN WINE. YOU WON'T FIND SHRIMP THIS FRESH IN THE GROCERY STORE.
AND THIS FLOUNDER MEUNIÈRE LOOKS DELICIOUS, DOESN'T IT? I PICKED OUT ALL THE BONES ONE BY ONE WITH TWEEZERS.

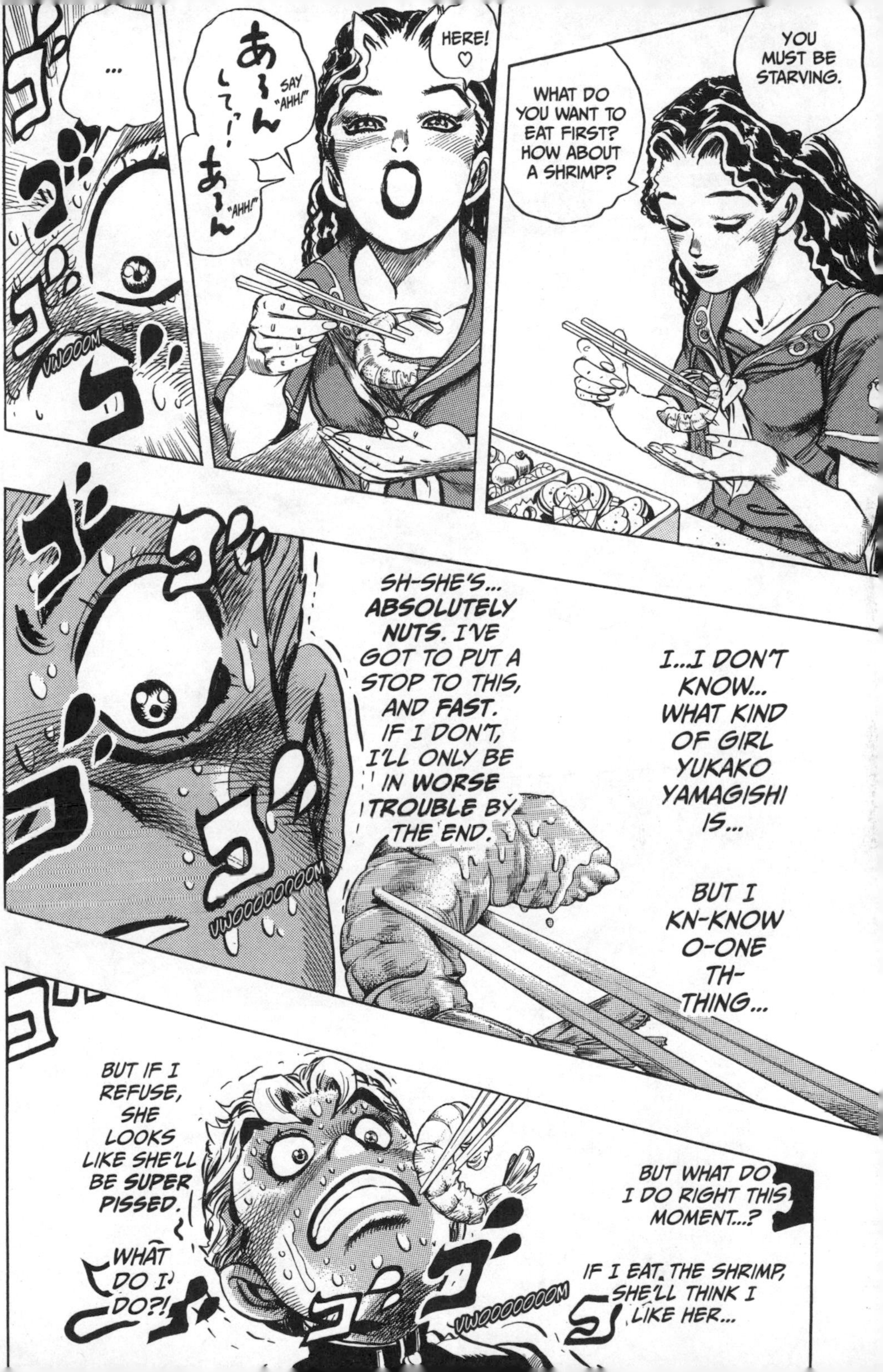

YOU MUST BE STARVING.
WHAT DO YOU WANT TO EAT FIRST? HOW ABOUT A SHRIMP?
HERE! ♡
あ～んして…！
SAY "AHH!"
あ～ん
"AHH!"
...
VWOOOM
I...I DON'T KNOW... WHAT KIND OF GIRL YUKAKO YAMAGISHI IS...
BUT I KN-KNOW O-ONE TH-THING...
SH-SHE'S... ABSOLUTELY NUTS. I'VE GOT TO PUT A STOP TO THIS, AND FAST. IF I DON'T, I'LL ONLY BE IN WORSE TROUBLE BY THE END.
VWOOOOOOOOM
BUT WHAT DO I DO RIGHT THIS MOMENT...?
IF I EAT THE SHRIMP, SHE'LL THINK I LIKE HER...
VWOOOOOOOOM
BUT IF I REFUSE, SHE LOOKS LIKE SHE'LL BE SUPER PISSED.
WHAT DO I DO?!

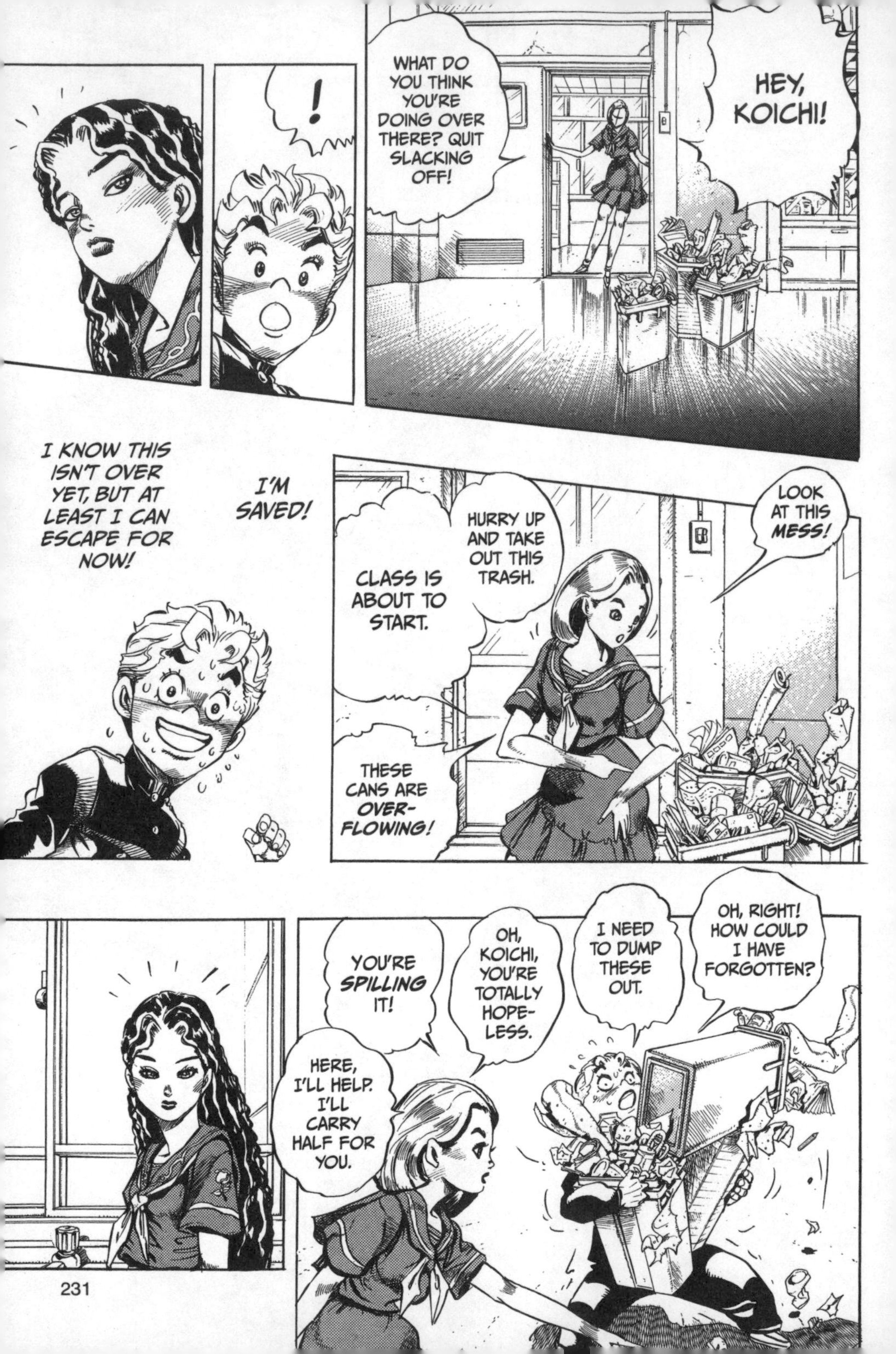
HEY, KOICHI!
WHAT DO YOU THINK YOU'RE DOING OVER THERE? QUIT SLACKING OFF!
!
LOOK AT THIS *MESS!*
HURRY UP AND TAKE OUT THIS TRASH.
CLASS IS ABOUT TO START.
THESE CANS ARE *OVER-FLOWING!*
I'M SAVED!
I KNOW THIS ISN'T OVER YET, BUT AT LEAST I CAN ESCAPE FOR NOW!
OH, RIGHT! HOW COULD I HAVE FORGOTTEN?
I NEED TO DUMP THESE OUT.
OH, KOICHI, YOU'RE TOTALLY HOPE-LESS.
YOU'RE *SPILLING* IT!
HERE, I'LL HELP. I'LL CARRY HALF FOR YOU.

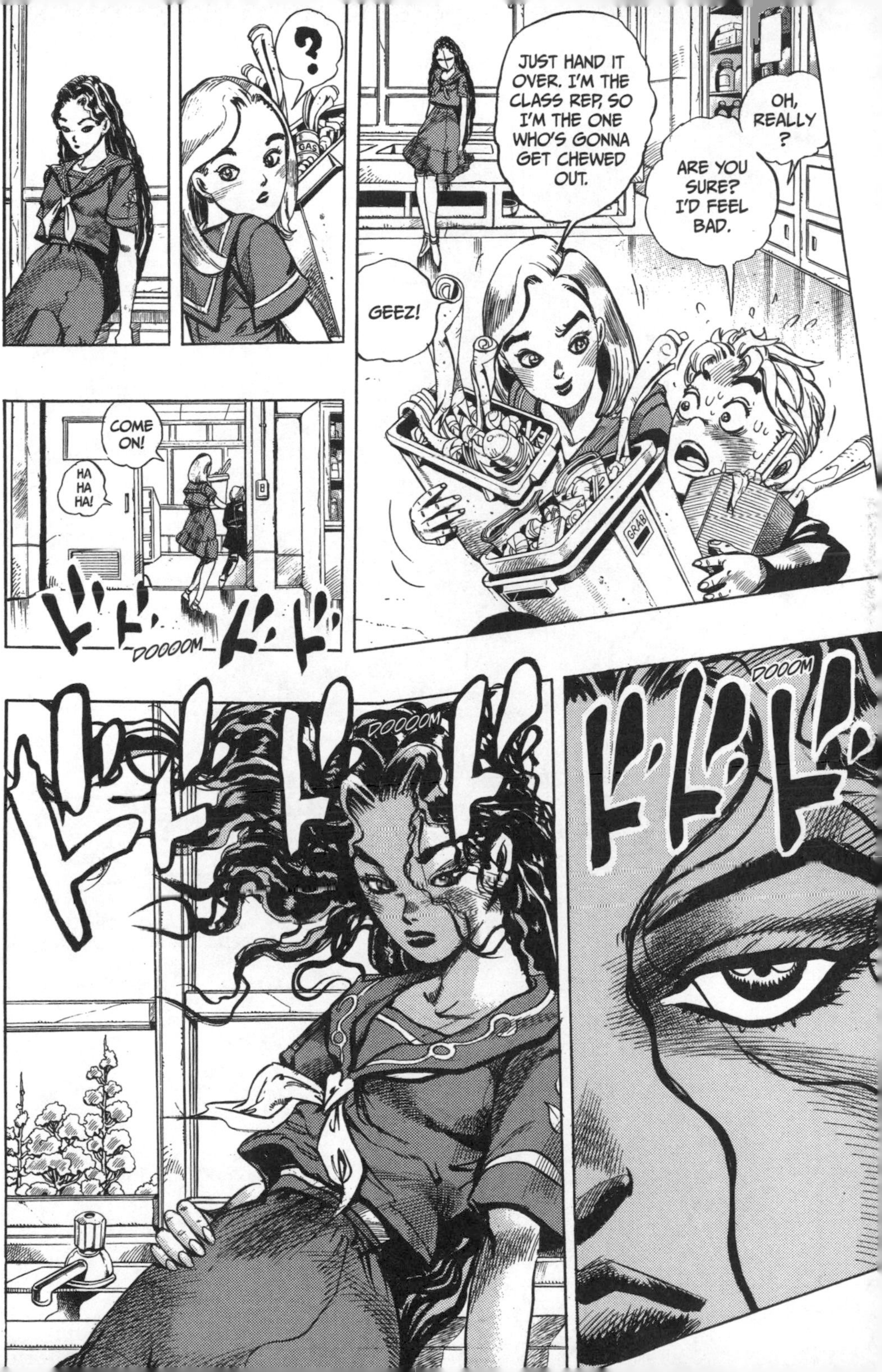
JUST HAND IT OVER. I'M THE CLASS REP, SO I'M THE ONE WHO'S GONNA GET CHEWED OUT.
OH, REALLY?
ARE YOU SURE? I'D FEEL BAD.
GEEZ!
GRAB
?
GAS
COME ON!
HA HA HA!
DOOOOM
DOOOM
DOOOOM

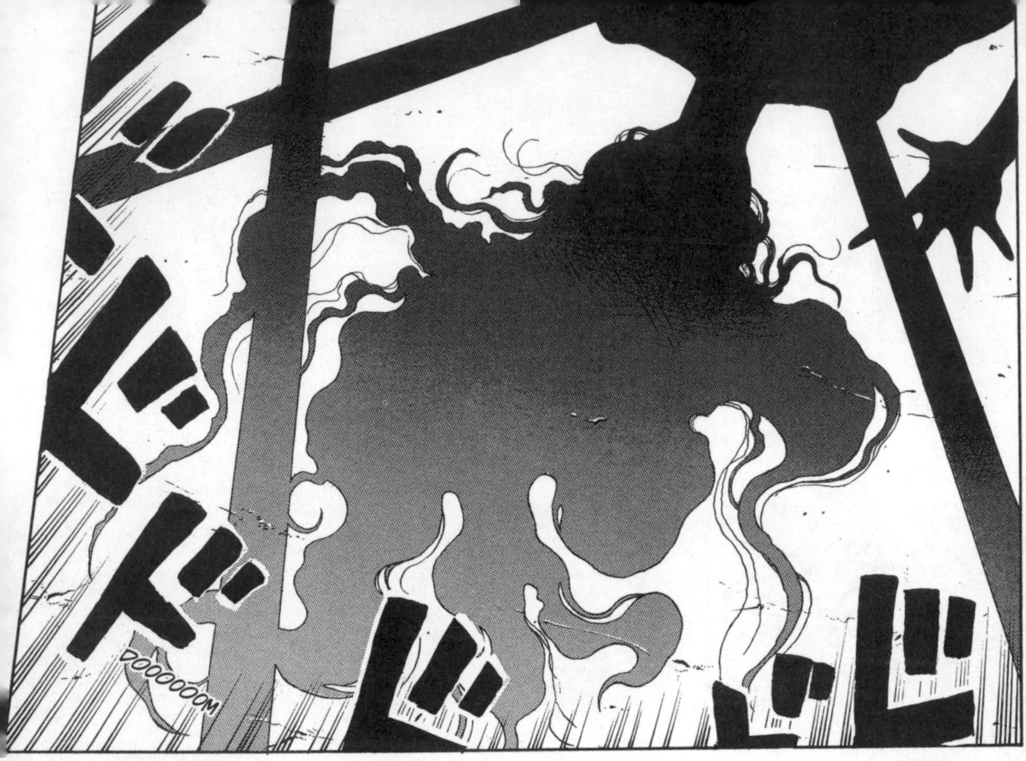
DOOOOOOOM

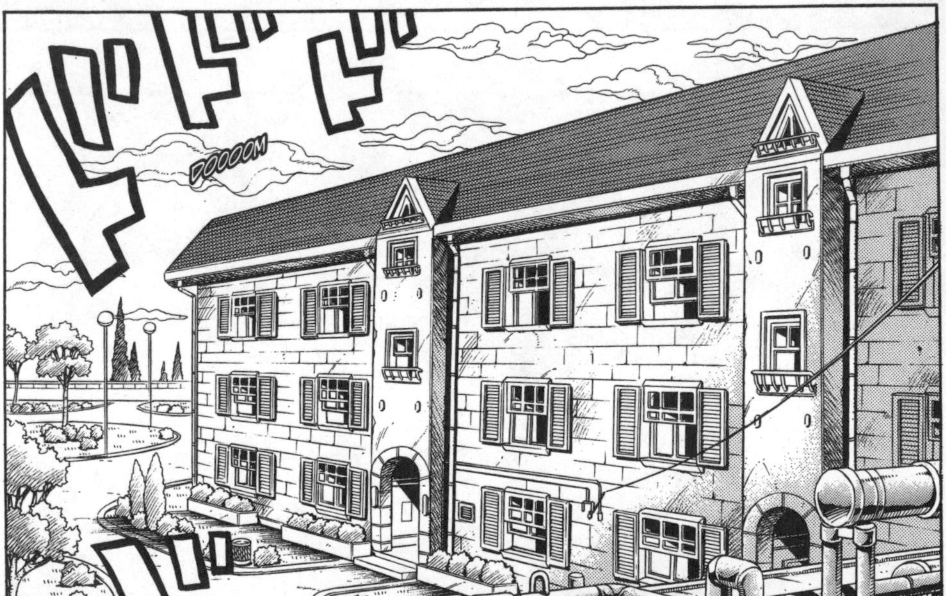
DOOOOM

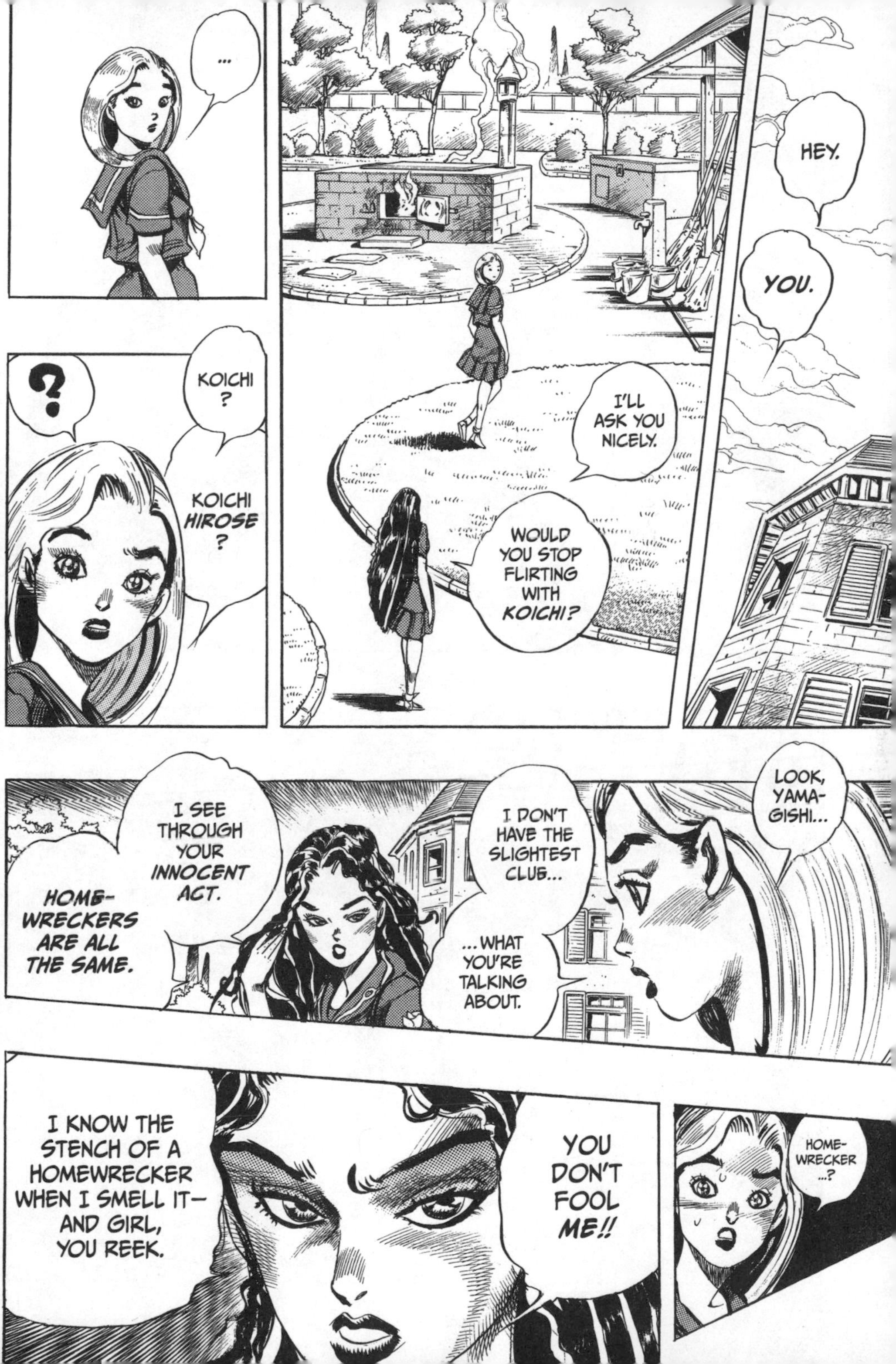
HEY.
YOU.
I'LL ASK YOU NICELY.
WOULD YOU STOP FLIRTING WITH KOICHI?
...
?
KOICHI?
KOICHI HIROSE?
LOOK, YAMAGISHI...
I DON'T HAVE THE SLIGHTEST CLUE...
...WHAT YOU'RE TALKING ABOUT.
I SEE THROUGH YOUR INNOCENT ACT.
HOMEWRECKERS ARE ALL THE SAME.
HOMEWRECKER...?
YOU DON'T FOOL ME!!
I KNOW THE STENCH OF A HOMEWRECKER WHEN I SMELL IT—AND GIRL, YOU REEK.

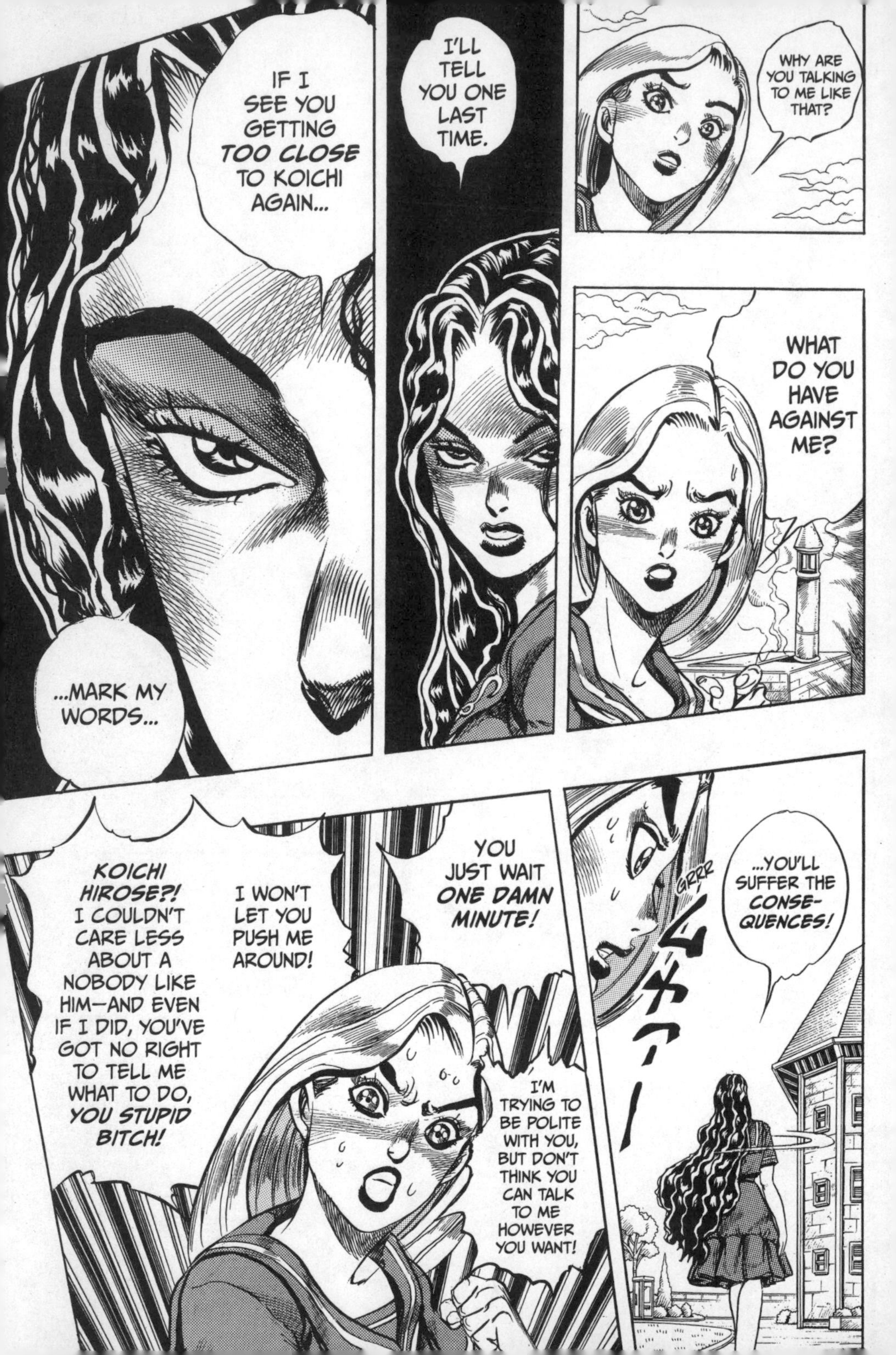
WHY ARE YOU TALKING TO ME LIKE THAT?
WHAT DO YOU HAVE AGAINST ME?
I'LL TELL YOU ONE LAST TIME.
IF I SEE YOU GETTING *TOO CLOSE* TO KOICHI AGAIN...
...MARK MY WORDS...
...YOU'LL SUFFER THE *CONSE-QUENCES!*
GRRR
ムカァーー
YOU JUST WAIT *ONE DAMN MINUTE!*
I'M TRYING TO BE POLITE WITH YOU, BUT DON'T THINK YOU CAN TALK TO ME HOWEVER YOU WANT!
I WON'T LET YOU PUSH ME AROUND!
KOICHI HIROSE?! I COULDN'T CARE LESS ABOUT A NOBODY LIKE HIM—AND EVEN IF I DID, YOU'VE GOT NO RIGHT TO TELL ME WHAT TO DO, *YOU STUPID BITCH!*

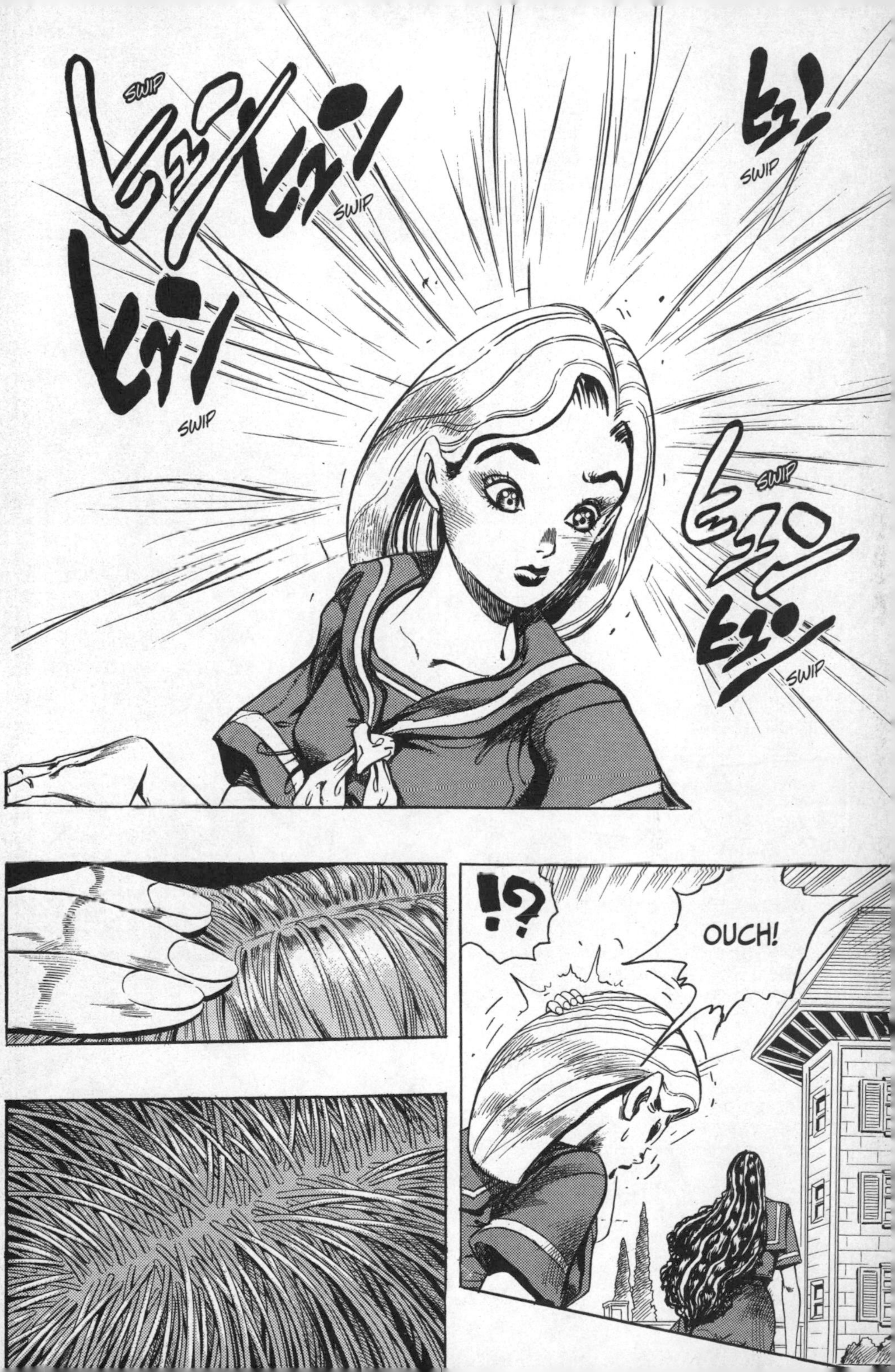
SWIP
SWIP
SWIP
SWIP
SWIP
SWIP
!?
OUCH!

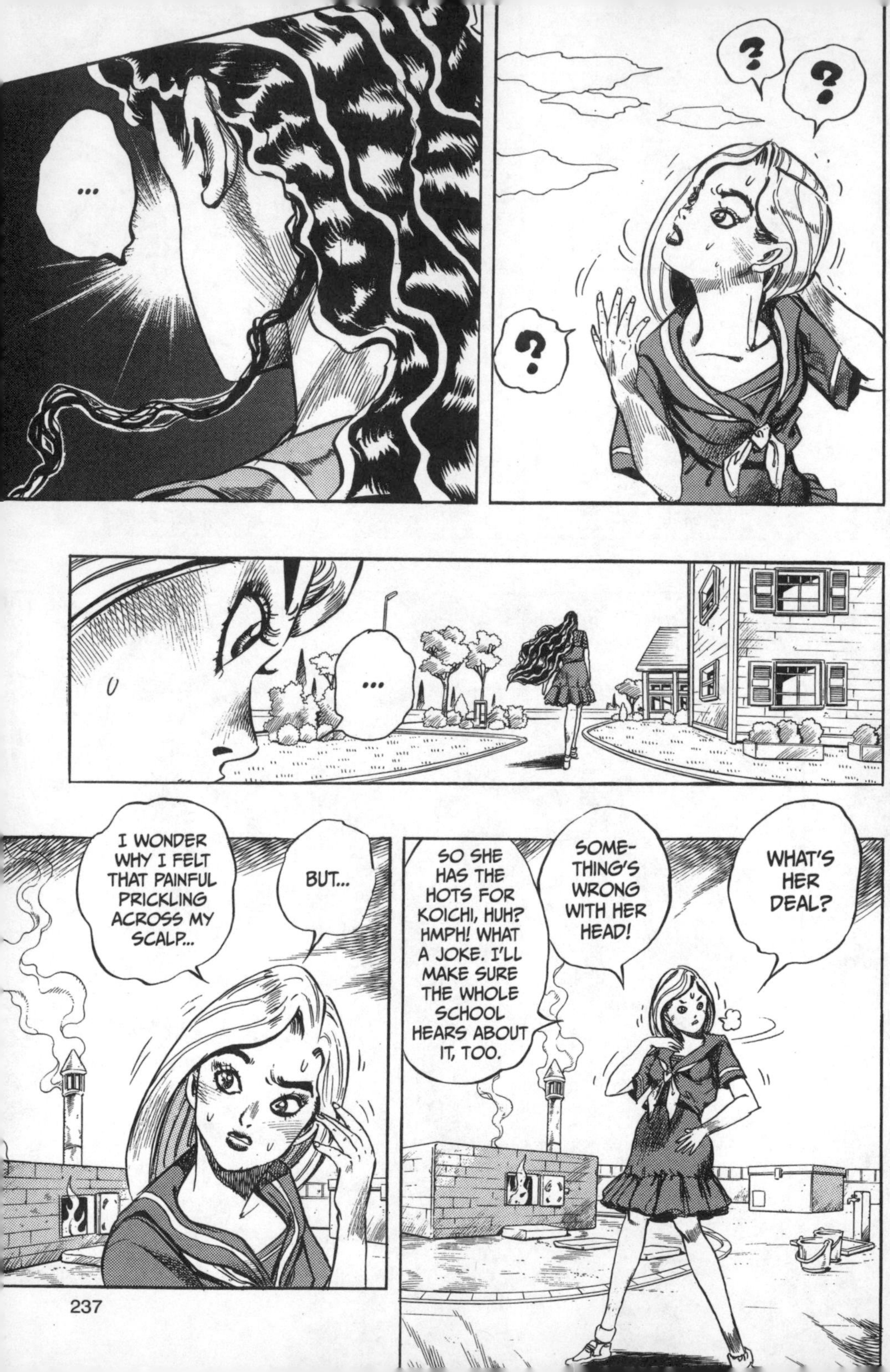
?
?
?
...
...
WHAT'S HER DEAL?
SOME-THING'S WRONG WITH HER HEAD!
SO SHE HAS THE HOTS FOR KOICHI, HUH? HMPH! WHAT A JOKE. I'LL MAKE SURE THE WHOLE SCHOOL HEARS ABOUT IT, TOO.
BUT...
I WONDER WHY I FELT THAT PAINFUL PRICKLING ACROSS MY SCALP...

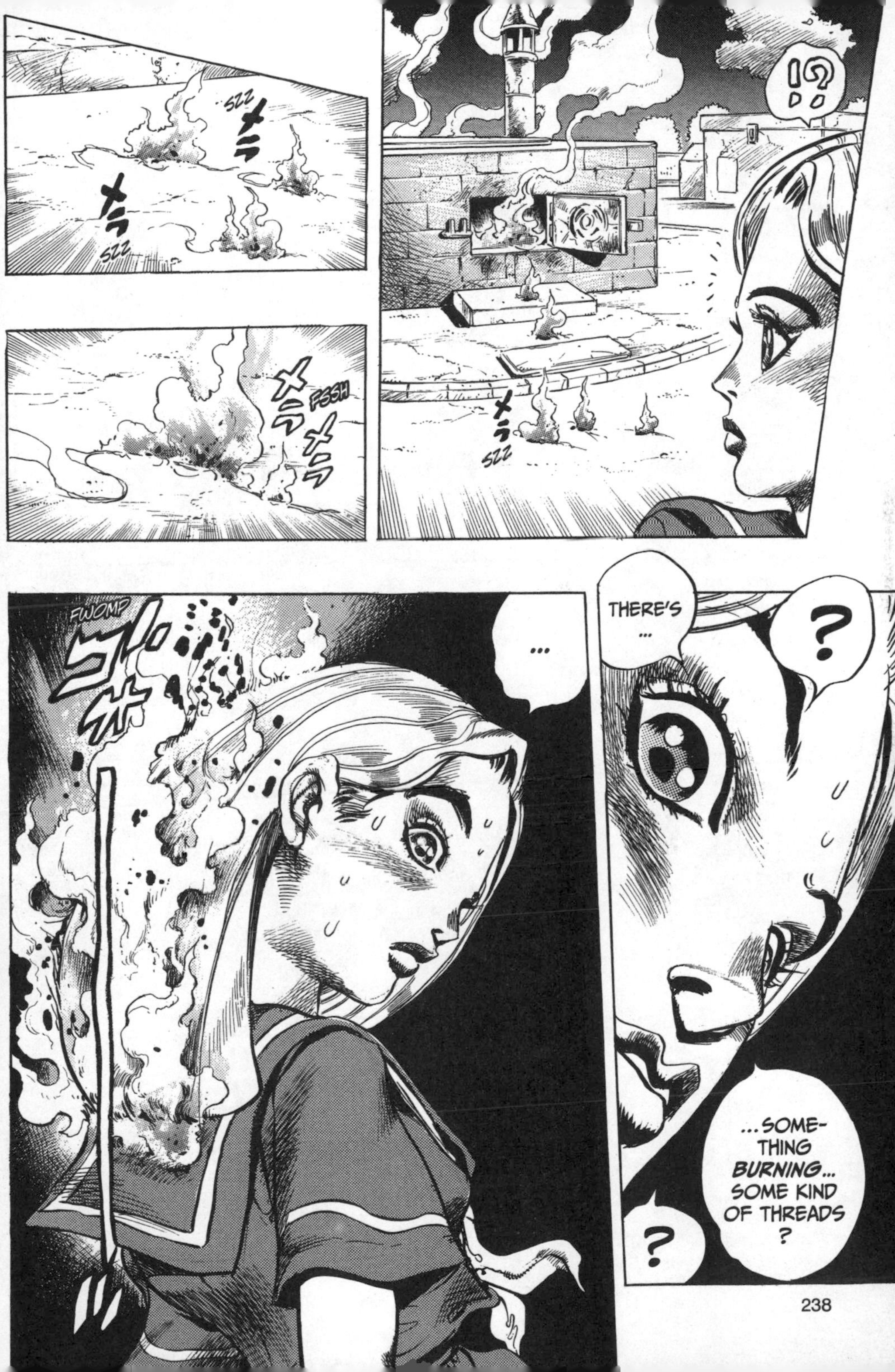
!?
SZZ
SZZ
SZZ
FSSH
THERE'S ...
?
...SOMETHING BURNING... SOME KIND OF THREADS ?
?
FWOMP
...

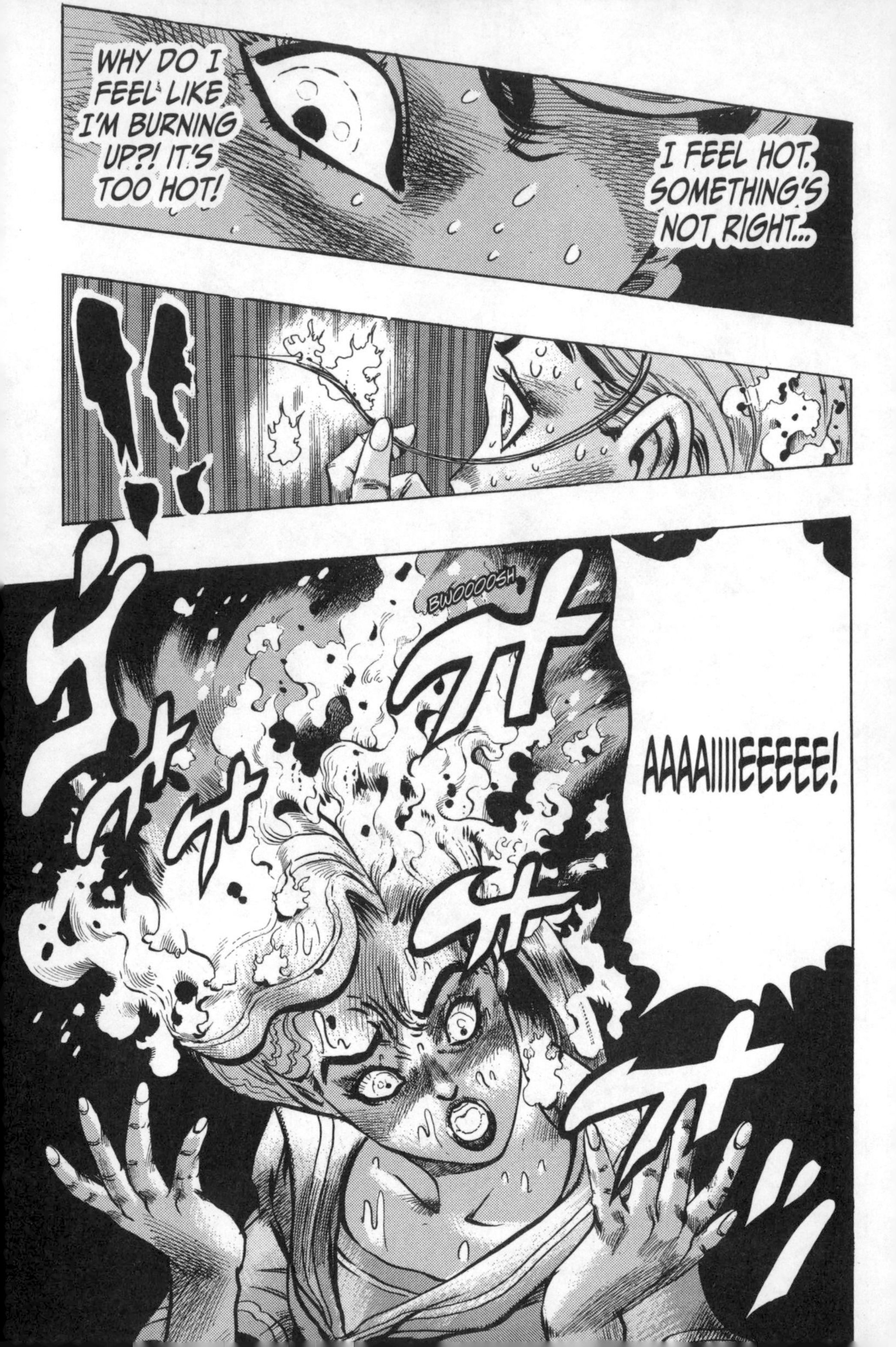
WHY DO I FEEL LIKE I'M BURNING UP?! IT'S TOO HOT!
I FEEL HOT. SOMETHING'S NOT RIGHT...
BWOOOOSH
AAAAIIIIIEEEEE!

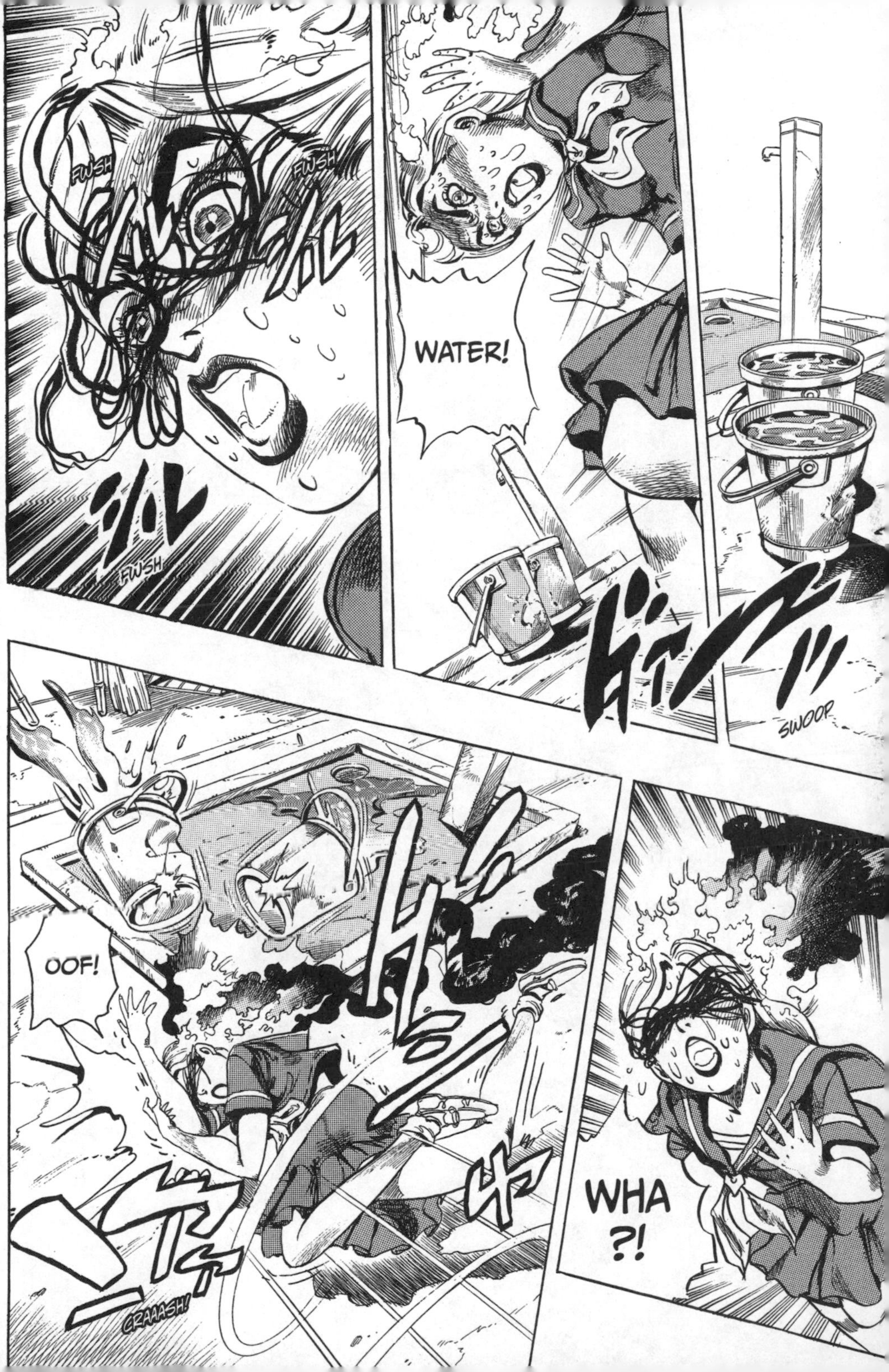
SWOOP
WATER!
FWSH
FWSH
FWSH
WHA
?!
OOF!
CRAAASH!

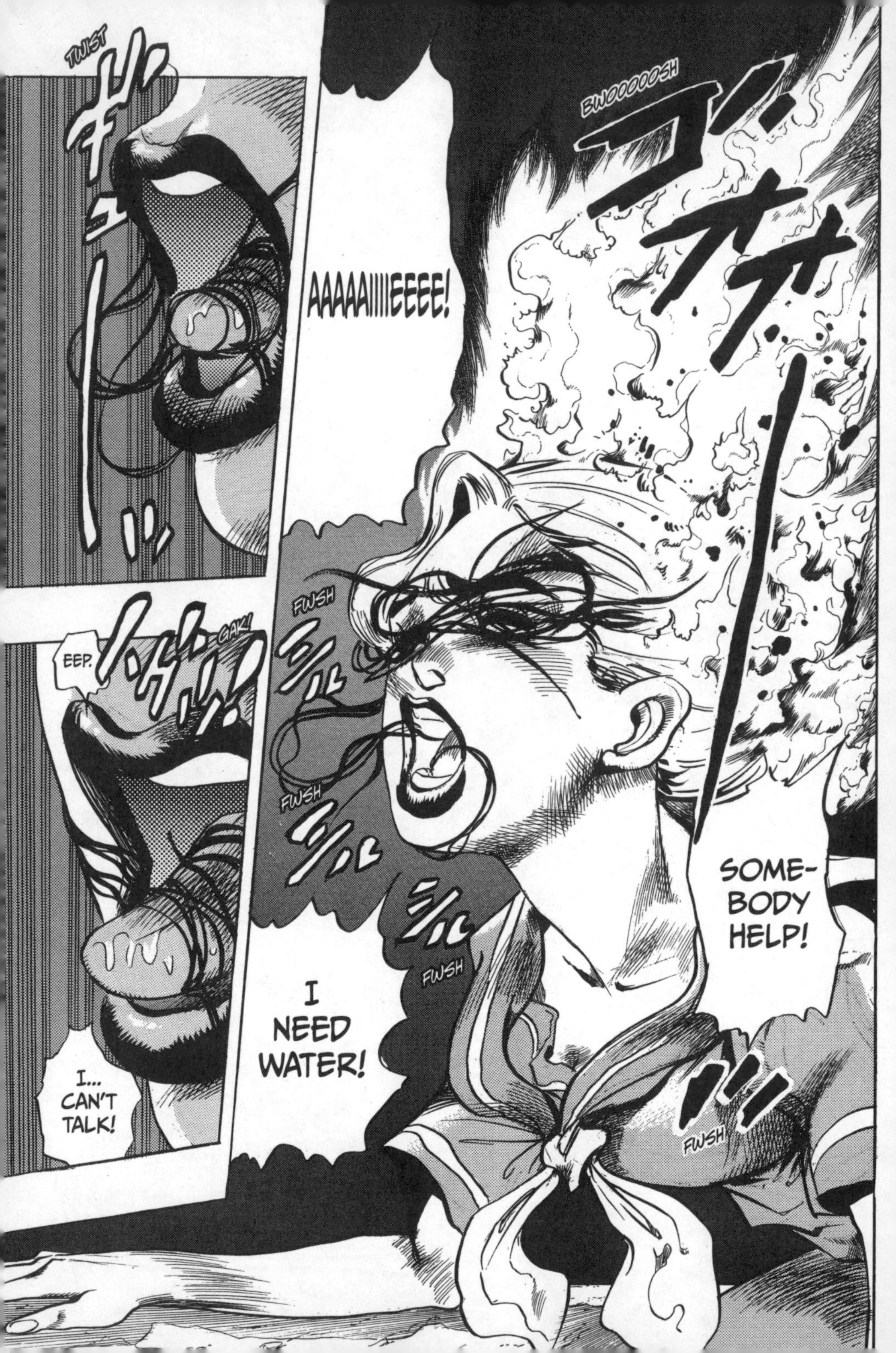
BWOOOOOOSH
AAAAAIIIIEEEE!
FWSH
FWSH
SOME-BODY HELP!
FWSH
I NEED WATER!
FWSH
TWIST
GAK!
EEP.
I... CAN'T TALK!

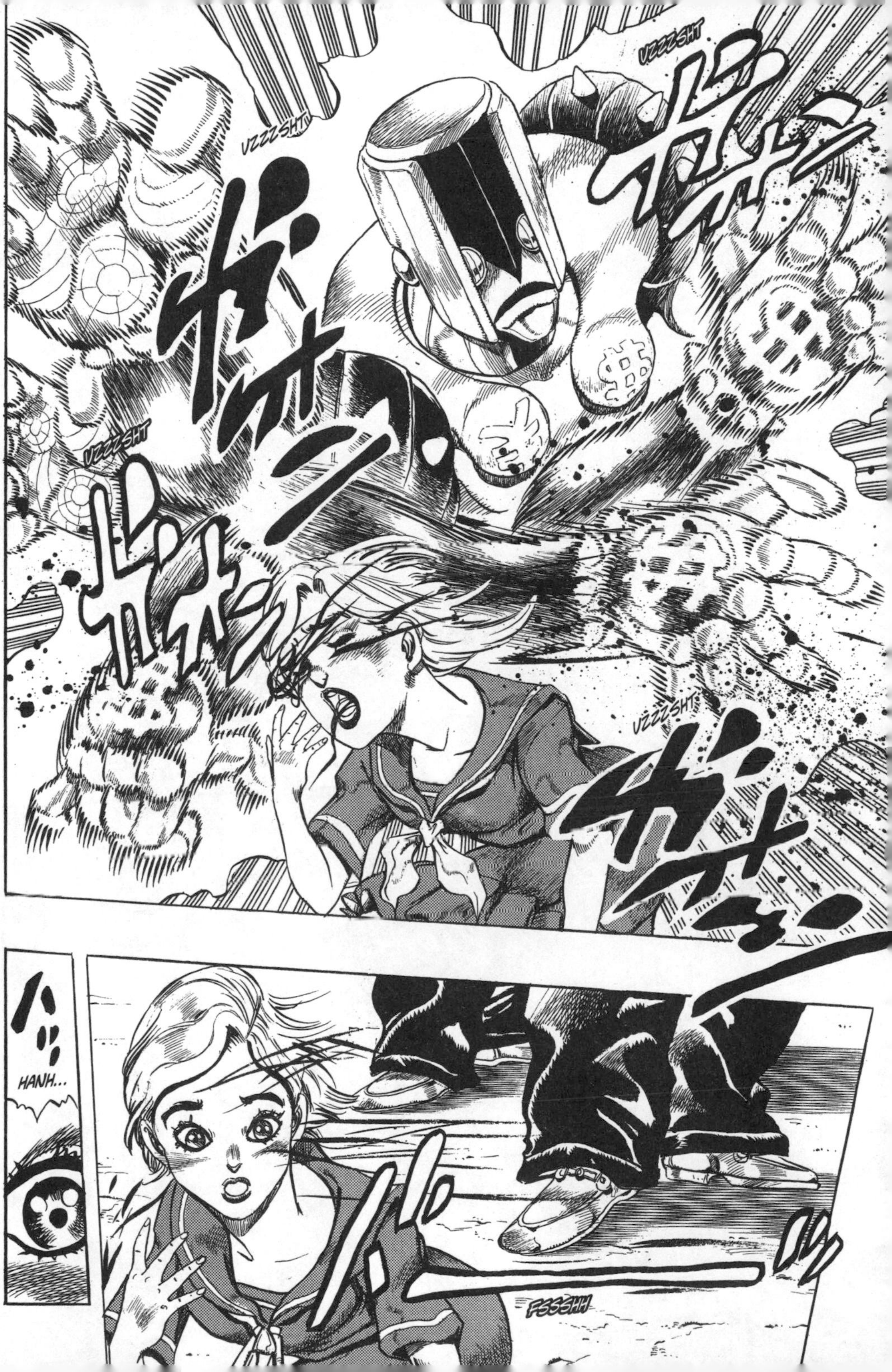
VZZZSHT
VZZZSHT
VZZZSHT
VZZZSHT
FSSSHH
HANH...

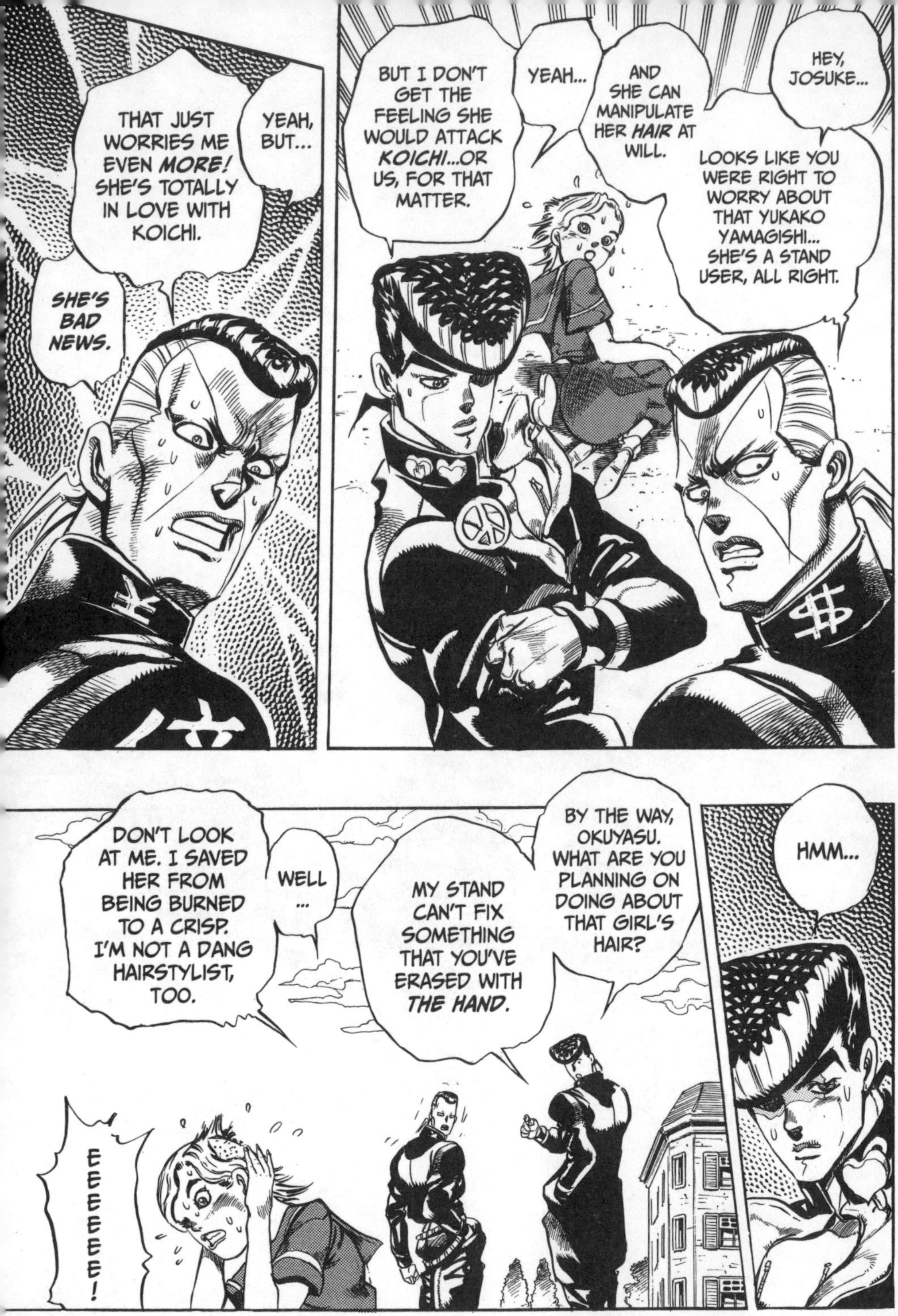
HEY, JOSUKE...
LOOKS LIKE YOU WERE RIGHT TO WORRY ABOUT THAT YUKAKO YAMAGISHI... SHE'S A STAND USER, ALL RIGHT.
AND SHE CAN MANIPULATE HER *HAIR* AT WILL.
YEAH...
BUT I DON'T GET THE FEELING SHE WOULD ATTACK *KOICHI*...OR US, FOR THAT MATTER.
YEAH, BUT...
THAT JUST WORRIES ME EVEN *MORE!* SHE'S TOTALLY IN LOVE WITH KOICHI.
SHE'S BAD NEWS.
HMM...
BY THE WAY, OKUYASU. WHAT ARE YOU PLANNING ON DOING ABOUT THAT GIRL'S HAIR?
MY STAND CAN'T FIX SOMETHING THAT YOU'VE ERASED WITH *THE HAND*.
WELL ...
DON'T LOOK AT ME. I SAVED HER FROM BEING BURNED TO A CRISP. I'M NOT A DANG HAIRSTYLIST, TOO.
EEEEEEE!

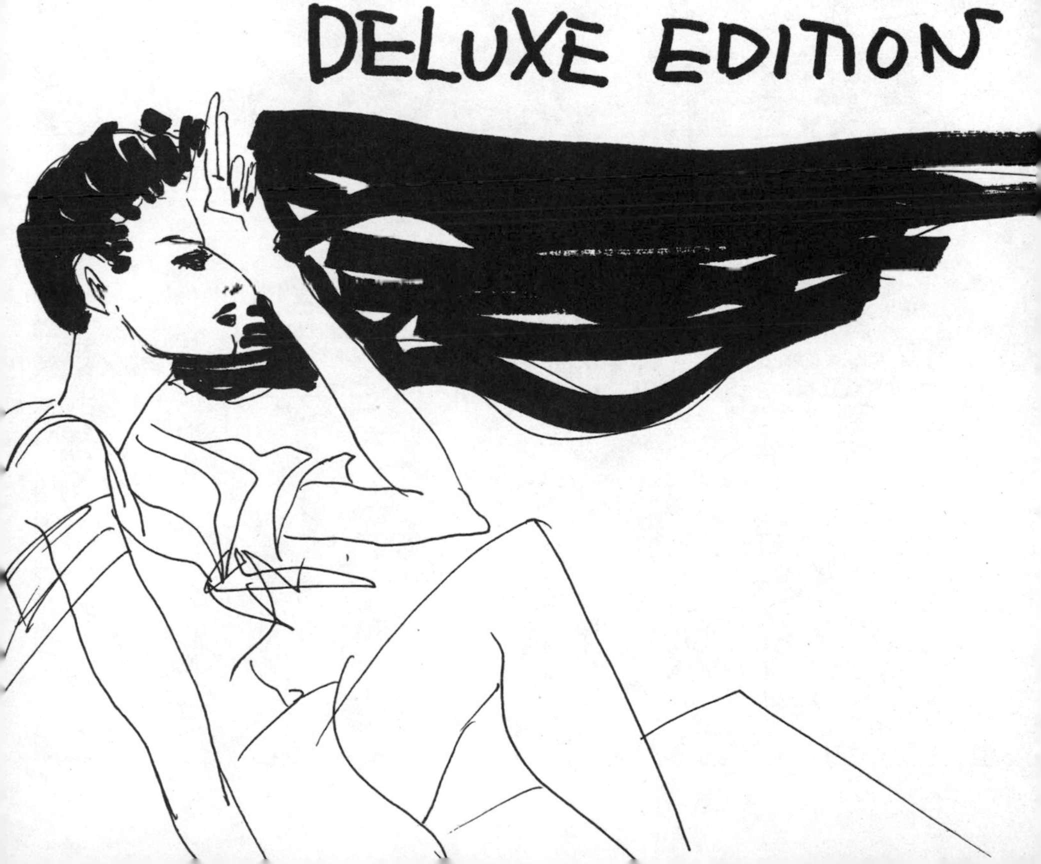
DELUXE EDITION

CHAPTER 31

YUKAKO YAMAGISHI FALLS IN LOVE, PART 3

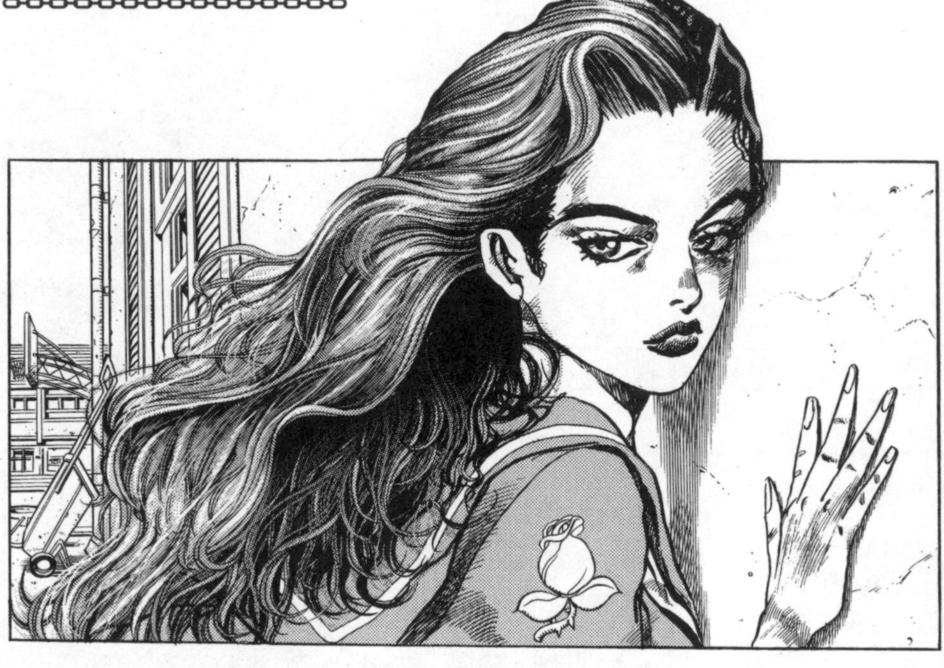

EVERYTHING KOICHI, JOSUKE AND OKUYASU KNOW ABOUT YUKAKO YAMAGISHI

①——Yukako Yamagishi is a Stand user.

②——Her Stand, Love Deluxe, allows her to manipulate her hair at will. Its strength is unknown, but its range appears to be at least tens of meters.

③——Yukako Yamagishi is in love with Koichi. She is not approaching him as an enemy or with the intent to harm.

④——Yukako Yamagishi is an unstable girl, prone to quickly leaping to conclusions, whether or not they are based on reality.

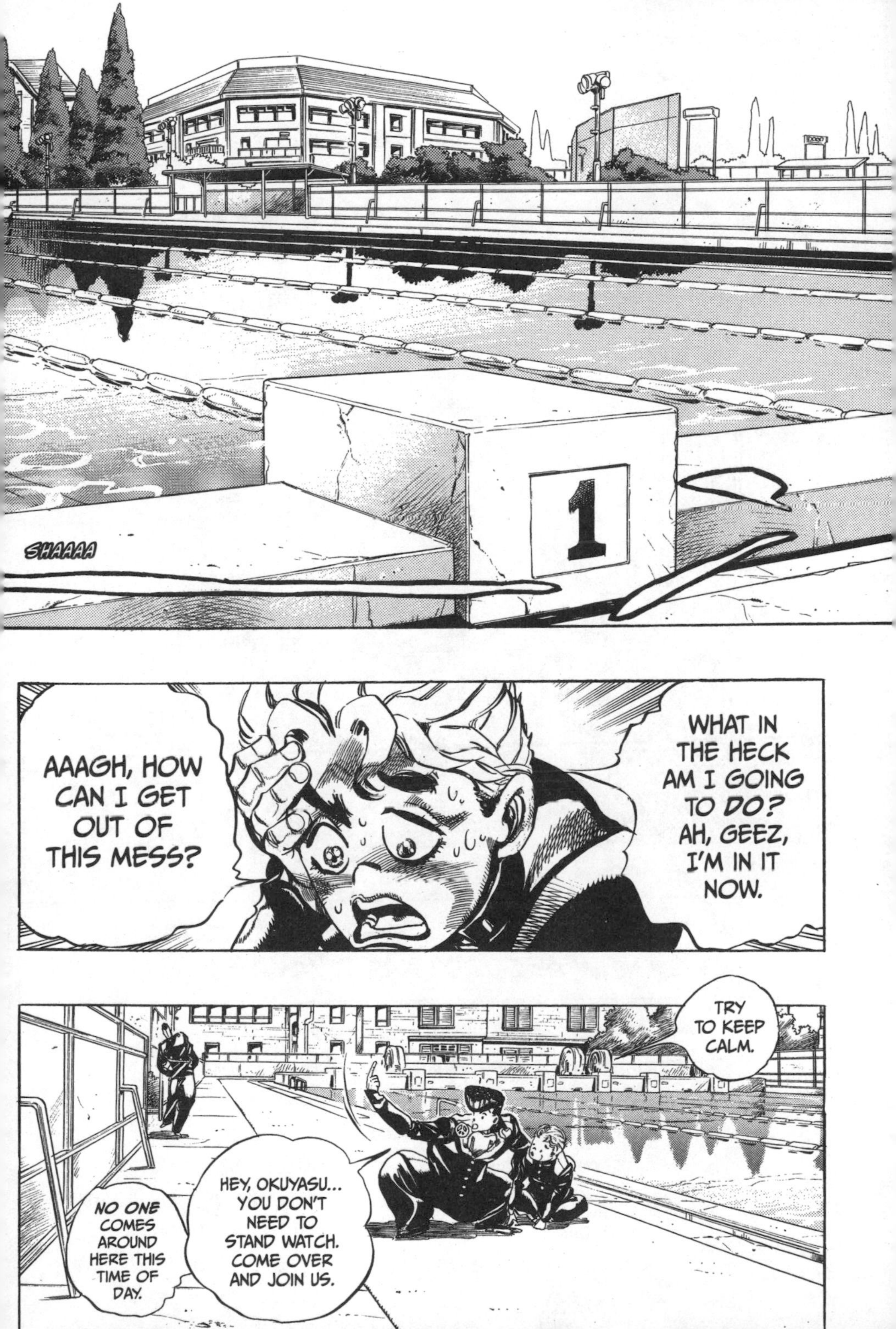
SHAAAA
WHAT IN THE HECK AM I GOING TO *DO?* AH, GEEZ, I'M IN IT NOW.
AAAGH, HOW CAN I GET OUT OF THIS MESS?
TRY TO KEEP CALM.
HEY, OKUYASU... YOU DON'T NEED TO STAND WATCH. COME OVER AND JOIN US.
NO ONE COMES AROUND HERE THIS TIME OF DAY.

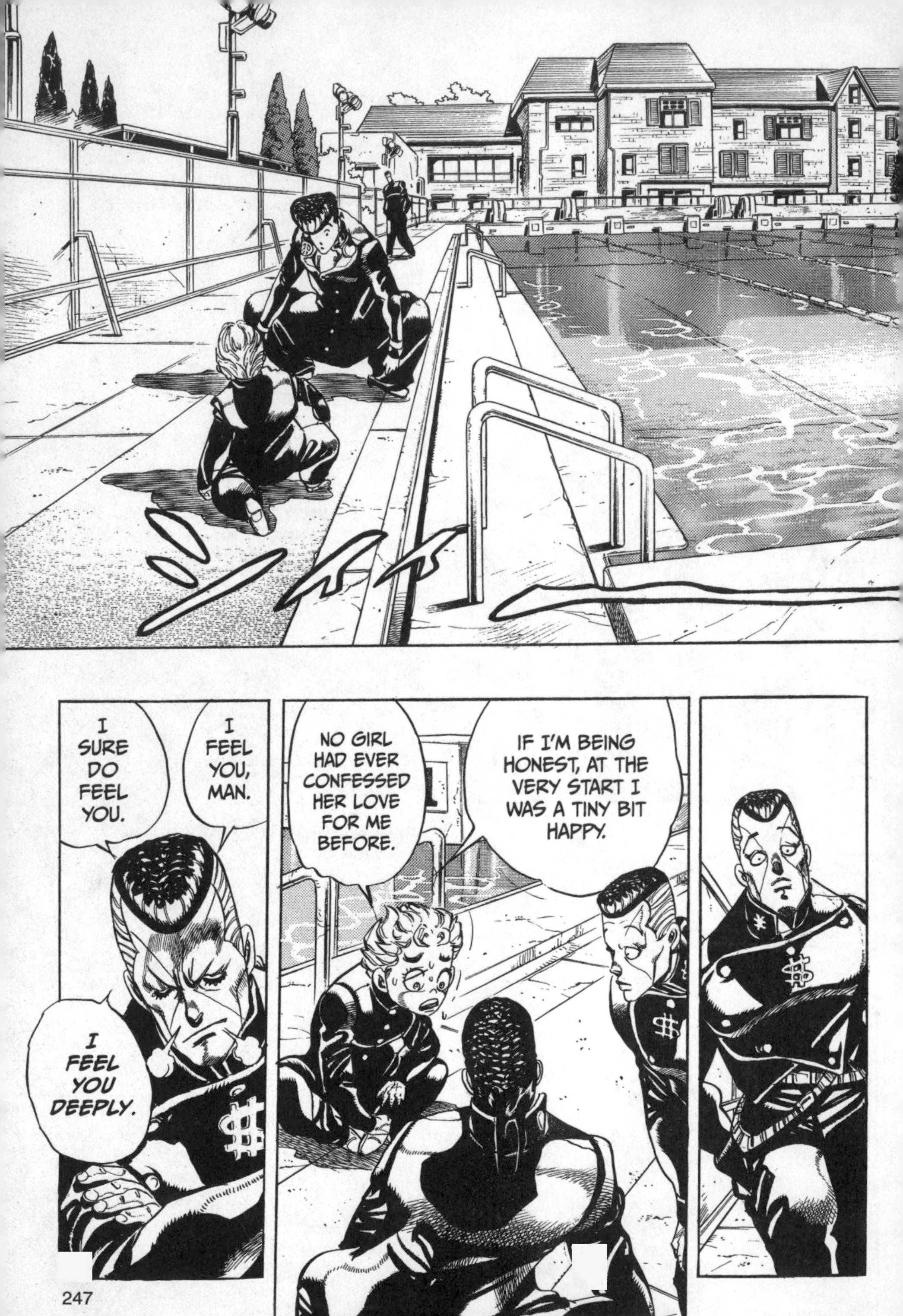
IF I'M BEING HONEST, AT THE VERY START I WAS A TINY BIT HAPPY.
NO GIRL HAD EVER CONFESSED HER LOVE FOR ME BEFORE.
I FEEL YOU, MAN.
I SURE DO FEEL YOU.
I FEEL YOU DEEPLY.

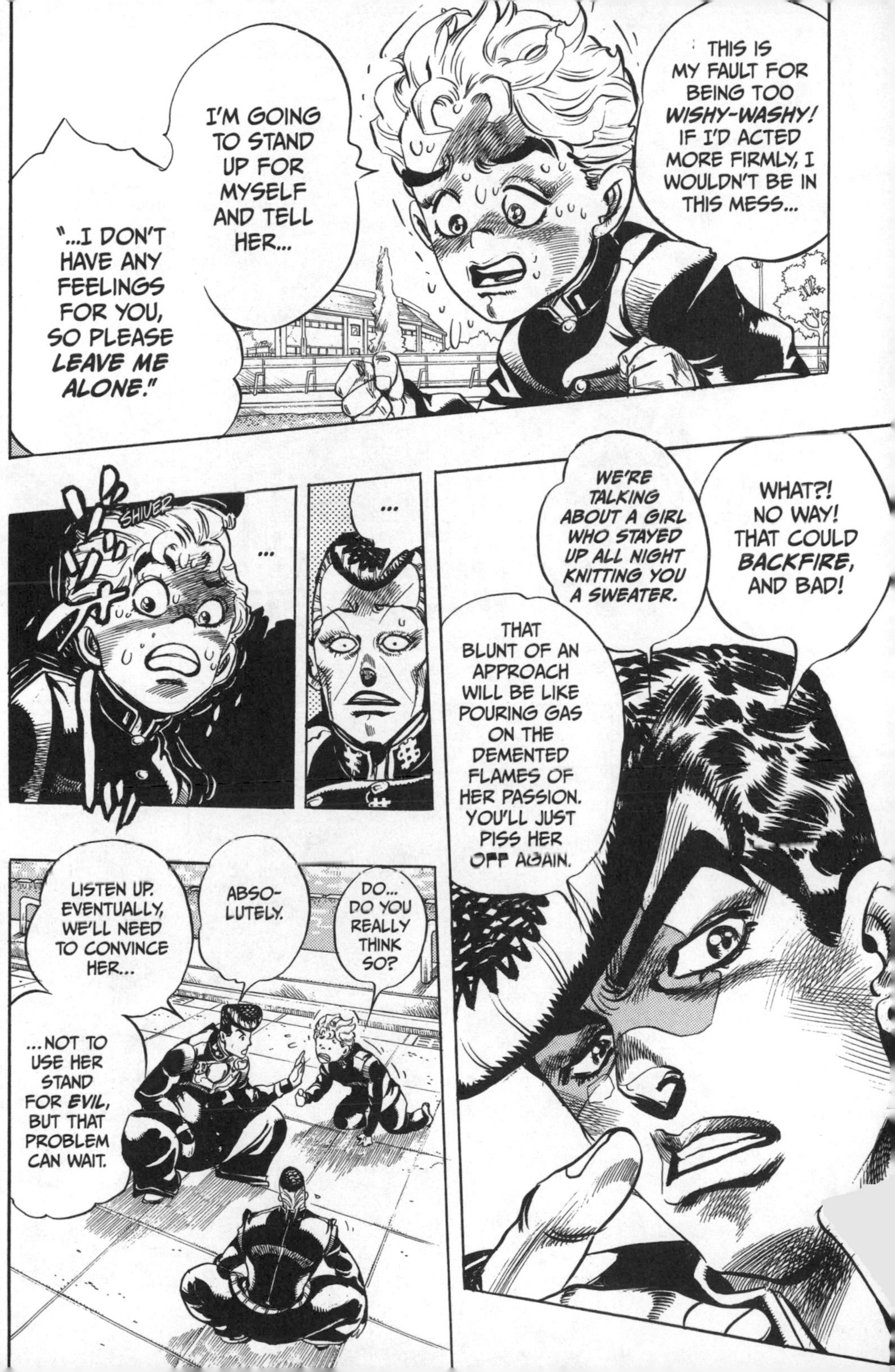
THIS IS MY FAULT FOR BEING TOO *WISHY-WASHY!* IF I'D ACTED MORE FIRMLY, I WOULDN'T BE IN THIS MESS...
I'M GOING TO STAND UP FOR MYSELF AND TELL HER...
"...I DON'T HAVE ANY FEELINGS FOR YOU, SO PLEASE *LEAVE ME ALONE.*"
WHAT?! NO WAY! THAT COULD *BACKFIRE,* AND BAD!
WE'RE TALKING ABOUT A GIRL WHO STAYED UP ALL NIGHT KNITTING YOU A SWEATER.
THAT BLUNT OF AN APPROACH WILL BE LIKE POURING GAS ON THE DEMENTED FLAMES OF HER PASSION. YOU'LL JUST PISS HER OFF AGAIN.
...
SHIVER
...
DO... DO YOU REALLY THINK SO?
ABSO-LUTELY.
LISTEN UP. EVENTUALLY, WE'LL NEED TO CONVINCE HER...
...NOT TO USE HER STAND FOR *EVIL,* BUT THAT PROBLEM CAN WAIT.

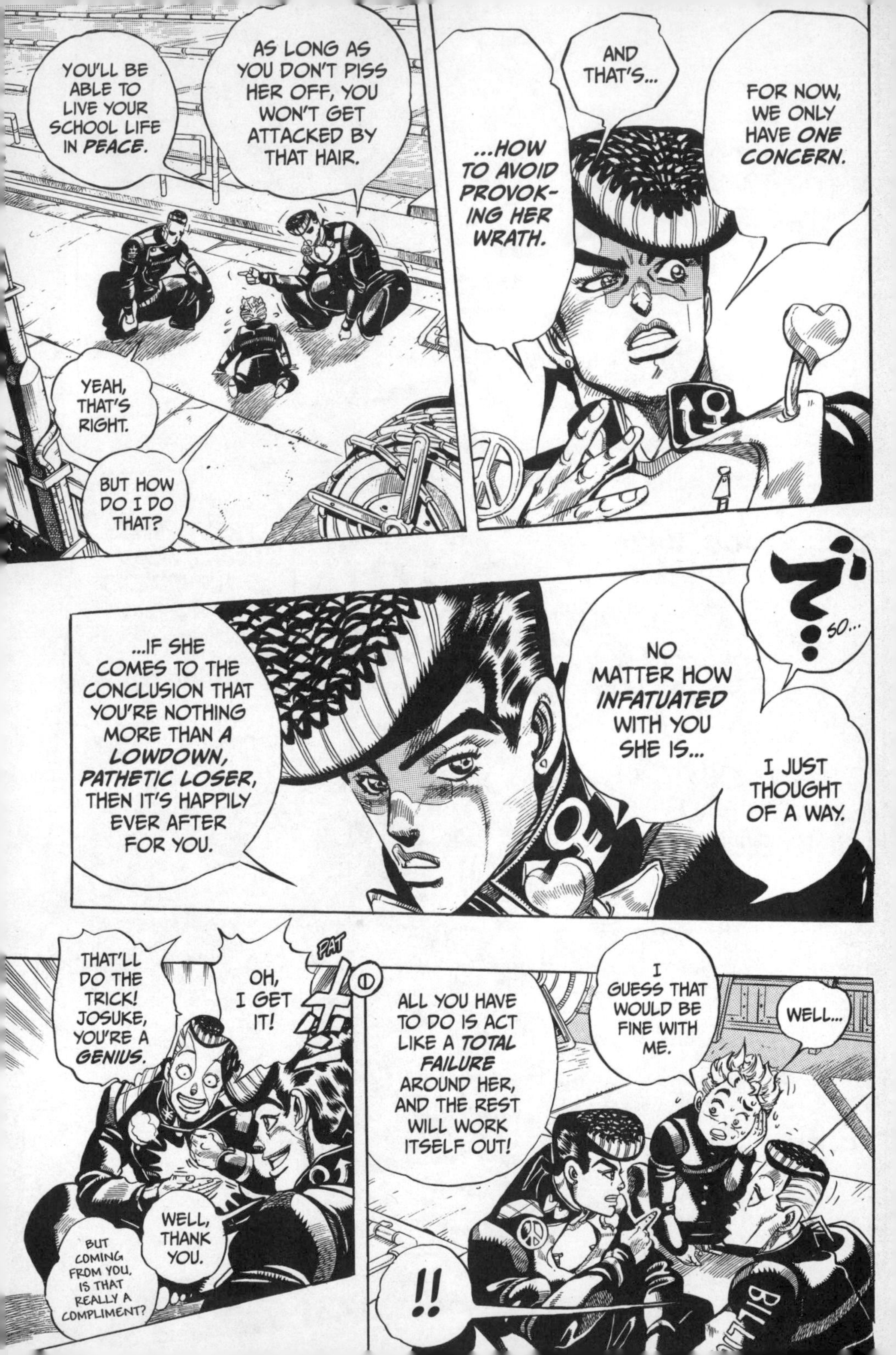
FOR NOW, WE ONLY HAVE ONE CONCERN.
AND THAT'S...
...HOW TO AVOID PROVOKING HER WRATH.
AS LONG AS YOU DON'T PISS HER OFF, YOU WON'T GET ATTACKED BY THAT HAIR.
YOU'LL BE ABLE TO LIVE YOUR SCHOOL LIFE IN PEACE.
YEAH, THAT'S RIGHT.
BUT HOW DO I DO THAT?
? SO...
I JUST THOUGHT OF A WAY.
NO MATTER HOW INFATUATED WITH YOU SHE IS...
...IF SHE COMES TO THE CONCLUSION THAT YOU'RE NOTHING MORE THAN A LOWDOWN, PATHETIC LOSER, THEN IT'S HAPPILY EVER AFTER FOR YOU.
ALL YOU HAVE TO DO IS ACT LIKE A TOTAL FAILURE AROUND HER, AND THE REST WILL WORK ITSELF OUT!
!!
WELL...
I GUESS THAT WOULD BE FINE WITH ME.
PAT
OH, I GET IT!
THAT'LL DO THE TRICK! JOSUKE, YOU'RE A GENIUS.
WELL, THANK YOU.
BUT COMING FROM YOU, IS THAT REALLY A COMPLIMENT?

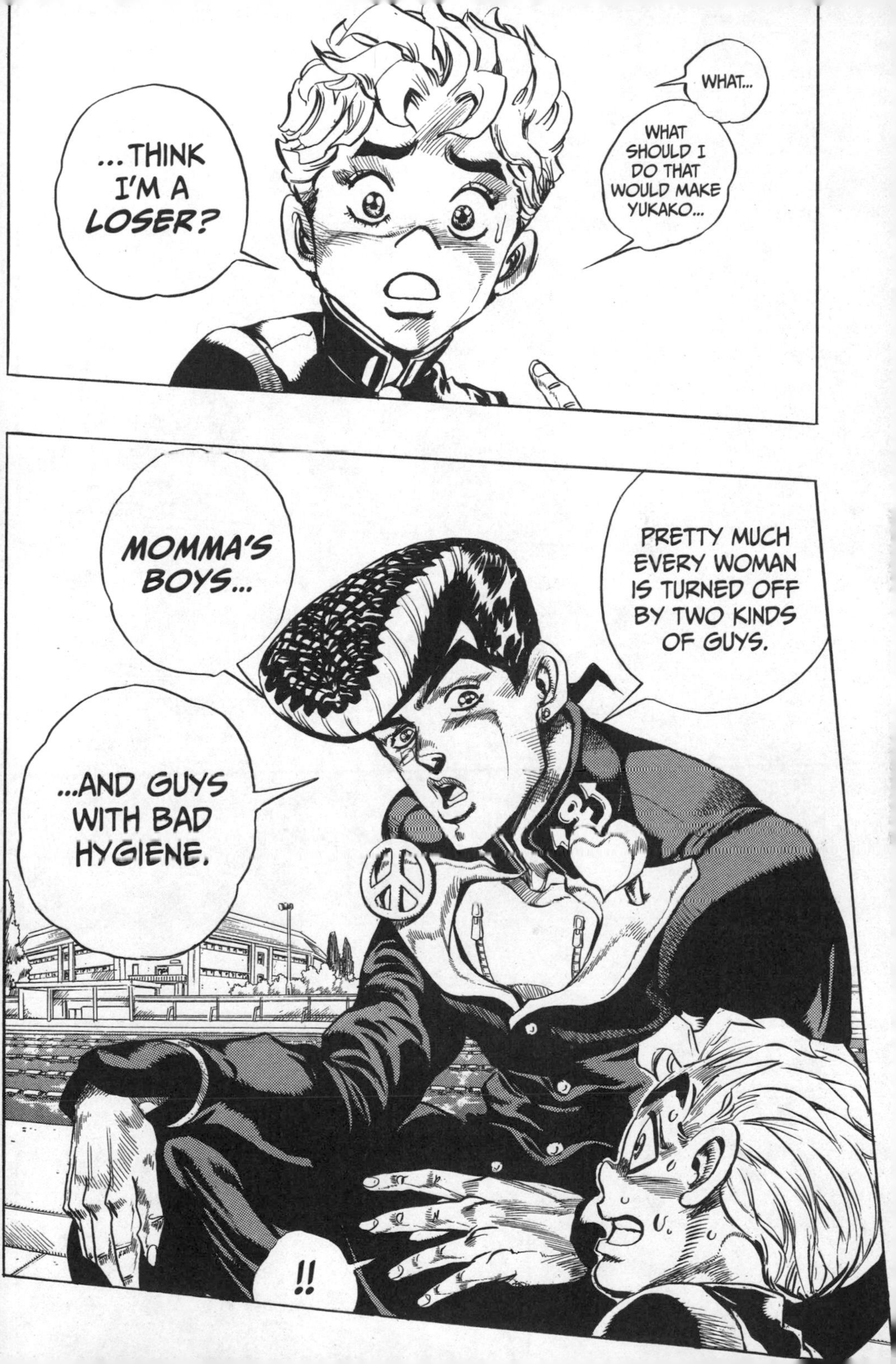
WHAT...
WHAT SHOULD I DO THAT WOULD MAKE YUKAKO...
...THINK I'M A LOSER?
PRETTY MUCH EVERY WOMAN IS TURNED OFF BY TWO KINDS OF GUYS.
MOMMA'S BOYS...
...AND GUYS WITH BAD HYGIENE.
!!

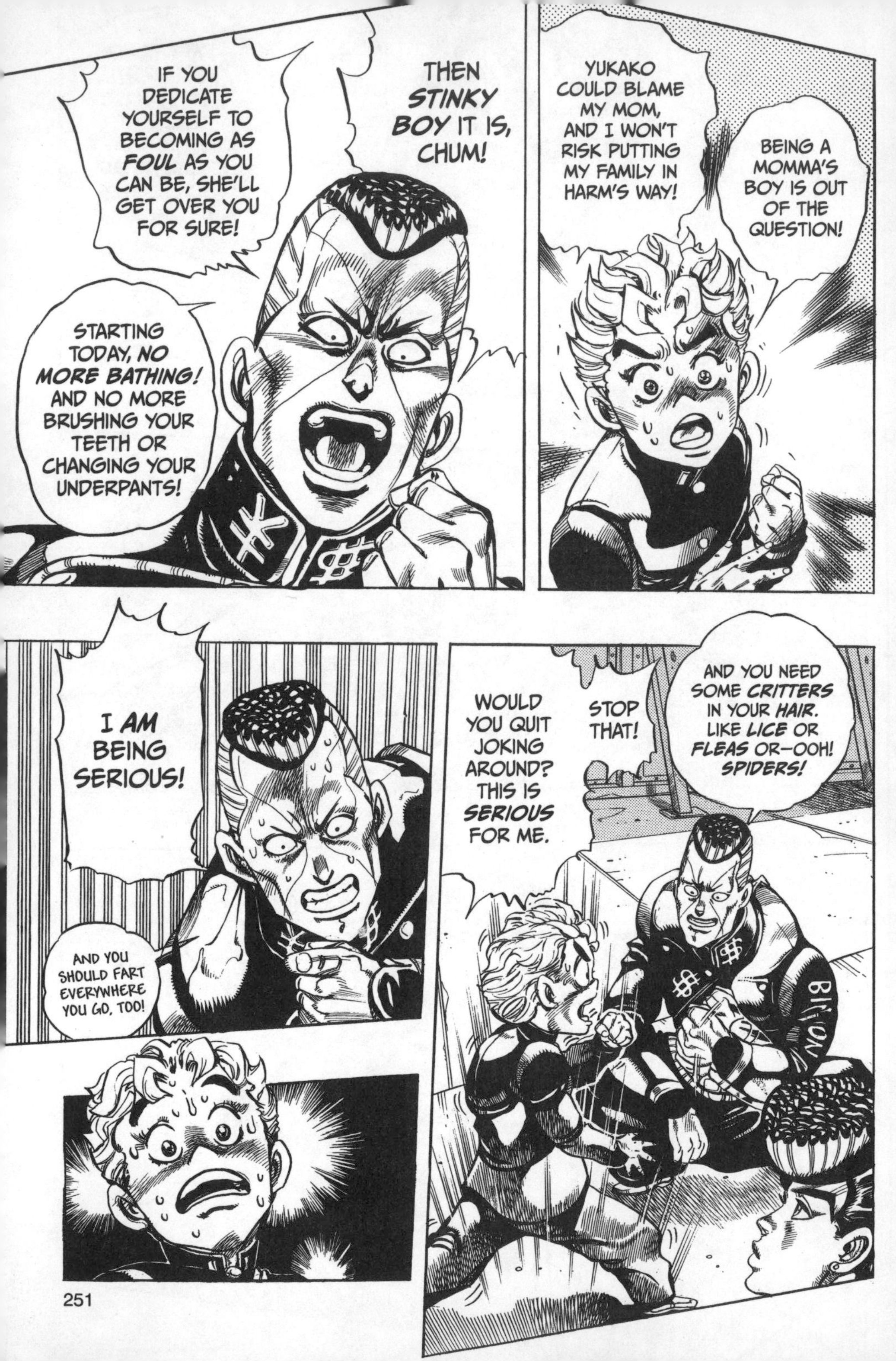
BEING A MOMMA'S BOY IS OUT OF THE QUESTION!
YUKAKO COULD BLAME MY MOM, AND I WON'T RISK PUTTING MY FAMILY IN HARM'S WAY!
THEN STINKY BOY IT IS, CHUM!
IF YOU DEDICATE YOURSELF TO BECOMING AS FOUL AS YOU CAN BE, SHE'LL GET OVER YOU FOR SURE!
STARTING TODAY, NO MORE BATHING! AND NO MORE BRUSHING YOUR TEETH OR CHANGING YOUR UNDERPANTS!
AND YOU NEED SOME CRITTERS IN YOUR HAIR. LIKE LICE OR FLEAS OR—OOH! SPIDERS!
STOP THAT!
WOULD YOU QUIT JOKING AROUND? THIS IS SERIOUS FOR ME.
I AM BEING SERIOUS!
AND YOU SHOULD FART EVERYWHERE YOU GO, TOO!

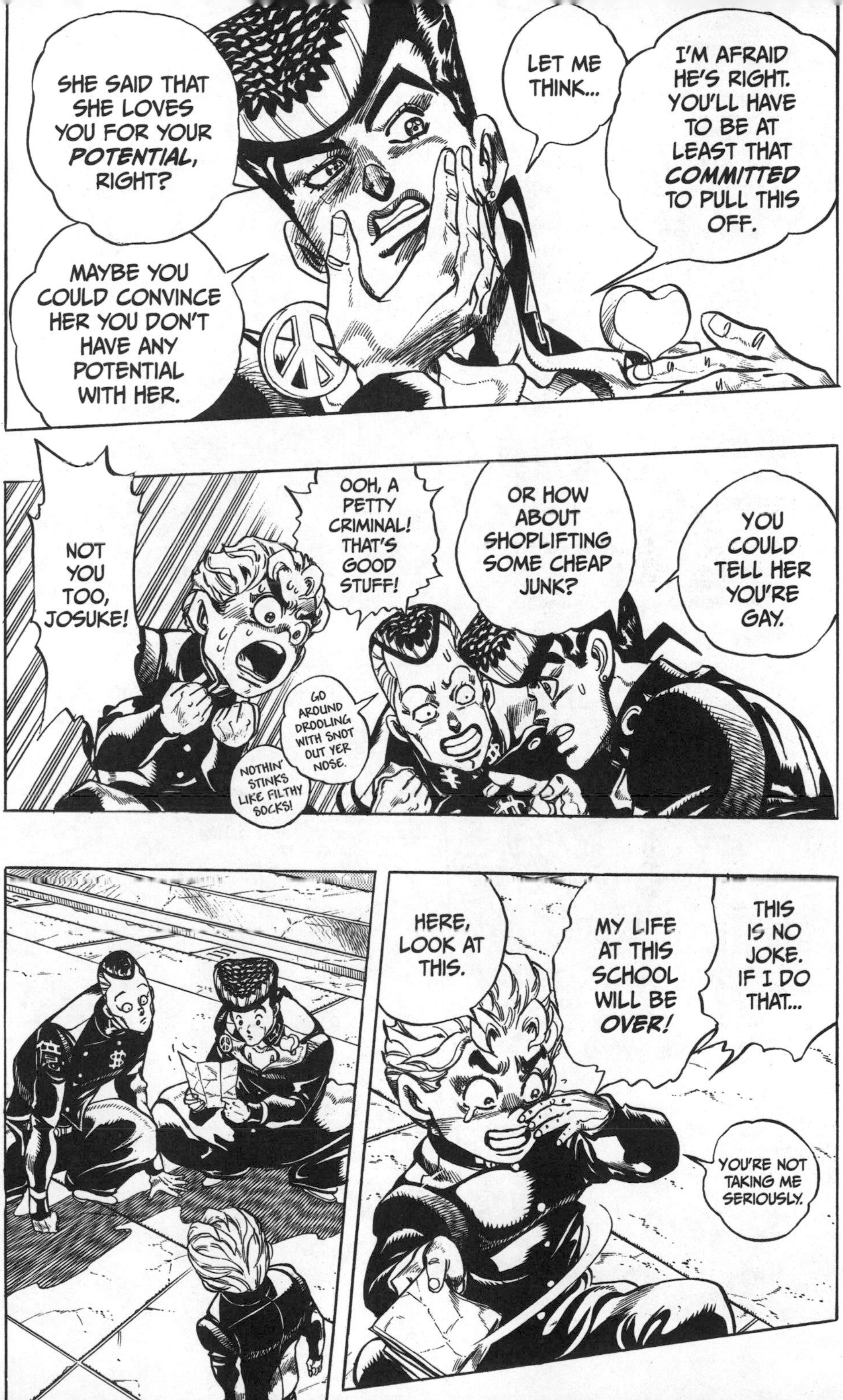
I'M AFRAID HE'S RIGHT. YOU'LL HAVE TO BE AT LEAST THAT *COMMITTED* TO PULL THIS OFF.
LET ME THINK...
SHE SAID THAT SHE LOVES YOU FOR YOUR *POTENTIAL*, RIGHT?
MAYBE YOU COULD CONVINCE HER YOU DON'T HAVE ANY POTENTIAL WITH HER.
YOU COULD TELL HER YOU'RE GAY.
OR HOW ABOUT SHOPLIFTING SOME CHEAP JUNK?
OOH, A PETTY CRIMINAL! THAT'S GOOD STUFF!
GO AROUND DROOLING WITH SNOT OUT YER NOSE.
NOTHIN' STINKS LIKE FILTHY SOCKS!
NOT YOU TOO, JOSUKE!
THIS IS NO JOKE. IF I DO THAT...
MY LIFE AT THIS SCHOOL WILL BE *OVER!*
HERE, LOOK AT THIS.
YOU'RE NOT TAKING ME SERIOUSLY.

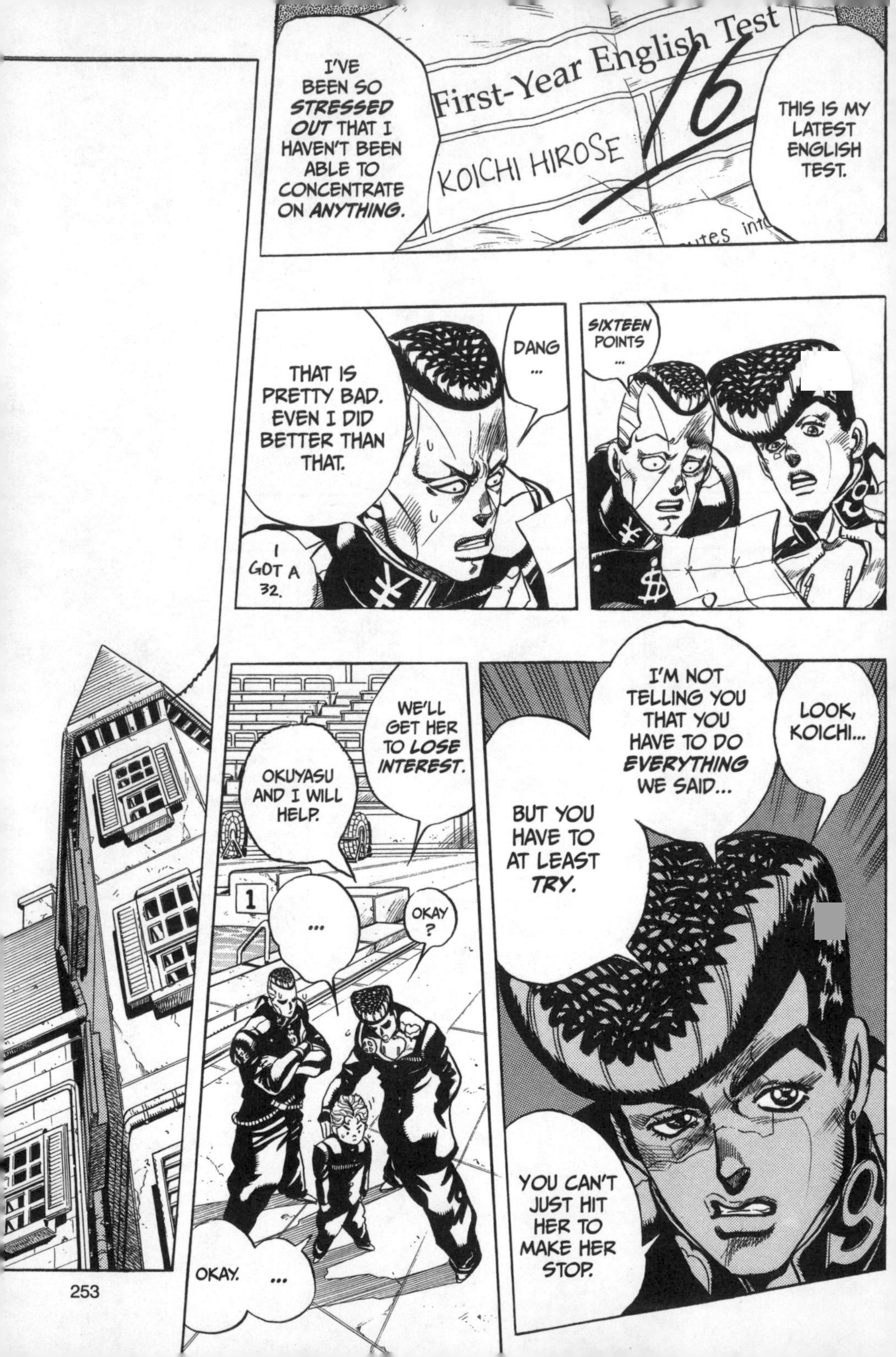

First-Year English Test
16
KOICHI HIROSE
THIS IS MY LATEST ENGLISH TEST.
I'VE BEEN SO STRESSED OUT THAT I HAVEN'T BEEN ABLE TO CONCENTRATE ON ANYTHING.
SIXTEEN POINTS ...
DANG ...
THAT IS PRETTY BAD. EVEN I DID BETTER THAN THAT.
I GOT A 32.
LOOK, KOICHI...
I'M NOT TELLING YOU THAT YOU HAVE TO DO EVERYTHING WE SAID...
BUT YOU HAVE TO AT LEAST TRY.
YOU CAN'T JUST HIT HER TO MAKE HER STOP.
WE'LL GET HER TO LOSE INTEREST.
OKUYASU AND I WILL HELP.
OKAY ?
...
1
OKAY. ...

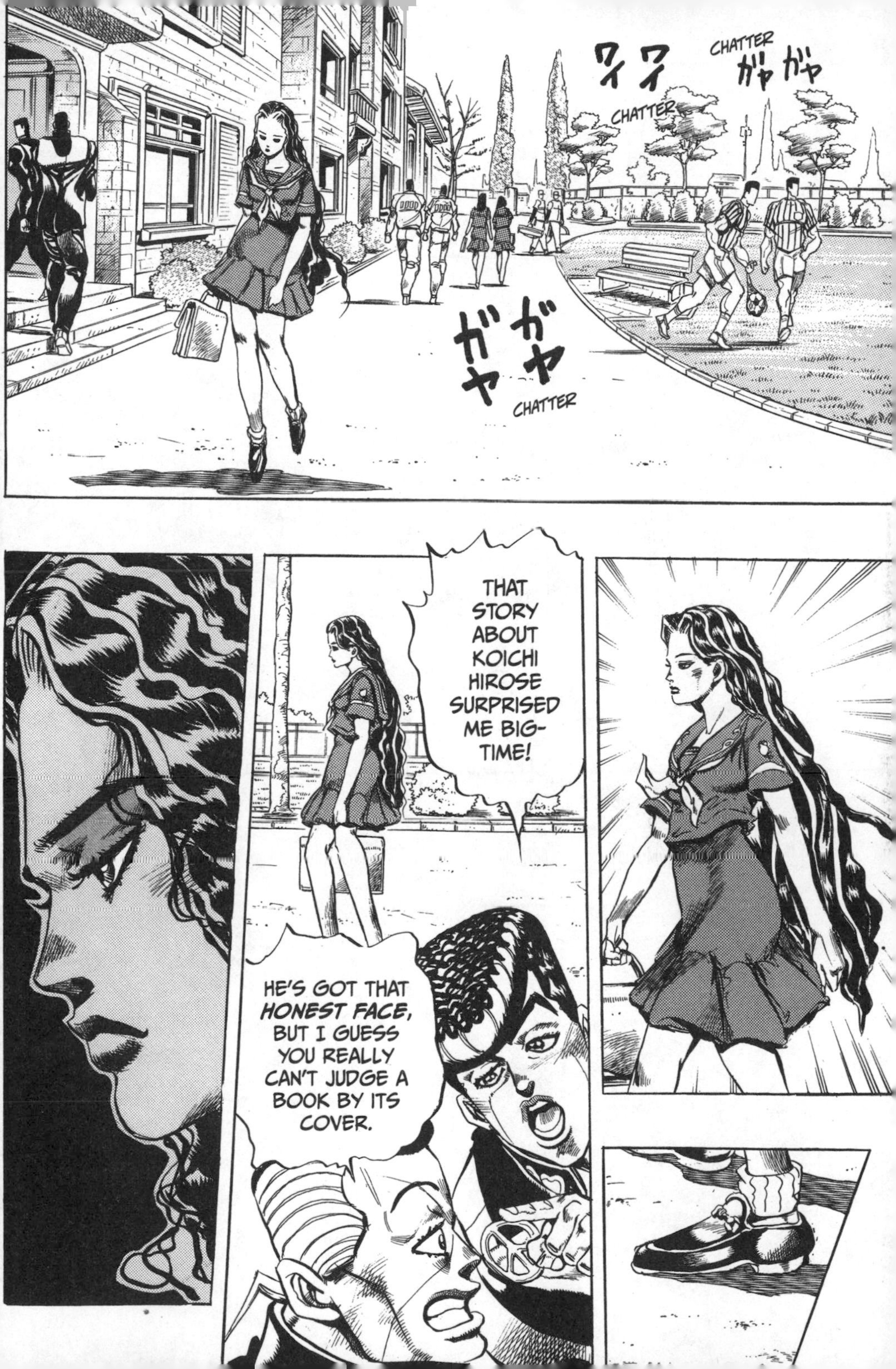
ガャガャ
CHATTER
ワイワイ
CHATTER
ガヤガヤ
CHATTER
THAT STORY ABOUT KOICHI HIROSE SURPRISED ME BIG-TIME!
HE'S GOT THAT ***HONEST FACE***, BUT I GUESS YOU REALLY CAN'T JUDGE A BOOK BY ITS COVER.

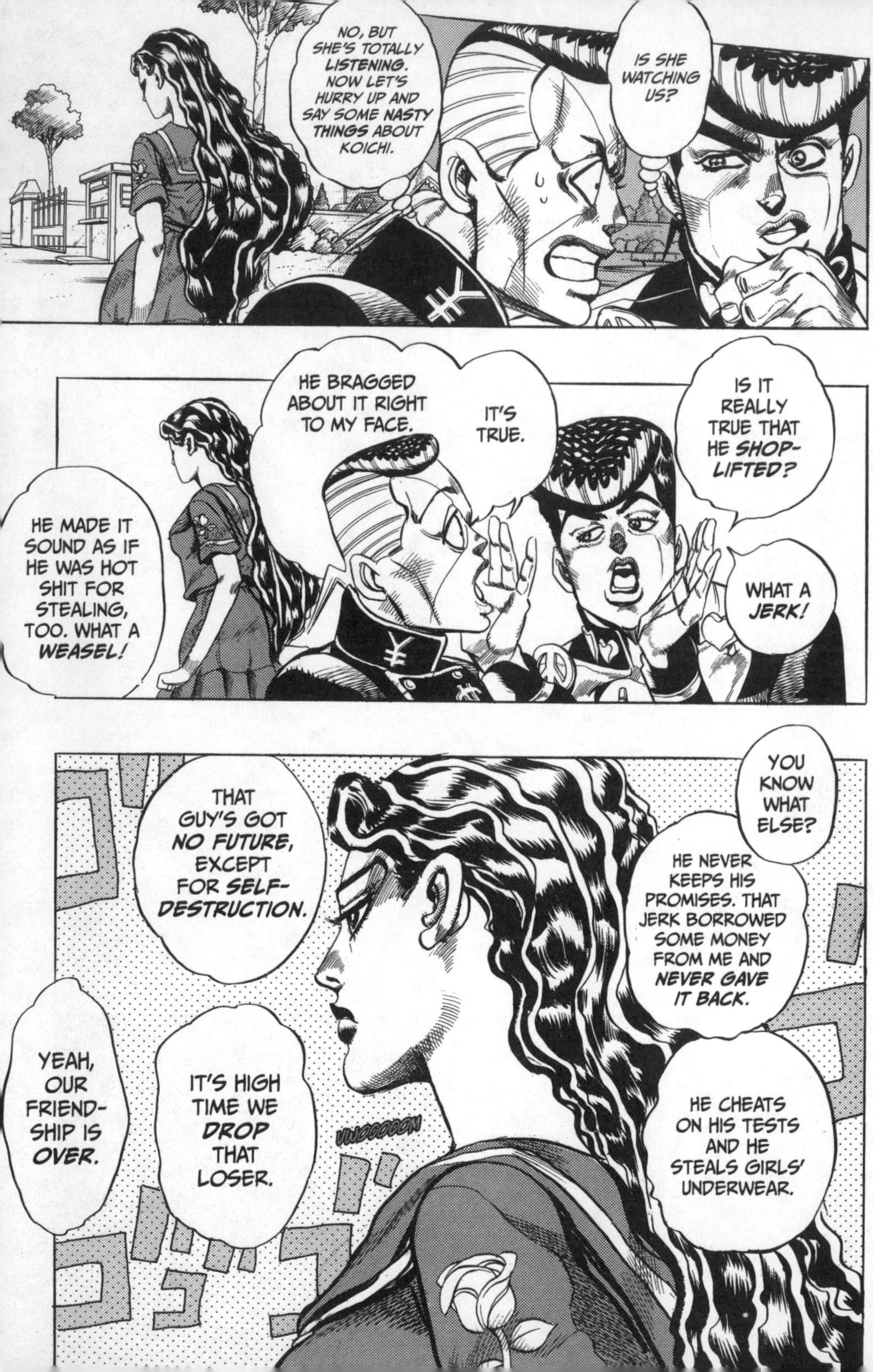
IS SHE WATCHING US?
NO, BUT SHE'S TOTALLY LISTENING. NOW LET'S HURRY UP AND SAY SOME NASTY THINGS ABOUT KOICHI.
IS IT REALLY TRUE THAT HE SHOP-LIFTED?
IT'S TRUE.
HE BRAGGED ABOUT IT RIGHT TO MY FACE.
WHAT A JERK!
HE MADE IT SOUND AS IF HE WAS HOT SHIT FOR STEALING, TOO. WHAT A WEASEL!
YOU KNOW WHAT ELSE?
HE NEVER KEEPS HIS PROMISES. THAT JERK BORROWED SOME MONEY FROM ME AND NEVER GAVE IT BACK.
THAT GUY'S GOT NO FUTURE, EXCEPT FOR SELF-DESTRUCTION.
HE CHEATS ON HIS TESTS AND HE STEALS GIRLS' UNDERWEAR.
IT'S HIGH TIME WE DROP THAT LOSER.
YEAH, OUR FRIEND-SHIP IS OVER.

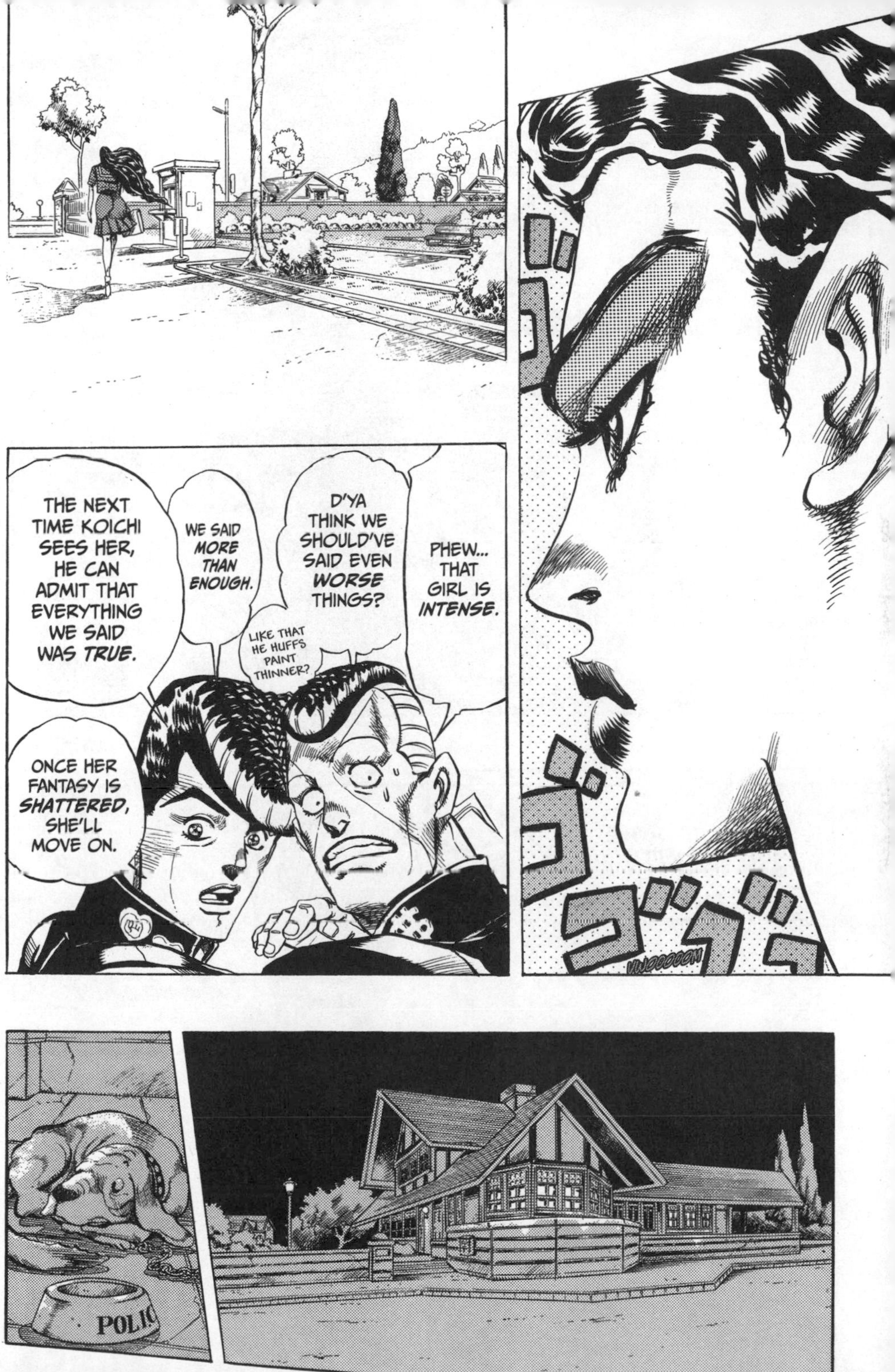
VWOOOOOM
PHEW... THAT GIRL IS *INTENSE*.
D'YA THINK WE SHOULD'VE SAID EVEN *WORSE* THINGS?
LIKE THAT HE HUFFS PAINT THINNER?
WE SAID *MORE THAN ENOUGH*.
THE NEXT TIME KOICHI SEES HER, HE CAN ADMIT THAT EVERYTHING WE SAID WAS *TRUE*.
ONCE HER FANTASY IS *SHATTERED*, SHE'LL MOVE ON.
POLIC

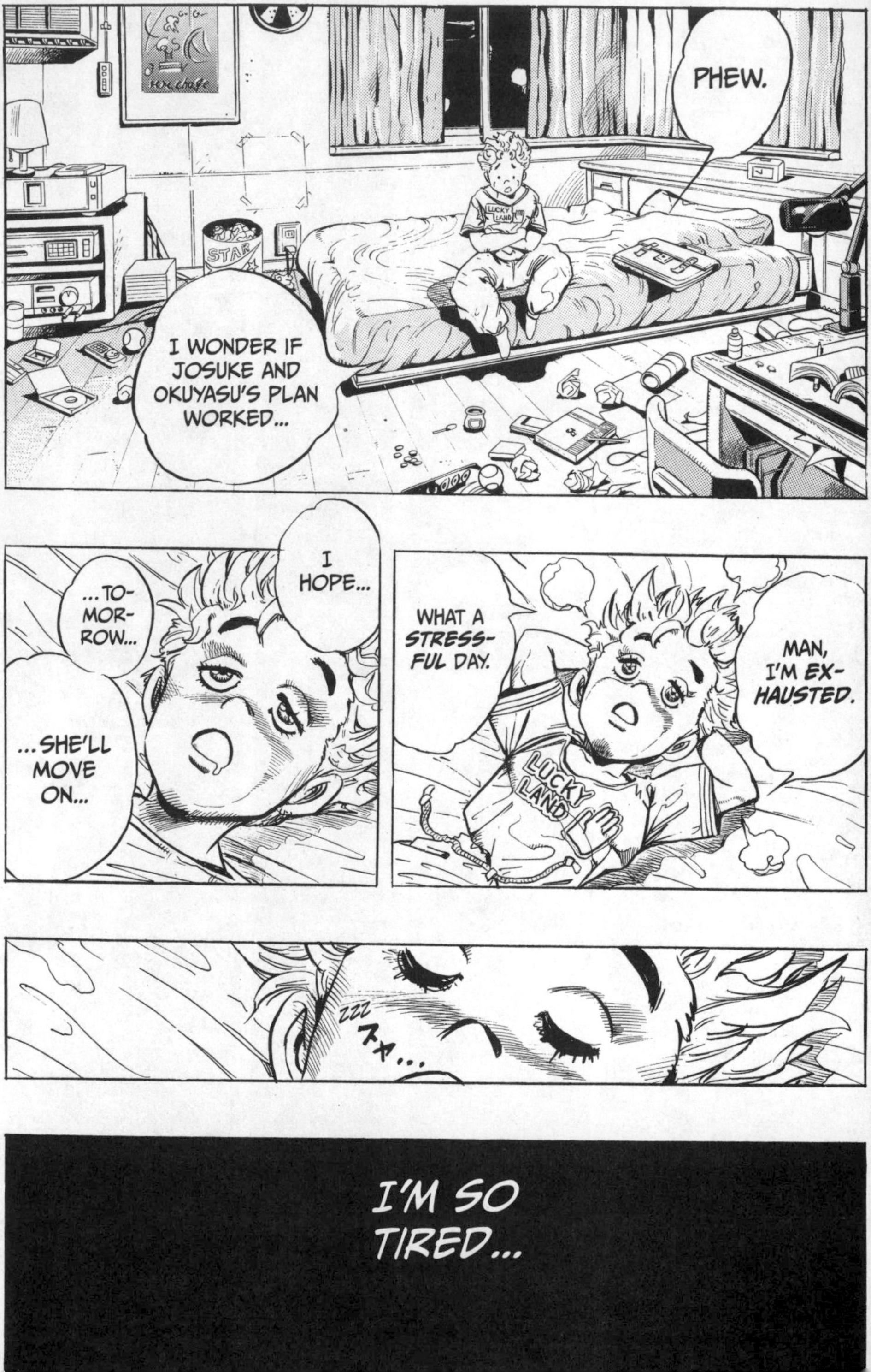
PHEW.
I WONDER IF JOSUKE AND OKUYASU'S PLAN WORKED...
MAN, I'M EX-HAUSTED.
WHAT A STRESS-FUL DAY.
I HOPE...
...TO-MOR-ROW...
...SHE'LL MOVE ON...
ZZZ スャ...
I'M SO TIRED...

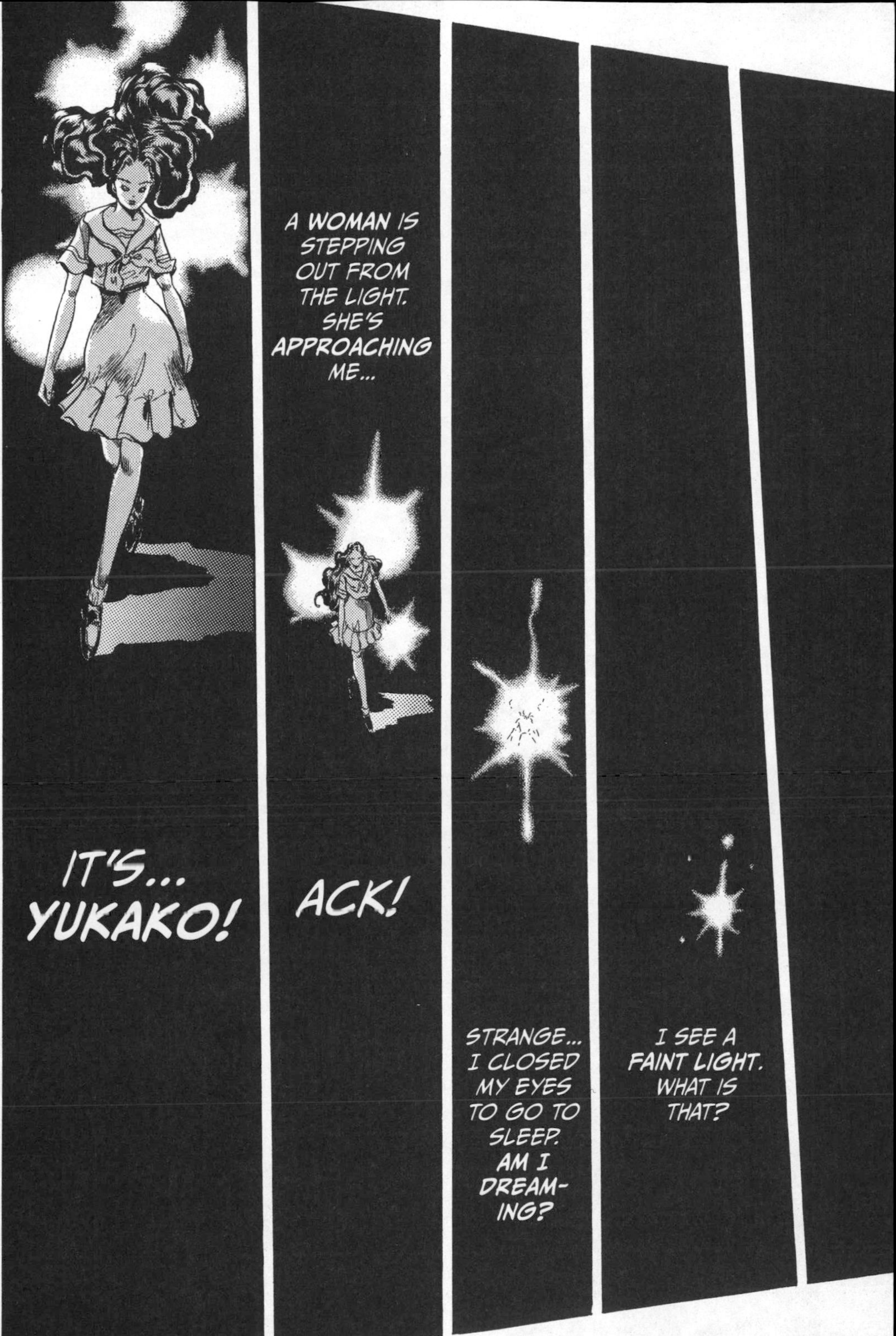
I SEE A FAINT LIGHT. WHAT IS THAT?
STRANGE... I CLOSED MY EYES TO GO TO SLEEP. AM I DREAMING?
A WOMAN IS STEPPING OUT FROM THE LIGHT. SHE'S APPROACHING ME...
ACK!
IT'S... YUKAKO!

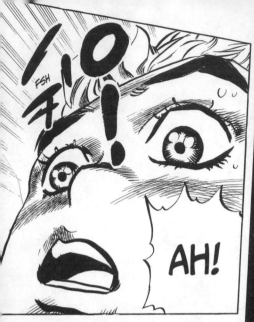

FSH

AH!

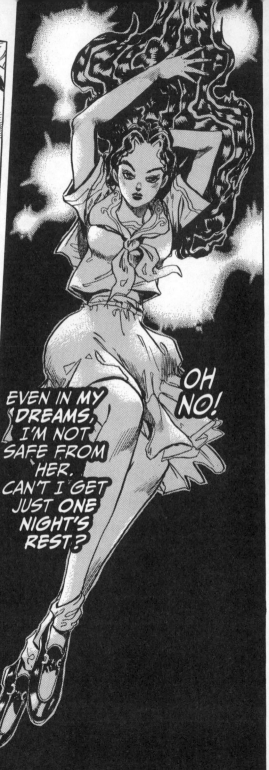

OH NO!

EVEN IN MY DREAMS, I'M NOT SAFE FROM HER. CAN'T I GET JUST ONE NIGHT'S REST?

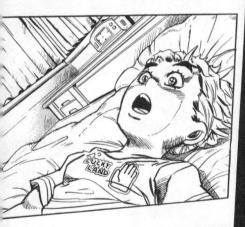

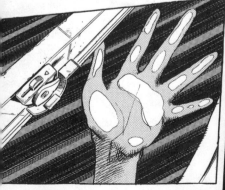

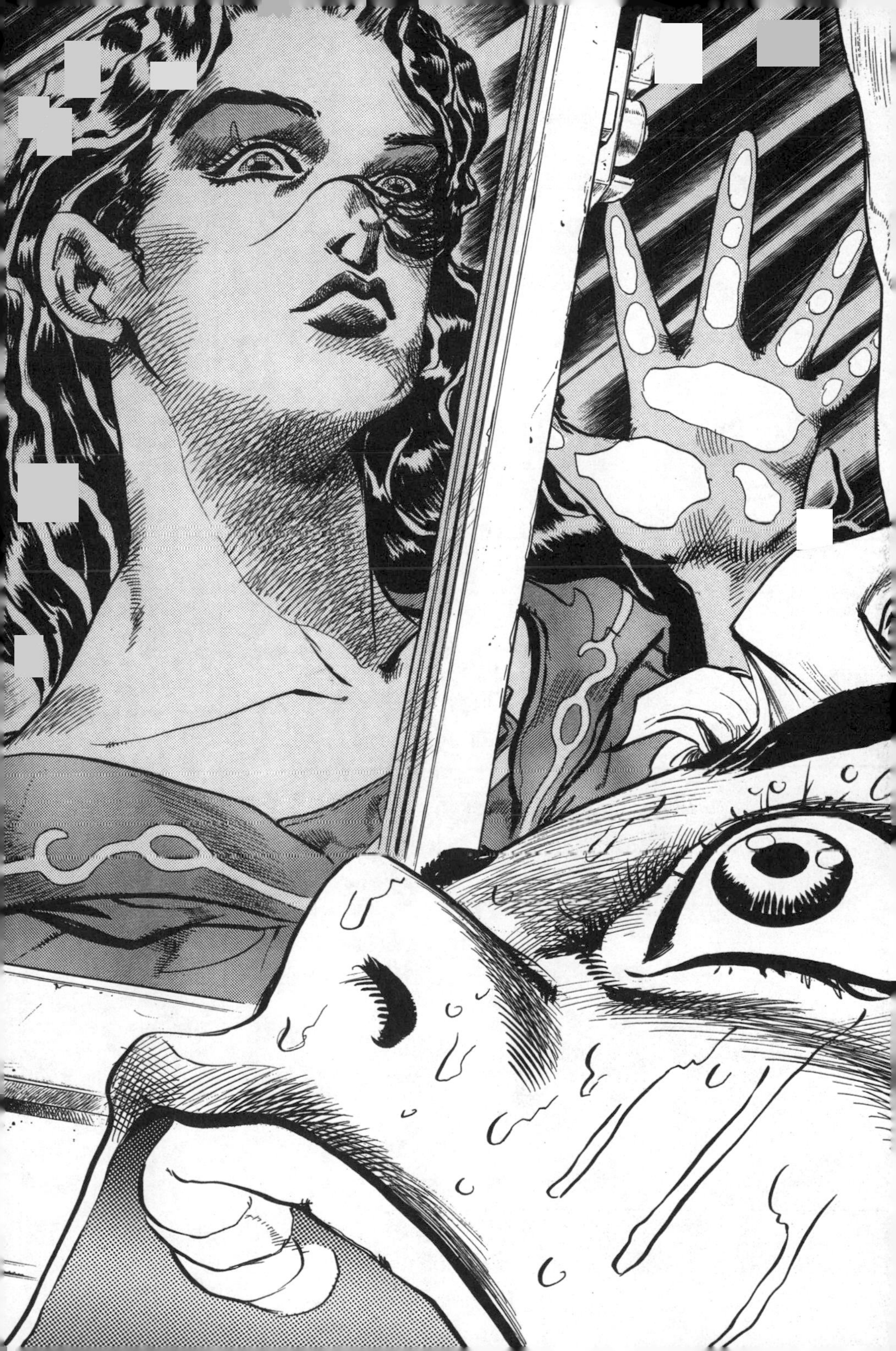

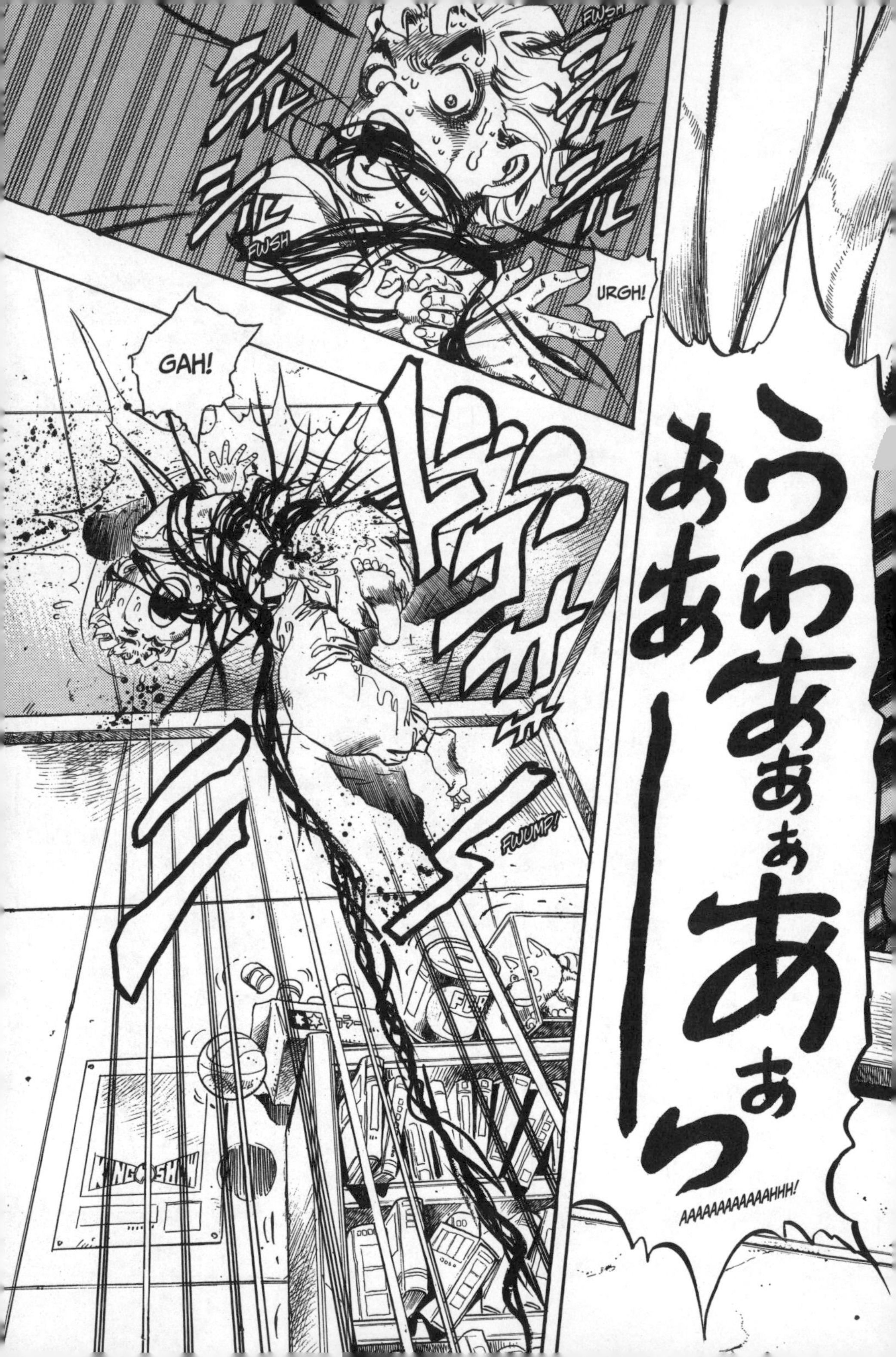
AAAAAAAAAAAAHHH!
FWSH
FWSH
URGH!
GAH!
FWUMP!

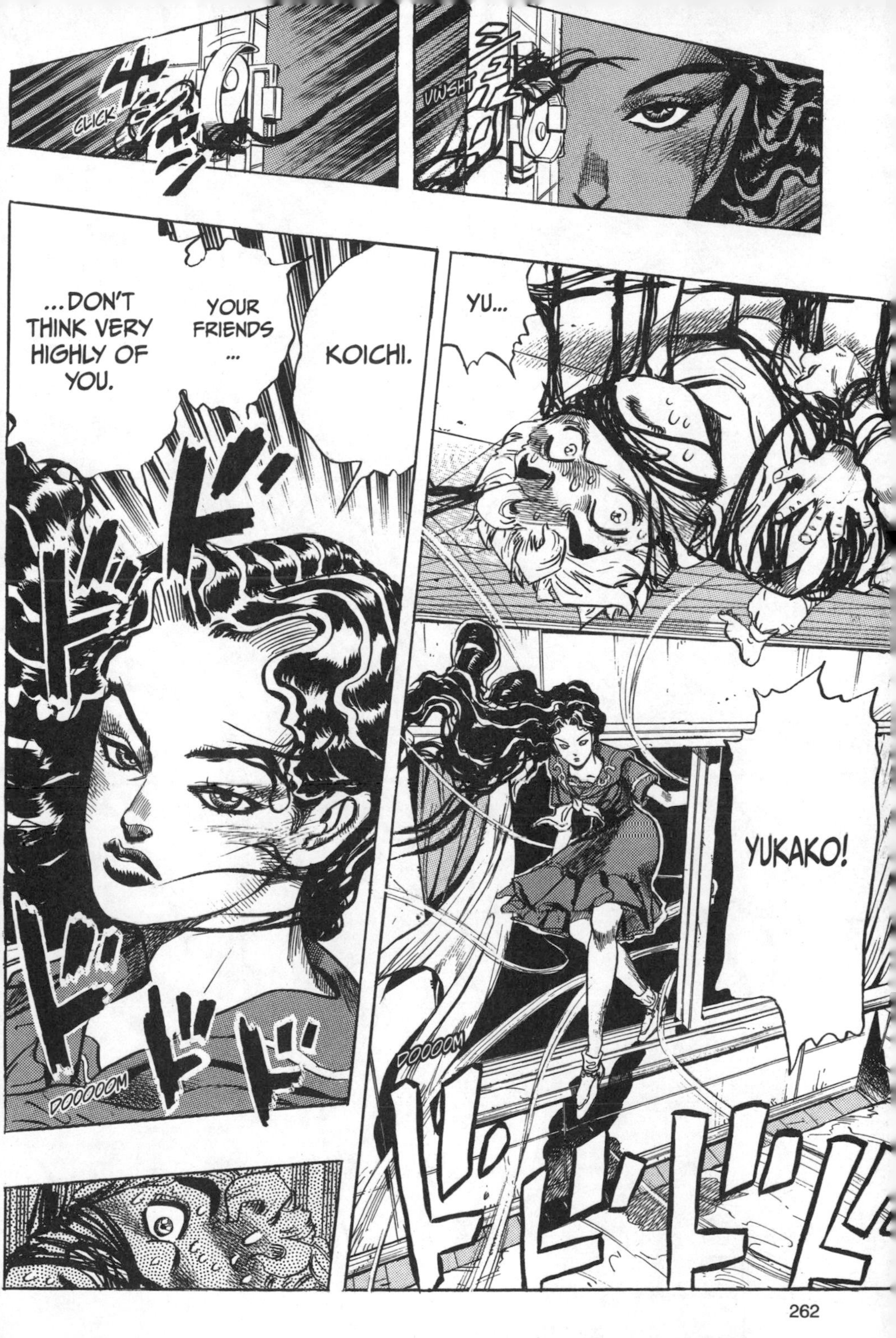
UWSHT
CLICK
YU...
YUKAKO!
DOOOOM
KOICHI.
YOUR FRIENDS ...
...DON'T THINK VERY HIGHLY OF YOU.
DOOOOOM

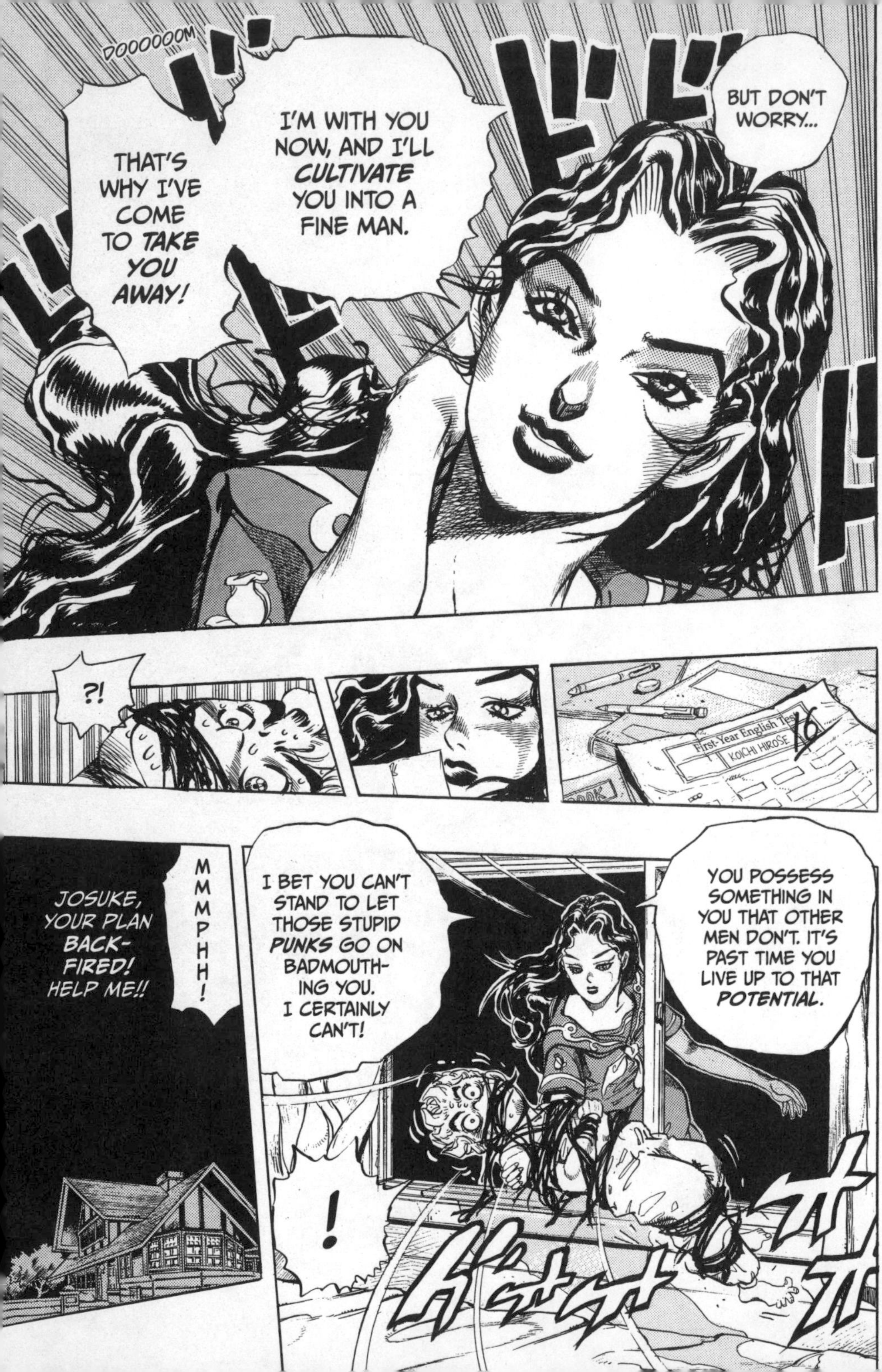
DOOOOOOM
BUT DON'T WORRY...
I'M WITH YOU NOW, AND I'LL *CULTIVATE* YOU INTO A FINE MAN.
THAT'S WHY I'VE COME TO *TAKE YOU AWAY!*
First-Year English Test
KOICHI HIROSE
16
?!
YOU POSSESS SOMETHING IN YOU THAT OTHER MEN DON'T. IT'S PAST TIME YOU LIVE UP TO THAT *POTENTIAL.*
I BET YOU CAN'T STAND TO LET THOSE STUPID *PUNKS* GO ON BADMOUTHING YOU. I CERTAINLY CAN'T!
!
MMMPHH!
JOSUKE, YOUR PLAN BACKFIRED! HELP ME!!

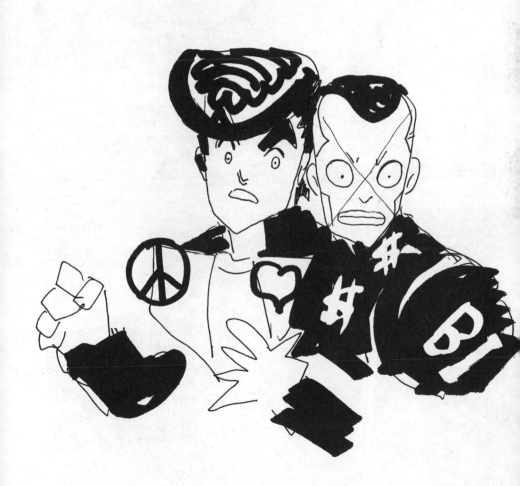

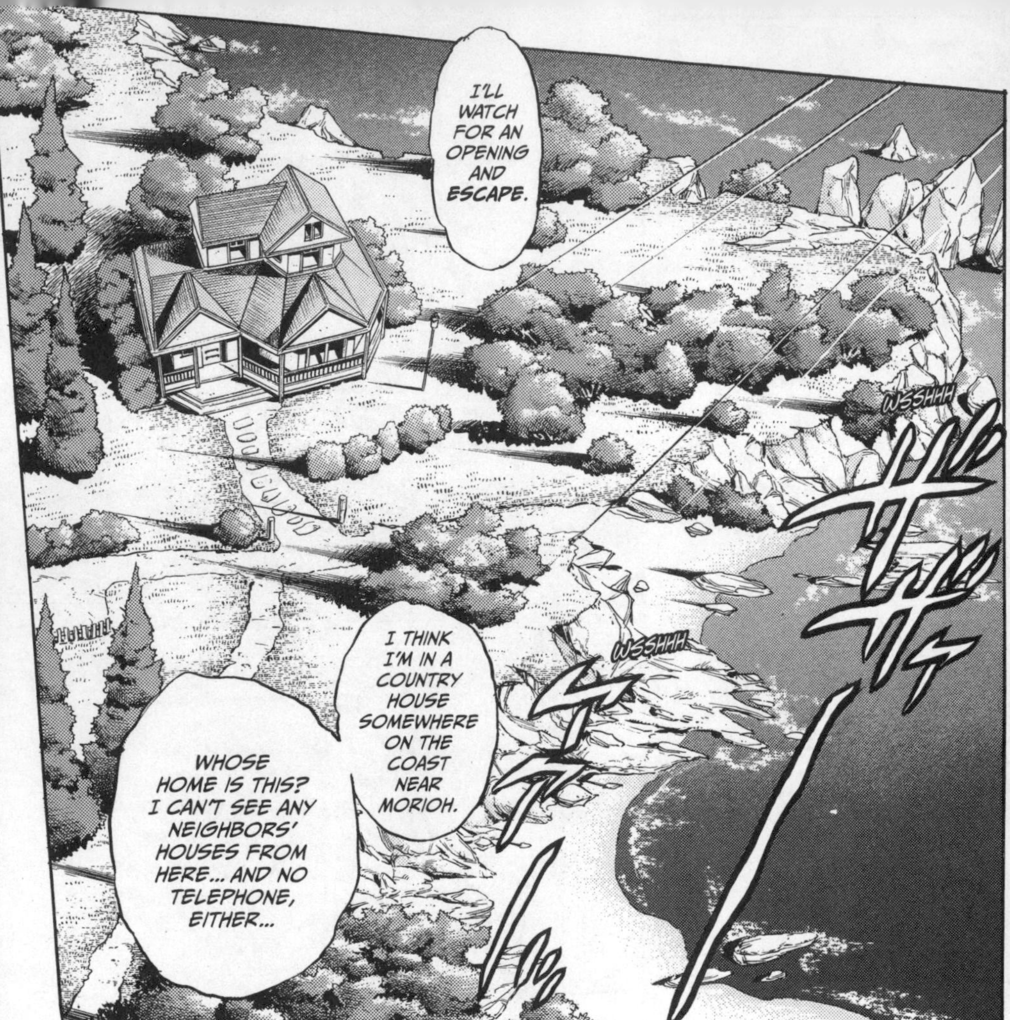
I'LL WATCH FOR AN OPENING AND ESCAPE.
WSSHHH
I THINK I'M IN A COUNTRY HOUSE SOMEWHERE ON THE COAST NEAR MORIOH.
WSSHHH
WHOSE HOME IS THIS? I CAN'T SEE ANY NEIGHBORS' HOUSES FROM HERE... AND NO TELEPHONE, EITHER...

CHAPTER 32

YUKAKO YAMAGISHI FALLS IN LOVE, PART 4

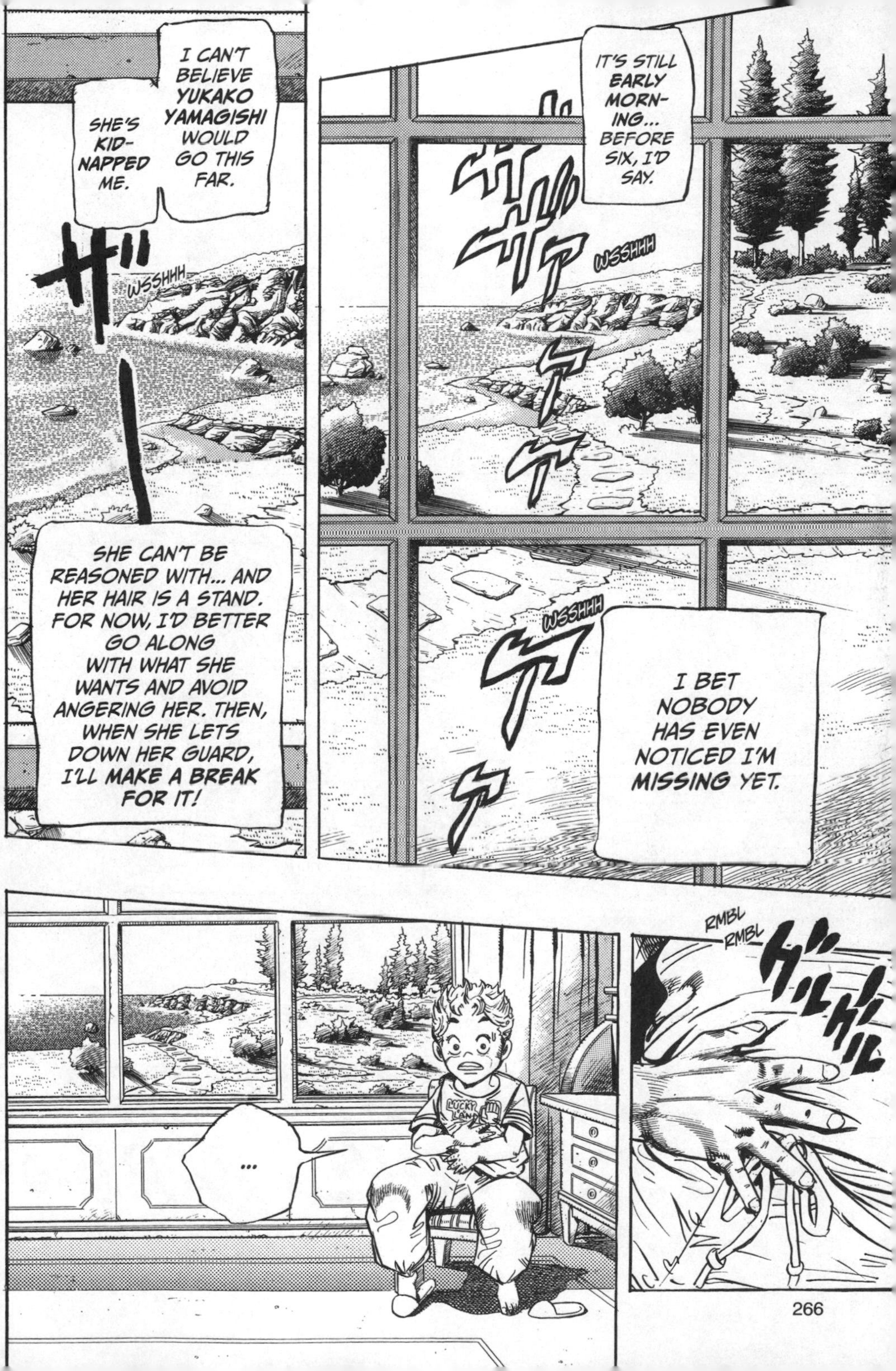
IT'S STILL EARLY MORN-ING... BEFORE SIX, I'D SAY.
WSSHHH
WSSHHH
I BET NOBODY HAS EVEN NOTICED I'M MISSING YET.
I CAN'T BELIEVE YUKAKO YAMAGISHI WOULD GO THIS FAR.
SHE'S KID-NAPPED ME.
WSSHHH
SHE CAN'T BE REASONED WITH... AND HER HAIR IS A STAND. FOR NOW, I'D BETTER GO ALONG WITH WHAT SHE WANTS AND AVOID ANGERING HER. THEN, WHEN SHE LETS DOWN HER GUARD, I'LL MAKE A BREAK FOR IT!
RMBL RMBL
LUCKY LAND
...

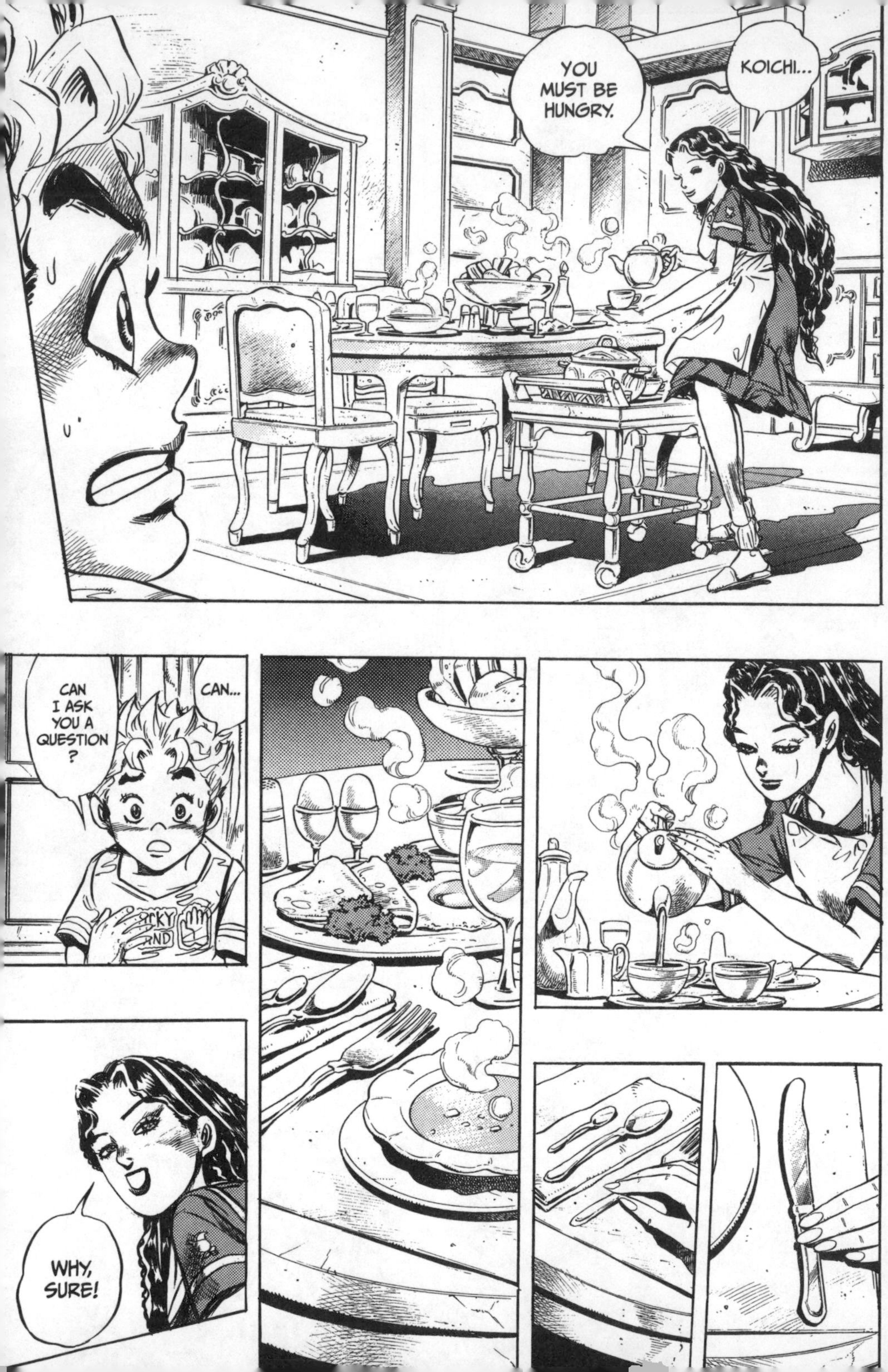

KOICHI...
YOU MUST BE HUNGRY.
CAN...
CAN I ASK YOU A QUESTION?
WHY, SURE!

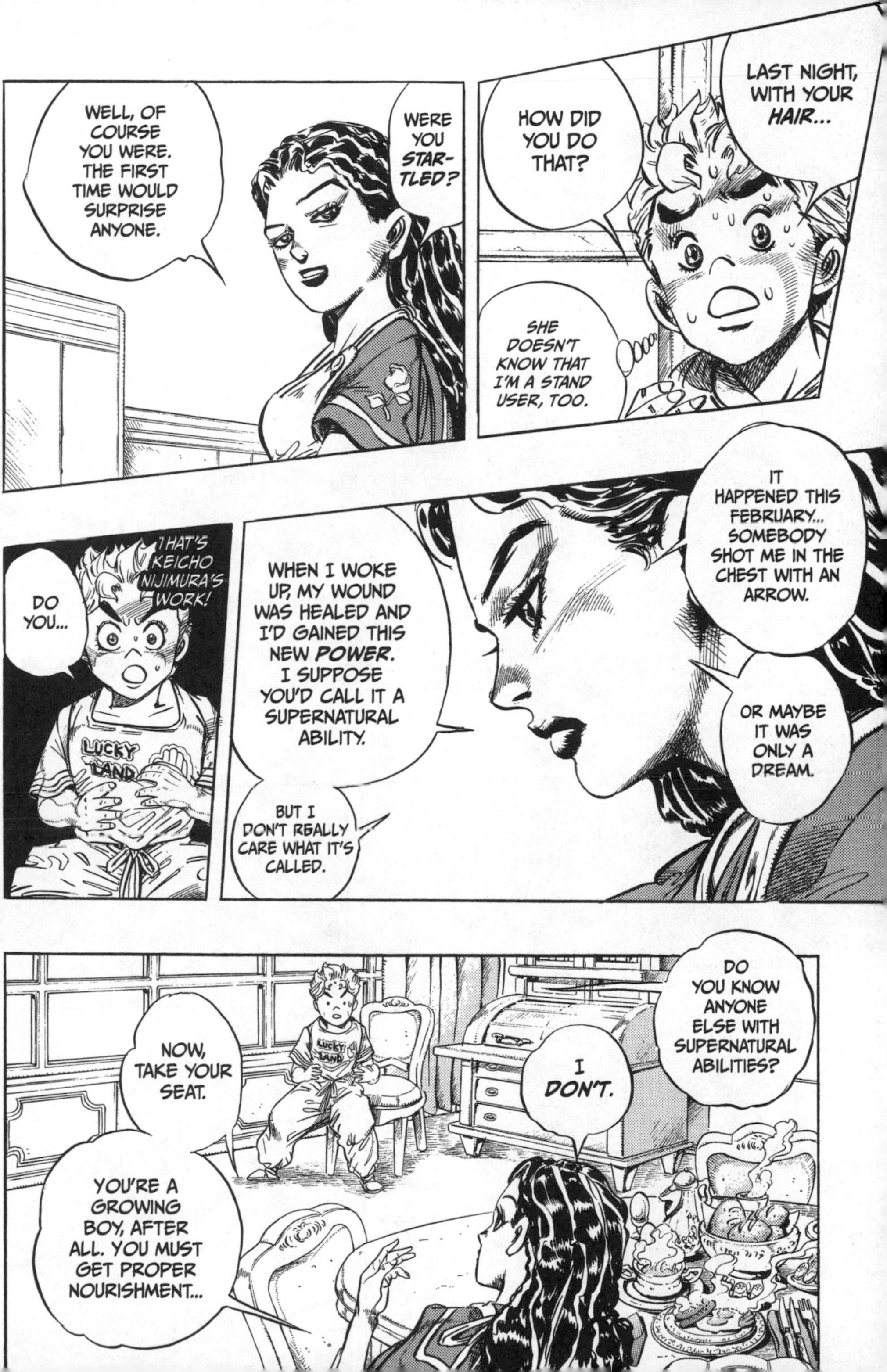
LAST NIGHT, WITH YOUR *HAIR*...
HOW DID YOU DO THAT?
SHE DOESN'T KNOW THAT I'M A STAND USER, TOO.
WERE YOU *STARTLED?*
WELL, OF COURSE YOU WERE. THE FIRST TIME WOULD SURPRISE ANYONE.
IT HAPPENED THIS FEBRUARY... SOMEBODY SHOT ME IN THE CHEST WITH AN ARROW.
OR MAYBE IT WAS ONLY A DREAM.
WHEN I WOKE UP, MY WOUND WAS HEALED AND I'D GAINED THIS NEW *POWER*. I SUPPOSE YOU'D CALL IT A SUPERNATURAL ABILITY.
BUT I DON'T REALLY CARE WHAT IT'S CALLED.
THAT'S KEICHO NIJIMURA'S WORK!
DO YOU...
LUCKY LAND
DO YOU KNOW ANYONE ELSE WITH SUPERNATURAL ABILITIES?
I *DON'T.*
NOW, TAKE YOUR SEAT.
YOU'RE A GROWING BOY, AFTER ALL. YOU MUST GET PROPER NOURISHMENT...

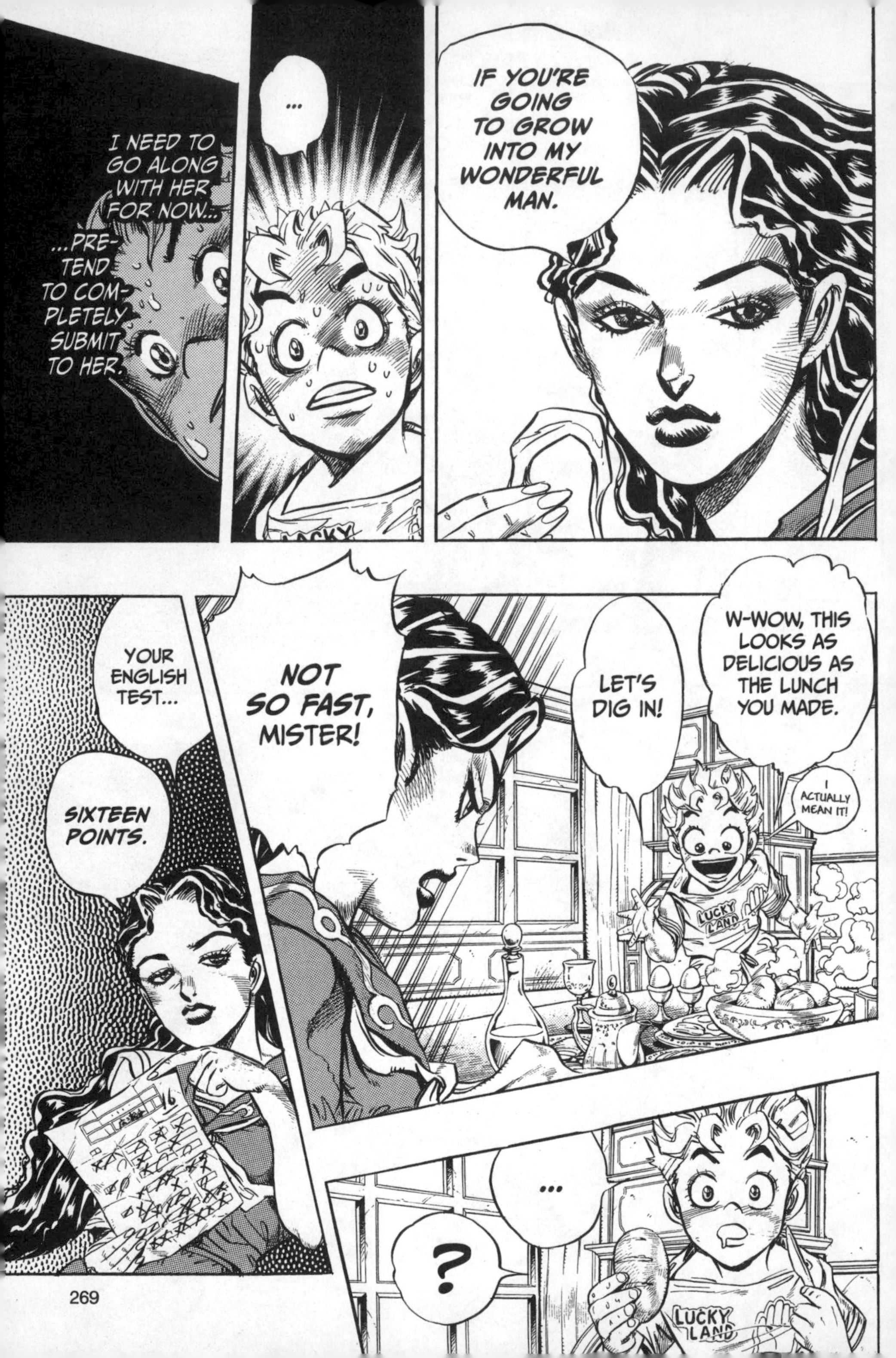
IF YOU'RE GOING TO GROW INTO MY WONDERFUL MAN.
...
I NEED TO GO ALONG WITH HER FOR NOW...
...PRE-TEND TO COM-PLETELY SUBMIT TO HER.
W-WOW, THIS LOOKS AS DELICIOUS AS THE LUNCH YOU MADE.
I ACTUALLY MEAN IT!
LUCKY LAND
LET'S DIG IN!
NOT SO FAST, MISTER!
...
?
LUCKY LAND
YOUR ENGLISH TEST...
SIXTEEN POINTS.

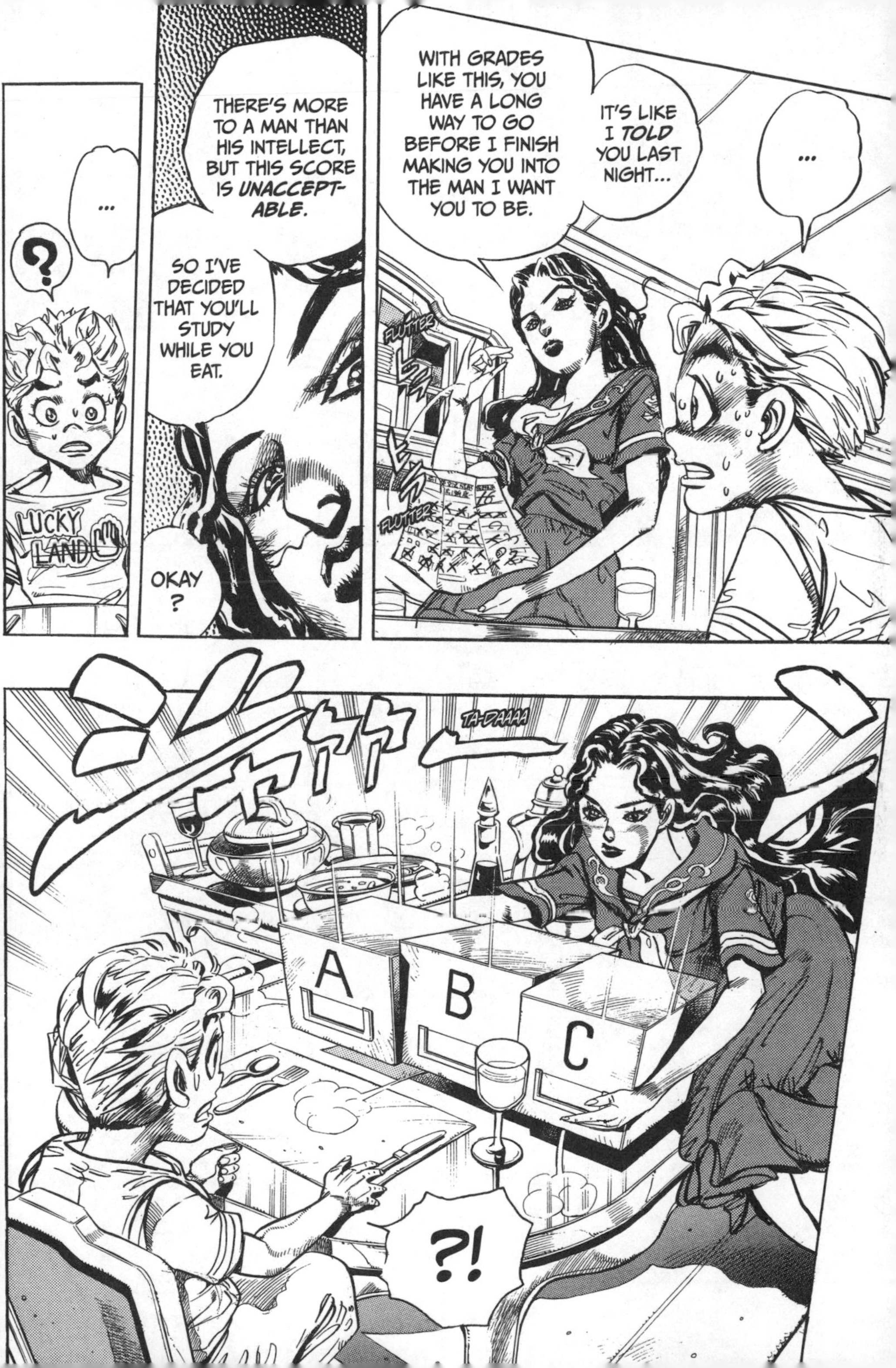
...
IT'S LIKE I *TOLD* YOU LAST NIGHT...
WITH GRADES LIKE THIS, YOU HAVE A LONG WAY TO GO BEFORE I FINISH MAKING YOU INTO THE MAN I WANT YOU TO BE.
FLUTTER
FLUTTER
THERE'S MORE TO A MAN THAN HIS INTELLECT, BUT THIS SCORE IS *UNACCEPTABLE*.
SO I'VE DECIDED THAT YOU'LL STUDY WHILE YOU EAT.
OKAY?
...
?
LUCKY LAND
TA-DAAAA
A
B
C
?!

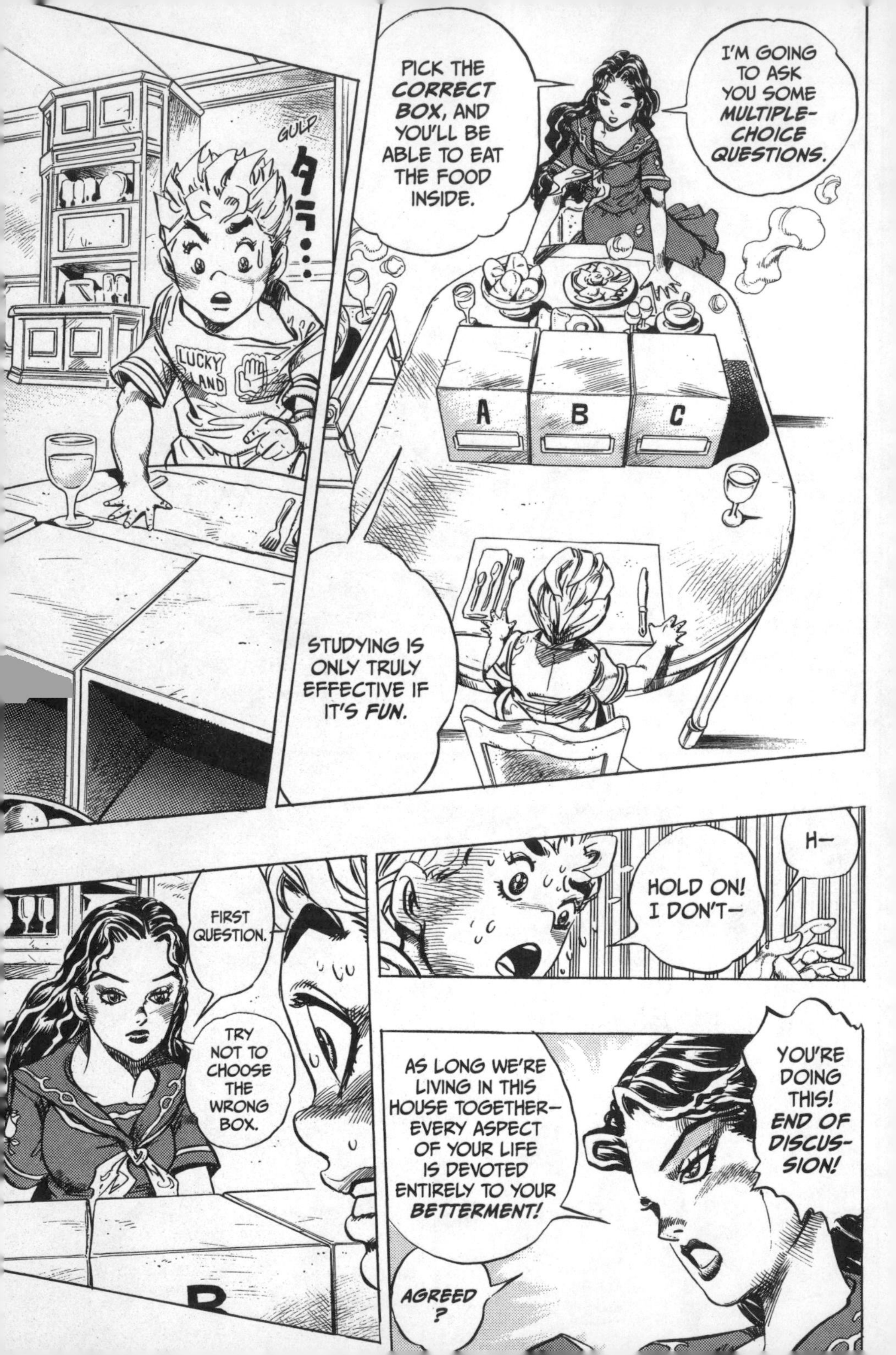
I'M GOING TO ASK YOU SOME MULTIPLE-CHOICE QUESTIONS.
PICK THE CORRECT BOX, AND YOU'LL BE ABLE TO EAT THE FOOD INSIDE.
A
B
C
STUDYING IS ONLY TRULY EFFECTIVE IF IT'S FUN.
GULP
タラ…
H—
HOLD ON! I DON'T—
YOU'RE DOING THIS! END OF DISCUSSION!
AS LONG WE'RE LIVING IN THIS HOUSE TOGETHER—EVERY ASPECT OF YOUR LIFE IS DEVOTED ENTIRELY TO YOUR BETTERMENT!
AGREED?
FIRST QUESTION.
TRY NOT TO CHOOSE THE WRONG BOX.

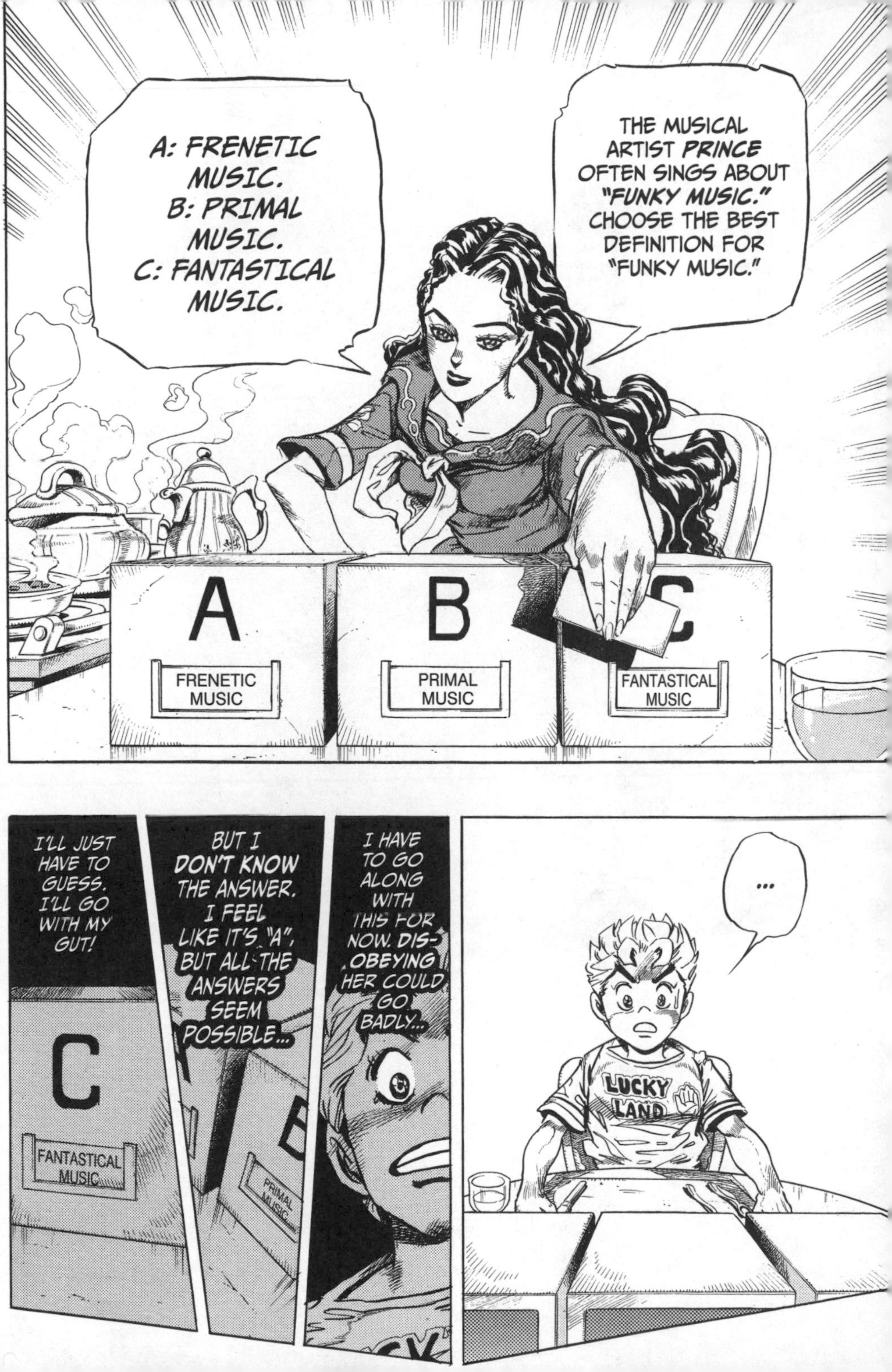
THE MUSICAL ARTIST PRINCE OFTEN SINGS ABOUT "FUNKY MUSIC." CHOOSE THE BEST DEFINITION FOR "FUNKY MUSIC."
A: FRENETIC MUSIC. B: PRIMAL MUSIC. C: FANTASTICAL MUSIC.
A
FRENETIC MUSIC
B
PRIMAL MUSIC
C
FANTASTICAL MUSIC
...
LUCKY LAND
I HAVE TO GO ALONG WITH THIS FOR NOW. DISOBEYING HER COULD GO BADLY...
BUT I DON'T KNOW THE ANSWER. I FEEL LIKE IT'S "A", BUT ALL THE ANSWERS SEEM POSSIBLE...
B
PRIMAL MUSIC
I'LL JUST HAVE TO GUESS. I'LL GO WITH MY GUT!
C
FANTASTICAL MUSIC

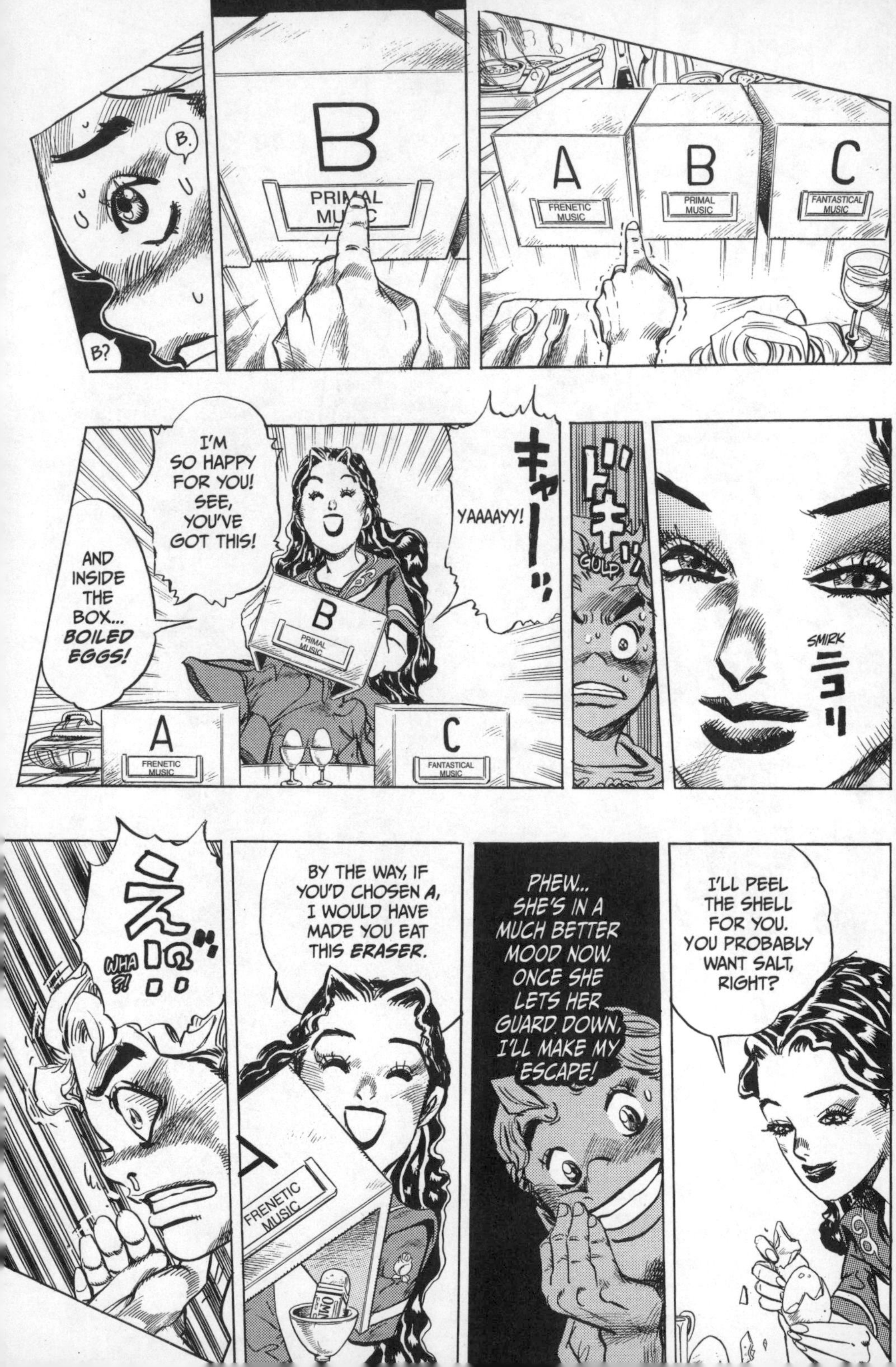
A
FRENETIC MUSIC
B
PRIMAL MUSIC
C
FANTASTICAL MUSIC
B
PRIMAL MUSIC
B.
B?
SMIRK
ニコリ
ドキッ
GULP
YAAAAYY!
キャーッ
I'M SO HAPPY FOR YOU! SEE, YOU'VE GOT THIS!
AND INSIDE THE BOX... BOILED EGGS!
B
PRIMAL MUSIC
A
FRENETIC MUSIC
C
FANTASTICAL MUSIC
I'LL PEEL THE SHELL FOR YOU. YOU PROBABLY WANT SALT, RIGHT?
PHEW... SHE'S IN A MUCH BETTER MOOD NOW. ONCE SHE LETS HER GUARD DOWN, I'LL MAKE MY ESCAPE!
BY THE WAY, IF YOU'D CHOSEN A, I WOULD HAVE MADE YOU EAT THIS ERASER.
FRENETIC MUSIC
え!?
WHA?!

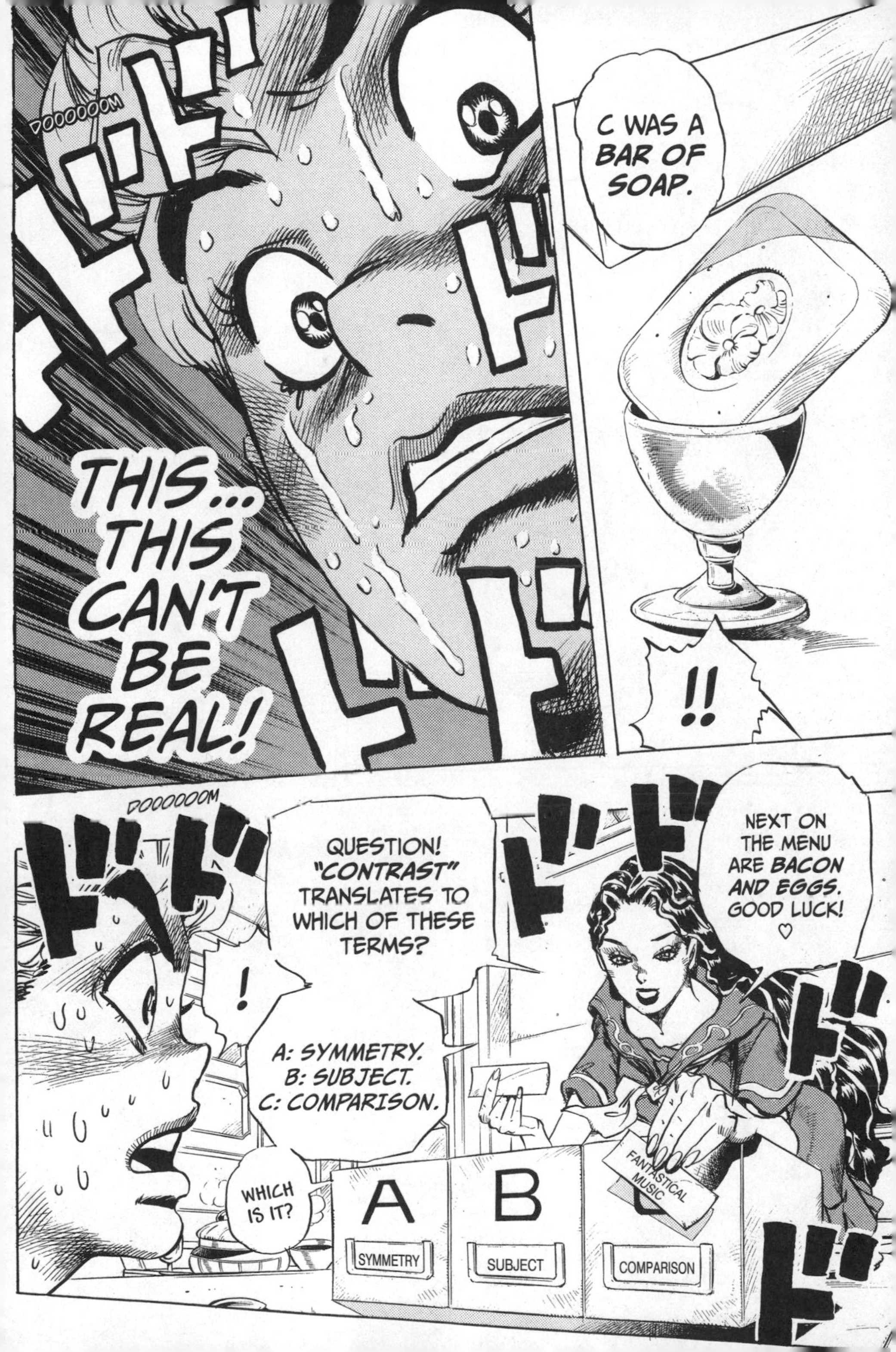
C WAS A BAR OF SOAP.
!!
DOOOOOOM
THIS... THIS CAN'T BE REAL!
NEXT ON THE MENU ARE *BACON AND EGGS.* GOOD LUCK! ♡
QUESTION! *"CONTRAST"* TRANSLATES TO WHICH OF THESE TERMS?
A: SYMMETRY.
B: SUBJECT.
C: COMPARISON.
DOOOOOOM
!
WHICH IS IT?
FANTASTICAL MUSIC
A
B
SYMMETRY
SUBJECT
COMPARISON

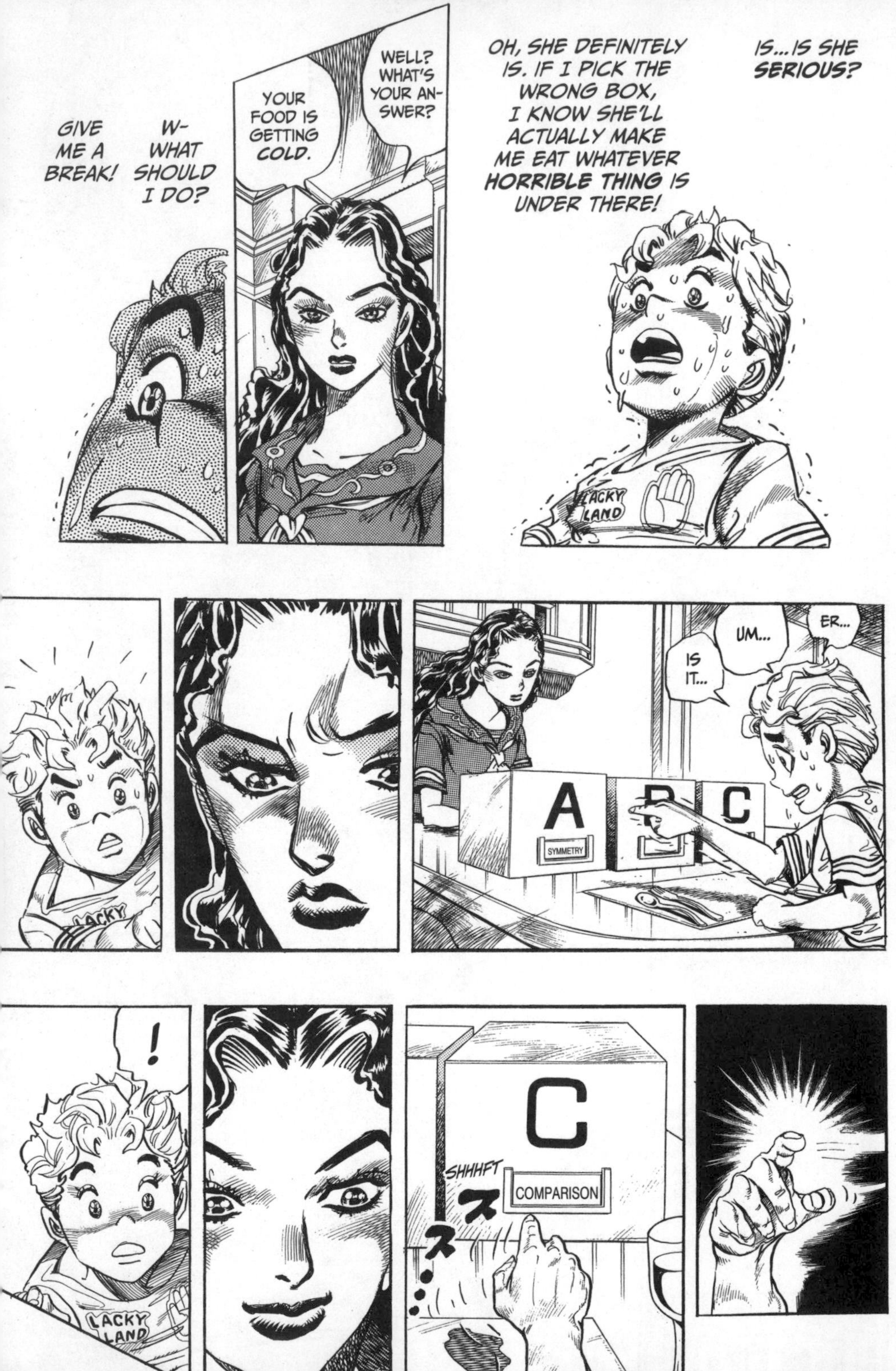
IS...IS SHE SERIOUS?
OH, SHE DEFINITELY IS. IF I PICK THE WRONG BOX, I KNOW SHE'LL ACTUALLY MAKE ME EAT WHATEVER HORRIBLE THING IS UNDER THERE!
LACKY LAND
WELL? WHAT'S YOUR AN-SWER?
YOUR FOOD IS GETTING COLD.
W-WHAT SHOULD I DO?
GIVE ME A BREAK!
ER...
UM...
IS IT...
A
C
SYMMETRY
LACKY
C
COMPARISON
SHHHFT
ス
ス
!
LACKY LAND

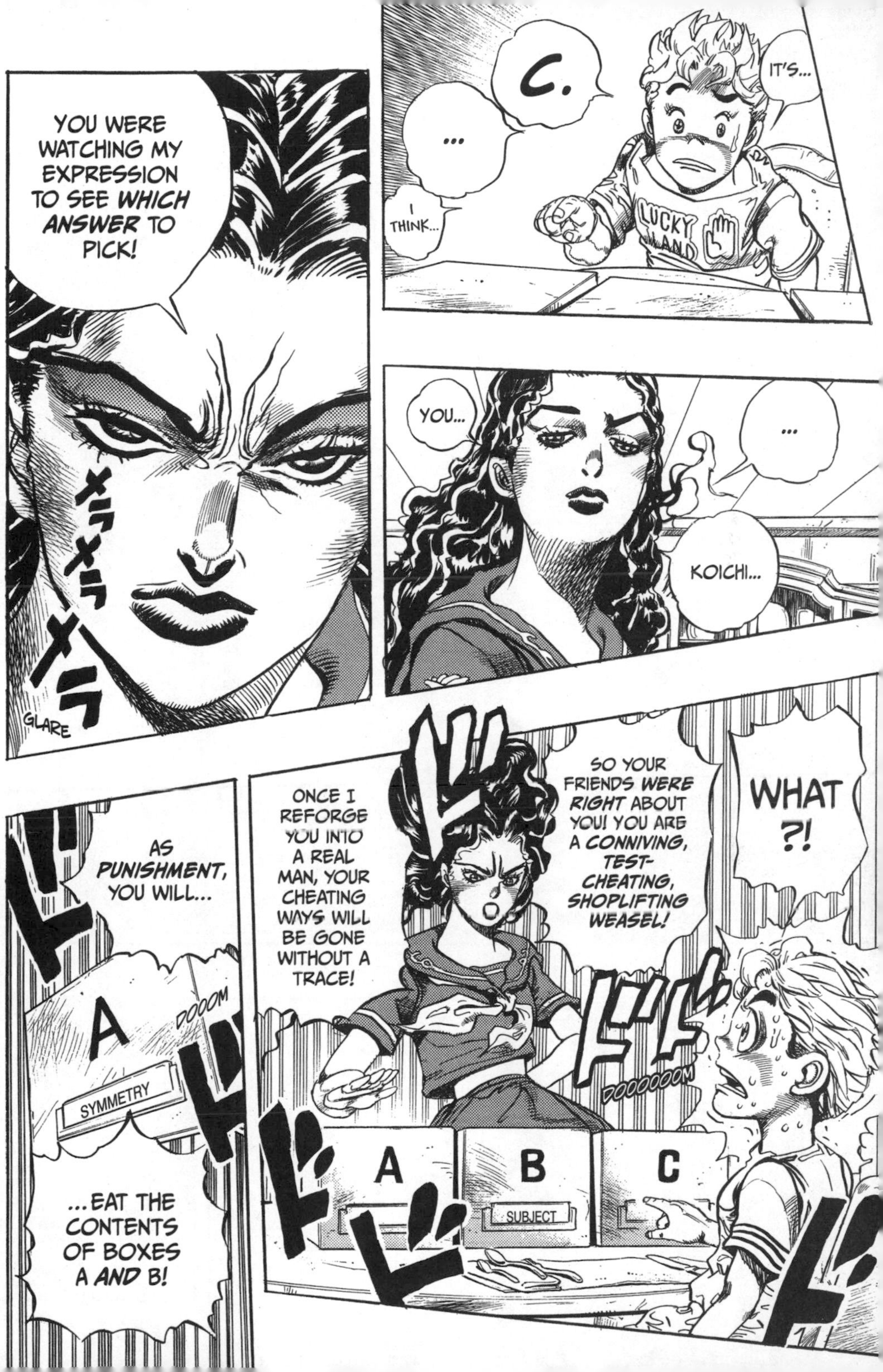
IT'S...
C.
...
I THINK...
...
KOICHI...
YOU...
YOU WERE WATCHING MY EXPRESSION TO SEE WHICH ANSWER TO PICK!
メラメラメラメラ
GLARE
WHAT?!
SO YOUR FRIENDS WERE RIGHT ABOUT YOU! YOU ARE A CONNIVING, TEST-CHEATING, SHOPLIFTING WEASEL!
ONCE I REFORGE YOU INTO A REAL MAN, YOUR CHEATING WAYS WILL BE GONE WITHOUT A TRACE!
ドドド
DOOOOOOM
A
B
C
SUBJECT
AS PUNISHMENT, YOU WILL...
DOOOM
A
SYMMETRY
...EAT THE CONTENTS OF BOXES A AND B!

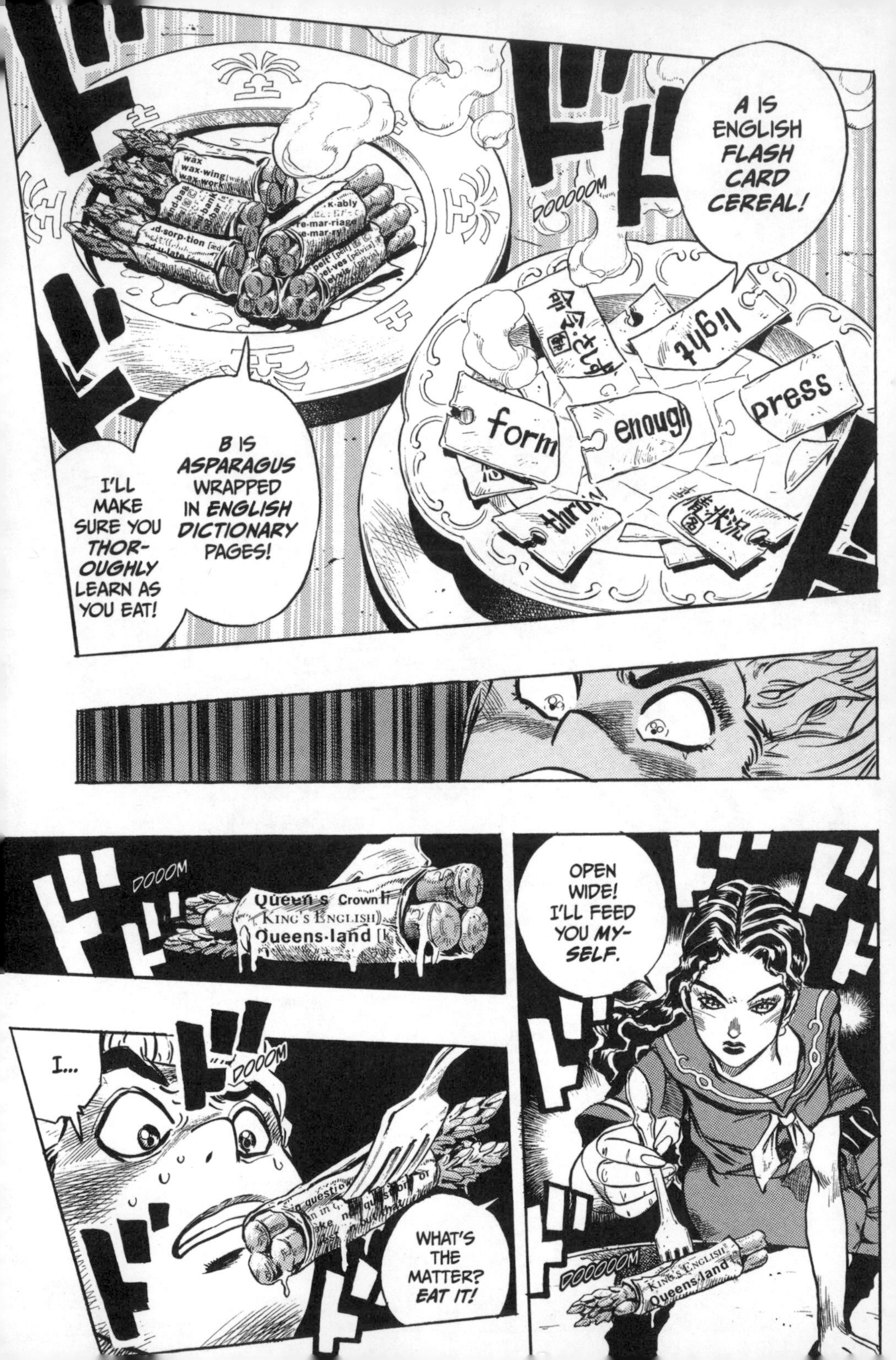
A IS ENGLISH FLASH CARD CEREAL!
DOOOOOM
light
press
enough
form
B IS ASPARAGUS WRAPPED IN ENGLISH DICTIONARY PAGES!
I'LL MAKE SURE YOU THOROUGHLY LEARN AS YOU EAT!
OPEN WIDE! I'LL FEED YOU MYSELF.
DOOOOOM
DOOOM
I...
DOOOM
WHAT'S THE MATTER? EAT IT!

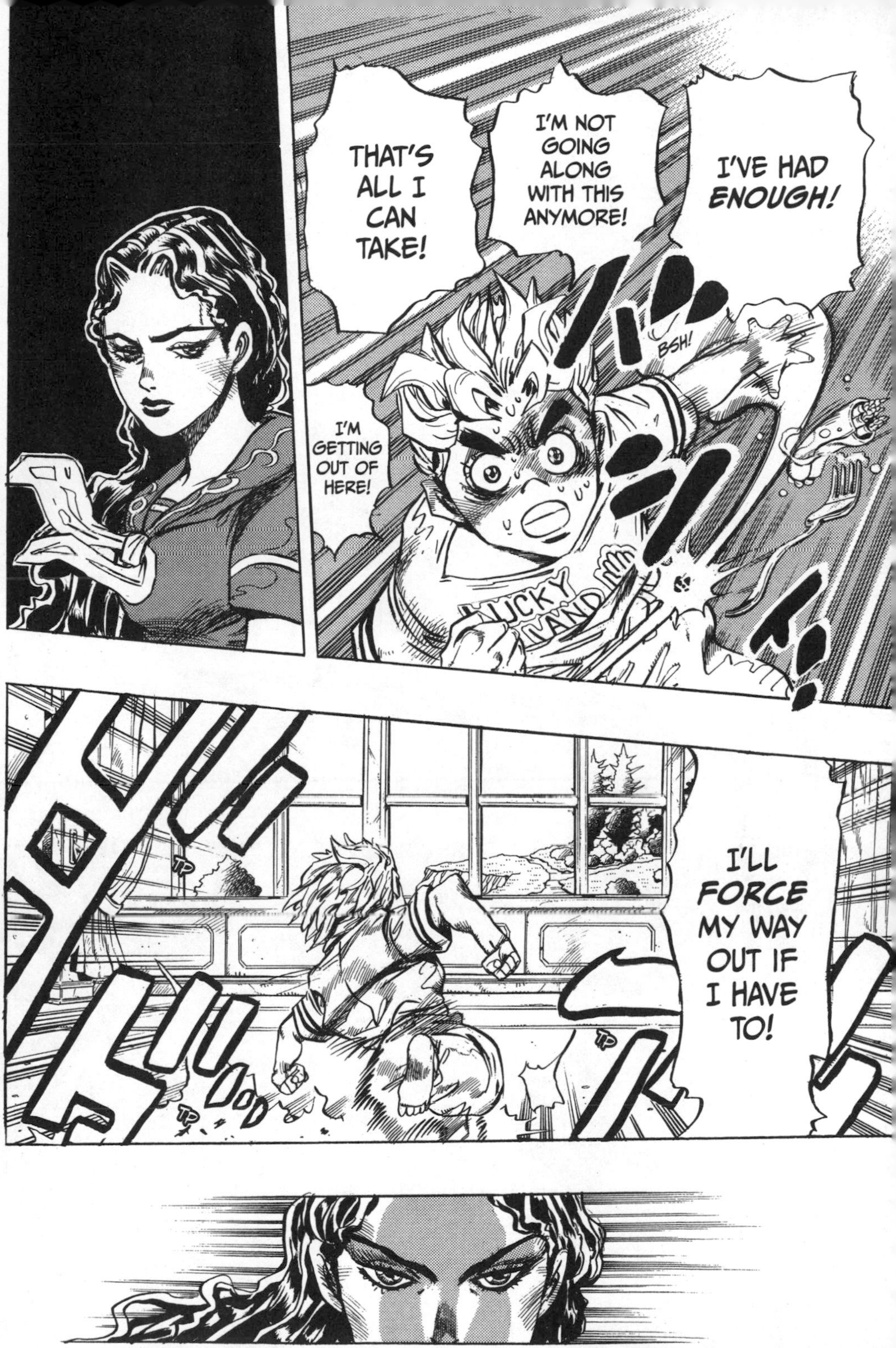
I'VE HAD ENOUGH!
I'M NOT GOING ALONG WITH THIS ANYMORE!
THAT'S ALL I CAN TAKE!
BSH!
LUCKY LAND
I'M GETTING OUT OF HERE!
I'LL FORCE MY WAY OUT IF I HAVE TO!
TP
TP
TP

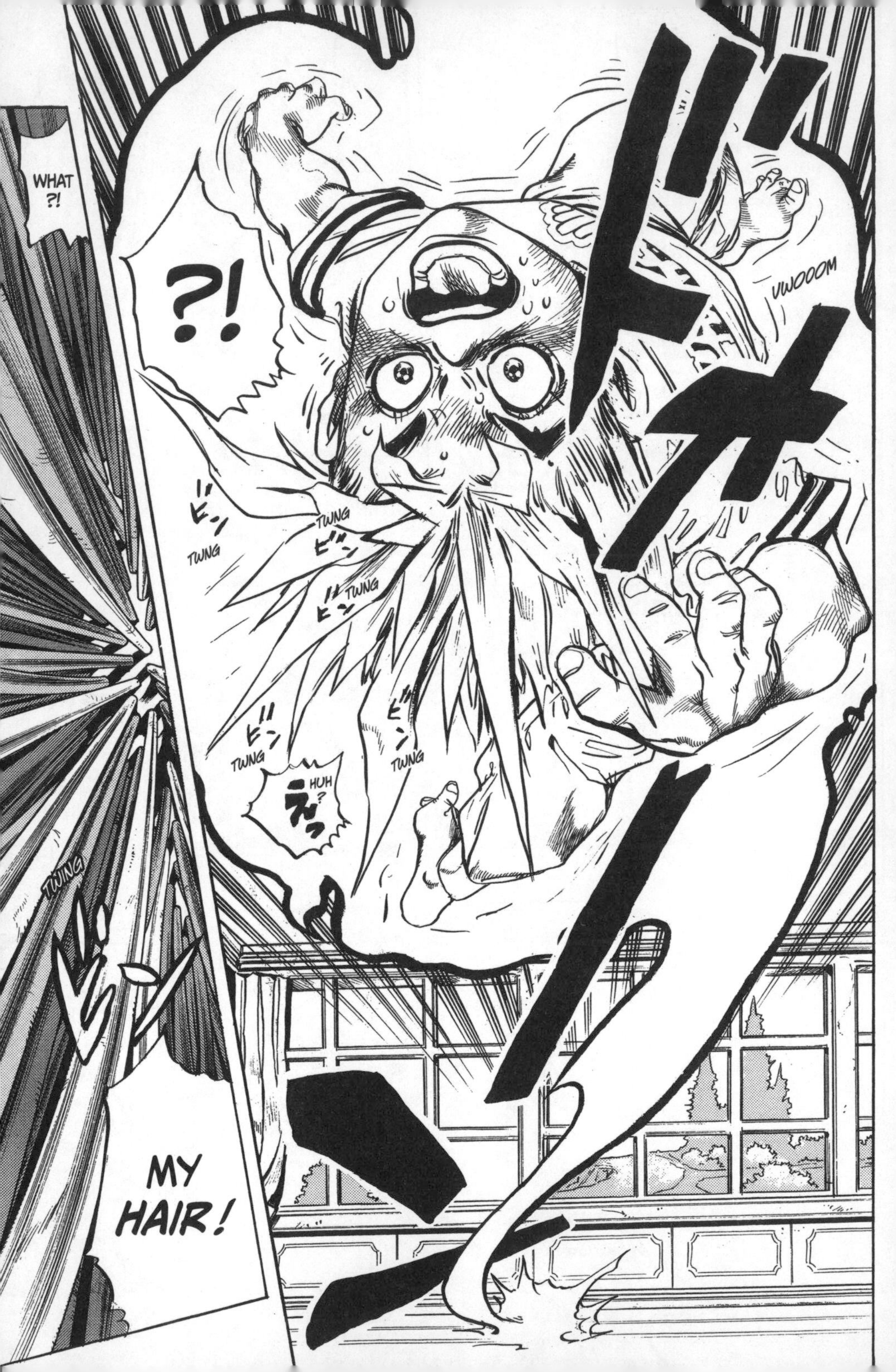
VWOOOM
?!
TWNG
TWNG
TWNG
TWNG
TWNG
HUH ?
えっ
WHAT ?!
TWING
MY HAIR!

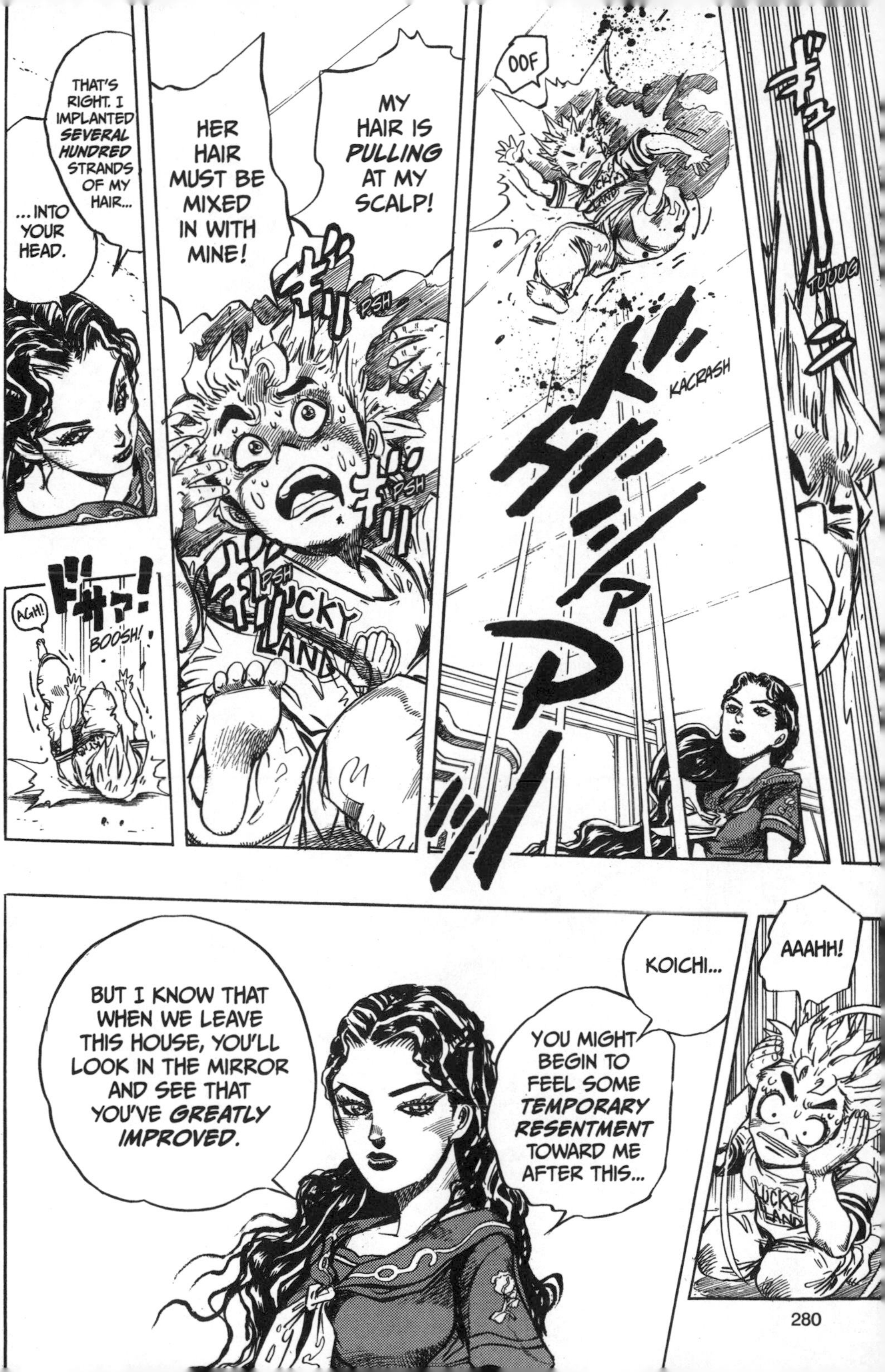
TUUUG
OOF
KACRASH
MY HAIR IS PULLING AT MY SCALP!
HER HAIR MUST BE MIXED IN WITH MINE!
PSH
PSH
PSH
THAT'S RIGHT. I IMPLANTED SEVERAL HUNDRED STRANDS OF MY HAIR...
...INTO YOUR HEAD.
AGH!
BOOSH!
AAAHH!
KOICHI...
YOU MIGHT BEGIN TO FEEL SOME TEMPORARY RESENTMENT TOWARD ME AFTER THIS...
BUT I KNOW THAT WHEN WE LEAVE THIS HOUSE, YOU'LL LOOK IN THE MIRROR AND SEE THAT YOU'VE GREATLY IMPROVED.

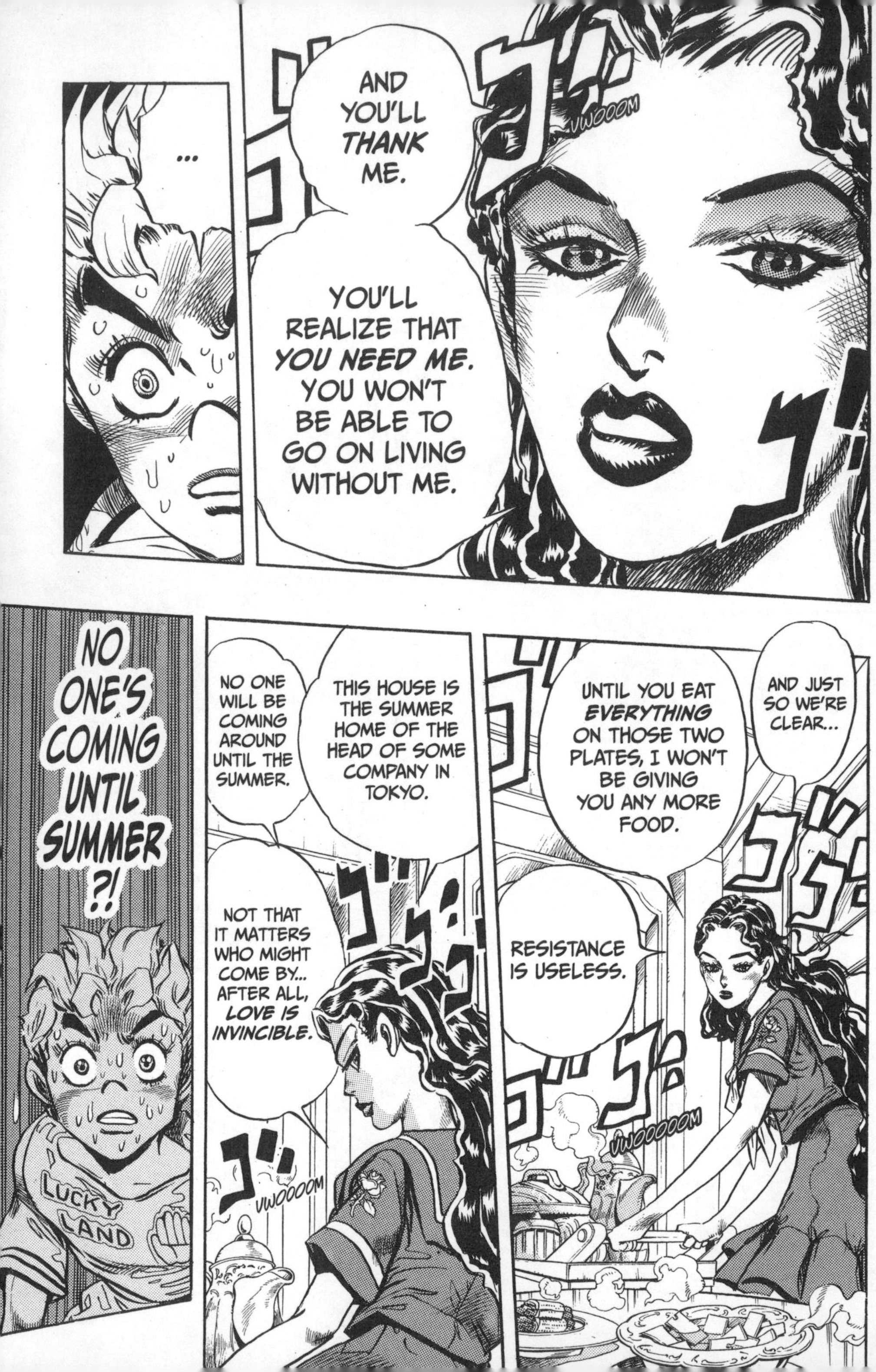
AND YOU'LL *THANK* ME.
VWOOOM
YOU'LL REALIZE THAT *YOU NEED ME.* YOU WON'T BE ABLE TO GO ON LIVING WITHOUT ME.
...
AND JUST SO WE'RE CLEAR...
UNTIL YOU EAT *EVERYTHING* ON THOSE TWO PLATES, I WON'T BE GIVING YOU ANY MORE FOOD.
RESISTANCE IS USELESS.
VWOOOOOM
THIS HOUSE IS THE SUMMER HOME OF THE HEAD OF SOME COMPANY IN TOKYO.
NO ONE WILL BE COMING AROUND UNTIL THE SUMMER.
NOT THAT IT MATTERS WHO MIGHT COME BY... AFTER ALL, *LOVE IS INVINCIBLE.*
VWOOOOM
NO ONE'S COMING UNTIL SUMMER?!
LUCKY LAND

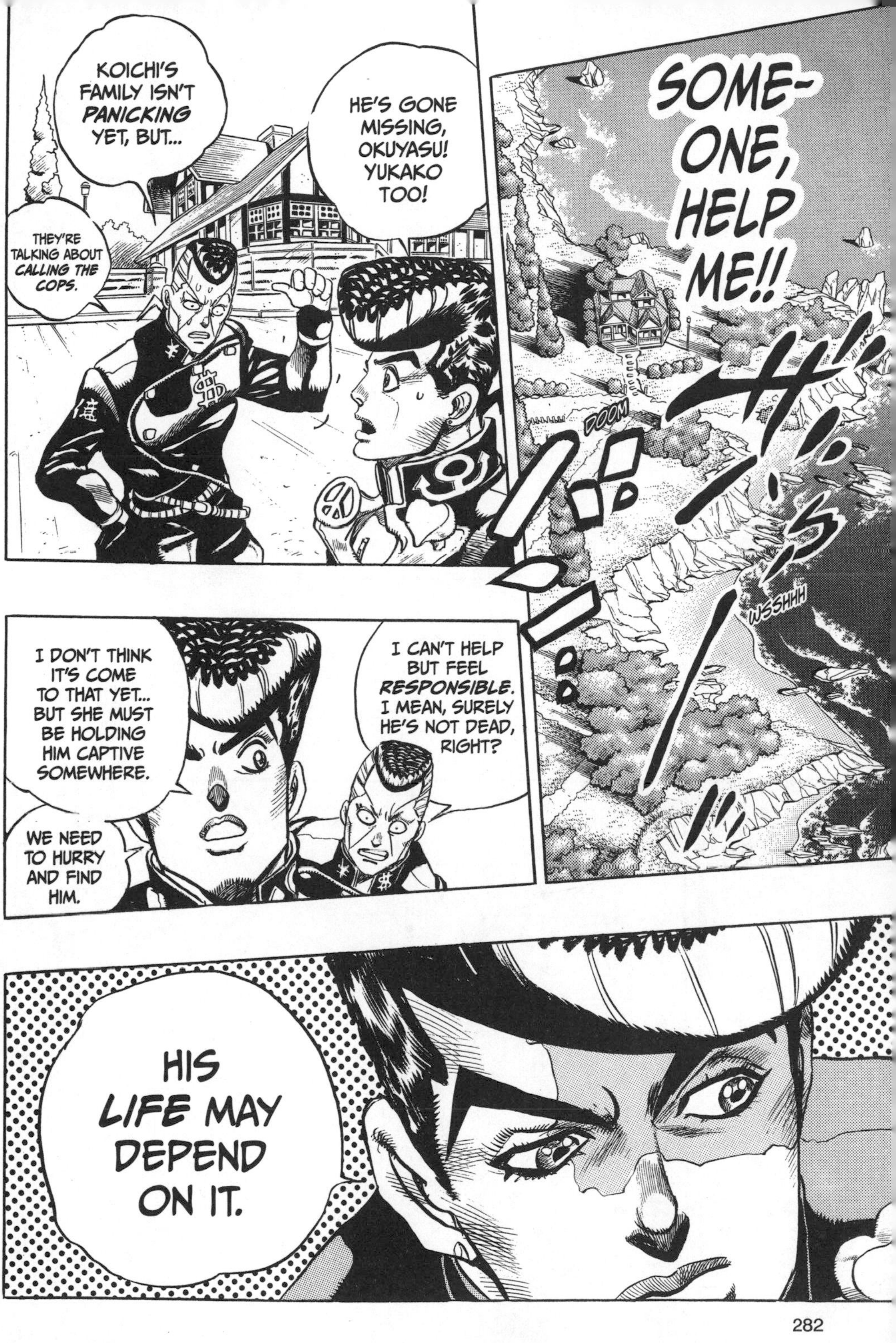
SOME-ONE, HELP ME!!
DOOM
WSSHHH
HE'S GONE MISSING, OKUYASU! YUKAKO TOO!
KOICHI'S FAMILY ISN'T PANICKING YET, BUT...
THEY'RE TALKING ABOUT CALLING THE COPS.
I CAN'T HELP BUT FEEL RESPONSIBLE. I MEAN, SURELY HE'S NOT DEAD, RIGHT?
I DON'T THINK IT'S COME TO THAT YET... BUT SHE MUST BE HOLDING HIM CAPTIVE SOMEWHERE.
WE NEED TO HURRY AND FIND HIM.
HIS LIFE MAY DEPEND ON IT.

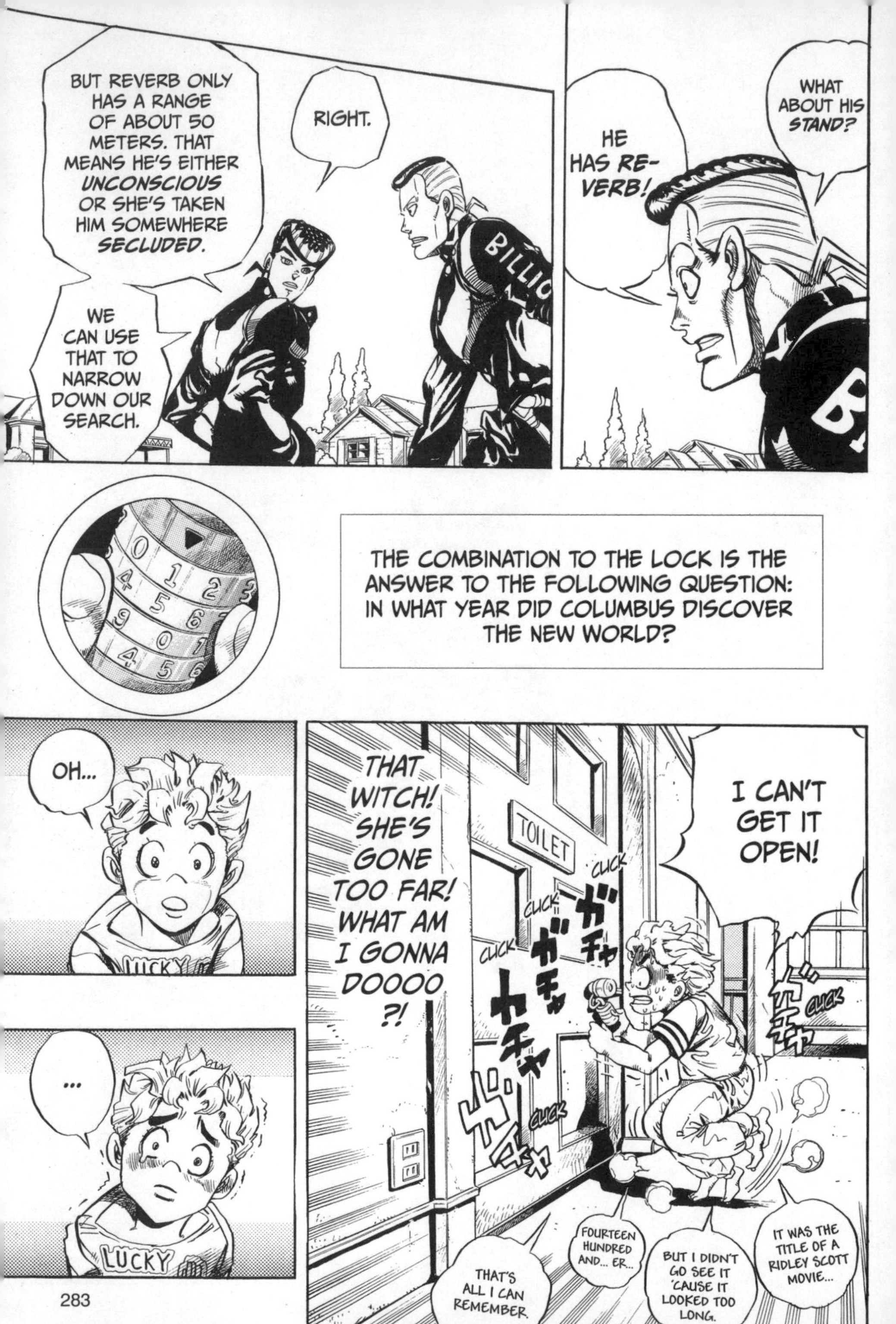
WHAT ABOUT HIS STAND?
HE HAS RE-VERB!
RIGHT.
BUT REVERB ONLY HAS A RANGE OF ABOUT 50 METERS. THAT MEANS HE'S EITHER UNCONSCIOUS OR SHE'S TAKEN HIM SOMEWHERE SECLUDED.
WE CAN USE THAT TO NARROW DOWN OUR SEARCH.
BILLIO
THE COMBINATION TO THE LOCK IS THE ANSWER TO THE FOLLOWING QUESTION: IN WHAT YEAR DID COLUMBUS DISCOVER THE NEW WORLD?
I CAN'T GET IT OPEN!
CLICK
THAT WITCH! SHE'S GONE TOO FAR! WHAT AM I GONNA DOOOO?!
TOILET
CLICK
CLICK
CLICK
CLICK
IT WAS THE TITLE OF A RIDLEY SCOTT MOVIE...
BUT I DIDN'T GO SEE IT 'CAUSE IT LOOKED TOO LONG.
FOURTEEN HUNDRED AND... ER...
THAT'S ALL I CAN REMEMBER.
OH...
LUCKY
...
LUCKY

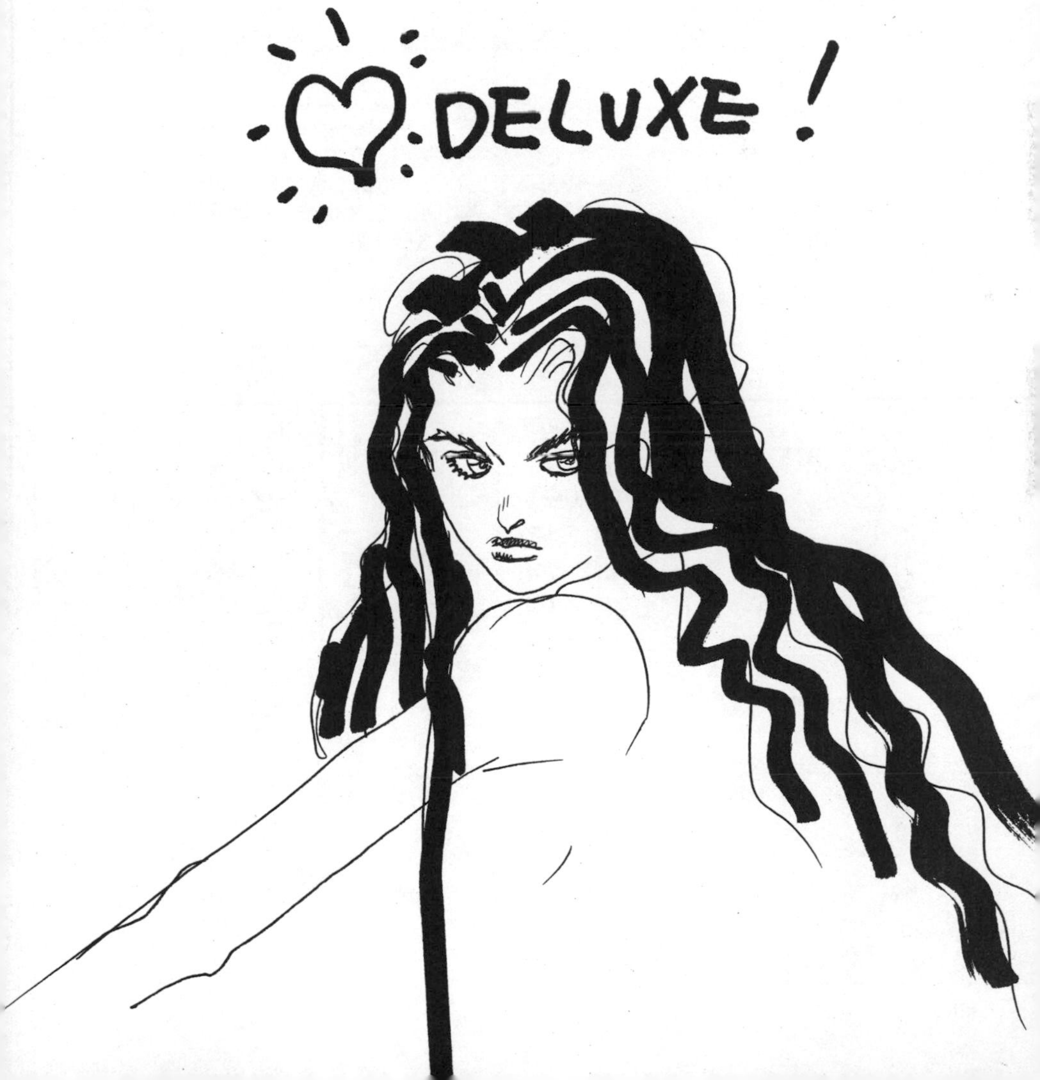
DELUXE!

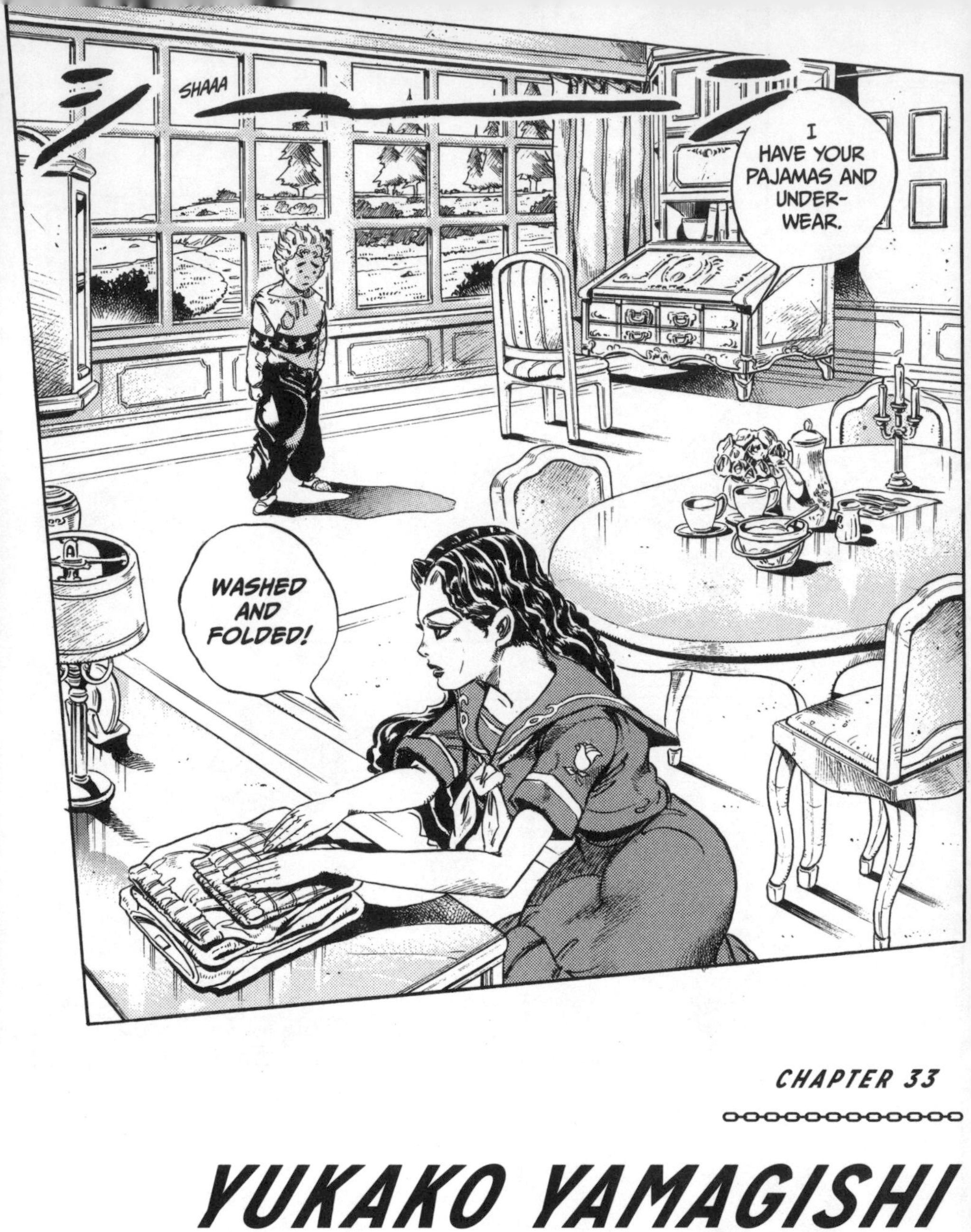
I HAVE YOUR PAJAMAS AND UNDER-WEAR.
SHAAA
WASHED AND FOLDED!

CHAPTER 33

YUKAKO YAMAGISHI FALLS IN LOVE, PART 5

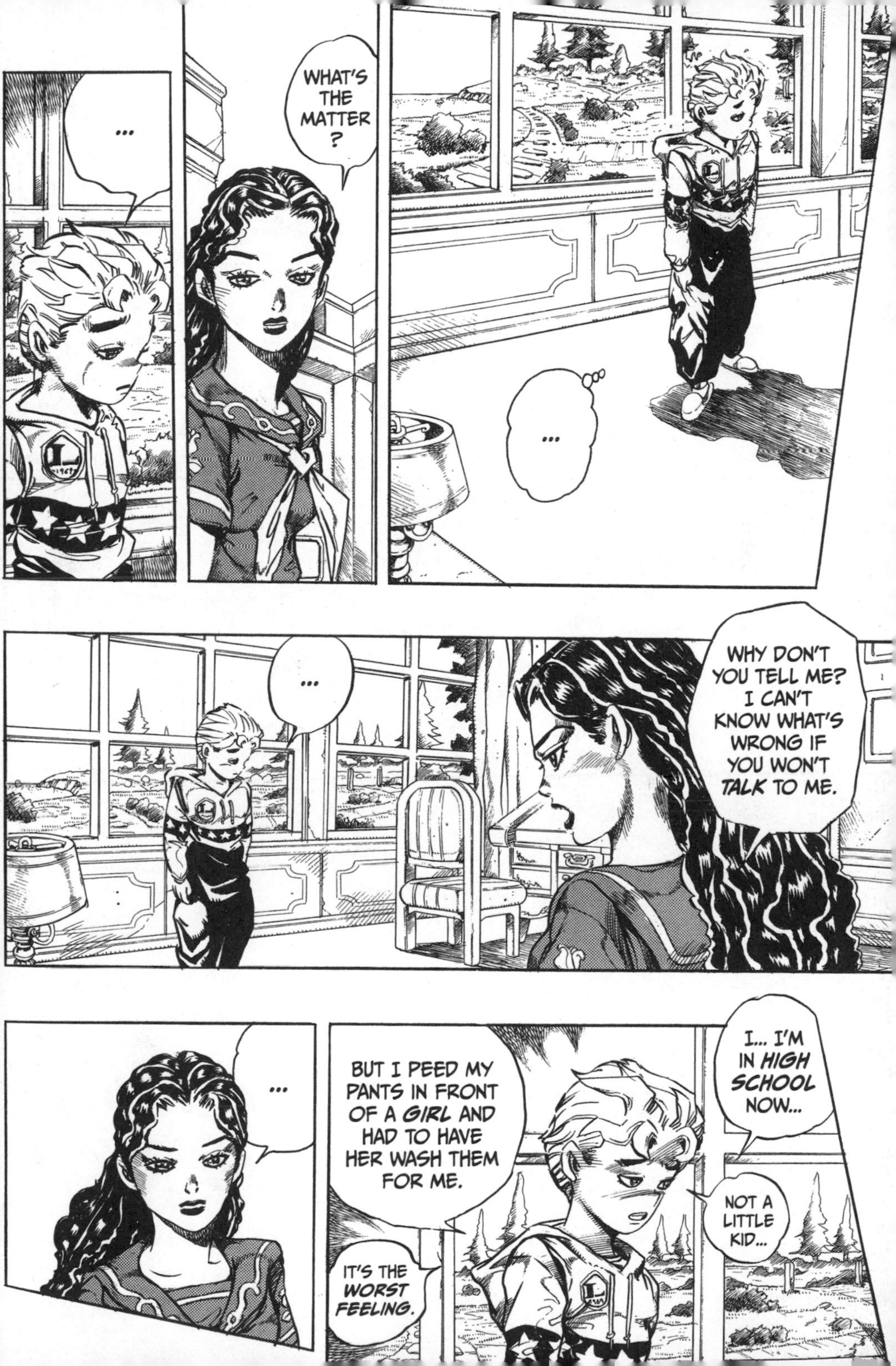
...
WHAT'S THE MATTER?
...
WHY DON'T YOU TELL ME? I CAN'T KNOW WHAT'S WRONG IF YOU WON'T TALK TO ME.
...
I... I'M IN HIGH SCHOOL NOW...
NOT A LITTLE KID...
BUT I PEED MY PANTS IN FRONT OF A GIRL AND HAD TO HAVE HER WASH THEM FOR ME.
IT'S THE WORST FEELING.
...

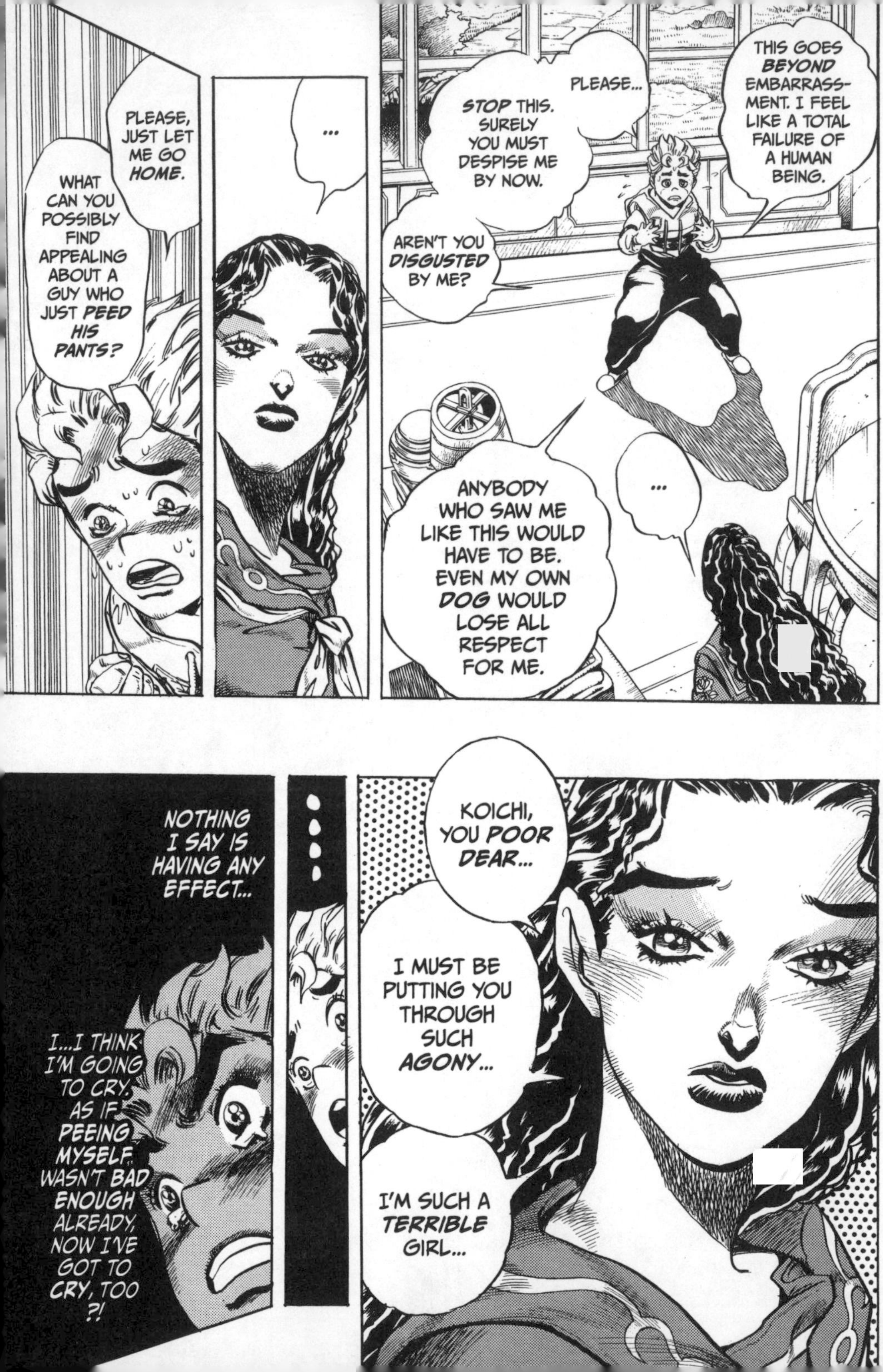
THIS GOES BEYOND EMBARRASSMENT. I FEEL LIKE A TOTAL FAILURE OF A HUMAN BEING.
PLEASE... STOP THIS. SURELY YOU MUST DESPISE ME BY NOW.
AREN'T YOU DISGUSTED BY ME?
...
ANYBODY WHO SAW ME LIKE THIS WOULD HAVE TO BE. EVEN MY OWN DOG WOULD LOSE ALL RESPECT FOR ME.
...
PLEASE, JUST LET ME GO HOME.
WHAT CAN YOU POSSIBLY FIND APPEALING ABOUT A GUY WHO JUST PEED HIS PANTS?
KOICHI, YOU POOR DEAR...
I MUST BE PUTTING YOU THROUGH SUCH AGONY...
I'M SUCH A TERRIBLE GIRL...
NOTHING I SAY IS HAVING ANY EFFECT...
I...I THINK I'M GOING TO CRY. AS IF PEEING MYSELF WASN'T BAD ENOUGH ALREADY, NOW I'VE GOT TO CRY, TOO?!

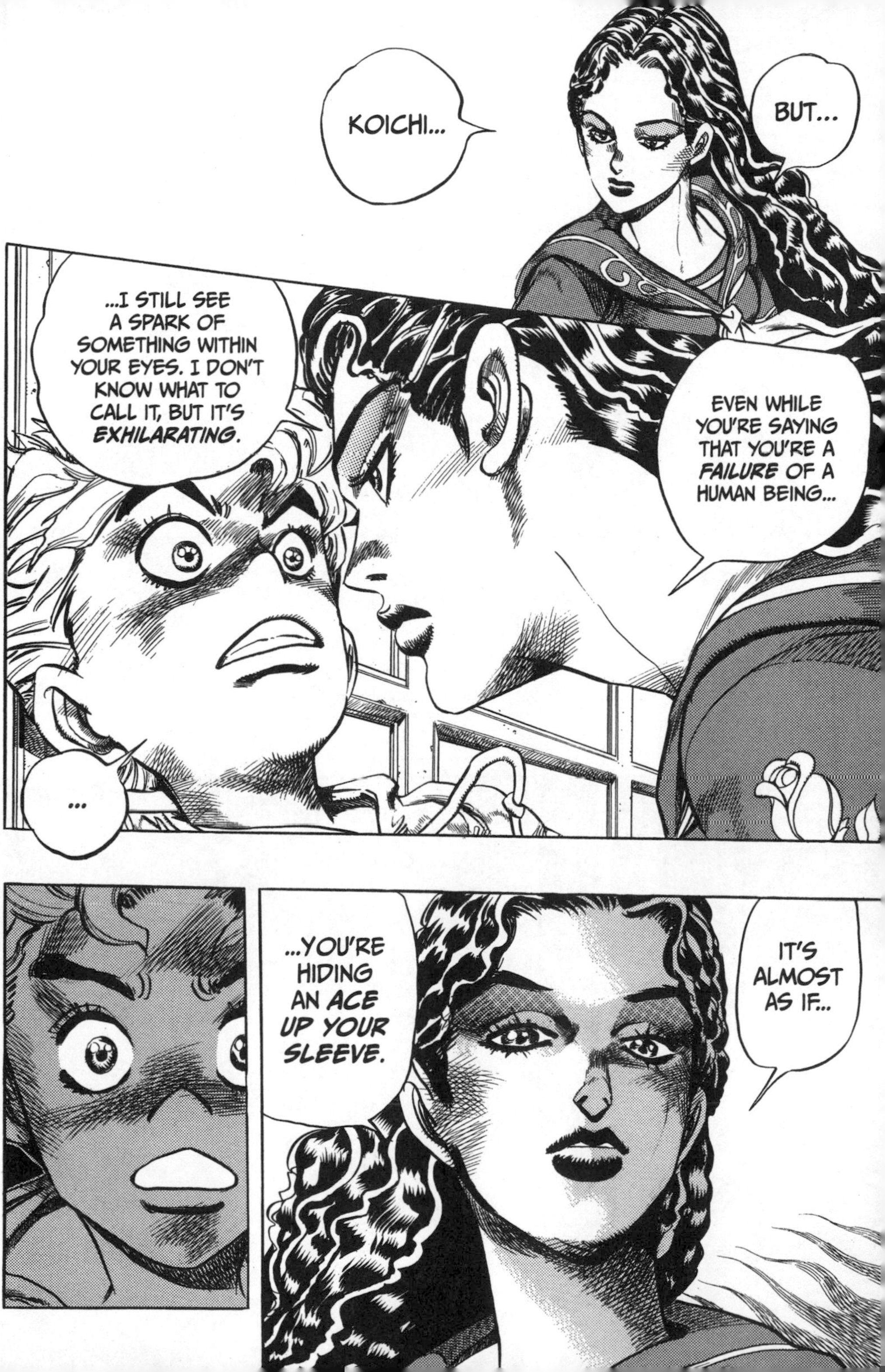
BUT...
KOICHI...
EVEN WHILE YOU'RE SAYING THAT YOU'RE A *FAILURE* OF A HUMAN BEING...
...I STILL SEE A SPARK OF SOMETHING WITHIN YOUR EYES. I DON'T KNOW WHAT TO CALL IT, BUT IT'S *EXHILARATING.*
...
IT'S ALMOST AS IF...
...YOU'RE HIDING AN *ACE UP YOUR SLEEVE.*

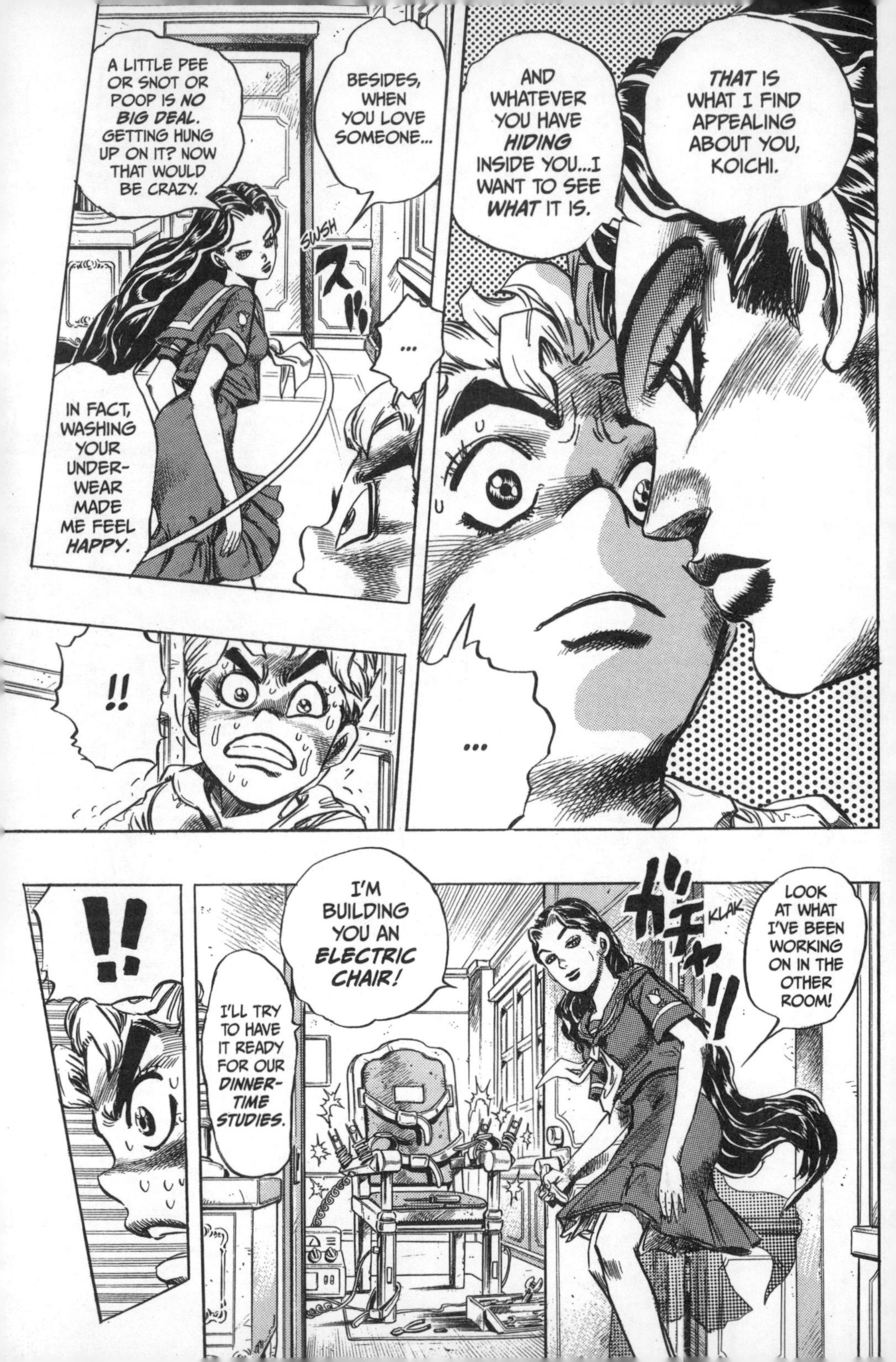
THAT IS WHAT I FIND APPEALING ABOUT YOU, KOICHI.
AND WHATEVER YOU HAVE HIDING INSIDE YOU...I WANT TO SEE WHAT IT IS.
...
BESIDES, WHEN YOU LOVE SOMEONE...
A LITTLE PEE OR SNOT OR POOP IS NO BIG DEAL. GETTING HUNG UP ON IT? NOW THAT WOULD BE CRAZY.
SWSH
...
IN FACT, WASHING YOUR UNDERWEAR MADE ME FEEL HAPPY.
!!
KLAK
LOOK AT WHAT I'VE BEEN WORKING ON IN THE OTHER ROOM!
I'M BUILDING YOU AN ELECTRIC CHAIR!
I'LL TRY TO HAVE IT READY FOR OUR DINNER-TIME STUDIES.
!!

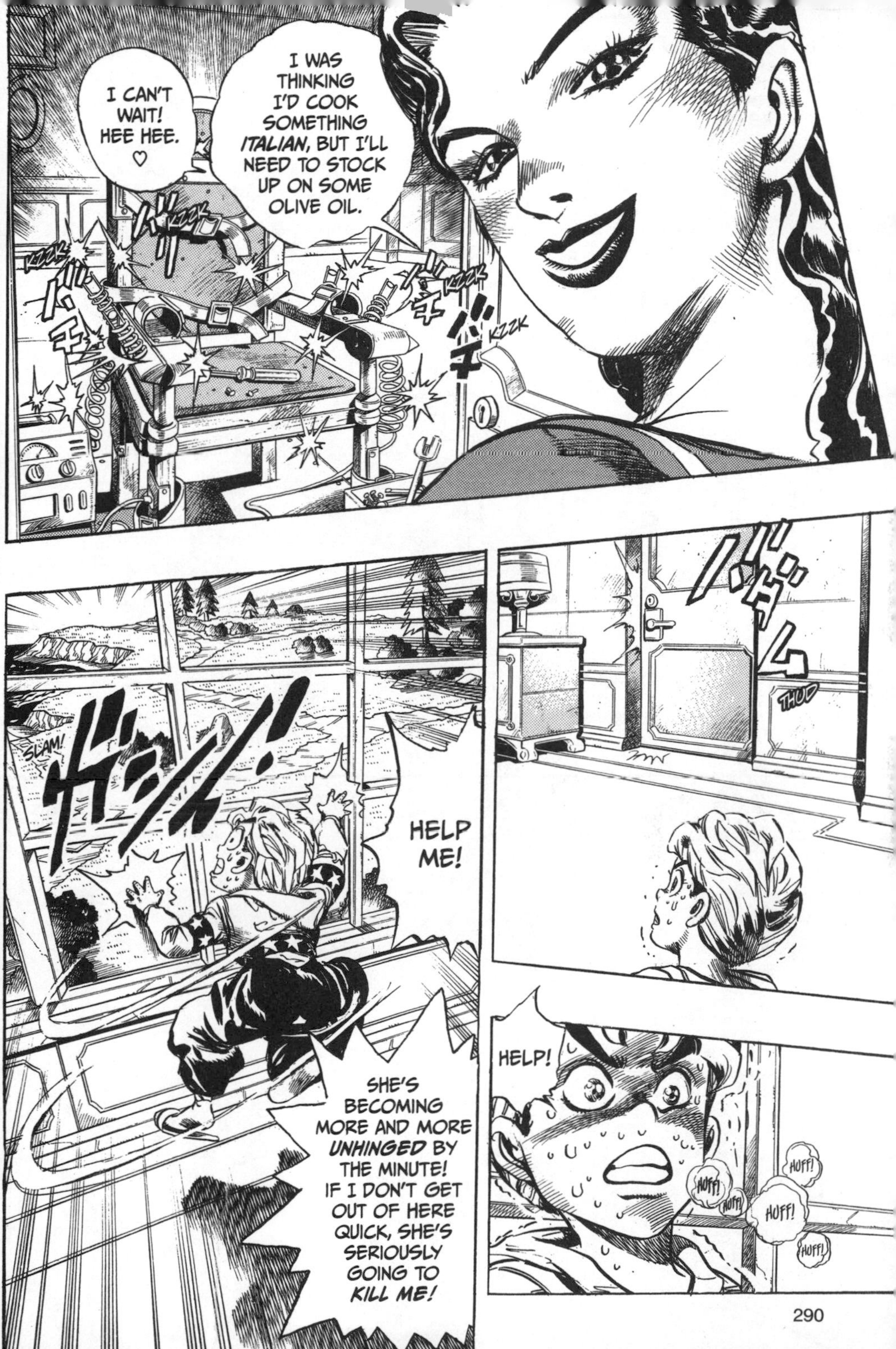

I WAS THINKING I'D COOK SOMETHING *ITALIAN*, BUT I'LL NEED TO STOCK UP ON SOME OLIVE OIL.
I CAN'T WAIT! HEE HEE. ♡
KZZK
KZZK
KZZK
KZZK
THUD
HELP!
HUFF!
HUFF!
HUFF!
HUFF!
HUFF!
SLAM!
HELP ME!
SHE'S BECOMING MORE AND MORE *UNHINGED* BY THE MINUTE! IF I DON'T GET OUT OF HERE QUICK, SHE'S SERIOUSLY GOING TO *KILL ME!*

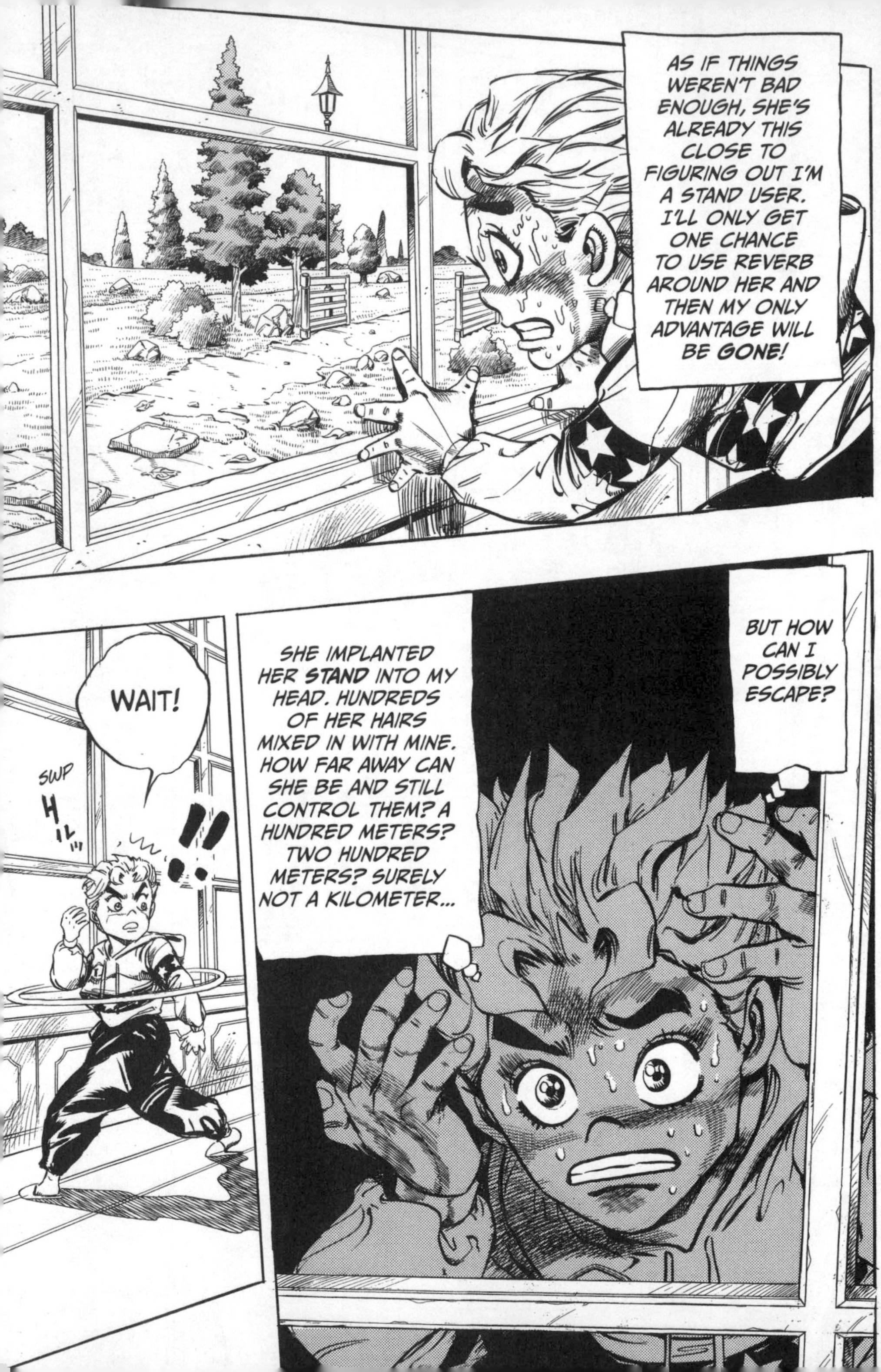
AS IF THINGS WEREN'T BAD ENOUGH, SHE'S ALREADY THIS CLOSE TO FIGURING OUT I'M A STAND USER. I'LL ONLY GET ONE CHANCE TO USE REVERB AROUND HER AND THEN MY ONLY ADVANTAGE WILL BE GONE!
BUT HOW CAN I POSSIBLY ESCAPE?
SHE IMPLANTED HER STAND INTO MY HEAD. HUNDREDS OF HER HAIRS MIXED IN WITH MINE. HOW FAR AWAY CAN SHE BE AND STILL CONTROL THEM? A HUNDRED METERS? TWO HUNDRED METERS? SURELY NOT A KILOMETER...
WAIT!
SWP
!!

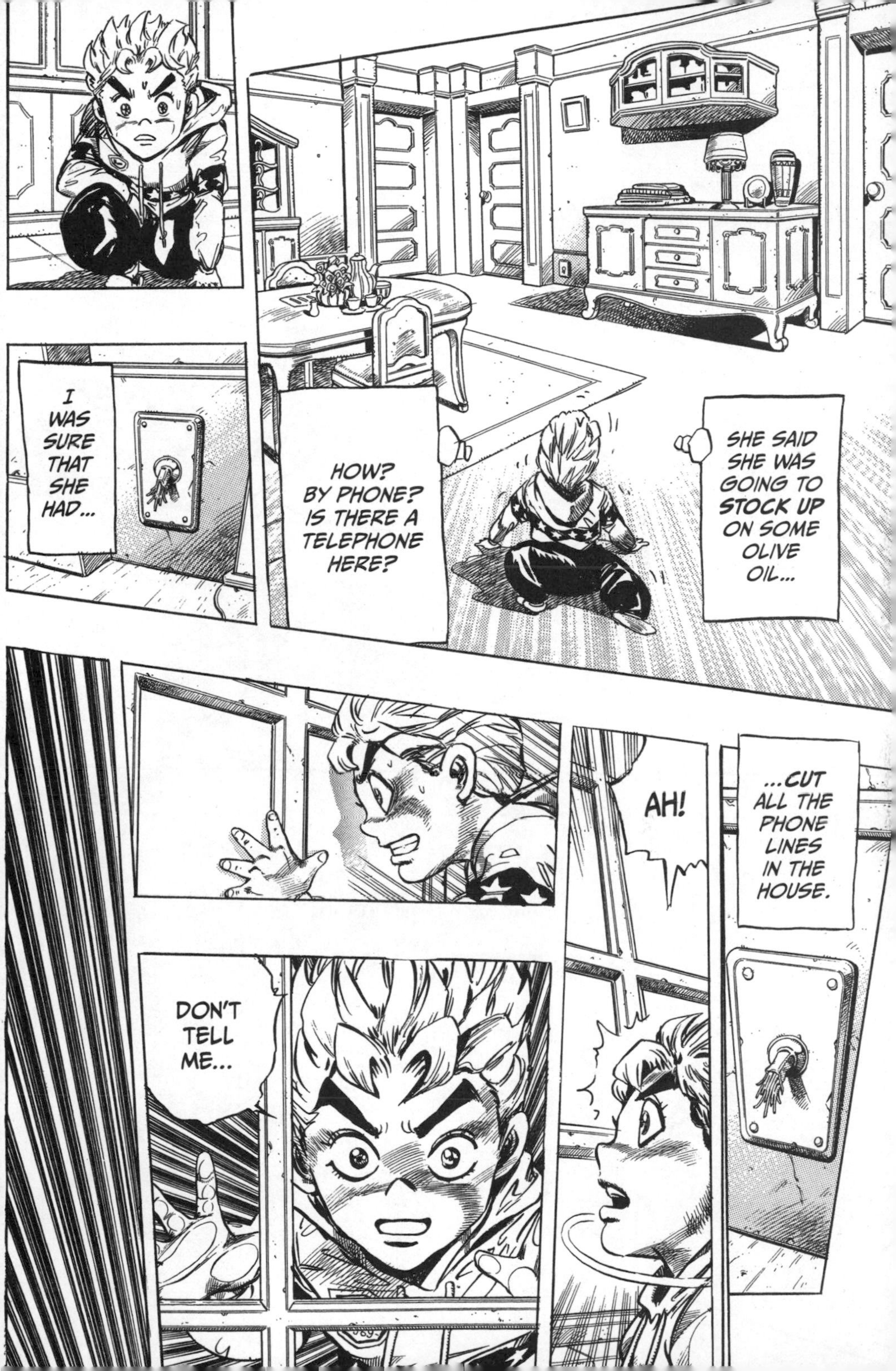
SHE SAID SHE WAS GOING TO STOCK UP ON SOME OLIVE OIL...
HOW? BY PHONE? IS THERE A TELEPHONE HERE?
I WAS SURE THAT SHE HAD...
...CUT ALL THE PHONE LINES IN THE HOUSE.
AH!
DON'T TELL ME...

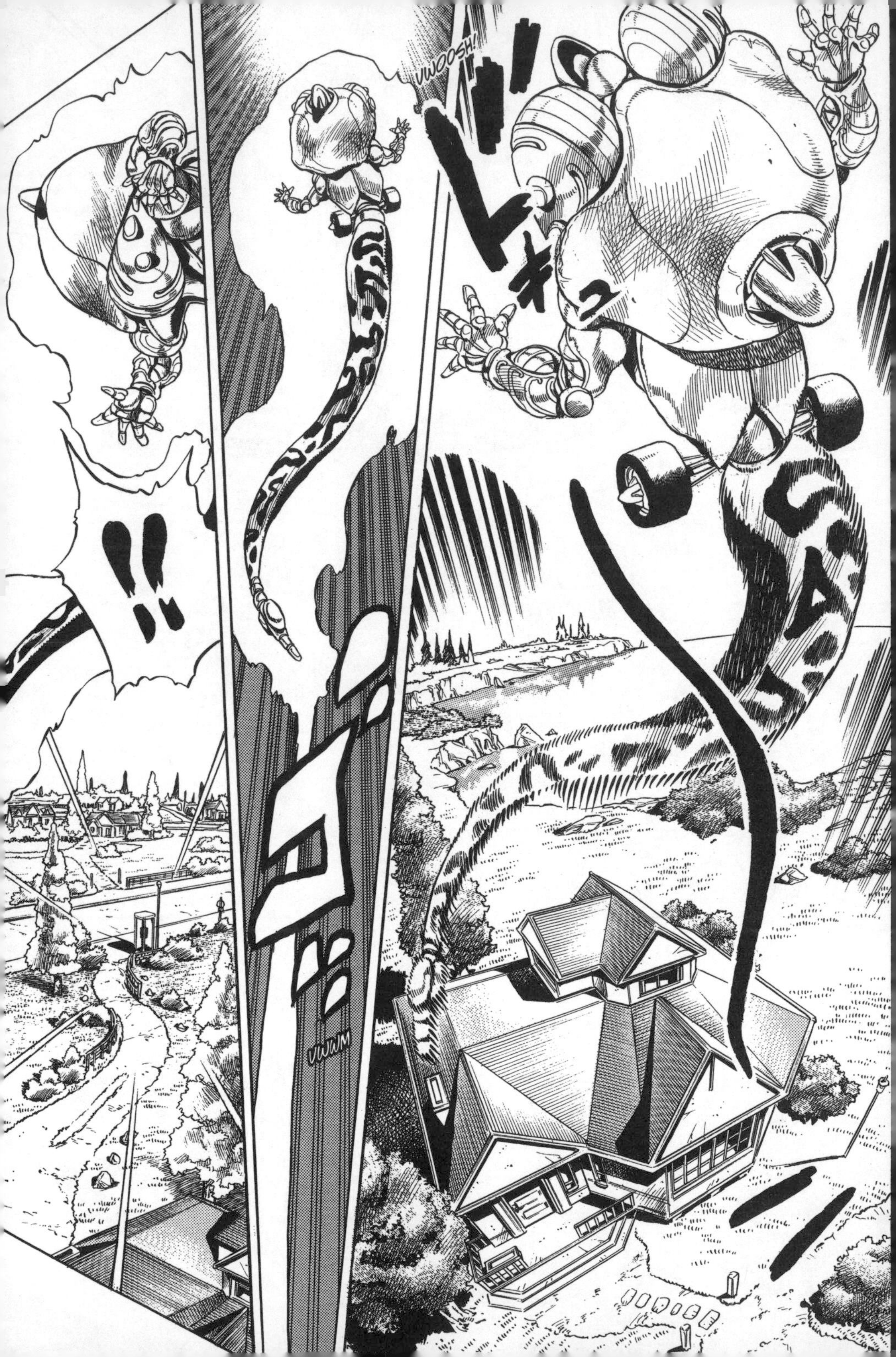
VWOOSH!
VWWM

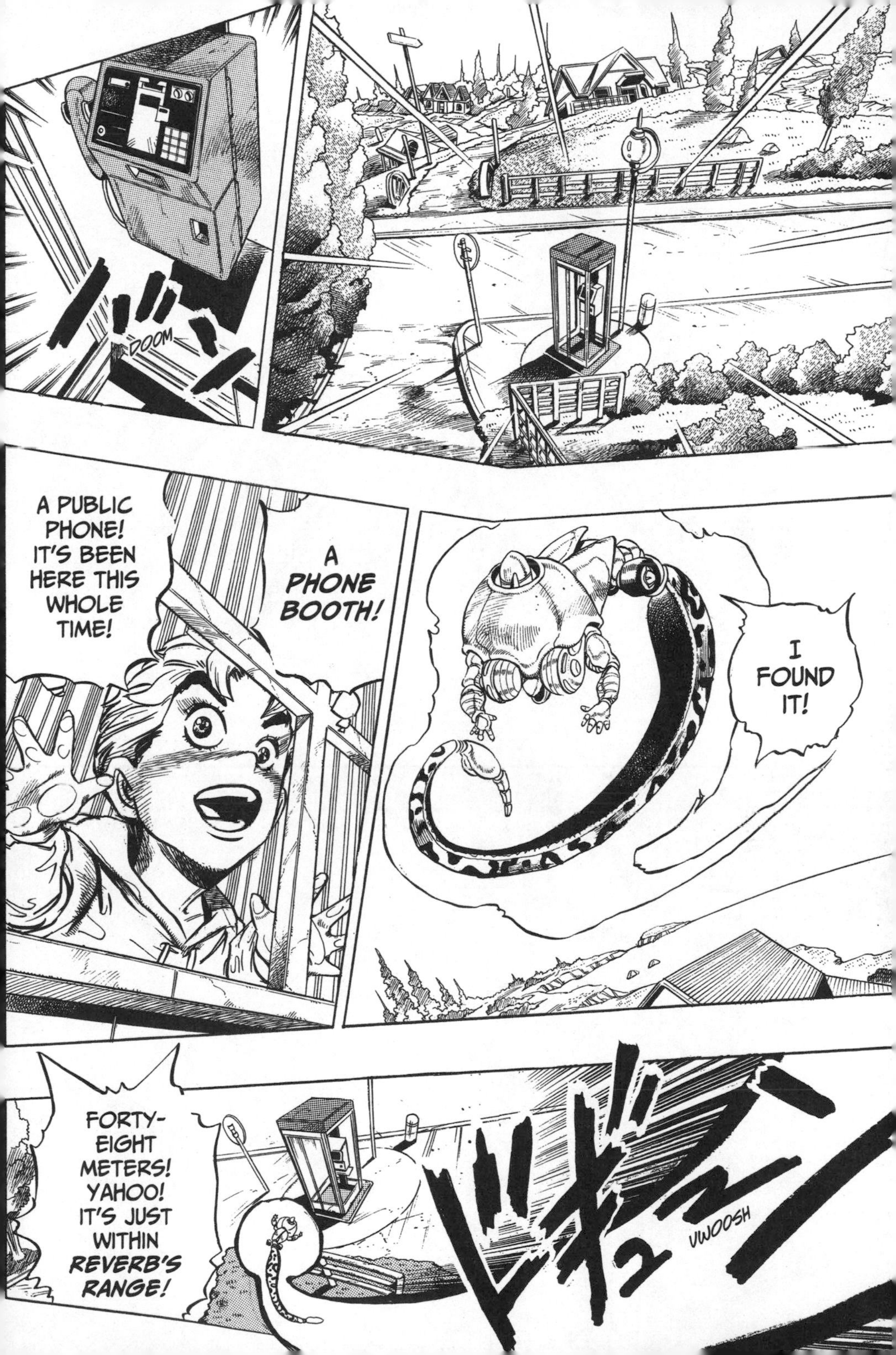
DOOM
I FOUND IT!
A PHONE BOOTH!
A PUBLIC PHONE! IT'S BEEN HERE THIS WHOLE TIME!
FORTY-EIGHT METERS! YAHOO! IT'S JUST WITHIN REVERB'S RANGE!
VWOOSH

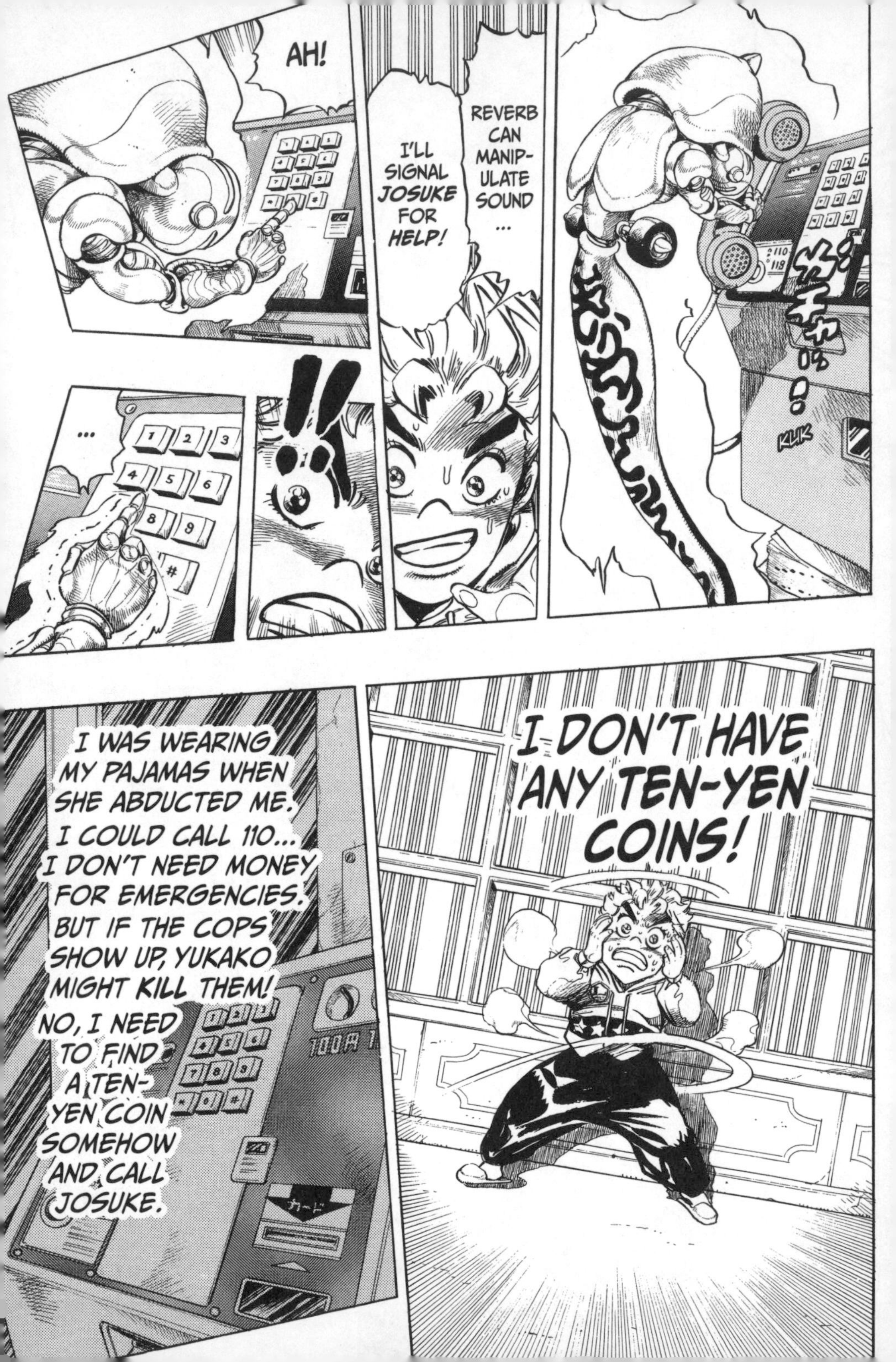
KUK
REVERB CAN MANIPULATE SOUND ...
I'LL SIGNAL JOSUKE FOR HELP!
AH!
!!
...
I DON'T HAVE ANY TEN-YEN COINS!
I WAS WEARING MY PAJAMAS WHEN SHE ABDUCTED ME.
I COULD CALL 110... I DON'T NEED MONEY FOR EMERGENCIES.
BUT IF THE COPS SHOW UP, YUKAKO MIGHT KILL THEM!
NO, I NEED TO FIND A TEN-YEN COIN SOMEHOW AND CALL JOSUKE.

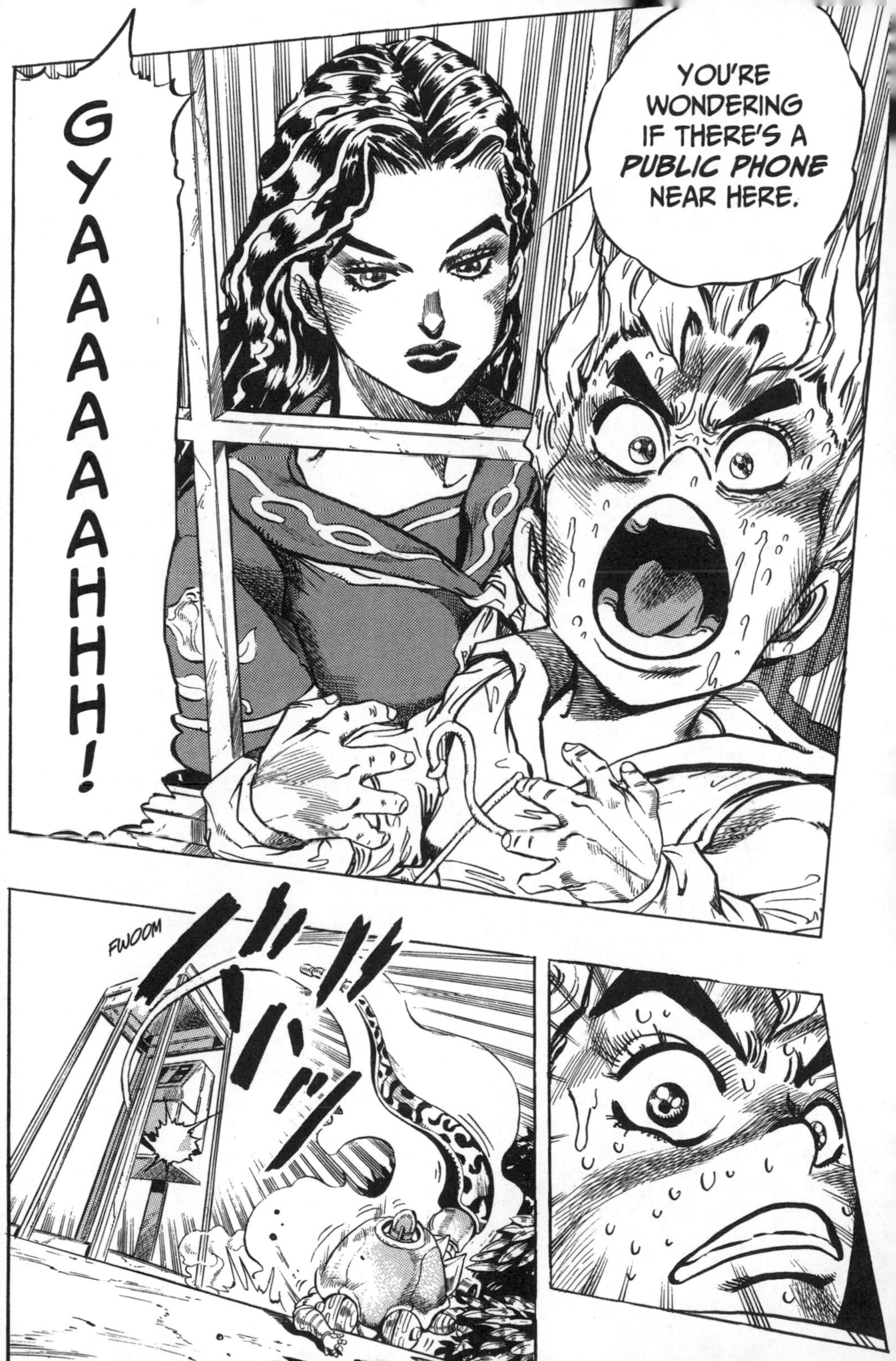
YOU'RE WONDERING IF THERE'S A *PUBLIC PHONE* NEAR HERE.
GYAAAAAAAHHH!
FWOOM

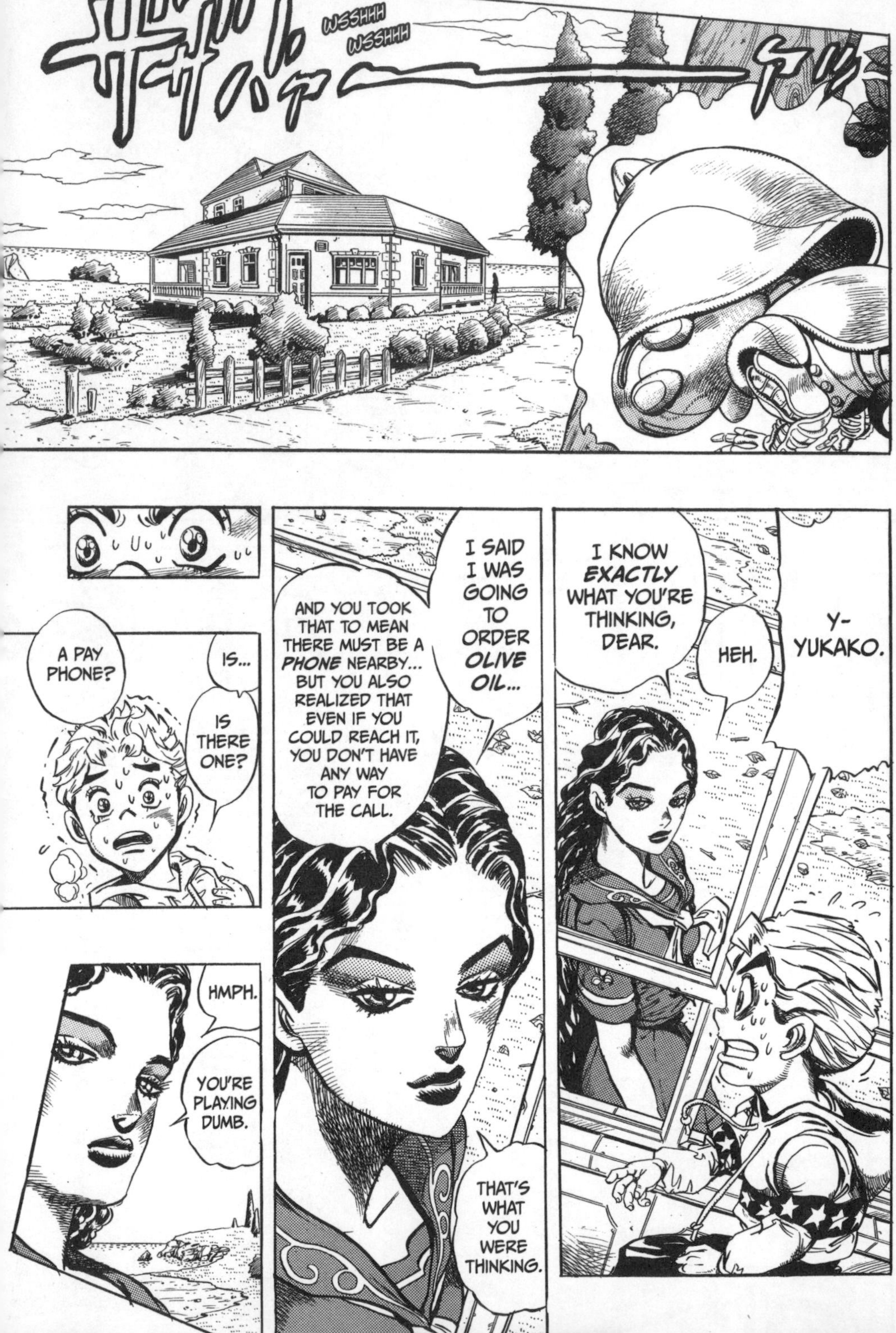
WSSHHH
WSSHHH
Y-YUKAKO.
HEH.
I KNOW EXACTLY WHAT YOU'RE THINKING, DEAR.
I SAID I WAS GOING TO ORDER OLIVE OIL...
AND YOU TOOK THAT TO MEAN THERE MUST BE A PHONE NEARBY... BUT YOU ALSO REALIZED THAT EVEN IF YOU COULD REACH IT, YOU DON'T HAVE ANY WAY TO PAY FOR THE CALL.
THAT'S WHAT YOU WERE THINKING.
IS...
IS THERE ONE?
A PAY PHONE?
HMPH.
YOU'RE PLAYING DUMB.

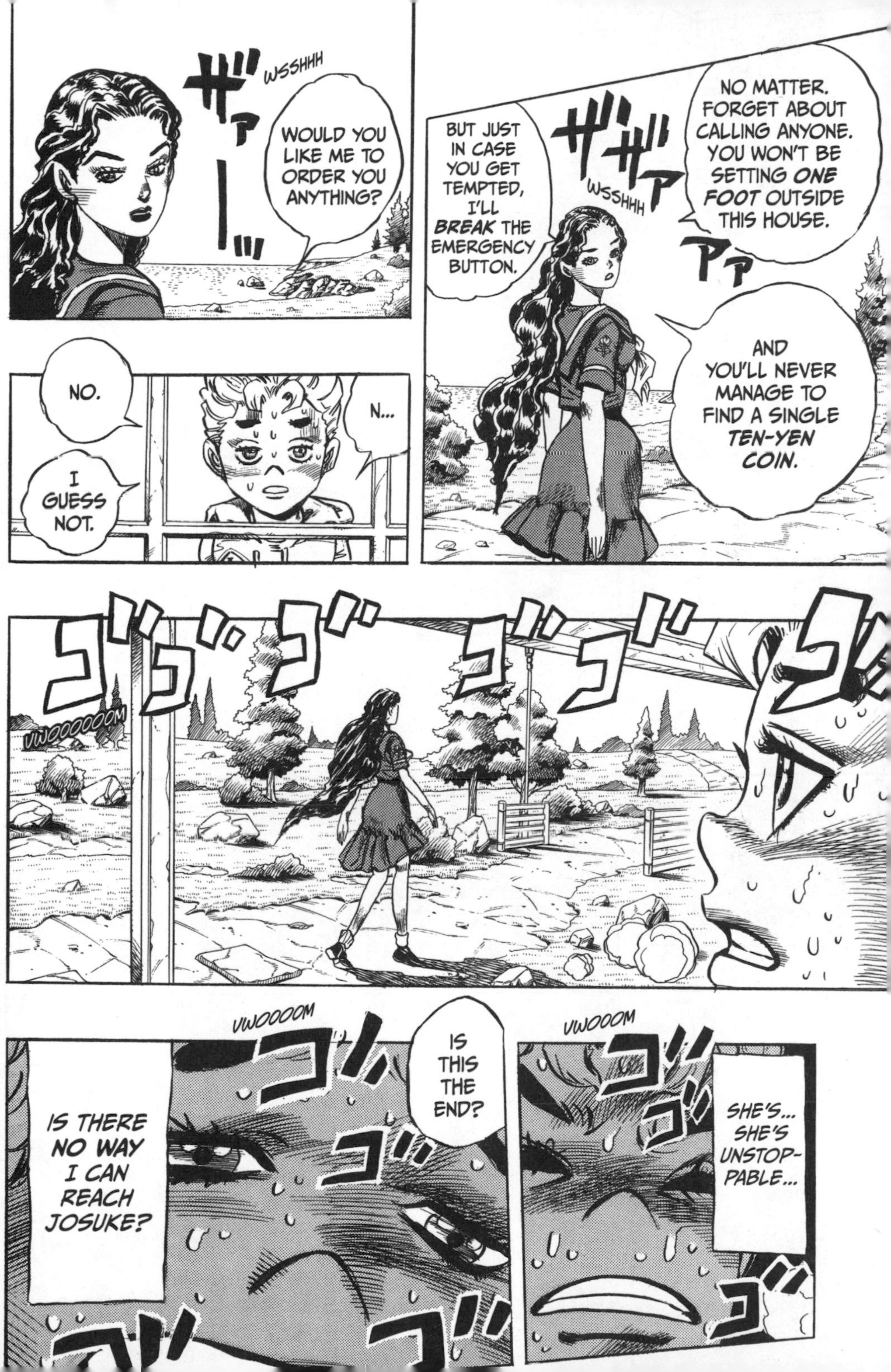
NO MATTER. FORGET ABOUT CALLING ANYONE. YOU WON'T BE SETTING *ONE FOOT* OUTSIDE THIS HOUSE.
WSSHHH
BUT JUST IN CASE YOU GET TEMPTED, I'LL *BREAK* THE EMERGENCY BUTTON.
AND YOU'LL NEVER MANAGE TO FIND A SINGLE *TEN-YEN COIN.*
WSSHHH
WOULD YOU LIKE ME TO ORDER YOU ANYTHING?
N...
NO.
I GUESS NOT.
VWOOOOOOOM
VWOOOM
SHE'S... SHE'S UNSTOPPABLE...
IS THIS THE END?
VWOOOOM
IS THERE NO WAY I CAN REACH JOSUKE?

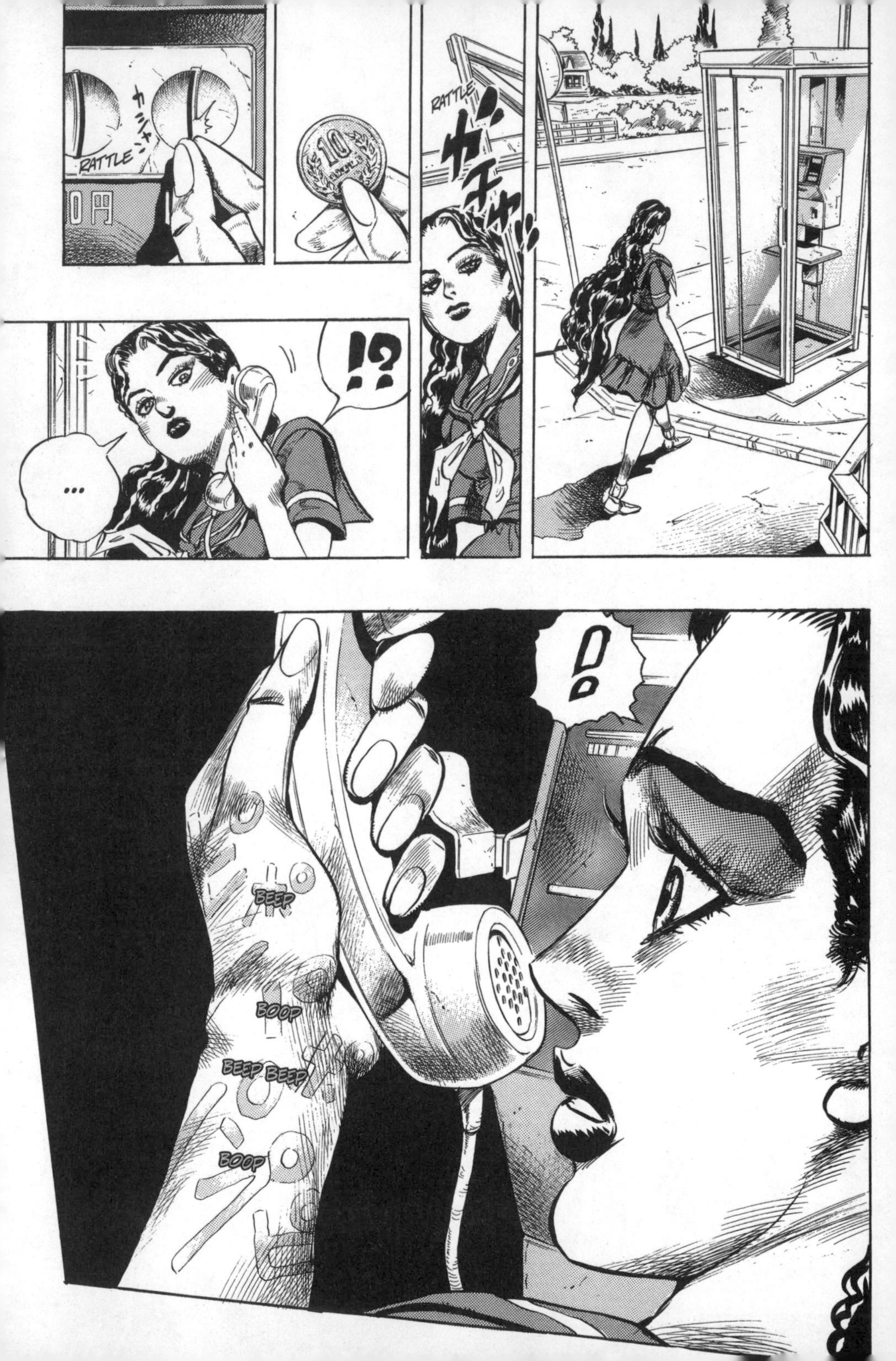

RATTLE
ガチャ
カシャン
RATTLE
!?
...
!
BEEP
BOOP
BEEP BEEP
BOOP

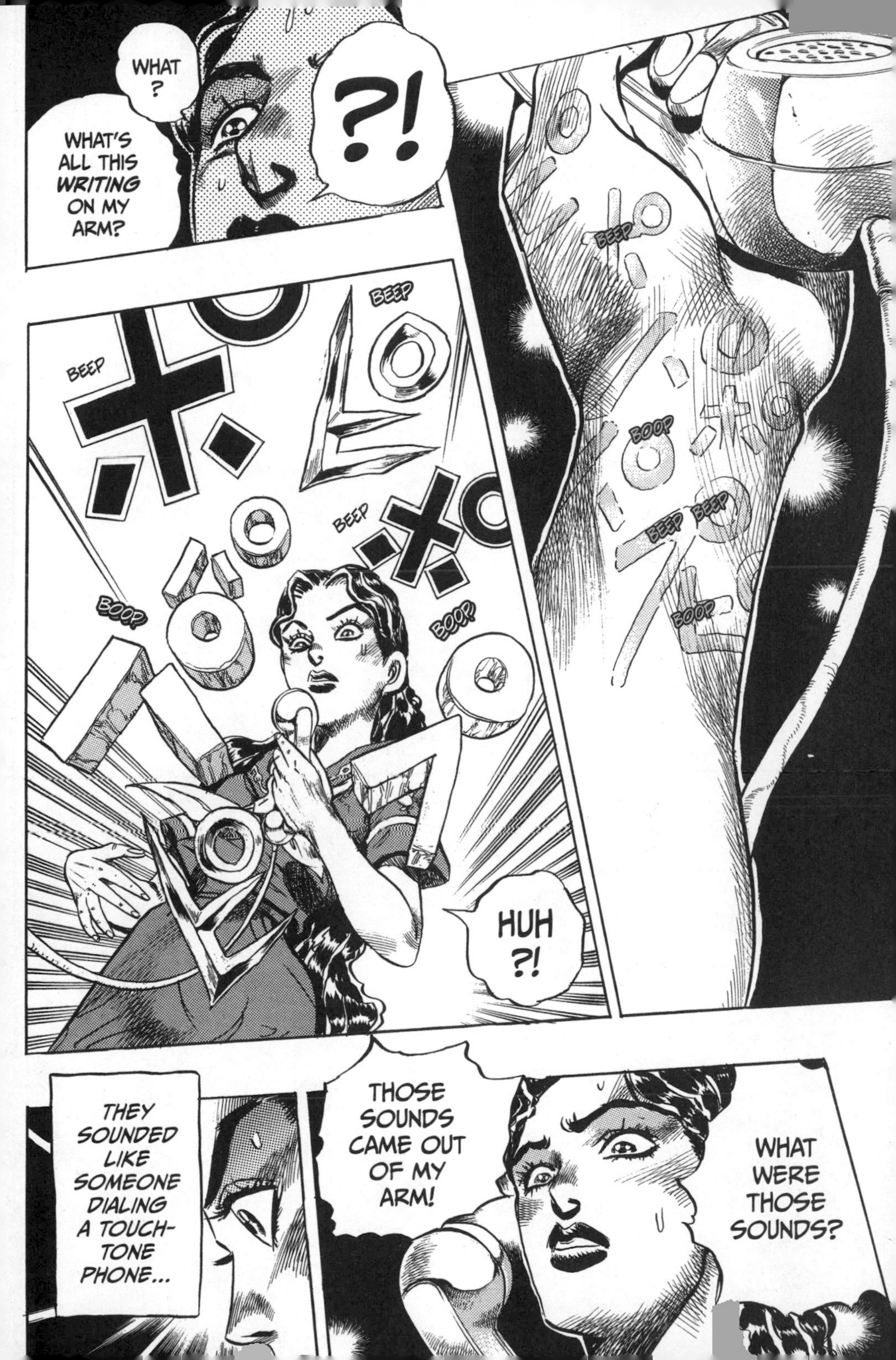
BEEP
BOOP
BEEP BEEP
BOOP
?!
WHAT ?
WHAT'S ALL THIS WRITING ON MY ARM?
BEEP
BEEP
BEEP
BOOP
BOOP
HUH ?!
WHAT WERE THOSE SOUNDS?
THOSE SOUNDS CAME OUT OF MY ARM!
THEY SOUNDED LIKE SOMEONE DIALING A TOUCH-TONE PHONE...

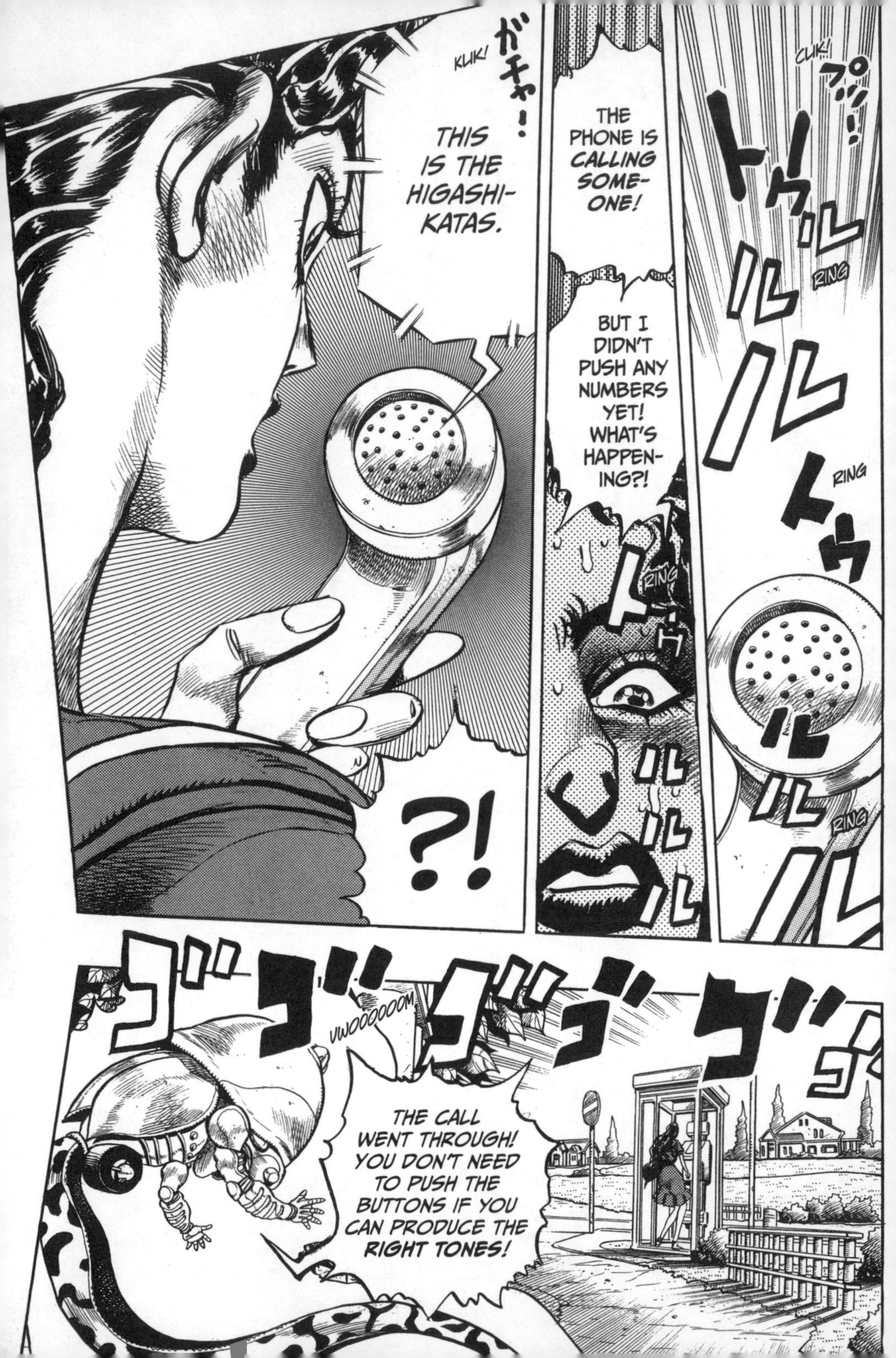
CUK!
RING
RING
RING
THE PHONE IS CALLING SOMEONE!
BUT I DIDN'T PUSH ANY NUMBERS YET! WHAT'S HAPPENING?!
RING
KUK!
ガチャ!
THIS IS THE HIGASHIKATAS.
?!
VWOOOOOOM
THE CALL WENT THROUGH! YOU DON'T NEED TO PUSH THE BUTTONS IF YOU CAN PRODUCE THE RIGHT TONES!

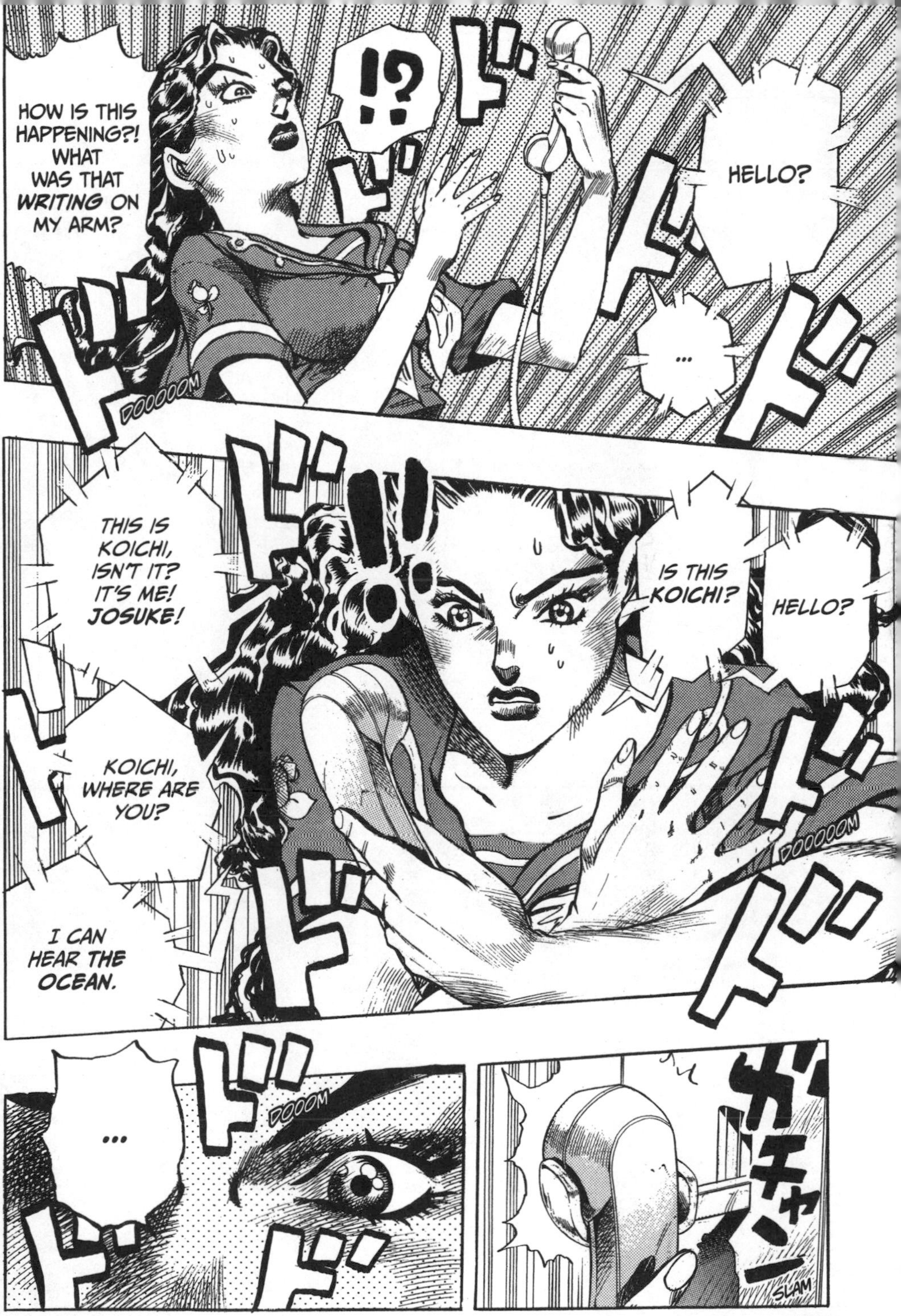
HELLO?
...
!?
HOW IS THIS HAPPENING?! WHAT WAS THAT *WRITING* ON MY ARM?
DOOOOOM
HELLO?
IS THIS KOICHI?
THIS IS KOICHI, ISN'T IT? IT'S ME! JOSUKE!
KOICHI, WHERE ARE YOU?
I CAN HEAR THE OCEAN.
DOOOOOM
SLAM
...
DOOOM

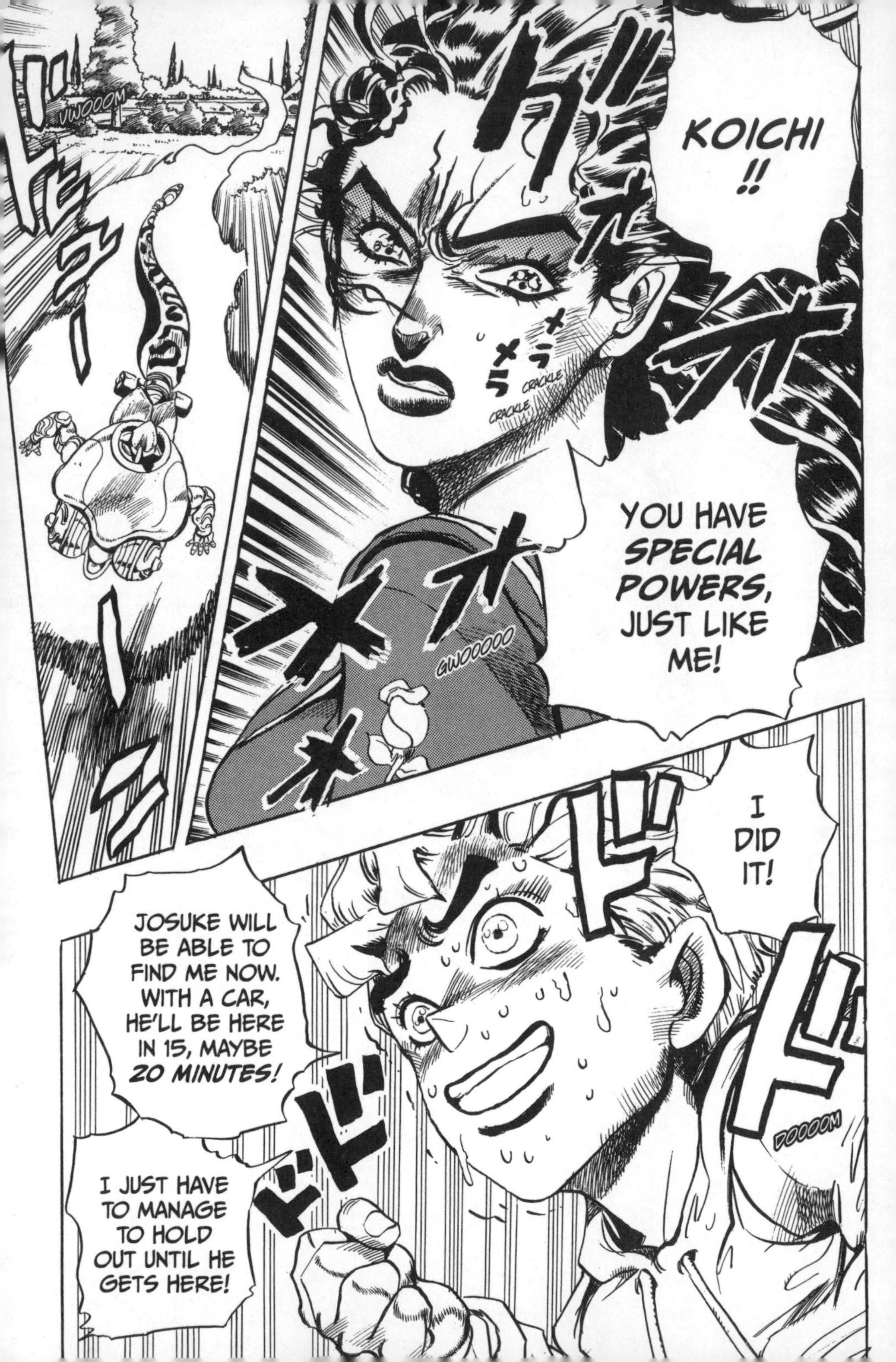
KOICHI !!
メラ メラ
CRACKLE
CRACKLE
YOU HAVE SPECIAL POWERS, JUST LIKE ME!
GWOOOOO
VWOOOM
I DID IT!
DOOOOM
JOSUKE WILL BE ABLE TO FIND ME NOW. WITH A CAR, HE'LL BE HERE IN 15, MAYBE 20 MINUTES!
I JUST HAVE TO MANAGE TO HOLD OUT UNTIL HE GETS HERE!

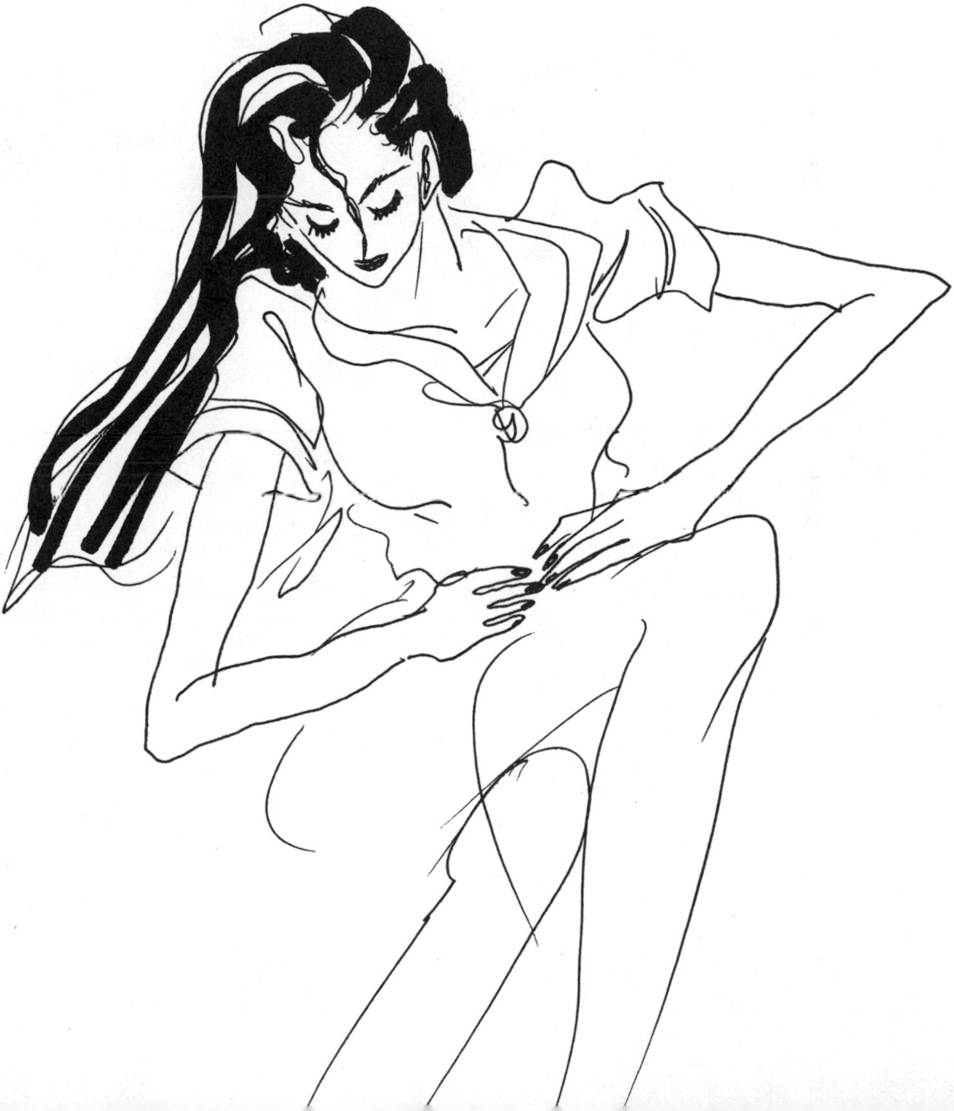

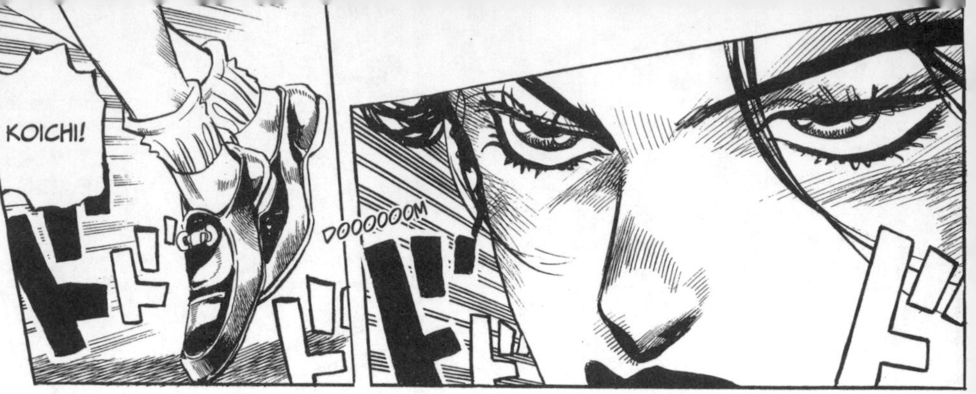
DOOOOOOM
KOICHI!

CHAPTER 34

YUKAKO YAMAGISHI FALLS IN LOVE, PART 6

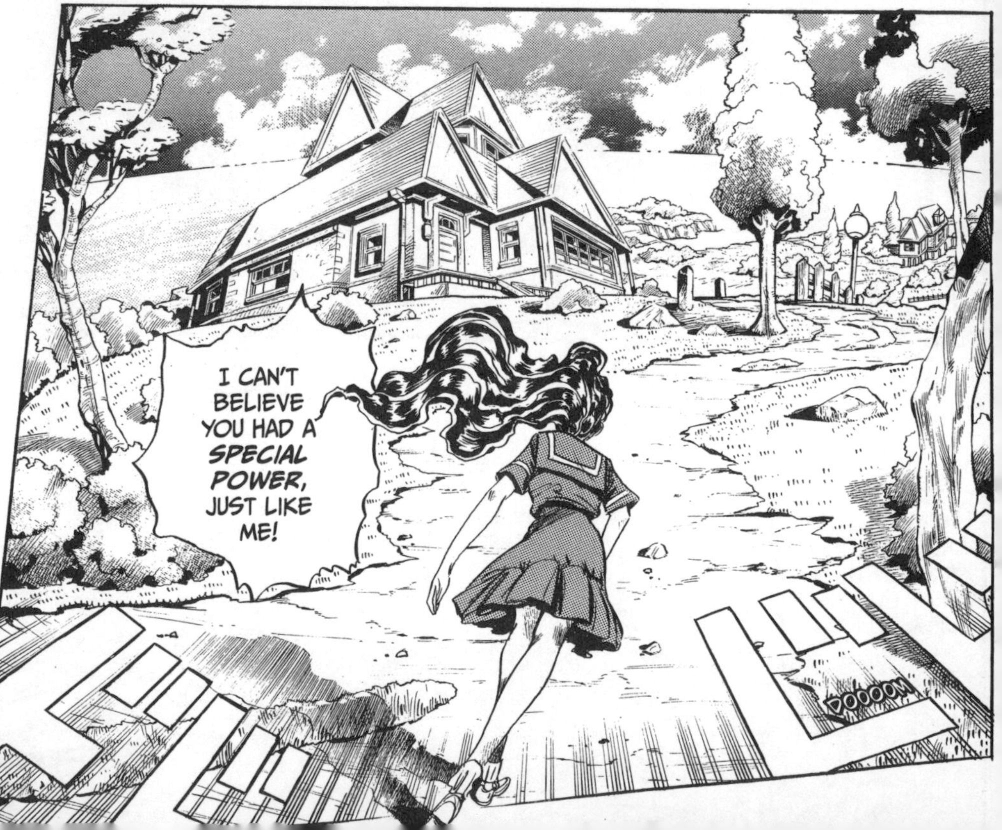
I CAN'T BELIEVE YOU HAD A *SPECIAL POWER*, JUST LIKE ME!
DOOOOM

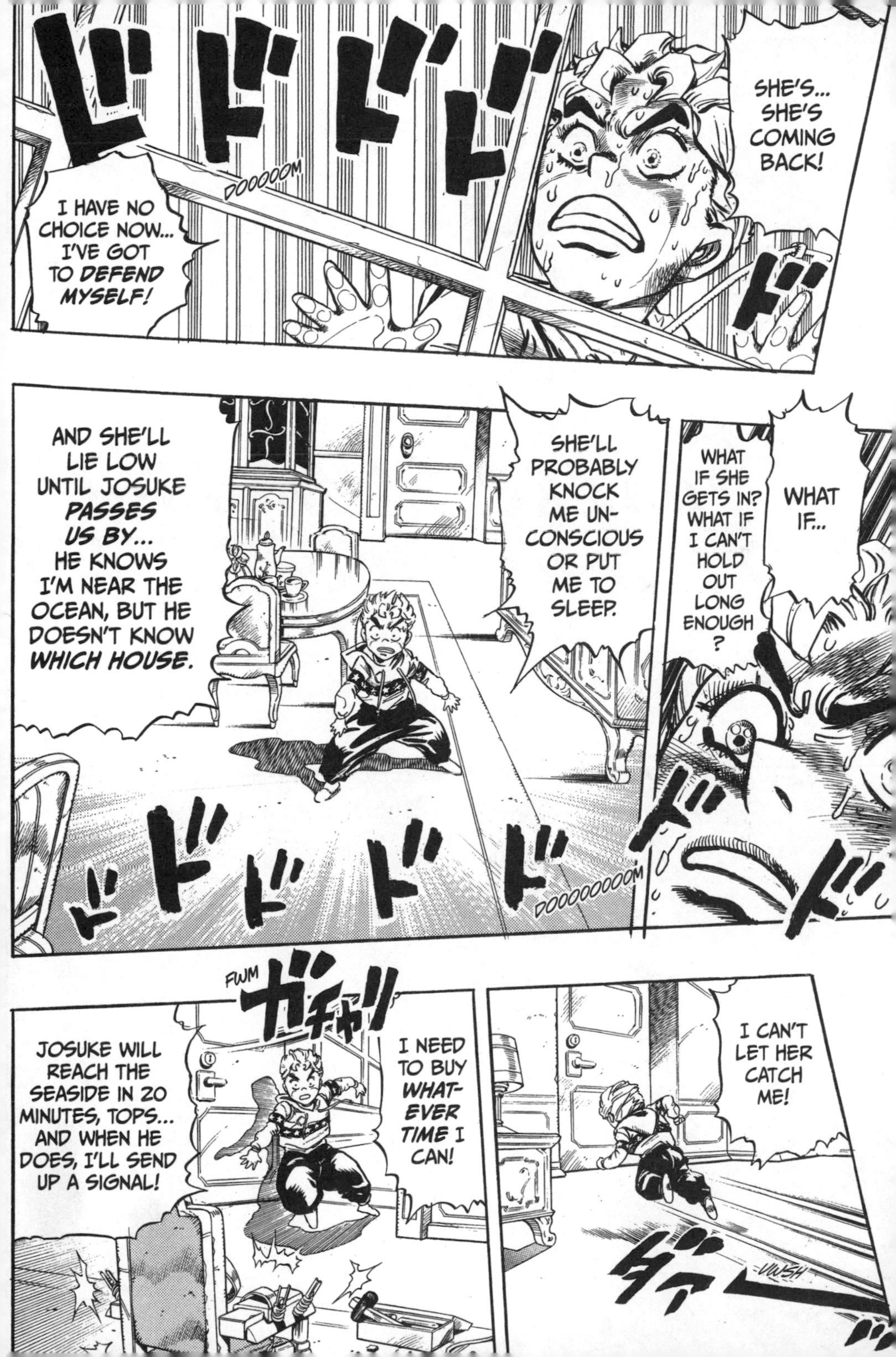
SHE'S... SHE'S COMING BACK!
ドドドドド
DOOOOOM
I HAVE NO CHOICE NOW... I'VE GOT TO DEFEND MYSELF!
WHAT IF...
WHAT IF SHE GETS IN? WHAT IF I CAN'T HOLD OUT LONG ENOUGH?
ドドド
SHE'LL PROBABLY KNOCK ME UN-CONSCIOUS OR PUT ME TO SLEEP.
AND SHE'LL LIE LOW UNTIL JOSUKE PASSES US BY... HE KNOWS I'M NEAR THE OCEAN, BUT HE DOESN'T KNOW WHICH HOUSE.
ドドドドド
DOOOOOOOOM
I CAN'T LET HER CATCH ME!
VWSH
FWUM
I NEED TO BUY WHATEVER TIME I CAN!
JOSUKE WILL REACH THE SEASIDE IN 20 MINUTES, TOPS... AND WHEN HE DOES, I'LL SEND UP A SIGNAL!

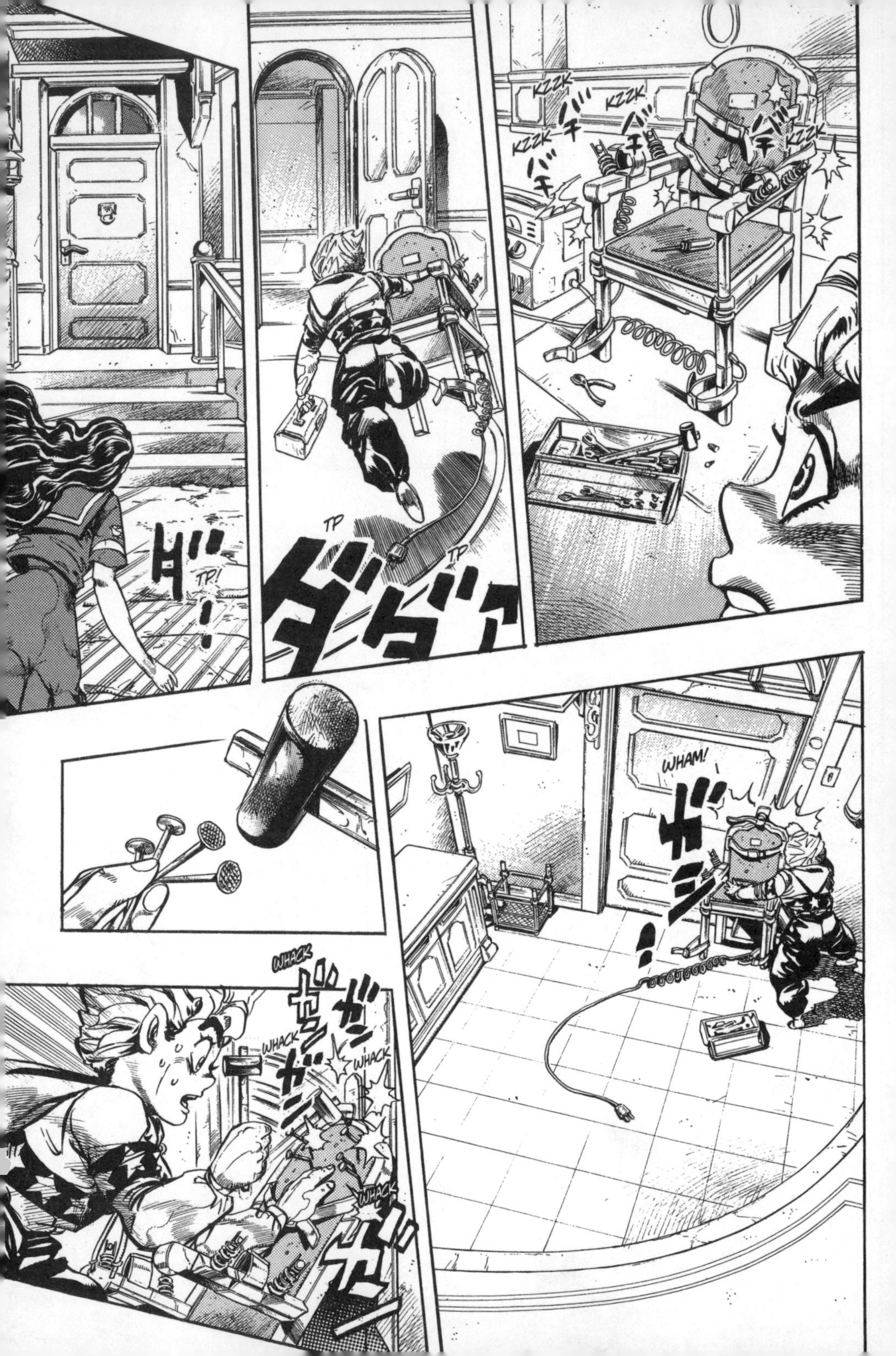
KZZK
KZZK
KZZK
KZZK
TP
TP
TP!
WHAM!
WHACK
WHACK
WHACK
WHACK

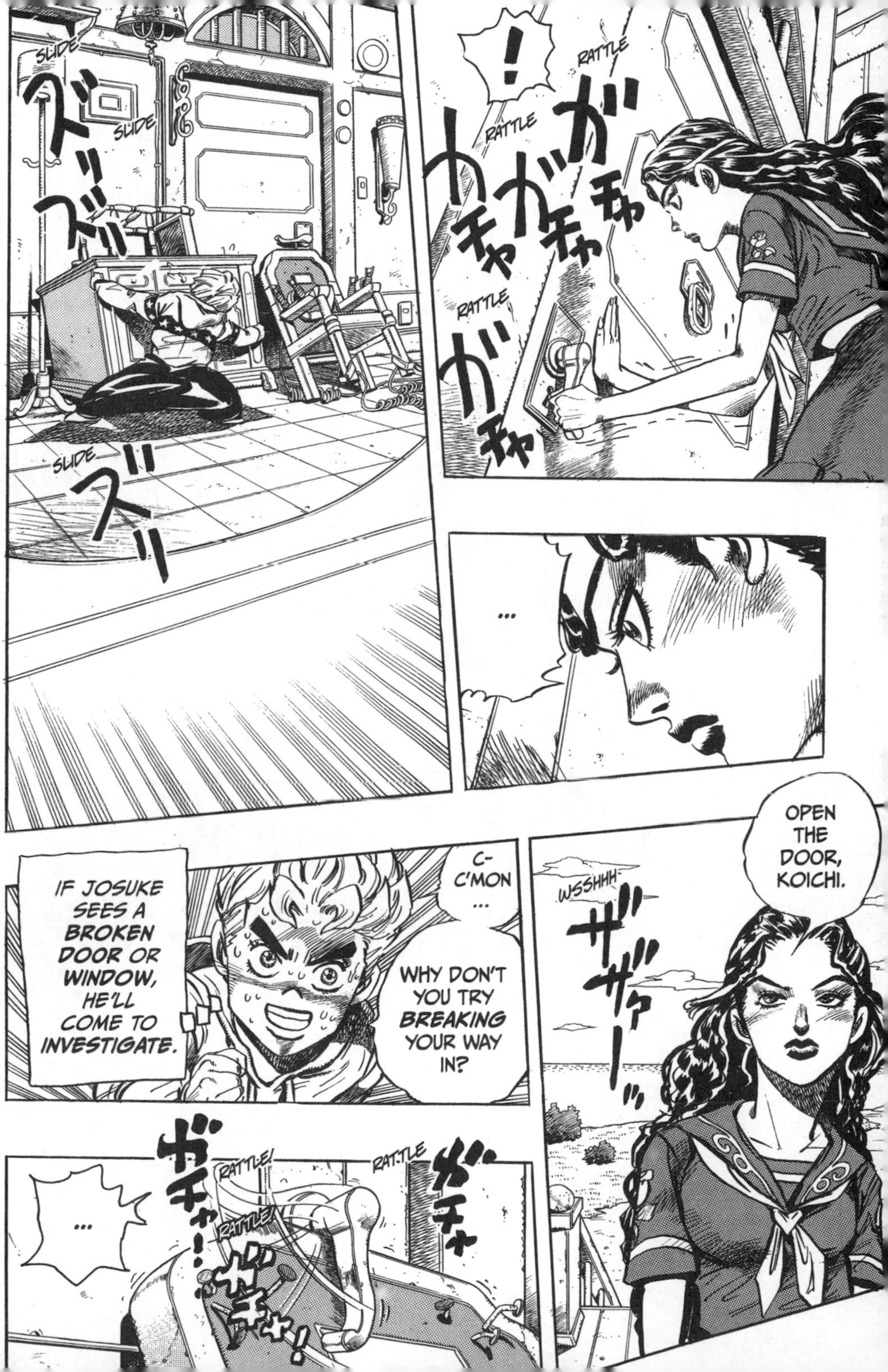
!
RATTLE
RATTLE
RATTLE
ガチャガチャ
ガチャ
...
SLIDE
SLIDE
SLIDE
OPEN THE DOOR, KOICHI.
WSSHHH
ザザァー
C-C'MON...
WHY DON'T YOU TRY BREAKING YOUR WAY IN?
IF JOSUKE SEES A BROKEN DOOR OR WINDOW, HE'LL COME TO INVESTIGATE.
RATTLE
ガチャ
RATTLE!
ガチャ!!
RATTLE!
ガチャ!
...

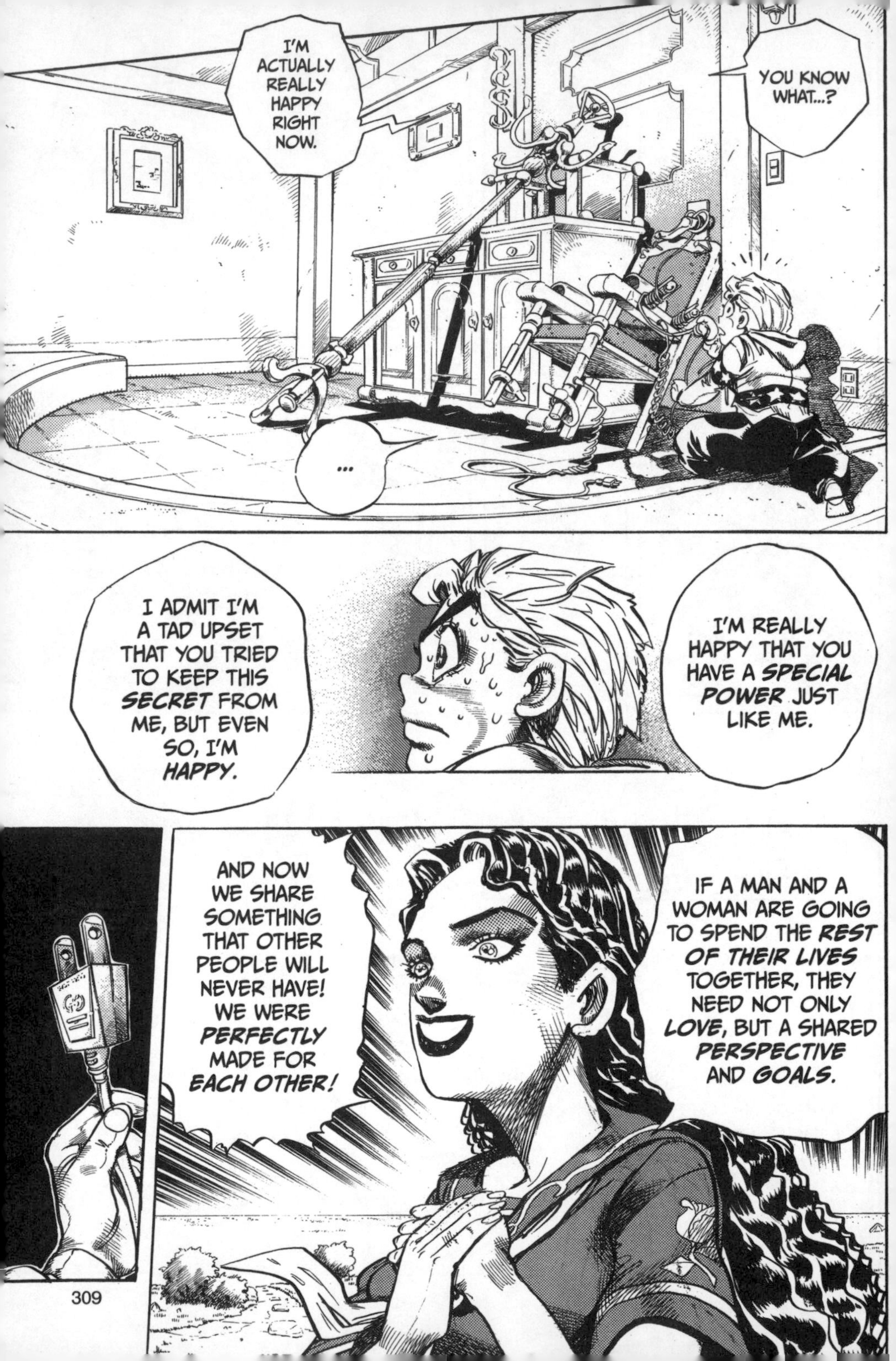
YOU KNOW WHAT...?
I'M ACTUALLY REALLY HAPPY RIGHT NOW.
...
I'M REALLY HAPPY THAT YOU HAVE A SPECIAL POWER JUST LIKE ME.
I ADMIT I'M A TAD UPSET THAT YOU TRIED TO KEEP THIS SECRET FROM ME, BUT EVEN SO, I'M HAPPY.
IF A MAN AND A WOMAN ARE GOING TO SPEND THE REST OF THEIR LIVES TOGETHER, THEY NEED NOT ONLY LOVE, BUT A SHARED PERSPECTIVE AND GOALS.
AND NOW WE SHARE SOMETHING THAT OTHER PEOPLE WILL NEVER HAVE! WE WERE PERFECTLY MADE FOR EACH OTHER!

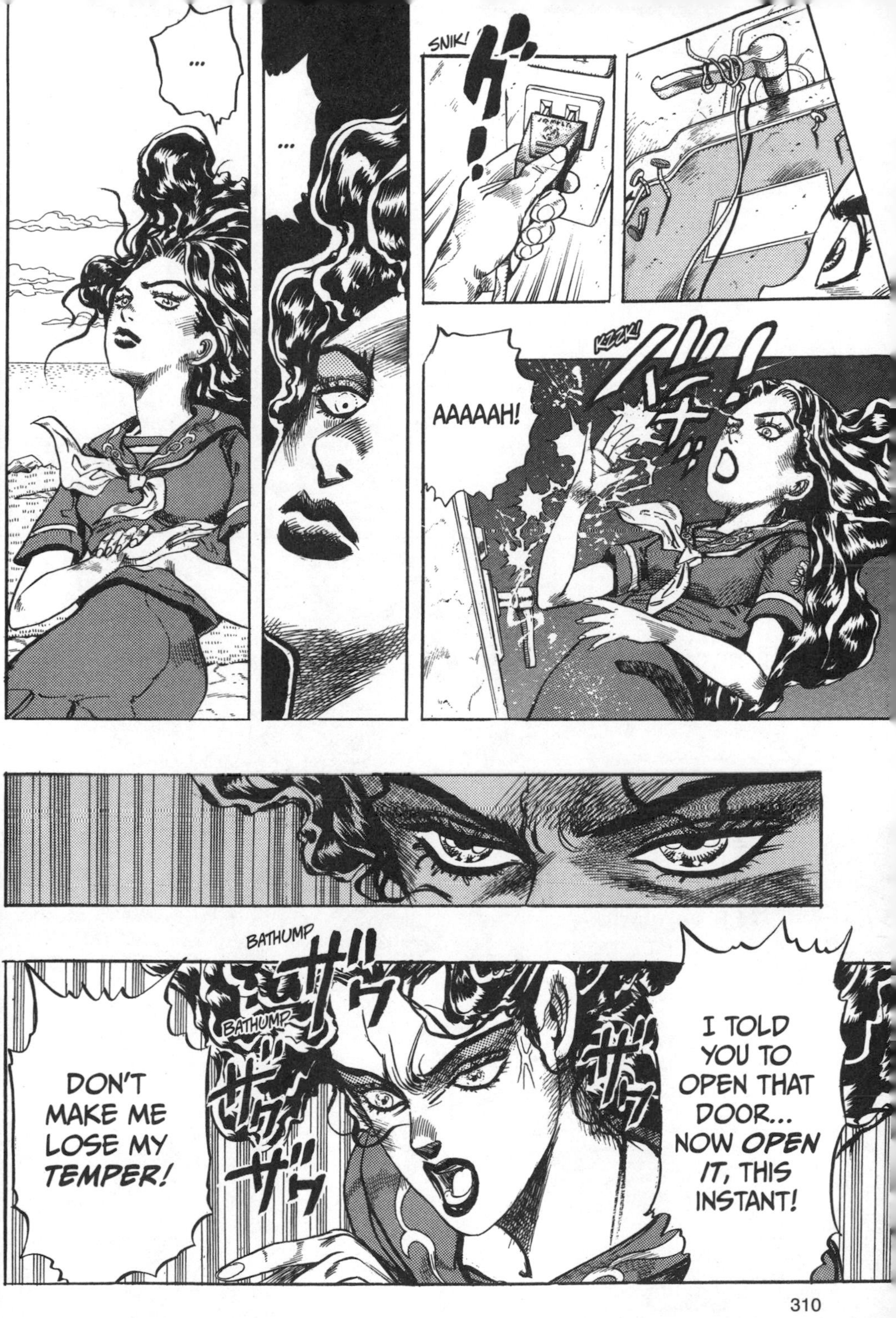
SNIK!
KZZK!
AAAAAH!
...
...
I TOLD YOU TO OPEN THAT DOOR... NOW *OPEN IT*, THIS INSTANT!
BATHUMP
BATHUMP
DON'T MAKE ME LOSE MY *TEMPER!*

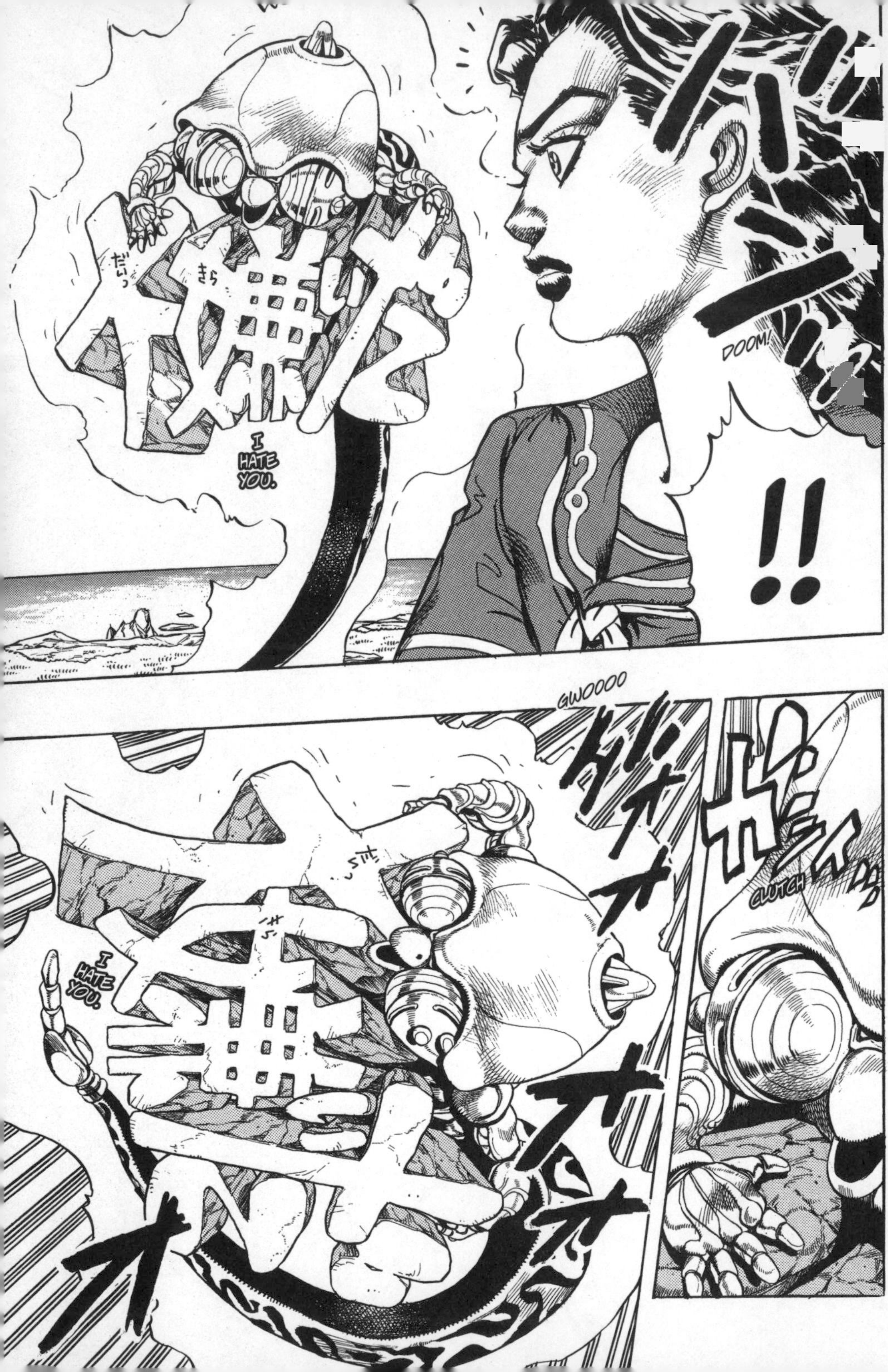
DOOM!
!!
だいっ
きら
I HATE YOU.
CLUTCH
GWOOOO
I HATE YOU.

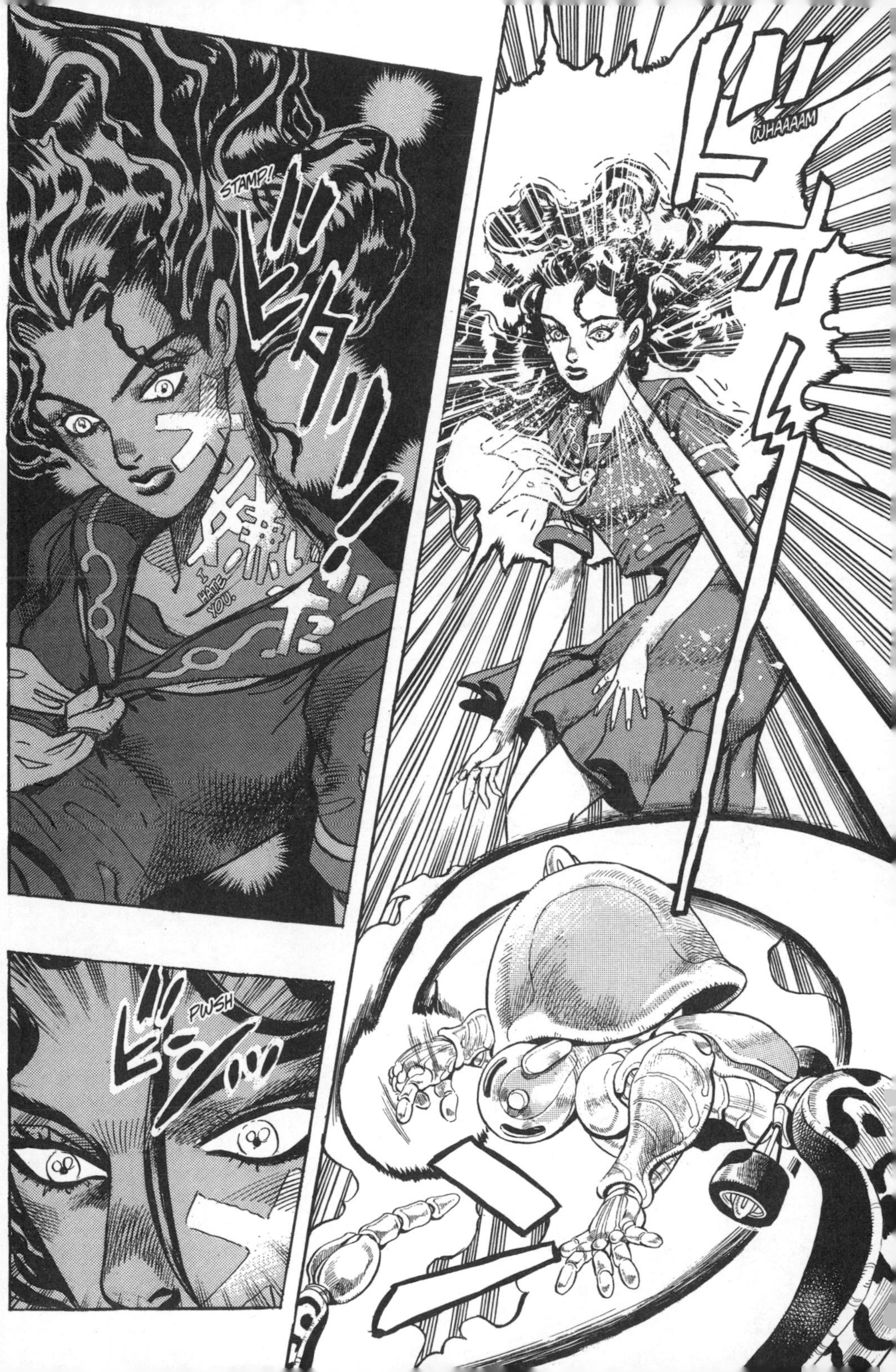
WHAAAAM
STAMP!
I HATE YOU.
PWSH

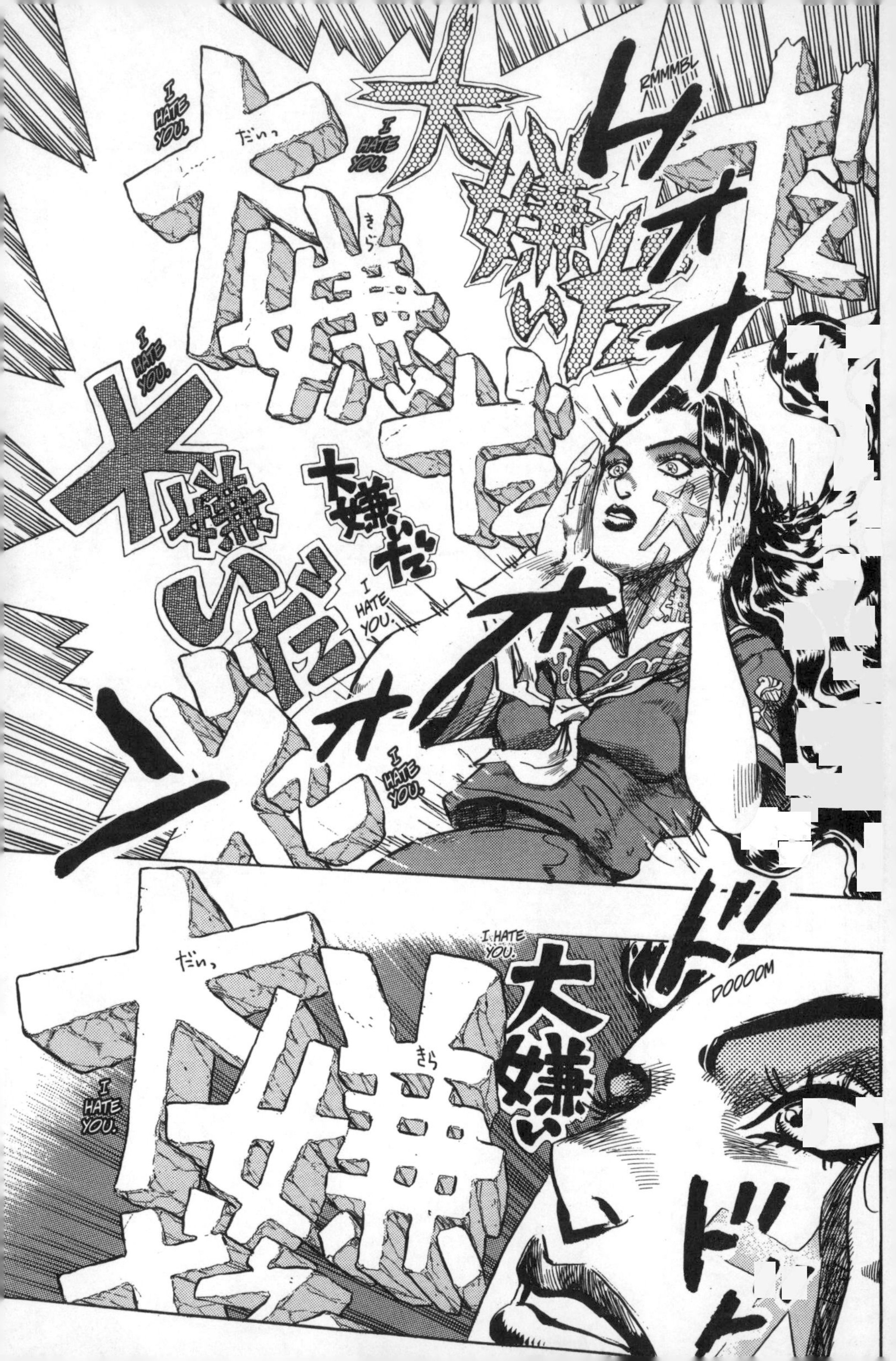

RMMMBL
I HATE YOU.
I HATE YOU.
I HATE YOU.
I HATE YOU.
I HATE YOU.
DOOOOM
I HATE YOU.
I HATE YOU.

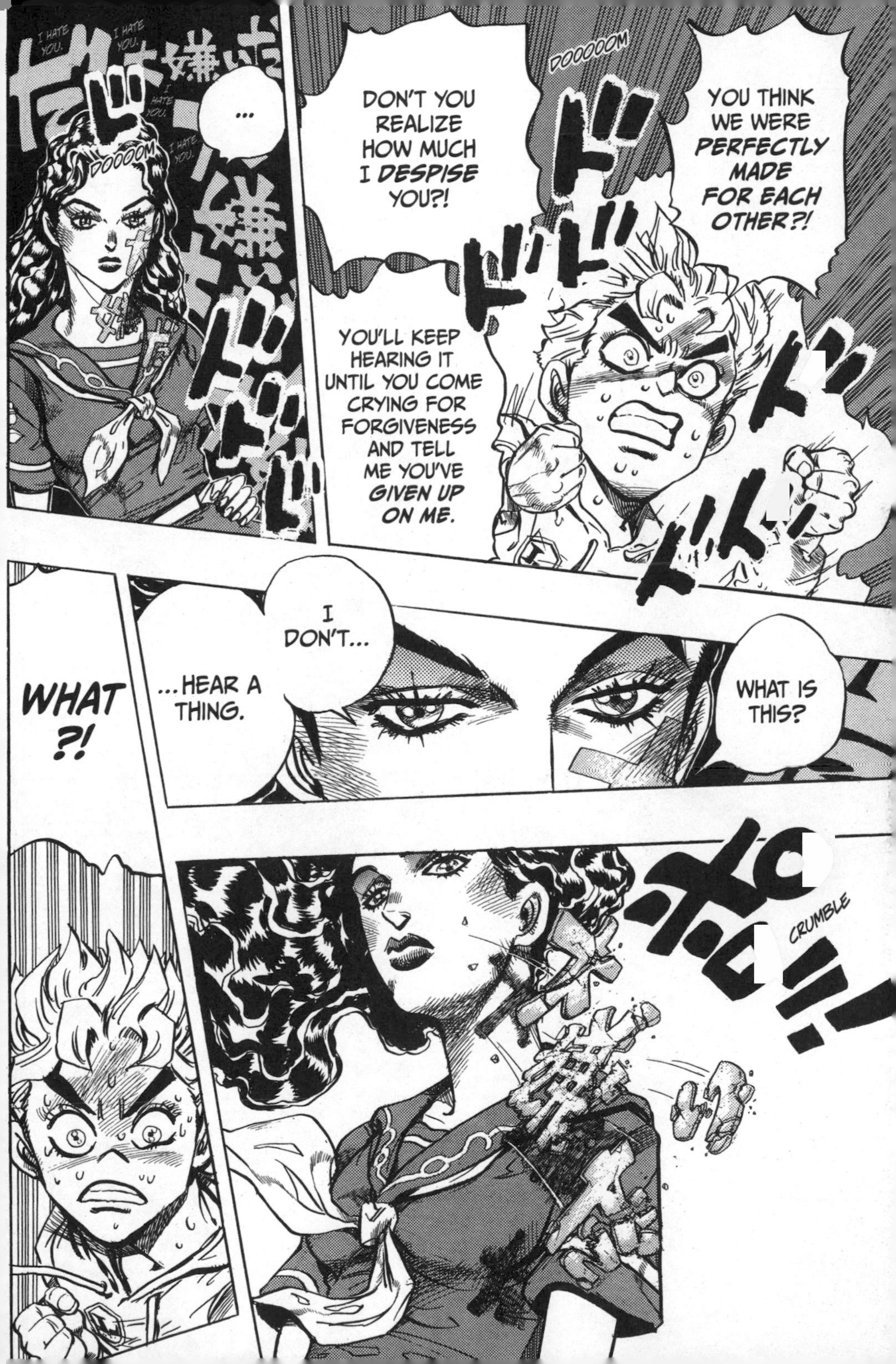
DOOOOOM
YOU THINK WE WERE PERFECTLY MADE FOR EACH OTHER?!
DON'T YOU REALIZE HOW MUCH I DESPISE YOU?!
YOU'LL KEEP HEARING IT UNTIL YOU COME CRYING FOR FORGIVENESS AND TELL ME YOU'VE GIVEN UP ON ME.
I HATE YOU.
I HATE YOU.
I HATE YOU.
I HATE YOU.
...
DOOOOM
WHAT IS THIS?
I DON'T...
...HEAR A THING.
WHAT ?!
CRUMBLE

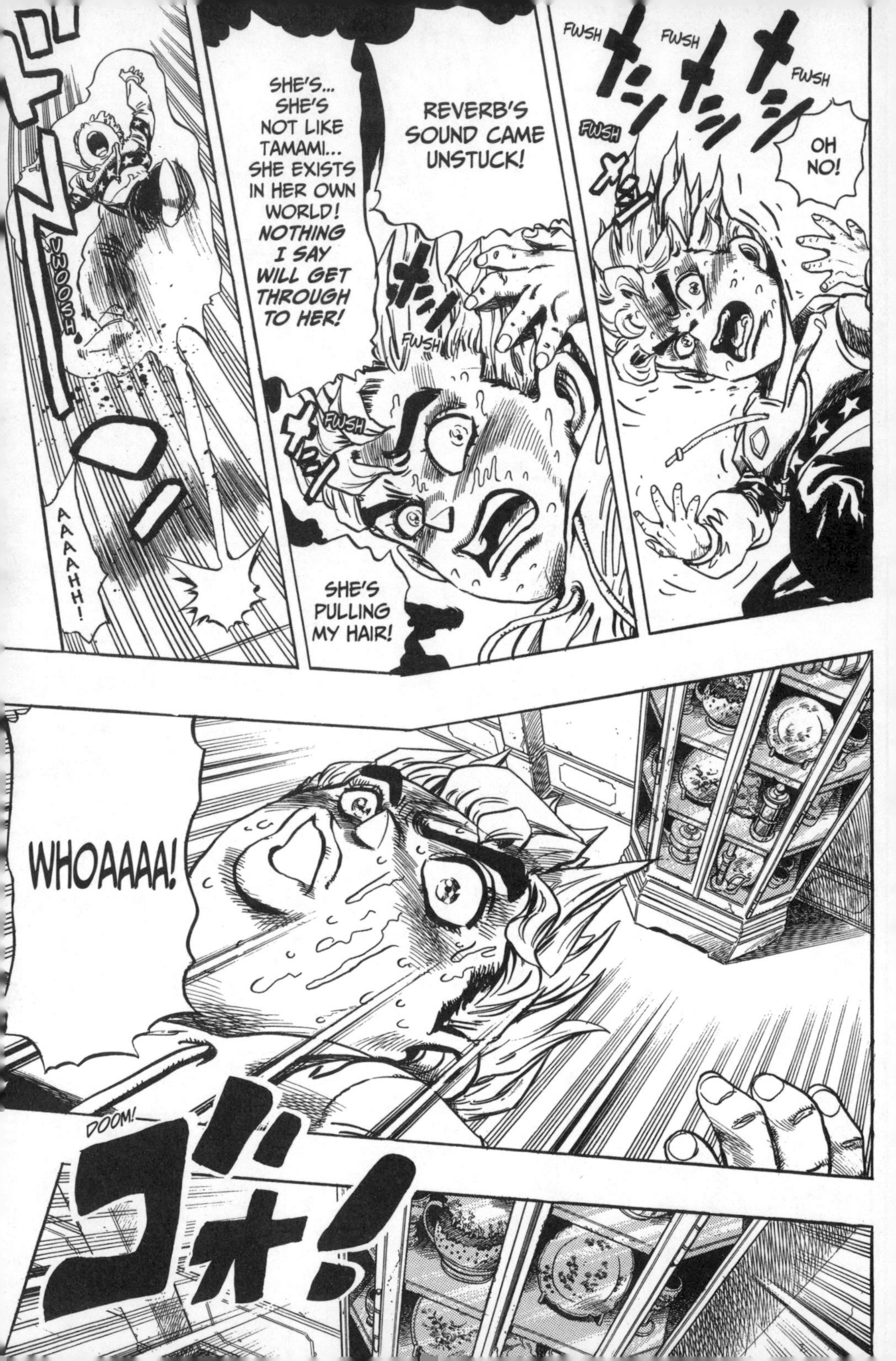
FWSH
FWSH
FWSH
FWSH
OH NO!
REVERB'S SOUND CAME UNSTUCK!
SHE'S... SHE'S NOT LIKE TAMAMI... SHE EXISTS IN HER OWN WORLD! *NOTHING I SAY WILL GET THROUGH TO HER!*
FWSH
FWSH
SHE'S PULLING MY HAIR!
WHOOSH
AAAAAHH!
WHOAAAA!
DOOM!

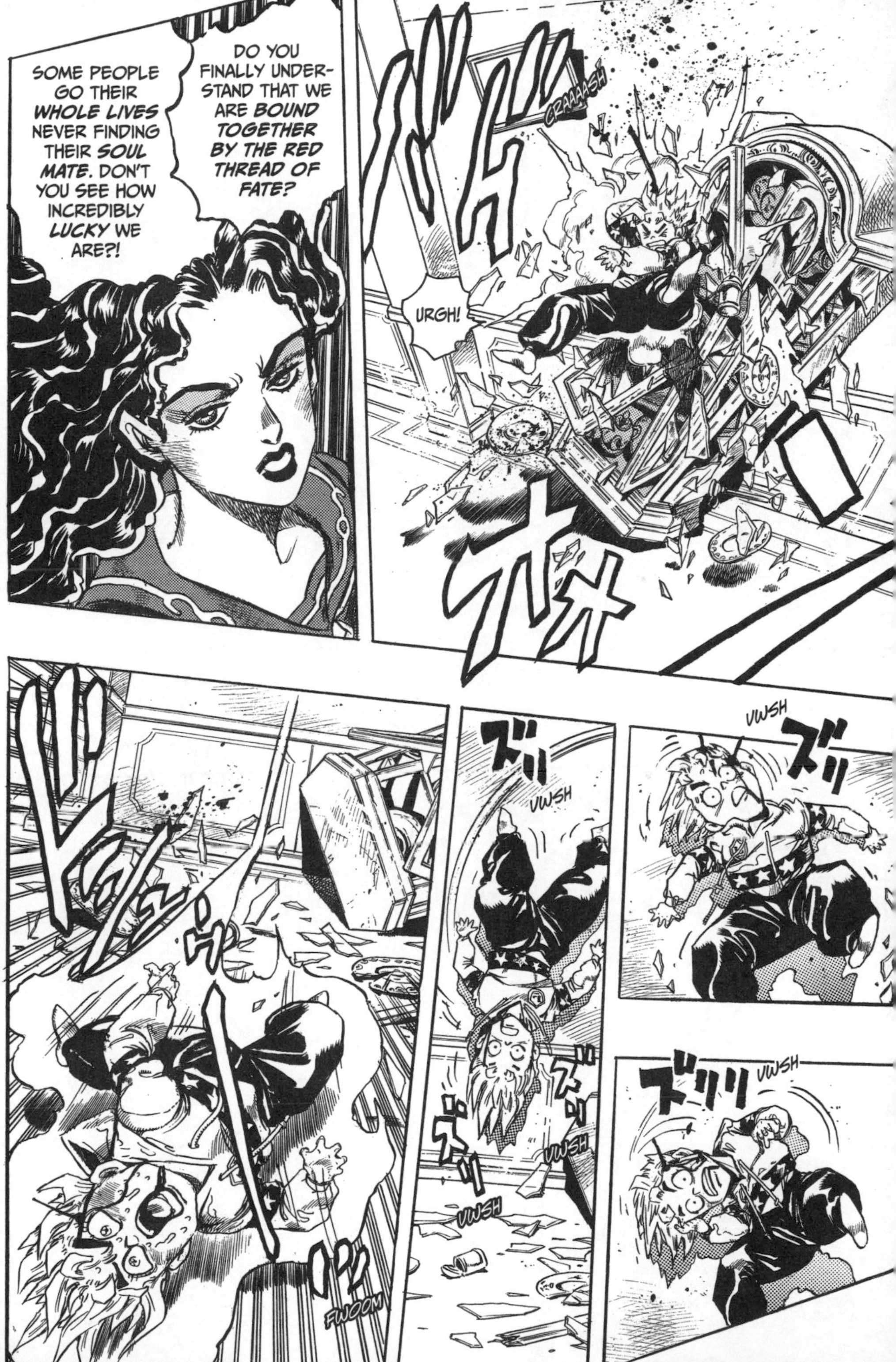
CRAAAASH
URGH!
DO YOU FINALLY UNDERSTAND THAT WE ARE BOUND TOGETHER BY THE RED THREAD OF FATE?
SOME PEOPLE GO THEIR WHOLE LIVES NEVER FINDING THEIR SOUL MATE. DON'T YOU SEE HOW INCREDIBLY LUCKY WE ARE?!
VWSH
VWSH
VWSH
VWSH
VWSH
FWOOM

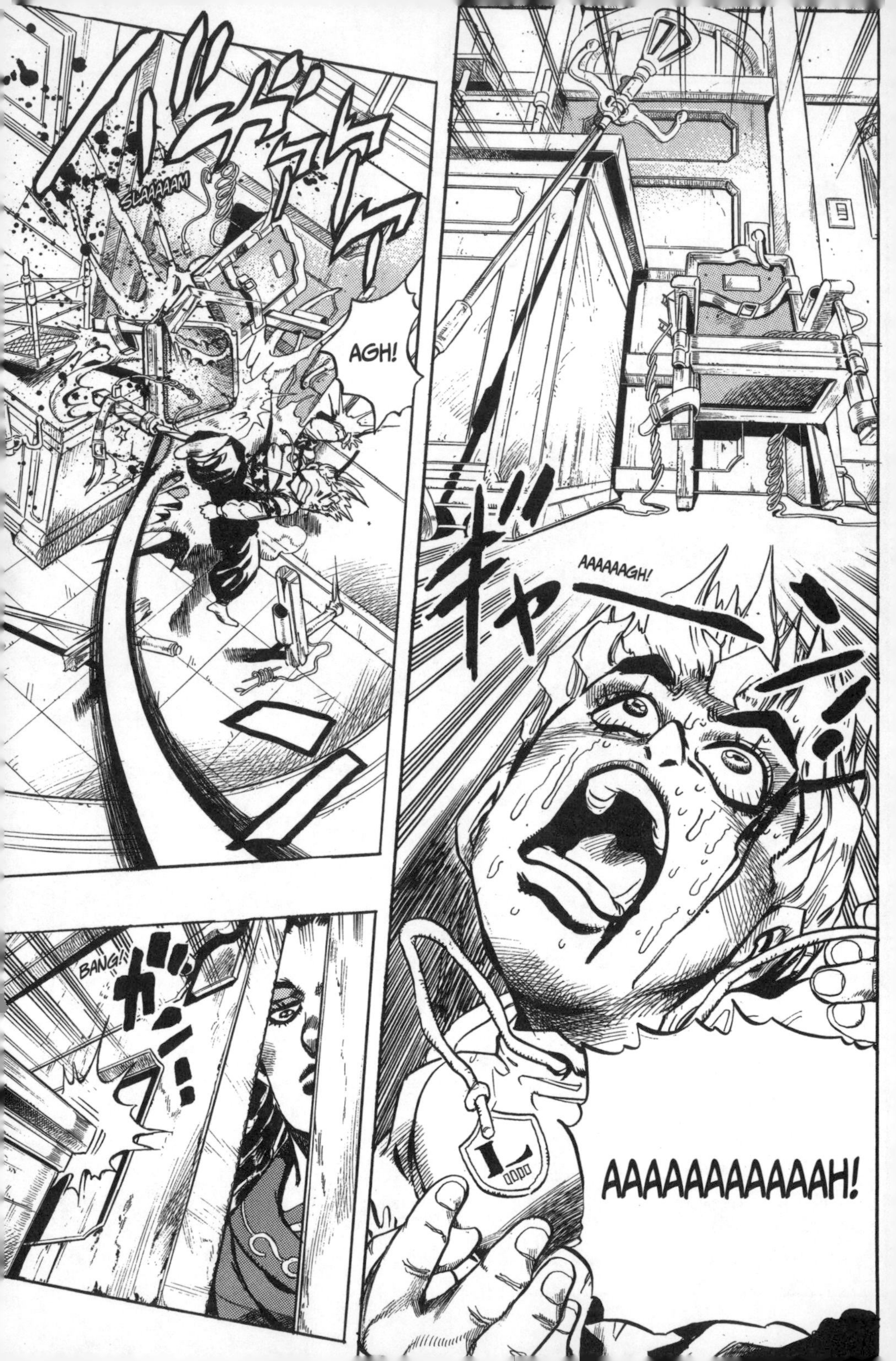
AAAAAAGH!
AAAAAAAAAAAH!
SLAAAAAM
AGH!
BANG!

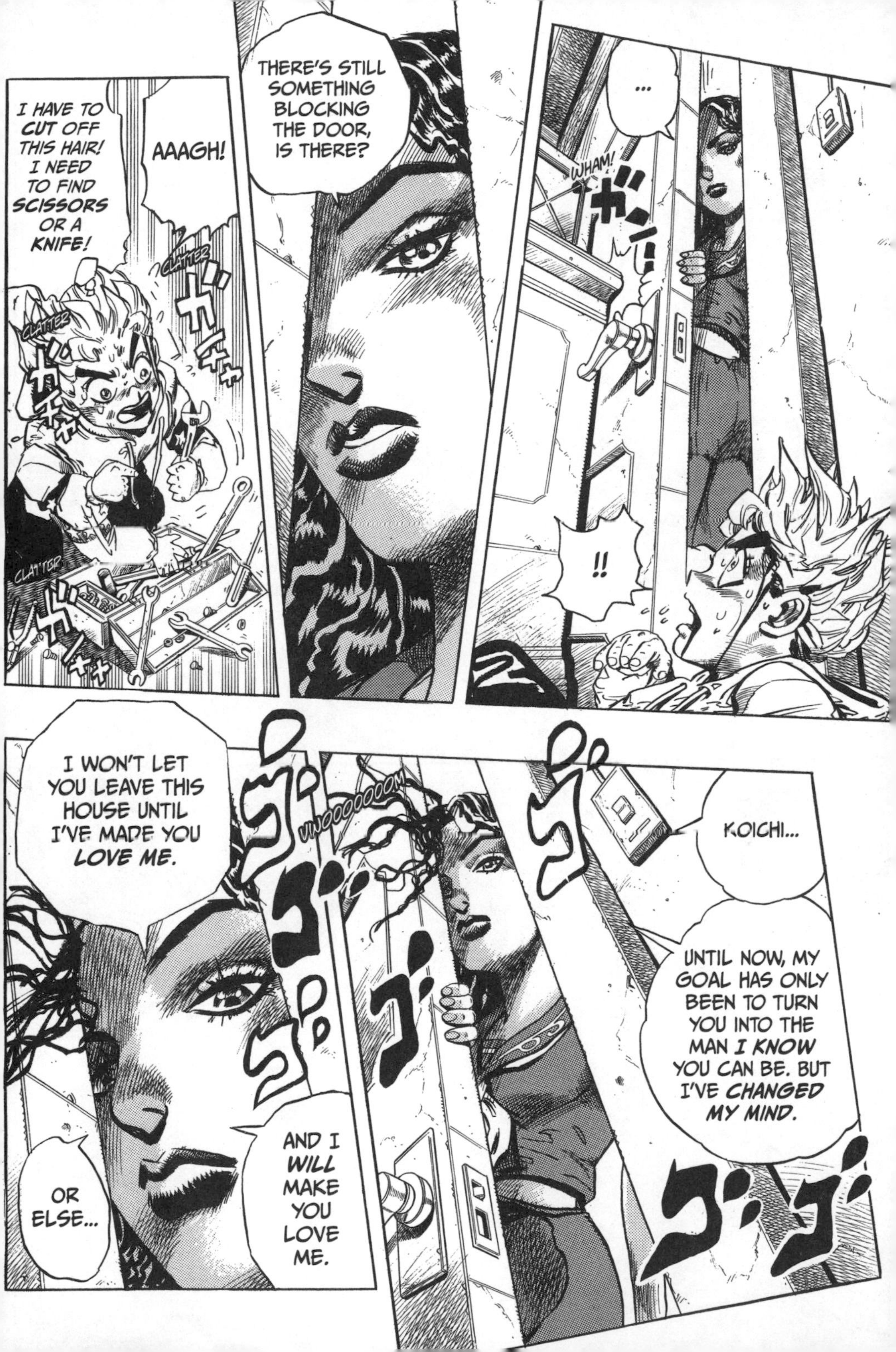
...
WHAM!
!!
THERE'S STILL SOMETHING BLOCKING THE DOOR, IS THERE?
AAAGH!
I HAVE TO CUT OFF THIS HAIR! I NEED TO FIND SCISSORS OR A KNIFE!
CLATTER
CLATTER
CLATTER
KOICHI...
UNTIL NOW, MY GOAL HAS ONLY BEEN TO TURN YOU INTO THE MAN I KNOW YOU CAN BE. BUT I'VE CHANGED MY MIND.
UWOOOOOOOM
I WON'T LET YOU LEAVE THIS HOUSE UNTIL I'VE MADE YOU LOVE ME.
AND I WILL MAKE YOU LOVE ME.
OR ELSE...

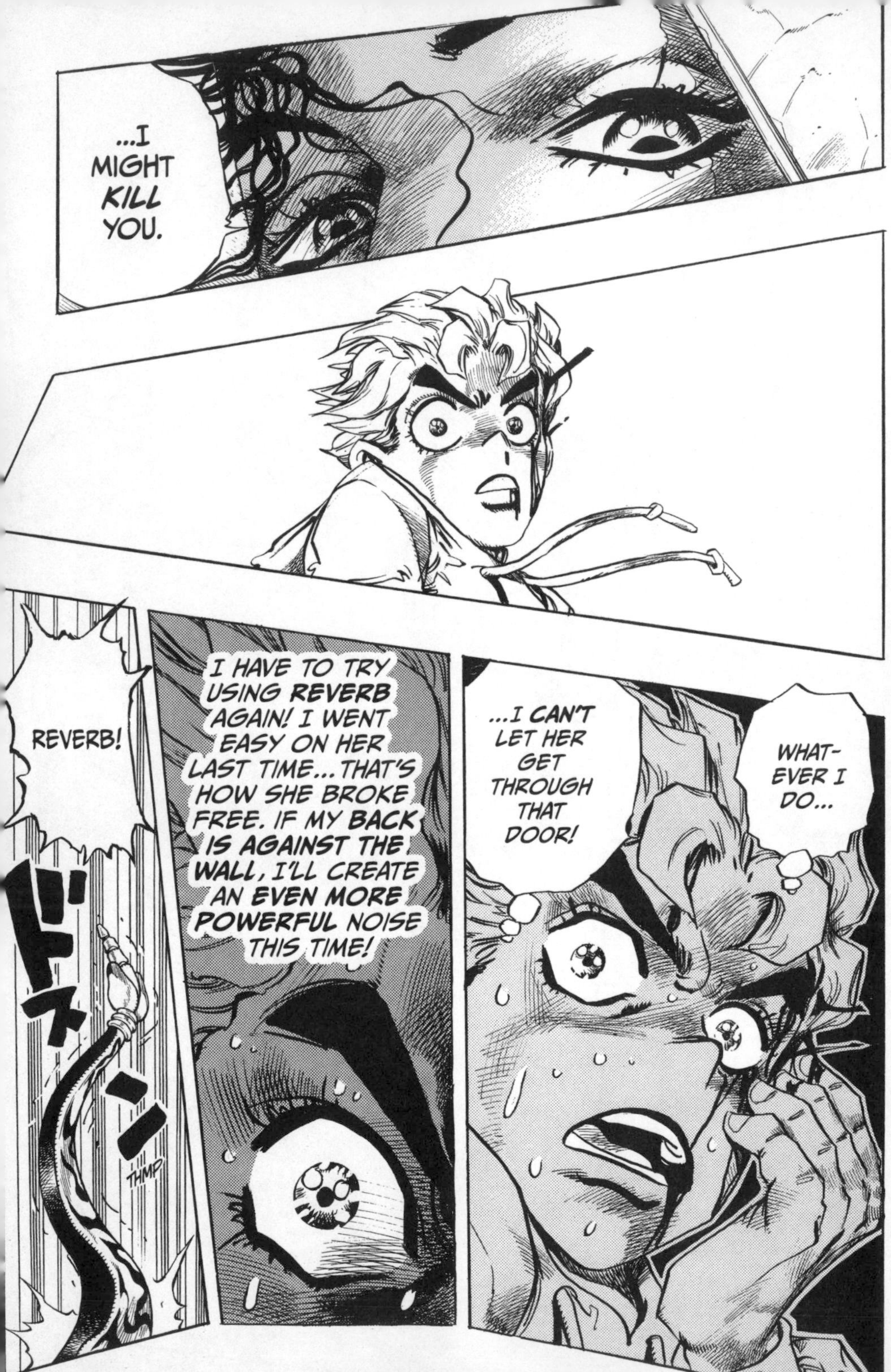
...I MIGHT KILL YOU.
WHAT-EVER I DO...
...I CAN'T LET HER GET THROUGH THAT DOOR!
I HAVE TO TRY USING REVERB AGAIN! I WENT EASY ON HER LAST TIME...THAT'S HOW SHE BROKE FREE. IF MY BACK IS AGAINST THE WALL, I'LL CREATE AN EVEN MORE POWERFUL NOISE THIS TIME!
REVERB!
ドスン
THMP

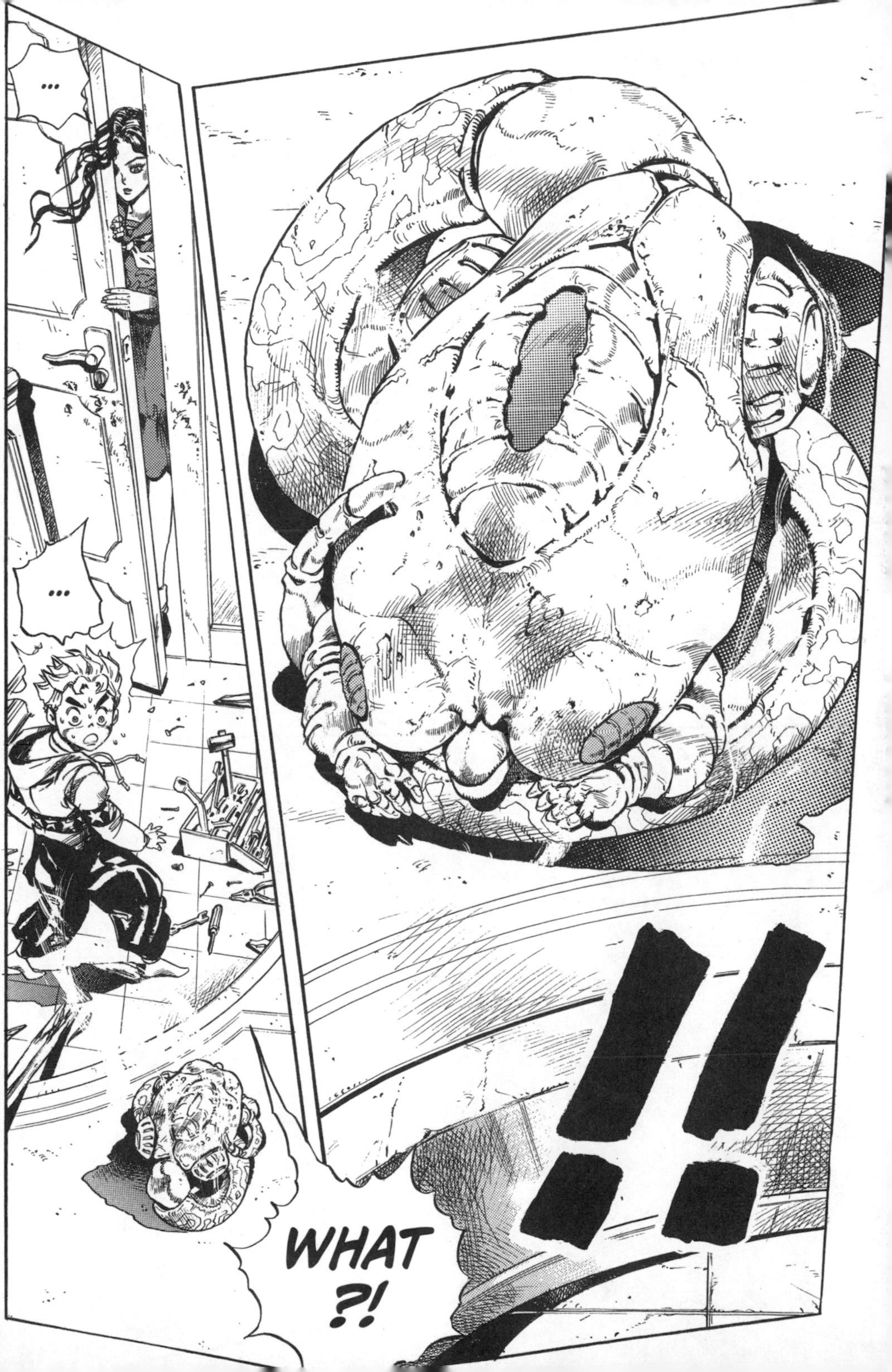
!!
...
...
WHAT ?!

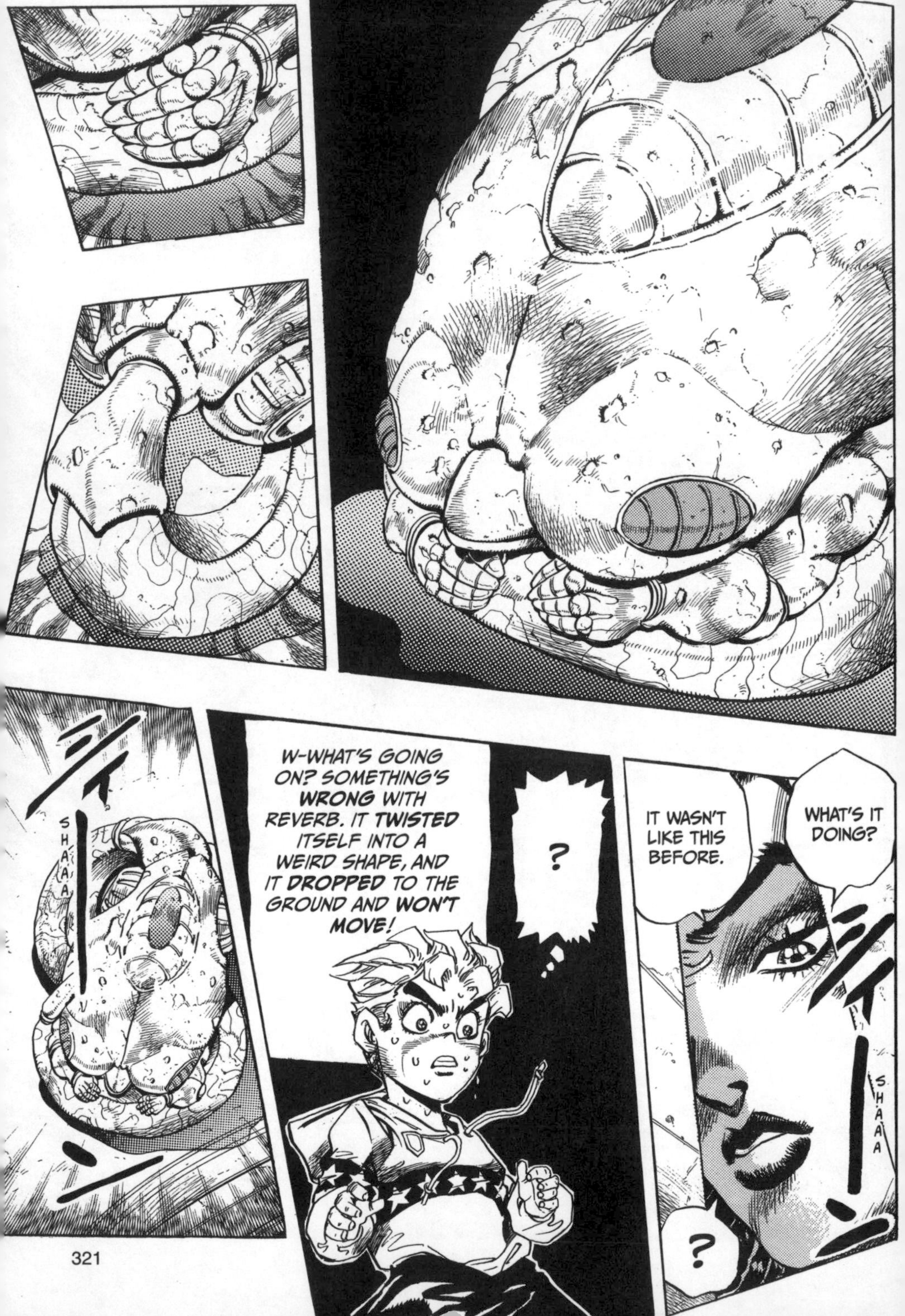
WHAT'S IT DOING?
IT WASN'T LIKE THIS BEFORE.
SHAAA
?
?
W-WHAT'S GOING ON? SOMETHING'S **WRONG** WITH REVERB. IT **TWISTED** ITSELF INTO A WEIRD SHAPE, AND IT **DROPPED** TO THE GROUND AND **WON'T MOVE!**
SHAAA

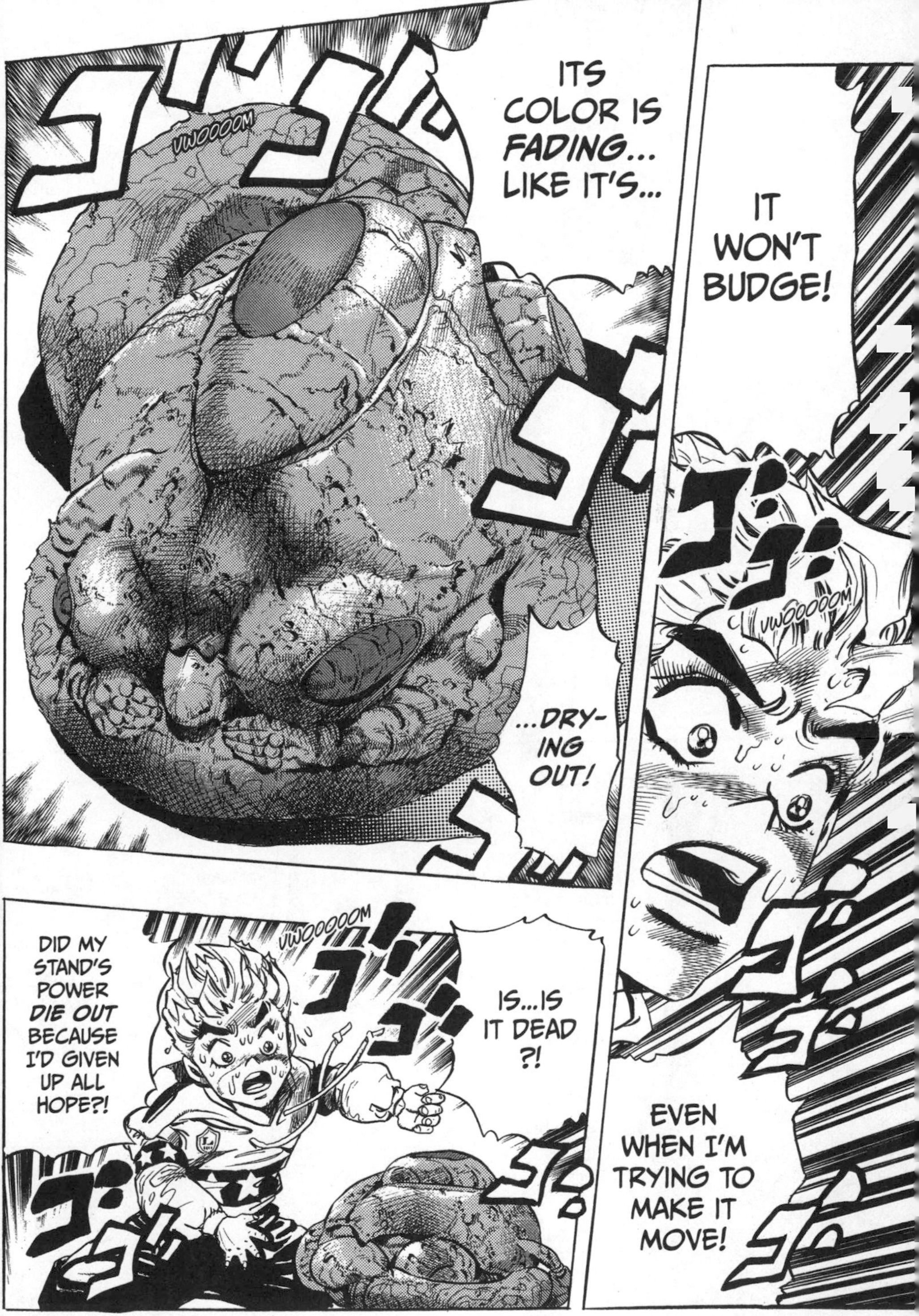
IT WON'T BUDGE!
VWOOOOOM
EVEN WHEN I'M TRYING TO MAKE IT MOVE!
ITS COLOR IS *FADING*... LIKE IT'S...
VWOOOOM
...*DRYING OUT!*
IS...IS IT DEAD ?!
VWOOOOOM
DID MY STAND'S POWER *DIE OUT* BECAUSE I'D GIVEN UP ALL HOPE?!

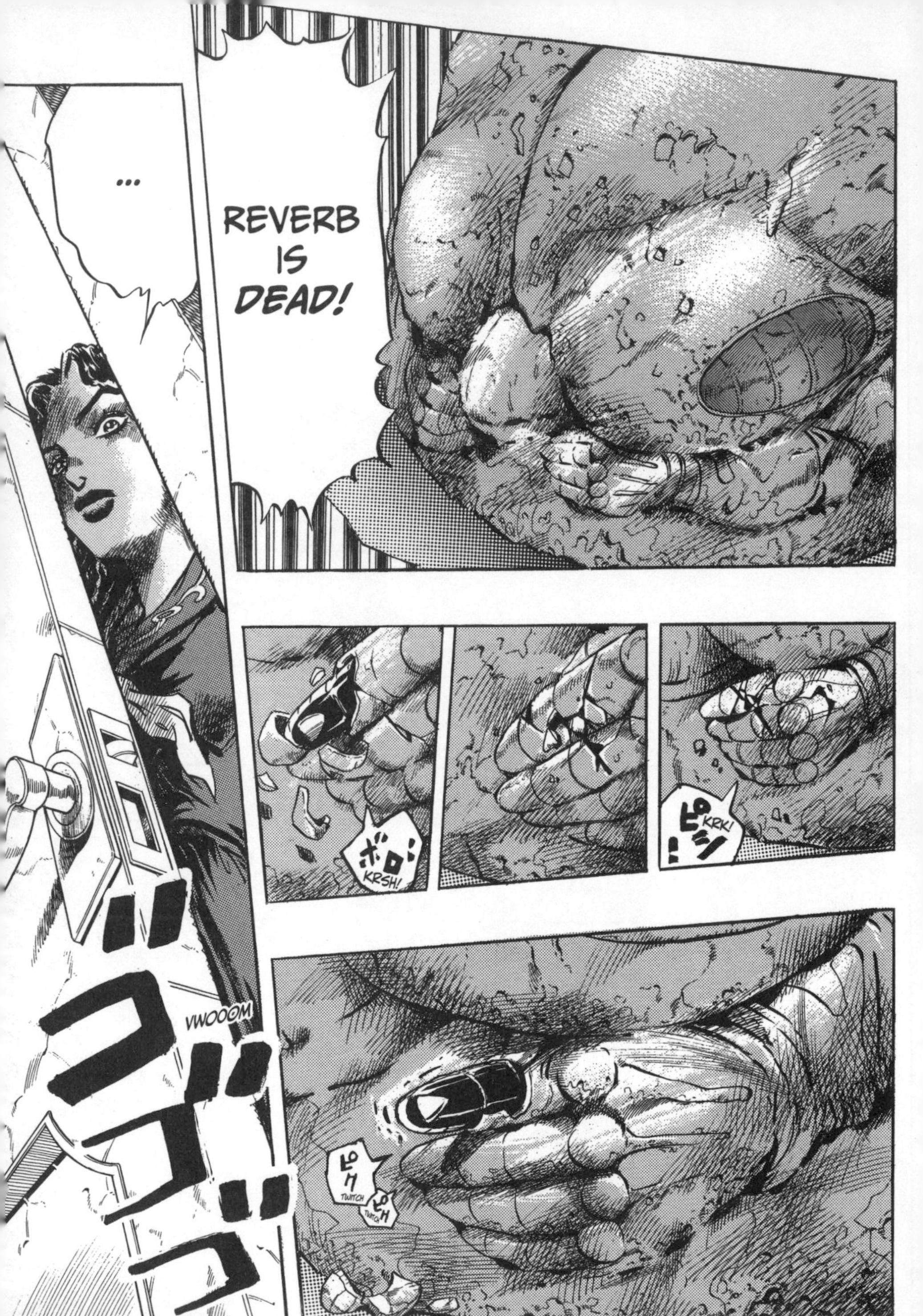
REVERB IS DEAD!
KRK!
KRSH!
TWITCH
TWITCH
...
VWOOOM

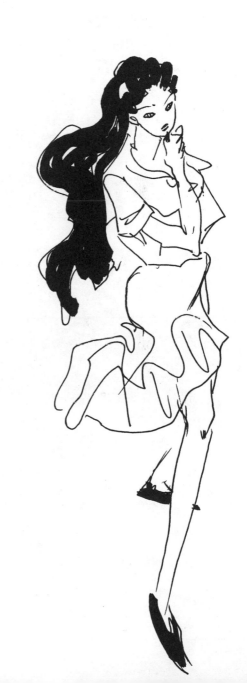

CHAPTER 35

YUKAKO YAMAGISHI FALLS IN LOVE, PART 7

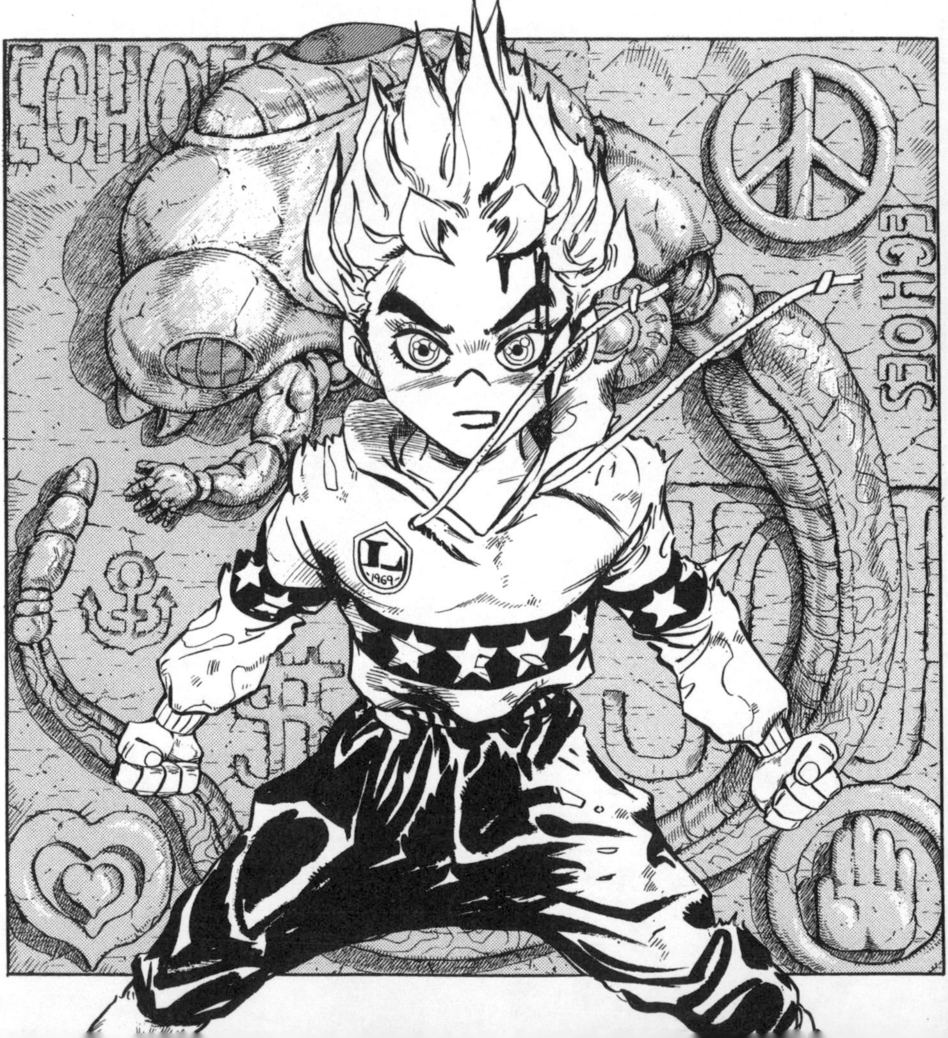
ECHOES

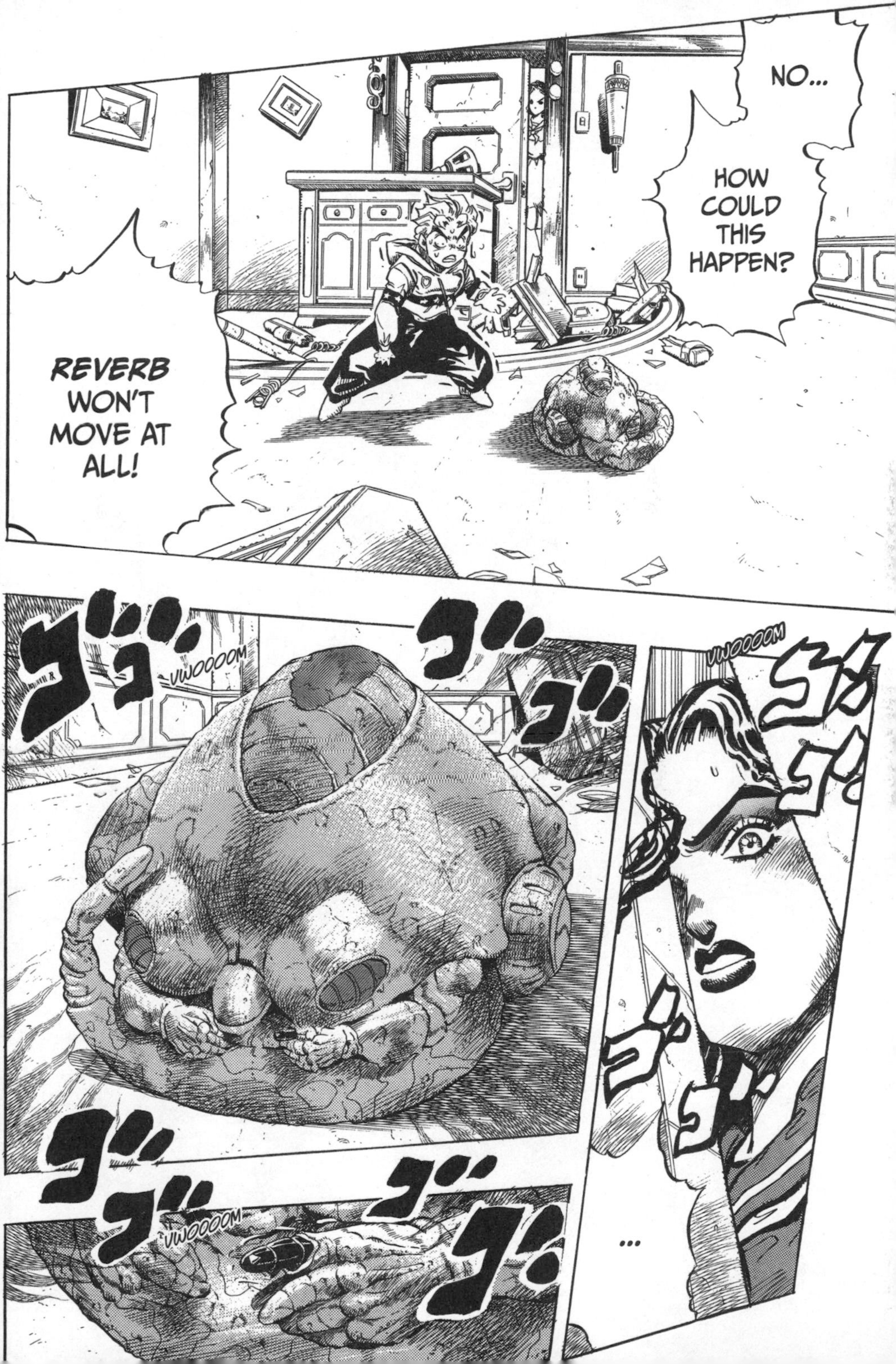
NO...
HOW COULD THIS HAPPEN?
REVERB WON'T MOVE AT ALL!
VWOOOOM
...
VWOOOOM
VWOOOOM
VWOOOOM

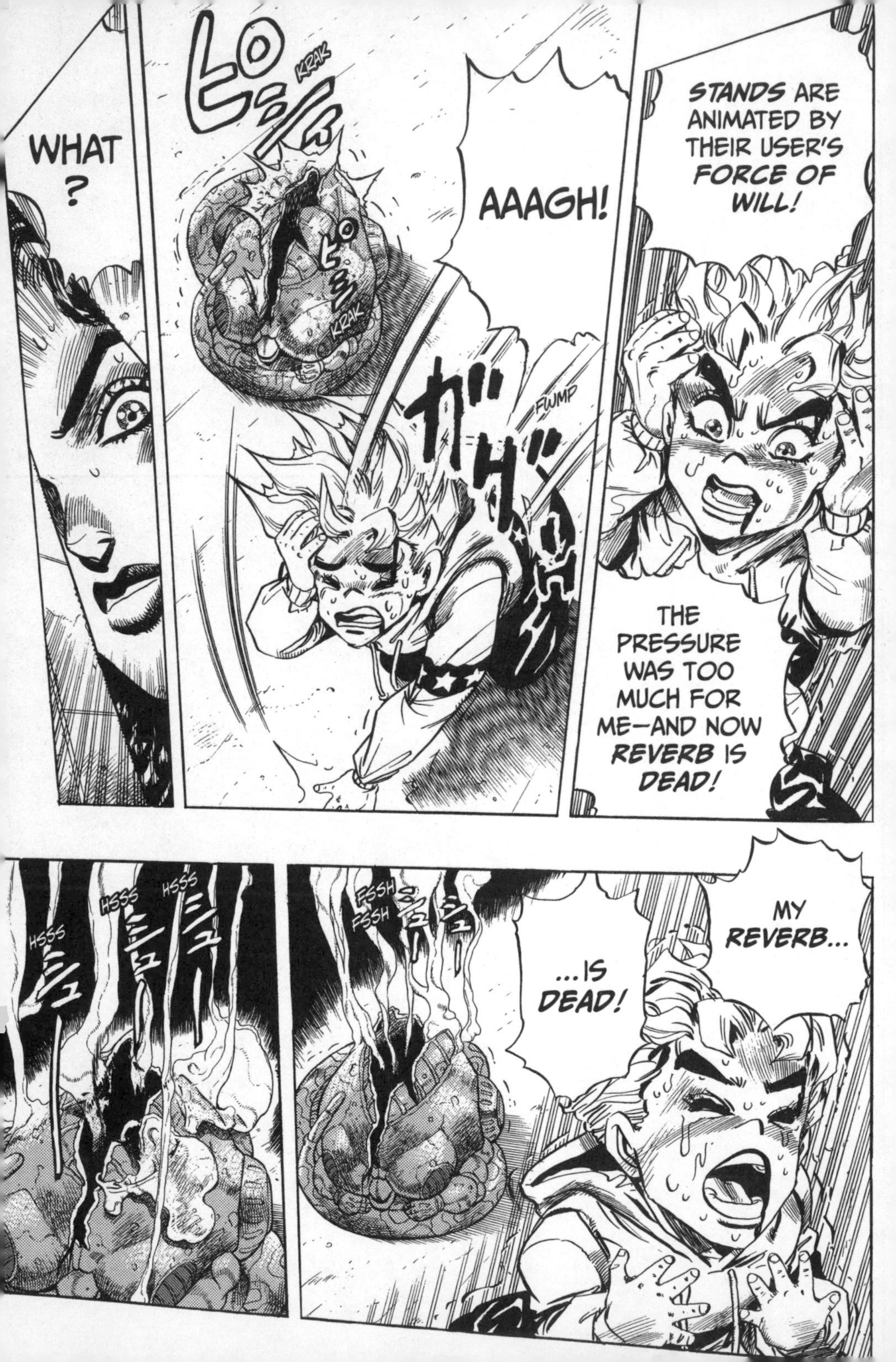
STANDS ARE ANIMATED BY THEIR USER'S FORCE OF WILL!
THE PRESSURE WAS TOO MUCH FOR ME—AND NOW REVERB IS DEAD!
AAAGH!
KRAK
KRAK
FWUMP
WHAT ?
MY REVERB...
...IS DEAD!
FSSH
FSSH
HSSS
HSSS
HSSS

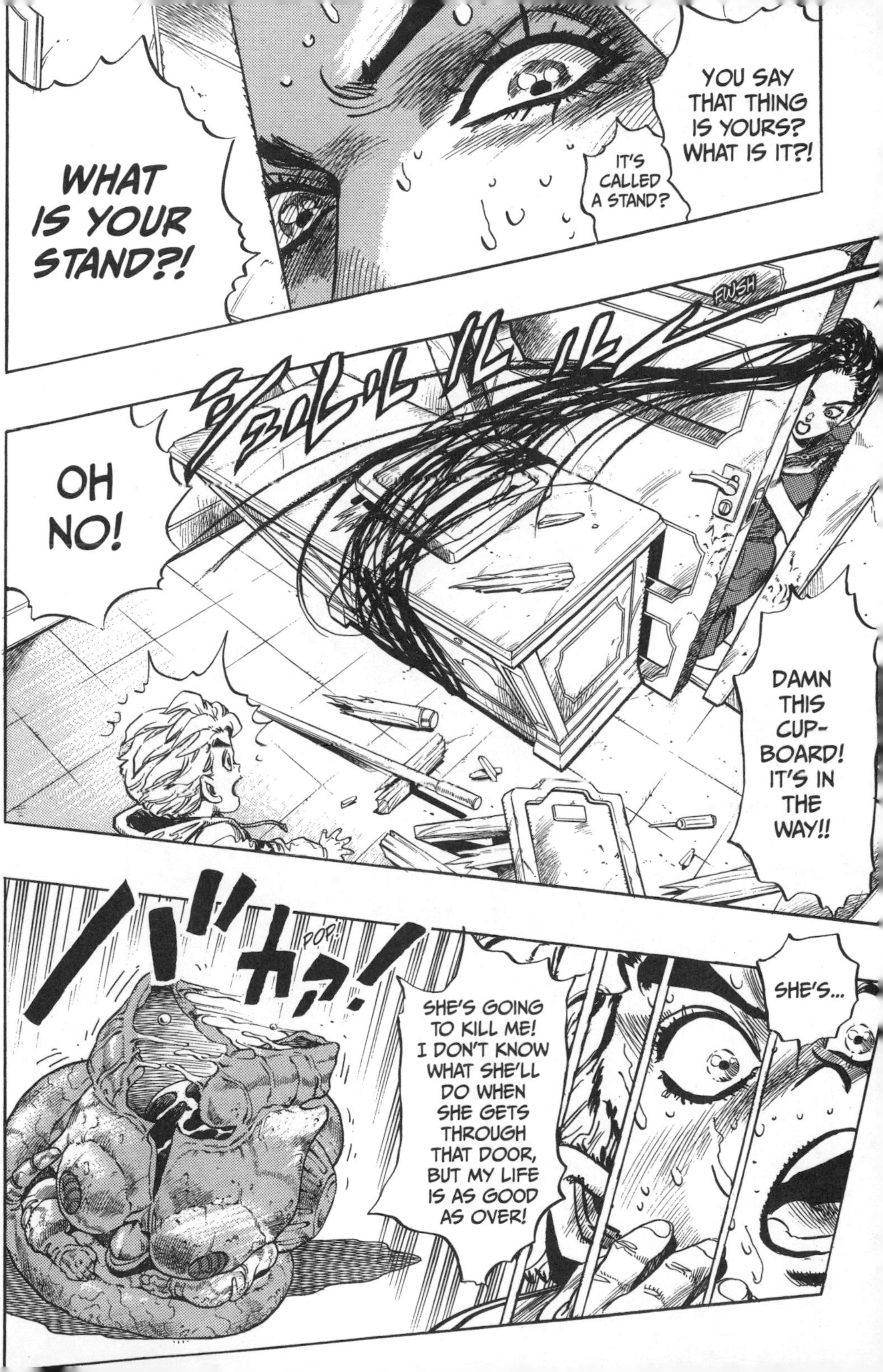
YOU SAY THAT THING IS YOURS? WHAT IS IT?!
IT'S CALLED A STAND?
WHAT IS YOUR STAND?!
FWSH
DAMN THIS CUP-BOARD! IT'S IN THE WAY!!
OH NO!
SHE'S...
SHE'S GOING TO KILL ME! I DON'T KNOW WHAT SHE'LL DO WHEN SHE GETS THROUGH THAT DOOR, BUT MY LIFE IS AS GOOD AS OVER!
POP!

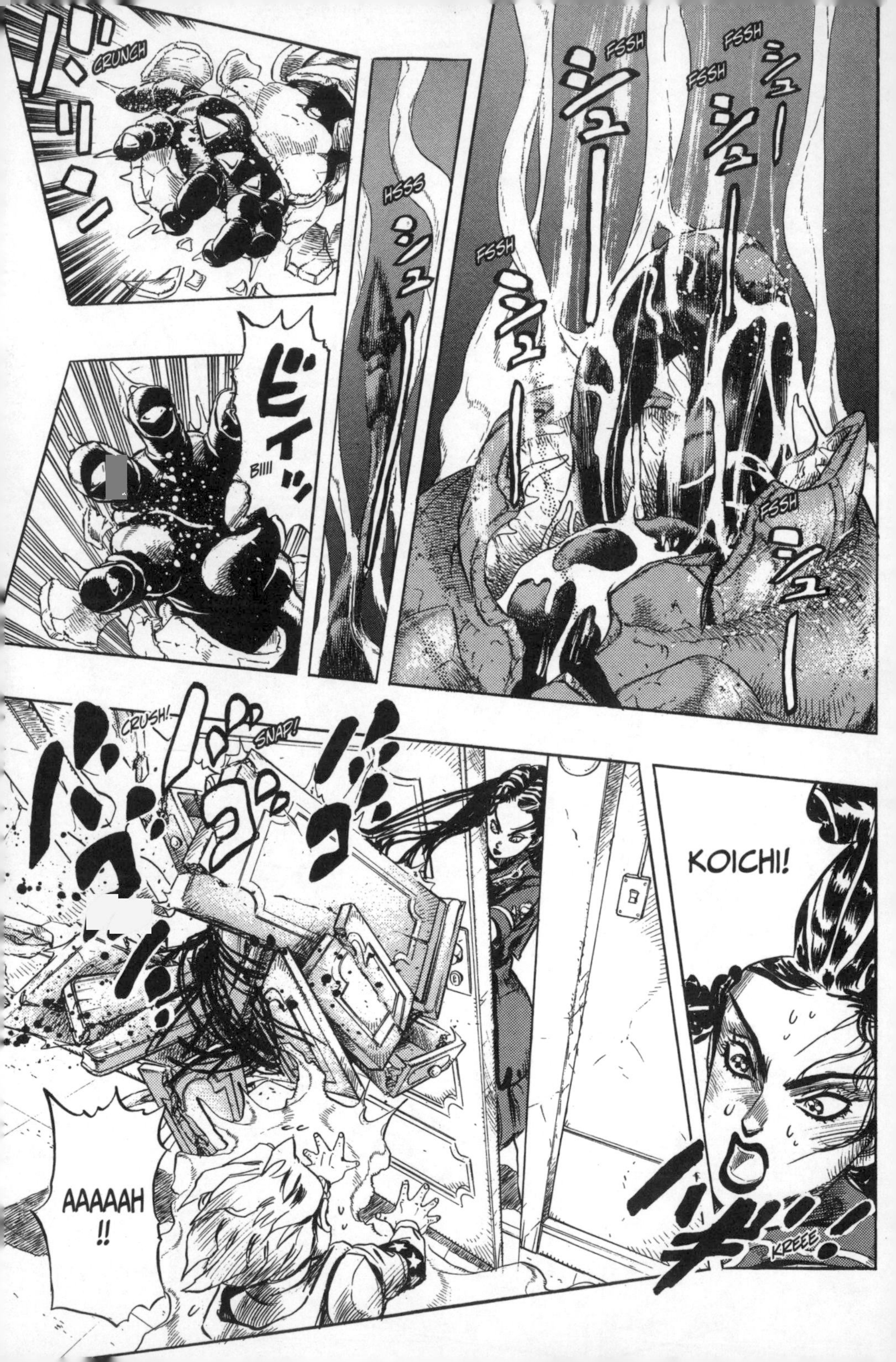

FSSH
FSSH
FSSH
FSSH
HSSS
FSSH
CRUNCH
BIIII
KOICHI!
KREEE!
CRUSH!
SNAP!
AAAAAH!!

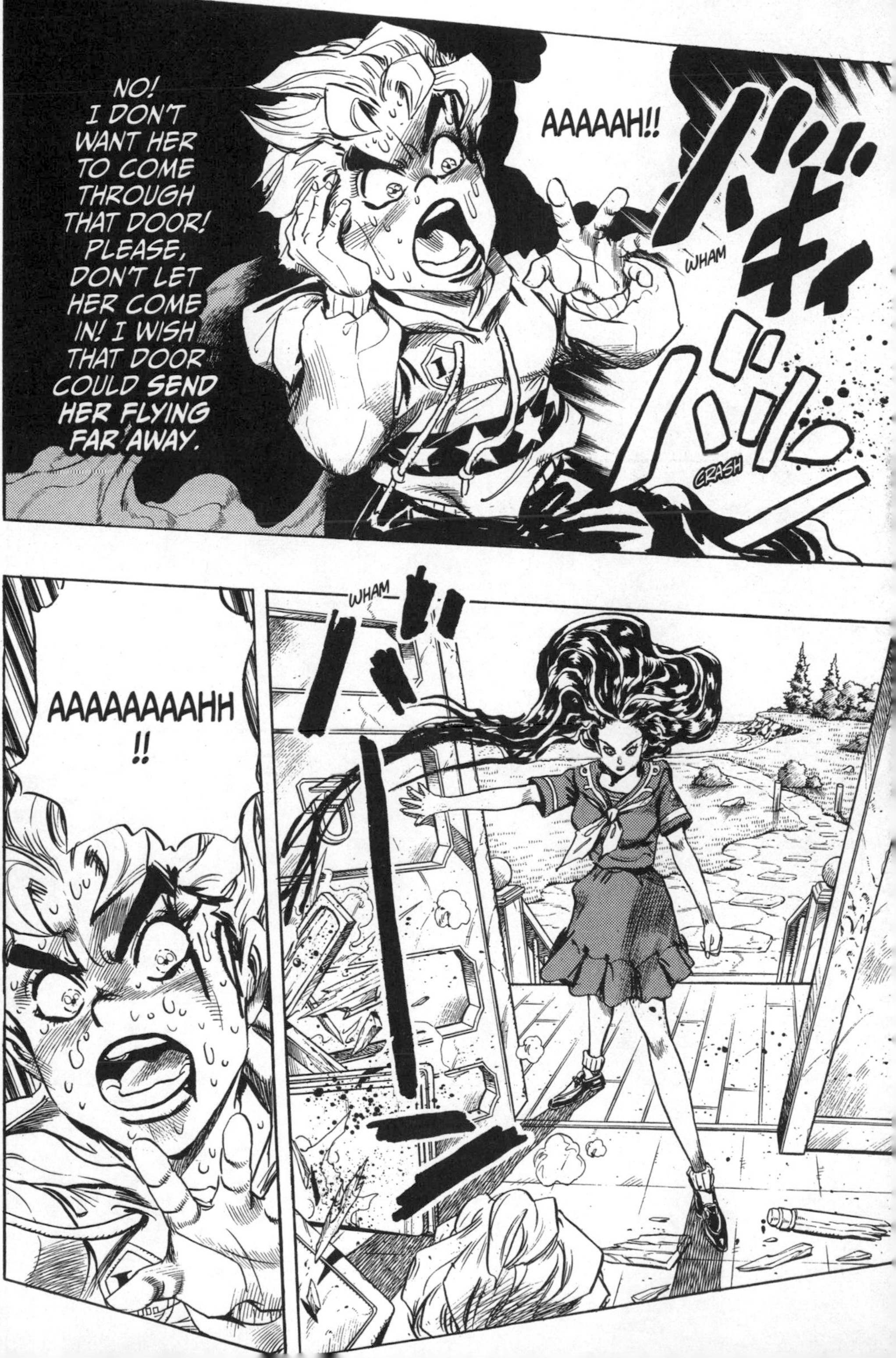
AAAAAH!!
WHAM
CRASH
NO! I DON'T WANT HER TO COME THROUGH THAT DOOR! PLEASE, DON'T LET HER COME IN! I WISH THAT DOOR COULD SEND HER FLYING FAR AWAY.
WHAM
AAAAAAAAHH !!

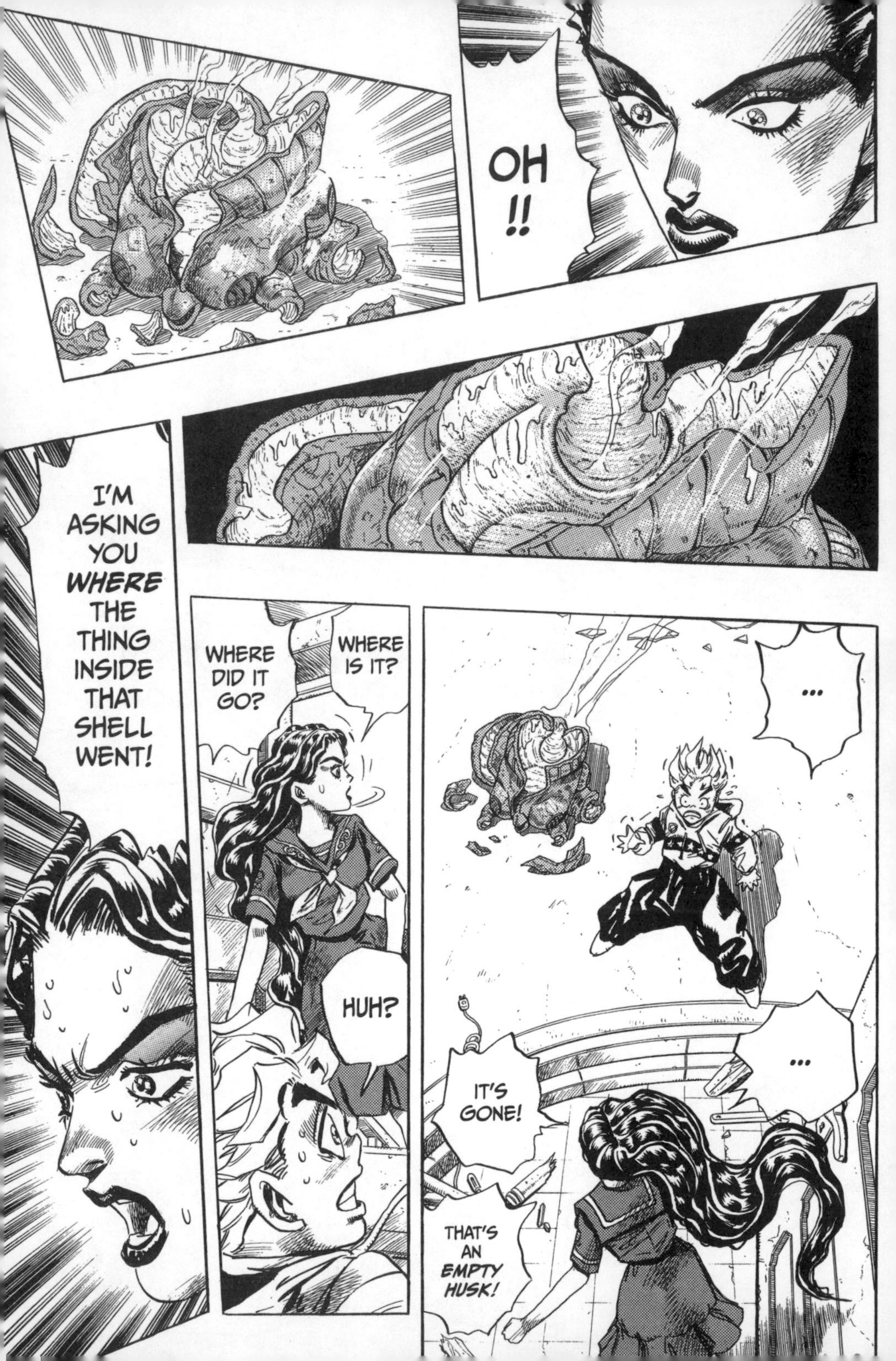
OH !!
...
...
IT'S GONE!
THAT'S AN EMPTY HUSK!
WHERE IS IT?
WHERE DID IT GO?
HUH?
I'M ASKING YOU WHERE THE THING INSIDE THAT SHELL WENT!

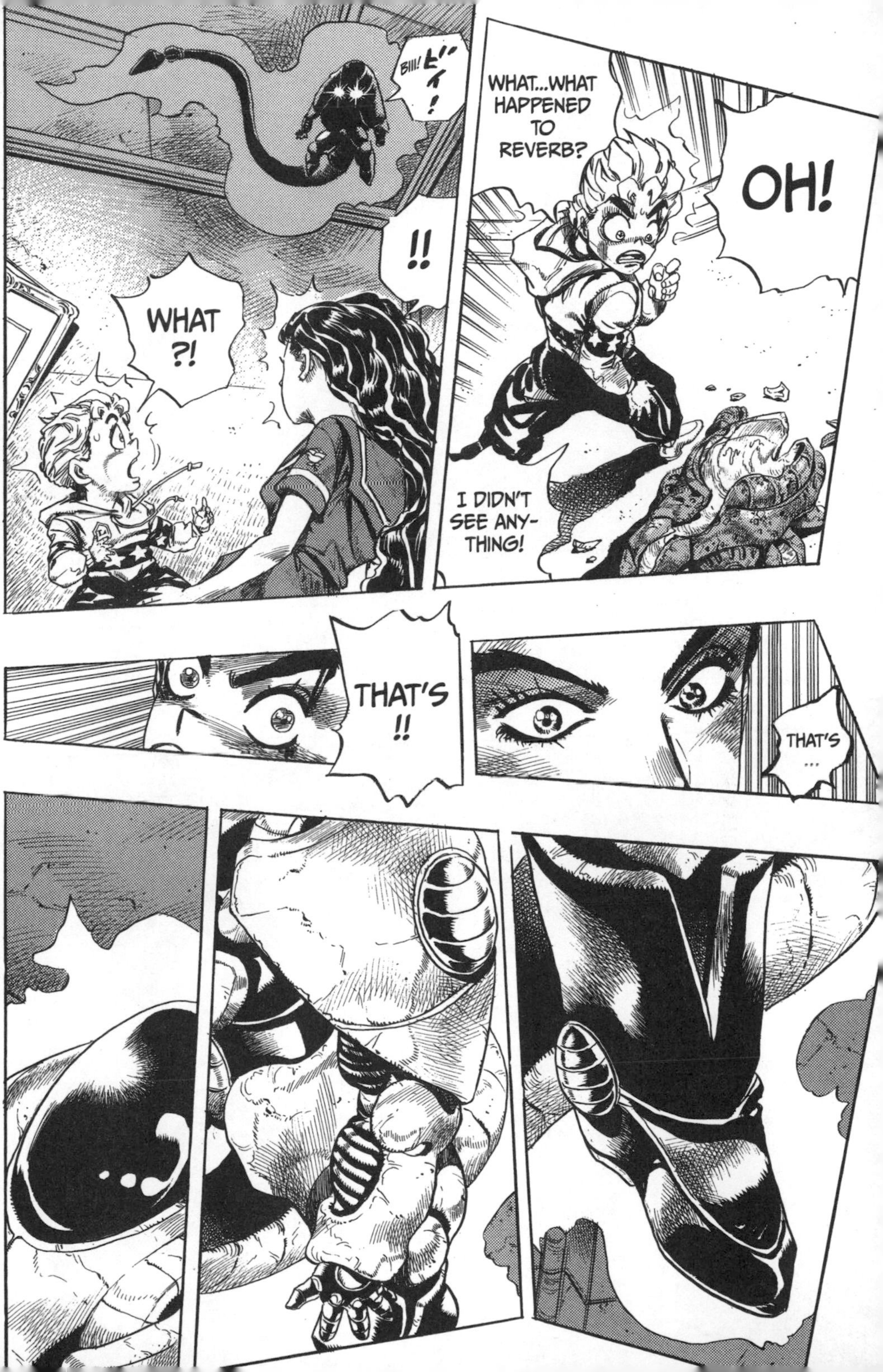

WHAT...WHAT HAPPENED TO REVERB?
OH!
I DIDN'T SEE ANY-THING!
BIII! ビイ!
!!
WHAT ?!
THAT'S ...
THAT'S !!

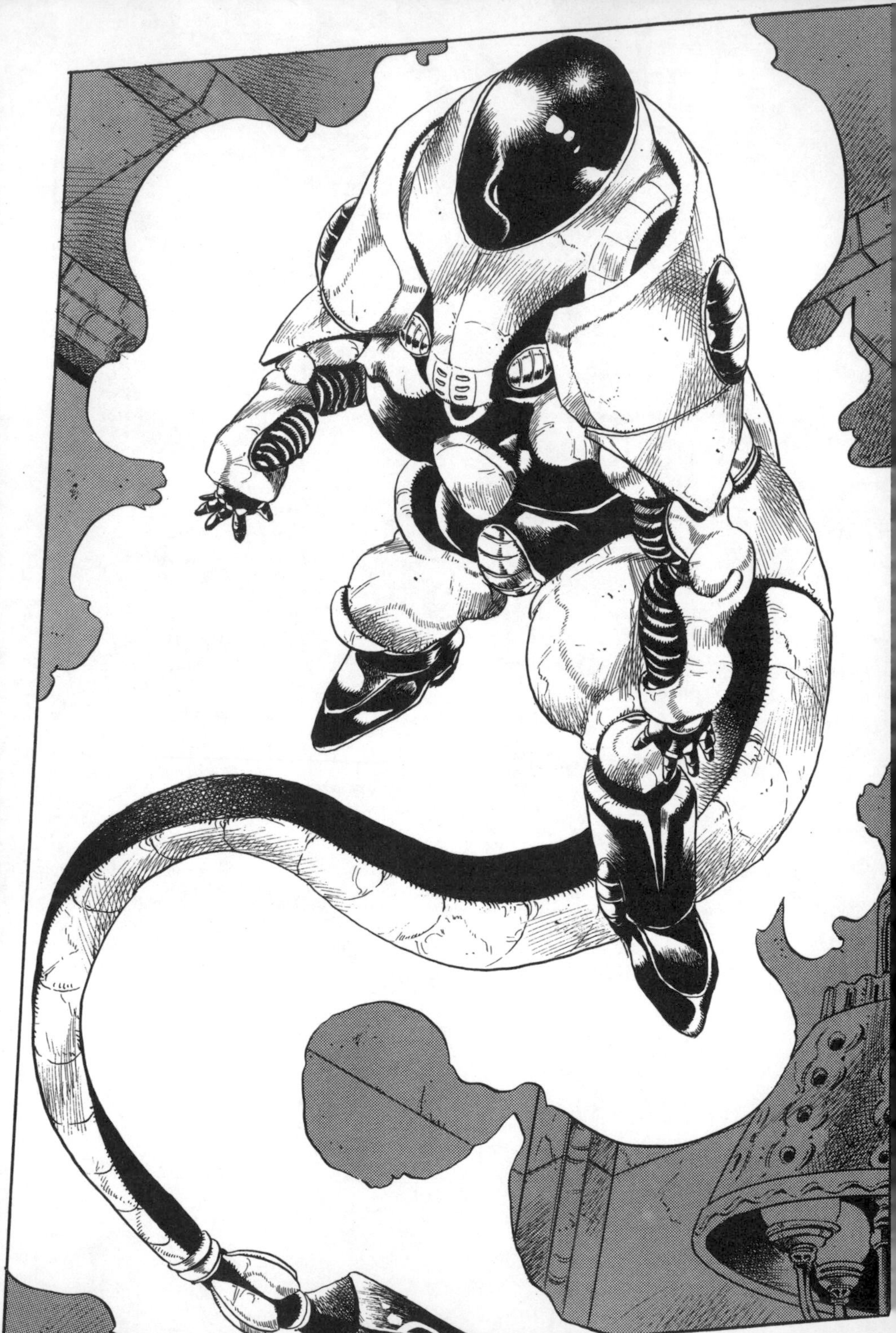

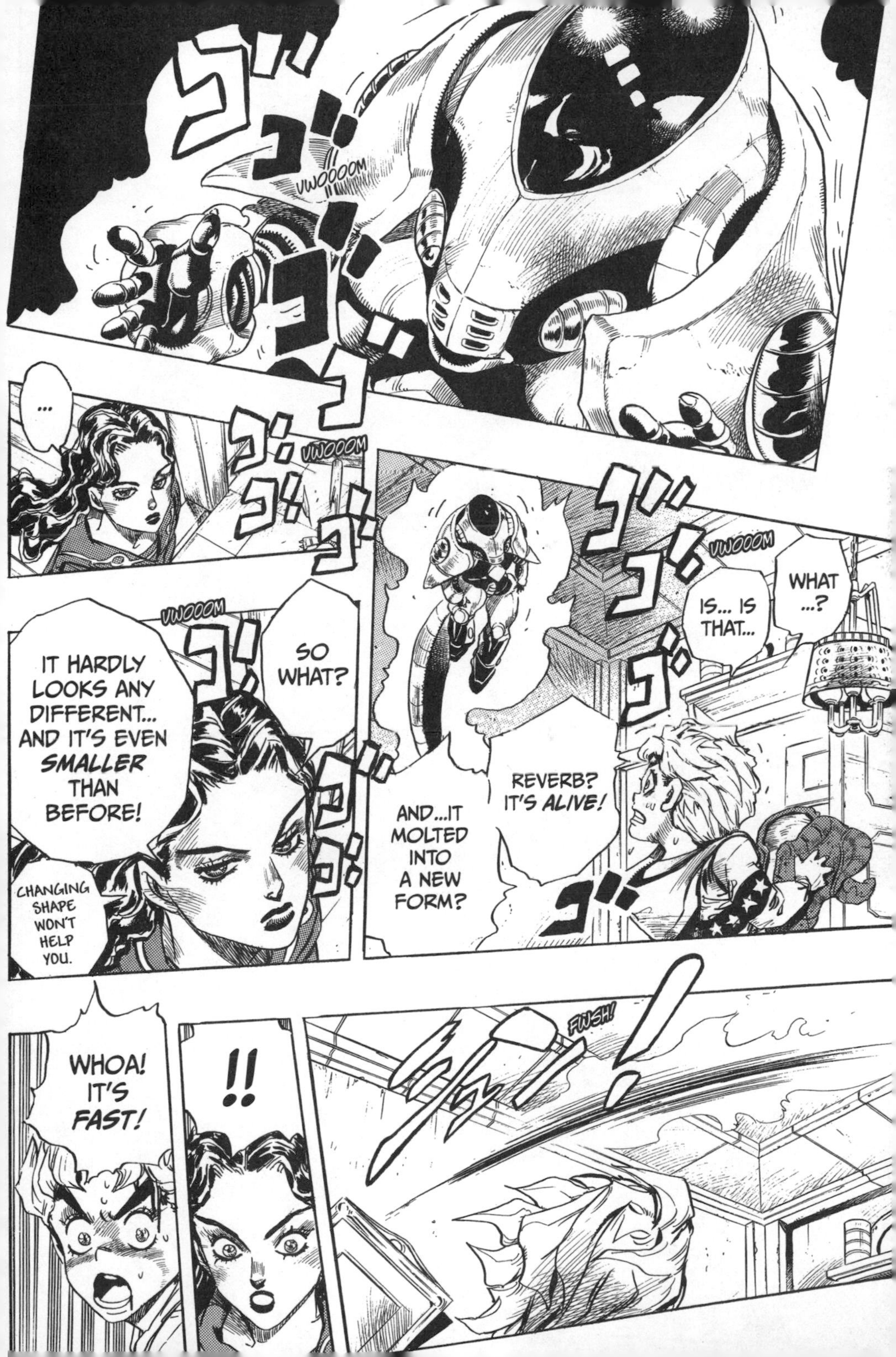
VWOOOM
VWOOOM
WHAT ...?
IS... IS THAT...
REVERB? IT'S *ALIVE!*
AND...IT MOLTED INTO A NEW FORM?
...
VWOOOM
VWOOOM
SO WHAT?
IT HARDLY LOOKS ANY DIFFERENT... AND IT'S EVEN ***SMALLER*** THAN BEFORE!
CHANGING SHAPE WON'T HELP YOU.
FWSH!
!!
WHOA! IT'S *FAST!*

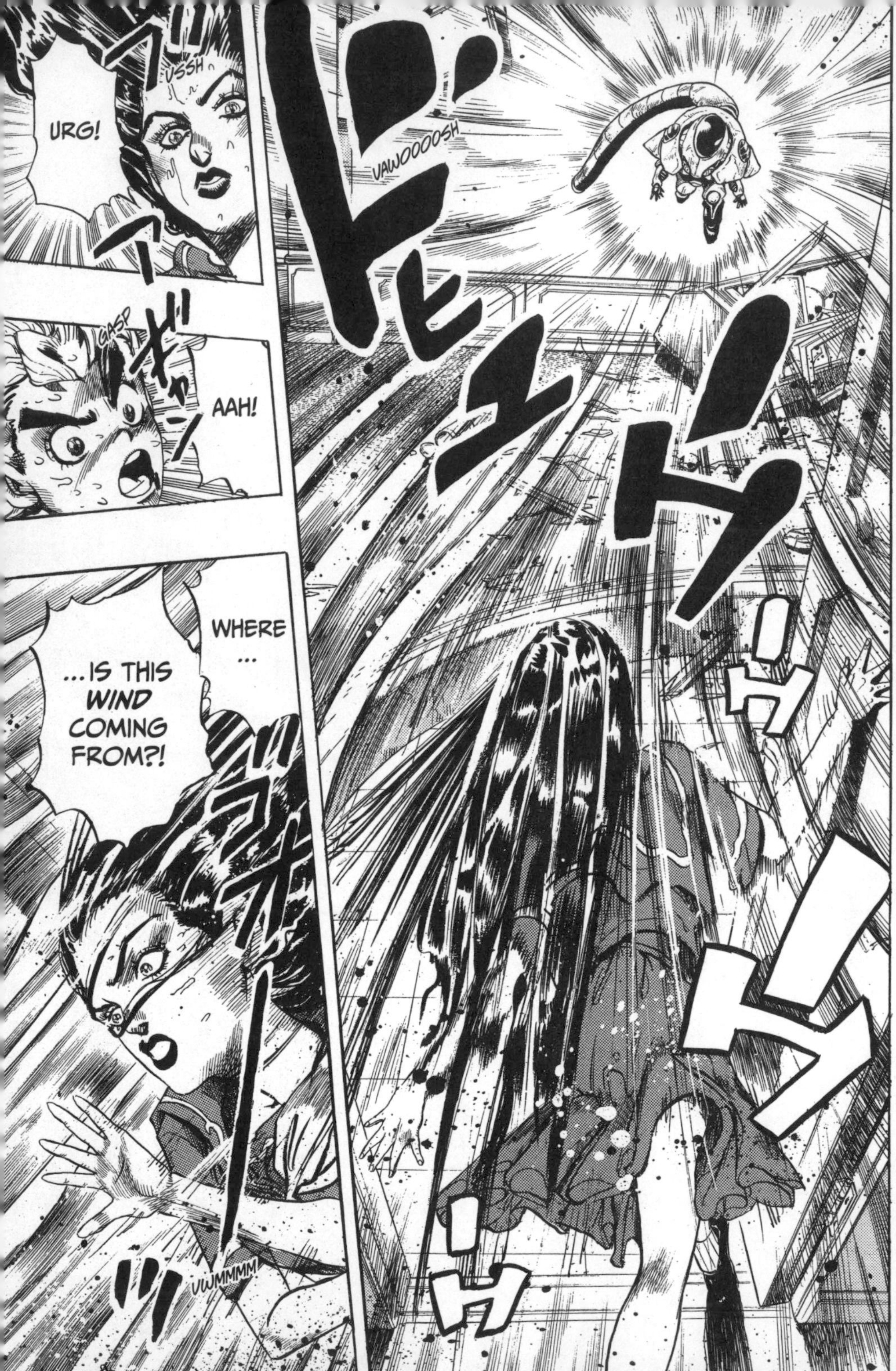
VAWOOOOSH
USSH
URG!
GASP
AAH!
WHERE ...
...IS THIS WIND COMING FROM?!
UWMMMM

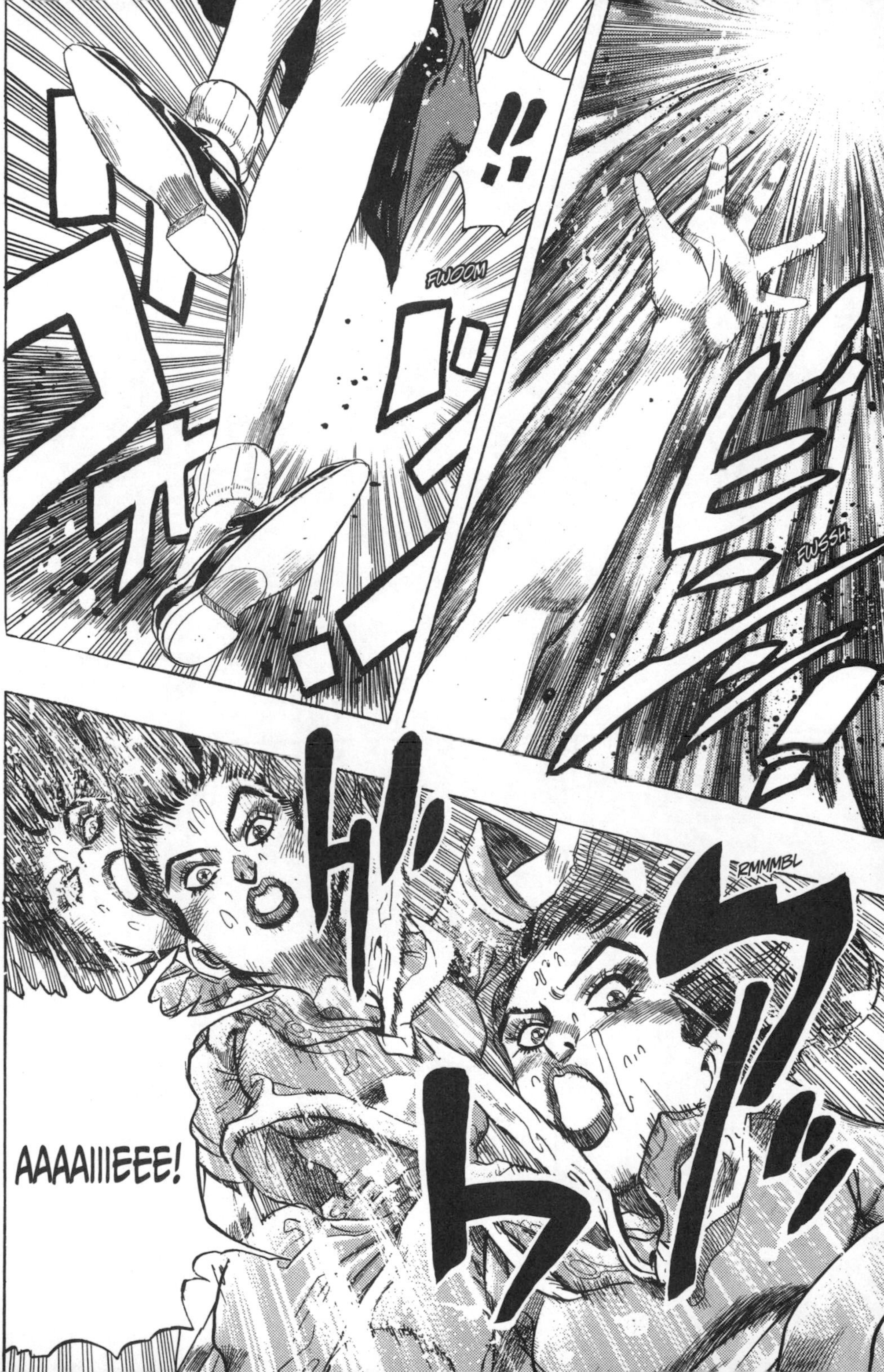
FWUSSH
FWOOM
RMMMBL
AAAAIIIEEE!

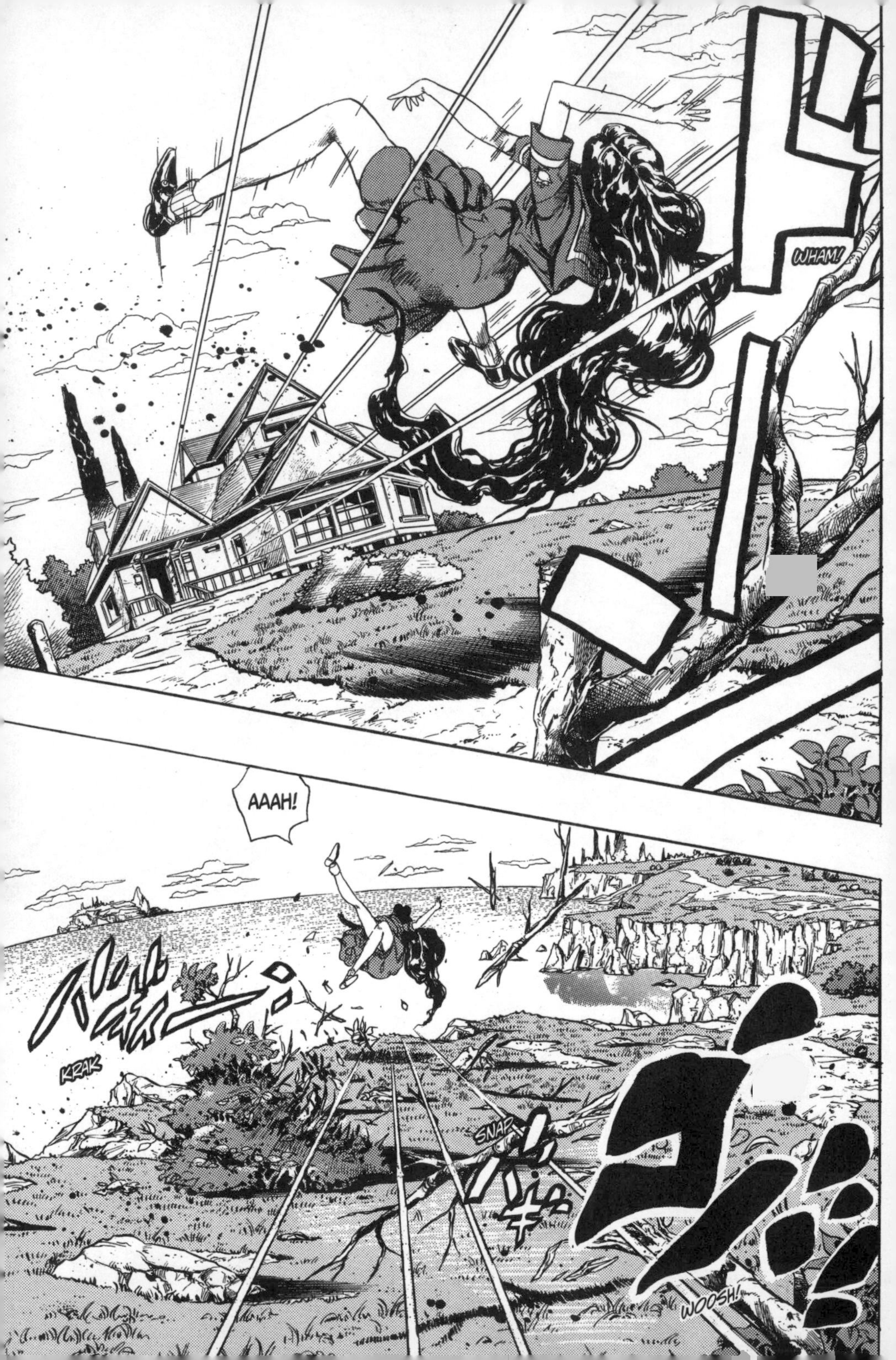
WHAM!
AAAH!
WOOSH!
SNAP
KRAK

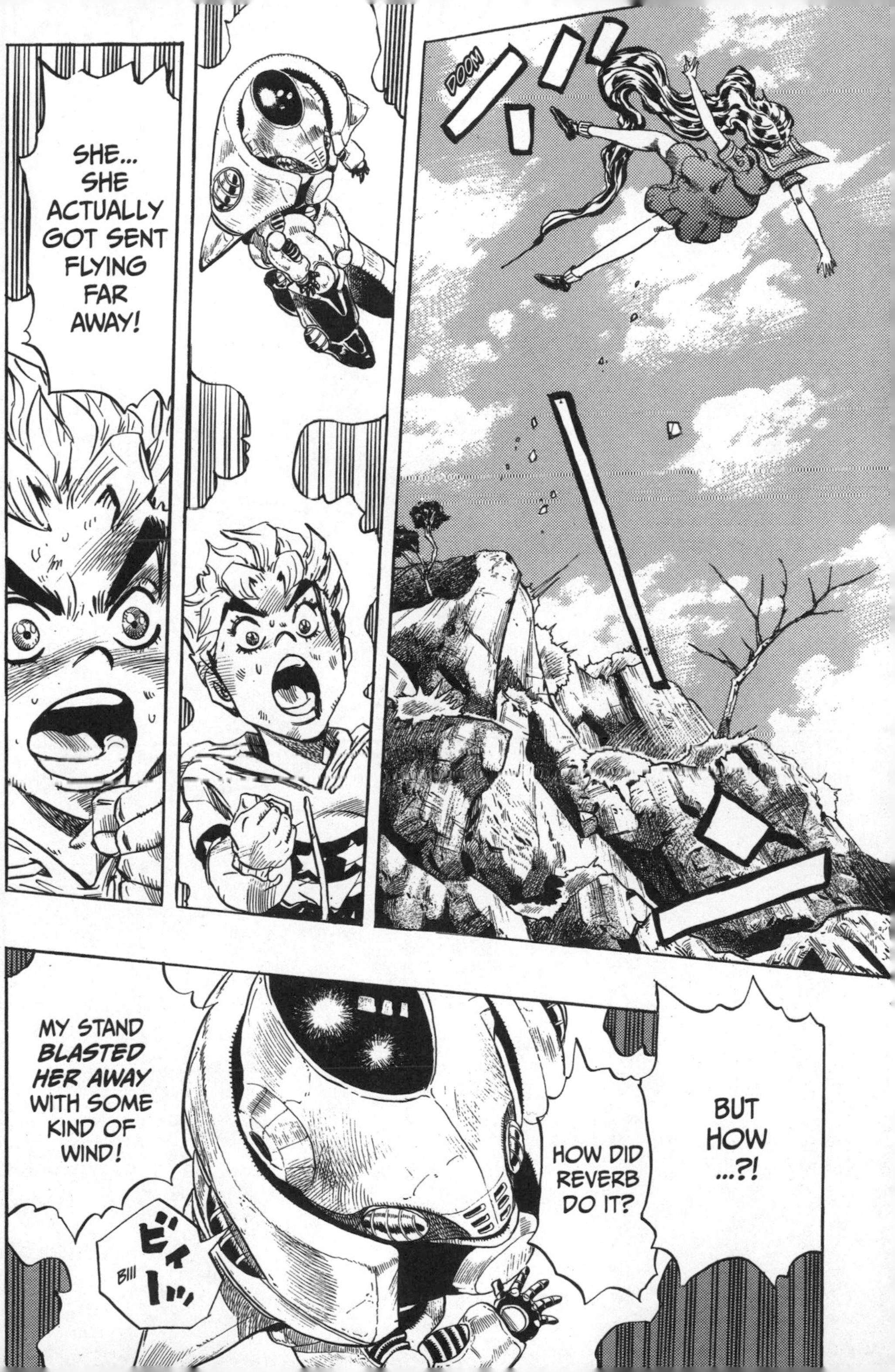
DOOM
SHE... SHE ACTUALLY GOT SENT FLYING FAR AWAY!
BUT HOW ...?!
HOW DID REVERB DO IT?
MY STAND BLASTED HER AWAY WITH SOME KIND OF WIND!
ビイーッ
BIII

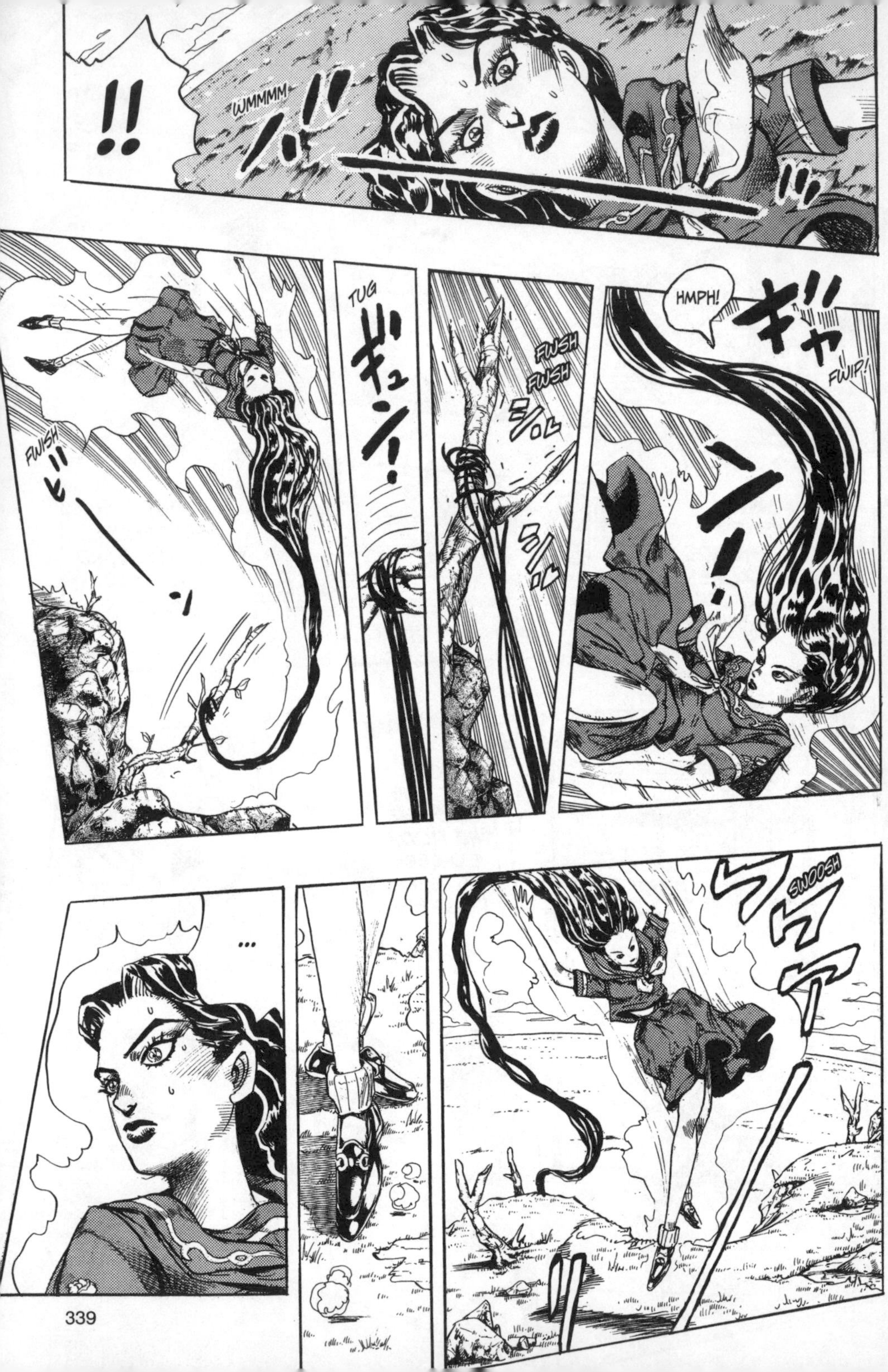
WMMMM
!!
HMPH!
FWIP!
FWSH
FWSH
TUG
FWISH
SWOOSH
...

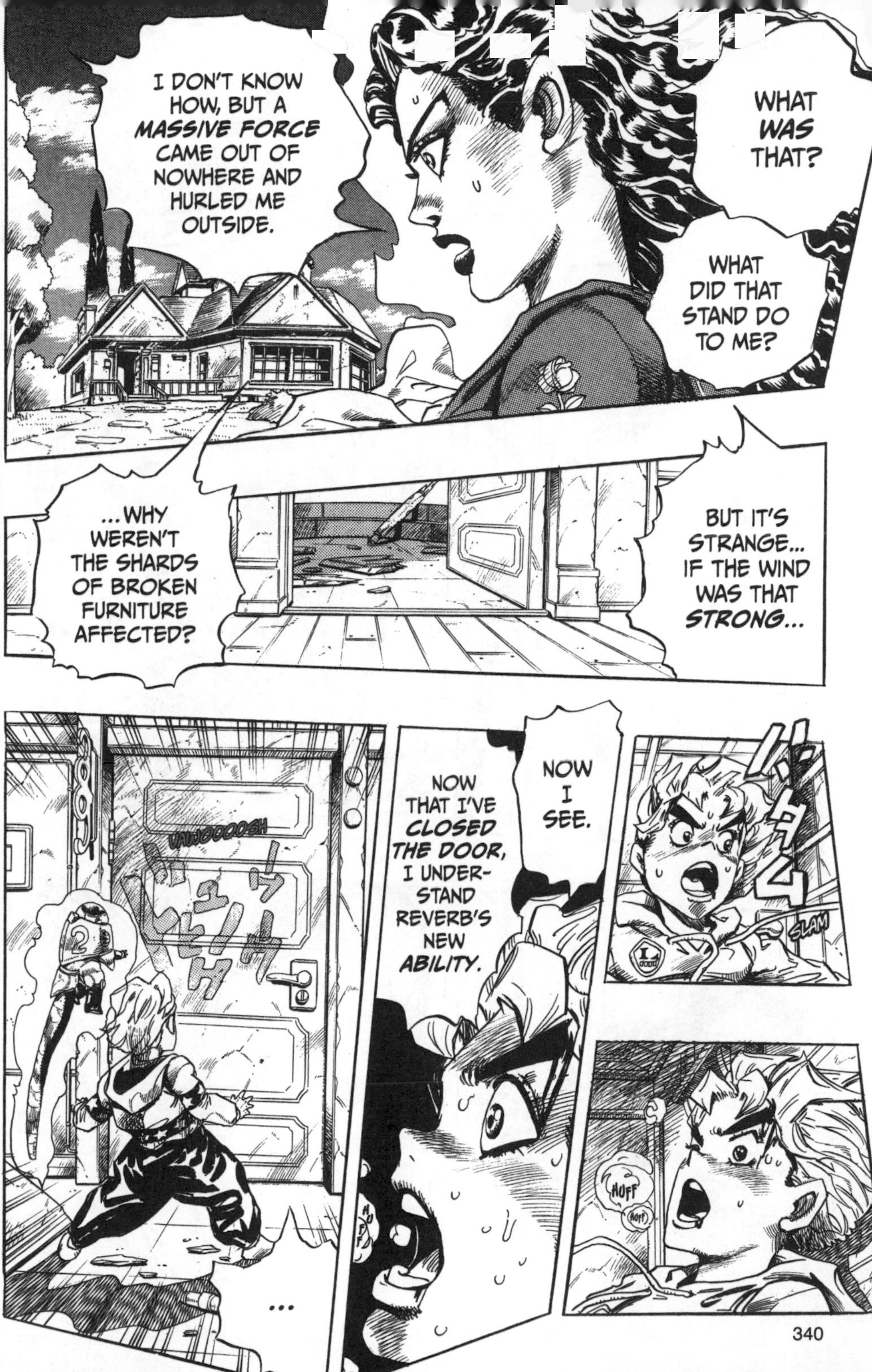
WHAT *WAS* THAT?
WHAT DID THAT STAND DO TO ME?
I DON'T KNOW HOW, BUT A *MASSIVE FORCE* CAME OUT OF NOWHERE AND HURLED ME OUTSIDE.
BUT IT'S STRANGE... IF THE WIND WAS THAT *STRONG*...
...WHY WEREN'T THE SHARDS OF BROKEN FURNITURE AFFECTED?
SLAM
HUFF
HUFF
NOW I SEE.
NOW THAT I'VE *CLOSED THE DOOR*, I UNDERSTAND REVERB'S NEW *ABILITY*.
HUFF
VAWOOOOOSH
...

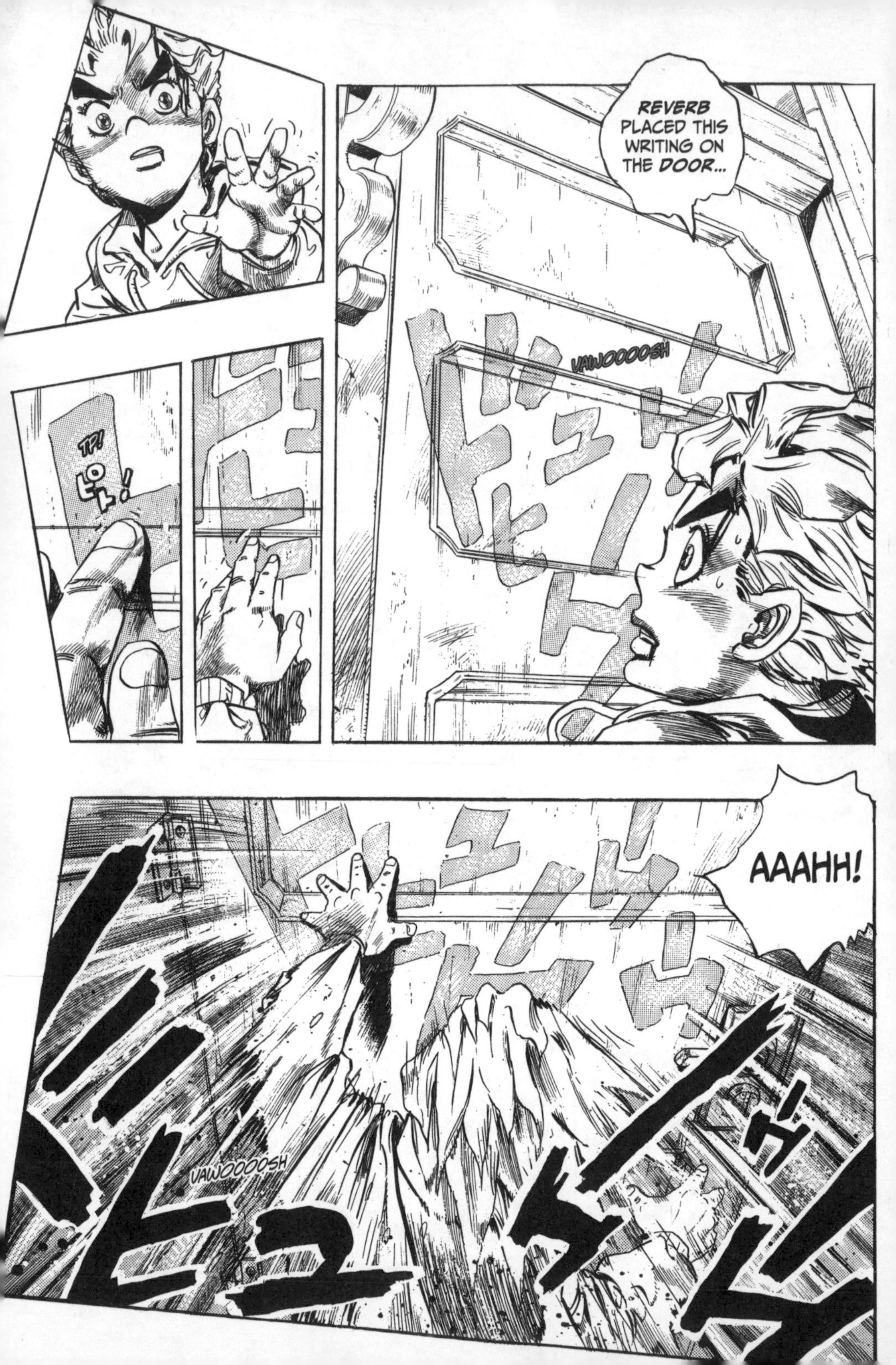
REVERB PLACED THIS WRITING ON THE DOOR...
VAWOOOOSH
TP!
ピタッ!
AAAH!
VAWOOOOSH

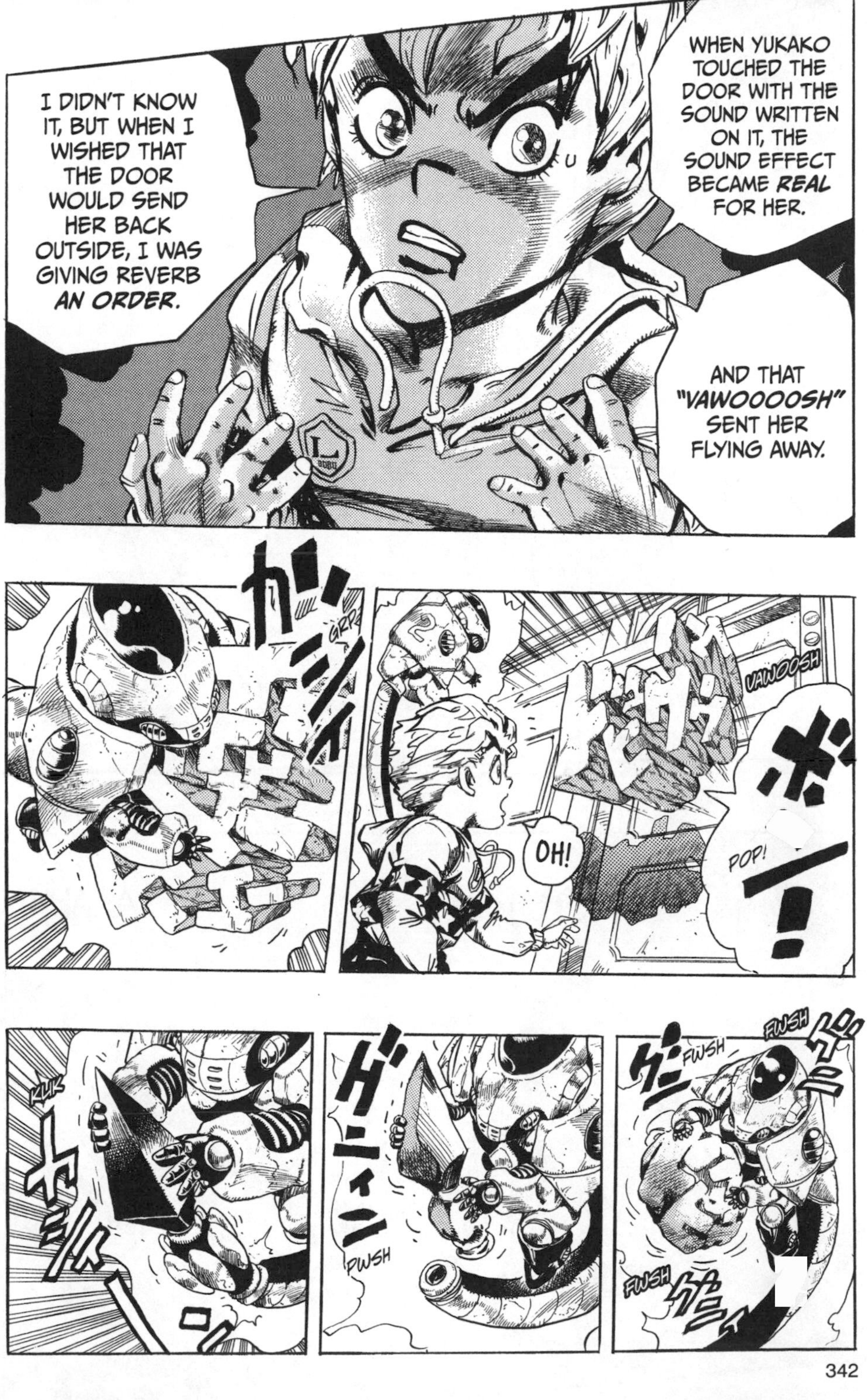
WHEN YUKAKO TOUCHED THE DOOR WITH THE SOUND WRITTEN ON IT, THE SOUND EFFECT BECAME *REAL* FOR HER.
I DIDN'T KNOW IT, BUT WHEN I WISHED THAT THE DOOR WOULD SEND HER BACK OUTSIDE, I WAS GIVING REVERB *AN ORDER.*
AND THAT *"VAWOOOOSH"* SENT HER FLYING AWAY.
VAWOOSH
POP!
OH!
GRP
FWSH
FWSH
FWSH
PWSH
KLIK

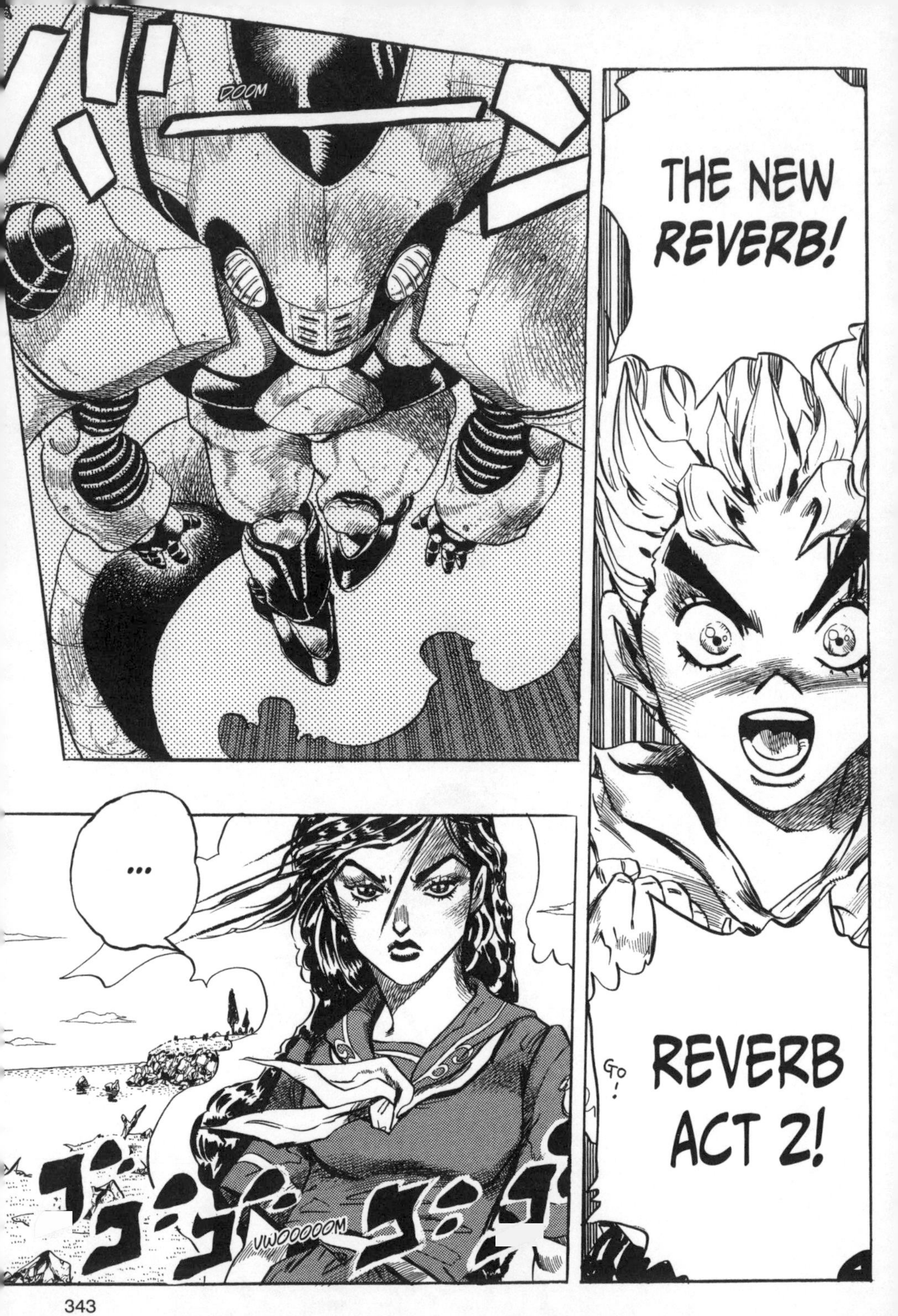
THE NEW REVERB!
GO!
REVERB ACT 2!
DOOM
...
VWOOOOOM

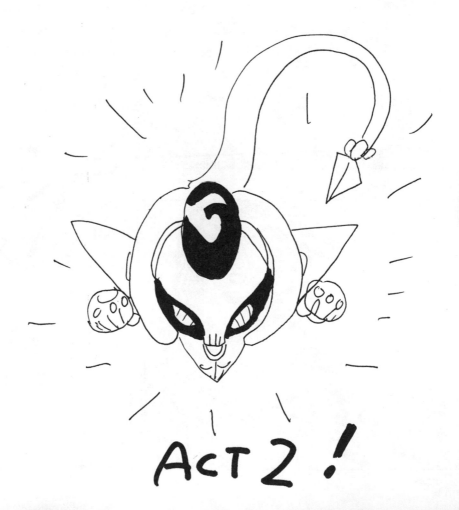

ACT 2 !

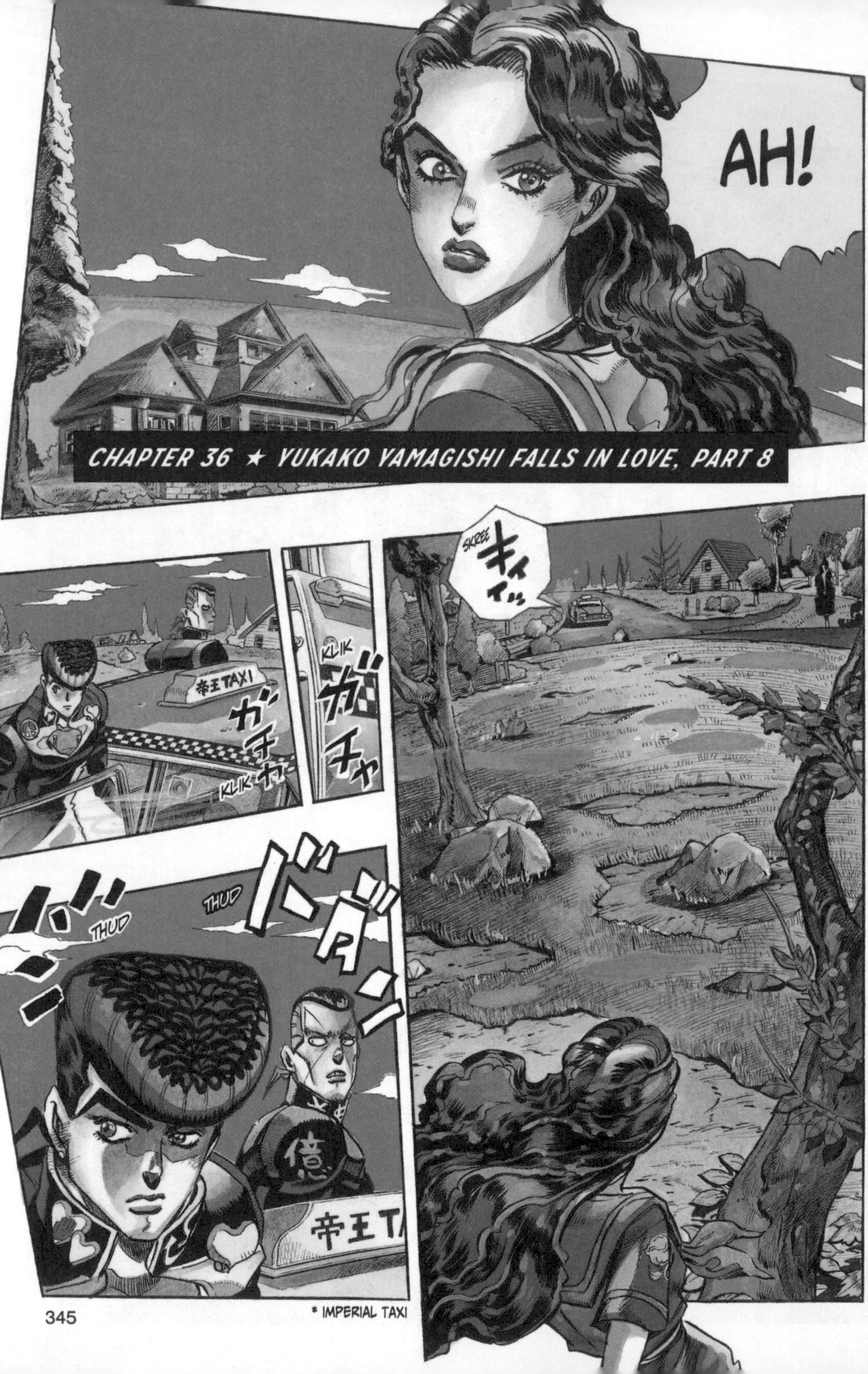
AH!
CHAPTER 36 ★ YUKAKO YAMAGISHI FALLS IN LOVE, PART 8
SKREE
キィイッ
KLIK
ガチャ
帝王TAXI
KLIK
ガチャ
THUD
THUD
帝王TA

* IMPERIAL TAXI

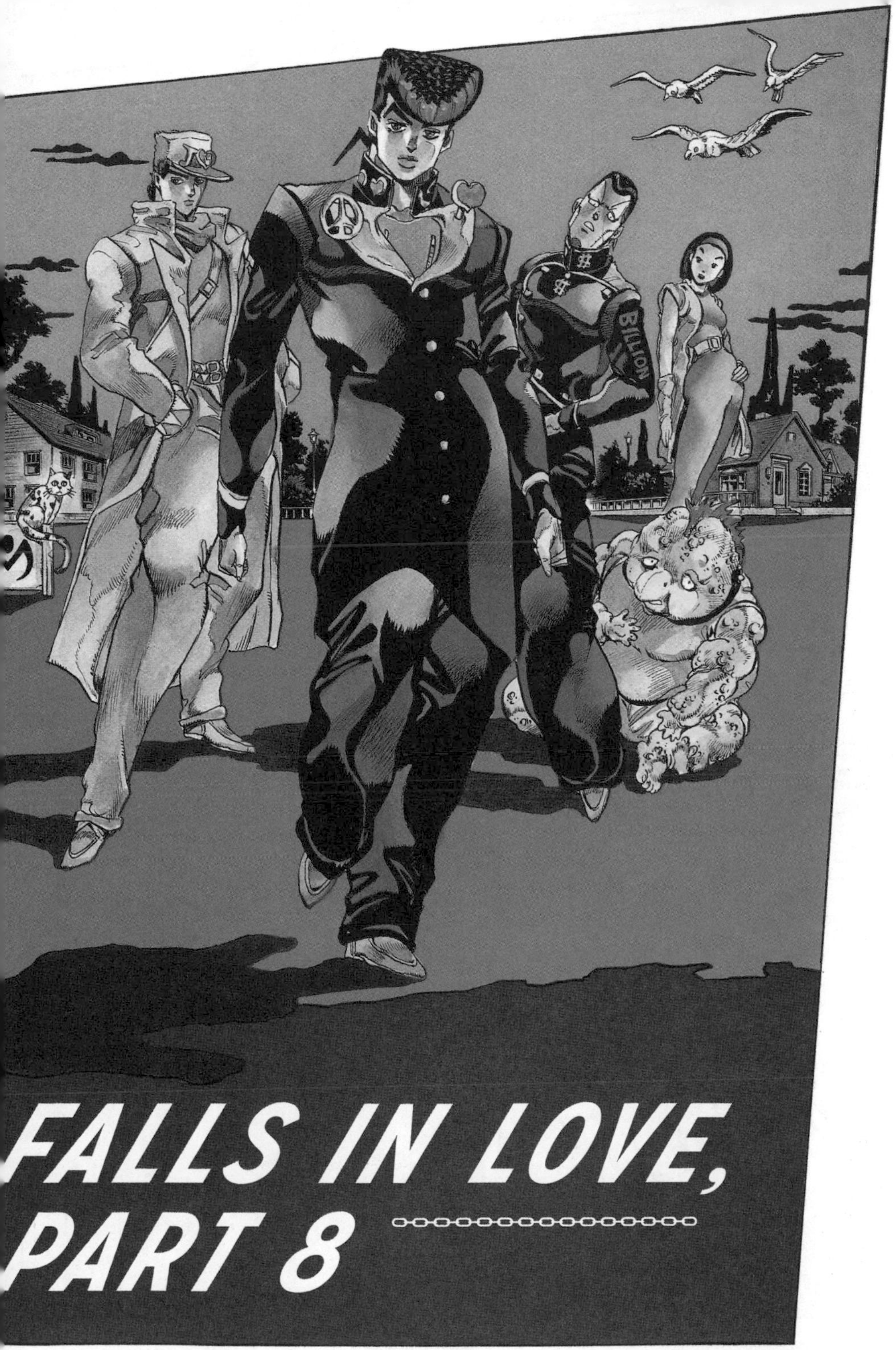
BILLION

FALLS IN LOVE, PART 8

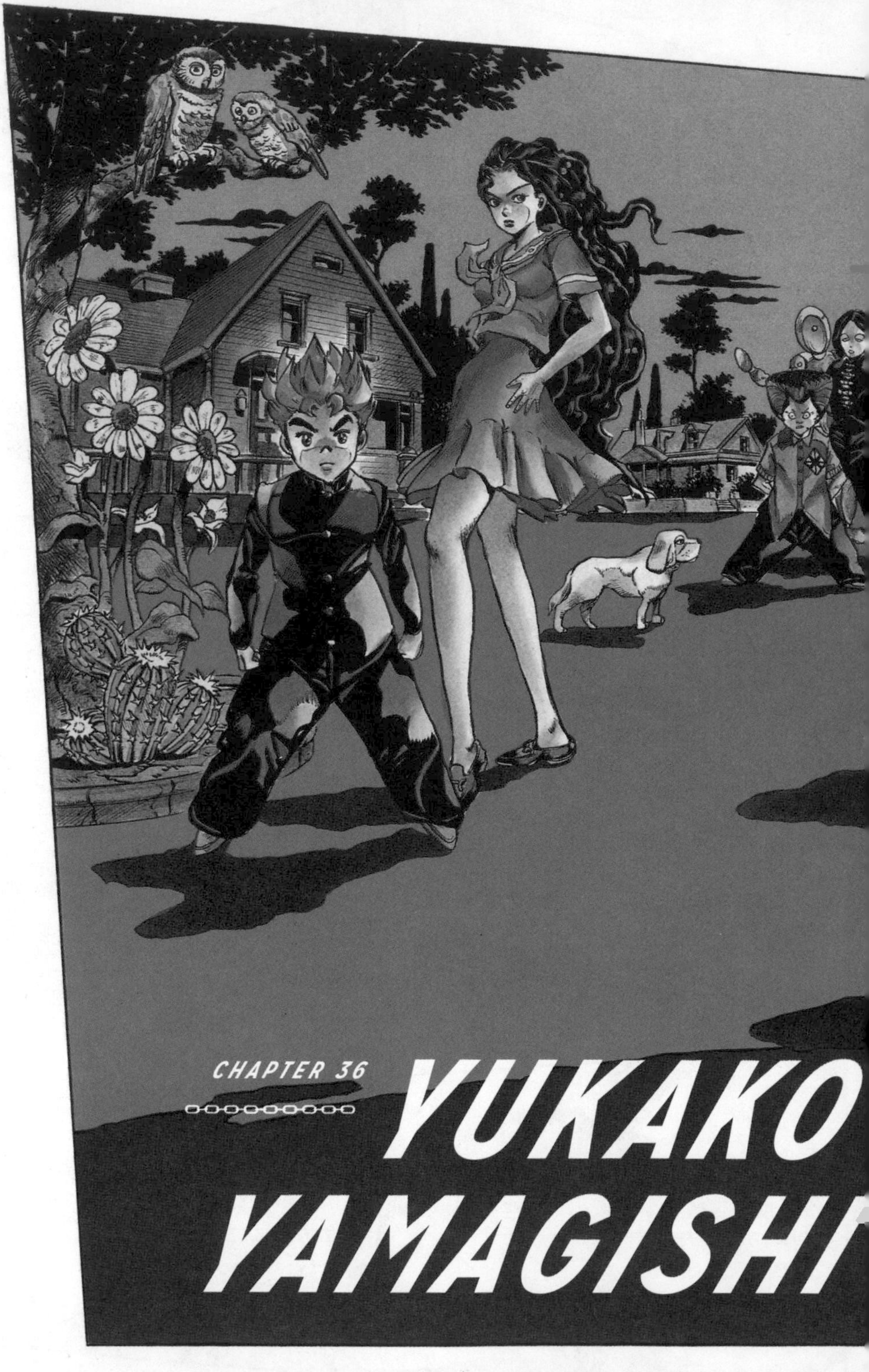
CHAPTER 36
YUKAKO YAMAGISHI

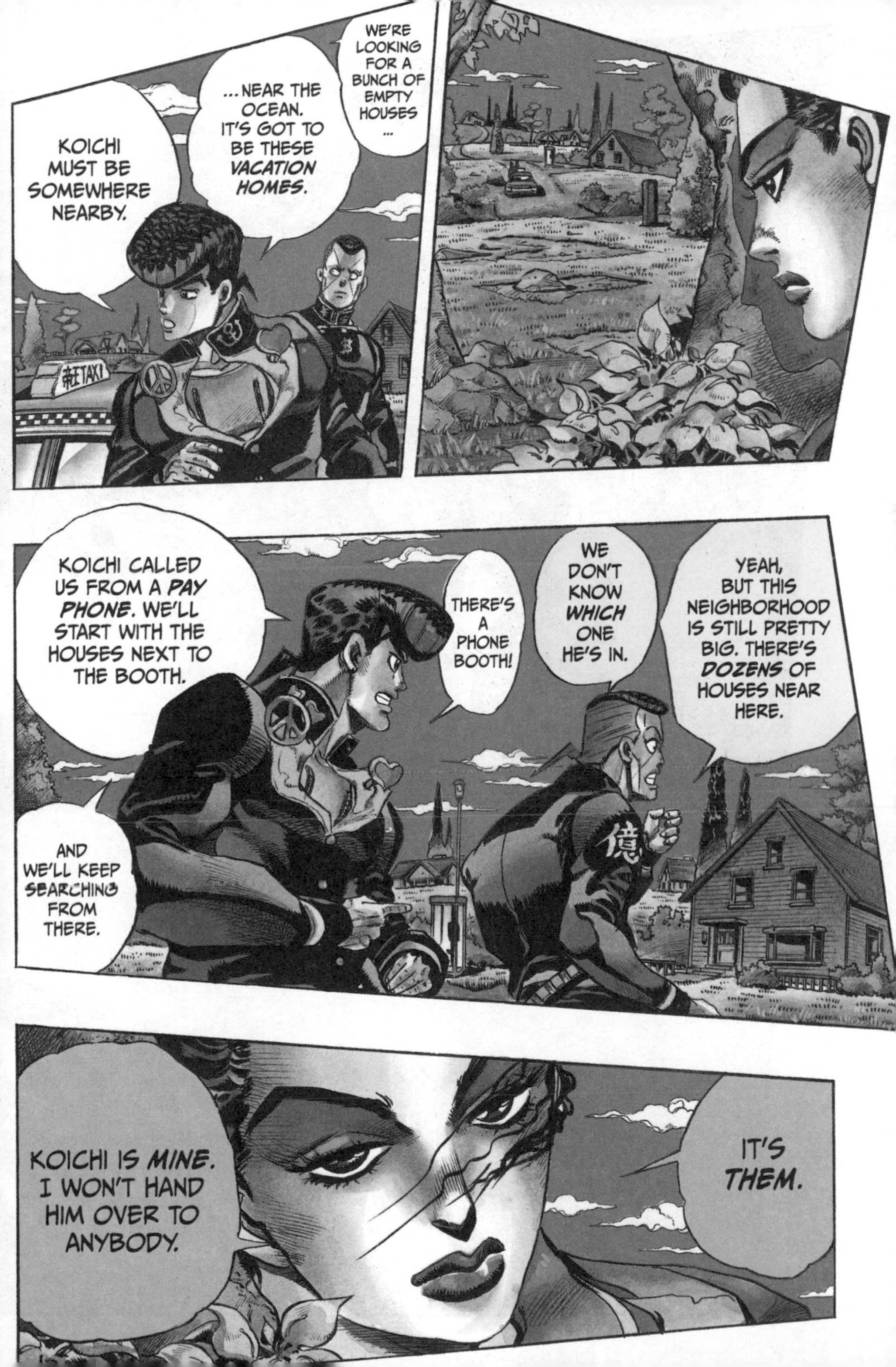
WE'RE LOOKING FOR A BUNCH OF EMPTY HOUSES ...
...NEAR THE OCEAN. IT'S GOT TO BE THESE *VACATION HOMES*.
KOICHI MUST BE SOMEWHERE NEARBY.
YEAH, BUT THIS NEIGHBORHOOD IS STILL PRETTY BIG. THERE'S *DOZENS* OF HOUSES NEAR HERE.
WE DON'T KNOW *WHICH* ONE HE'S IN.
THERE'S A PHONE BOOTH!
KOICHI CALLED US FROM A *PAY PHONE*. WE'LL START WITH THE HOUSES NEXT TO THE BOOTH.
AND WE'LL KEEP SEARCHING FROM THERE.
IT'S *THEM*.
KOICHI IS *MINE*. I WON'T HAND HIM OVER TO ANYBODY.

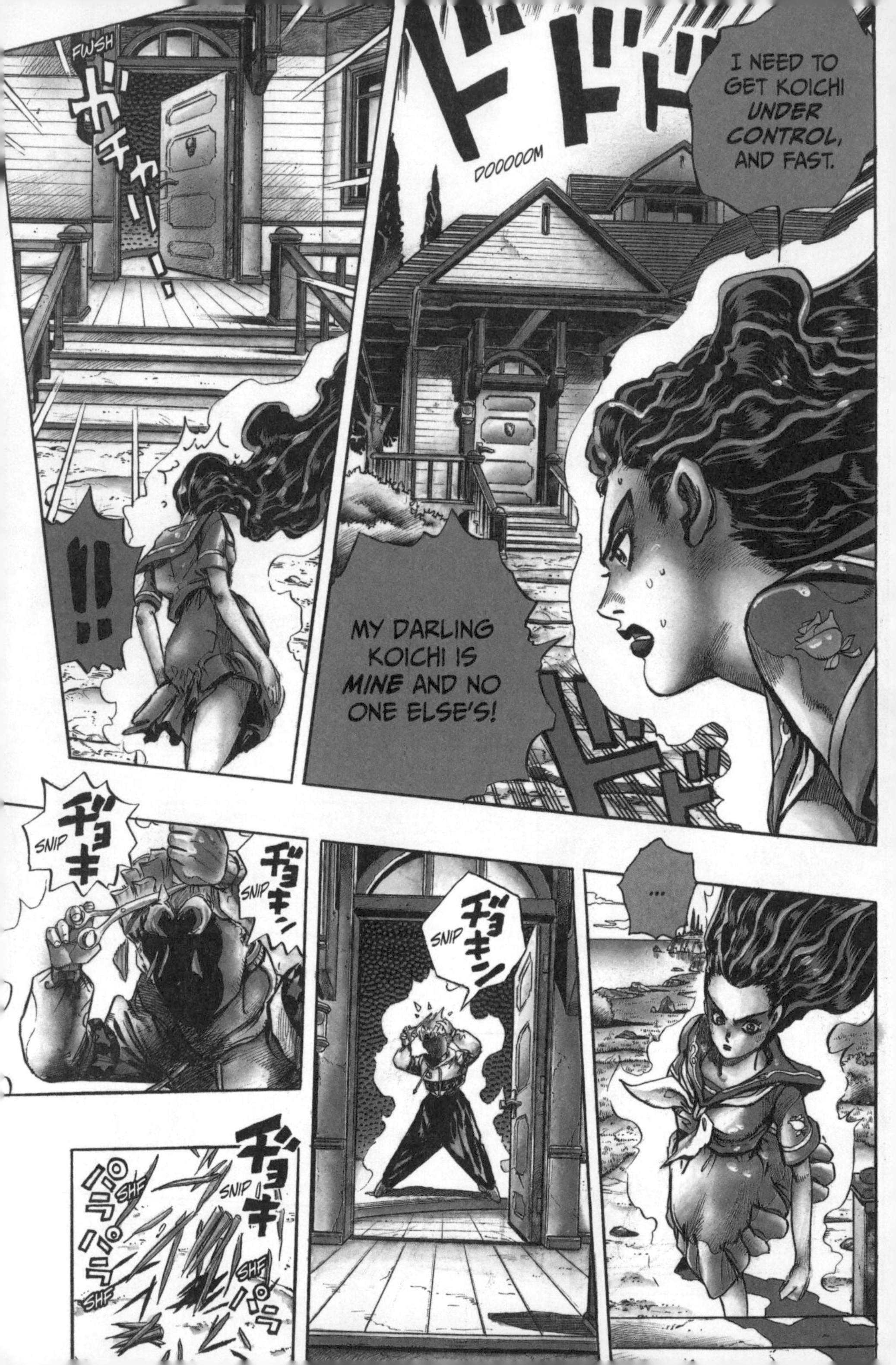

DOOOOOM
I NEED TO GET KOICHI *UNDER CONTROL*, AND FAST.
MY DARLING KOICHI IS *MINE* AND NO ONE ELSE'S!
FWSH
!!
...
SNIP
SNIP
SNIP
SNIP
SHF
SHF
SHF

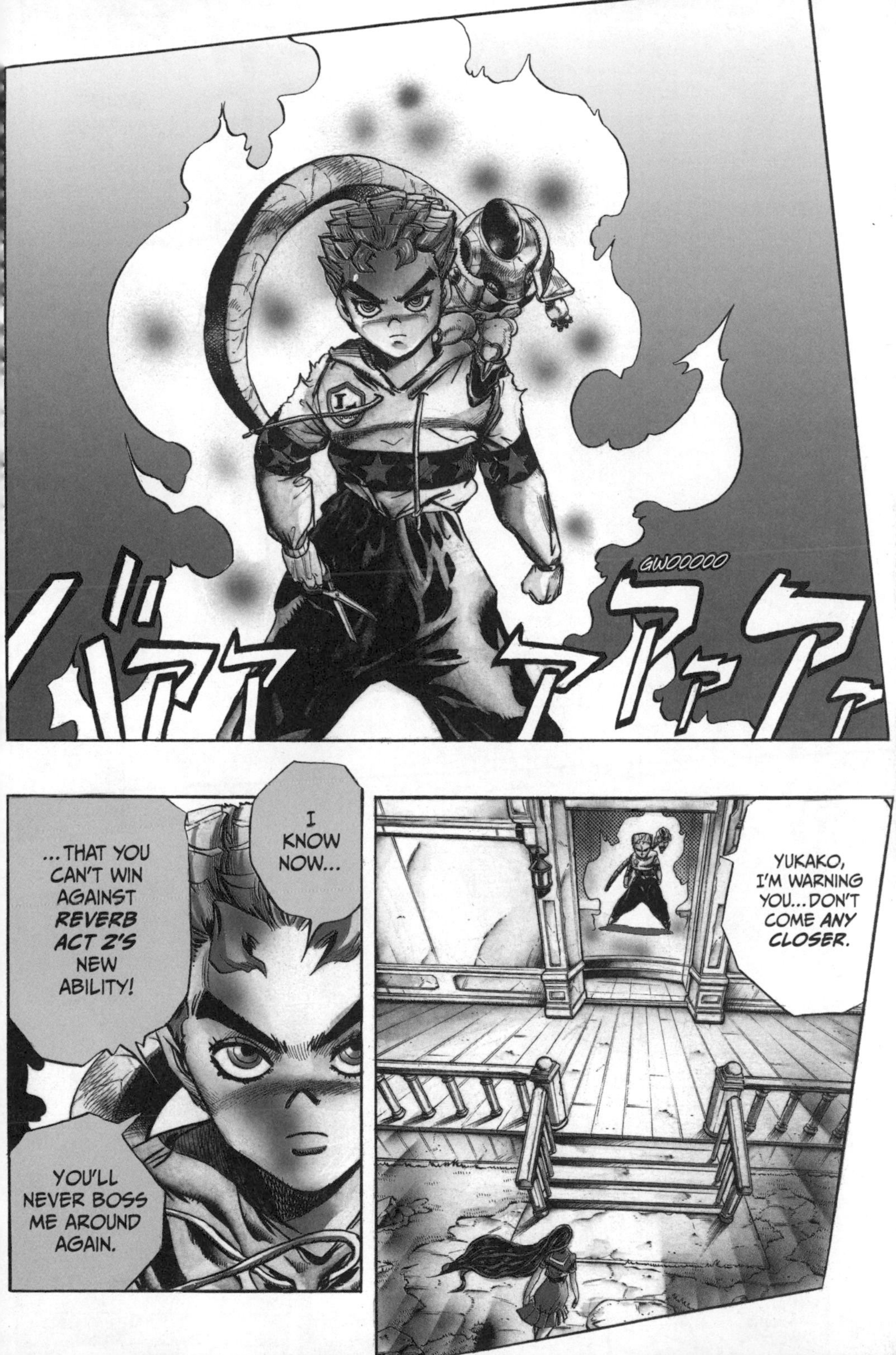
GWOOOOO
YUKAKO, I'M WARNING YOU...DON'T COME ANY CLOSER.
I KNOW NOW...
...THAT YOU CAN'T WIN AGAINST REVERB ACT 2'S NEW ABILITY!
YOU'LL NEVER BOSS ME AROUND AGAIN.

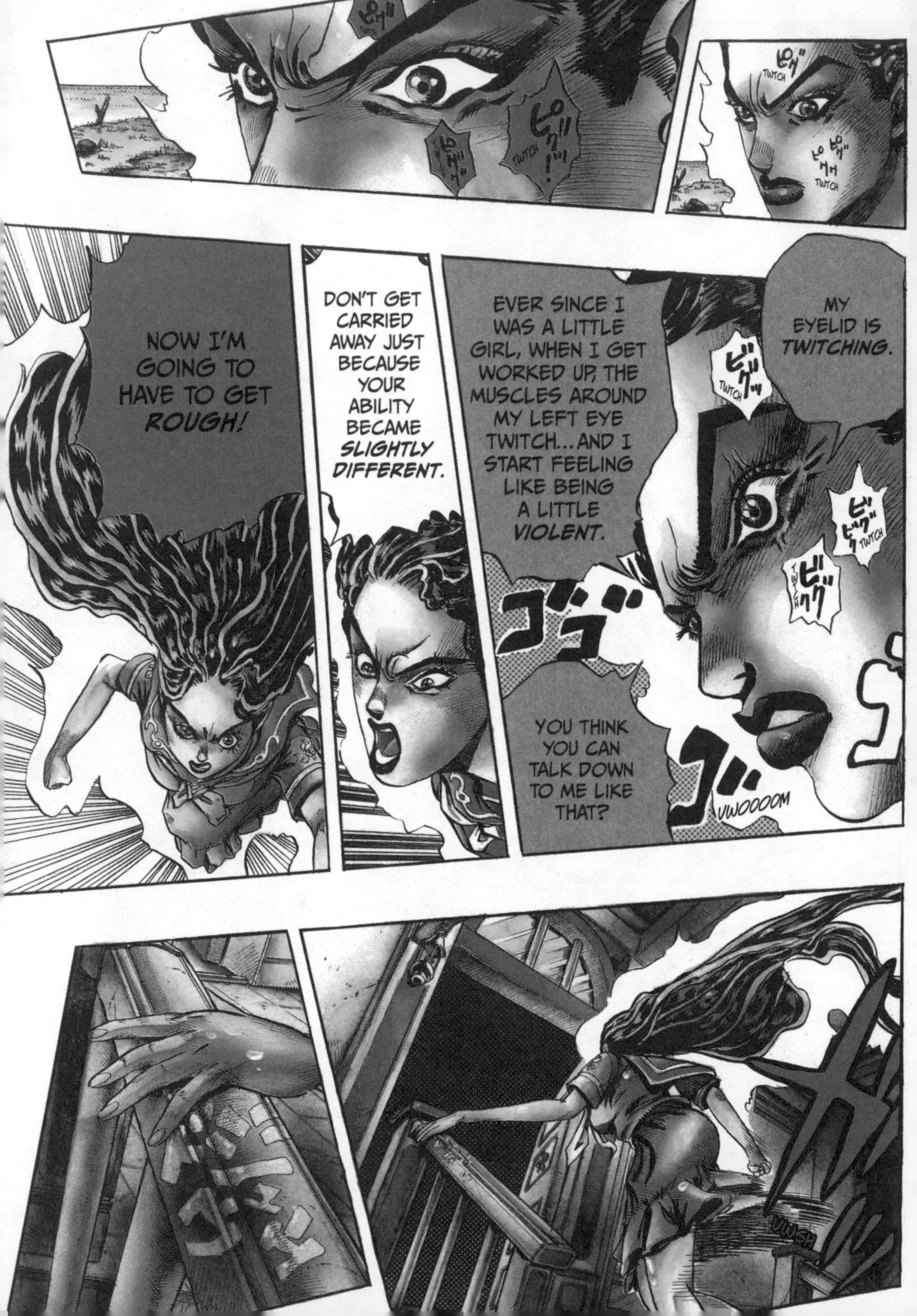

TWITCH
TWITCH
TWITCH
MY EYELID IS *TWITCHING.*
TWITCH
EVER SINCE I WAS A LITTLE GIRL, WHEN I GET WORKED UP, THE MUSCLES AROUND MY LEFT EYE TWITCH... AND I START FEELING LIKE BEING A LITTLE *VIOLENT.*
TWITCH
YOU THINK YOU CAN TALK DOWN TO ME LIKE THAT?
VWOOOOM
DON'T GET CARRIED AWAY JUST BECAUSE YOUR ABILITY BECAME *SLIGHTLY DIFFERENT.*
NOW I'M GOING TO HAVE TO GET *ROUGH!*
VWISH

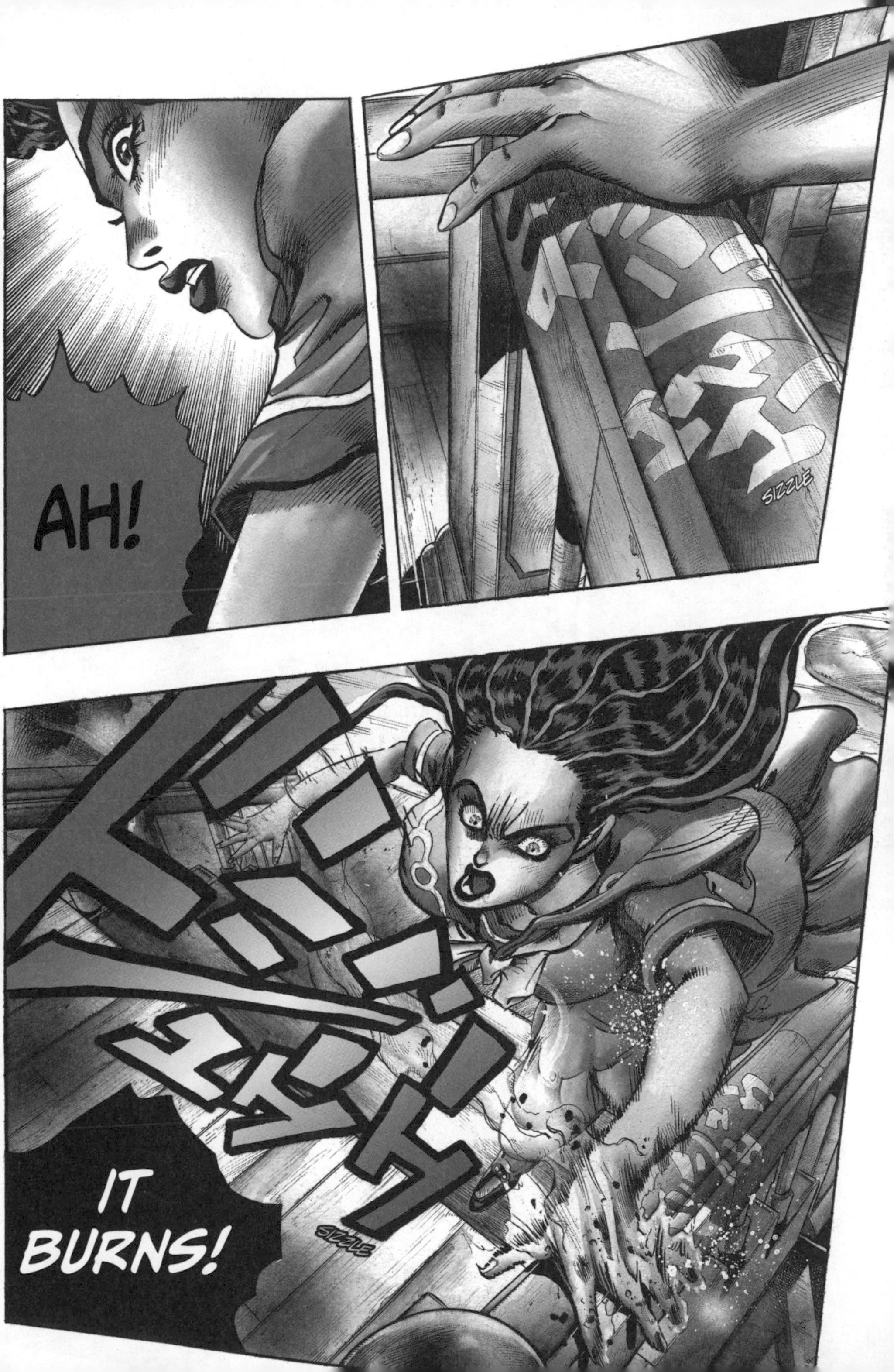
SIZZLE
AH!
IT BURNS!
SIZZLE

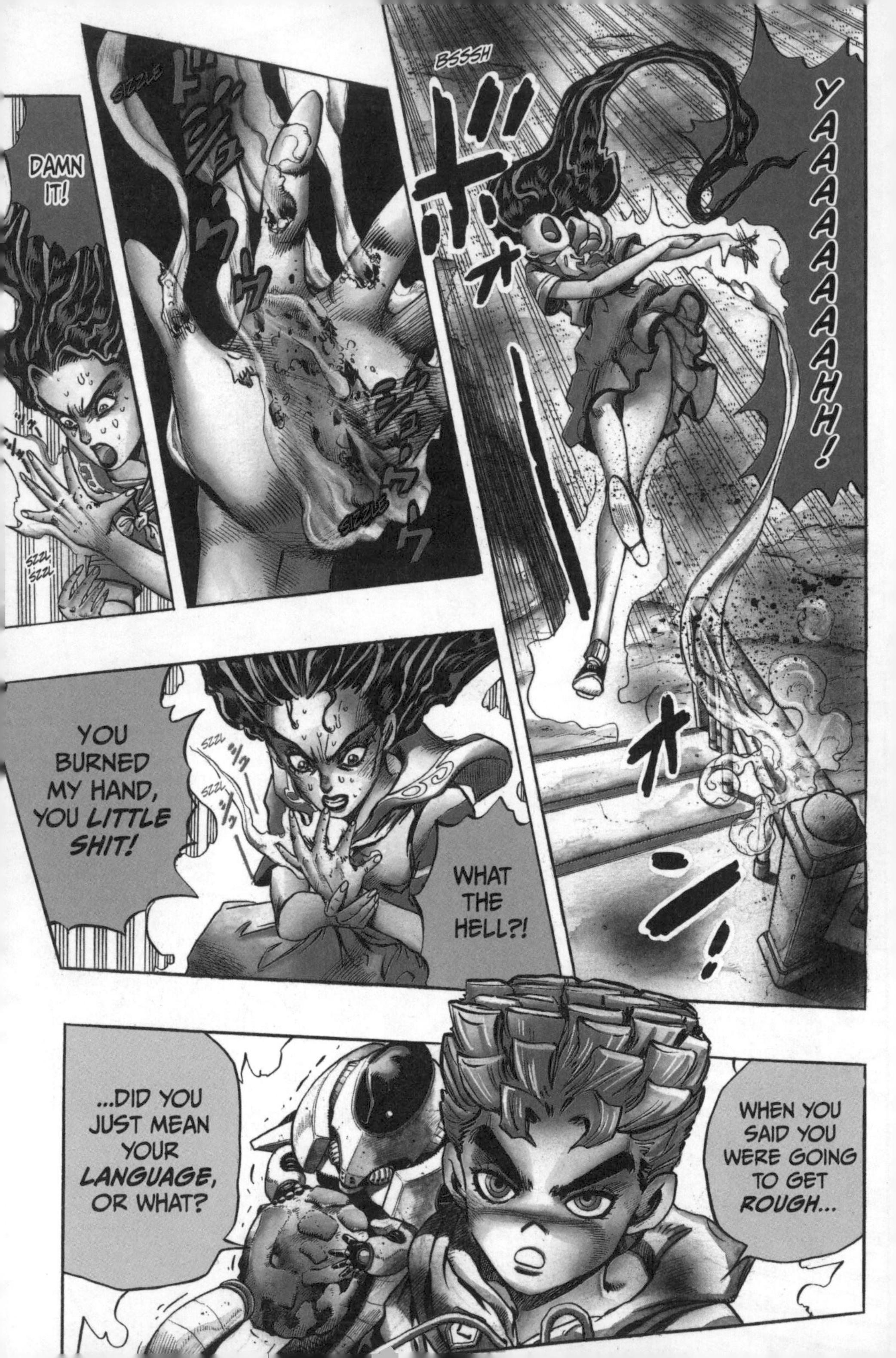
BSSSH
YAAAAAAAAAAAHH!
SIZZLE
SIZZLE
DAMN IT!
SZZL SZZL
WHAT THE HELL?!
YOU BURNED MY HAND, YOU *LITTLE SHIT!*
SZZL
SZZL
WHEN YOU SAID YOU WERE GOING TO GET *ROUGH*...
...DID YOU JUST MEAN YOUR *LANGUAGE*, OR WHAT?

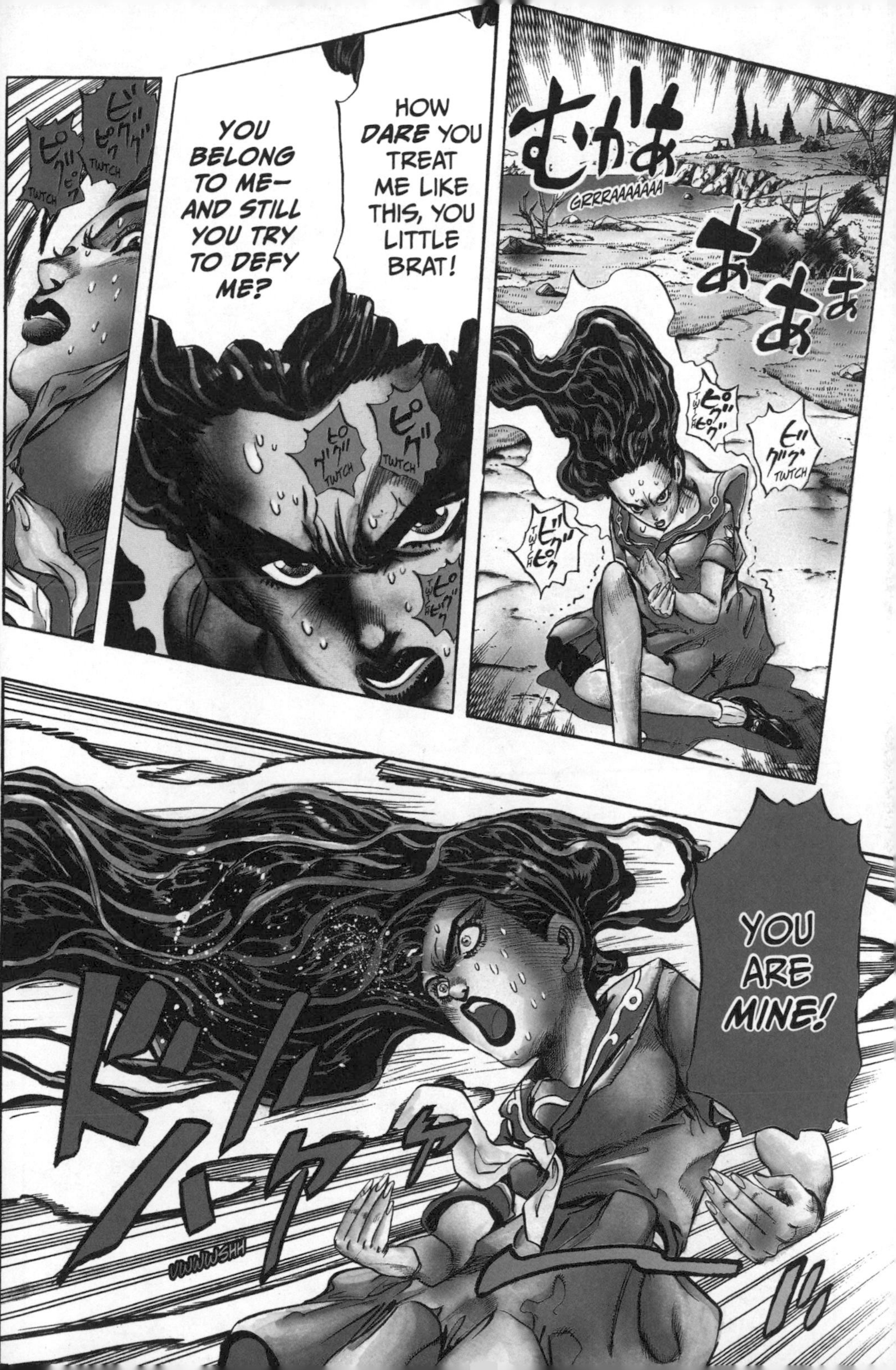

GRRRAAAAAAA
TWITCH
TWITCH
TWITCH
HOW DARE YOU TREAT ME LIKE THIS, YOU LITTLE BRAT!
YOU BELONG TO ME—AND STILL YOU TRY TO DEFY ME?
TWITCH
TWITCH
TWITCH
TWITCH
TWITCH
YOU ARE MINE!
VWWWSHH

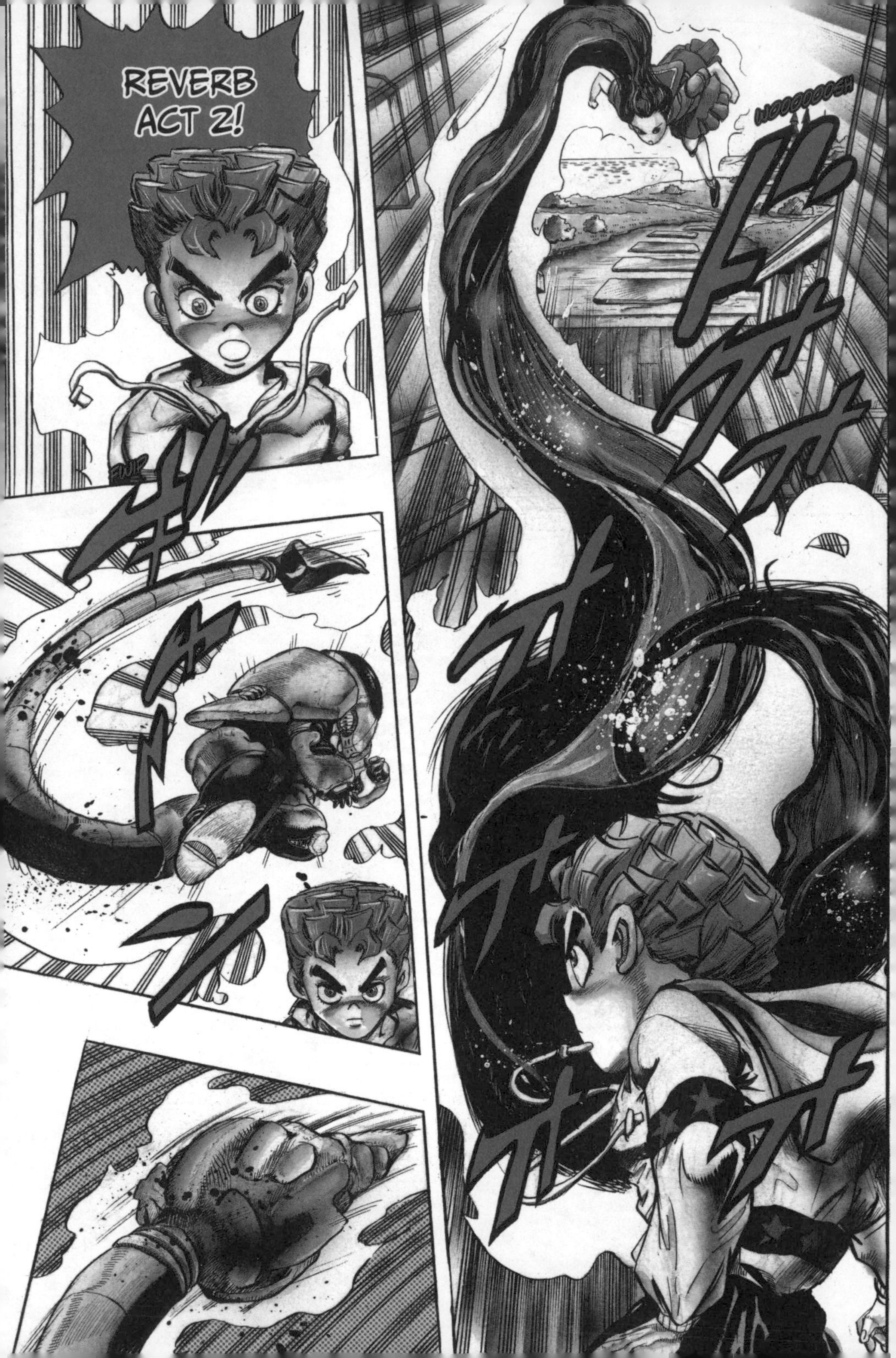
WOOOOOOOSH
REVERB ACT 2!
FWIP

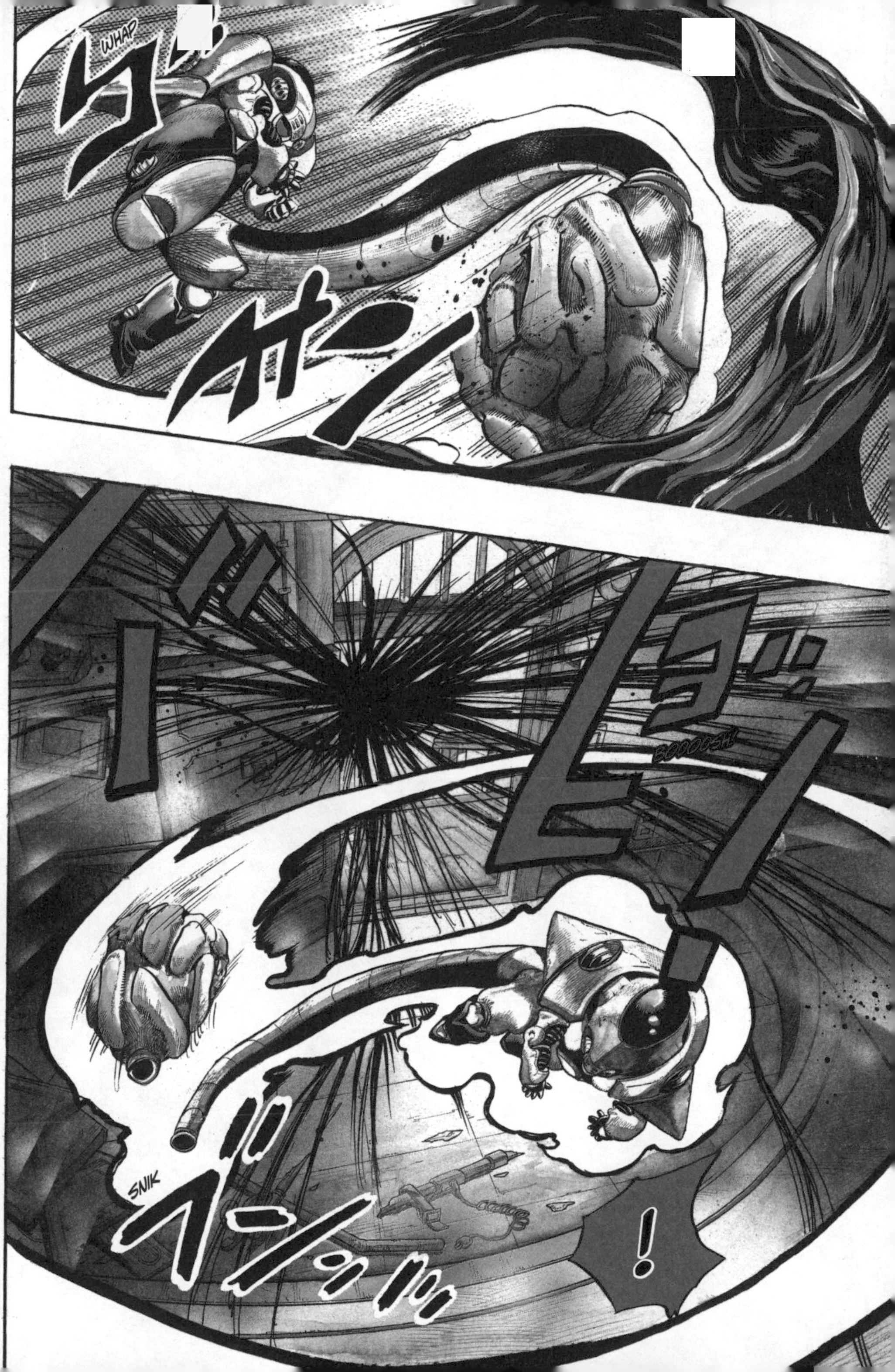
WHAP
BOOOOOSH
SNIK
!

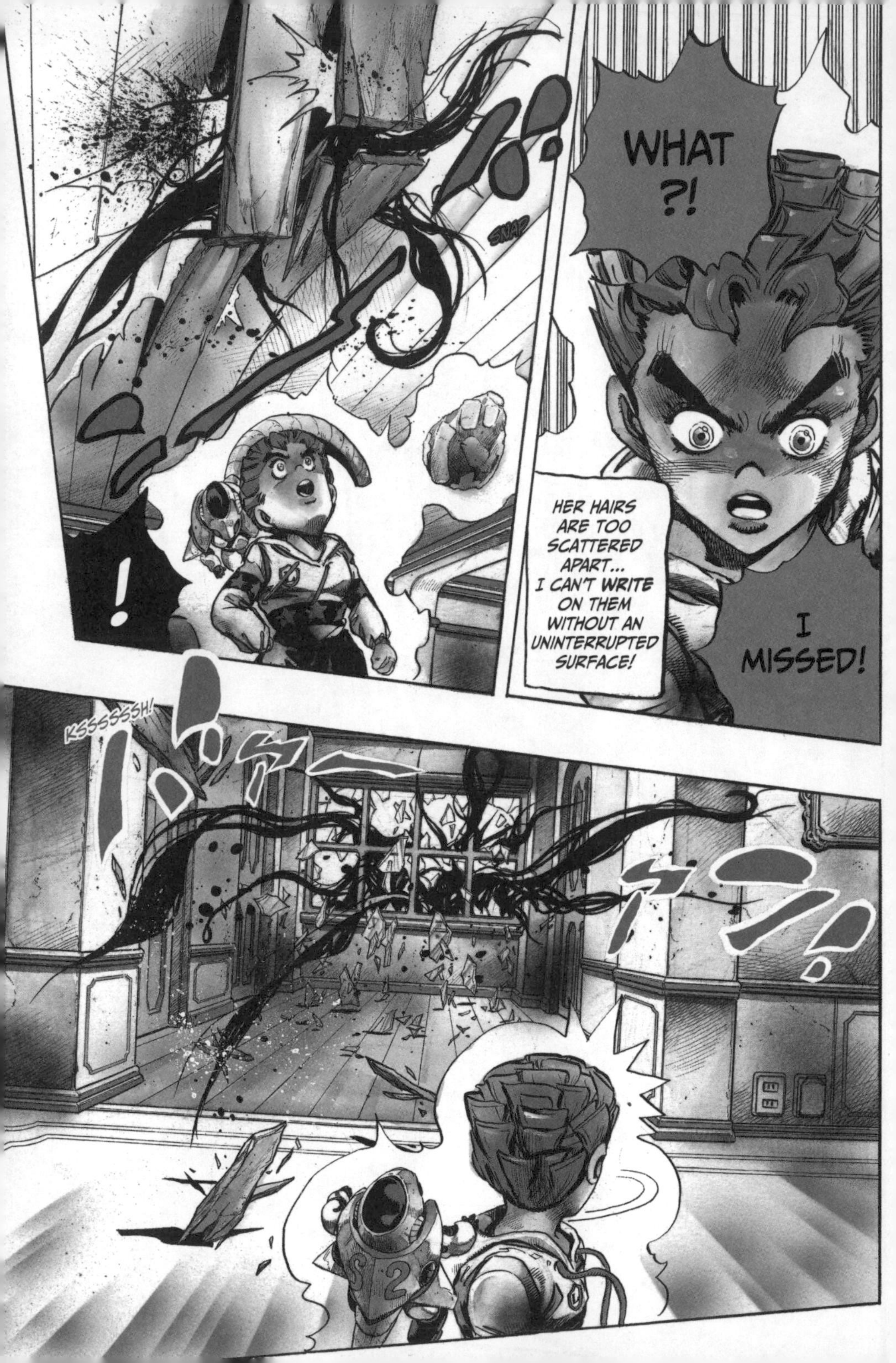
WHAT ?!
HER HAIRS ARE TOO SCATTERED APART... I CAN'T WRITE ON THEM WITHOUT AN UNINTERRUPTED SURFACE!
I MISSED!
SNAP
!
KSSSSSSH!

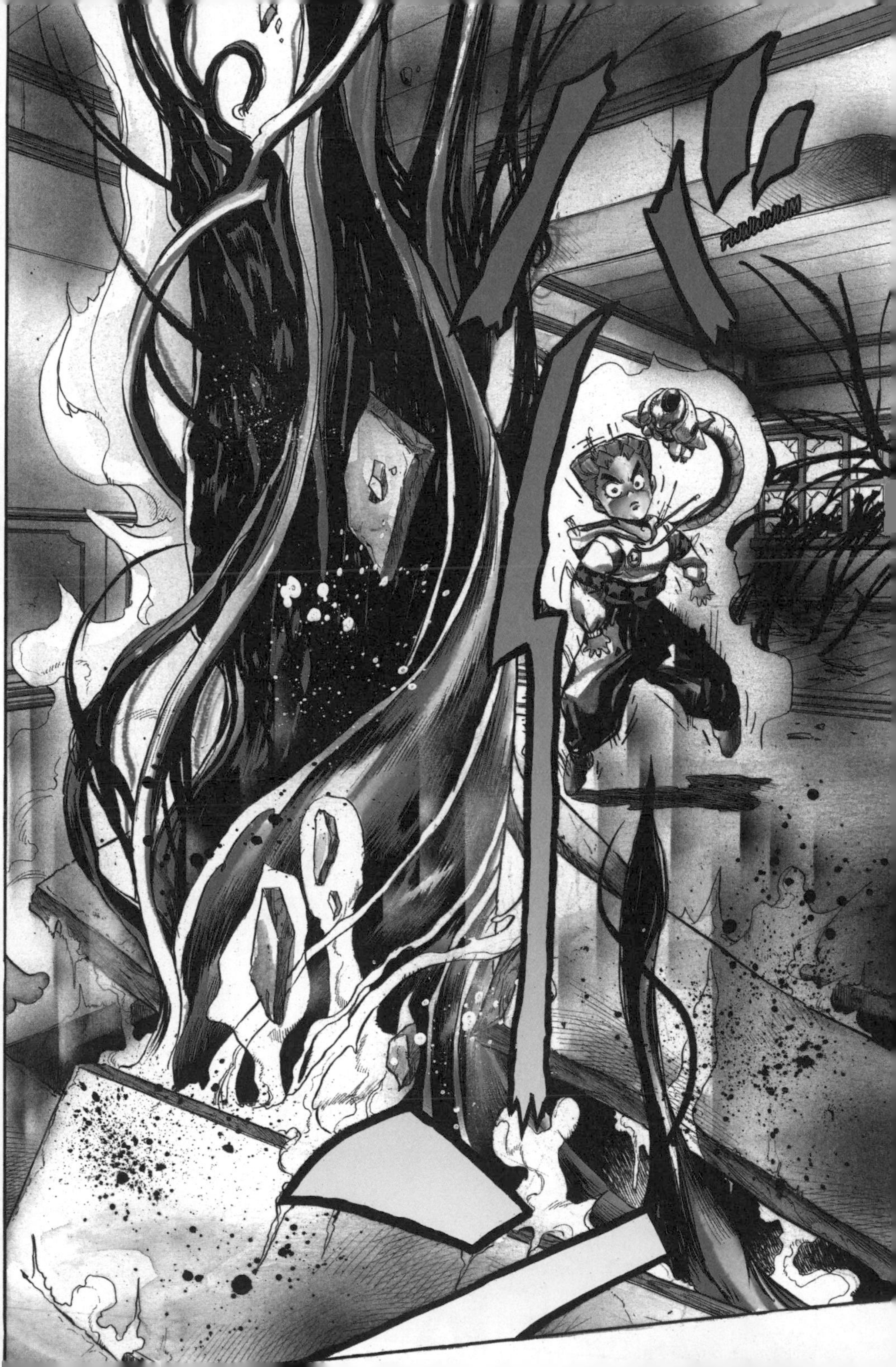

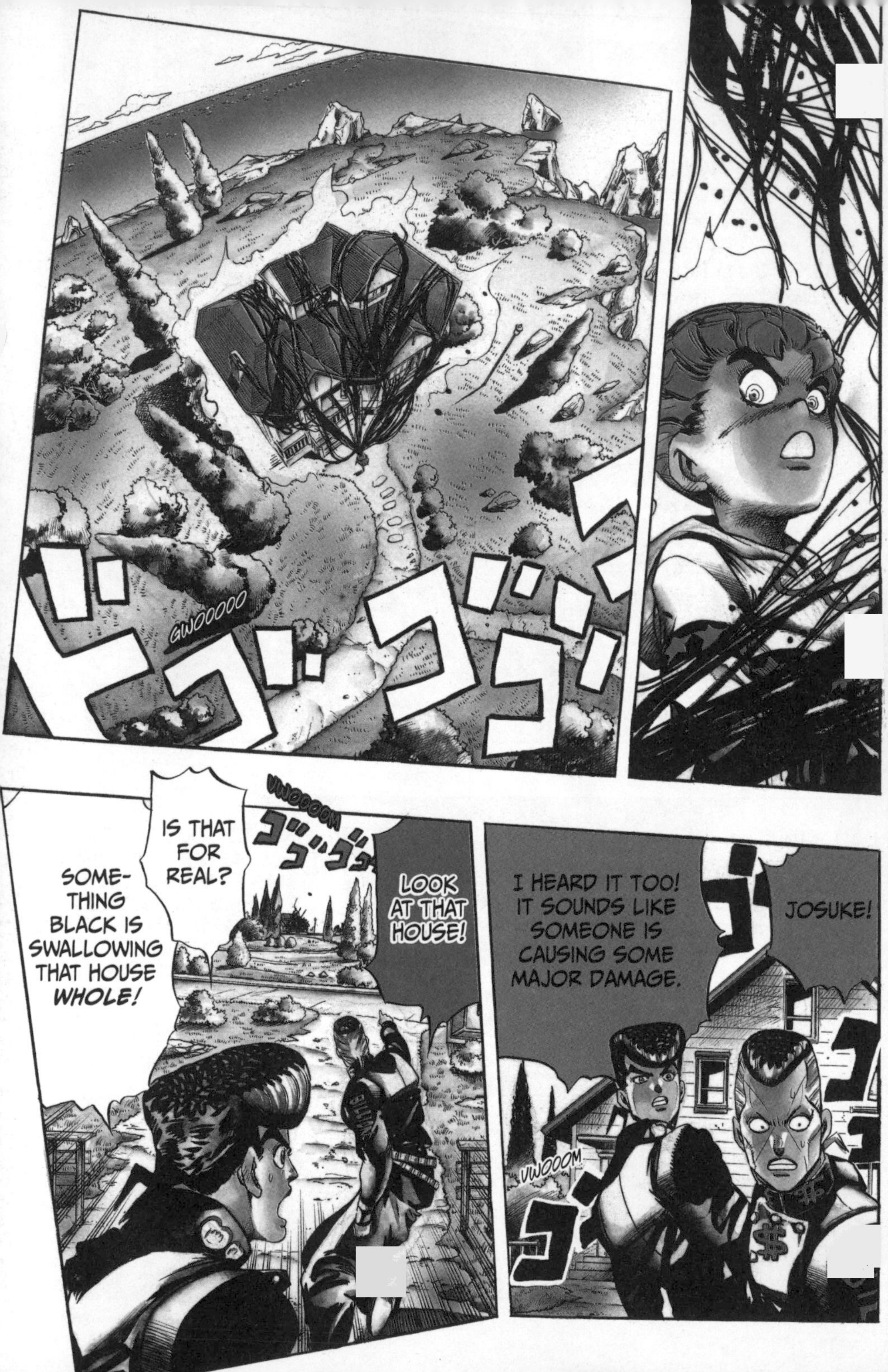
GWOOOOO
JOSUKE!
I HEARD IT TOO! IT SOUNDS LIKE SOMEONE IS CAUSING SOME MAJOR DAMAGE.
VWOOOM
VWOOOOM
LOOK AT THAT HOUSE!
IS THAT FOR REAL?
SOMETHING BLACK IS SWALLOWING THAT HOUSE *WHOLE*!

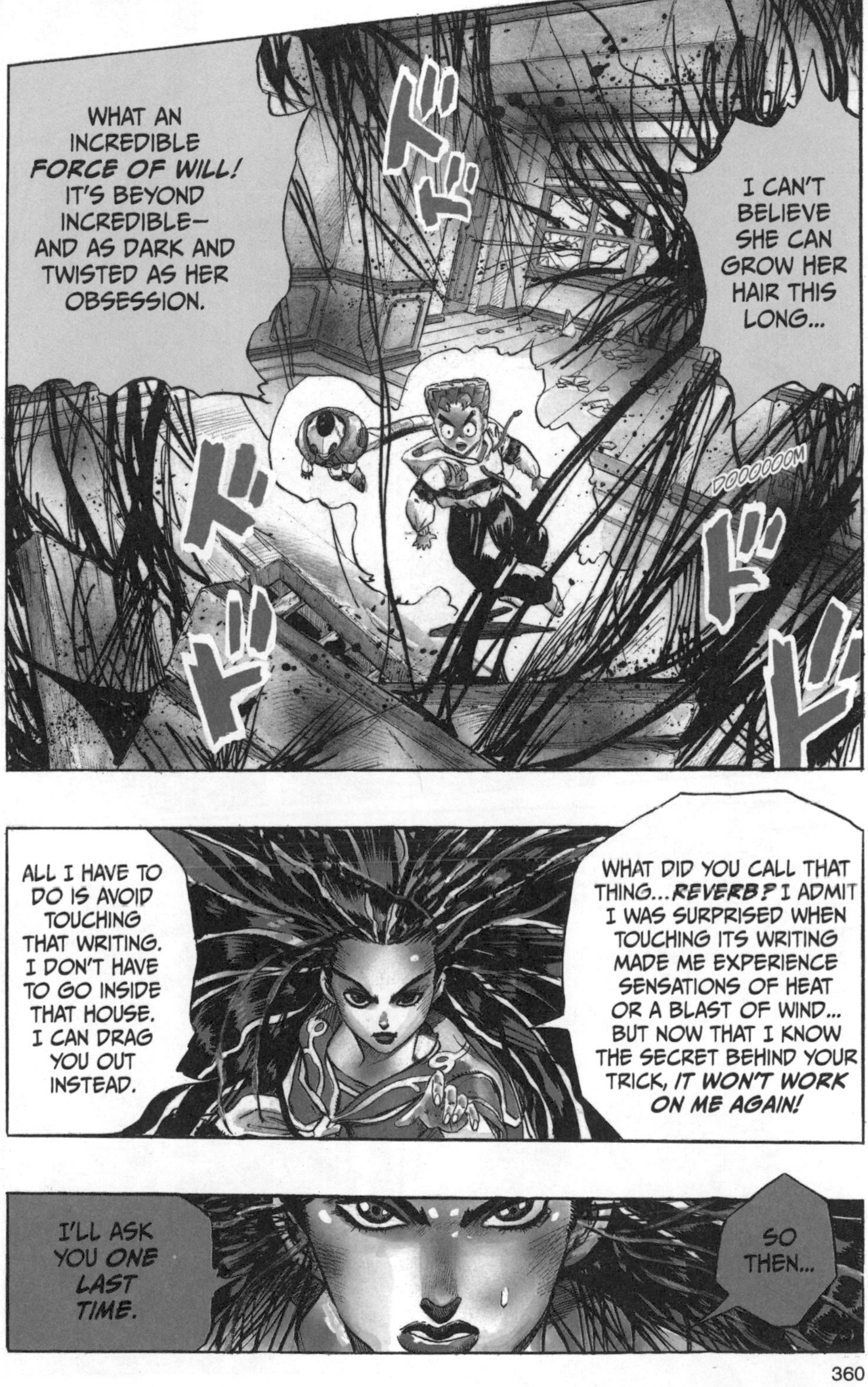
I CAN'T BELIEVE SHE CAN GROW HER HAIR THIS LONG...
WHAT AN INCREDIBLE *FORCE OF WILL!* IT'S BEYOND INCREDIBLE— AND AS DARK AND TWISTED AS HER OBSESSION.
DOOOOOOM
WHAT DID YOU CALL THAT THING... *REVERB?* I ADMIT I WAS SURPRISED WHEN TOUCHING ITS WRITING MADE ME EXPERIENCE SENSATIONS OF HEAT OR A BLAST OF WIND... BUT NOW THAT I KNOW THE SECRET BEHIND YOUR TRICK, *IT WON'T WORK ON ME AGAIN!*
ALL I HAVE TO DO IS AVOID TOUCHING THAT WRITING. I DON'T HAVE TO GO INSIDE THAT HOUSE. I CAN DRAG YOU OUT INSTEAD.
SO THEN...
I'LL ASK YOU *ONE LAST TIME.*

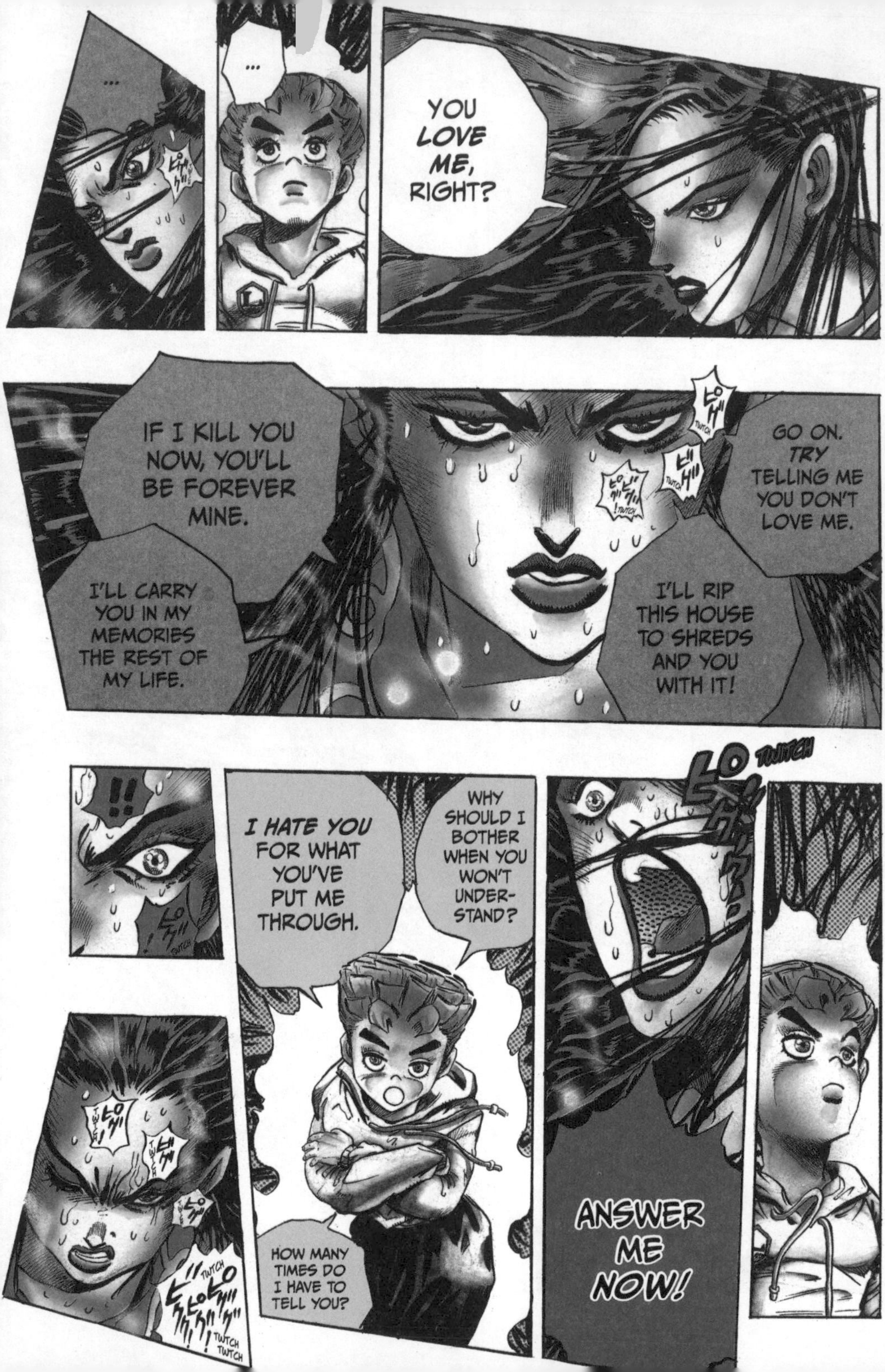
YOU LOVE ME, RIGHT?
...
...
GO ON. TRY TELLING ME YOU DON'T LOVE ME.
TWITCH
TWITCH
TWITCH
I'LL RIP THIS HOUSE TO SHREDS AND YOU WITH IT!
IF I KILL YOU NOW, YOU'LL BE FOREVER MINE.
I'LL CARRY YOU IN MY MEMORIES THE REST OF MY LIFE.
TWITCH
ANSWER ME NOW!
WHY SHOULD I BOTHER WHEN YOU WON'T UNDER-STAND?
I HATE YOU FOR WHAT YOU'VE PUT ME THROUGH.
HOW MANY TIMES DO I HAVE TO TELL YOU?
!!
TWITCH
TWITCH
TWITCH TWITCH

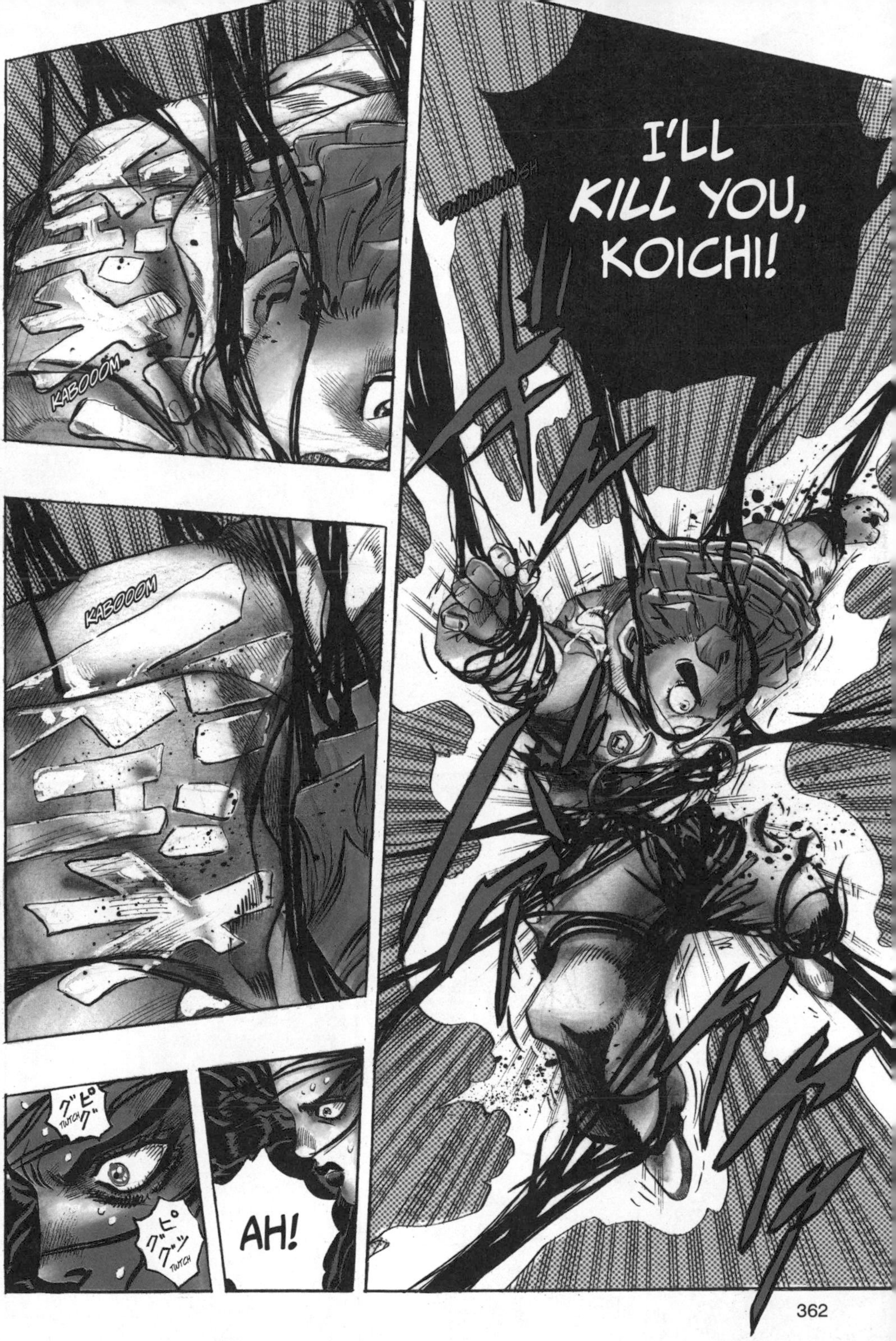

I'LL KILL YOU, KOICHI!
KABOOOM
KABOOOM
AH!
ピクッ
TWITCH
ピクッ
TWITCH

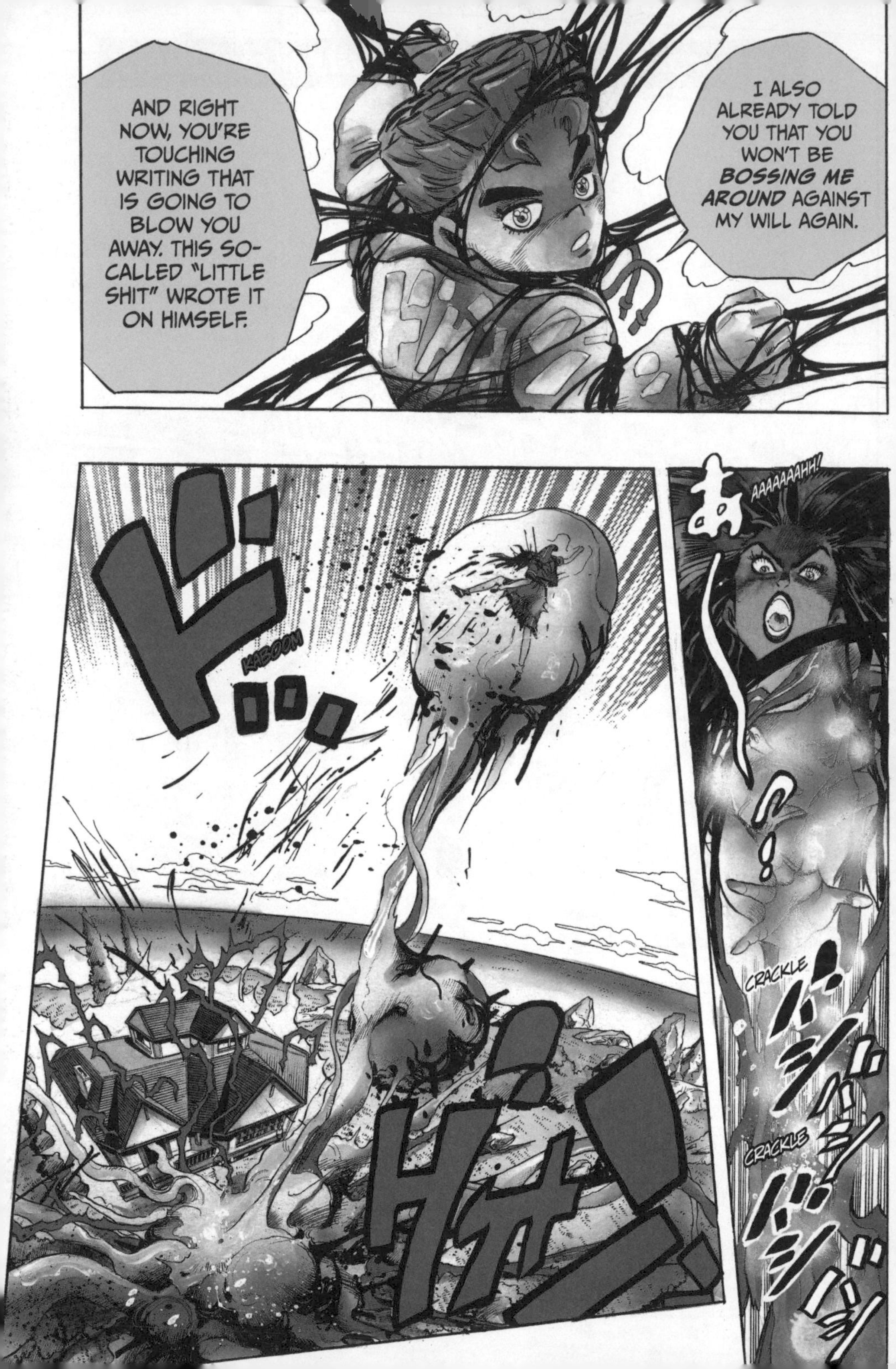
I ALSO ALREADY TOLD YOU THAT YOU WON'T BE ***BOSSING ME AROUND*** AGAINST MY WILL AGAIN.
AND RIGHT NOW, YOU'RE TOUCHING WRITING THAT IS GOING TO BLOW YOU AWAY. THIS SO-CALLED "LITTLE SHIT" WROTE IT ON HIMSELF.
あ
AAAAAAAHH!
CRACKLE
CRACKLE
KABOOM

CHAPTER 37 ★ YUKAKO YAMAGISHI FALLS IN LOVE, PART 9

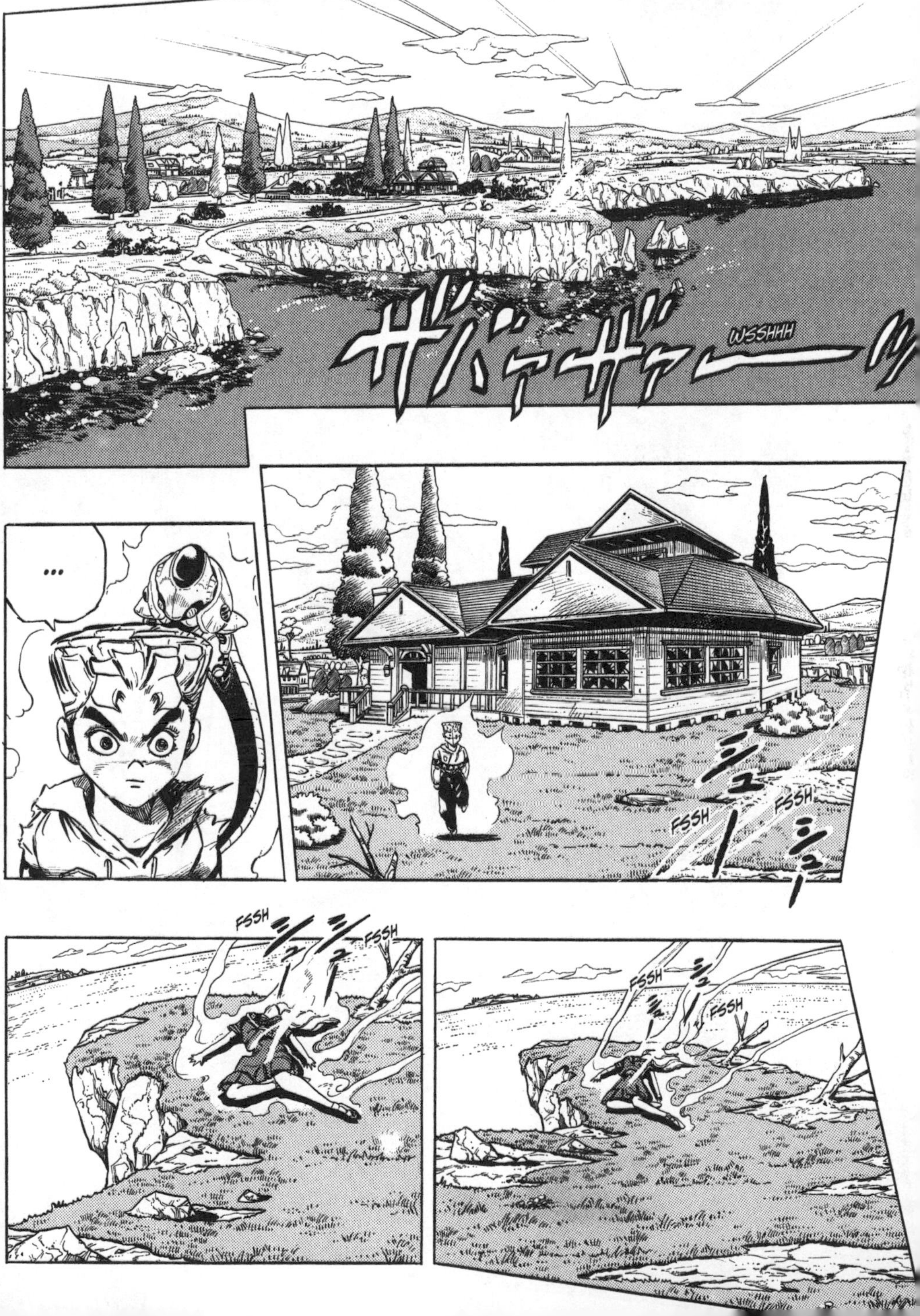
ザバァザァーッ
WSSHHH
シュー
FSSH
FSSH
シュー
...
シュ
FSSH
FSSH
シュ
FSSH
FSSH

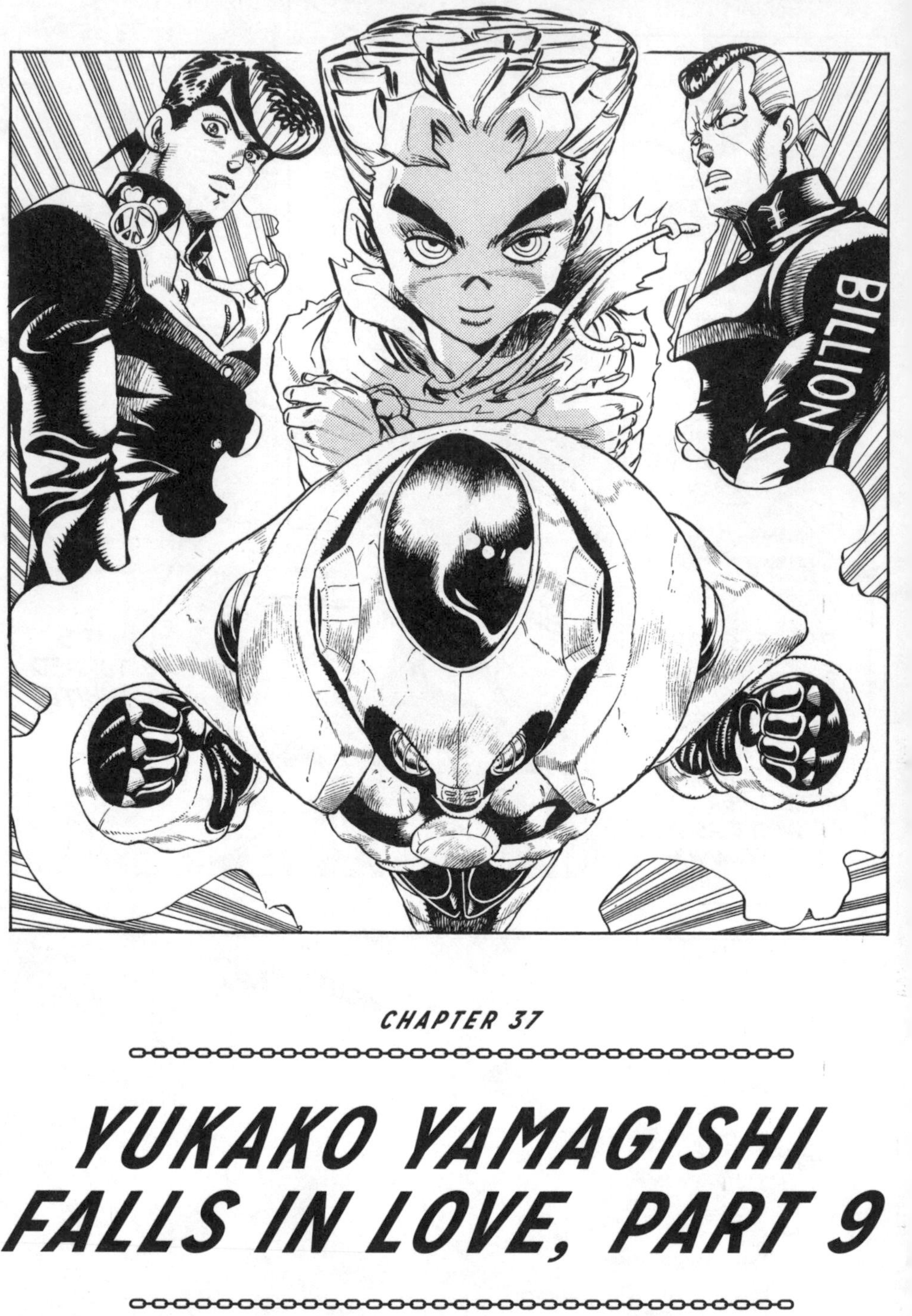
BILLION

CHAPTER 37

YUKAKO YAMAGISHI FALLS IN LOVE, PART 9

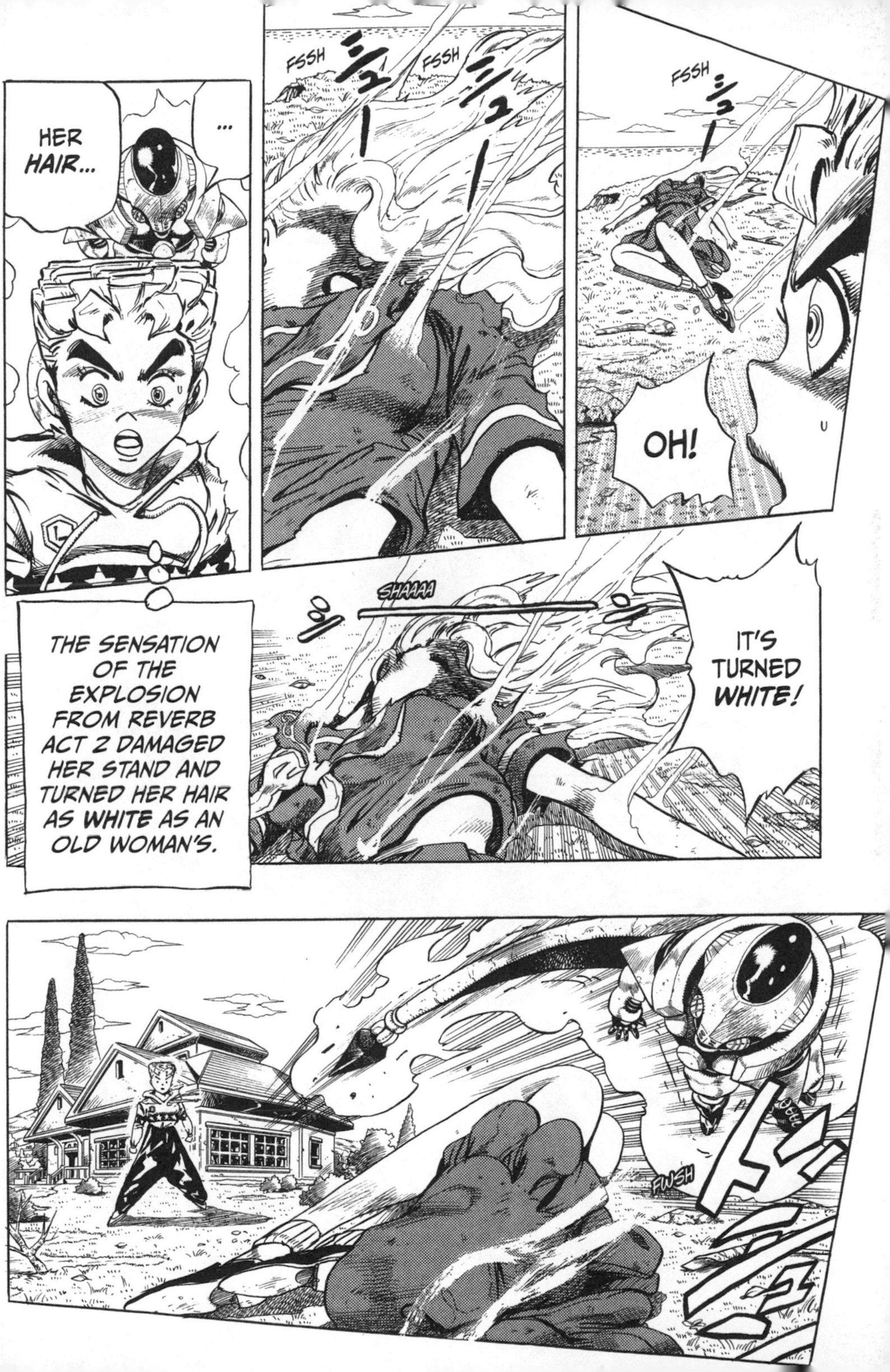
FSSH
OH!
FSSH
FSSH
...
HER HAIR...
IT'S TURNED WHITE!
SHAAAA
THE SENSATION OF THE EXPLOSION FROM REVERB ACT 2 DAMAGED HER STAND AND TURNED HER HAIR AS WHITE AS AN OLD WOMAN'S.
FWSH

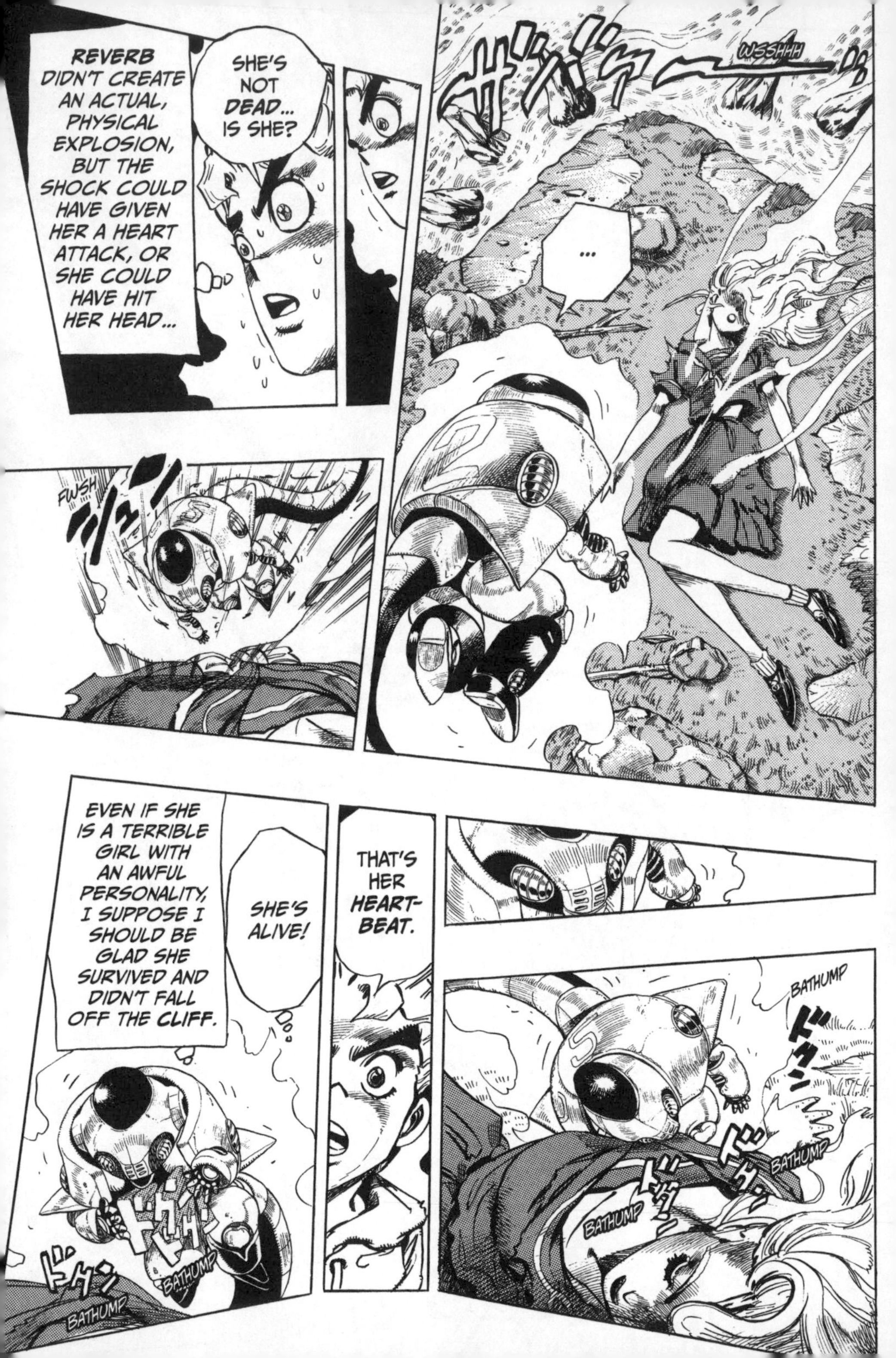
WSSHHH
...
SHE'S NOT DEAD... IS SHE?
REVERB DIDN'T CREATE AN ACTUAL, PHYSICAL EXPLOSION, BUT THE SHOCK COULD HAVE GIVEN HER A HEART ATTACK, OR SHE COULD HAVE HIT HER HEAD...
FWSH
BATHUMP
BATHUMP
BATHUMP
THAT'S HER HEART-BEAT.
SHE'S ALIVE!
EVEN IF SHE IS A TERRIBLE GIRL WITH AN AWFUL PERSONALITY, I SUPPOSE I SHOULD BE GLAD SHE SURVIVED AND DIDN'T FALL OFF THE CLIFF.
BATHUMP
BATHUMP

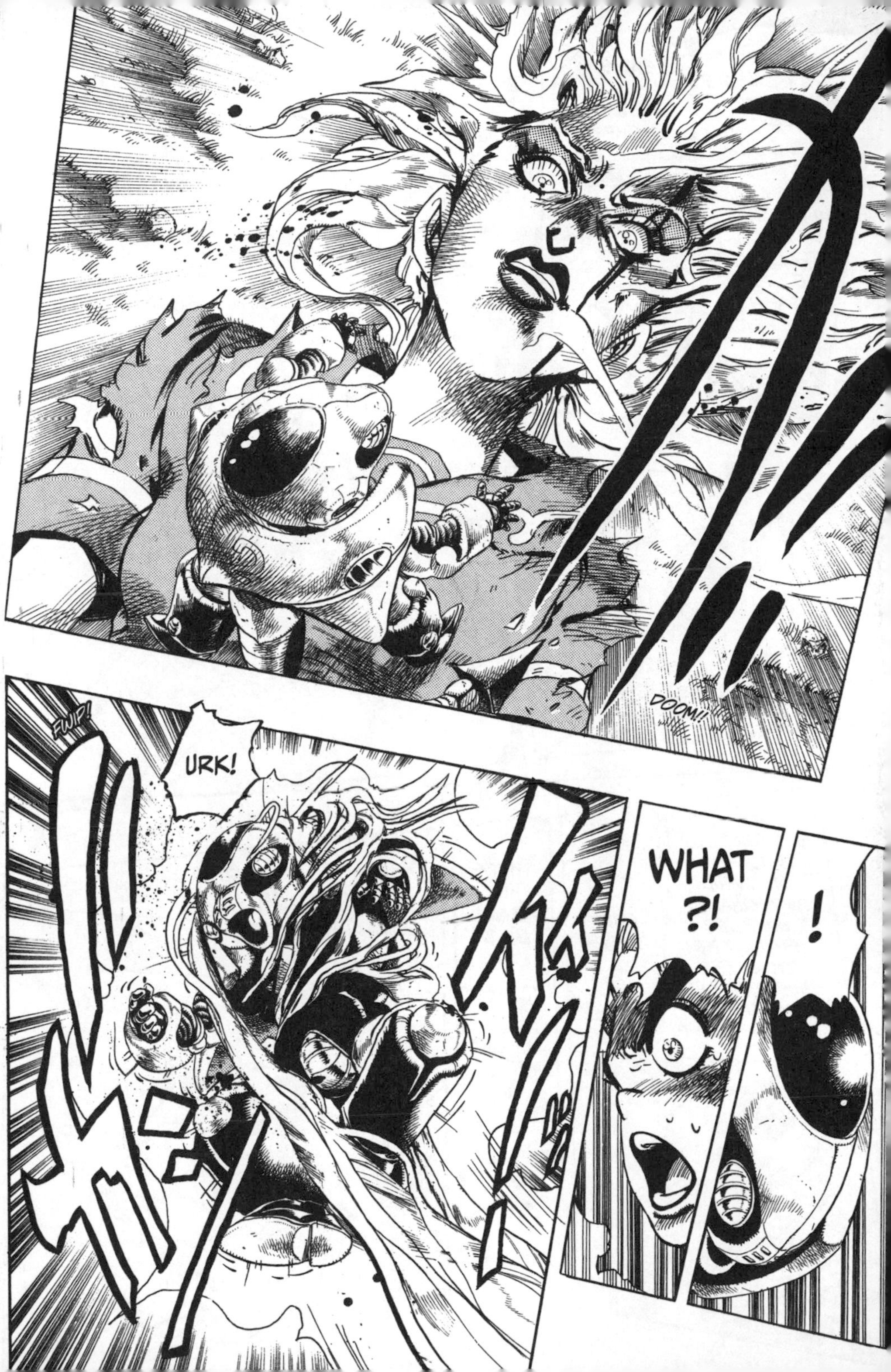
DOOM!!
!
WHAT ?!
URK!
FWIP!

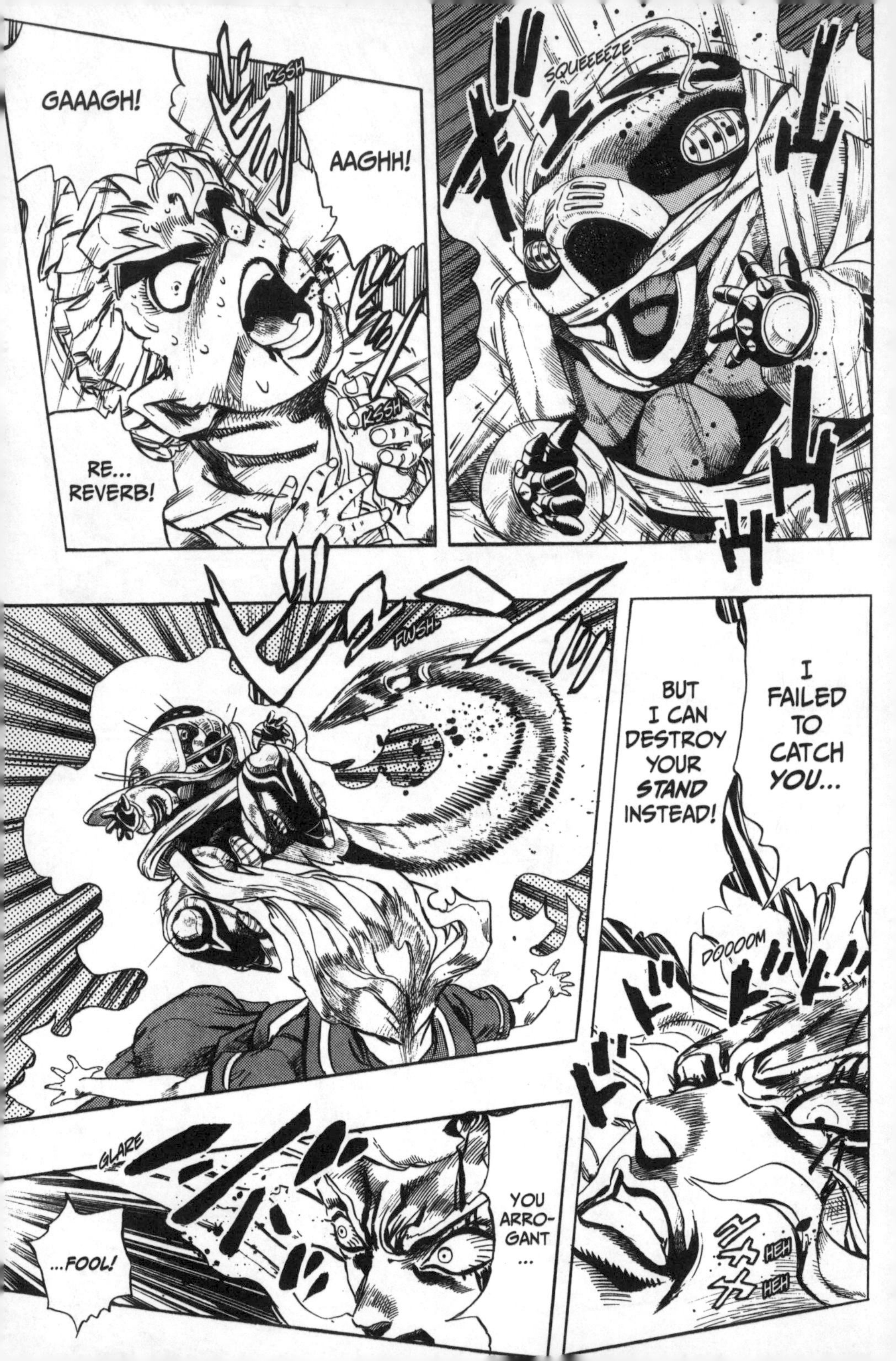
SQUEEEEZE
GAAAGH!
AAGHH!
KSSH
KSSH
RE... REVERB!
I FAILED TO CATCH YOU...
BUT I CAN DESTROY YOUR STAND INSTEAD!
DOOOOM
HEH
HEH
FWSH
GLARE
YOU ARROGANT...
...FOOL!

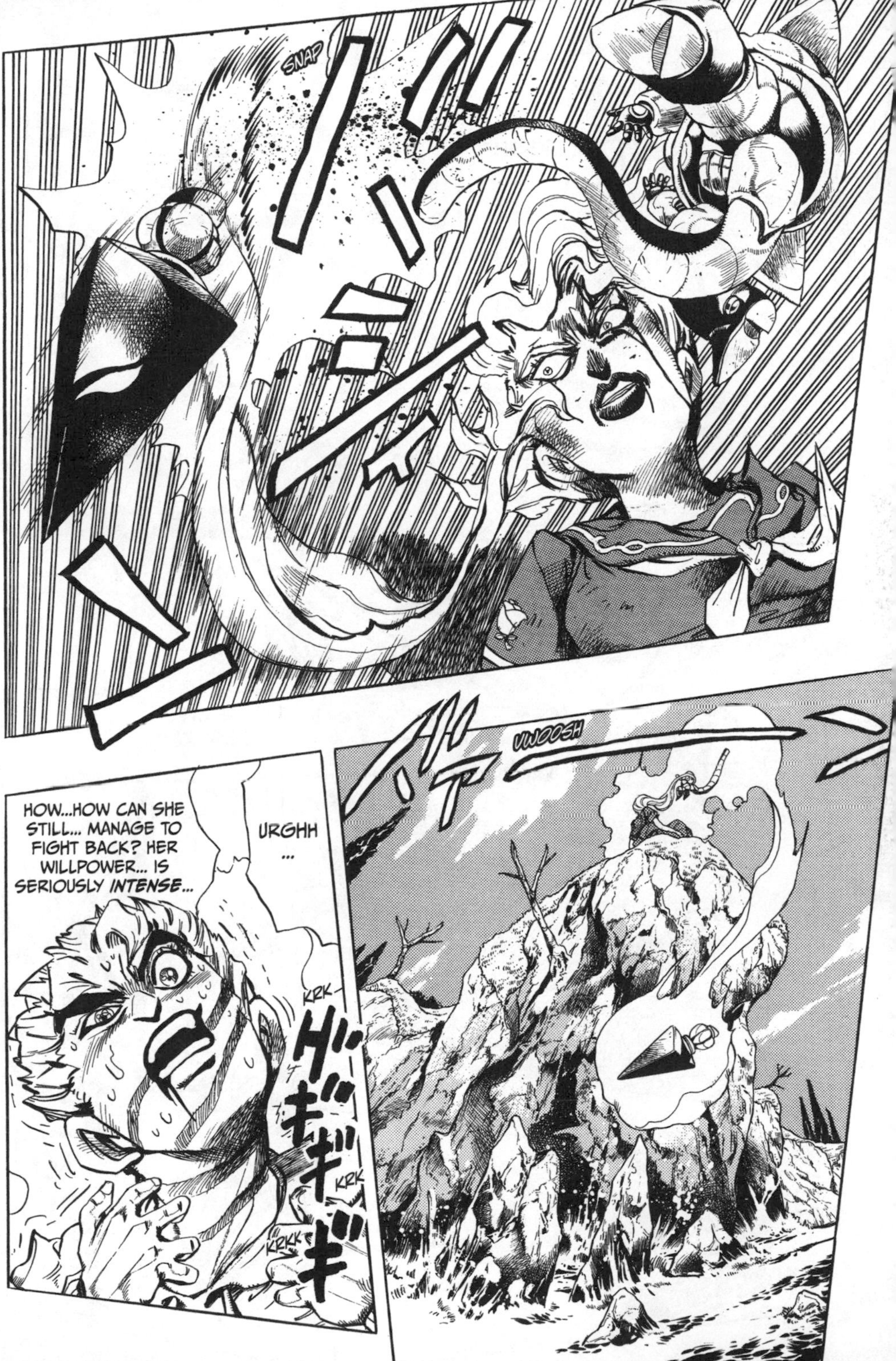
SNAP
VWOOSH
URGHH
...
HOW...HOW CAN SHE STILL... MANAGE TO FIGHT BACK? HER WILLPOWER... IS SERIOUSLY *INTENSE*...
KRK
KRK
KRKK

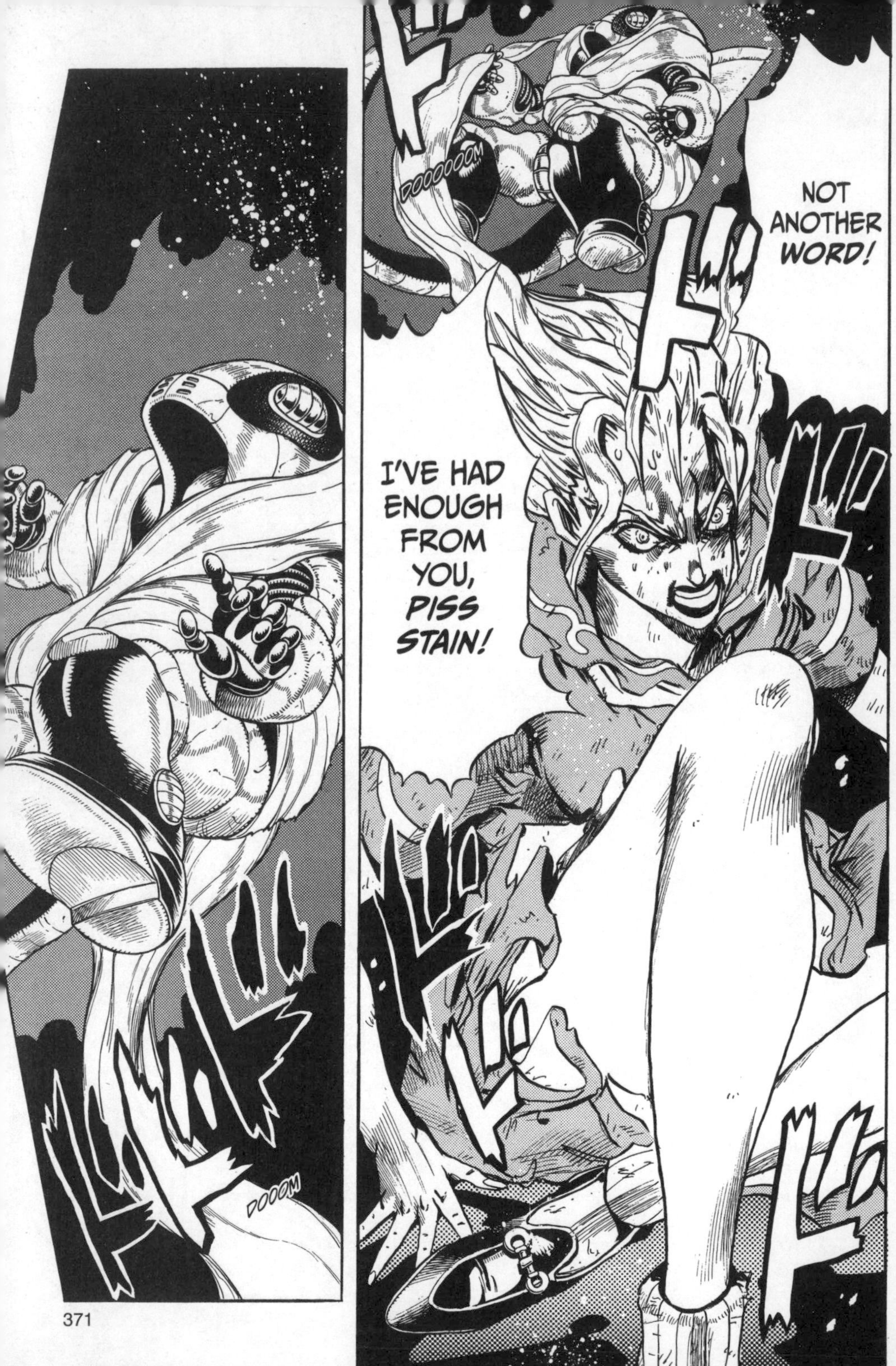
NOT ANOTHER WORD!
DOOOOOOOM
I'VE HAD ENOUGH FROM YOU, PISS STAIN!
DOOOM

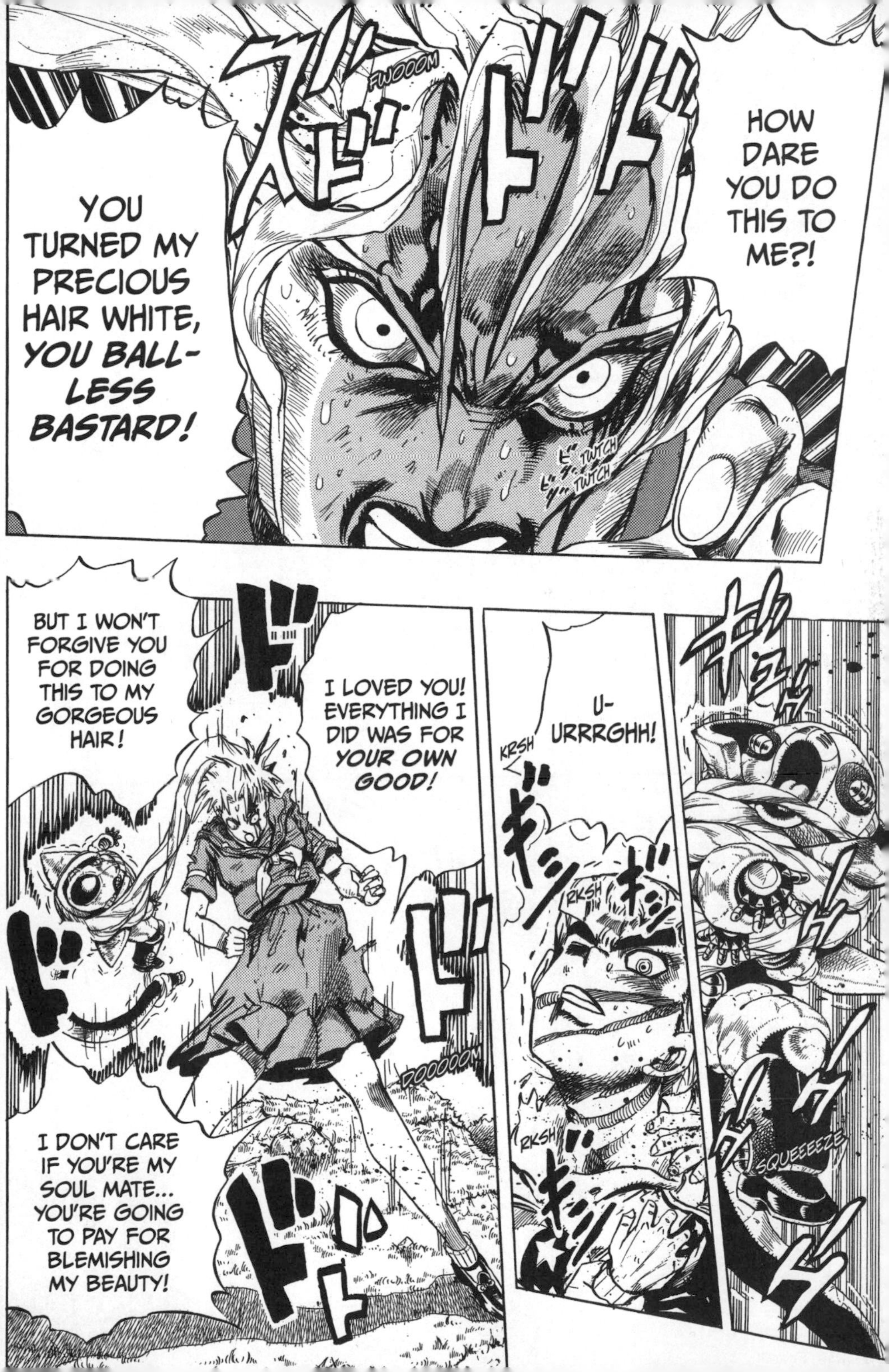
FWOOOM
HOW DARE YOU DO THIS TO ME?!
YOU TURNED MY PRECIOUS HAIR WHITE, YOU BALL-LESS BASTARD!
TWITCH TWITCH
SQUEEEEZE
U-URRRGHH!
KRSH
RKSH
RKSH
I LOVED YOU! EVERYTHING I DID WAS FOR YOUR OWN GOOD!
BUT I WON'T FORGIVE YOU FOR DOING THIS TO MY GORGEOUS HAIR!
DOOOOOM
I DON'T CARE IF YOU'RE MY SOUL MATE... YOU'RE GOING TO PAY FOR BLEMISHING MY BEAUTY!

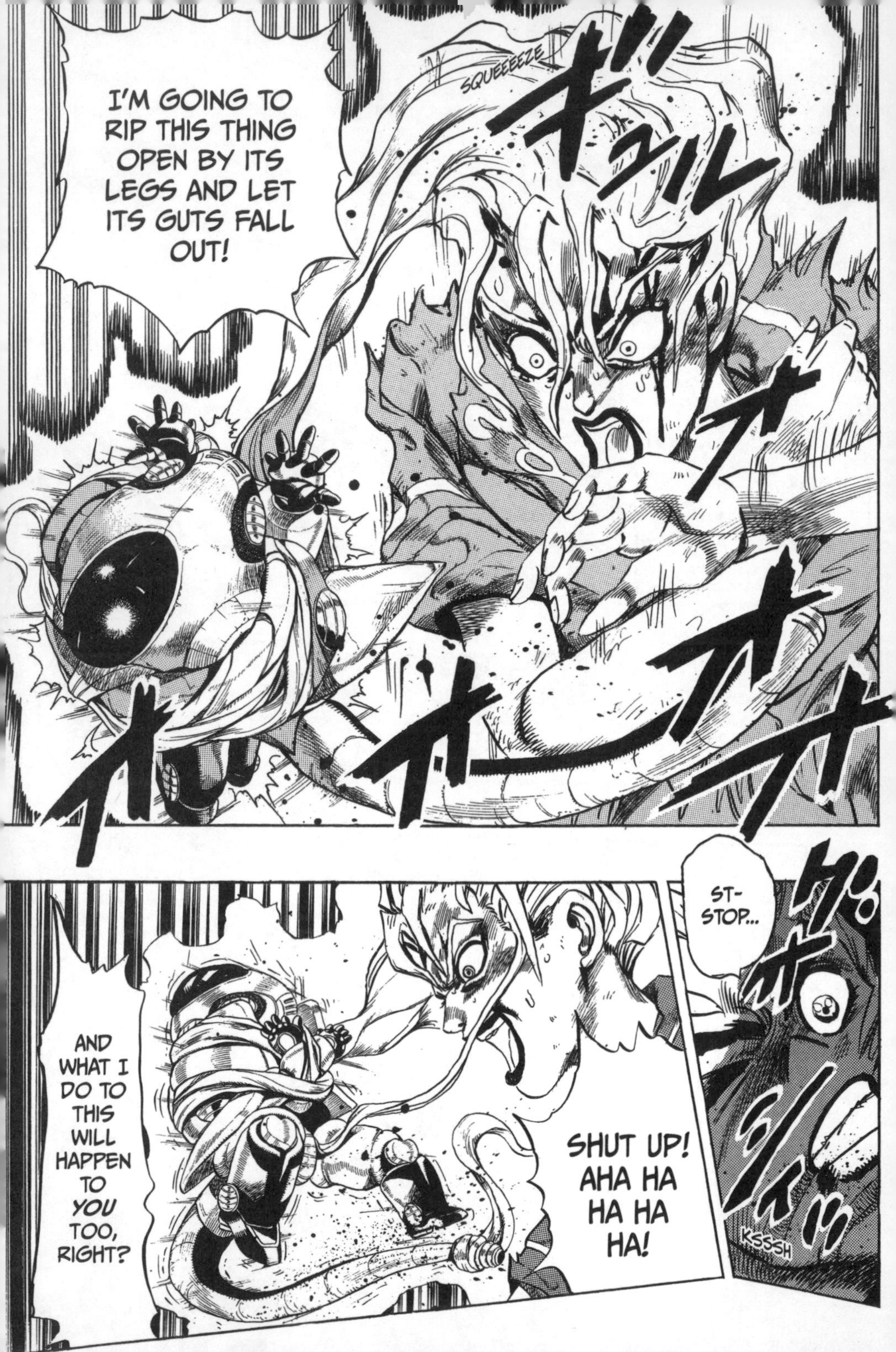
SQUEEEEZE
I'M GOING TO RIP THIS THING OPEN BY ITS LEGS AND LET ITS GUTS FALL OUT!
ST- STOP...
KSSSH
SHUT UP! AHA HA HA HA HA!
AND WHAT I DO TO THIS WILL HAPPEN TO *YOU* TOO, RIGHT?

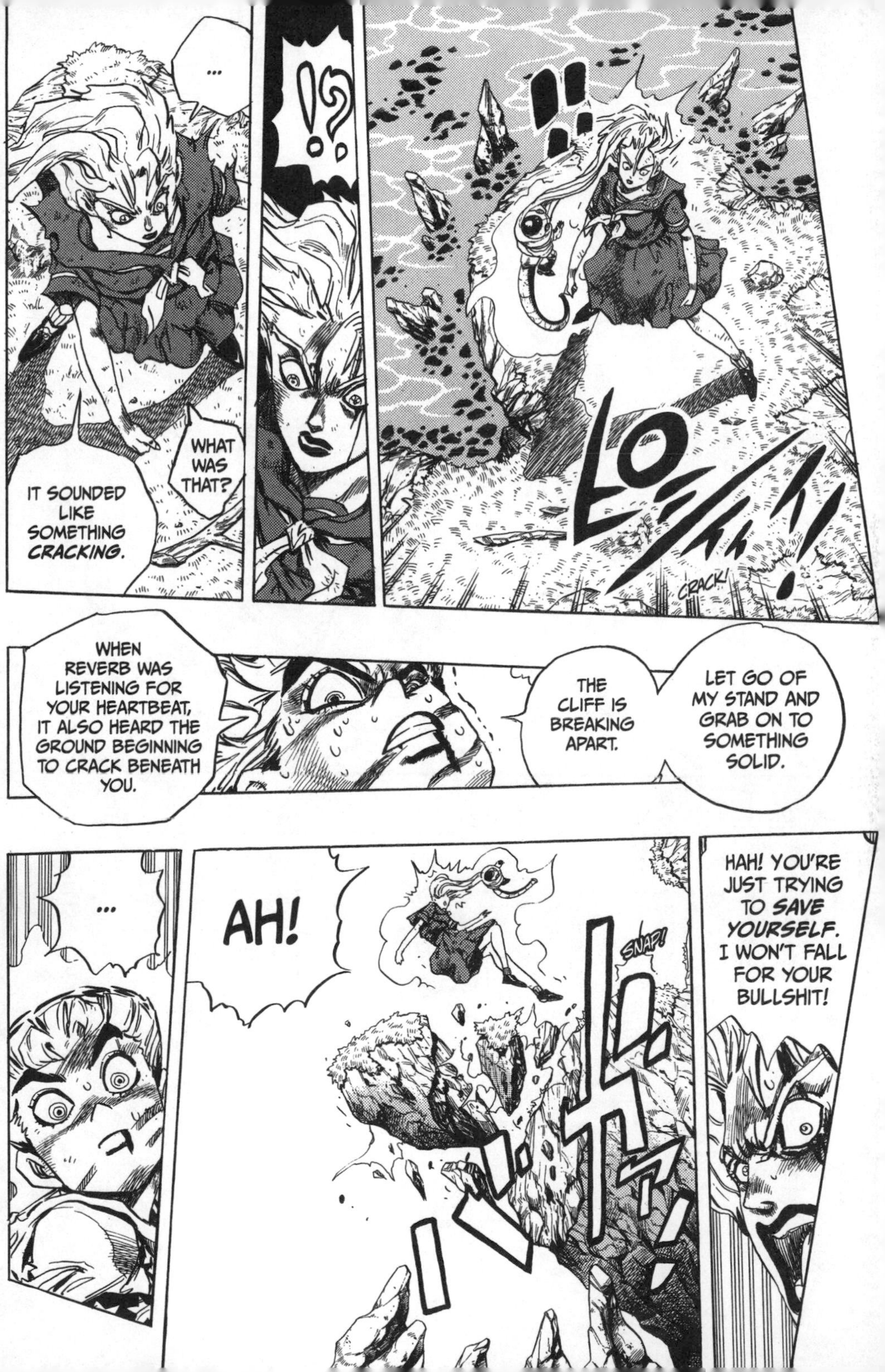

!!
CRACK!
!?
...
WHAT WAS THAT?
IT SOUNDED LIKE SOMETHING *CRACKING*.
LET GO OF MY STAND AND GRAB ON TO SOMETHING SOLID.
THE CLIFF IS BREAKING APART.
WHEN REVERB WAS LISTENING FOR YOUR HEARTBEAT, IT ALSO HEARD THE GROUND BEGINNING TO CRACK BENEATH YOU.
HAH! YOU'RE JUST TRYING TO *SAVE YOURSELF*. I WON'T FALL FOR YOUR BULLSHIT!
SNAP!
AH!
...

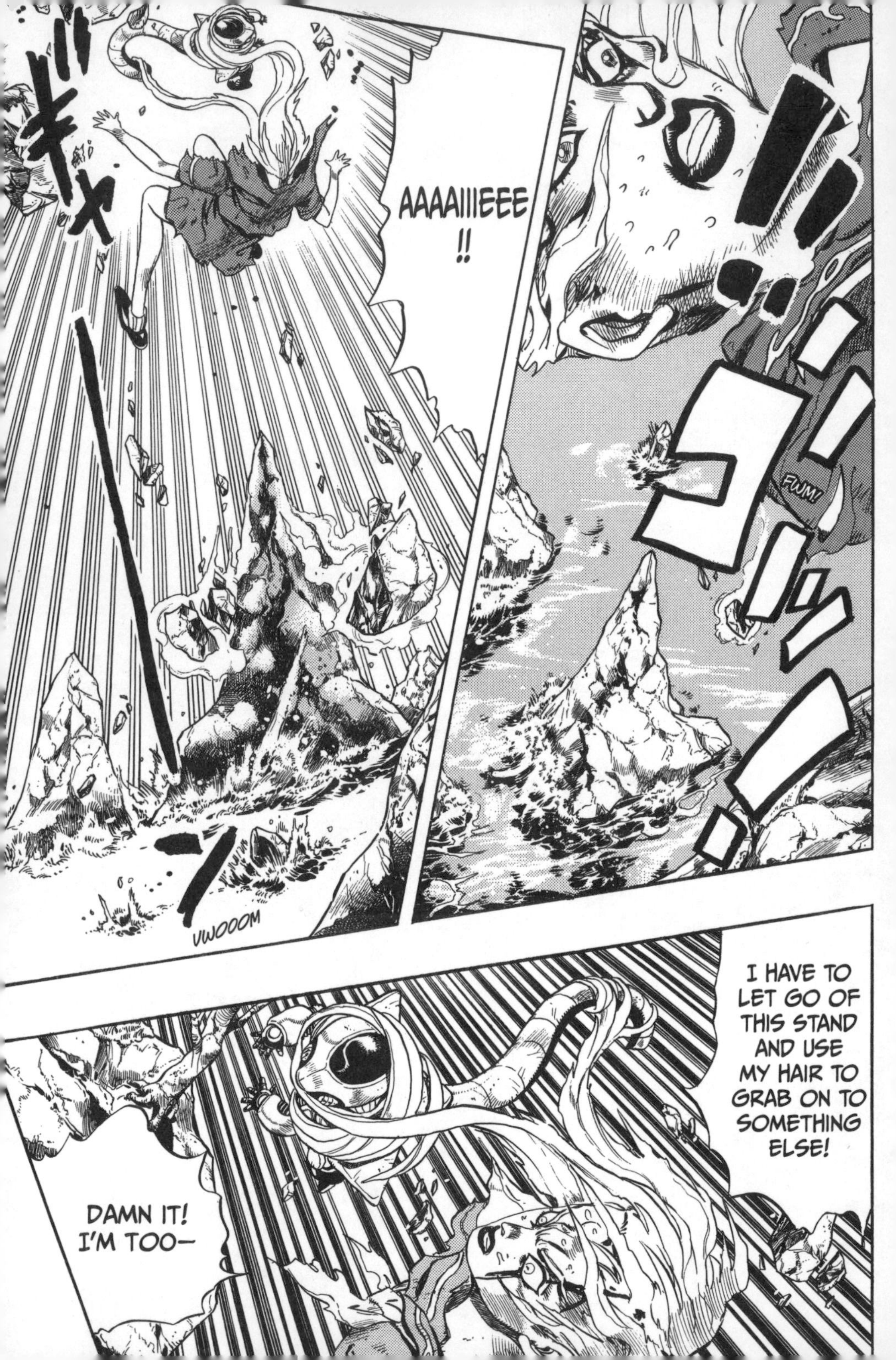
FWM!
ドギャ
AAAAIIIEEE!!
VWOOOM
I HAVE TO LET GO OF THIS STAND AND USE MY HAIR TO GRAB ON TO SOMETHING ELSE!
DAMN IT! I'M TOO—

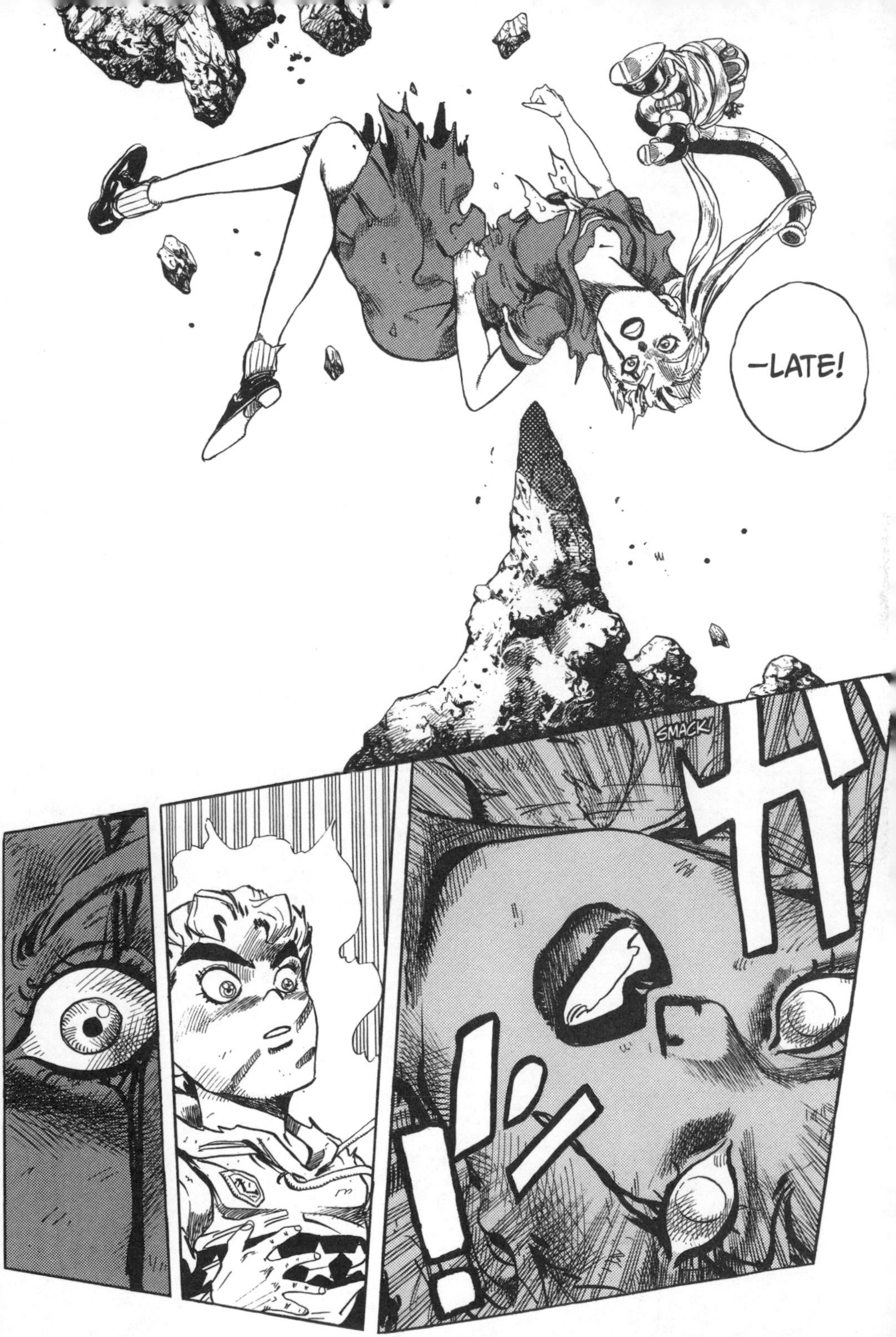
—LATE!
SMACK!

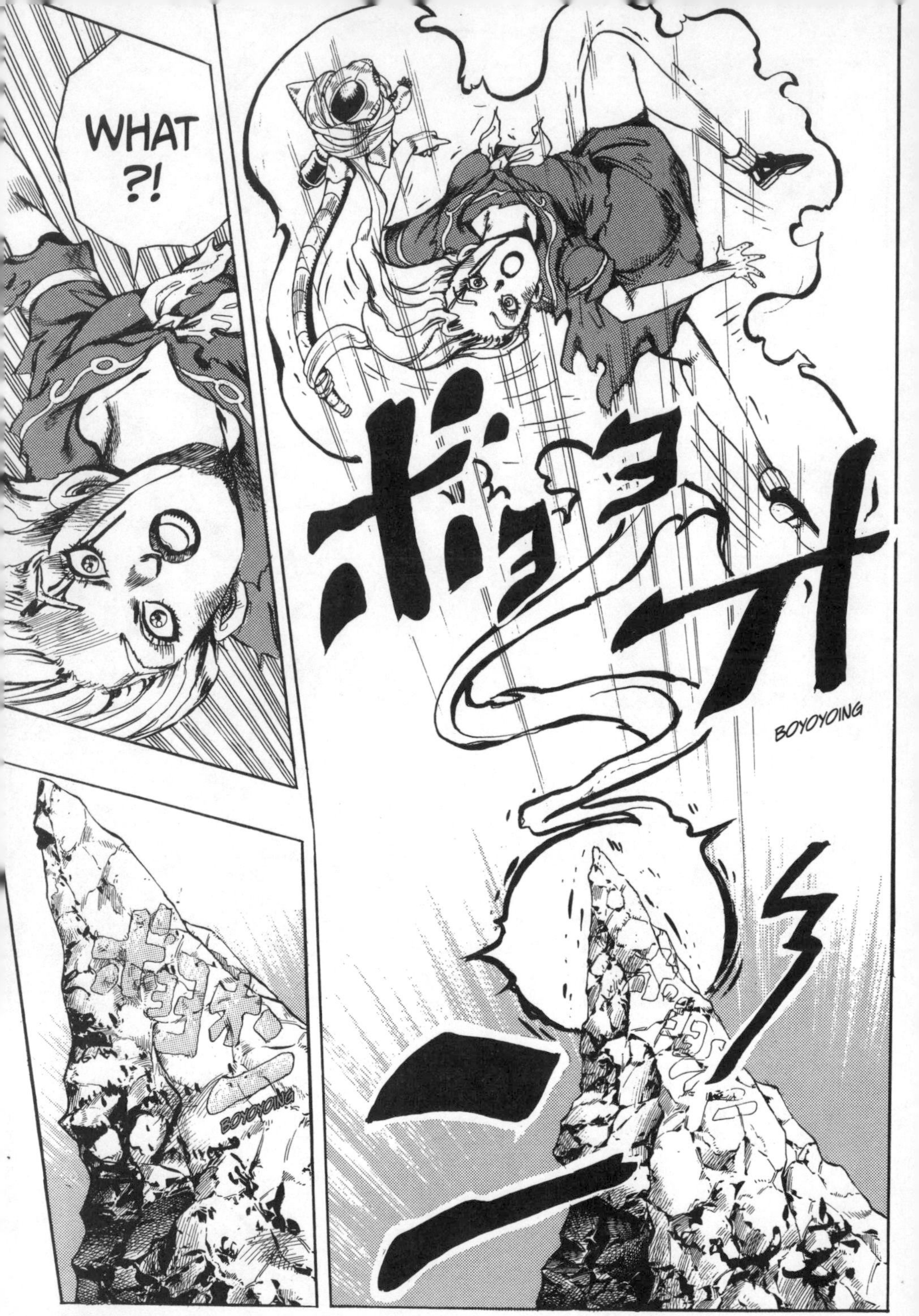
BOYOYOING
WHAT ?!
BOYOYOING

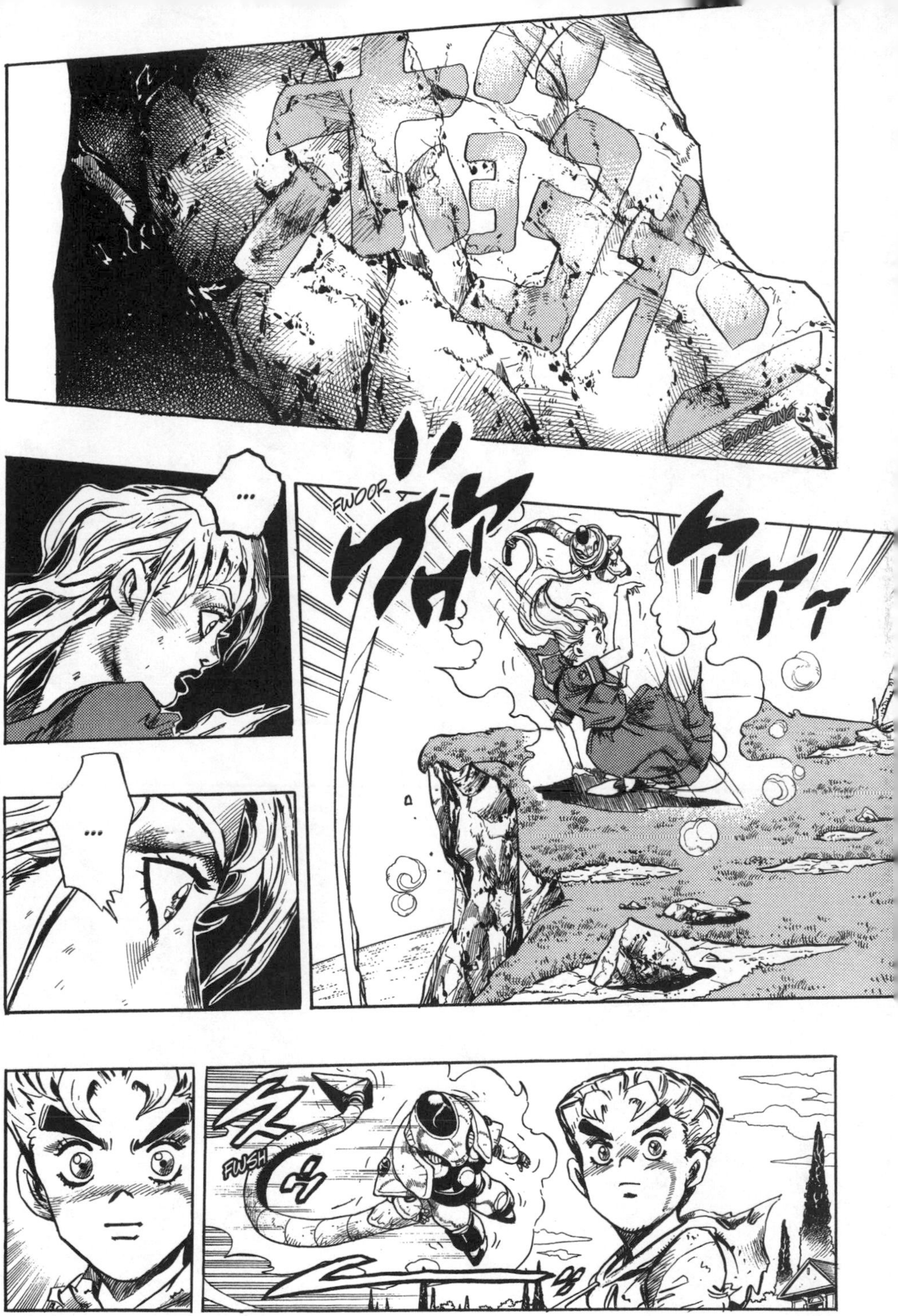
BOYOYOING
FWOOP
...
...
FWISH

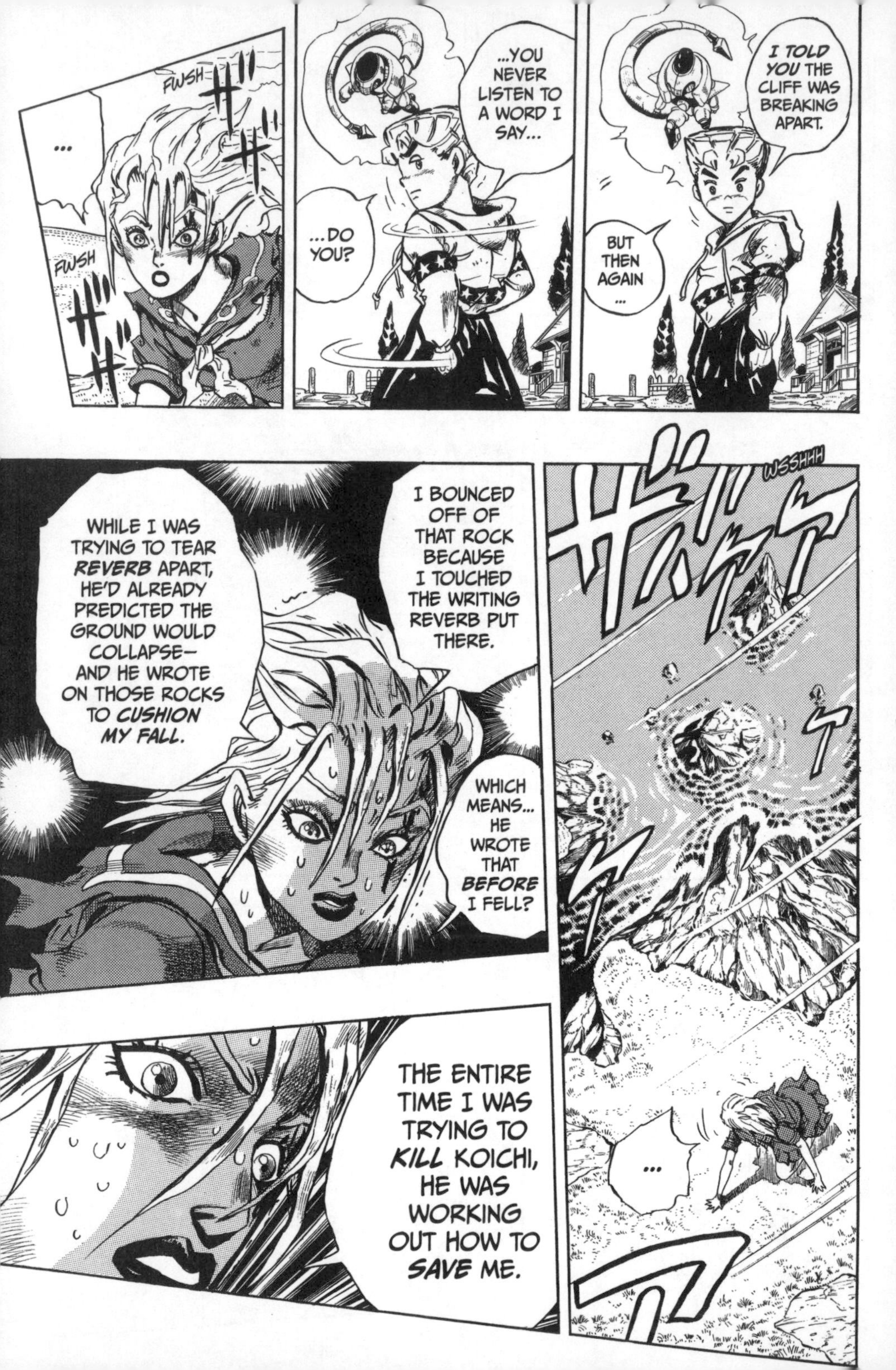
I TOLD YOU THE CLIFF WAS BREAKING APART.
BUT THEN AGAIN...
...YOU NEVER LISTEN TO A WORD I SAY...
...DO YOU?
FWSH
...
FWSH
WSSHHH
...
I BOUNCED OFF OF THAT ROCK BECAUSE I TOUCHED THE WRITING REVERB PUT THERE.
WHILE I WAS TRYING TO TEAR REVERB APART, HE'D ALREADY PREDICTED THE GROUND WOULD COLLAPSE—AND HE WROTE ON THOSE ROCKS TO CUSHION MY FALL.
WHICH MEANS... HE WROTE THAT BEFORE I FELL?
THE ENTIRE TIME I WAS TRYING TO KILL KOICHI, HE WAS WORKING OUT HOW TO SAVE ME.

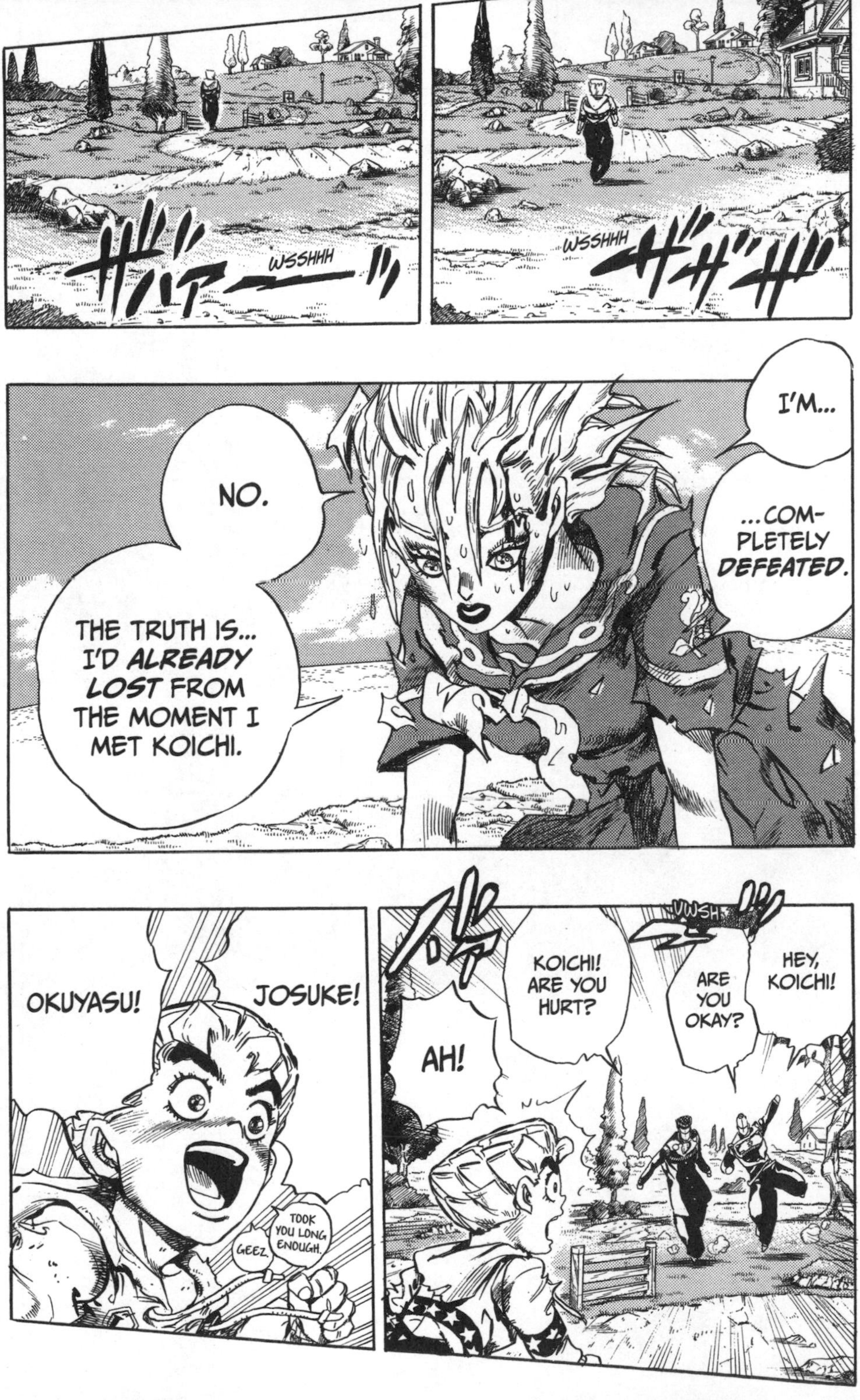
WSSHHH
WSSHHH
I'M...
...COM-PLETELY DEFEATED.
NO.
THE TRUTH IS... I'D ALREADY LOST FROM THE MOMENT I MET KOICHI.
VWSH
HEY, KOICHI!
ARE YOU OKAY?
KOICHI! ARE YOU HURT?
AH!
JOSUKE!
OKUYASU!
TOOK YOU LONG ENOUGH.
GEEZ.

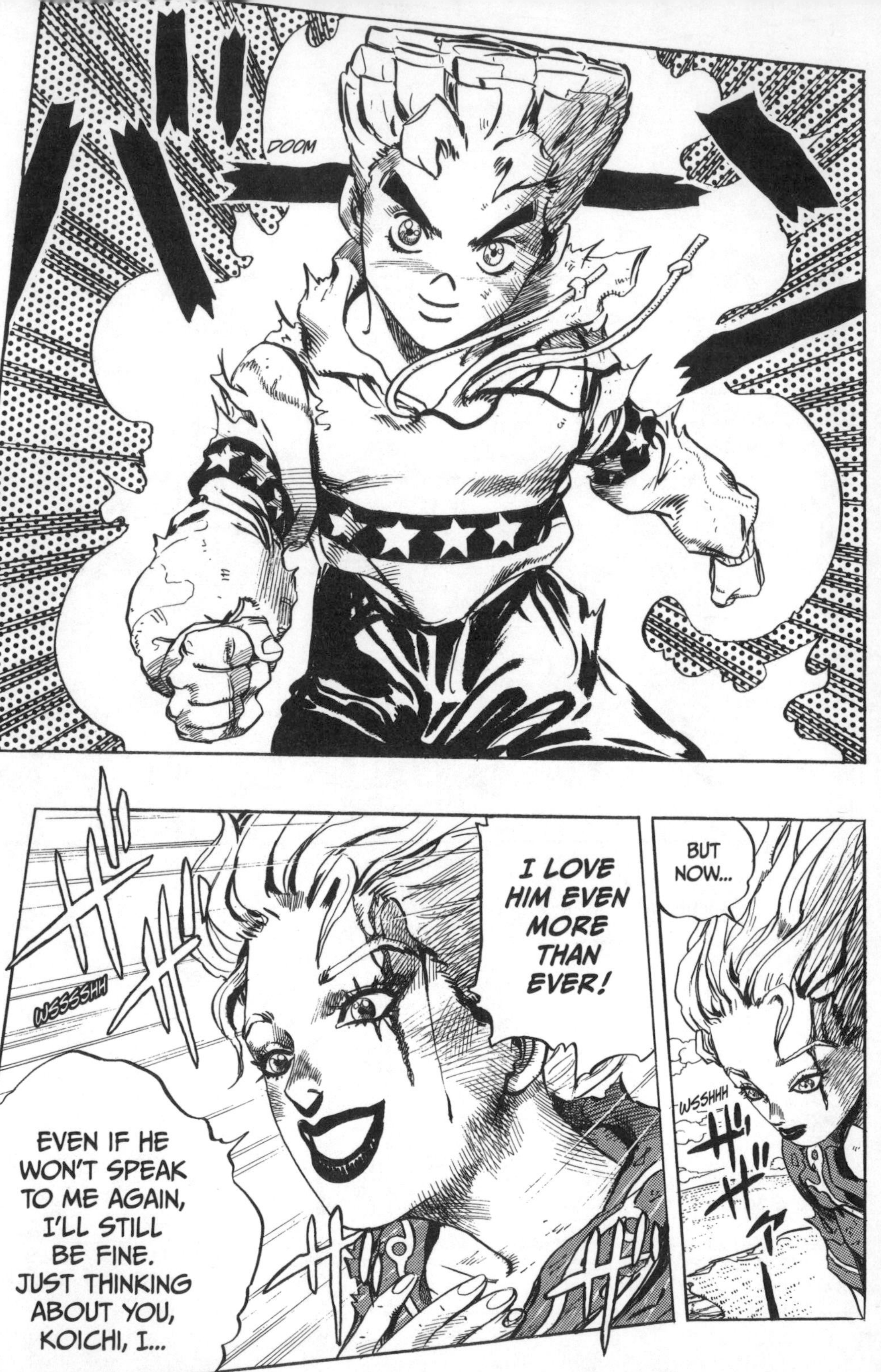
DOOM
BUT NOW...
WSSHHH
I LOVE HIM EVEN MORE THAN EVER!
WSSSSHH
EVEN IF HE WON'T SPEAK TO ME AGAIN, I'LL STILL BE FINE. JUST THINKING ABOUT YOU, KOICHI, I...

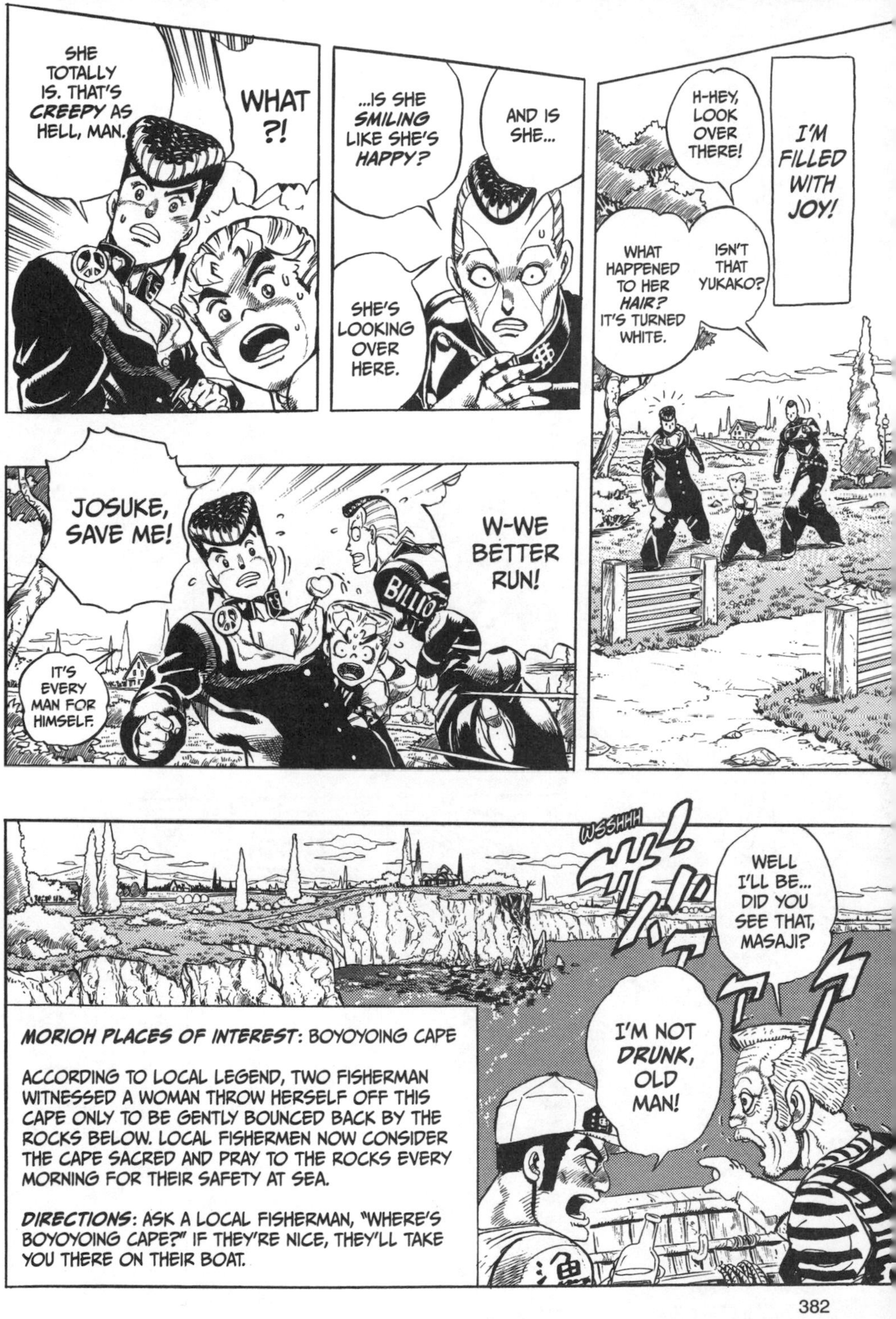
I'M FILLED WITH JOY!
H-HEY, LOOK OVER THERE!
ISN'T THAT YUKAKO?
WHAT HAPPENED TO HER HAIR? IT'S TURNED WHITE.
AND IS SHE...
...IS SHE SMILING LIKE SHE'S HAPPY?
SHE'S LOOKING OVER HERE.
WHAT ?!
SHE TOTALLY IS. THAT'S CREEPY AS HELL, MAN.
W-WE BETTER RUN!
JOSUKE, SAVE ME!
IT'S EVERY MAN FOR HIMSELF.
WSSHHH
WELL I'LL BE... DID YOU SEE THAT, MASAJI?
I'M NOT DRUNK, OLD MAN!
MORIOH PLACES OF INTEREST: BOYOYOING CAPE
ACCORDING TO LOCAL LEGEND, TWO FISHERMAN WITNESSED A WOMAN THROW HERSELF OFF THIS CAPE ONLY TO BE GENTLY BOUNCED BACK BY THE ROCKS BELOW. LOCAL FISHERMEN NOW CONSIDER THE CAPE SACRED AND PRAY TO THE ROCKS EVERY MORNING FOR THEIR SAFETY AT SEA.
DIRECTIONS: ASK A LOCAL FISHERMAN, "WHERE'S BOYOYOING CAPE?" IF THEY'RE NICE, THEY'LL TAKE YOU THERE ON THEIR BOAT.

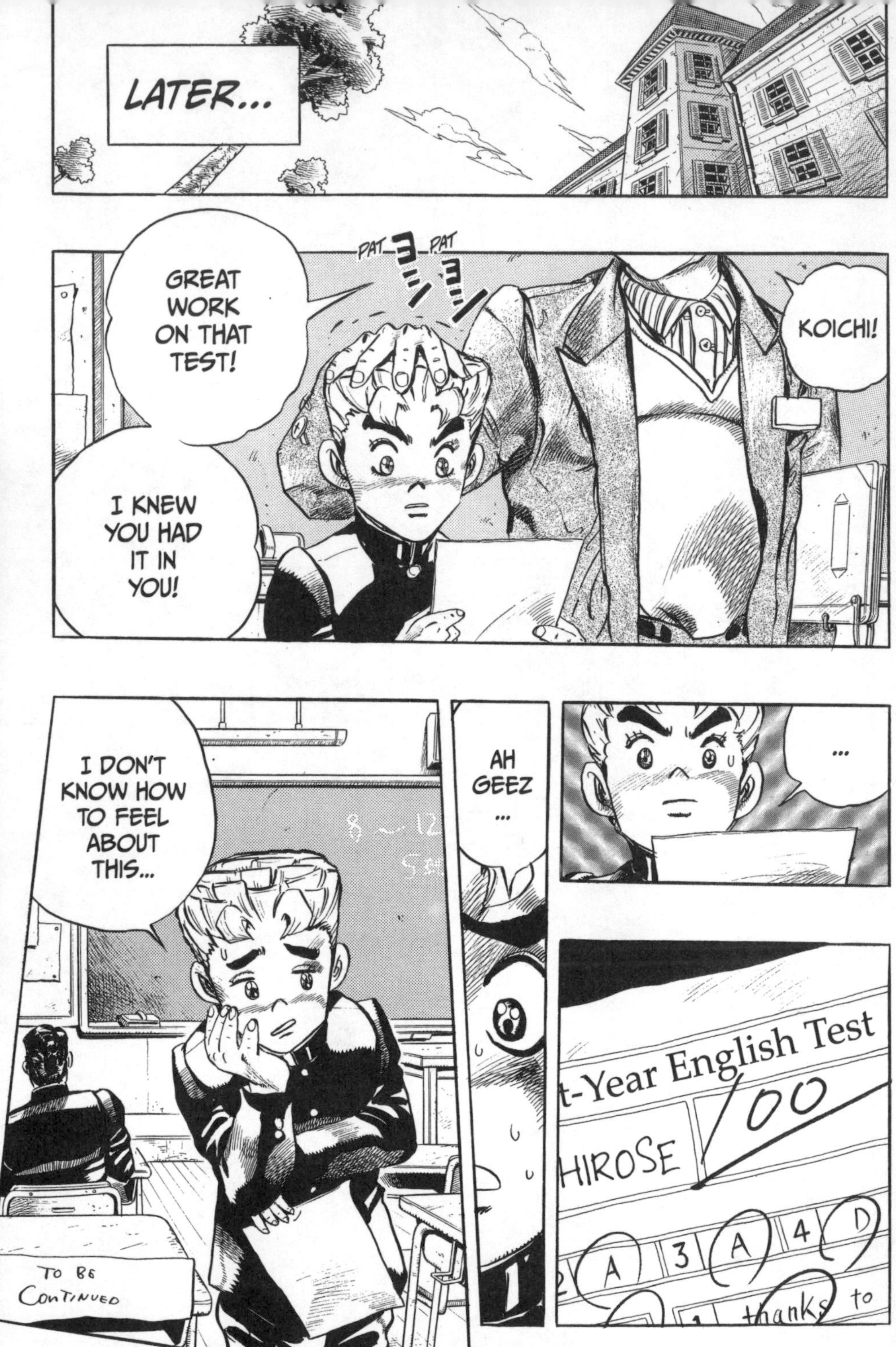
LATER...
KOICHI!
PAT PAT
GREAT WORK ON THAT TEST!
I KNEW YOU HAD IT IN YOU!
...
t-Year English Test
HIROSE
100
2 A 3 A 4 D
1 thanks to
AH GEEZ ...
I DON'T KNOW HOW TO FEEL ABOUT THIS...
TO BE CONTINUED

PART 4, VOLUME 2 / END

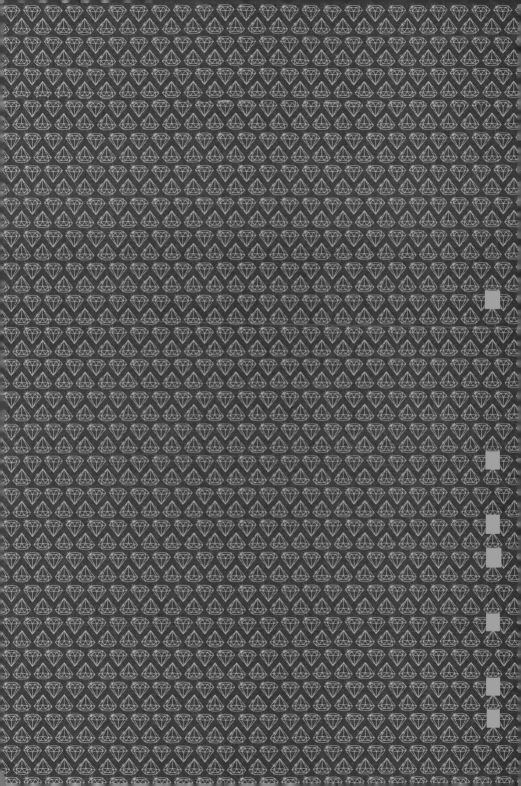

AUTHOR'S COMMENTS

I listen to a lot of music and that sometimes has an unfortunate side effect: a melody getting stuck in my head. The most serious case was a song called "Otoko to Onna" ("Man and Woman"), with its "ba ba da ba da" repeating relentlessly for three days straight. I was in school at the time and I remember thinking, "I can't study like this!"

I also went through a period when I would hear Kiyoko Suizenji's "365 Steps March" every time I started walking, in a Pavlovian sort of response that had me entirely at its mercy.

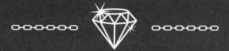

HIROHIKO ARAKI'S TOP 10 MOVIES
THAT HAD HIM SQUIRMING IN HIS SEAT

(The ten best movies I wished would stop but I kept watching anyway.)

#1 *Night of the Living Dead*
#2 *Jaws*
#3 *Johnny Got His Gun*
#4 *Mississippi Burning*
#5 *Platoon*
#6 *Papillon*
#7 *Halloween 4*
#8 *Lord of the Flies*
#9 *Silence of the Lambs*
#10 *Alien*

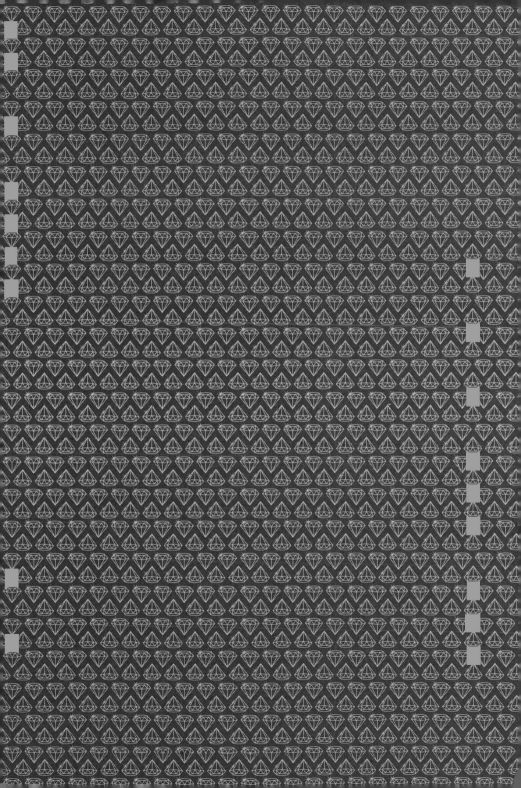

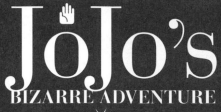

JoJo's
BIZARRE ADVENTURE

PART 4: DIAMOND IS UNBREAKABLE
VOLUME 2
BY HIROHIKO ARAKI

DELUXE HARDCOVER EDITION
Translation: Nathan A. Collins
Touch-Up Art & Lettering: Mark McMurray
Design: Adam Grano
Editor: David Brothers

Printed in the U.S.A.

Published by VIZ Media, LLC
P.O. Box 77010
San Francisco, CA 94107

10 9 8 7 6 5 4 3 2 1
First printing, August 2019

viz.com   shonenjump.com

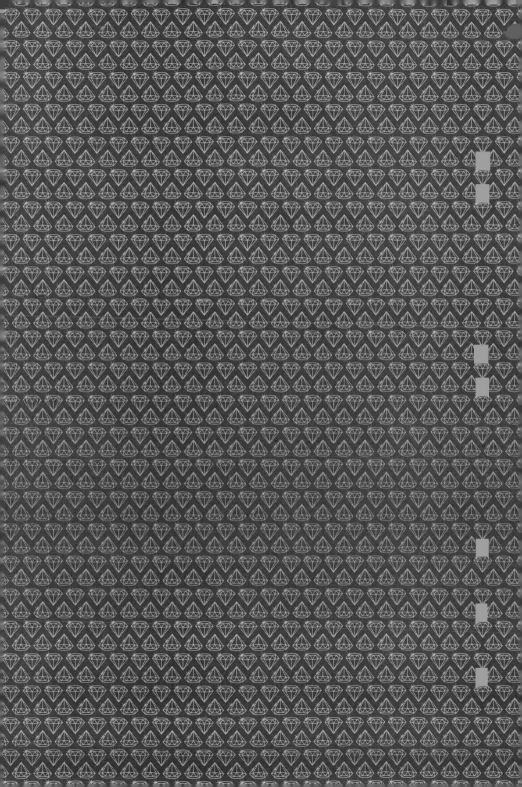

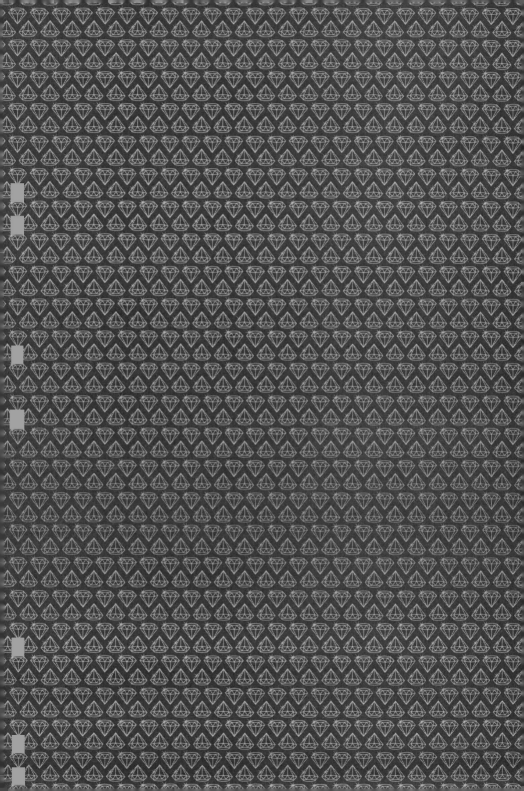

THIS IS THE LAST PAGE

JoJo's BIZARRE ADVENTURE

has been printed in the original
Japanese format in order to preserve
the orientation of the original artwork.

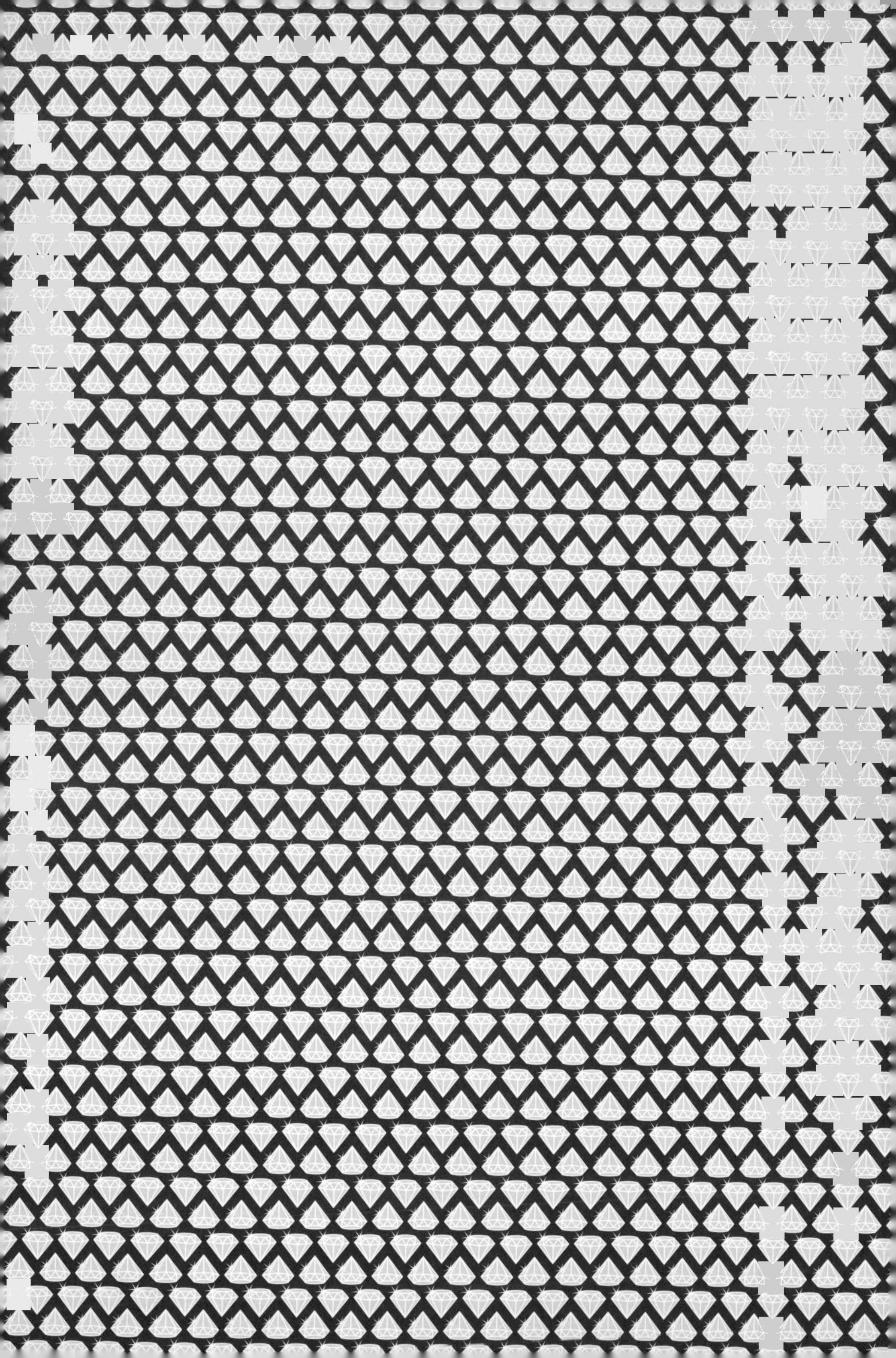

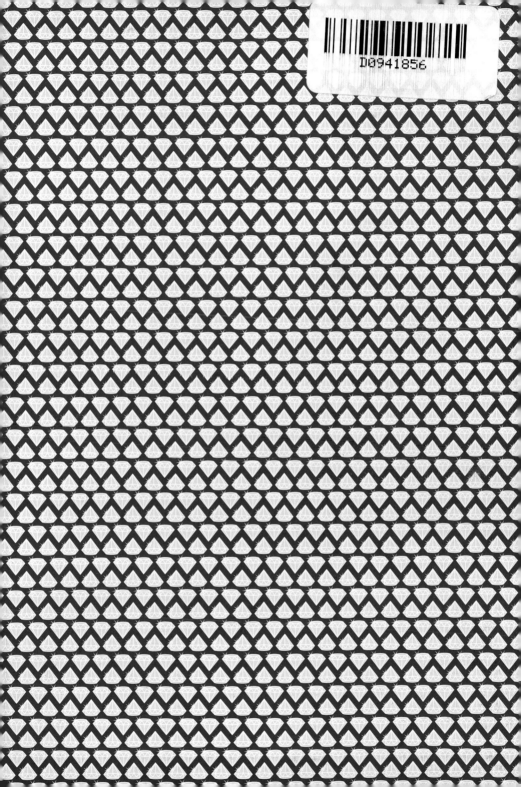